PassKey EA Review Complete:

Individuals, Businesses, and Representation

IRS Enrolled Agent Exam Study Guide
2013-2014 Edition

Authors:
Collette Szymborski, CPA
Richard Gramkow, EA
Christy Pinheiro, EA ABA®

PassKey Publications
Elk Grove, CA 95758

Editor: Cynthia Willett Sherwood, EA, MSJ

PassKey EA Review, Complete: Individuals, Businesses and Representation IRS Enrolled Agent Exam Study Guide, 2013-2014 Edition

ISBN: 978-1-935664-21-5

First Printing. PassKey EA Review
PassKey EA Review® is a U.S. Registered Trademark

Tammy the Tax Lady® is a U.S. registered trademark of PassKey Publications.

PassKey Publications, PO Box 580465, Elk Grove, CA 95758

www.PassKeyPublications.com

Recent Praise for the PassKey EA Review Series

Kari Hutchens (Canon City, Colorado)
I passed all three exams! Easy to understand and comprehensive. Even from Part 1 of the book (Individuals), I learned so much that I am going to amend two prior year tax returns and get over $1,000 back. Passing all three parts of the EA exam on the first try and getting some extra cash in my pocket gets this book an A+!

Ken Smith (Chicago, Illinois)
I studied like crazy, night and day, and passed all three parts of the EA exam in just eight days. And I passed on the first try!

Michael Mirth (North Las Vegas, Nevada)
I am happy to say I am now an enrolled agent. This was the only source I used to study besides some extra practice tests. The way the book presented the materials made it easy to comprehend. If you are looking for a detailed study guide, this one is for you.

E. Dinetz (Mt. Laurel, New Jersey)
This book is very informative. I have an accounting degree and have done taxes in the past and I learned many new things from this book. I like the fact that after each concept they have a multiple choice quiz/review.

Oliver Douglass
I found this book to be the least expensive and the best guide around. The tests are on the money and the explanations are so easy to comprehend. Thanks for a great book.

Baiye Zebulone
Great books. Straight to the point, and very good examples for SEE preparations. I used all three parts to prepare for the SEE and passed Parts 1 and 3 on the first sitting and Part 2 on the second sitting. I will recommend it to anybody who wants to pass the rigorous EA examination.

Carl Ganster (Wyomissing, Pennsylvania)
I passed all my tests on the first try in five months using the PassKey books. Every topic is covered. It is easy reading, with plenty of examples. I have recommended the books to others who have to take the test. Thanks, PassKey, for writing great test guides. So many of the ones out there are hard to understand.

Do you want to test yourself?
Then get the PassKey EA Exam Workbook, newly expanded for tax year 2012!

PassKey EA Review Workbook:
Six Complete Enrolled Agent Practice Exams

Thoroughly revised and updated for tax year 2012, this workbook features **six complete** enrolled agent practice exams, with detailed answers, to accompany the PassKey EA Review study guides. This workbook includes two full exams for each of the three parts of the EA exam: Individuals, Businesses, and Representation.

You can learn by testing yourself on 600 questions, with all of the answers clearly explained in the back of the book.

Test yourself, time yourself, and learn!

Table of Contents

Introduction

Congratulations on taking the first step toward becoming an enrolled agent, a widely respected professional tax designation. The Internal Revenue Service licenses enrolled agents, known as EAs, after candidates pass a three-part exam testing their knowledge of federal tax law.

This PassKey study guide is designed to help you study for the EA exam, which is formally called the *IRS Special Enrollment Examination* or *"SEE."* The exam covers all aspects of federal tax law, including the taxation of individuals; corporations, partnerships, and exempt entities; ethics; and IRS collection and audit procedures. This guide is designed for the 2013 to 2014 testing season, which begins May 1, 2013 and closes February 28, 2014. Anyone taking the EA exam during this time period will be tested on 2012 tax law.

Exam Basics

The EA exam consists of three parts, which candidates typically take on different dates that do not need to be consecutive. The exam is exclusively administered by the testing company Prometric. You can find valuable information and register online at: *http://www.prometric.com/IRS*

The yearly pass rates for the SEE vary by exam. In the 2011-2012 testing period, an average of more than 80% of test-takers passed Parts 1 and 3. The pass rate for Part 2 was much lower, averaging about 60%.

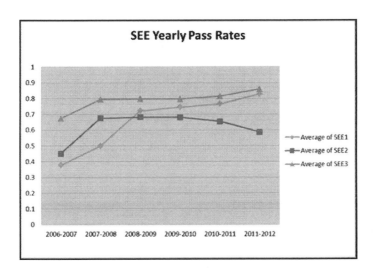

The computerized exam is offered only at Prometric testing centers. The format is multiple choice, with no questions requiring written answers. The length of each part of the exam is 3.5 hours, not including a pre-exam tutorial and post-exam survey.

Computerized EA Exam Format
Part 1 - Individual Taxation-100 Questions
Part 2 - Business Taxation-100 Questions
Part 3 - Representation, Practice, and Procedures-100 Questions

Testing Center Procedures

The testing center is designed to be a secure environment. The following are procedures you'll need to follow on test day:

1. Check in about a half-hour before your appointment time, and bring a current government-issued ID with both a photo and signature. If you don't have valid ID, you'll be turned away and you'll have to pay for a new exam appointment.
2. You'll be given a locker for your wallet, phone, and other personal items. You won't be able to bring any reference materials or other items into the testing room, with the exception of soft earplugs. The center supplies noise-blocking headphones.
3. No food, water, or other beverages are allowed in the testing room.
4. You'll be given scratch paper and a pencil to use, which will be collected after the exam.
5. You'll be able to use an onscreen calculator during the exam, or Prometric will provide you with a handheld calculator. You cannot bring your own.
6. Before going into the testing room, you'll be scanned with a metal detector wand.
7. You'll need to sign in and out every time you leave the testing room. Bathroom breaks are permitted, but the test timer will continue to count down.
8. You're not allowed to talk or communicate with other test-takers in the exam room. Prometric continuously monitors the testing via video, physical walk-throughs, and an observation window.

Violation of any of these procedures may result in the disqualification of your exam. In cases of cheating, the IRS says candidates may be subject to a variety of consequences, including civil and criminal penalties.

Exam-takers who require special accommodations under the Americans with Disabilities Act (ADA) must contact Prometric at 888-226-9406 to obtain an accommodation request form. A language barrier is not considered a disability. [1]

Exam Content

The IRS introduces multiple versions of new EA exams each May. If you fail a particular part of the exam and need to retake it, don't expect to see the identical questions the next time.

The IRS no longer releases new test questions and answers, although old exam questions from 1999 to 2005 are available on the IRS website for review. (Be aware that tax law changes every year, so make sure you are familiar with recent updates and don't rely too heavily on these sample questions and answers.) Prometric includes broad exam content outlines for each exam part; however, not all of the topics will appear on the exam and there may be other topics that are included.

Your PassKey study guides present an overview of all the major areas of federal taxation that enrolled agents typically encounter in their practices and that are likely to appear on the exam. Although the PassKey guides are designed to be comprehensive, we suggest you review IRS publications and try to learn as much as you can about tax law in general so that you're well-equipped to take the exam. In addition to this study guide, we highly recommend that all exam candidates read:

---

[1] *Candidate Information Bulletin* for the Enrolled Agent Special Enrollment Examination.

- **Publication 17,** *Your Federal Income Tax* (for Part 1 of the exam), and
- **Circular 230,** *Regulations Governing the Practice of Attorneys, Certified Public Accountants, Enrolled Agents, Enrolled Actuaries, and Appraisers before the Internal Revenue Service* (for Part 3 of the exam).

Anyone may download these publications for free from the IRS website.

> **Note:** Some exam candidates take Part 3, *Representation, Practice, and Procedures,* first, rather than taking the tests in order, since the material in Part 3 is considered less complex. The IRS discourages taking the tests out of order by including multiple questions (5% or more at times) of material that relates to taxation of *Individuals* and *Businesses.*

Exam Strategy

Each multiple choice question provides four choices for an answer. There are several different multiple choice formats used:[2]

Format One- Direct question

Which of the following entities are required to file Form 709, United States Gift Tax Return?

A. An individual

B. An estate or trust

C. A corporation

D. All of the above

Format Two-Incomplete sentence

Supplemental wages are compensation paid in addition to an employee's regular wages. They **do not** include payments for_____.

A. Accumulated sick leave

B. Nondeductible moving expenses

C. Vacation pay

D. Travel reimbursements paid at the federal government per diem rate

Format Three-All of the following EXCEPT

There are five tests which must be met for you to claim an exemption for a dependent. Which of the following is **not** a requirement?

A. Citizen or Resident Test

B. Member of Household or Relationship Test

C. Disability Test

D. Joint Return Test

There may also be a limited number of questions on the exam that have four choices, with three of them incorrect statements or facts and only one that is a correct statement or

---

[2] Candidate Information Bulletin for the Enrolled Agent Special Enrollment Examination.

fact, which you would select as the right answer.[3] All four of these question-and-answer formats appear in your PassKey study guides. During the EA exam, you need to make sure you read each question thoroughly to understand exactly what is being asked.

Your exam may also include some experimental questions that will not be scored. You won't know which ones they are—the IRS uses them to gather statistical information on the questions before they're added to the exam as scored items.

To familiarize yourself with the computerized testing format, there's a tutorial on the Prometric website. If you're not sure of an answer, you may mark it for review and return to it later. Try to eliminate clearly wrong answers of the four possible choices to narrow your odds of selecting the right answer. But be sure to answer every question, even if you have to guess, because all answers left incomplete will be marked as incorrect. Each question is weighted equally.

In the 3.5 hours of the exam, you'll have 210 minutes to answer questions, or slightly more than two minutes per question. Try to answer the questions you're sure about quickly, so you can devote more time to those that include calculations or that you're not as sure about. Remember that the clock doesn't stop for bathroom breaks, so try to allocate your time wisely.

Scoring

After you finish your exam and submit your answers, you'll learn immediately from a Prometric staff member whether you passed or failed. In either case, you won't receive a printout of the questions you answered correctly or missed.

The IRS determines scaled scores by calculating the number of questions answered correctly from the total number of questions in the examination and converting to a scale that ranges from 40 to 130. The IRS has set the scaled passing score at 105, which corresponds to the minimum level of knowledge deemed acceptable for EAs. Under its testing system, the IRS does not release the percentage of questions that you need to answer correctly in order to pass.

If you pass, you'll receive a score report showing a passing designation, but not your actual score. The IRS considers all candidates who pass as qualified, but does not rank *how* qualified each person may be.

If you fail, you'll receive a scaled score between 40 and 104, so you'll be able to see how close you are to the minimum score of 105. You'll also receive diagnostic information to help you know subject areas you need to focus on when retaking the exam:

- 1: Area of weakness where additional study is necessary. It is important for you to focus on this domain as you prepare to take the test again. You may want to consider taking a course or participating actively in a study group on this topic.
- 2: May need additional study.
- 3: Clearly demonstrated an understanding of subject area.[4]

---

[3] 1-31-13: Telephone interview with Larry Orozco, IRS director of competency and standards.
[4] *Candidate Information Bulletin* for the Enrolled Agent Special Enrollment Examination.

If necessary, you may take each part of the exam up to four times during the May 1 and February 28 testing window. You'll need to re-register with Prometric and pay fees for each new time you take an exam part.

You can carry over passing scores for individual parts of the exam up to two years from the date you took them.

After Passing

Once you've passed the exam, you must apply for enrollment as an EA, which includes an IRS review of your tax compliance history. Failure to timely file or pay personal income taxes can be grounds for denial of enrollment. You may not practice as an EA until the IRS approves your application and issues you a Treasury Card.

Successfully passing the EA exam can launch you into a fulfilling and lucrative new career. The exam requires intense preparation and diligence, but with the help of Passkey's comprehensive *EA Review*, you'll have the tools you need to learn how to become an enrolled agent.

We wish you much success.

Ten Steps for the IRS EA Exam

STEP 1-Learn

Learn more about the enrolled agent designation and explore the career opportunities that await you after passing your three-part EA exam. In addition to preparing taxes for individuals and businesses, EAs can represent people before the IRS, just like attorneys and CPAs. Many people who use the PassKey study guides have had no previous experience in preparing taxes, but go on to rewarding new professional careers.

STEP 2-Gather information

Gather more information before you launch into your studies. The IRS publishes basic information about becoming an EA on its website at www.irs.gov/Tax-Professionals/Enrolled-Agents. You'll also find valuable information about the exam itself on the Prometric testing website at www.prometric.com/see. Be sure to download the *Candidate Information Bulletin*, which takes you step-by-step through the registration and testing process.

STEP 3-Obtain a PTIN

A PTIN stands for "Preparer Tax Identification Number." Before you can register for your EA exam, you must obtain a PTIN, which is issued by the IRS.[5] The sign-up system can be found at www.irs.gov/ptin. You'll need to create an account, complete an on-line application, and pay a required fee.

STEP 4-Sign up with Prometric

Once you have your PTIN, you may register for your exam on the Prometric website. After creating an account and paying the required testing fee, you can complete the registration process by clicking on "Scheduling."

STEP 5-Schedule a time, date, and location

You'll be able to choose a test site and time and date that are convenient for you. Prometric has test centers in most major metropolitan areas of the United States, as well as certain other parts of the world. You may schedule as little as two days in advance—space permitting—through the website or by calling 800-306-3926 Monday through Friday. Be aware that the website and the phone line have different inventory of available times and dates, so you may want to check the other source if your preferred date is already full.

STEP 6-Adopt a study plan

Focus on one exam part at a time, and adopt a study plan that covers all the tax topics on the EA exam. You'll need to develop an individualized study program based on your current

---

[5] Foreign-based candidates do not need a PTIN to register to take the exam.

level of tax knowledge. For those without prior tax experience, a good rule of thumb is to study at least 60 hours for each of the three exam sections, committing at least 15 hours per week. Start well in advance of the exam date.

STEP 7-Get plenty of rest, exercise, and good nutrition

Get plenty of rest, exercise, and good nutrition prior to the EA exam. You'll want to be at your best on exam day.

STEP 8-Test day has arrived!

On test day, make sure you remember your government-issued ID and arrive early at the test site. Prometric advises to arrive at least 30 minutes before your scheduled examination time. If you miss your appointment and are not allowed to test, you'll forfeit your exam fee and have to pay for a new appointment.

STEP 9-During the exam

This is when your hard work finally pays off. Focus, don't worry if you don't know every question, but make sure you allocate your time appropriately. Give your best answer to every question. All questions left blank will be marked as wrong.

Step 10-Congratulations. You passed!

After celebrating your success, you need to apply for your EA designation. The quickest way is by filling out Form 23, *Application for Enrollment to Practice Before the Internal Revenue Service*, directly on the IRS website. Once your application is approved, you'll be issued a Treasury card, and you'll be official—a brand new enrolled agent!

Essential Tax Figures for Tax Year 2012
Part One: Individuals

Here is a quick summary of all the tax figures for the current exam cycle:

Income Tax Return Filing Deadline: April 15, 2013

The Personal Exemption: $3,800 (up $100 from 2011)
*Note: In the 2012 tax year, the personal exemption and itemized deductions do not phase out at higher income levels.

Social Security Taxable Wage Base: $110,100

Medicare Taxable Wage Base: No limit

Standard Deduction Amounts:
- Married filing jointly (or qualifying widow/widower) $11,900
- Head of household $8,700
- Single $5,950
- Married filing separately $5,950
- Dependents $950
- Blind taxpayers and senior citizens (over 65) qualify for an increased standard deduction. Additional amounts for 2012 per taxpayer are:
  - $1,450 for single or head of household
  - $1,150 for married filing jointly, married filing separately, or qualifying widow

Retirement Plan Contribution Limits: Traditional or Roth IRA: $5,000 ($6,000 for taxpayers age 50 or over by the end of 2012.)

Roth IRA Phase-out AGI limits:
- Married filing jointly: $173,000 to $183,000
- Single or head of household: $110,000 to $125,000
- Married filing separately: $0 to $10,000

Earned Income Credit (EIC) Income Thresholds:
Earned income and adjusted gross income must each be less than:
- $45,060 ($50,270 MFJ) with three or more qualifying children
- $41,952 ($47,162 MFJ) with two qualifying children
- $36,920 ($42,130 MFJ) with one qualifying child
- $13,980 ($19,190 MFJ) with no qualifying children

Maximum EIC credit (for all taxpayers except MFS):
- $5,891 with three or more qualifying children
- $5,236 with two qualifying children
- $3,169 with one qualifying child
- $475 with no qualifying children

Investment income must be $3,200 or less for the year in order to qualify for the EIC.

Alternative Minimum Tax Exemption (AMT):
- $78,750 (MFJ or QW)
- $50,600 (Single or HOH)
- $39,375 (MFS)

Estate and Gift Tax Exclusion Amount: $5,120,000 (up from $5 million in 2011)

Gift Tax Annual Exclusion: $13,000

Non-Citizen Marital Threshold for Gift Tax: $139,000

Kiddie Tax Unearned Income Threshold: $1,900

"Nanny Tax" Threshold: $1,800

Foreign Earned Income Exclusion: $95,100

Child Tax Credit: $1,000 per child

Adoption Credit: $12,650 nonrefundable (credit was refundable in 2011)

Education Credits and Deductions:
- Hope/American Opportunity Credit: maximum of $2,500 per student
- Lifetime Learning Credit: maximum of $2,000 per return
- Tuition and fees deduction: maximum of $4,000
- Student loan interest deduction: maximum of $2,500

Mileage Rates:
- Business miles: 55.5¢ per mile
- Medical or moving miles: 23¢ per mile
- Charitable purposes: 14¢ per mile

Section 179 Expense: $500,000 of qualified expenditures/phase-out at $2 million

New 2012 Tax Law Affecting Individuals

The American Taxpayer Relief Act of 2012 extended a majority of tax cuts already in place. The legislation also made permanent certain other tax provisions that had been temporary. The major changes are as follows:

- **Alternative minimum tax:** The exemption amount on the AMT on individuals is permanently indexed for inflation starting in 2013. The AMT exemption amounts were increased for 2012.
- **Marriage penalty relief:** The increased size of the 15% bracket and the increased standard deduction for married taxpayers filing jointly has been made permanent.
- **Personal exemption phase-out:** This repeals the personal exemption phase-out and the limitation on itemized deductions for taxpayers with adjusted gross income at or below a certain threshold.
- **Reduced rates on capital gains and dividends:** The current maximum tax rate of 15% (or 0% for those below the 25% bracket) has been extended permanently, except that the rate will be 20% for taxpayers above a certain threshold starting in 2013.
- **Child and Dependent Care Credit:** The rules allowing the credit to be calculated based on up to $3,000 for one dependent or up to $6,000 for one has been made permanent.
- **Child Tax Credit:** The $1,000 credit per child was made permanent.
- **American Opportunity Credit:** This credit was extended through 2017.
- **Adoption Tax Credit:** This credit was made permanent. It is nonrefundable for tax year 2012.
- **Education tax relief:** An increase in the annual contribution to Coverdell Education Savings Accounts; an extension of the exclusion for employer-provided educational assistance; and an increase in the phaseout ranges for the student loan interest deduction have all been made permanent.
- **Estate and gift tax:** The estate tax portability election has been made permanent. This is when the surviving spouse's exemption amount is increased by the deceased spouse's unused exemption amount.

Individual provisions extended retroactively to 2012 include the following:

Deduction for certain teacher expenses; exclusion from gross income of discharge of qualified principal residence indebtedness; deduction for mortgage insurance; parity for exclusion from income for employer-provided mass transit and parking benefits; deduction of state and local general sales taxes; above-the-line deduction for qualified tuition and related expenses; the credit for energy-efficient existing homes; the credit for two-or-three-wheeled plug-in electric vehicles; and the credit for installing alternative vehicle refueling property in a main home; and in some cases, the American Taxpayer Relief Act of 2012 Act modified certain provisions of these items.

Also for 2012:

- Schedule 8812 is now also used for the Additional Child Tax Credit, replacing Form 8812.
- Taxpayers who converted amounts to a Roth IRA or designated Roth account in 2010 must report half of the resulting taxable income on their 2012 returns, unless they reported the full amount on their 2011 returns.
- An employee's W-2 must now report both the employer and employee portion of health care insurance costs for 2012.

Essential Tax Figures for 2012

Part Two: Businesses

Here is a quick summary of key tax figures related to business for the current exam cycle:

2012 Social Security Taxable Wage Base: $110,100. In 2012, the Social Security portion of the FICA tax for employees only is reduced from 6.2% to 4.2%. The employer's portion remains 6.2%. The Social Security tax rate for self-employed persons is similarly reduced, from 12.4% to 10.4%. Therefore, the tax rate for self-employment income earned in calendar year 2012 is 13.3% (10.4% for Social Security and 2.9% for Medicare).

2012 Medicare Taxable Wage Base: No limit.

Section 179 Expense: $500,000 of qualified expenditures/phase-out at $2 million; up to $250,000 in expense for qualified leasehold improvement, restaurant, and retail improvement property.

Bonus Depreciation: Up to 50% for new assets placed in service in 2012.

Mileage Rates:
- Business miles: 55.5¢ per mile
- Medical or moving miles: 23¢ per mile
- Charitable purposes: 14¢ per mile

Exclusion for Employer-Provided Mass Transit:
- $240 per month for parking benefits
- $240 per month in combined highway vehicle transportation and transit passes (increased retroactively for 2012)

Employer Contribution Limits to 401(k) Participant's Plan: $17,000 maximum.
Estate and Gift Tax Exclusion Amount: $5,120,000 (up from $5 million in 2011).
Gift Tax Annual Exclusion: $13,000

New Rules for Businesses: 2012 Tax Year

S Corporation Built-In Gains Tax (BIG tax): The American Taxpayer Relief Act of 2012 extends the reduced five-year recognition period to sales occurring in 2012 and 2013. The Act also provides that gain on installment sales during these years are subject to the five-year recognition period when it is recognized in future years.

Business Credits: The American Taxpayer Relief Act of 2012 extends and in some cases modifies many credits, including the following:

- Research and Experimentation Credit
- Work Opportunity Tax Credit (expanded target groups that qualify for 2012)
- Employer Credit for Differential Military Pay
- Indian Employment Tax Credit
- New Markets Tax Credit
- Empowerment Zone Employment Credit
- Low Income Housing Credit
- Credit for Alternative Fuel Vehicle Refueling Property
- Credit for Construction of New Energy Efficient Homes
- Credit for Manufacture of Energy Efficient Appliances
- Various credits for producing cellulosic biofuel, alternative fuel mixtures, and wind electricity

Other Extensions Under the Taxpayer Relief Act:
- Enhanced charitable deduction for contributions of food inventory
- Special rules allowing U.S. film and television producers to expense up to $15 million of production costs incurred in the United States ($20 million in economically depressed areas in the U.S.)

Estate and Gift Tax: The estate tax portability election has been made permanent. This is when the surviving spouse's exemption amount is increased by the deceased spouse's unused exemption amount. The single lifetime exemption extending unification of the estate and gift tax has been made permanent.

Other 2012 Business-Related Tax Changes

1. **W-2s:** An employee's W-2 must now report both the employer and employee portion of health care insurance costs for 2012.
2. **Farmers' Tax Deadline:** Because of delays created by the late tax changes of the fiscal cliff legislation, the IRS will waive penalties for farmers and fishermen who miss the March 1, 2013 tax filing deadline, so long as they file their returns and pay the tax due by April 15.
3. **Cell Phones:** The value of employer-provided cell phones has been ruled as excludable as a de minimis fringe benefit, if provided primarily for noncompensatory business reasons.
4. **Nonprofit Relief:** Small organizations that lost their tax-exempt status by failing to file e-postcards were eligible for transitional relief in 2012, including possible retroactive reinstatement and a reduced user fee.
5. **Reporting of Nontaxable Exchanges of Property:** Both the corporation and certain stockholders involved in a nontaxable exchange of property for stock must attach to their income tax returns a complete statement of all facts pertinent to the exchange. The reporting requirement now applies to stockholders that own 5% or more of a public company or 1% or more of a privately held company.

New Tax Preparer Information For 2012
Part Three: Representation

RTRP Program Suspended: On January 18, 2013, the U.S. District Court for the District of Columbia directed the IRS to stop enforcing the requirements for registered tax return preparers. In accordance with this order, RTRPs are not required to complete competency testing or secure continuing education. This ruling does not affect the practice requirements for other enrolled practitioners (CPAs, attorneys, enrolled agents, enrolled retirement plan agents, or enrolled actuaries). The IRS has stated that they plan to appeal this decision.[6]

Mandatory PTIN Requirement: Beginning in 2011 all paid preparers were required to have a Preparer Tax Identification Number (PTIN) *before* preparing returns. The mandatory PTIN requirement was suspended for a short time due to pending litigation, and was reinstated February 1, 2013.

PTIN Helpline: PTIN applicants can obtain (and renew) their PTIN online using the IRS website (www.irs.gov/ptin). The fee is $64.25. The PTIN helpline is 1-877-613-7846.

OPR Mailbox Suspended: Effective in 2012, the former OPR e-mail address is no longer in operation. This is because many preparers were receiving fraudulent e-mails that purported to be from the Office of Professional Responsibility.

Reporting Preparer Violations: Starting in 2012, taxpayers are able to report tax preparers in violation of Circular 230 guidelines using the new Form 14157, *Complaint: Tax Return Preparer*. This form is appropriate for reporting violations of both enrolled and unenrolled preparers.

TAC Refusing Bulk Returns: Starting in 2012, IRS offices will no longer accept bulk returns for processing. The IRS wants to eliminate the practice of tax preparers dropping off completed returns for processing, especially during peak operating periods. However, TACs will still accept returns with imminent statute implications, with remittances or other time-sensitive situations.

ITIN/SSN Mismatch: For tax year 2012, it is now possible to e-file returns with an ITIN/SSN mismatch. The IRS made this change on June 22, 2012.

ITIN Application Requirements Changed: Starting in 2012, Forms W-7, *Application for IRS Individual Taxpayer Identification Number*, must include **original** documentation such as passports and birth certificates. Notarized copies or photocopies of documentation are no longer sufficient.

Stockpiling: The IRS announced on January 4, 2013 that the stockpiling of 2012 returns is allowed. The Internal Revenue Service temporarily lifted its prohibition against stockpiling tax returns before e-filing due to the late tax law changes.[7]

---

[6] Sabina Loving, et al. vs. Internal Revenue Service.
[7] The American Taxpayer Relief Act of 2012, better known as the "fiscal cliff" legislation.

Part 1: Individuals

Tammy the Tax Lady®

Let me get this straight... you only accept cash, and your official job description is "underground pharmaceutical rep?"

Unit 1: Tax Returns for Individuals

> **More Reading:**
> Publication 17, *Your Federal Income Tax*
> Publication 501, *Exemptions, Standard Deduction, and Filing Information*
> Publication 519, *U.S. Tax Guide for Aliens*
> Publication 552, *Recordkeeping for Individuals*

Overview of EA Exam Part 1: Individuals

For Part 1 of the enrolled agent exam, you will be expected to know a broad range of information related to preparing tax returns for individual taxpayers. This information includes the basics of filing status, requirements, and due dates; deductions, credits, and adjustments to income; items that affect future returns such as carryover and operating losses; taxable and nontaxable income; retirement income; determining the basis of property; figuring capital gains and losses; rental income; estate and gift taxes, and much more.

Although the focus is on individual taxes, some of the material concerns issues that affect self-employed business persons and deal with business-related income, so there is a degree of overlap with Part 2 of the EA exam: Businesses.

We begin with the preliminary work tax preparers are expected to do in order to prepare accurate tax returns.

Taxpayer Biographical Information

Tax preparers are expected to collect essential biographical information from their clients. The following information is required in order to prepare an accurate tax return:

- Legal name
- Date of birth
- Marital status
- Nationality
- Dependents
- Social Security Number or other acceptable Taxpayer Identification Number

Taxpayer biographical information is considered highly sensitive and confidential. Wrongful disclosure of taxpayer information is a criminal offense.

Use of Prior Years' Returns for Comparison

When enrolled agents and other tax professionals prepare tax returns for clients, they are expected to perform due diligence[8] in collecting, verifying, and gathering taxpayer data. EAs are also expected to review prior year tax returns for compliance, accuracy, and completeness.

A tax professional is required by law to notify a taxpayer of an error on his tax return and to notify the taxpayer of the consequences of *not* correcting the error. However, a tax professional is not required to actually correct the error.

---

[8] The responsibilities of tax preparers are dealt with extensively in Part 3 of the EA exam: Representation, Practices, and Procedures, as detailed in the study guide for PassKey EA Review Part 3.

The use of prior year returns can help prevent major mathematical errors and alert a tax preparer to issues specific to a particular client. In addition, by reviewing a prior year return, a tax preparer can determine whether there are items that affect the current year's return.

Example: Janice is an EA with a new client named Terrence who has always prepared his own tax returns. When Terrence makes his tax interview appointment, Janice tells him to bring his prior year Form 1040. At the appointment, Janice notices that Terrence made a large error when calculating his mortgage interest deduction. Janice is required to notify Terrence of the error, as well as the consequences of not correcting the error. She encourages him to file an amended tax return in order to fix the mistake. Terrence declines because he does not want to pay for an amended tax return. Janice notes in her work papers that Terrence has declined to amend his return, even though she has warned him of the consequences. She has therefore fulfilled her professional obligation to notify the taxpayer of the prior year error.

Recordkeeping for Individuals

Whether a professional tax return preparer is involved or not, a taxpayer is responsible for keeping copies of tax returns and maintaining other records for as long as they may be needed for the "administration of any provision of the Internal Revenue Code."[9] The IRS does not require taxpayers to keep records in any particular way, but says individuals need good records to:

- **Identify sources of income:** Taxpayers receive money or property from a variety of sources. Individuals need this information to separate business from nonbusiness income and taxable from nontaxable income.
- **Keep track of expenses:** Tracking expenses as they occur helps taxpayers identify expenses that can be used to claim deductions.
- **Keep track of the basis of property:** Taxpayers need to retain records showing the original cost or other basis of property they own and any improvements made to them.
- **Prepare tax returns:** Good records help taxpayers, and their preparers, file accurate returns more quickly.
- **Support items reported on tax returns:** If the IRS has questions about items on a return, a taxpayer should have the records to substantiate those items.

Even if a tax professional prepares an individual's tax return, the taxpayer is ultimately responsible for the accuracy of its contents.

The IRS allows taxpayers to maintain records in any way that will help determine the correct tax. A checkbook can serve as a record of income and expenses, along with documents such as receipts and sales slips to help prove particular deductions.

Electronic records are acceptable, so long as a taxpayer can reproduce the records in a legible and readable format. Basic records that everyone should keep include items related to:

- **Income:** Forms W-2, Forms 1099, bank statements, brokerage statements, Forms K-1.

---

[9] IRS Publication 552, *Recordkeeping for Individuals*.

- **Expenses:** Sales slips, invoices, receipts, canceled checks or other proof of payment, written communications from qualified charities, Forms 1098 to support mortgage interest and real estate taxes paid.
- **Home:** Closing statements, purchase and sales invoices, proof of payment, insurance records, receipts for improvement costs.
- **Investments:** Brokerage statements, mutual fund statements, Forms 1099, Forms 2439.

Taxpayers should keep copies of tax returns and records until the statute of limitations runs out for their return.[10]

Taxpayer Identification Numbers (TINs)

IRS regulations require that each individual listed on a federal income tax return has a valid Taxpayer Identification Number (TIN).[11] That includes the taxpayer, his or her spouse (if married), and any dependents.

The types of TINs are:

- Social Security Number (SSN)
- Individual Taxpayer Identification Number (ITIN)
- Adoption Taxpayer Identification Number (ATIN)

Although it is not required, the IRS calls it a "best practice"[12] for a preparer to ask to see a Social Security card for each person who will be listed on the return.

Taxpayers who cannot obtain an SSN must apply for an ITIN if they file a U.S. tax return or are listed on a tax return as a spouse or dependent. These taxpayers must file Form W-7, *Application for Individual Taxpayer Identification Number*, and supply documentation that will establish foreign status and true identity.

The issuance of an ITIN also does not confirm an individual's immigration status or give him the right to work in the United States.

> **Example:** Kamala is a U.S. citizen and has a Social Security Number. In January 2012, Kamala marries José Martinez, a citizen of Mexico. José has one daughter from a prior marriage. Kamala decides to file jointly with José in 2012 and also claim her stepdaughter as a dependent. In order to file jointly and claim the child, they must request ITINs for José and his daughter.

An ITIN is also required when a soldier marries a foreign spouse and brings him or her to the United States. In order to file a joint return, the couple would need to request an ITIN for the foreign spouse. Taxpayers with an ITIN are not eligible to receive Social Security benefits or the Earned Income Credit. In the case of adopted children who do not yet have an SSN, a taxpayer may request an Adoption Taxpayer Identification Number (ATIN) from the IRS if he is adopting a child *and* meets all of the following qualifications:

- The child is placed in the taxpayer's home for legal adoption.

---

[10] Unit 2, *Tax Rates, Estimates, and Due Dates,* has specific details related to statute of limitations for tax returns and claims for refunds.

[11] The Preparer Tax Identification Number (PTIN) is also an identifying number, but it is used exclusively by tax preparers to identify themselves on a taxpayer's return. It is not an identifying number for taxpayer use.

[12] http://www.eitc.irs.gov/rptoolkit/faqs/duediligence/.

- The adoption is a domestic adoption or the adoption is a legal foreign adoption and the child has a permanent resident alien card or certificate of citizenship.
- The taxpayer cannot obtain the child's existing SSN even though he has made a reasonable attempt to obtain it from the birth parents, the placement agency, and other persons.
- The taxpayer cannot obtain an SSN for other reasons, such as the adoption not yet being final.

The taxpayer needs the ATIN to claim the adopted child as a dependent or to be eligible for a child care credit, but an ATIN cannot be used to obtain the Earned Income Credit.

There is *one* narrow exception to the rule that requires all dependents to have an SSN, ITIN, or ATIN. If a child is born *and* dies within the same tax year and is not granted an SSN, the taxpayer may still claim that child as a dependent.

The tax return must be filed on paper and the birth and death certificate attached to the return. The birth certificate must show that the child was born alive, as a stillborn infant does not qualify. The taxpayer enters "DIED" in the space for the dependent's Social Security Number on the tax return.

Example: Alice gave birth to a son on October 1, 2012. The baby had health problems and died within three days. He was issued a death certificate and a birth certificate, but not a Social Security Number. Alice may claim her son as a qualifying child in 2012, even though he only lived a short time.

Filing Requirements and Thresholds

Not every person is required to file a tax return. A taxpayer is required to file a tax return if his 2012 income exceeds the *combined total* of the standard deduction and personal exemption amounts.[13] Sometimes, a taxpayer is required to file even though none of his income is taxable. To determine whether a person should file a return, a tax preparer must check the taxpayer's Form W-2, and/or Form(s) 1099.

There are different requirements for taxpayers who are self-employed. Generally, a taxpayer is required to file a tax return if he has self-employment earnings of $400 or more. In order to determine whether someone must file a tax return, the tax practitioner must also determine if:

- The person can be claimed as a dependent on another taxpayer's return
- Special taxes might be owed on different types of income
- Some of the taxpayer's income is excludable (or exempt)

The filing requirements listed below apply mainly to wage earners. There will be numerous examples later in the unit in order to demonstrate different filing scenarios. In the case of an individual taxpayer, filing requirements vary based on gross income, age, and filing status.

---

[13] See the tables at the beginning of the book for the standard deduction and personal exemption amounts.

2012 Filing Requirements for Most Taxpayers

Here are the 2012 filing requirement thresholds:

- Single: $9,750
- Single, 65 or over: $11,200
- Head of household (HOH): $12,500
- Head of household, 65 or over: $13,950
- Married filing jointly (MFJ): $19,500
    - *Over 65, one spouse (MFJ): $20,650
    - *Over 65, both spouses (MFJ): $21,800
- Married filing separately (MFS): $3,800 (any age)
- Qualifying widow/widower with dependent child: $15,700
    - *65 or over (QW): $16,850[14]

Example: Laurel is 36 years old, single, and her gross income was $17,500 last year. She does not have any children. She is required to file a tax return status since her income was over $9,750. She will use the single filing status.
Example: Arlene and Marvin are married and plan to file jointly. Frances is 64 and had a gross income of $12,225 for the tax year. Marvin is 66 and his gross income was $6,500 for the year. Since their combined gross income was $18,725, they are not required to file a tax return. The filing requirement threshold for joint filers when one spouse is over 65 is $20,650 in 2012.
Example: Wallace is 67 years old and single. No one can claim him as a dependent. His gross income was $11,900 during the tax year. Based only on this information, Wallace is required to file a return because his gross income is over the filing threshold, ($11,200 for 2012) for single taxpayers who are over 65.
Example: Rita is 66 years old, married, and had $9,500 of wage income in 2012. Her husband, Roger, also 66, had $10,000 in wage income. They have no dependents. Normally, Roger and Rita would not have a filing requirement because their gross income is under the filing threshold for MFJ taxpayers over 65. However, Rita has decided that she wants to file separately from her husband in 2012. She is therefore required to file a tax return because the filing threshold for MFS is $3,800. Roger must also file a tax return, because his filing status is also MFS by default. Roger cannot choose to file jointly with his wife unless she agrees, since both spouses are required to sign a joint return.

There are special rules for dependents with taxable income, self-employed persons, and nonresident aliens.

A dependent is required to file when he has *any* of the following:

- Unearned income[15] of *more than* $950 (such as interest income)
- Earned income of *more than* $5,950 (such as wages)
- Gross income of *more than* the larger of:
    - $950, or

---

[14] Detailed information about the various filing statuses and who may use them can be found in Unit 3.

[15] Unearned income is all income that is not earned, such as prizes, inheritances, interest income, and dividends. Earned income is money that is earned by the taxpayer, such as wages or self-employment income.

- Earned income (up to $5,650) plus $300

Example: Cesar is a 16-year-old high school student who is claimed as a dependent on his parents' tax return. He works as a pizza delivery boy ten hours a week and earned $3,200 in wages in 2012. He also had $1,100 of interest income from a certificate of deposit that his grandmother gave him. Cesar is required to file a tax return because his unearned income exceeds $950.

Example: Taryn is 15 and is claimed as a dependent on her mother's tax return. Taryn babysat full-time over the summer, worked at an ice cream parlor during the school year, and earned a total of $6,100. She had no other income. Taryn must file a tax return because her total earned income is more than $5,950.

Example: Marc is 20, single, and a full-time college student. Marc's parents claim him on their joint tax return. Marc received $200 in interest income and earned $2,750 in wages from a part-time job. Marc does not have to file a tax return because his total income of $2,950 is below the filing threshold for dependents.

Generally, if a dependent child who must file a tax return cannot file it for any reason, such as age, then the parent or other legal guardian must file it on the child's behalf. Not all income is taxable. There are many types of income that are *reportable*, but not taxable, to the recipient. Even if a taxpayer is not legally required to file a tax return, he should—if eligible to receive a refund. Taxpayers should still file tax returns if any of the following are true:

- They had income tax withheld from their pay.
- They made estimated tax payments or had a prior year overpayment.
- They qualify for the Earned Income Credit.
- They qualify for any other refundable tax credits.

Example: Holly is single, has a four-year-old child, and qualifies for head of household filing status. In 2012, she earns $8,500 in wages and $700 in self-employment income from cleaning houses on the side. Although Holly makes less than the filing threshold for head of household filing status, she is required to file a tax return because her self-employment earnings exceed $400. Even if Holly did not have self-employment earnings, she should still file a tax return, because she likely qualifies for the Earned Income Credit. The EIC is a refundable credit for low income wage earners, which could give Holly a nice refund.

Other Odd Filing Requirement Situations

Sometimes a taxpayer is required to file a tax return when the gross income threshold is not met, such as in the previous example of self-employment earnings of $400 or more. Other examples include the following:

- Church employees who are *exempt* from employers' Social Security and Medicare taxes and have wages of $108.28 or more. (Note: This odd exception has shown up on prior exams.)
- If the taxpayer owes Social Security tax or Medicare tax on tips not reported to his employer.
- If the taxpayer must pay the alternative minimum tax.

- If the taxpayer owes additional tax on a qualified plan, including an IRA, health savings account, or other tax-favored health plan.
- If the taxpayer received Medicare Advantage MSA or health savings account distributions.
- If the taxpayer owes household employment taxes for a household worker such as a nanny.
- If the taxpayer must recapture an education credit, investment credit, or other credit.

Basic Tax Forms for Individuals: A Summary

Form 1040EZ

Of the tax return forms, Form 1040EZ is the simplest. The one-page form is designed for single and joint filers with *no dependents*. It shows the taxpayer's filing status, income, adjusted gross income, standard deduction, taxable income, tax, Earned Income Credit, amount owed or refund, and signature. A taxpayer may use the 1040EZ if:

- Taxable income is below $100,000
- The filing status is single or married filing jointly
- The taxpayer is under age 65 and not blind
- The taxpayer is not claiming any dependents
- Interest income is $1,500 or less
- The taxpayer claims no adjustments to income or credits other than the Earned Income Credit.

Form 1040A

Form 1040A is a two-page form. Page one shows the filing status, exemptions, income, and adjusted gross income. Page two shows standard deduction, exemption amount, taxable income, tax, credits, payments, amount owed or refund, and signature.

Taxable income must be less than $100,000, and there can be no self-employment income. A taxpayer may not itemize deductions when using Form 1040A, and is limited to certain adjustments to income and credits.

Form 1040

This form is also called the "long form." It is a two-page form that contains all specialized entries for additional types of income, itemized deductions, and other taxes. If a taxpayer cannot use Form 1040EZ or Form 1040A, he must use Form 1040. Form 1040 is designed to report all types of income, deductions, and credits.

Among the most common reasons why taxpayers must use Form 1040 are:

- Their taxable income exceeds $100,000.
- They want to itemize their deductions. [16]
- They are reporting self-employment income.
- They are reporting income from the sale of property (such as the sale of stock or rental property).

---

[16] Remember that when a married couple chooses to file separately, if one spouse itemizes deductions, the other must do so as well, meaning they both must use Forms 1040.

Form 1040NR

This is the form used by nonresident aliens to report their U.S. source income. It is used by investors overseas, as well as nonresident taxpayers who earn money while in the U.S. The 1040NR is not used by U.S. citizens or U.S. residents.

Example: Cisco Ramos is a boxing champion, and a legal citizen and resident of Mexico. Cisco receives a non-immigrant visa in order to attend and participate in a boxing match in the United States, where he earns $500,000 for his appearance. After his appearance, he returns to Mexico. Cisco is not eligible for an SSN and must request an ITIN in order to report his U.S. income. Without the ITIN, Cisco would be subject to automatic backup withholding[17] on his U.S. earnings. Cisco's income is subject to a special treaty provision and his tax accountant reports his income and his tax on Form 1040NR.

Example: Yao Lee is a Chinese citizen. He has never been to the United States. Yao owns various U.S. investments, on which he earns dividends and capital gains income. He is not eligible for an SSN. In order to prevent backup withholding on his earnings, Yao requests an ITIN. His tax preparer files Form 1040NR every year to report Yao's U.S.-source income.

Nonresidents

A tax preparer is required to determine a taxpayer's residency in order to determine whether or not the taxpayer is considered a *resident* or *nonresident*.

For tax purposes, an alien is an individual who is not a U.S. citizen. Aliens are further classified as nonresident aliens and resident aliens. Tax preparers must determine a taxpayer's correct status because the two groups are taxed in different ways:

- Resident aliens are generally taxed on their worldwide income, the same as U.S. citizens.
- Nonresident aliens are taxed only on their income from sources within the United States and on certain income connected with the conduct of a trade or business in the U.S.

Residency for IRS purposes is not the same as legal immigration status. An individual may still be considered a U.S. resident for tax purposes based upon the *physical* time he spends in the United States, regardless of immigration status.

A nonresident can be someone who lives outside the U.S. and simply invests in U.S. property or stocks, and is therefore required to file a tax return in order to correctly report his earnings. Each year, thousands of nonresident aliens are gainfully employed in the United States. Thousands more own rental property or earn interest or dividends from U.S. investments, and are therefore required to file U.S. tax returns.

How to Determine Alien Tax Status

If the taxpayer is an alien, he is considered a *nonresident* for tax purposes *unless* he meets at least ONE of two tests:

1. The Green Card Test, or

2. The Substantial Presence Test.

---

[17] Backup withholding is when an entity is required to withhold certain amounts from a payment and remit the amounts to the IRS.

The Green Card Test

A taxpayer is considered a U.S. resident if he is a "lawful permanent resident" of the United States at any time during calendar year 2012. A taxpayer generally has this status if he is a lawful immigrant and has been issued an alien registration card, also known as a green card. An alien who has been present in the United States at *any time* during a calendar year as a lawful permanent resident may choose to be treated as a resident alien for the entire calendar year.[18]

The Substantial Presence Test

The substantial presence test is based on a calendar year. A taxpayer will be considered a U.S. resident for tax purposes only if he meets the substantial presence test for the calendar year. To meet this test, the taxpayer must be physically present in the United States on at least:

- 31 days during the current year (2012), and
- 183 days during the three-year period that includes the current year (2012) and the two years immediately before that, counting:

All the days he was present in the current year (2012), and

- 1/3 of the days he was present in the first year before the current year (2011), and
- 1/6 of the days he was present in the second year before the current year (2010).

Note: An individual who meets the requirements of the "substantial presence" test is, for tax purposes, a resident alien of the United States. This status applies even though the person may be an undocumented alien. Remember: Filing a tax return as a resident does **not affect** or alter immigration status.

There are numerous exceptions to the substantial presence test. Days in the United States are not counted if the alien taxpayer:

- Regularly commutes to work in the U.S. from a residence in Canada or Mexico.
- Is in the U.S. as a crew member of a foreign vessel.
- Is unable to leave the U.S. because of a medical condition that arose while in the United States.
- Is an exempt individual. Exempt individuals include aliens who are:
- Foreign government-related individuals who are in the U.S. temporarily, such as diplomats.
- A teacher or trainee on a temporary visa.
- A student on a temporary visa who does not intend to reside permanently in the U.S.

---

[18] In some cases, an alien taxpayer can choose to be treated as both a nonresident alien and a resident alien during the same tax year. This usually occurs in the year the person arrives or departs from the United States. If so, some taxpayers may elect to be treated as a dual-status alien for this taxable year and a resident alien for the next taxable year if they meet certain tests.

- A professional athlete in the U.S. to compete in a charitable sports event. These athletes exclude only the days in which they actually competed in the sports event, but do not exclude practice, travel, or promotional events.[19]

If the taxpayer does *not* meet either the green card test or the substantial presence test, then the taxpayer is considered a nonresident for tax purposes. Unlike U.S. citizens and U.S. residents, nonresident aliens are subject to U.S. income tax *only* on their U.S. source income.

Example: Juliana is a Brazilian citizen who was physically present in the United States for 15 days in each of the years 2010, 2011, and 2012. She is not a green card holder. Juliana earned $32,000 in 2012 as a Portuguese translator for the U.S. government. Since the total days she was present in the U.S. for the three-year period does not meet the substantial presence test, Juliana is not considered a resident for tax purposes for 2012 and her earnings are taxed as a nonresident. Juliana is required to file a nonresident tax return in 2012 (Form 1040NR, *U.S. Nonresident Alien Income Tax Return*). If she does not file a U.S. tax return, then income tax will be withheld at the highest rate. This is called backup withholding.[20]

---

*Special rule for nonresident spouses: Nonresident alien individuals who are *married* to U.S. citizens or green card holders may choose to be treated as resident aliens for income tax purposes.

Example: Lola and Bruno are married and both are nonresident aliens at the beginning of the year. In February, Bruno becomes a legal U.S. resident alien and obtains a green card and a Social Security Number. Lola and Bruno may both choose to be treated as resident aliens for tax purposes by attaching a statement to their joint return. Lola is not eligible for a Social Security Number, so she must apply for an Individual Tax Identification Number (ITIN). Lola and Bruno must file a joint return for the year they make the election, but they can file either joint or separate returns for later years.

Due Dates for Nonresident Aliens

Nonresident aliens who have income that is not subject to U.S. withholding are required to file a tax return by June 15, two months *after* the regular filing deadline for individuals.

However, nonresident employees (such as a nonresident alien who earns money while living or visiting the U.S.) who received wages that are subject to U.S. income tax withholding must file Form 1040NR by the due date.

---

[19] These exceptions may seem minor, but they have appeared on EA exams in the past.

[20] In most cases, a foreign person is subject to tax on his U.S. source income. Most types of U.S. source income received by a foreign person are subject to U.S. tax of 30%. A reduced rate, including exemption, may apply if there is a tax treaty between the foreign person's country of residence and the United States. Nonresidents who do not provide a TIN (either an SSN or ITIN) are generally subject to automatic backup withholding on their U.S. source income.

Unit 1: Questions

1. Generally, every taxpayer who files a tax return must use an identifying number. All of the following are Taxpayer Identification Numbers for IRS purposes except_____:

A. Social Security Number (SSN).
B. Adoption Taxpayer Identification Number (ATIN).
C. Individual Tax Identification Number (ITIN).
D. Preparer Tax Identification Number (PTIN).

The answer is D. A Preparer Tax Identification Number (PTIN) is used by preparers to identify themselves on a taxpayer's return. It is not an identifying number for taxpayer use. ###

2. Which of the following taxpayers is required to have an Individual Taxpayer Identification Number (ITIN)?

A. A nonresident alien with an SSN who moves outside the U.S.
B. A nonresident alien who must file a return and is not eligible for a valid SSN.
C. Anyone who does not have a Social Security Number.
D. All nonresident and resident aliens.

The answer is B. If a taxpayer must file a U.S. tax return or is listed on a tax return as a spouse or dependent and is not eligible for an SSN, he must apply for an ITIN. ###

3. Ray and Maggie are married, but he and his wife are filing MFS. Their combined income was $100,000. Ray earned $60,000 in wage income and plans to itemize his deductions. Maggie has $40,000 in self-employment income and has nothing to itemize. Which is the simplest form that Maggie can use for her tax return?

A. Form 1040.
B. Form 1040A.
C. Form 1040EZ.
D. Either Form 1040 or Form 1040A.

The answer is A. Maggie will be forced to file Form 1040 for two reasons: she had self-employment income and because Ray plans to itemize deductions. When a married couple files separate returns and one spouse chooses to itemize deductions, the other spouse cannot claim the standard deduction and therefore must itemize. If Maggie has no itemized deductions, then her deduction would be zero. ###

4. The issuance of an ITIN does not:

A. Entitle the recipient to Social Security benefits or the Earned Income Credit.
B. Create a presumption regarding the individual's immigration status.
C. Give the individual the right to work in the United States.
D. All of the above.

The answer is D. An ITIN is for reporting purposes only and does not entitle the taxpayer to the EIC or to Social Security benefits. An ITIN also does not create a presumption about the taxpayer's immigration or work status. ###

5. All of the following statements regarding the ATIN are correct except_____:

A. An ATIN may be used to claim the Earned Income Credit.
B. The ATIN may not be used to claim the Earned Income Credit.
C. An ATIN may be requested by a taxpayer who is unable to secure a Social Security Number for a child until his adoption is final.
D. An ATIN can be obtained even if an adoption has not been finalized.

The answer is A. An ATIN may not be used to claim the Earned Income Credit. If the taxpayer is unable to secure a Social Security Number for a child until the adoption is final, he may request an ATIN. ###

6. Steven and Rochelle had a child on December 2, 2012. The child only lived for an hour and died before midnight. Which of the following statements is true?

A. They may not claim the child as a dependent on their tax return, because the child did not live with them for the entire tax year.
B. They may not claim the child as a dependent on their tax return unless they obtain a Social Security Number for the child.
C. They may claim the child as a dependent on their tax return, even if they are unable to get a Social Security Number.
D. They may not claim the child as a dependent on their tax return for 2012, but they may do so for tax year 2013.

The answer is C. If a child is born and died in the same tax year, an SSN is not required in order to take the dependency exemption in that tax year. The tax return must be filed on paper, and the taxpayer must enter the word "DIED" in the space normally reserved for the SSN. ###

7. Helen, age 65, and Edward, age 72, were married in 2012. They have no dependents. Helen had gross income of $2,000 and Edward had gross income of $28,000 for the year. Edward wants to file jointly, but Helen wants to file separately. Which of the following statements is true?

A. Edward is required to file a tax return, using the MFS status. Helen is not required to file a return.
B. Edward may still file jointly with Helen and sign on her behalf, so long as he notifies her in writing.
C. Edward and Helen are both required to file tax returns, and they must both file MFS.
D. Edward and Helen may both file single.

The answer is A. Since Edward and Helen are married, they must either file jointly or separately. Since Helen does not agree to file jointly with Edward, Edward is forced to file MFS. Helen is not required to file a tax return because her gross income in 2012 was $2,000. The filing requirement threshold for married filing separately is $3,800 for any age. ###

8. Janet and Harry are married and file jointly. During the tax year, Janet turned 67 and Harry turned 66. Janet's gross income was $19,000, and Harry's gross income from self-employment was $620. Harry had no other income. Based on this information, which of the following statements is true?

A. Janet and Harry are not required to file a tax return.
B. Janet and Harry are required to file a tax return.
C. Only Janet is required to file a tax return.
D. Only Harry is required to file a tax return.

The answer is B. Janet and Harry must both file a tax return. Normally, Janet and Harry would not be required to file because their combined gross income was less than $21,800 in 2012, and they are both over 65 (this threshold applies to taxpayers who are 65 or over, both spouses). However, they are required to file a tax return because they file jointly, and Harry's self-employment income exceeds $400. ###

9. Trinity, age 22, is single and a full-time college student who is claimed as a dependent on her father's tax return. In 2012, Trinity earned $5,975 in wages from her part-time job as an administrative assistant. She has no other income. Is she required to file a tax return?

A. Yes, she is required to file a tax return.
B. No, she is not required to file a tax return.
C. Trinity is only required to file a tax return if she is a full-time student.
D. Trinity should file a return because she will receive a refund, but she is not required to file.

The answer is A. A single dependent whose earned income was more than $5,950 in 2012 must file a return. ###

10. What is the minimum amount of time taxpayers should normally keep the supporting documents for their tax returns?

A. Five years.
B. Three years.
C. Two years.
D. One year.

The answer is B. Taxpayers should keep the supporting documentation for their tax returns for at least three years from the date the return was filed, or two years from the date the tax was paid, whichever is later. This includes applicable worksheets and forms. ###

11. Clark and Christy are both age 34 and will be filing jointly. They have no dependents. Their combined income was $31,000, which included $35 in interest income. The remainder of their income was from wages. They want to take the standard deduction. Which is the simplest form that Clark and Christy can use for their tax return?

A. Form 1040.
B. Form 1040A.
C. Form 1040EZ.
D. Form 1040NR.

The answer is C. Clark and Christy have no dependents, their combined income was less than $100,000, and they do not plan to itemize. Their interest income was also less than $1,500, so they may use Form 1040EZ to file their tax return. ###

12. Cynthia is divorced and files as head of household. She has two children she will claim as dependents. She works as a secretary and earned $35,000 in wages for the tax year. She plans to itemize her deductions. Which tax form should Cynthia use?

A. Form 1040.
B. Form 1040A.
C. Form 1040EZ.
D. Form 1040NR.

The answer is A. Since Cynthia plans to itemize her deductions, she must file Form 1040. ###

13. A taxpayer who claims a dependent can use any form except _____.

A. Form 1040.
B. Form 1040A.
C. Form 1040EZ.
D. None of the above. A taxpayer who is claiming a dependent can use any of these forms.

The answer is C. A taxpayer who is claiming a dependent cannot use Form 1040EZ. ###

14. Munir is a citizen of Pakistan who is granted a green card and comes to the U.S. to work as an engineer. Munir arrives in the U.S. on November 1, 2012. He earns $26,000 in U.S. wages in November and December. Which of the following is true?

A. Munir is not required to file a U.S. tax return.
B. Munir is required to file a U.S. tax return, and he must file using Form 1040NR.
C. Munir is required to file a U.S. tax return, and he may file using Form 1040.
D. Munir is not required to file a U.S. tax return in 2012, but he will be required to file a return in 2013.

The answer is C. Munir is required to file a U.S. tax return in 2012, and he may file using Form 1040. Munir is a green card holder, and therefore he may choose to be treated as a U.S. resident for tax purposes, regardless of how much time he has been present in the United States. An alien who has been present in the United States at any time during a calendar year as a "lawful permanent resident" may choose to be treated as a resident alien for the entire calendar year. As a resident alien, Munir will be taxed on income from worldwide sources, including any income he earned while he was in Pakistan. ###

15. A person who is not required to file a tax return should still file a return for any of the following reasons except to _____ .

A. Report self-employment net earnings of $400 or more.
B. Claim a refund of withheld taxes.
C. Claim the Earned Income Credit.
D. Claim the Additional Child Tax Credit.

The answer is A. Even if the thresholds indicate that a return does not have to be filed, an individual who wants to claim a tax refund, the EIC, or the Additional Child Tax Credit should still file a return. A taxpayer with self-employment earnings of $400 or more is *required* to file a tax return. ###

16. Angela's husband, Enzo, has neither a green card nor a visa, and he does not have a tax home in another country. He was physically present in the United States for 150 days in each of the years 2010, 2011, and 2012. Is Enzo a resident alien under the substantial presence test?

A. Yes, he is a resident for tax purposes.
B. No, he is a nonresident for tax purposes.
C. Enzo is a nonresident for tax purposes, but he may elect to file as a resident with his spouse.
D. None of the above is correct.

The answer is A. Enzo is a resident for tax purposes. He was present in the United States a total of 225 days. He meets the substantial presence test and is considered a resident alien for tax purposes. The full 150 days are counted for 2012; 50 days for 2011 (1/3 of 150); and 25 days for 2010 (1/6 of 150). ###

17. In order to prepare an accurate return, a tax preparer needs all of the following biographical information about a client except _____:

A. Date of birth.
B. National status.
C. SSN or other TIN.
D. Occupation.

The answer is D. To prepare an accurate return, a tax preparer must gather biographical information including a client's legal name, date of birth, marital status, nationality, dependents, and SSN or other TIN. A preparer does not need to know a client's occupation. ###

18. Kerstin is a professional tennis player from Germany who travels around the world to play in tournaments. In 2012, she comes to the United States on the following dates:

May 3: Travel from Frankfurt to New York.
May 4-5: Practice for the tournament.
May 6: Promotional event for the tournament.
May 7-9: Play in the tournament that benefits the American Cancer Society.
May 10-11: Vacation in New York.
May 12: Travel from New York to Frankfurt.
Sept. 5: Travel from Frankfurt to Atlanta.
Sept. 6-7: Practice for the tournament.
Sept. 8: Play in the tournament that benefits the Arthritis Foundation.
Sept. 9-10: Fly to Miami and vacation.
Sept. 11: Fly from Miami to Frankfurt.

Kerstin receives no compensation from playing in either tournament. How many days must she count toward the substantial presence test in 2012?

A. 4.
B. 8.
C. 13.
D. 17.

The answer is C. Kerstin is an exempt individual under the substantial presence rules. However, she may only exclude the days she is actually playing in a charitable sports events, which means days devoted to traveling, practice, promotion, or leisure do not count. She is in the United States a total of 17 days, but only plays in charity tournaments for four days, meaning she must count 13 days toward the substantial presence test. ###

19. Malik and his wife, Stacey, are married and file jointly. In 2012, she earned $4,600 in wages before she became pregnant and had to quit her job due to complications. Malik worked as a bartender and earned $11,000 in wages for the year. He owes Social Security and Medicare tax on $2,500 in tip income he did not report to his employer. Do Malik and Stacey have to file a tax return?

A. No, because their gross income is below the threshold for MFJ.
B. Yes, because their gross income is above the threshold for MFJ.
C. Yes, because Malik owes Social Security and Medicare tax on his unreported tip income.
D. Stacey is not required to file, if Malik files separately and chooses not to report the tip income.

The answer is C. Even though their gross income is below the MFJ filing threshold of $19,500 for 2012, the couple must file a tax return because Malik owes Social Security and Medicare tax on his unreported tip income. (A taxpayer who fails to disclose tip income to his employer as required is also subject to IRS penalties.) ###

20. All of the following are required to file an income tax return except:

A. A taxpayer who owes household employment tax for a nanny.
B. A church employee who is exempt from payroll taxes and who earned $106 in wages in 2012.
C. A 74-year-old qualifying widower who earned $17,000 in 2012.
D. A single taxpayer who earned $6,500 in 2012 and who owes tax on a Health Savings Account.

The answer is B. Church employees who are exempt from Social Security and Medicare taxes and have wages of $108.28 or more for the year are required to file a tax return. In Answer "B," the church employee's wages were below that threshold. In all of the other answers, the taxpayer would be required to file a return. ###

21. Kylie is an 18-year-old senior in high school. She works as a grocery store bagger on weekends and earned $1,400 in 2012. She also received $1,000 for a winning scratch-off lottery ticket. Her parents claim her as a dependent on their tax return. Does Kylie have to file her own return?

A. Yes, because of the amount of her unearned income.
B. Yes, because of the amount of her unearned and earned income combined.
C. No, because her earned income is below the threshold for a dependent.
D. No, because it is illegal for a high school student to play the lottery.

The answer is A. Kylie has to file a tax return because of the amount of her unearned income: the $1,000 lottery prize. A dependent with unearned income of more than $950 is required to file a tax return. Her earned income—$1,400—was not high enough to trigger a filing requirement. In 2012, dependents with earned income of more than $5,950 are required to file.

Unit 2: Tax Rates, Estimates, and Due Dates

More Reading:
Publication 505, *Tax Withholding and Estimated Tax*
Tax Topic 556, *Alternative Minimum Tax*
Publication 594, *Understanding the Collection Process*
Publication 3, *Armed Forces' Tax Guide*

Tax Rates

An individual's income is taxed at progressive rates in the United States. The more taxable income a taxpayer has, the higher the percentage of that income he pays in taxes. The IRS groups individuals by their taxable income levels and places them into different tax rates, or "brackets." Each tax rate applies to a specific range of taxable income, which is income after various deductions have been subtracted.

In 2012, there are six tax brackets for individuals: 10%, 15%, 25%, 28%, 33%, and 35%. Each year, the IRS adjusts these income ranges for inflation and issues tax tables that show how much tax is owed for specific income levels depending upon a taxpayer's filing status.

For example, in 2012 a single taxpayer with $8,000 in taxable income would be in the 10% tax bracket. If he had $50,000 in taxable income, he would be in the 25% tax bracket, while a taxpayer with $400,000 in taxable income would be in the highest tax bracket of 35%.

However, this does not mean that taxpayers in the highest income ranges owe a full 35% of tax on all their taxable income. The *marginal tax rate* applies tax to any additional dollars of taxable income earned. The tax rate does not increase for a taxpayer's entire income, merely dollar for dollar for taxable income over a certain threshold.

> **Example:** Jamie is single and has $35,500 in taxable income for 2012. For the first $8,700 she is taxed at a 10% rate. From $8,701 to $35,350 she is taxed at a 15% rate. It is only for the remaining $149 in income (on $35,351 to $35,500) that she is taxed at a 25% rate.

Alternative Minimum Tax

Federal tax law gives special treatment to certain types of income and allows deductions and credits for certain types of expenses. Taxpayers who benefit from this special treatment may have to pay at least a minimum amount of tax through an additional alternative minimum tax (AMT). First enacted in 1969, the AMT was adopted by Congress in an attempt to ensure that individuals and corporations pay at least a minimum amount of tax.[21]

The AMT is the excess of the tentative minimum tax over the regular tax. Thus, the AMT is owed only if the tentative minimum tax is greater than the regular tax. The tentative minimum tax is calculated separately from the regular tax. In general, the tentative minimum tax is computed by:

---

[21] The American Taxpayer Relief Act retroactively increased the AMT exemption amounts for 2012. Lawmakers also created a permanent fix to the AMT, which has been modified 19 times since 1969. Going forward, the AMT will be indexed to inflation, meaning the income threshold for being subject to the AMT will rise automatically each year.

1. Starting with AGI less itemized deductions, or with AGI for taxpayers who are not claiming itemized deductions, for regular tax purposes,
2. Eliminating or reducing certain exclusions, deductions, and credits that are allowed in computing the regular tax, to derive alternative minimum taxable income (AMTI),
3. Subtracting the AMT exemption amount,
4. Multiplying the amount computed in (3) by the AMT rate, and
5. Subtracting the AMT Foreign Tax Credit.

When calculating the AMT using this formula, the following "tax preference items" must be included, many of which apply more to business taxpayers than to individuals: depletion, excess intangible drilling costs, interest on private activity bonds, accelerated depreciation on property placed in service before 1987, and exclusion of gain on qualified small business stock.

When figuring the AMT, an individual taxpayer cannot claim deductions for miscellaneous expenses; certain mortgages used to refinance other mortgages; for tax payments to state, local, or foreign governments; and for medical expenses except to the extent they exceed 10% of AGI (as opposed to the 7.5% floor under the regular income tax). Also, deductions for expenses are limited to net investment income.

For 2012, the AMT exemption amounts are as follows, and they are phased out at a rate of 25% when the alternative minimum tax income is within the indicated ranges:

Filing Status	AMT Exemption	Exemption Phase-out Range
MFJ or QW	$78,750	$150,000 to $465,000
MFS	$39,375	$75,000 to $232,500
Single or HOH	$50,600	$112,500 to $314,900

A credit may be available for alternative minimum tax paid in prior years that relates to certain of the items above that create special treatment for regular tax purposes. In general, a portion of the AMT paid in a given year and credit carried forward from earlier years can be used in the following year to the extent that the taxpayer's regular tax is greater than his tentative minimum tax. For example, if a taxpayer paid AMT in 2011, in 2012 he may be able to calculate a credit on Form 8801, *Credit for Prior Year Minimum Tax*, which can be used on Form 1040.

Due Dates and Extensions

The regular due date for individual tax returns is usually April 15; if April 15 falls on a Saturday, Sunday, or legal holiday, the due date will be delayed until the next business day. This year's due date is Monday, April 15, 2013.

If a taxpayer cannot file his tax return by the due date, he may request an extension by filing IRS Form 4868, *Application for Automatic Extension of Time to File*, which may be filed electronically. Extended individual tax returns are due by October 15, 2013.

An extension will grant a taxpayer an additional six months to file his individual tax return. An extension will give a taxpayer extra time to file his return, but it does not extend the time to pay any tax due.

A taxpayer will owe interest on any unpaid amount that is not paid by the filing deadline, plus a late payment penalty if he has not paid at least 90% of his total tax due by that date. Taxpayers are expected to estimate and pay the amount of tax due by the filing deadline.

The IRS will accept a postmark as proof of a timely-filed return. For example, if the tax return is postmarked on April 14 but does not arrive at the IRS Service Center until April 18, the IRS will accept the tax return as having been filed on time.

E-filed tax returns are also given an "electronic postmark" to indicate the day that they are transmitted. You should memorize the due dates for tax returns and extensions for the EA exam.

IRS Penalties in General

If a taxpayer does not file on time, he will face a *failure-to-file* penalty.

If a taxpayer does not pay on time, he will face a *failure-to-pay* penalty.

Penalties and Interest on Late Filing

An extension only grants a taxpayer additional time to file, not additional time to pay. Interest and penalties will continue to accrue on any unpaid balance until the taxpayer finally files his tax return and pays any amounts that are owed. There are two separate penalties:

- Failure-to-file penalty (the failure to file on time)
- Failure-to-pay penalty (the failure to pay on time)

Taxpayers may also be assessed interest on the delinquent amount due.

---

*Note: Penalties are tested on all three parts of the EA exam. Be sure you memorize the most common types of taxpayer and preparer penalties.

Failure to File

The failure-to-file penalty is much greater than the failure-to-pay penalty. The IRS recommends that even if a taxpayer cannot pay all the taxes he owes, he should still file his tax return on time. The penalty for late filing is usually 5% of the unpaid taxes for each month (or part of a month) that a return is late. This penalty will not exceed 25% of the unpaid tax on the return. The failure-to-file penalty is calculated based on the time from the due date of the return to the date the taxpayer actually files. This penalty is calculated on the amount due on the return, so if the taxpayer is due a refund or has no tax liability, then this penalty will not be assessed.[22]

However, if a taxpayer files his return more than 60 days after the due date (or extended due date), the *minimum* penalty is the smaller of:

- $135, or
- 100% of the unpaid tax.

Failure to Pay

If the taxpayer does not pay his taxes by the due date, he will have to pay a failure-to-pay penalty. This is 0.5% (½ of 1 percent) of the unpaid tax for each month after the due date that the taxes are not paid. This penalty will not exceed 25% of the unpaid tax.

---

[22] We are only talking about penalties for individual taxpayers at this point. The penalties for entities are different and will be covered in Part 2: Businesses.

If a taxpayer files a request for an extension of time to file and pays *at least* 90% of the actual tax liability by the original due date, he will not be faced with a failure-to-pay penalty if the remaining balance is paid by the *extended* due date.

If both of these penalties apply in any month, the 5% failure-to-file penalty is reduced by the failure-to-pay penalty.

A taxpayer will not be assessed either penalty if he can show that he failed to file or pay on time because of reasonable cause and not because of willful neglect.[23]

Interest is charged on any unpaid tax from the due date of the return until the date of payment. The interest rate is determined quarterly and is the federal short-term rate plus 3%, compounded daily.

Penalty	Dollar Amount
Failure to file	• 5% of unpaid balance per month, up to a maximum of 25%. • More than 60 days late, the smaller of $135 or 100% of the tax due on the return. • No penalty if the taxpayer is due a refund. • The failure-to-file penalty is reduced by the failure-to-pay penalty if both apply to the same tax return.
Failure to pay	• 0.5% of unpaid balance per month, up to a maximum of 25%. • 0.25% of the unpaid balance while an installment agreement is in place.

Estimated Tax Payments

The federal income tax is a "pay-as-you-go" tax. A taxpayer must pay taxes as he earns or receives income throughout the year. If a taxpayer earns income that is not subject to withholding, such as self-employment income, rents, and alimony), he will often be required to make estimated tax payments each quarter of the tax year. Estimated tax is used to pay not only income tax, but self-employment tax and alternative minimum tax as well. Taxes are generally not withheld from payments that are made to independent contractors (1099 income).

Taxes are withheld from wages, salaries, and pensions. Taxpayers can avoid making estimated tax payments by ensuring they have enough tax withheld from their income. A taxpayer must make estimated tax payments if:

- He expects to owe at least $1,000 in tax (after subtracting withholding and tax credits)
- He expects the total amount of withholding and tax credits to be less than the smaller of:
  - 100% of the tax shown on the taxpayer's prior year return
  - 90% of the tax shown on the taxpayer's current year return

A U.S. citizen or U.S. resident is not required to make estimated tax payments if he had zero tax liability in the prior year.[24]

---

[23] There are exceptions to the general deadlines for filing a return and paying tax. One exception is for armed forces personnel serving in a combat zone. The second is for citizens or resident aliens working abroad.

[24] This rule only applies to U.S. citizens or residents; it does not apply to nonresident aliens.

> **Example**: Cassius, who is single and 25 years old, was unemployed for most of 2011. He earned $2,700 in wages before he was laid off, and he received $1,500 in unemployment compensation afterward. He had no other income. Even though he had gross income of $4,200, he did not have to pay income tax because his gross income was less than the filing requirement. In 2012, Cassius began working as a carpenter, but made no estimated tax payments during the year. Even though he owed $3,000 in tax at the end of the year, Cassius does not owe the underpayment penalty for 2012 because he had zero tax liability in the prior year.

A taxpayer will not face an underpayment penalty if the total tax shown on his return (minus the amount paid through withholding) is less than $1,000. This safe harbor only applies to individual taxpayers and not to entities.

> **Example:** Dominique has a full-time job as a secretary. She also earns money part-time as a self-employed manicurist. In 2012, she did not make estimated payments. However, Dominique made sure to increase her withholding at her job in order to cover any amounts that she would have to pay on her self-employment earnings. When she files her tax return, she discovers that she owes $750. She will not owe an underpayment penalty, because the total tax shown on her return was less than $1,000.

Safe Harbor Rule for Estimated Payments

The majority of taxpayers who pay estimated tax rely on the "safe harbor rule" in order to avoid any potential penalties.

There will be no underpayment penalty if the taxpayer pays at least 90% of whatever the current year's tax bill turns out to be. Since it is often difficult to guess what a person or business will earn during the year, most taxpayers find it easier to use the safe harbor rule.

The first safe harbor applies to taxpayers whose adjusted gross income is $150,000 or less. The taxpayer will not be assessed penalties in 2012 if the taxpayer pays *at least* the amount of the tax liability on his previous year's tax return (the amount on line 60 of Form 1040 reduced by any tax credits).

> **Example:** Gerald earned $95,000 in 2011. His overall tax liability for the tax year was $8,200, after taking into account his deductions and credits. Although Gerald expects his income to increase in 2012, he will not be assessed a penalty for underpayment of estimated taxes so long as he pays at least $8,200 in estimated tax during the year.

> ***Note:** For high income taxpayers with adjusted gross income of over $150,000 ($75,000 if MFS), the safe harbor amount is 110% of the previous year's tax liability.

Estimated Payment Due Dates (Quarterly Payments)

The year is divided into four payment periods for estimated taxes, each with a specific payment due date. Taxpayers generally must have made their first estimated tax payment for the year by April 15.

If the due date falls on a Saturday, Sunday, or legal holiday, the due date is the next business day. If a payment is mailed, the date of the U.S. postmark is considered the date of payment.

First Payment Due: April 15
Second Payment Due: June 15
Third Payment Due: September 15
Fourth Payment Due: January 15 (of the following year)

Special Exception for Farmers and Fishermen

Farmers and fishermen are not required to pay estimated taxes throughout the year. Unlike other taxpayers, farmers and fishermen may choose to pay all their estimated tax in one installment.

Qualified farmers and fishermen only have one due date for estimated taxes (if they choose). They have two choices:

- They may pay all of their 2012 estimated taxes by January 15, 2013, or
- If they are able to file their 2012 tax return by March 1, 2013 and pay all the tax they owe, they do not need to make an estimated tax payment. They may file and pay their tax along with the return.[25]

Example #1: Jay is the self-employed owner of a commercial fishing vessel. One hundred percent of his income is from commercial fishing, so Jay is not required to pay quarterly estimated taxes. Jay's records are incomplete, so he asks his tax accountant to file an extension on his behalf. Since Jay is unable to file his tax return by March 1, 2013, his enrolled agent notifies Jay that he is required to pay his estimated taxes in a lump sum by January 15, 2013.

Example #2: Karla earns 100 percent of her income from growing organic strawberries. She is not required to pay quarterly estimated taxes. Karla filed her tax return on February 20, 2013 and enclosed a check for her entire balance due, which was $4,900. Since she filed before the March 1 deadline, she will not be subject to any penalty.

In order to qualify for this special treatment, the farmer or fisherman must have at least two-thirds of his total gross income from farming or fishing. For purposes of this rule, qualified "farming" income includes:

- Gross farming income from Schedule F, *Profit or Loss From Farming*
- Gross farming rental income
- Gains from the sale of livestock used for draft, breeding, sport, or dairy purposes
- Crop shares for the use of a farmer's land

Qualifying gross income from farming does not include:

- Gains from sales of farmland and/or depreciable farm equipment
- Income received from contract harvesting and hauling with workers and machines furnished by the taxpayer

*Note: Income from wages received as a farm employee is not considered farm income for purposes of this special estimated tax treatment.

---

[25] For the 2012 tax year, the IRS is waiving estimated tax penalties for farmers and fishermen who file by April 15, 2013. Since Congress did not finalize the tax rules for 2012 until early 2013, the IRS could not guarantee that common IRS forms that farmers use would be ready by March 1, so it extended the due date for avoiding the penalty.

> **Example:** Dennis owns a dairy farm and files a Schedule F showing 2012 farm income of $95,000. He also had $3,500 in interest income and $41,500 in rental income from an unrelated business. Dennis's total gross income for the year was $140,000 ($3,500 + $41,500 + $95,000). Dennis qualifies to use the special estimated tax rules for qualified farmers, since 67.9% (at least two-thirds) of his gross income is from farming ($95,000 ÷ $140,000 = .679).

Backup Withholding

Sometimes individuals will be subject to backup withholding. This is when an entity is required to withhold certain amounts from a payment and remit the amounts to the IRS. Most U.S. taxpayers are exempt from backup withholding. However, the IRS requires backup withholding if a taxpayer's name and Social Security Number on Form W-9, *Request for Taxpayer Identification Number and Certification*, does not match its records.

> **Example:** Heath owns a number of investments through the Top Finances Corporation. In 2012, the IRS notifies Top Finances that Heath's Social Security Number is incorrect. Top Finances notifies Heath by mail that the company needs his correct Social Security Number, or it will have to start automatic backup withholding on his investment income. Heath ignores the notice and never updates his SSN. Top Finances is forced to begin backup withholding on Heath's investment income.

The IRS will sometimes require mandatory backup withholding if a taxpayer has a delinquent tax debt, or if he fails to report all his interest, dividends, and other income. Payments that may be subject to backup withholding include interest, dividends, rents, and royalties, payments to independent contractors for services, and broker payments. The current backup withholding rate is 28% for all U.S. citizens and legal U.S. residents. Under the backup withholding rules, the business or bank must withhold on a payment if:

- The individual did not provide the payer with a valid Taxpayer Identification Number or Social Security Number.
- The IRS notified the payer that the TIN or SSN is incorrect.
- The IRS has notified the payer to start withholding on interest and dividends because the payee failed to report income in prior years.
- The payee failed to certify that it was not subject to backup withholding for underreporting of interest and dividends.

If a taxpayer wishes to change his withholding amounts from his wages, he must use Form W-4, *Employee's Withholding Allowance Certificate* and submit it to his employer, not to the IRS.

Oddball Situations: Exceptions to the Normal Deadlines

There are special rules that are favorable for taxpayers who live outside the United States. A taxpayer will be granted an automatic two-month extension to file **and pay any tax due** if the taxpayer is a U.S. citizen or legal U.S. resident, and

- The taxpayer is living outside the United States and his main place of business is outside the United States; or
- The taxpayer is on active military service duty outside the U.S.

Taxpayers Serving in a Combat Zone

Additionally, the deadline for filing a tax return, claim for refund, and deadline for tax owed will be automatically extended for any service member, Red Cross personnel, accredited correspondents, or contracted civilians serving in a combat zone. In fact, taxpayers serving in a combat zone have all of their tax deadlines suspended until they leave the combat zone.

> **Example:** Philip is a Marine who has been serving in a combat zone since March 1. He is entitled to an extension of time for filing and paying his federal income taxes. In addition, IRS deadlines for assessment and collections are suspended while Philip is serving in the combat zone, plus another 180 days after his last day in the combat zone. During this period, Philip will not be charged interest or penalties attributable to the extension period.

The deadline extensions also apply to spouses of armed services members serving in combat zones.

Statute of Limitations

Generally, the taxpayer must file a claim for a credit or refund within three years from the date the original return was filed or two years from the date the taxpayer paid the tax, whichever is later.[26]

There is no penalty for failure to file if the taxpayer is due a refund. However, the taxpayer may have many legal deductions that the IRS does not know about. In order to claim a refund and avoid possible collection action, a tax return must be filed. If the taxpayer does not file a claim for a refund within this three-year period, he usually will not be entitled to the refund.

> **Example:** Juan has not filed a tax return for a long time, and now he wants to file six years of delinquent tax returns: 2007 through 2012. Juan files the returns and realizes that he had refunds for each year. If Juan files all the back tax returns by April 15, 2013, he will receive the refunds for his 2009, 2010, 2011, and 2012 tax returns. His refunds for 2007 and 2008, however, have expired.

> **Example:** David made estimated tax payments of $1,000 and filed an extension to file his 2009 income tax return. When he filed his return on August 15, 2010, he paid an additional $200 tax due. He later finds an error on the return and files an amendment. Three years later, on August 15, 2013, David files an amended return and claims a refund of $700.

> **Example:** Aisha's 2009 tax return was due April 15, 2010. She filed it on March 20, 2010. In 2012, Aisha discovered that she missed a big deduction on her 2009 return. Now she wants to amend that return, expecting the correction to result in a large refund. If she gets it postmarked on or before April 15, 2013, it will be within the three-year limit and the return will be accepted. But if the IRS receives the amended 2009 return after that date, it will fall outside the three-year period and Aisha will not receive the refund.

The same statute of limitations applies on refunds being claimed on amended returns. In general, if a refund is expected on an amended return, taxpayers must file the return within three years from the due date of the original return, or within two years after the date they paid the tax, whichever is later.

---

[26] Section 6511 (three-year refund statute).

Special Cases (Extended Statute for Claiming Refunds)

In some cases, a request for a tax refund will be honored past the normal three-year deadline. These special cases are:

- A bad debt from a worthless security (up to **seven years** prior)
- A payment or accrual of foreign tax
- A net operating loss carryback
- A carryback of certain tax credits
- Exceptions for military personnel
- For taxpayers in presidentially declared disaster areas
- For taxpayers who have been affected by a "terroristic or military action"

Time periods for claiming a refund are also extended when a taxpayer is "financially disabled." This usually requires that the taxpayer be mentally or physically disabled to the point that he is unable to manage his financial affairs. If the taxpayer qualifies, he may file a refund after the three-year period of limitations.

Statute of Limitations for IRS Assessment

The IRS is required to assess tax or audit a taxpayer's return within three years after the return is filed.[27] If a taxpayer files his tax return late, then the IRS has the later of three years from:

- The due date of the return, or
- The date the return was actually filed.

If a taxpayer never files a return, the statute remains open. If a taxpayer files his return prior to the return deadline, the time is measured from the April 15 deadline.

The IRS has additional time—six years—to assess tax on a return if a "substantial understatement" is identified. A substantial understatement is defined as 25% or more of the income shown on the return.

There is an exception for outright fraud: If the taxpayer files a fraudulent tax return, the statute for IRS audit never expires. However, the burden of proof switches to the IRS in cases where the statute has expired.

Example: Caroline filed her 2009 tax return on February 27, 2010. The three-year statute period for an audit began April 15, 2010 (the filing deadline) and will stop on April 15, 2013. After that date, the IRS must be able to prove fraud or a substantial understatement of income in order to audit the tax return.

Statute of Limitations for IRS Collections

The statute of limitations for IRS collection is ten years.[28] However, the clock only starts ticking when the tax return is filed. The statute of limitations on a tax assessment begins on the day *after* the taxpayer files his tax return. So, if a taxpayer never files a return, the IRS can attempt to collect indefinitely. In other words, there is no statute of limitations for assessing and collecting tax if no return has been filed.

---

[27] Internal Revenue Code, section 6501 (three-year audit statute).
[28] Section 6502 (ten-year debt collection statute).

Statute of Limitations: Snapshot	
Claims for a refund	Three years from the time the original return was filed, or two years from the time the tax was paid, whichever is later.
IRS assessment	Three years after the return is considered filed. Exceptions apply in cases of fraud, failure to file, and substantial understatement.
Substantial understatement	If a substantial understatement is discovered (25% or more income is omitted on the return), the statute for IRS assessment is six years.
Fraud	No limit.
Unfiled returns	No limit.
Collections	The statute of limitations for IRS collections is 10 years from the day after a tax return is filed.

Unit 2: Questions

1. Theo forgot to file his tax return, and mailed his return more than 60 days late. He did not file an extension. Theo owed $120 with his return. What is his minimum penalty for late filing?

A. $0.
B. $120.
C. $135.
D. $220.

The answer is B. If a return is filed more than 60 days late, the minimum penalty for late filing is the smaller of $135 or 100% of the tax owed. Since he owed $120 with the return, his penalty is 100% of the amount due. ###

2. All of the statements about estimated tax payments are correct except_____:

A. An individual whose only income is from self-employment will have to pay estimated payments.
B. If insufficient tax is paid through withholding, estimated payments may still be necessary.
C. Estimated tax payments are required when the withholding taxes are greater than the overall tax liability.
D. Estimated tax is used to pay not only income tax, but self-employment tax and alternative minimum tax as well.

The answer is C. If a taxpayer's withholding exceeds his tax liability, no estimated payments would be required. The taxpayer would receive a refund of the overpaid tax when he files his tax return. ###

3. Which of the following is not an acceptable reason for extending the statute of limitations for a refund past the normal deadline?

A. A bad debt from a worthless security.
B. Living in a presidentially declared federal disaster area.
C. Exceptions for military personnel.
D. Living outside the country for three years.

The answer is D. Living outside the country is not a valid excuse for extending the statute of limitations for claiming a refund. In some cases, a request for a tax refund will be honored past the normal three-year deadline. Exceptions include those for military personnel, individuals who are "financially disabled," taxpayers who live in presidentially declared disaster areas, and taxpayers who have bad debts from worthless securities. ###

4. Dottie is a U.S. resident who paid estimated tax in 2012 totaling $2,500. In 2013, Dottie quit her business as a self-employed contractor and is now unemployed. She expects to have zero tax liability in 2013. Which of the following statements is true?

A. Dottie is still required to make estimated tax payments in 2013.
B. Dottie is not required to make estimated tax payments in 2013.
C. Dottie must pay a minimum of $2,500 in estimated tax in 2013, or she will be subject to a failure-to-pay penalty.
D. Dottie must make a minimum of $2,250 (90% X $2,500) in estimated tax payments in 2013, or she will be subject to an underpayment penalty.

The answer is B. A taxpayer is not required to pay estimated tax if she expects to have zero tax liability. ###

5. Charles had a $4,500 tax liability in 2012. In 2013, Charles expects to owe approximately $3,200 in federal taxes. He has $1,200 in income tax withheld from his paycheck. Which of the following statements is true?

A. Charles is required to make estimated tax payments in 2013.
B. Charles is not required to pay estimated taxes in 2013.
C. Charles is required to adjust his withholding. He cannot make estimated tax payments because he is an employee.
D. None of the above.

The answer is A. Charles is required to make estimated tax payments because his expected tax liability for 2013 exceeds $1,000. His withholding is insufficient to cover his tax liability. Charles could elect to adjust his withholding with his employer so the taxes are taken out of his pay automatically. If Charles does not adjust his withholding, he will be required to make estimated tax payments. If he does not make estimated tax payments, then he will be subject to a penalty. ###

6. Which of the following statements is true regarding the filing of Form 4868, *Application for an Automatic Extension of Time to File U.S. Individual Income Tax Return?*

A. Form 4868 provides the taxpayer with an automatic six-month extension to file and pay.
B. Even though a taxpayer files Form 4868, he will owe interest and may be charged a late payment penalty on the amount owed if the tax is not paid by the due date.
C. Interest is not assessed on any income tax due if Form 4868 is filed.
D. A U.S. citizen, who is out of the country on vacation on the due date, will be allowed an additional twelve months to file so long as "Out of the Country" is written across the top of Form 1040.

The answer is B. Even though a taxpayer files Form 4868, he will owe interest and a late payment penalty on the amount owed if he does not pay the tax due by the regular due date. ###

7. What is the statute of limitations for IRS assessment on a tax return in which more than 25% of the taxpayer's income was omitted?

A. There is no statute of limitations on a return where income was omitted.
B. Three years from the date the return was filed.
C. Six years from the date the return was filed.
D. Ten years from the date the return was filed.

The answer is C. If a taxpayer omitted 25% of his income or more, the IRS has up to six years to assess a deficiency. ###

8. Todd is a self-employed architect and must make estimated tax payments. What is the due date for his third estimated tax payment for tax year 2012?

A. June 15, 2012.
B. August 15, 2012.
C. September 15, 2012.
D. October 15, 2012.

The answer is C. The third-quarter payment for estimated tax is due September 15, 2012. For estimated tax payments, a year is divided into four quarterly payment periods. Each period has a due date. The payments are due as follows:

Periods	Due Date
Jan. 1-March 31	April 15
April 1-May 31	June 15
June 1-Aug. 31	September 15
Sept. 1-Dec. 31	January 15 (following year)

###

9. Logan had the following gross income amounts in 2012:

1. Taxable interest: $3,000
2. Dividends: $42,000
3. Farm income (Schedule F): $80,000

Is Logan allowed to use the special estimated tax rules for farmers and fishermen?

A. Unable to determine based on the information given.
B. Logan is a farm employee.
C. Yes, Logan is a qualified farmer.
D. No, Logan is not a qualified farmer, and he must make quarterly estimated tax payments.

The answer is D. Based on his income, Logan does not qualify to use the special estimated tax rules for qualified farmers. At least two-thirds of his gross income (66.6%) must be from farming in order to qualify. Logan's gross farm income is 64% of his total gross income ($80,000 ÷ $125,000 = 0.64). Therefore, Logan is not a qualified farmer. ###

10. Which of the following best describes AMT?

A. The excess of regular tax over tentative minimum tax.
B. The tax calculated by applying the regular tax rate to alternative minimum tax income.
C. An additional tax payable to the extent that calculated minimum tax exceeds the regular tax.
D. The excess of regular tax over the AMT exemption amount.

The answer is C. The AMT is the excess of the tentative minimum tax over the regular tax. Thus, the AMT is owed only if the tentative minimum tax is greater than the regular tax. The tentative minimum tax is calculated separately from the regular tax. Congress passed the AMT in an attempt to ensure that individuals and corporations that benefit from certain exclusions, deductions, or credits pay at least a minimum amount of tax. ###

Unit 3: Filing Status

More Reading:
Publication 501, *Exemptions, Standard Deduction, and Filing Information*

In order to file a tax return, a tax preparer must identify the taxpayer's filing status. There are five filing statuses, and for the EA exam you must clearly understand the rules governing each. There are also special rules for annulled marriages and widows/widowers.

In general, a taxpayer's status depends on whether he is married or unmarried. For federal tax purposes, a marriage means only a legal union between a man and a woman as husband and wife. The word "spouse" means a person of the opposite sex who is a husband or a wife.[29]

1. Single or "Considered Unmarried"

A taxpayer is considered single for the *entire tax year* if, on the last day of the tax year, he or she was:

- Unmarried
- Legally separated or divorced, or
- Widowed (and not remarried during the year).

Example: Kenneth and Jennifer legally divorced on December 31, 2012. They do not have any dependents. They may not file a joint return for tax year 2012, but instead must each file SINGLE.

*Special Note: Annulled Marriages (Single): If a marriage is annulled, then it is considered *never to have existed.* Annulment is a legal procedure for declaring a marriage null and void. Unlike divorce, an annulment is retroactive. If a taxpayer obtains a court degree of annulment that holds no valid marriage ever existed, the couple is considered unmarried even if they filed joint returns for earlier years.

Taxpayers who have annulled their marriage must file amended returns (Form 1040X) claiming single (or head of household status, if applicable) for all the tax years affected by the annulment that are not closed by the statute of limitations. The statute of limitations for filing generally does not expire until *three years* after an original return was filed or the date the return was due, whichever is later.

Example: Sarah and Robert were granted an annulment on October 31, 2012. They were married for two years. They do not have any dependents. They must each file single for 2012, and the prior two years' tax returns must be amended to reflect single as their filing status.

---

[29] This is true even in states where marriage is legal between same-sex couples. However, the Supreme Court is going to weigh in on the issue, so the current law may change. In the spring of 2013, the court will hear arguments on whether a same-sex partner can claim the estate tax marital deduction. The decision, which is expected by late June 2013, also should settle whether same sex-sex couples may file jointly. Regardless of how justices rule, it will not affect tax law for 2012, the basis of the current EA exam.

2. Married Filing Jointly (MFJ)

Taxpayers may use the MFJ status if they are married and:

- Live together as husband and wife
- Live together in a common law marriage recognized in the state where they now reside or in the state where the common law marriage began
- Live apart but are not legally separated or divorced
- Are separated under an interlocutory (not final) divorce decree
- The taxpayer's spouse died during the year and the taxpayer has not remarried

A U.S. resident or U.S. citizen who is married to a nonresident alien can elect to file a joint return as long as both spouses agree to be taxed on their worldwide income.

On a joint return, spouses report all of their combined income, allowable expenses, exemptions, and deductions. Spouses can file a joint return even if only one spouse had income. Both husband and wife must agree to sign the return and are responsible for any tax owed, even if all the income was earned by only one spouse.

A subsequent divorce usually does not relieve either spouse of the liability associated with the original joint return.

Note: In certain situations, one spouse may be relieved of joint responsibility for tax on a joint return for items that the other spouse incorrectly reported. There are three types of relief: innocent spouse relief; separation of liability (available only to joint filers who are divorced, widowed, legally separated, or who have not lived together for 12 months ending on the date the relief request is filed); and equitable relief.[30]

3. Married Filing Separately (MFS)

The MFS status is for taxpayers who are married and either:

- Choose to file separate returns, or
- Do not agree to file a joint return.

If one spouse chooses to file MFS, the other is forced to do the same, since a joint return must be signed by both spouses.

Example: Jerry and Danielle usually file jointly. However, Danielle has chosen to separate her finances from her husband. Jerry wishes to file jointly with Danielle, but she has refused. Danielle files using married filing separately as her filing status; therefore, Jerry is forced to file MFS as well.

The MFS filing status means the husband and wife report their own incomes, exemptions, credits, and deductions on separate returns, even if one spouse had no income. This filing status may benefit a taxpayer who wants to be responsible only for his own tax, or if it results in less tax than filing a joint return. Typically, however, a spouse will pay more when filing MFS than he would by filing MFJ.

Special rules apply to the MFS filing status, including:

- The tax rate is generally higher than on a joint return.

---

[30] This type of relief from liability is covered extensively in Part 3 of the PassKey EA Review. For Part 1 of the EA exam, you should be familiar with the terms and know that this type of relief exists in certain cases.

- The exemption amount for figuring the alternative minimum tax is half that allowed on a joint return.
- Various credits, including the Earned Income Credit and ones for child care expenses, education, adoption, and retirement savings, are generally not allowed or are much more limited than on a joint return.
- The capital loss deduction is limited to $1,500, half that allowed on a joint return.
- The standard deduction is half the amount allowed on a joint return, and cannot be claimed if the taxpayer's spouse itemizes deductions.

Example: Tom and Judith keep their finances separate and choose to file MFS. Tom plans to itemize his casualty losses, so then Judith is forced to either itemize her deductions or claim a zero standard deduction.

One common reason taxpayers choose the MFS filing status is to avoid an offset of their refund against their current spouse's outstanding prior debt. This includes past due child support, past due student loans, or a tax liability a spouse incurred before the marriage.

Example: Dinesh and Maya were married in 2012. Dinesh owes past due taxes from a prior year. Maya chooses to file separately from Dinesh, so her refund will not be offset by his overdue tax debt. If they were to file jointly, their refund would be retained in order to pay the debt.

There are rules for when married taxpayers are allowed to change their filing status. To change from a separate return to a joint return, a taxpayer must:
- File an amended return using Form 1040X.
- Make the change any time within three years from the due date of the separate[31] returns.

A taxpayer cannot change from a joint return to a separate return after the due date of the return. So, for example, if a married couple filed their joint 2012 tax return on March 13, 2013 and one of the spouses decides to file MFS, then they only have until April 15, 2013 to elect (or amend to) MFS filing status.

*Exception: A personal representative for a decedent (deceased taxpayer) can change from a joint return elected by the surviving spouse to a separate return for the decedent, up to a year *after* the filing deadline.

Example: Kurt and his wife Susan have always filed jointly. Susan dies suddenly in 2012, and her will names Harriet, her daughter from a previous marriage, as the executor for her estate and all her legal affairs. Kurt files a joint return with Susan in 2012, but Harriet, as the executor, decides that it would be better for Susan's estate if her tax return was filed MFS. Harriet files an amended return claiming MFS status for Susan, and signs the return as the executor.

4. Head of Household (HOH)

The HOH status is available to taxpayers who meet all three of the following requirements:
- The taxpayer must be single, divorced, or legally separated on the last day of the year, or meet the tests for married persons living apart with dependent children.

---

[31] Besides MFS returns, a "separate" return also refers to returns with the single and head of household filing status.

- The taxpayer must have paid more than half the cost of keeping up a home for the year. head
- The taxpayer must have had a qualifying person living in his home for *more* than half the year. (Exceptions exist for temporary absences, such as school, and for a qualifying parent, who does not have to live with the taxpayer.)

Taxpayers who qualify to file as head of household will usually have a lower tax rate than the rates for single or MFS, and will receive a higher standard deduction.

For the HOH status, a taxpayer must either be unmarried or "considered unmarried" on the last tax day of the year. To be "considered unmarried," a taxpayer must meet the following conditions:

- File a separate return.
- Pay more than half the cost of keeping up the home for the tax year.
- Not live with his spouse in the home during the last six months of the tax year.
- The home must be the main residence of the qualifying child, stepchild, or foster child for more than half the year.
- Be able to claim an exemption for the child.

Valid household expenses used to calculate whether a taxpayer is paying more than half the cost of maintaining a home include:

- Rent, mortgage interest, property taxes
- Home insurance, repairs, utilities
- Food eaten in the home

Costs do not include clothing, education, medical treatment, vacations, life insurance, or transportation. Welfare payments are not considered amounts that the taxpayer provides to maintain a home.

*Special Rule for Dependent Parents: If a taxpayer's qualifying person is a dependent *parent*, the taxpayer may still file HOH even if the parent *does not live* with the taxpayer. The taxpayer must pay more than half the cost of keeping up a home that was the parent's main home for the entire year. This rule also applies to a parent in a rest home.

Example: Sharon is 54 years old and single. She pays the monthly bill for Shady Pines Nursing Home, where her 75-year-old mother lives. Sharon's mother has lived at Shady Pines for two years and has no income. Since Sharon pays more than half of the cost of her mother's living expenses, Sharon qualifies to use the head of household filing status.
Example: Tina is single and financially supports her mother, Rue, who lives in her own apartment. Rue dies suddenly on September 15, 2012. Tina may still claim her mother as a dependent and file HOH in 2012.

This rule also applies to parents, stepparents, grandparents, etc. who are related to the taxpayer by blood, marriage, or adoption (other examples include a stepmother or father-in-law).

*Special Rule for a Death or Birth during the Year: A taxpayer may still file as HOH if the qualifying individual is born or dies during the year. The taxpayer must have provided more than half of the cost of keeping up a home that was the individual's main home while the person was alive.

Example: Tony and Velma have a child in September 2012 who dies after a few weeks. Tony and Velma may still claim the child on their tax return as a qualifying child. That is because a dependent can still be claimed, even though the child only lived a short while.

For purposes of the HOH status, a "qualifying person" is defined as:

- A qualifying child,
- A married child who can be claimed as a dependent, or
- A dependent parent.

The taxpayer's qualifying child includes the taxpayer's child or stepchild (whether by blood or adoption); foster child, sibling, or stepsibling; or a descendant of any of these. For example, a niece or nephew, stepbrother, foster child, or a grandchild may all be eligible as "qualifying persons" for the HOH filing status.

Example: Lewis's unmarried son, Lincoln, lived with him all year. Lincoln turned 18 at the end of the year. Lincoln does not have a job, did not provide any of his own support, and cannot be claimed as a dependent of anyone else. As a result, Lincoln is Lewis's qualifying child. Lewis may claim the HOH filing status.

The qualifying person for HOH filing status must always be related to the taxpayer either by blood or marriage (with the exception of a foster child, who also qualifies if the child was legally placed in the home by a government agency or entity).

Example: Jeffrey has lived with his girlfriend, Patricia, and her son, Nolan, for five years. Jeffrey pays all of the costs of keeping up their home. Patricia is unemployed and does not contribute to the household costs. Jeffrey is not related to Nolan and cannot claim him as a dependent. No one else lives in the household. Jeffrey cannot file as HOH because neither Patricia nor Nolan is a qualifying person for Jeffrey.

An unrelated individual may still be considered a "qualifying relative" for a dependency exemption[32], but will not be a qualifying person for the HOH filing status.

Example: Since her husband died five years ago, Joan has lived with her friend, Wilson. Joan is a U.S. citizen, is single, and lived with Wilson all year. Joan had no income and received all of her financial support from Wilson. Joan falls under the definition of a qualifying relative, and Wilson can claim Joan as a dependent on his return. However, Joan does not qualify Wilson to file as head of household.

Special Rule for Divorced or Noncustodial Parents

In order for a taxpayer to file as HOH, a qualifying child does not have to be a dependent of the taxpayer (unless the qualifying person is married). That means a taxpayer may still file as HOH and not claim the qualifying person as his dependent. This happens most often with divorced parents.

Example: George and Elizabeth Garcia have been divorced for five years. They have one child, a 12-year-old daughter named Rebecca, who lives with her mother and only sees her father on weekends. Therefore, Elizabeth is the custodial parent. They agree, however, to allow George to claim the dependency exemption for Rebecca on his tax return. In 2012, George correctly files single and claims Rebecca as his dependent. Elizabeth may still file as HOH, as shown in the following example.

---

[32] The rules regarding dependency exemptions are covered in detail in Unit 4, *Exemptions and Dependents*.

The "considered unmarried" rules apply in determining who may claim a child for dependency and HOH purposes. Couples, even if not formally separated or divorced, must live apart for more than half the year in order to claim HOH status.

Example: Luke and Pauline separated in February 2012 and lived apart for the rest of the year. They do not have a written separation agreement and are not yet divorced. Their six-year-old daughter, Kennedy, lived with Luke all year, and he paid more than half the cost of keeping up the home. Luke files a separate tax return and claims Kennedy as a dependent because he is the custodial parent. Luke can also claim HOH status for 2012. Although Luke is still legally married, he can file as HOH because he meets all the requirements to be "considered unmarried."

Example: Janine and Richard separated on July 10, but were not yet divorced at the end of the year. They have one minor child, Madeline, age 8. Even though Janine lived with Madeline and supported her for the remainder of the year, Janine does not qualify for HOH filing status because she and Richard **did not live apart** for the last six months of the year.

---

*Special Rule for Nonresident Alien Spouses: A taxpayer who is married to a *nonresident alien* spouse may elect to file as HOH even if both spouses lived together throughout the year.

Example: In 2011, Tim Bianchi met and married Aom Mookja, a nonresident alien. Aom is a citizen and resident of Thailand. The couple lived together in Thailand while Tim was on sabbatical from his university teaching position. They have a son who was born in 2012. Tim may still file as HOH, even though Tim and Aom lived together all year, because Aom is a nonresident alien.

---

5. Qualifying Widow(er) With a Dependent Child

"Qualifying widow(er)" is the least common filing status. However, because of its complexity, it is still often tested on the EA exam.

This filing status yields a tax rate *equal to* MFJ. What this means is that surviving spouses receive the same standard deduction and tax rates as taxpayers who are married filing jointly.

In the year of the spouse's death, a taxpayer can file a joint return. For the following two years after death, the surviving spouse can use the qualifying widow(er) filing status as long as he or she has a qualifying dependent. After two years, the taxpayer's filing status converts to single or HOH, whichever applies.

For example, if the taxpayer's spouse died in 2011 and the surviving spouse did not remarry, he or she can use the "qualifying widow(er)" filing status for 2012 and 2013.

Example: Barbara's husband dies on December 3, 2012. She has one dependent child, a 15-year-old daughter. Barbara does not remarry. Therefore, Barbara's filing status for 2012 is MFJ (the last year her husband was alive). She can file as a qualifying widow in 2013 and 2014, which is a more favorable filing status than single or HOH.

However, if a surviving spouse *remarries* before the end of the year, MFS must be used for the decedent's final return.

Example: Shelly and her husband, Rodney, have an infant son. Rodney dies of cancer in January 2012. Shelly remarries in December 2012. Since she remarried in the same year her former husband died, she no longer qualifies for the joint return filing status with her deceased husband. Shelly does qualify for MFJ with her *new* spouse. It also means that Rodney's filing status for 2012 would be considered MFS.

To qualify for the qualifying widow(er) filing status, the taxpayer must:

- Not have remarried before the end of the tax year.
- Have been eligible to file a joint return for the year the spouse died; it does not matter if a joint return was actually filed.
- Have a qualifying child for the year.
- Have furnished over half the cost of keeping up the child's home for the entire year.

Example: Hazel's husband, Randy, died on July 20, 2010. Hazel has a dependent daughter who is three. Hazel files a joint return with Randy in 2010, and in 2011 she correctly files as a qualifying widow with dependent child. In 2012, however, Hazel remarries, so she no longer qualifies for the qualifying widow filing status. She must now file jointly with her new husband, or file MFS.

After a Spouse's Death

The chart shows which filing status to use for a widowed taxpayer who does not remarry and has a qualifying dependent.

Tax Year	Filing Status	Exemption for Deceased Spouse?
The year of death	Married filing jointly or married filing separately	Yes
First year after death	Qualifying widow(er)	No
Second year after death	Qualifying widow(er)	No
After second year of death	Head of household	No

Unit 3: Questions

1. Which of the following statements is true regarding the head of household filing status?

A. The taxpayer must be single on the first day of the year in order to qualify for head of household filing status.
B. The taxpayer's spouse must live in the home during the tax year.
C. The taxpayer's dependent parent does not have to live with the taxpayer in order to qualify for head of household.
D. The taxpayer must have paid less than half of the cost of keeping up the house for the entire year.

The answer is C. Parents do not have to live with a taxpayer in order for the taxpayer to elect the head of household filing status. This is a special rule for dependent parents. This rule also applies to parents or grandparents who are related to the taxpayer by blood, marriage, or adoption. A taxpayer must pay more than half of the household costs in order to qualify for this filing status. ###

2. The person who qualifies a taxpayer as head of household must be _____.

A. A minor child.
B. A blood relative.
C. The taxpayer's dependent or the taxpayer's qualifying child.
D. A minor child or a full-time student.

The answer is C. The taxpayer must claim the person as a dependent unless the noncustodial parent claims the child as a dependent. Answer A is incorrect, because a qualifying dependent does not have to be a minor in many cases. Answer B is incorrect because a qualifying dependent may be related by blood, marriage, or adoption. Answer D is incorrect because a dependent parent may also qualify a taxpayer for HOH status. ###

3. Clarence takes care of his 10-year-old grandson. How long must his grandson live in Clarence's home in order for Clarence to qualify for head of household status?

A. At least three months.
B. More than half the year.
C. The entire year.
D. More than 12 months.

The answer is B. The relative must have lived with the taxpayer more than half the year (over six months) and be the taxpayer's dependent. The exception is that a taxpayer's dependent parent does not have to live with the taxpayer. ###

4. Dana's husband died on January 24, 2012. She has one dependent son who is eight years old. What is Dana's best filing status for tax year 2012?

A. Married filing jointly.
B. Single.
C. Qualifying widow.
D. Head of household.

The answer is A. If a taxpayer's spouse died during the year, the taxpayer is considered married for the whole year and may file as "MFJ." So Dana may file a joint return with her husband in 2012, which is the year he died. ###

5. When may a taxpayer amend a joint tax return from "married filing jointly" to "married filing separately" after the filing deadline?

A. Never.
B. Only within the statute of limitations for filing amended returns.
C. Only in the case of annulled marriages.
D. Only when an estate's personal representative changes a joint return elected by the surviving spouse to a separate return for the decedent.

The answer is D. This is the only exception to the rule that prevents a taxpayer from amending his MFJ return to a MFS return. ###

6. Victor is 39 years old and has been legally separated from his wife, Eleanor, since February 1, 2012. Their divorce was not yet final at the end of 2012. They have two minor children. Since they separated, one child has lived with Victor and the other with Eleanor. Victor provides all of the support for the minor child living with him. Eleanor refuses to file jointly with Victor this year. Therefore, the most beneficial filing status that Victor qualifies for is:

A. Married filing separately.
B. Single.
C. Head of household.
D. Qualifying widower with a dependent child.

The answer is C. Victor qualifies for head of household filing status. His child lived with him for more than six months, and he did not live with his spouse the last half of the year. Victor may file as HOH because he is "considered unmarried" for tax purposes, and he paid more than half the cost of keeping up a home for the year for a qualifying child. Victor cannot file jointly with Eleanor, if she does not agree. ###

7. Lisa married Stuart in 2009. Stuart died in 2011. Lisa never remarried and has one dependent child. Which filing status should Lisa use for her 2012 tax return?

A. Single.
B. Married filing jointly.
C. Head of household.
D. Qualifying widow with dependent child.

The answer is D. In 2012, Lisa is eligible for qualifying widow with dependent child filing status. Lisa and Stuart qualified to file MFJ in 2011, the year he died, with Lisa signing the tax return as a surviving spouse. The year of death is the last year for which a taxpayer can file jointly with a deceased spouse. Then, in 2012, Lisa would be eligible to file as a qualifying widow with dependent child. ###

8. Sean is single. His mother, Clara, lives in an assisted living facility. Sean provides all of Clara's support. Clara died on June 1, 2012. Clara had no income. Which of the following is true?

A. Sean may file as head of household and may also claim his mother as a dependent on his 2012 tax return.
B. Sean must file single in 2012, and he cannot claim his mother as a dependent on his tax return.
C. Sean may claim his mother as a dependent on his tax return, but he cannot claim head of household status for 2012.
D. Sean may claim head of household status for 2012, but he cannot claim his mother as a dependent.

The answer is A. Because Sean paid more than half the cost of his mother's care in a care facility from the beginning of the year until her death, then he is entitled to claim an exemption for her, and he can also file as head of household. ###

9. Mary and Troy are married and live together. Mary earned $7,000 in 2012, and Troy earned $42,000. Mary wants to file a joint return, but Troy refuses to file with Mary and instead files a separate return. Which of the following statements is true?

A. Mary may file a joint amended tax return and sign Troy's name.
B. Mary and Troy must both file separate returns.
C. Mary may file as single because Troy refuses to sign a joint return.
D. Mary does not have a filing requirement.

The answer is B. In this case, both spouses are required to file a tax return because both are above the earnings threshold for MFS. Married couples must agree to file jointly. If one spouse does not agree to file jointly, they must file separately. ###

10. Kathy's marriage was annulled on February 25, 2013. She was married to her husband in 2010 and filed jointly with him in 2010 and 2011. She has not yet filed her 2012 return. Kathy has no dependents. Which of the following statements is true?

A. Kathy must file amended returns, claiming single filing status for all open years affected by the annulment.
B. Kathy is not required to file amended returns, and she may file jointly with her husband in 2012.
C. Kathy is not required to file amended returns, and she must file married filing separately on her 2012 tax return.
D. Kathy is not required to file amended returns, and she should file as single on her 2012 tax return.

The answer is A. Kathy must file amended tax returns for 2010 and 2011. She cannot file jointly with her husband in 2012. If a couple obtains a court decree of annulment, the taxpayer must file amended returns (Form 1040X) claiming single or head of household status for all tax years affected by the annulment that are not closed by the statute of limitations for filing a tax return. ###

11. The two filing statuses that generally result in the lowest tax amounts are married filing jointly and _____.

A. Married filing separately.
B. Head of household.
C. Qualifying widow(er) with dependent child.
D. Single.

The answer is C. The qualifying widow(er) with dependent child filing status generally yields the same tax amount as married filing jointly. ###

12. Which of the following is not a valid filing status?

A. Married filing jointly.
B. Qualifying widow(er) with dependent child.
C. Head of household.
D. Annulled.

The answer is D. There is no such thing as an "annulled" filing status. There are five filing statuses: married filing jointly, qualifying widow(er) with dependent child, head of household, single, and married filing separately.###

13. Dwight and Angela are married, but they choose to file separate tax returns for tax year 2012, because Dwight is being investigated by the IRS for a previous tax issue. Dwight and Angela file their separate tax returns on time. A few months later, after the investigation is over and Dwight is cleared of all wrongdoing, he wishes to file amended returns and file jointly with his wife in order to claim the Earned Income Credit. Which of the following is true?

A. Dwight is prohibited from changing his filing status in order to claim this credit.
B. Dwight and Angela may amend their MFS tax returns to MFJ in order to claim the credit.
C. Dwight may amend his tax return to MFJ filing status, but he may not claim the credit.
D. Angela may not file jointly with Dwight after she has already filed a separate tax return.

The answer is B. Dwight and Angela are allowed to amend their separate returns to a joint return in order to claim the credit. If a taxpayer files a separate return, the taxpayer may elect to amend the filing status to married filing jointly at any time within three years from the due date of the original return. This does not include any extensions. However, the same does not hold true in reverse. Once a taxpayer files a joint return, the taxpayer cannot choose to file a separate return for that year after the due date of the return (with a rare exception for deceased taxpayers). ###

14. Carol and Raul were married four years ago and have no children. They split up in 2011, but did not file for divorce. Although they lived apart during all of 2012, they are neither divorced nor legally separated. Which of the following filing statuses can they use?

A. Single or married filing separately.
B. Married filing jointly or married filing separately.
C. Married filing separately or head of household.
D. Single or qualifying widow(er).

The answer is B. As long as they are married and are neither divorced nor legally separated, Carol and Raul can file a joint return, or they can choose to file separately. They cannot file single. ###

15. Which dependent relative may qualify a taxpayer for head of household filing status?

A. An adult stepdaughter supported by the taxpayer who lives across town.
B. A family friend who lives with the taxpayer all year.
C. A parent who lives in his own home and not with the taxpayer.
D. A child who lived with the taxpayer for three months of the tax year.

The answer is C. A parent is the only dependent relative who does not have to live with the taxpayer in order for the taxpayer to claim head of household status. ###

16. Samantha is divorced and provided over half the cost of keeping up a home. Her five-year-old daughter, Mollie, lived with her for seven months last year. Samantha allows her ex-husband, Jim, to claim Mollie as a dependent. Which of the following statements is true?

A. Jim may take Mollie as his dependent and also file as head of household.
B. Jim may take Mollie as his dependent, and Samantha may still file as head of household.
C. Neither parent qualifies for head of household filing status because Mollie did not live with either parent for the entire year.
D. Samantha cannot release the dependency exemption to Jim, because their daughter did not live with Jim for over six months.

The answer is B. Samantha may use head of household status because she is not married and she provided over half the cost of keeping up the main home of her dependent child for more than six months. However, because Samantha's ex-husband claims Mollie as his dependent, the preparer must write Mollie's name on line 4 of the filing status section of Form 1040 or Form 1040A. ###

17. Madison and Todd are not married and do not live together, but they have a two-year-old daughter named Amanda. Madison and her daughter lived together all year while Todd lived alone in his own apartment. Madison earned $13,000 working as a clothing store clerk. Todd earned $48,000 managing a hardware store. He paid over half the cost of Madison's apartment for rent and utilities. He also gave Madison extra money for groceries. Todd does not pay any expenses or support for any other family member. Which of the following is true?

A. Todd may file as head of household.
B. Madison may file as head of household.
C. Todd and Madison may file jointly.
D. Neither may claim head of household filing status.

The answer is D. Todd provided over half the cost of maintaining a home for Madison and Amanda, but he cannot file head of household since Amanda did not live with him for more than half the year. Madison cannot file HOH either, because she did not provide more than one-half the cost of keeping up the home for her daughter. However, either Todd or Madison may still claim Amanda as their dependent. ###

18. Louisa legally separated from her husband during 2012. They have a 10-year-old son. Which of the following would prevent Louisa from filing as head of household?

A. Louisa has maintained a separate residence from her husband since November 2011.
B. Her son's principal home is with Louisa.
C. Louisa's parents assisted with 40% of the household costs.
D. Her son lived with Louisa from July 3, 2012 to December 31, 2012.

The answer is D. For Louisa to file as head of household, her home must have been the main home of her qualifying child for *more than half* the tax year. Since her son started living with her in July, he would not have been in the household sufficient time to qualify for this filing status. ###

19. Alexandra's younger brother, Sebastian, is seventeen years old. Sebastian lived with friends in January and February of 2012. From March through July of 2012, he lived with Alexandra. On August 1, Sebastian moved back in with his friends and stayed with them the rest of the year. Since Sebastian did not have a job, Alexandra gave him money every month. Alexandra had no other dependents. Which of the following statements is true?

A. Alexandra may file as head of household for 2012.
B. Alexandra may file jointly with Sebastian in 2012.
C. Alexandra cannot file as head of household in 2012.
D. Sebastian may file as head of household in 2012.

The answer is C. Alexandra cannot claim head of household status because Sebastian lived with her for only five months, which is less than half the year. ###

20. Taxpayers are considered to be married for the entire year if:

A. One spouse dies during the year and the surviving spouse does not remarry.
B. The spouses are legally separated under a separate maintenance decree.
C. The spouses are divorced on December 31 of the tax year.
D. The spouses had their marriage annulled December 31 of the tax year.

The answer is A. Taxpayers are considered "married" for the entire year if:
- They were married on the last day of the tax year, or
- The spouse died during the year and the surviving spouse has not remarried. ###

21. A U.S. resident or citizen who is married to a nonresident alien can file a joint return so long as both spouses _____.

A. Sign the return and agree to be taxed on their worldwide income.
B. Are living overseas.
C. Have valid Social Security Numbers
D. Are physically present in the United States.

The answer is A. A U.S. resident or citizen who is married to a nonresident alien can elect to file a joint return so long as both spouses agree to sign the return and be taxed on their worldwide income. A Social Security Number is not required, because a nonresident spouse that is ineligible for a Social Security Number may request an ITIN. ###

22. The married filing separately (MFS) status is for taxpayers who:

A. Are legally divorced on the last day of the year.
B. Are married and choose to file separate returns.
C. Are unmarried, but engaged to be married.
D. Are unmarried, but have a dependent child.

The answer is B. The married filing separately (MFS) status is for taxpayers who are married and either:
- Choose to file separate returns, or
- Cannot agree to file a joint return. ###

23. The MFS filing status typically results in a higher tax. However, in which of the following instances may it be beneficial for spouses to file separately?

A. When the taxpayer has significant capital losses to deduct.
B. When the taxpayer is claiming the Earned Income Credit.
C. When the taxpayer is claiming the standard deduction.
D. When the taxpayer's spouse has a past due student loan that was incurred prior to the marriage.

The answer is D. The MFS filing status generally has a tax rate that is higher than that of MFJ, and has many restrictions, including which credits a taxpayer may claim. However, when a taxpayer's spouse has an outstanding tax liability such as past due student loans, the other spouse might benefit from the MFS status. If filing jointly, the couple would have the prior debt offset against their refund. By filing separately, a spouse could protect his or her share of the refund. ###

Unit 4: Exemptions and Dependents

> **More Reading:**
> **Publication 501, *Exemptions, Standard Deduction, and Filing Information***

Taxpayers are allowed to take an exemption for themselves and also for their dependents. The 2012 exemption amount is $3,800 per person. The personal exemption is just like a tax deduction. It can reduce a person's taxable income to zero.

Taxpayers may qualify to claim two kinds of exemptions:

- **Personal exemptions,** which taxpayers claim for themselves
- **Dependency exemptions,** which taxpayers claim for their dependents

On a joint tax return, a married couple is allowed *two* personal exemptions, one for each spouse. A spouse is never considered the "dependent" of the other spouse. However, taxpayers may claim a personal exemption for their spouse simply because they are married, regardless of whether only one spouse had income during the year. If a taxpayer's spouse dies during the year and the surviving spouse files a joint return, the surviving spouse can claim an exemption for the deceased spouse.

Only one exemption is allowed per person. So, for example, a married couple with one child would claim three exemptions on a jointly filed return.

Example: Jenny married Rick in April of 2012. Neither Jenny nor Rick can be claimed as a dependent on another taxpayer's return. Jenny and Rick may claim two personal exemptions on their jointly filed return.

Example: Hao and Bình are married and have four dependent children. On their jointly filed return, they may claim a total of six exemptions: four dependency exemptions for their children and two personal exemptions for themselves.

Basic Rules for All Dependents

A taxpayer can claim one dependency exemption for each qualified dependent, thereby reducing his taxable income. Some examples of dependents include a child, stepchild, brother, sister, or parent.

If a taxpayer can claim another person as a dependent—even if the taxpayer does not actually do so—the dependent *cannot* take a personal exemption on his own tax return. The dependent is only entitled to one personal exemption, whether he files his own return or is listed as a dependent on someone else's return.

A dependent may still be required to file a tax return. This happens most often with teenagers who have jobs. They are usually claimed as dependents on their parents' tax return, but they also file their own return to report their wage income and receive a refund of income tax withheld.

Example: Cole is a 16-year-old high school student who also works part-time for his city's recreation department. In 2012, he earned $4,210 from his part-time job. Cole still lives with his parents, who file jointly and claim him as a dependent on their return. Although his income is below the 2012 filing requirement, Cole files his own tax return in order to obtain a refund of the income taxes that were withheld at his job. He does not claim a personal exemption for himself because his parents already claimed his exemption on their joint return. However, Cole is still entitled to the standard deduction for single taxpayers. This wipes out all of his taxable income, and he receives a refund of the income tax that was withheld on his Form W-2.

Whether or not a dependent is required to file is determined by the amount of the dependent's earned income, unearned income, and gross income. Even though a dependent child may lose a personal exemption, most dependent children usually owe little or no tax on their individual returns because they can still offset a small amount of income with the standard deduction. In actual practice, it is rare to see a dependent who owes a large amount of tax.

There are certain rules that must be followed in order to claim a dependent on a tax return. Dependency rules are extremely complex and frequently tested on the EA exam. A dependent is always defined as either a:

- Qualifying child, or a
- Qualifying relative

The following sections discuss these rules in detail.

The Primary Tests for Dependency

In order to determine if a taxpayer may claim a dependency exemption for another person, it must first be determined if the dependent can legally be claimed on the taxpayer's return. There are four main tests to determine this:

- **Citizenship or Residency Test**
- **Joint Return Test**
- **Qualifying Child of More Than One Person Test**
- **Dependent Taxpayer Test**

1. Citizenship or Residency Test

In order for a taxpayer to claim a dependency exemption for someone, the "citizen, national, or resident test" must be met. To qualify the dependent must be a citizen of the United States, a resident of the United States, or a citizen or resident of Canada or Mexico. There is also an exception for foreign-born adopted children.

Example: Horatio is an American citizen. He provides all of the financial support for his mother, who is a resident of Canada. Horatio may claim his mother as a dependent. (***Note:** She does not have to live with him, since she is a dependent parent). Horatio may need to request an ITIN number for his mother if she does not have a valid Social Security Number.

2. Joint Return Test

A dependent cannot file a joint return with his spouse. In other words, once an individual files a joint return, that individual cannot be taken as a dependent by another taxpayer.

> **Example:** Ellen is 18 years old and had no income in 2012. She got married on November 1, 2012. Ellen's new husband had $26,700 income and they file jointly, claiming two personal exemptions on their tax return. Ellen's father supported her throughout the year and even paid for their wedding. However, her father cannot claim Ellen as his dependent because she already filed a joint return with her new husband.

However, the Joint Return Test does *not apply* if the joint return is filed by the dependent only to claim a refund and no tax liability exists for either spouse, even if they filed separate returns.

> **Example:** Greg and Taylor are both 18 and married. They live with Taylor's mother, Michelle. In 2012, Greg had $1,800 of wage income from a part-time job and no other income. Neither Greg nor Taylor is required to file a tax return. Taxes were taken out of Greg's wages due to regular withholding, so they file a joint return only to obtain a refund of the withheld taxes. The exception to the Joint Return Test applies, so Michelle may claim exemptions for both Greg and Taylor on her tax return, as long as all the other tests for dependency are met.

3. Qualifying Child of More Than One Person Test

Sometimes a child meets the rules to be a qualifying child of more than one person. However, only one person can claim that dependent on his tax return.

> **Example:** Dan and Linda live together with their daughter, Savannah. They are not married. Savannah is a qualifying child for both Dan and Linda, but only one of them can claim her as a dependent on their tax return.

4. Dependent Taxpayer Test

If a person can be claimed as a dependent by another taxpayer, that person cannot claim *anyone else* as a dependent. A person who is claimed as a dependent on *someone else's* return cannot claim a dependency exemption on *his own* return.

> **Example:** Eva is a 17-year-old single mother who has an infant son. Eva is claimed as a dependent by her parents. Therefore, since Eva is a dependent of her parents, she is prohibited from claiming her infant son as a dependent on her own tax return.

Qualifying Child or Qualifying Relative?

Once the preparer determines that a dependent may be claimed on a taxpayer's return, then he must decide the type of dependency relationship the dependent has with the taxpayer. There are only two types of dependents, a **qualifying child** and a **qualifying relative**, with very specific tests for identifying the difference between the two.

Tests for a Qualifying Child

The tests for a qualifying child are more stringent than the tests for a qualifying relative. A qualifying child entitles a taxpayer to numerous tax credits, including the Earned Income Credit and the Child Tax Credit. A qualifying relative, on the other hand, does not qualify a taxpayer for the EIC. There are five tests for a qualifying child:

- **Relationship Test**
- **Age Test**
- **Residency Test**
- **Support Test**
- **Tie-breaker Test (for a qualifying child of more than one person)**

1. Relationship Test

The qualifying child must be related to the taxpayer by blood, marriage, or legal adoption. Qualifying children include:

- A child or stepchild
- An adopted child
- A sibling or stepsibling
- A descendant of one of the above (such as a grandchild, niece, or nephew)
- An eligible foster child

2. Age Test

In order to be a qualifying child, the dependent must be:

- Under the age of 19 at the end of the tax year, or
- Under the age of 24 *and* a full-time student, or
- Permanently and totally disabled at any time during the year (of any age).

A child is considered a full-time student if he attends a qualified educational institution full-time at least five months out of the year.

> **Example:** Andrew is 45 years old and totally disabled. Karen, his 37-year-old sister, provides all of Andrew's support and cares for him in her home, where he lives with her full-time. Although Andrew does not meet the age test, since he is **completely disabled,** he is still considered a *qualifying child* and a dependent for tax purposes. Karen may claim Andrew as her qualifying child, and also file as head of household.

Also, a child who is claimed as a dependent must be *younger than* the taxpayer who is claiming him, except in the case of dependents who are disabled. For taxpayers filing jointly, the child must be *younger* than *one spouse* listed on the return, but does not have to be younger than both spouses.

> **Example #1:** Owen and Sydney are both 22 years old and file jointly. Sydney's 23-year-old brother, Parker, is a full-time student, unmarried, and lives with Owen and Sydney. Parker is not disabled. Owen and Sydney are both younger than Parker. Therefore, Parker is not their qualifying child, even though he is a full-time student.

Example #2: Lucius, age 34, and Paige, age 20, are married and file jointly. Paige's 23-year-old nephew, Jason, is a full-time student, unmarried, and lives with Lucius and Paige. Lucius and Paige provide all of Jason's support. In this case, Lucius and Paige may claim Jason as a qualifying child on their joint tax return because he is *younger than* Lucius. Jason is a full-time student, so he is a qualifying child for tax purposes.

3. Support Test

A qualifying child cannot provide more than one-half of his own support. A full-time student does not take scholarships (whether taxable or nontaxable) into account when calculating the support test.

Example #1: Samuel has an 18-year-old daughter named Tiffany. Samuel provided $4,000 toward his teenage daughter's support for the year. Tiffany also has a part-time job and provided $13,000 of her own support. Therefore, Tiffany provided over half of *her own support* for the year. Tiffany does not pass the support test, and consequently, she is not Samuel's qualifying child. Tiffany can file a tax return as "single" and claim her own exemption.

Example #2: Penelope is 15 years old and had a small role in a television series. She earned $40,000 as a child actor, but her parents put all the money in a trust fund to pay for college. She lived at home all year. Penelope meets the support test since her earnings were not used for her own support. Since she meets the tests for a qualifying child, Penelope can be claimed as a dependent by her parents.

Foster Care Payments

Payments received for the support of a foster child from a child placement agency are considered support provided by the agency (not support provided by the child).

Example: Gina is a foster parent who provided $3,000 toward her 10-year-old foster child's support for the year. The state government provided $4,000, which was considered support provided by the state, not by the child. Gina's foster child did not provide more than half of her own support for the year. Therefore, the child may be claimed as a qualifying child by Gina if all the other tests are met.

4. Residence Test

A qualifying child must live with the taxpayer for more than half the tax year (over six months). Exceptions apply for children of divorced parents, kidnapped children, temporary absences, and for children who were born or died during the year.[33]

A *temporary absence* includes illness, college, vacation, military service, and incarceration in a juvenile facility. It must be reasonable to assume that the absent child will return to the home after the temporary absence.

The taxpayer must continue to maintain the home during the absence.

---

[33] A taxpayer cannot claim an exemption for a stillborn child. The child must be born alive, even if he or she lives only for a short time.

Example: Douglas and Andrea file jointly. They have one daughter named Isabella who is 29 years old. In March of 2012, Isabella lost her job and moved back in with her parents. Isabella earned $4,000 at the beginning of 2012 before she was laid off. Douglas and Andrea therefore provided the majority of Isabella's support for the rest of the year. Isabella got a new job in December and moved out. Isabella is not a qualifying child for federal tax purposes. Although Isabella meets the relationship, residence, and support test, she *does not* meet the age test.

Example: Scott is unmarried and lives with his 10-year-old son, Elijah. Scott provides all of Elijah's support. In 2012, Elijah became very ill and was hospitalized for seven months. Elijah is still considered Scott's qualifying child, because the illness and hospitalization count as a temporary absence from home. Scott may claim Elijah as his qualifying child and also file for head of household status.

*Special rules: Kidnapped child

A taxpayer can treat a kidnapped child as meeting the residency test, but both of the following must be true:

- The child is presumed to have been kidnapped by someone who is not a family member.
- In the year the kidnapping occurred, the child lived with the taxpayer for more than half of the year before the kidnapping.

This special tax treatment applies for all years until the child is returned. However, the last year this treatment can apply is the earlier of:

- The year there is a determination that the child is dead, or
- The year the child would have reached age 18.

5. The Tie-Breaker Test

Only one person can claim the same qualifying child, even if the child would qualify more than one person. If two taxpayers disagree on who gets to claim a child as their qualifying child and more than one person attempts to claim the same child, then the tie-breaker rules apply.

Under the tie-breaker rule, the child is treated as a qualifying child only by:

- The parents, if they file a joint return.
- The parent, if only one of the persons is the child's parent.
- The parent with whom the child lived the longest during the year.
- The parent with the highest AGI if the child lived with each parent for the same amount of time during the tax year and they do not file a joint return together.
- The person with the highest AGI, if no parent can claim the child as a qualifying child.
- A person with the higher AGI than any parent who can also claim the child as a qualifying child but does not.

Example: Sophia, who is single, has a three-year-old son named Orlando. They live with Sophia's father, Theodore (the child's grandfather). Sophia claims Orlando as her qualifying child, which means the child may not be treated as a qualifying child of the grandfather, Theodore.

Example: Penny and her sister, Rosa, live together. They also live and take care of their seven-year-old niece, Brianna, who lived with her aunts all year because Brianna's mother is incarcerated. Penny's AGI is $12,600. Rosa's AGI is $19,000. Brianna is a qualifying child of both Penny and Rosa because she meets the relationship, age, residency, and joint return tests for both aunts. However, Rosa has the primary right to claim Brianna as her qualifying child because her AGI is higher than Penny's.

Tests for Qualifying Relatives

A person who is not a qualifying child may still qualify as a dependent under the rules for qualifying relatives.

There is a six-part test for qualifying relatives. Under these tests, even an individual who is not a family member can still be a qualifying relative. Unlike a qualifying child, a qualifying relative can be any age.

*Note: There is no age test for a qualifying relative, and the support test and relationship test have different criteria.

In order to be claimed as a qualifying relative, the dependent must meet all of the following criteria:

- **Relationship (or Member of Household) Test**
- **Gross Income Test**
- **Total Support Test**
- **Joint Return Test**
- **Citizenship or Residency Test**

1. Relationship Test (or Member of Household)

The dependent must be related to the taxpayer in certain ways. A family member who is related to the taxpayer in any of the following ways *does not* have to live with the taxpayer to meet this test:

- A child, stepchild, foster child, or a descendant of any of them (for example, a grandchild).
- A sibling, stepsibling, or a half sibling.
- A parent, grandparent, stepparent, or other direct ancestor (but this does not include foster parents).
- A niece or nephew, a son-in-law, daughter-in-law, father-in-law, mother-in-law, brother-in-law, or sister-in-law[34].

---

[34] ***Note:** The listing of family members for the relationship test does not include cousins. A cousin must live with the taxpayer for the entire year and also meet the gross income test in order to qualify as a dependent. In that respect, the IRS treats a cousin just like an unrelated person.

- *Or the dependent **must have lived with** the taxpayer the entire tax year.

This means that an unrelated person who lived with the taxpayer for the entire year can also meet the member of household or relationship test.

> ***Note:** If a relationship violates local laws, this test is not met. For example, if a taxpayer's state prohibits cohabitation, then that person cannot be claimed as a dependent, even if all other criteria are met.

> **Example:** Isaac's 12-year-old grandson, Josh, lived with him for three months in 2012. For the rest of the year, Josh lived with his mother, Natalie, in another state. Natalie is Isaac's 32-year-old daughter. Even though Josh and Natalie lived in another state, Isaac still provided all of their financial support. Josh is not Isaac's *qualifying child* because he does not meet the residency test (Josh did not live with Isaac for more than half the year). However, Josh is Isaac's *qualifying relative*.

*Note: Any of these relationships that are established by marriage are *not ended* by death or divorce. So, for example, if a taxpayer supports his mother-in-law, he can continue to claim her as a dependent even if he and his ex-spouse are divorced or if he becomes widowed.

> **Example #1**: Mia and Caleb have always financially supported Mia's elderly mother, Gertrude, and claim her as their dependent on their jointly filed returns. However, in 2010, Mia dies and Caleb becomes a widower. Caleb remarries in 2012, but continues to support his former mother-in-law. Caleb can continue to claim Gertrude on his tax returns, even though he has remarried. This is because of the special rule that dependency relationships established by marriage do not end by death or divorce.

> **Example #2:** Todd has lived all year with his girlfriend, Ava, and her two children in his home. Their cohabitation does not violate local laws. Ava does not work and is not required to file a 2012 tax return. Ava and her two children pass the "not a qualifying child test" to be Todd's qualifying relatives. Todd can claim them as dependents if he meets all the other tests.

2. Gross Income Test

A *qualifying relative* cannot earn more than the personal exemption amount. In 2012, the personal exemption amount is $3,800. For purposes of this test, gross income includes:

- All taxable income in the form of money, property, or services
- Gross receipts from rental property
- A partner's share of gross partnership income (not net)
- Unemployment compensation
- Taxable scholarships and grants

For purposes of this test, gross income does not include:

- Tax-exempt income
- Income earned by a disabled person at a sheltered workshop

3. Total Support Test

In order to claim an individual as a qualifying relative, the taxpayer must provide over half of the dependent's total support during the year. "Support" includes amounts from Social Security and welfare payments, even if that support is nontaxable. "Support" does not include amounts received from nontaxable scholarships. Support can include the fair market value of lodging.

Example #1: Ella is 78 and lives in her own apartment. She received $7,000 in Social Security benefits in 2012, which she used to pay for her apartment. Ella's daughter, Laurie, provided $2,200 in support to her mother by paying her utility bills and buying her groceries. Even though Ella's Social Security benefits are not taxable and she does not have a filing requirement, Laurie cannot claim her mother as a dependent because Ella provided over one-half of her own support.

Example #2: Nicholas lives with Gavin, who is an old army buddy of his. Nicholas provided all of the support for Gavin, who lived with Nicholas all year in his home. Gavin has no income and does not file a 2012 tax return. Nicholas can claim Gavin as his qualifying relative if all of the other tests are met.

Example #3: Morgan provided $4,000 toward her father's support during the year. In 2012, Morgan's father earned income of $600, had nontaxable Social Security benefits of $4,800, and tax-exempt interest of $200. He uses all these for his support. Morgan cannot claim an exemption for her father because the $4,000 she provides is not more than half of her father's total support of $9,600 ($4,000 + $600 + $4,800 + $200).

Multiple Support Agreements

There are special rules for claiming a dependency exemption for a qualifying relative when a taxpayer has a *multiple support* agreement. A multiple support agreement is when two or more people agree to join together to provide a person's support. This happens commonly with adult children who are taking care of their parents.

In order for the dependency exemption to apply under a multiple support agreement, family members together must pay more than half of the person's total support, but no one member individually may pay more than half. In addition, the taxpayer who claims the dependent must provide *more than 10%* of the person's support. Only one of the family members can claim the dependency exemption. A different qualifying family member can claim the dependency exemption each year.

Example: Benjamin, Matthew, and Pamela are siblings who support their disabled mother, Abigail. Abigail is 83 and lives with Benjamin. In 2012, Abigail receives 20% of her financial support from Social Security, 40% from Matthew, 30% from Benjamin, and 10% from Pamela. Under IRS rules for multiple support agreements, either Matthew or Benjamin can take the exemption for their mother if the other signs a statement agreeing not to do so. Pamela may not claim the dependency exemption because she does not provide *more than* 10% of the support for her mother.

> **Example:** Graciela and Pilar are sisters who help support their 64-year-old father, Alonso. Each provides 20% of his care. The remaining 60% is provided equally by two persons not related to Alonso. He does not live with them. Because more than half of his support is provided by persons who cannot claim an exemption for him, no one can take the exemption.

4. Joint Return Test

If the dependent is married, he cannot file a joint return with his spouse, unless the return is filed solely to obtain a refund of withheld income taxes. (With the Joint Return Test, the same exceptions apply for a qualifying relative as for qualifying children.)

5. Citizenship or Residency Test

A qualifying relative must be either a citizen or resident alien of:

- The United States,
- Canada, or
- Mexico.

This means that a child who lives in Canada or Mexico may still be a *qualifying relative* of a U.S. taxpayer.

Even If the child does not live with the taxpayer at all during the tax year, the child may still be eligible to be claimed as a *qualifying relative*.

> **Example:** Manuel provides all the financial support of his children, ages 6 and 12, who live in Mexico with Manuel's mother, their grandmother. Manuel is unmarried and lives in the United States. He is a legal U.S. resident alien and has a valid Social Security Number. Manuel's children are citizens of Mexico and do not have SSNs. Regardless, both his children are still qualifying relatives for tax purposes. Manuel may claim them as dependents if all the tests are met. He may also be able to claim his mother as a dependent if all the tests are met.

Special Rules for Children of Divorced or Separated Parents

Generally, to claim a child as a dependent, the child must live with the taxpayer for over half the year (over six months). There is an exception to this rule for divorced/separated parents.

If the child did not live with the taxpayer, the custodial parent may still allow the noncustodial parent to claim the dependency exemption. The noncustodial parent must attach IRS Form 8332 in order to claim the dependency exemption.

If a divorce decree does not specify which parent is the custodial parent or which parent receives the dependency exemption, the exemption will automatically go to the parent who has physical custody for the majority of the year.

> **Example**: Alexis and Nathan are divorced. They have one child named Dylan. In 2012, Dylan lived with Alexis for 300 nights and with Nathan for 65 nights. Therefore, Alexis is the custodial parent. Alexis has the right to claim Dylan on her tax return as her qualifying child. However, Alexis may choose to release the exemption to Nathan by signing Form 8332.

> ***Note:** Even if the custodial parent releases the dependency exemption to the noncustodial parent, the custodial parent still has the right to claim head of household status, the Earned Income Credit, and dependent care credit.

Example: Gary and Frieda are divorced, and have one minor child named Sunny. Frieda is the custodial parent, but she agrees to release the dependency exemption for their child over to Gary by signing Form 8332. Gary will file as single and claim Sunny as his dependent. Frieda may still file as head of household even though she does not claim the dependency exemption for Sunny. That is because Frieda is the parent who lived with Sunny and maintained the home in which her child lived for most of the year.

The "Nanny" Tax (Household Employees)

A taxpayer *may not* claim a dependency exemption for a household employee such as a nanny, even if the employee lived with the taxpayer.

However, a taxpayer who has household employees may need to pay employment taxes, commonly referred to as the "nanny tax." The tax applies to any taxpayer who pays wages of $1,800 or more in 2012 to any one household employee. The worker is the taxpayer's employee if the taxpayer can control not only what work is done but how it is done, regardless of whether the work is full-time or part-time; the employee is paid on an hourly, daily, weekly, or per job basis; or the employee is hired through an agency. Examples of household employees include babysitters, housekeepers, private nurses, yard workers, and drivers. A self-employed worker, such as a daycare provider who cares for several children from different families in her own home, is not a taxpayer's household employee.

If a taxpayer pays a household employee $1,800 or more in 2012, he must withhold and pay Social Security and Medicare taxes. The employer's share of the tax is 7.65% and the employee's is 5.65% in 2012.

If a taxpayer pays wages of $1,000 or more to a household employee in any one quarter in 2012, he must also pay federal unemployment tax. The tax is 6% of cash wages. Wages over $7,000 a year per employee are not taxed.

Wages paid to a taxpayer's spouse, parent, or child under the age of 21 are exempt from the nanny tax rules.

Taxpayers who pay household income taxes must file a Schedule H along with their Form 1040.

The Kiddie Tax

The "kiddie tax" deals with the taxation of unearned income of children. Years ago, wealthy families would transfer investments to their minor children and save thousands of dollars in investment income because the money would be taxed at a lower rate. This was completely legal until Congress closed this tax loophole, and now investment income earned by dependent children is taxed at the parents' marginal rate.

This law became known as the "kiddie tax." The kiddie tax does not apply to wages or self-employment income—it applies to *investment income* only. Examples of unearned income include bank interest, dividends, and capital gains distributions.

Part of a children's investment income may be taxed at the parent's tax rate if:

- The child's investment income was more than $1,900 in 2012.

- The child is under the age of 19 or a full-time college student under the age of 24.
- The child is required to file a tax return for the end of the tax year.
- The child does not file a joint return for the tax year.

For 2012, the first $950 of unearned income a child or college student earns is offset by the $950 standard deduction for dependents (assuming the child has no earned income), and the next $950 is taxed at the child's rate. All of the child's unearned income in excess of $1,900 is taxed at the parent's rate.

> **Example:** Bill and Donna have one 14-year-old son named Jack. In 2012, Jack has $2,900 of interest income from a CD that his grandfather gave him. He does not have any other income. The first $950 of investment income is not taxable, because the standard deduction for dependents is $950. The next $950 is taxed at the 10% income tax rate. The remainder, $1,000, is taxed at the parents' tax rate.

Parents can avoid paying the kiddie tax only if the child has enough *earned* income to provide greater than half of his own support. In that case, the child's unearned income would be based on the child's tax rates, and not the parents.

Unit 4: Questions

1. Dan is unmarried and lives alone. His mother received $5,600 in Social Security benefits and $100 in taxable interest income in 2012. She paid $4,000 for living expenses and $400 for recreation. She also put $1,300 in a savings account. Dan also spent $4,800 of his own money on his mother's support in 2012, which paid her rent for the entire year. Dan and his mother did not live together. Which of the following is true?

A. Dan may claim his mother as a dependent, and also file as head of household.
B. Dan may not claim his mother as a dependent, but he may file as head of household.
C. Dan may claim his mother as a dependent, but he may not file as head of household.
D. Dan may not claim his mother as a dependent, and he cannot file as head of household.

The answer is A. Dan may claim his mother as a dependent, and also file as head of household. Even though Dan's mother received a total of $5,700 ($5,600 + $100), she spent only $4,400 ($4,000 + $400) for her own support. Since Dan spent more than $4,400 for her support and no other support was received, Dan has provided more than half of her support. Also, Dan paid for all her rental expenses, so he paid more than half the cost of keeping up a home that was the main home for the entire year for his parent. Therefore, Dan is also eligible to file as head of household. ###

2. Roy is a client who tells you that his wife died in February 2012. Based on this information, Roy can claim _____.

A. Only the personal exemption for himself.
B. Only the personal exemption for his wife.
C. Personal exemptions for both himself and for his wife.
D. A personal exemption for himself and a partial exemption for his wife.

The answer is C. In 2012, Roy can claim a personal exemption for his deceased wife, along with a personal exemption for himself. A taxpayer whose spouse dies during the year may file jointly in the year of death. ###

3. Alyssa is 18 years old and a full-time student. She comes into your office with some questions about her tax return. She says that she is claimed as a dependent on her parents' tax return. Over the summer, she worked in a clothing boutique and earned $7,000. Alyssa wants to file a tax return to report her wage income and get a refund. How many exemptions may she claim on her tax return?

A. Zero.
B. One.
C. Two.
D. Three.

The answer is A. Since Alyssa is claimed as a dependent on her parents' tax return, she cannot claim an exemption for herself. Therefore, her total number of exemptions is zero. She can still file a tax return in order to claim a refund of taxes withheld. ###

4. John is the sole support of his mother. To claim her as a dependent on his Form 1040, John's mother must be a resident or citizen of which of the following countries?

A. United States.
B. Mexico.
C. Canada.
D. Any of the above.

The answer is D. To qualify as a dependent, the dependent must be a citizen or resident alien of the United States, Canada, or Mexico. ###

5. In a multiple support agreement, what is the minimum amount of support that a taxpayer can provide and still claim the dependent?

A. 11% support.
B. 15% support.
C. 50% support.
D. 75% support.

The answer is A. The law provides for multiple support agreements, which usually exist when family members collectively support a relative, often a parent. The taxpayer can claim the dependent as a qualifying relative if he paid *more than* 10% of the support. The taxpayer would not be entitled to the exemption if someone else provided more than 50% of support of the family member. ###

6. Joseph, 52, is a single father who lives with an adopted son named Wyatt who has Down syndrome. Wyatt is 32 years old and permanently disabled. Wyatt had $800 in interest income and $5,000 in wages from a part-time job in 2012. Which of the following statements is true?

A. Joseph can file as head of household, with Wyatt as his qualifying child.
B. Joseph does not qualify for head of household, but he could still claim Wyatt as his qualifying relative, because Wyatt does not meet the age test for a qualifying child.
C. Joseph can file as head of household, with Wyatt as his qualifying relative.
D. Joseph must file single and he cannot claim Wyatt, because Wyatt earned more than the standard deduction amount.

The answer is A. Even though Wyatt is over the normal age threshold for a qualifying child, he is still considered a qualifying child for tax purposes. This is because Wyatt is permanently disabled and Joseph provides his financial support and care. Since Wyatt is disabled, he is therefore also a "qualifying child" for purposes of head of household filing status. ###

7. Clifford and Lily divorced in 2011 and they have one child together. Clifford's child lived with him for ten months of the year in 2012. The child lived with Lily for the other two months. The divorce decree states that Lily is supposed to be the custodial parent, not Clifford. Who is considered the custodial parent for IRS purposes?

A. Clifford.
B. Lily.
C. Neither.
D. Both.

The answer is A. For IRS purposes, the "custodial parent" is the parent with whom the child lived for the greater part of the year. The other parent is the noncustodial parent. If the parents divorced or separated during the year and the child lived with both parents before the separation, the custodial parent is the one with whom the child lived for the greater part of the rest of the year. ###

8. Haley is 23 and a full-time college student. During the year, Haley lived at home with her parents for four months and lived in the dorm for the remainder of the year. During the tax year, Haley worked part-time and earned $6,000, but that income did not amount to half of her total support. Can Haley's parents still claim her as a dependent?

A. No, because Haley earned more than the personal exemption amount.
B. No, because Haley did not live with her parents for more than half the year, and she does not meet the age test.
C. Yes, Haley's parents can claim her as a qualifying child.
D. Yes, Haley's parents can claim her as a dependent, but only as a qualifying relative, not as a qualifying child.

The answer is C. Haley meets all the qualifying child tests: the relationship test; the age test (because she is under 24 and was a full-time student); the residence test (because the time spent at college is a legitimate temporary absence); and the support test (because she did not provide over half of her own support). ###

9. Carson has a 12-year-old daughter named Emma. In 2012, Emma had $925 in interest income from a bank account. Which of the following statements regarding Emma's unearned income is correct?

A. Tax will be assessed to Carson and is calculated using Emma's tax rate.
B. Emma is not required to file a return, and Carson is not required to report his daughter's income on his own tax return.
C. Emma is required to file a tax return, and income tax will be assessed at a flat rate of 10%.
D. Carson may elect to report Emma's interest income on his own tax return. Her income will be taxed at the parent's highest marginal rate.

The answer is B. Emma is not required to file a tax return, because her unearned income is less than the standard deduction amount for dependents. The first $950 of investment income (which is equal to the dependent's standard deduction) escapes income tax. Emma has no filing requirement, and her father is not required to report the income on his own return. ###

10. Cheryl is 46 and unmarried. Her nephew, Bradley, lived with her all year and was 18 years old at the end of the year. Bradley did not provide more than half of his own support. He had $4,200 in income from wages and $1,000 in investment income. Which of the following is true?

A. Bradley qualifies as Cheryl's qualifying child for tax purposes.
B. Bradley is not a qualifying child; however, he can be claimed by Cheryl as a qualifying relative.
C. Bradley is not a qualifying child or qualifying relative, because he had income that exceeded the personal exemption amount.
D. Cheryl can claim Bradley only if he is a full-time student, since he is no longer a minor child.

The answer is A. Bradley is Cheryl's qualifying child because he meets the age test, support test, and relationship test. Also, because Bradley is single, he is a qualifying person for Cheryl to claim head of household filing status. Bradley is not required to be a full-time student, because the IRS says that any child under the age of 19 at the end of the tax year will be treated as a qualifying child if all the other tests are met. Bradley is only 18 years old, and therefore he passes the age test. ###

11. There are many tests that must be met for a taxpayer to claim an exemption for a dependent as a qualifying relative. Which of the following is not a requirement?

A. Citizen or resident test.
B. Member of household or relationship test.
C. Disability test.
D. Joint return test.

The answer is C. There is no such thing as a "disability test" for a qualifying relative. ###

12. Tony and Isabelle are the sole support of all the following individuals. (All are U.S. citizens but none lives with them, files a tax return, or has any income.)

1. Jennie, Tony's grandmother.
2. Julie, Isabelle's stepmother.
3. Jonathan, father of Tony's first wife.
4. Timothy, Isabelle's cousin.

How many exemptions may Tony and Isabelle claim on their joint return?

A. 3.
B. 4.
C. 5.
D. 6.

The answer is C. They may take three dependency exemptions on their tax return, and two personal exemptions for themselves. Tony and Isabelle may take dependency exemptions for all the dependents listed, except for Timothy, since he is Isabelle's cousin. Timothy would have to live with Tony and Isabelle all year in order for them to claim him as their dependent. Parents (or grandparents, in-laws, stepparents, etc.) do not have to live with a taxpayer in order to qualify as dependents. Tony can claim Jonathan, because Jonathan was once his father-in-law. ###

13. Ted and Sharon are married and are the sole support of their 23-year-old son, Ashton, who lives with them. Ashton is not a student and not disabled. He was unable to find steady work in 2012, but received $4,900 from a charitable foundation for painting a mural. Which of the following statements is true?

A. Ted and Sharon may claim Ashton as a qualifying child on their federal income tax return.
B. Ted and Sharon may claim Ashton as a qualifying relative on their federal income tax return.
C. Ted and Sharon may only claim Ashton if they file MFS.
D. Ted and Sharon may not claim Ashton as a dependent.

The answer is D. Ashton is not a minor, not a student, and not disabled, and therefore does not qualify as a qualifying child. He does not qualify as a qualifying relative, either, because he fails the gross income test. A qualifying relative cannot earn more than the personal exemption amount. In 2012, the personal exemption amount is $3,800. Since Ashton earned $4,900 in 2012, he cannot be claimed as a dependent. ###

14. Peter filed for divorce in 2012, and he and his wife moved into separate residences on April 20. Peter's 10-year-old daughter lived with him for the entire year. Peter owns the home and pays all the costs of upkeep for it. Which of the following is true?

A. Peter must file jointly with his wife in 2012, since they are still legally married. They may claim their daughter as a dependent on their jointly filed return.
B. Peter must file single in 2012.
C. Peter must file MFS in 2012.
D. Peter qualifies for HOH filing status.

The answer is D. Peter qualifies for head of household filing status. Since Peter and his wife lived in separate residences for the last six months of the year and Peter had a qualifying child, he may file as head of household. ###

15. Tyler is single and 17 years old. He works a part-time job at night and goes to school full-time. His total income for 2012 was $10,500. Tyler lives with his parents, who provided the majority of Tyler's support. Tyler's parents are claiming him as a dependent on their 2012 tax return. Which of the following statements is true?

A. Tyler is required to file his own return, and he may also take an exemption for himself.
B. Tyler is not required to file his own return.
C. Tyler's parents may not claim him as a dependent because Tyler earned more than the standard deduction amount for 2012.
D. His parents may claim Tyler as their qualifying child. Tyler is required to file a tax return, but he cannot claim a personal exemption for himself. He is still entitled to the standard deduction for single filers.

The answer is D. Tyler's parents may claim him as their qualifying child because he is under the age of 19 and does not provide more than half of his own support. Tyler is required to file a tax return but cannot claim an exemption for himself. ###

16. A child has investment income. What is the income limit threshold for when the kiddie tax kicks in?

A. $0.
B. $950.
C. $1,900.
D. $3,700.

The answer is C. In 2012, a child's unearned income in excess of $1,900 is subject to the kiddie tax rules. ###

17. Frank provided $4,000 toward his 17-year-old son's support for the year. Frank's son has a part-time job and provided $16,000 to his own support. Which of the following is true?

A. Frank may claim his son as a qualifying child on his return.
B. Frank may claim his son as his business partner on his return.
C. Frank may not claim his son as a dependent on his return.
D. None of the above is correct.

The answer is C. Frank's son provided more than half of his *own support* for the year. Therefore, he is not Frank's qualifying child. ###

18. Persons who can be claimed as a dependent may file a tax return, but they cannot:

A. Claim any deductions.
B. Claim any exemptions.
C. File a claim for a refund.
D. File an amended return.

The answer is B. Persons who can be claimed as a dependent may file a tax return, but they cannot claim any exemptions. If a taxpayer can claim another person as a dependent—even if the taxpayer does not actually do so—the dependent cannot take a personal exemption on *his* tax return. ###

19. Mateo is a U.S. resident. He has a 10-year-old child named Rey, who is a legal resident of Mexico. Rey does not have an SSN. Mateo would like to claim Rey as a dependent on his tax return. Rey lived with Mateo for eight months and with his grandmother in Mexico for the remaining part of the year. Does Rey meet the requirements of the citizen or resident test?

A. No, because Rey does not have a valid SSN.
B. No, because Rey is a resident of Mexico.
C. Yes, Rey meets the requirements of the citizen or resident test.
D. None of the above.

The answer is C. Rey meets the requirements of the citizen or resident test. In order to meet this test, a person must be a U.S. citizen or resident, or a resident of Canada or Mexico for at least some part of the year. ###

20. Donna Wiley has three children: Luther, Tim, and Mary. Each child contributes toward Mrs. Wiley's support. Luther and Tim each provide 45%, and Mary provides 10%. Which of Mrs. Wiley's children would be eligible to claim a dependency exemption for her in 2012 under a multiple support agreement?

A. Luther or Tim.
B. Both Luther and Tim.
C. Luther, Tim, or Mary.
D. None of the three are eligible to claim the dependency exemption because no one child provided more than half of his or her mother's support.

The answer is A. Only Luther or Tim would be eligible to claim the exemption under a multiple support agreement in 2012. Answer "B" is incorrect because only a single taxpayer may claim the exemption in a tax year. Mary is not eligible in either case because she does not provide more than 10% of her mother's support. ###

21. In 2012, when does an employer have to withhold and pay Social Security and Medicare taxes for a household employee?

A. Whenever the taxpayer pays any employee for household services.
B. When the taxpayer pays a household employee $1,000 or more in wages a year.
C. When the taxpayer pays a household employee $1,800 or more in wages a year.
D. When the taxpayer pays his 20-year-old daughter to care for her younger siblings.

The answer is C. In 2012, the "nanny tax" kicks in when a taxpayer pays a household employee $1,800 or more in wages a year.

Unit 5: Taxable and Nontaxable Income

> **More Reading:**
> Publication 525, *Taxable and Nontaxable Income*
> Publication 504, *Divorced or Separated Individuals*
> Publication 4681, *Canceled Debts, Foreclosures, Repossessions, and Abandonments*
> Publication 544, *Sales and Other Dispositions of Assets*
> Publication 550, *Investment Income and Expenses*

For a taxpayer to determine how much tax he owes, he first needs to figure out his gross income. Gross income includes all money, goods, property, and services that are not exempt from tax. In addition to wages, salaries, commissions, fees, and tips, this includes other forms of compensation such as fringe benefits and stock options.

The IRS's position is that all income is taxable unless it is specifically excluded. An exclusion is not the same as a deduction, and it is important to understand the distinction because many deductions are phased out as a taxpayer's gross income increases. Excluded income, on the other hand, retains its character as excluded income no matter what the taxpayer's gross income is.

Most of the time, excluded income does not have to be reported on a tax return. There are other instances where excluded income must be reported, but it is still not taxable to the recipient.

> **Example:** Brock is a popular recording artist and makes more than $600,000 in wages per year. Because of his high income, Brock is phased out for many deductions. However, in 2012 Brock is involved in an auto accident where he sustains major injuries. Brock sues the other driver and receives a settlement of $80,000 from the insurance company. The insurance settlement is excluded income because compensation for physical injuries is not taxable to the recipient.

Sources of All Income

When taxpayers prepare a federal income tax return such as IRS Form 1040, they must calculate three levels of income:

1. **Gross Income:** This is the sum of all sources of taxable income that the taxpayer receives during the year.

2. **Adjusted Gross Income (AGI):** AGI is total income minus certain allowable deductions. These deductions include, but are not limited to, IRA contributions, qualified student loan interest, certain expenses for self-employed individuals, alimony payments, and moving expenses.

3. **Taxable Income:** This is the amount of income on which a taxpayer owes income taxes. It is calculated by subtracting any deductions and exemptions from AGI.

The Internal Revenue Code (IRC) describes types of income that are taxable and nontaxable. In this unit, we will cover the most common types of both.

How to Calculate Gross Individual Income (Tax Formula)

Start with GROSS INCOME

MINUS- Adjustments to Income ("Above the Line" Deductions)

= <u>ADJUSTED GROSS INCOME</u>

MINUS- Greater of Itemized Deductions or Standard Deduction

MINUS- Personal Exemptions

= TAXABLE INCOME

X Tax Rate

= GROSS TAX Liability

<u>MINUS- Credits</u>

= **NET TAX Liability or Refund Receivable**

Earned Income vs. Unearned Income

Earned income is received for services performed, such as wages, salaries, tips, or professional fees. *Unearned* income is also called "passive income," or investment income. Earned income (such as wages) is treated differently from passive income (such as dividends).

Earned income is generally subject to Social Security tax and Medicare tax (also called the FICA tax). Investment income and other passive income are generally not subject to FICA tax. Some income is variable, which means it is considered earned income for some taxpayers and unearned income for others.

The Doctrine of Constructive Receipt

The doctrine of constructive receipt is premised on the IRS position that taxpayers should be taxed on their income when it becomes available, regardless of whether it is actually in their physical possession.

For example, a check that a taxpayer receives before the end of the tax year is considered income constructively received in that year, even if the taxpayer does not deposit the check into his bank account until the next year. Taxpayers must include in income any amounts that are constructively received during the tax year.

Example: Jerrald is on vacation in Las Vegas. On December 30, 2012, the postal service delivers a check for $500 to his home mailbox in Boise, Idaho. Even though he did not have the check in his physical possession, he is still considered to have constructive receipt of it. Jerrald must include the $500 in gross income on his 2012 tax return.

If there are significant restrictions on the income or if the income is not accessible to the taxpayer, it is not considered to have been constructively received. If a taxpayer refuses income, such as a prize or an award, then the income also is not considered to have been constructively received.

Example: Opal won a big prize for concert tickets from a local radio station. The front-row concert tickets were valued at $1,200. This was a taxable award for Opal, and she is required to pay taxes on the fair market value of the tickets. However, on the day of the concert, the radio station does not receive the tickets in time from the promoter. Opal is not able to attend the concert. Since she never actually received the proceeds, the prize is not taxable to her. She never had constructive receipt of her prize.

Claim of Right Doctrine

Under the claim of right doctrine, income received without restriction—income the taxpayer has complete control over—must be reported in the year received, even if there is a possibility it may have to be repaid in a later year.

If there is a dispute and income is later repaid, the repayment is deductible in the year repaid. As a result, taxpayers are not required to amend their federal gross income for an earlier year based on a subsequent repayment of amounts held under a claim of right by filing an amended return.

Example: In 2012, a gallery owner named Courtney receives $25,000 from the sale of a painting. She properly includes $25,000 in her gross income and pays taxes on the income for the 2012 tax year. On March 1, 2013, the customer discovers that the painting is a forgery and returns it for a full refund of $25,000. Since Courtney pays back the $25,000 in tax year 2013, she is entitled to deduct the amount from her gross income in 2013. No further claim of right deduction is allowed.

However, this does not include income that has substantial restrictions applied to it. The issue usually lies with control over the income. Income received by an agent for a taxpayer is income constructively received in the year the agent received it.

If a taxpayer agrees by contract that a third party is to receive income for him, he must include the amount in his own income when the third party receives it.

Example: Holden's employer garnishes part of his salary for back child support. Since the amount would have normally been included in Holden's paycheck, he must still recognize the income as if he had received it himself. Holden must include that amount in his gross income, even though he never actually received it.

Prizes and Awards

Prizes and awards are usually taxable. If the prize or award is in a form other than cash, the FMV of the property is treated as the taxable amount. The winner may avoid taxation of the award by rejecting the prize. The taxpayer may also choose to transfer the prize to a charity or other nonprofit.

Example: Jerry is a college instructor. He is chosen as teacher of the year by a national education association. He is awarded $3,000, but he does not accept the prize. Instead, Jerry directs the association to transfer his winnings to a college scholarship fund. Jerry never receives a check or has control over the funds. Therefore, the award is not taxable to Jerry.

Some prizes and awards are excludable from income. An award recipient may exclude the FMV of the prize from gross income if:

- The amount received is in recognition of religious, scientific, charitable, or similar meritorious achievement (**Example**: a nonprofit charity awards a Christmas gift to a needy individual);
- The recipient is selected without action on his part;
- The receipt of the award is not conditioned on substantial future services; and
- The amount is paid by the organization making the award to a tax-exempt organization (including a governmental unit) designated by the recipient.

Employee Awards (Exclusion from Income)

There is also an exclusion for awards given to employees. Certain employee awards may qualify for exclusion from the employee's gross income as a nontaxable fringe benefit. A prize may also qualify for exclusion from income if it is a scholarship.

Amounts paid for employee awards are still deductible to the employer and not taxable to the employee if certain rules are followed.[35] A cash award is always taxable to the employee. An achievement award in the form of property, if given to the employee for length of service or as a safety achievement, is not taxable to the employee and is still deductible by the employer.

Employers can exclude from wages the value of achievement awards given to an employee from the employee's wages if the cost is not more than the amount the employer can deduct as a business expense for the year. The excludable annual amount is $1,600 for qualified plan awards per employee.

There is a $400 annual limit for nonqualified awards that are given to highly compensated executives, but not to rank-and-file employees.

Example: Space Corporation awards a set of golf clubs to an employee as a nonqualified plan employee achievement award. The FMV of the golf clubs is $750. The amount included in taxable wages to the employee is $350 ($750 – $400). If the award had been a qualified plan award, the employee would not have been taxed on the FMV of the award.
Example: Rowan received three employee achievement awards during the year: a watch valued at $250, a stereo valued at $1,000, and a set of golf clubs valued at $500. She received each of the awards for length of service and exceptional safety achievement. They are all qualified plan awards and would normally be excluded from her income, assuming that the other requirements for qualified plan awards are satisfied. However, because the $1,750 total value of the awards is more than $1,600, Rowan must include $150 ($1,750 – $1,600) in her income.

The employer must make the award as part of a meaningful presentation, and it cannot simply be disguised pay.

---

[35] Employee awards and fringe benefits are covered in more detail in Part 2. For Part 1 of the EA exam, you must understand the tax implications of how an employee award would be reported by an individual who receives the award (the employee). For Part 2 of the exam, you would need to understand the tax implications of employee awards from the perspective of the employer that offers the benefit.

Income from Canceled Debt

Generally, if a taxpayer's debt is canceled or forgiven, the taxpayer must include the canceled debt in his gross income. There is no income from a canceled debt if it is intended as a gift (for example, if a taxpayer owes his parents money but the parents choose to forgive the debt.)

Cancellation of debt can involve auto loans, credit card debt, medical care, professional services, installment purchases of furniture or other personal property, mortgages, and home equity loans. A debt includes any indebtedness for which a taxpayer is liable or which attaches to the taxpayer's property.

Taxpayers often question the taxability of canceled debt because they did not receive any actual money. In situations where property is surrendered or repossessed such as a foreclosure, taxpayers may feel that by giving up the property, they should be relieved from any further obligation. However, canceled debt is taxable because the benefit to the taxpayer is the relief from personal liability to pay the debt.

If the debt is a *nonbusiness* debt, the canceled debt amount should be reported as "other income" on line 21 of a taxpayer's Form 1040. If it is a business debt, it is reported on Schedule C of Form 1040.

When an entity cancels a debt of $600 or more, the taxpayer should receive a Form 1099-C, *Cancellation of Debt*.

Example: Phoebe borrows $10,000 to take a vacation and defaults on the loan after paying back only $2,000. She spends all the money and is unwilling to make payments on the loan. The lender is unable to collect the remaining amount of the loan. Phoebe is not insolvent. Therefore, there is a cancellation of debt of $8,000, which is taxable income to Phoebe. She must include it on her tax return as "other income."

If a financial institution offers a discount for the early payment of a mortgage loan, the amount of the discount is taxable as canceled debt. This occurs when a lender discounts or reduces the principal balance of a loan to reward an early payoff.

Recourse and Nonrecourse Debt

Knowing whether a loan is recourse or nonrecourse will often determine the taxability of a canceled debt.

Recourse debt holds the borrower personally liable for any amount not satisfied by the surrender of secured property. If a lender forecloses on property subject to a recourse debt and cancels the portion of the debt in excess of the FMV of the property, the canceled portion is treated as ordinary income. This amount must be included in gross income unless it qualifies for an exception or exclusion. In a recourse loan, the taxpayer must generally report two transactions:

1. The cancellation of debt income
2. Gain or loss on the sale or repossession

In addition to this cancellation of indebtedness income, the taxpayer may realize a gain or loss on the disposition of the property; this amount is generally the difference between the FMV of the property at the time of the foreclosure and the taxpayer's adjusted basis in the property.

*Note: If a personal vehicle is repossessed, then the repossession is treated as a sale, and the gain or loss must be computed. The loss would be nondeductible for personal vehicles.

Example: Zach lost his yacht because he could no longer make his payments. At the time of repossession, he owed a balance of $170,000 to the lender, and the FMV of the yacht was $140,000. Zach is personally liable for the debt (recourse loan), so the abandonment is treated as a sale. The "selling price" from the repossession is $140,000, and Zach must recognize $30,000 in debt forgiveness income.

Example: Doreen bought a new car for $15,000. She made a $2,000 down payment and borrowed the remaining $13,000 from her bank. Doreen is personally liable for the car loan (recourse debt). The bank repossessed her car because she stopped making payments. The balance due on the loan at the time of the repossession was $10,000. The FMV of the car when repossessed was only $9,000. Since a repossession is treated as a sale, the gain or loss must be computed. Doreen compares the amount realized ($9,000) with her adjusted basis ($15,000) to determine that she has a $6,000 nondeductible loss. She also has ordinary income from cancellation of debt. That income is $1,000 ($10,000 canceled debt − $9,000 FMV). Doreen must report the canceled debt as income on line 21 of her Form 1040.

A *nonrecourse* debt is a type of loan that is secured by collateral in which the borrower does not have liability for the loan. Many mortgages are nonrecourse. This means that if the borrower defaults, the lender can seize the home, but cannot seek out the borrower for any further compensation, even if the FMV of the home does not cover the full value of the loan amount.

If the taxpayer abandons property that secures debt for which the taxpayer is not personally liable (a nonrecourse loan), the abandonment is treated as a sale or exchange. If a loan is nonrecourse and the borrower does not retain the asset, then the borrower does not have to recognize cancellation of debt income.

Qualified Principal Residence Indebtedness (QPRI)

The *Mortgage Debt Relief Act of 2007* allows taxpayers to exclude income from the discharge of debt on their principal residence, which is defined as the home where the taxpayer ordinarily lives most of the time. This exception does not apply to second homes or vacation homes.

The provision applies to debt forgiven in 2007 through 2012, and has been extended through 2013 by the 2012 American Taxpayer Relief Act. Up to $2 million of forgiven debt is eligible for this exclusion ($1 million if MFS). The exclusion does not apply unless it is directly related to a decline in the home's value or the taxpayer's financial condition.

Normally, when a bank forecloses on a home and sells it for less than the borrower's outstanding mortgage, it forgives the unpaid mortgage debt. That canceled debt then becomes taxable income to the homeowner. The Mortgage Debt Relief Act, however, allows an exclusion of income realized as a result of loan modification or foreclosure of a taxpayer's principal residence. The taxpayer must report the amount of debt forgiven on his return by completing Form 982, *Reduction of Tax Attributes Due to Discharge of Indebtedness.*

"Qualified principal residence indebtedness" (QPRI) is a mortgage secured by a taxpayer's principal residence that was taken out to buy, build, or substantially improve that residence. QPRI cannot be more than the cost of the home plus improvements. QPRI also may include debt from refinancing.

*Note: A loss on the sale of a personal residence is not deductible.
Example: Adam's home is subject to a $320,000 mortgage debt. Adam's creditor forecloses in April 2012. Due to declining real estate values, the residence is sold for $280,000 in December 2012. Adam has $40,000 of income from discharge of indebtedness and may claim the exclusion by filing Form 982 with his 2012 tax return.

"Ordering Rule" for Principal Residence Indebtedness

If only a part of a loan is qualified principal residence indebtedness, the exclusion from income for QPRI applies only to the extent the amount canceled exceeds the amount of the loan that is not QPRI.

However, the remaining part of the loan may qualify for a different exclusion (such as the exclusion for insolvency).

Example: Ken incurred debt of $800,000 when he purchased his home for $880,000. He made a down payment of $80,000 and financed the rest. When the FMV of the property was $1 million, Ken refinanced the debt for $850,000. At the time of the refinancing, the balance of the original loan was $740,000. Ken used the $110,000 he obtained from the refinancing ($850,000 minus $740,000) to buy a luxury car and take a vacation to the Bahamas. Two years after the refinancing, Ken lost his job. Ken's home declined in value to $750,000. Based on Ken's circumstances, the lender agreed to a short sale of the property for $735,000 and to cancel the remaining $115,000 of the $850,000 debt. Under the "ordering rule," Ken can exclude only $5,000 of the canceled debt from his income using the exclusion for canceled QPRI ($115,000 canceled debt minus the $110,000 amount of the debt that was not QPRI—basically the money he spent on personal purchases). Ken must include the remaining $110,000 of canceled debt in income.

HAMP Loan Modifications

The Home Affordable Modification Program (HAMP) attempts to help financially distressed homeowners lower their monthly mortgage payments. If a borrower continues to make timely payments on the loan for three years, he can have his mortgage reduced by a predetermined amount (known as the PRA Forbearance Amount).

The loan holder is then reimbursed through incentive payments by the HAMP program administrator. To the extent the mortgage reduction exceeds the incentive payments, the borrower may be required to include the excess amount in gross income as a discharge of indebtedness. However, the borrower may be eligible to exclude the discharge of indebtedness income from gross income if:

- The mortgage loan is qualified principal residence indebtedness and the loan is modified before January 1, 2014, or
- The discharge of indebtedness occurs when the borrower is insolvent.

Any portion of the discharge of indebtedness that is excluded from income must also be reflected as a reduction in basis.

Canceled Debt that is Otherwise Deductible

If a taxpayer uses the cash method of accounting, he should not recognize canceled debt income if payment of the debt would have otherwise been a deductible expense.

Example: Jiao is a self-employed interior designer. She receives $2,200 in accounting services for her business on credit. Later, Jiao loses a major account and has trouble paying her debts, so her accountant forgives the amount she owes. Jiao does not include the canceled debt in her gross income because payment of the debt would have been deductible as a business expense anyway.

Nontaxable Canceled Debt

Besides the QPRI and HAMP rules already discussed, there are other types of canceled debt that qualify for exclusion from gross income. Among the most common are:

- Debt canceled in a Title 11 bankruptcy case
- Debt canceled during insolvency
- Cancellation of qualified farm indebtedness

Bankruptcy

Debts discharged through bankruptcy court in a Title 11 bankruptcy case are not considered taxable income. The taxpayer must attach Form 982 to his federal income tax return to report debt that is canceled in bankruptcy.

Insolvency

If a taxpayer is insolvent when the debt is canceled, the canceled debt is not taxable. A taxpayer is "insolvent" when total debts are more than the FMV of his total assets. For purposes of determining insolvency, assets include the value of everything the taxpayer owns, including the value of pensions and retirement accounts.

Example: In 2012, Darla had $5,000 in credit card debt, which she did not pay. She received a Form 1099-C from her credit card company showing canceled debt of $5,000. Darla's total liabilities immediately before the cancellation were $15,000, and the FMV of her total assets immediately before the cancellation was $7,000. This means that at the time the debt was canceled, Darla was insolvent to the extent of $8,000 ($15,000 total liabilities minus $7,000 FMV of her total assets). Therefore, Darla can exclude the entire $5,000 canceled debt from income.

Qualifying Farm Debts

If a taxpayer incurred the canceled debt in farming, it is generally not considered taxable income.

Certain Canceled Student Loans are Not Taxable

Certain student loans contain a provision that all or part of the debt incurred to attend a qualified educational institution will be canceled if the student later works for a specified period of time in certain professions. The canceled debt does not have to be recognized as income on a taxpayer's return.

> **Example:** Tatum is a medical student completing her residency. She agrees to work as a doctor in a state program in Minnesota serving rural and poor communities. Tatum agreed to take a job as a pediatrician in the state's rural towns for four years in return for the forgiveness of her student loans. The canceled debt qualifies for nonrecognition treatment, and the canceled debt does not have to be recognized as income.

529 Plans

529 plans (also known as "prepaid" qualified tuition programs) are operated by a state or an educational institution to provide tax advantages that make it easier for taxpayers to save for college for their designated beneficiaries. Earnings are not subject to federal income tax, though contributions to a 529 plan are not deductible.

Under a 529 plan, a taxpayer purchases tuition credits or waivers on behalf of a designated beneficiary that entitle the beneficiary to the waiver or payment of qualified higher education expenses. Expenses include tuition, fees, books, computer equipment and software, and room and board for any time the beneficiary is enrolled in college. A beneficiary may be whomever the taxpayer chooses: himself, a child, a grandchild, or an unrelated person.

Contributions cannot exceed the amount necessary to provide for the qualified education expenses of the beneficiary. There may also be gift tax considerations for the taxpayer, depending on how much he contributes to a 529 plan in a given year.

Gambling Winnings

Gambling winnings are fully taxable and must be reported on a taxpayer's return. Gambling winnings are reported on IRS Form W-2G, and will be sent if a taxpayer wins:

- $600 or more in winnings from gambling
- $1,200 or more in winnings from bingo or slot machines
- $1,500 or more in proceeds from keno
- Or any gambling winnings subject to federal income tax withholding

A taxpayer must report and pay tax on all gambling winnings, regardless of whether he receives a Form W-2G. Gambling income includes winnings from lotteries, raffles, horse races, and casinos. It also includes cash winnings and the fair market value of prizes such as cars and trips.

Gambling losses are deductible, but only on Schedule A as an itemized deduction. The amount of the deduction is limited to the amount of gambling winnings.

> **Example:** Yolanda had $1,000 in gambling winnings for the year. She had $3,000 in gambling losses. Her deduction for gambling losses cannot exceed $1,000, the amount of her gambling winnings. Yolanda must itemize and list her gambling losses on Schedule A (Form 1040.)

An accurate diary or similar record of gambling winnings and losses must be kept along with tickets, receipts, canceled checks, and other documentation. These supporting records need not be sent in with the tax return, but should be retained in case of an audit.

Gambling winnings are reported as "other income" on line 21 of Form 1040.

Self-Employment Income and SE Tax

Self-employment income is earned by taxpayers who work for themselves. Generally, these are small business owners. Any taxpayer who has self-employment income of $400 or more in a year must file a tax return and report the earnings to the IRS.

Most self-employed people report their income and loss on Schedule C, Form 1040. Self-employed farmers or fishermen report their earnings on Schedule F, Form 1040. Self-employment income also includes:

- Income of ministers, priests, and rabbis for the performance of services such as baptisms and marriages
- The distributive share of partnership income allocated to general partners or managers of a limited liability company, with the income reported to the partner on IRS Form K-1.

Self-employment tax (SE tax) is a tax consisting of Social Security and Medicare taxes primarily for self-employed individuals. It is similar to the Social Security and Medicare taxes withheld from the pay of most wage earners. If an employee is working for an employer, the employer pays half of these taxes and the employee pays the other half. But self-employed people are responsible for paying the entire amount of Social Security and Medicare taxes.

The SE tax rate for 2012 is 13.3% on self-employment income up to $110,100 of a taxpayer's combined wages, tips, and net earnings. If net earnings exceed $110,100, the taxpayer will continue to pay only the Medicare portion of the SE tax, which is 2.9%, on the rest of their earnings.

This SE tax rate for 2012 includes a temporary decrease in the employee's share of payroll tax, with Social Security taxed at a rate of 4.2% rather than the normal 6.2%, up to the Social Security wage limit of $110,100.[36]

There is no cap on the 2.9% Medicare tax, which is imposed on all net earnings no matter how high the income (true for both wage earners and self-employed individuals.) If a taxpayer has wages in addition to self-employment earnings, the Social Security tax on the wages is paid first.

There are two income tax deductions related to the self-employment tax that reduce overall taxes on a taxpayer with self-employment income.

---

[36] Congress has chosen not to extend this "payroll tax holiday." That means in tax year 2013 the Social Security tax rate for employees and self-employed individuals rose 2 percentage points to 6.2%. The self-employment tax rate increased from 13.3% to 15.3%, up to the $113,700 income threshold for tax year 2013.

- First, net earnings from self-employment are reduced by 7.65% of the total Social Security tax. This is similar to the way employees are treated under the tax laws, because the employer's share of the Social Security tax is not considered wages to the employee.
- Second, the taxpayer can deduct half of the Social Security tax on IRS Form 1040 as an adjustment to gross income.

Self-employment tax is calculated on IRS Schedule SE. If a taxpayer operates more than one business, he may combine the net incomes and use only one Schedule SE.

Example: In 2012, Devon has a full-time job and also makes money on weekends as a self-employed musician. In 2012, his wages from his job are $79,000. He also has $35,000 in net earnings from his music business for total income of $115,000. Devon does not pay dual Social Security taxes on his earnings that exceed $110,100. His employer withholds 5.65% in Social Security and Medicare taxes on his $79,000 in wages. That means Devon must pay 13.3% in Social Security and Medicare taxes on his first $31,100 in self-employment earnings and 2.9% in Medicare tax on the remaining $3,900 in earnings.

More than One Sole Proprietorship

If a taxpayer runs more than one business, then he will net the profit (or loss) from each to determine the total earnings subject to SE tax. Taxpayers cannot combine a spouse's income (or loss) to determine their individual earnings subject to SE tax. However, a single person with two sole proprietorships may combine income and losses from both businesses to figure self-employment tax.

Example: Tanner is a sole proprietor who owns a barbershop. He has $19,000 in net income for 2012. His wife, Erin, has a candle-making business, which has a loss of $12,000 in 2012. Tanner must pay self-employment tax on $19,000, regardless of how he and Erin choose to file. That is because married couples cannot offset each other's self-employment tax. The income of each business is allocated to the individual—not the gross amount shown on a joint tax return.

Example: Darren is a single taxpayer who is a sole proprietor with two small businesses, a computer repair shop and a car wash business. The computer business has net income of $45,000 in 2012, while the car wash has a net loss of $23,000 in 2012. Darren only has to pay self-employment tax on $22,000 ($45,000-$23,000) of income, because he may net the income and losses from both his businesses.

Employee Fringe Benefits (Taxable and Nontaxable)

Fringe benefits are offered to employees by employers as a condition of their employment. Some fringe benefits are taxable and some are not. This next section will cover each type of fringe benefit, both from the perspective of the individual (the employee receiving the benefits) and the business owner (the entity providing the benefits.) Common fringe benefits include health benefits, vacation pay, and parking passes. Although most employee fringe benefits are nontaxable, some benefits must be included in an employee's taxable income and are usually reported on the taxpayer's Form W-2. Examples of *taxable* fringe benefits include:

- Off-site athletic facilities and health club memberships.

- The value of employer-provided life insurance over $50,000.
- Any cash benefit or benefit in the form of a credit card or gift card.
- Season tickets to sporting events, although single tickets can be excluded in certain cases.
- Transportation benefits, if the value of a benefit for any month is more than the nontaxable limit. Employers cannot exclude the excess from the employee's wages as a *de minimis* transportation benefit.
- Employer-provided vehicles, if they are used for personal purposes.

Example: Tanning Town Inc. owns a tropical resort employees may use free of charge. Sam visits the resort with his family for two weeks. The fair market value of the stay is $5,000, which will be included in his taxable wages.

Nontaxable Employee Fringe Benefits

Most fringe benefits are not taxable and may be excluded from an employee's income. The following are some common types of nontaxable employee fringe benefits.

Cafeteria Plans

A *cafeteria plan* provides employees an opportunity to receive certain benefits on a pretax basis. An employer may choose to make benefits available to employees, their spouses, and dependents. Generally, qualified benefits under a cafeteria plan are not subject to FICA, FUTA, Medicare tax, or income tax withholding.

Employee contributions to the cafeteria plan are usually made via salary reduction agreements taken directly out of the employee's paycheck. The employee usually agrees to contribute a portion of his salary on a pretax basis to pay for a portion of the qualified benefits.

Participants in a cafeteria plan must be permitted to choose among at least one taxable benefit (such as cash) and one qualified benefit. A qualified benefit is a benefit that is nontaxable. Qualified benefits include:

- Accident, dental, vision, and medical benefits (but not Archer medical savings accounts or long-term care insurance)
- Adoption assistance
- Dependent care assistance
- Group-term life insurance coverage (up to $50,000 of life insurance coverage may be provided as a nontaxable benefit to an employee.)
- Health savings accounts

*Note: If an employer pays the cost of an accident insurance plan for an employee, then the amounts received under the plan are taxable to the employee. If a taxpayer pays the cost of an accident insurance plan for himself, then the benefits received under the plan are not taxable.

Flexible Spending Arrangement (FSA)

An FSA is a form of cafeteria plan benefit, funded by salary reduction, which reimburses employees for expenses incurred for certain qualified benefits. An FSA may be offered for dependent care assistance, adoption assistance, and medical care reimbursements. The benefits are subject to an annual maximum and an annual "use-or-lose" rule. An FSA cannot provide a cumulative benefit to the employee beyond the plan year. The employee must substantiate his expenses, and then the distributions to the employee are tax-free.

Dependent Care Assistance

An employee can generally exclude from gross income up to $5,000 in 2012 ($2,500 if MFS) of benefits received under a dependent care assistance program each year. Amounts paid directly to the taxpayer or to a daycare provider qualify for exclusion. The amount that qualifies for exclusion is limited to:

- The total amount of the dependent care benefits received
- The employee's earned income
- The spouse's earned income
- $5,000 ($2,500 if married filing separately)

Example: John's employer offers a cafeteria plan that allows for dependent care assistance. John files jointly with his wife, Cindy. John makes $50,000 in 2012. Cindy earns $4,500 as a part-time bookkeeper. They have $5,500 in daycare costs for 2012. The maximum amount that can be excluded in 2012 is $4,500, the amount of Cindy's earned income.

Example: Tina's employer provides a dependent care assistance flexible spending plan to its employees through a cafeteria plan. In addition, it provides occasional onsite dependent care to its employees at no cost. Tina had $4,500 deducted from her pay for the dependent care flexible spending arrangement. She also used the on-site dependent care several times. The FMV of the on-site care was $700. Tina's Form W-2 will report $5,200 of dependent care assistance ($4,500 flexible spending + $700 FMV of on-site dependent care.) Since the IRS only allows an exclusion of $5,000 in dependent care assistance per year, Boxes 1, 3, and 5 of her Form W-2 should include $200 (the amount in excess of the nontaxable assistance), and applicable taxes should be withheld on that amount.

De Minimis Employee Benefits

Some employee benefits are so small that it would be impractical for the employer to account for them. These are called *de minimis* benefits. The exclusion applies, for example, to the following items:

- Coffee, doughnuts, or soft drinks provided to employees
- Occasional meals while employees work overtime (100% of the cost)
- Occasional company picnics for employees
- Occasional use of the employer's copy machine
- Holiday gifts, other than cash, such as a Thanksgiving turkey
- An employer-provided cell phone

De Minimis Meals: Meals that are provided to an employee at his place of work and that are for the employer's convenience are not taxable to the employee. They are also 100% deductible by the employer and not subject to the normal 50% limit.[37] Meals that employers furnish to a restaurant employee during, immediately before, or after the employee's working hours are considered furnished for the employer's convenience.

Example: Ellen is a registered nurse who is not allowed to leave the hospital premises during her long shifts. She works in the emergency room and must be available to help patients immediately, so the hospital provides meals and a place for her to sleep during her shift. Ellen does not have to recognize the value of the meals as income. The hospital also does not have to add the FMV of Ellen's meals to her wages. In addition, the meals are 100% deductible by the hospital, not subject to the 50% limit, because they are provided as a condition of her employment and are for the convenience of her employer.

Example: A commuter ferry breaks down unexpectedly, and the engineers are required to work overtime to make repairs. After working eight hours, the engineers break for dinner because they will be working overtime until the engine is repaired. The supervisor gives each employee $10 for a meal. The meal is not taxable to the engineers because it was provided to permit them to work overtime in a situation that is not routine.

Employer-Provided Cell Phones

The value of the business use of an employer-provided cell phone is excludable from an employee's income to the extent that, if the employee paid for its use, the payment would be deductible. The IRS has ruled that there must be substantial "noncompensatory" reasons for use of a phone that relate to the employer's business.

Legitimate reasons include the employer's need to contact the employee at all times for work-related emergencies and the employee's need to be available to speak with clients away from the office. However, a cell phone provided simply to promote an employee's morale or to attract a prospective employee is not noncompensatory. In those cases, the value of a cell phone would no longer be a de minimis benefit and must be added to an employee's wages.

If an employer provides an employee with a cell phone primarily for noncompensatory business purposes, then personal use of the phone also is excludable from an employee's income as a *de minimis* fringe benefit.[38]

*NOTE: Most *cash* benefits or their equivalent (such as gift cards or credit cards) cannot be excluded as de *minimis* fringe benefits, except in certain cases of minimal amounts given for meals or transportation.

No-Additional-Cost Services

Nontaxable fringe benefits include services provided to employees that do not impose any substantial additional cost because the employer already offers those services in the ordinary course of doing business. Employees do not need to include these no-additional-cost

---

[37] Meals are generally 50% deductible. This means when a business pays for a meal, only 50% of its cost is normally deductible by the employer, except in certain situations such as those described above.
[38] IRS Notice 2011-72.

services in their income. An employer can offer discounts, as well as on-site benefits, such as an on-site gym. If an employee is provided with the free or low cost use of a health club on the employer's premises, the value is not included in the employee's compensation. The gym must be used primarily by employees, their spouses, and their dependent children. If the employer pays for a fitness program provided to the employee at an off-site resort hotel, country club, or athletic club, the value of the program is included in the employee's compensation.

> **Example:** Trey works for a local fitness club. He is allowed to work out for free as a condition of his employment. This is because this fringe benefit is a no-additional-cost service to his employer. Trey is also allowed a 10% discount on vitamins that the gym sells to patrons, so long as the vitamins are for his own use (Publication 15-B).

Typically, no-additional-cost services are excess capacity services, such as airline, bus, or train tickets; hotel rooms; or telephone services provided free or at a reduced rate to employees working in those lines of business.

> **Example:** Henrietta is a flight attendant with Jet Way Airlines. She is allowed to fly for free on stand-by flights when there is an extra seat. This is an example of a fringe benefit that is allowed for no additional cost to the employer and is therefore nontaxable to the employee.

Employer-Provided Educational Assistance

An employer-provided educational assistance program can be excluded up to a certain amount. The amounts must be for tuition, books, required fees, and supplies. Room and board do not qualify as educational expenses for purposes of an employer-sponsored educational assistance plan.

The maximum excluded educational benefit is $5,250 in 2012. If an employee receives these employer-provided benefits, he cannot use any of the tax-free education expenses as the basis for any other education-related deduction or credit.

Transportation Fringe Benefits

Employers may provide transportation benefits to their employees up to certain amounts without having to include the benefit in the employee's income. Qualified transportation benefits include transit passes, paid parking, a ride in a commuter highway vehicle between the employee's home and workplace, and qualified bicycle commuting reimbursement. In 2012, employees may exclude:

- $240 per month in combined commuter highway vehicle transportation and transit passes,[39] and
- $240 per month in parking benefits.

This nontaxable benefit is a combined maximum of $480 per month in 2012. Employees may receive transit passes and benefits for parking during the same month; they are not mutually exclusive.

---

[39] Congress's fiscal cliff legislation of January 1, 2013 retroactively reinstated parity between the benefits for parking and transit benefits for 2012. The parity had expired at the end of 2011, so that for all of 2012 employers had expected the amount excluded for commuter highway vehicles or transit passes to be $125 a month, not $240. The IRS has issued guidance on FICA tax refunds and W-2 adjustments for businesses that gave transit benefits of more than $125 a month in 2012. Employers that treated the excess as wages can make adjustments, but they will have to reimburse their employees for the over-collected FICA tax before doing so.

An employer may also reimburse an employee for a bicycle that is used for commuting purposes. A qualified bicycle commuting reimbursement is a reimbursement of up to $20 per month for reasonable expenses incurred by the employee in conjunction with his commute to work by bike.

However, the use of a company car for commuting purposes is a taxable benefit. So, if an employer allows an employee to use a company vehicle for commuting, then the value of the vehicle's use is taxable to the employee.

Personal use of an employer's vehicle is also considered taxable wages to the employee.

Example: Joe, an employee of Carsonville Lumber Company, uses an employer-provided pickup truck. He uses the truck on job sites, to haul equipment, and to deliver lumber to customers. In 2012, Joe drives the truck 20,000 miles, of which 4,000 were personal miles or 20% (4,000/20,000 = 20%). The truck has an annual lease value of $4,100. Personal use is therefore valued at $820 and is included in Joe's wages.

Accountable Plans

An accountable plan is a plan in which an employer reimburses employees for business-related expenses such as mileage, meals, and travel expenses. For expenses to qualify under an accountable plan, employees must meet all of the following requirements:

- Have incurred the expenses while performing services as employees
- Adequately account for the expenses within a reasonable period of time
- Adequately account for their travel, meals, and entertainment expenses
- Provide evidence of their employee business expenses, such as receipts or other records
- Return any excess reimbursement or allowance within a reasonable period of time

Under an accountable plan, a business may advance money to employees; however, certain conditions must be met. The cash advance must be reasonably calculated to equal the anticipated expenses. The business owner must make the advance within a reasonable period of time. If any expenses reimbursed under this arrangement are not substantiated, a business is not allowed to deduct them under an accountable plan.

Instead, the reimbursed expenses are considered a nonaccountable plan and become taxable to the employee.

Example: Donna is an EA who runs a tax preparation business. She advances $250 to her employee, Mel, so that he can become a notary. Mel spends $90 on a notary course and then another $100 to take the notary exam, which he passes. Mel returns the unused funds ($60) as well as copies of his receipts to Donna, his boss. The expenses are qualified expenses under an accountable plan. Donna may deduct the $190 ($90 + $100) as a business expense, and the amounts are not taxable to Mel.

Cash reimbursements are excludable if an employer establishes a bona fide reimbursement plan. This means there must be reasonable procedures to verify reimbursements and employees must substantiate the expenses using receipts or other substantiation.

Example: Mai Ling buys a parking permit for $240 each month in 2012. At the end of each month, she presents her used parking pass to her employer and certifies that she purchased and used it during the month. The employer reimburses her $240 in cash. The employer has established a bona fide reimbursement arrangement for purposes of excluding the $240 reimbursement from the employee's gross income in 2012. The reimbursement is not taxable to Mai Ling, and it is deductible by the employer.

Accountable Plans: Travel Reimbursements

Qualifying expenses for travel are excludable from an employee's income if they are incurred for *temporary* travel on business away from the area of the employee's tax home. Travel expenses paid in connection with an indefinite work assignment are not excludable. Any work assignment in excess of one year is considered "indefinite." Travel expense reimbursements include:

- Costs to travel to and from the business destination (flights, mileage reimbursements)
- Transportation costs while at the business destination (taxi fare, shuttles)
- Lodging, meals, and incidental expenses
- Cleaning, laundry, and other miscellaneous expenses

Example: Woody works for a travel agency in Detroit. He flies to Seattle to conduct business for an entire week. His employer pays the cost of transportation to and from Seattle, as well as lodging and meals while there. The reimbursements for substantiated travel expenses are excludable from Woody's income, and the reimbursements are deductible by his employer.

Employer-Provided Life Insurance as a Fringe Benefit

Employers may deduct the cost of life insurance premiums provided to employees. Employer-provided life insurance is a nontaxable fringe benefit only up to $50,000. Coverage amounts over $50,000 are taxable to the employee. The employer must calculate the taxable portion of the premiums for coverage that exceeds $50,000.

Example: Carol, a 47-year-old employee, receives $40,000 of life insurance coverage per year under a policy carried by her employer. Her employer agrees to pay the premiums on the first $40,000 of coverage as part of Carol's cafeteria plan. She may also elect another $100,000 of additional life insurance coverage. This optional coverage is also carried by her employer. The cost of $10,000 of this additional amount is excludable; the cost of the remaining $90,000 of coverage is included in income. Since only $50,000 of life insurance coverage can be nontaxable to the employee, Carol will be taxed on the difference between the premiums.

Employer-Provided Retirement Plan Contributions

Many employers contribute to their employees' retirement plans. This contribution is not taxable to the employee when it is made. The contribution only becomes taxable when the employee finally withdraws the funds from his retirement account.[40]

---

[40] The IRS has very detailed rules for retirement plans, and they are often tested on the EA exam. Retirement plans are covered extensively in Unit 14, *Individual Retirement Arrangements*.

This rule also applies to elected deferrals. Employees may elect to have part of their pretax compensation contributed to a retirement fund. An elective deferral is excluded from wages, but is still subject to Social Security and Medicare tax. Elective deferrals include contributions into the following retirement plans:

- 401(k) plans, 403(B) plans, section 457 plans
- SIMPLE plans
- Thrift Savings Plans for federal employees

Elective deferrals to a Roth retirement plan are taxable to the employee. That is because a Roth plan is always funded with post-tax income. Roth IRAs are tax-free when they are withdrawn.

Special Rules for Highly Compensated Employees (HCEs)

If a benefit plan favors highly compensated employees, the value of their benefits become taxable. There cannot be special rules that favor eligibility for HCEs to participate, contribute, or benefit from a cafeteria plan. This is to discourage companies from offering spectacular tax-free benefits to their highly compensated executives, while ignoring the needs of lower-paid employees.

An HCE is any of the following:

- an officer
- a shareholder who owns more than 5% of the voting power or value of all classes of the employer's stock
- an employee who is highly compensated based on the facts and circumstances; or
- a spouse or dependent of a person described above.

Employer-provided benefits also cannot favor "key employees," defined as:

- An officer with annual pay of more than $165,000 in 2012, or
- An employee who is either a 5% owner of the business or a 1% owner of the business whose annual pay was more than $150,000 in 2012.

The law for highly compensated employees includes a "look-back provision," so employees who were previously considered HCEs are generally still considered HCEs for 2012 plan year testing (Publication 15-B).

Example: Fengrew Inc. is a C Corporation with 300 employees, 45 of whom are considered "highly compensated employees." Fengrew's cafeteria plan is available to all the employees; therefore, the discrimination rules do not apply, and the employees' benefits are not taxable.

If a plan favors HCE or key employees, the employer is required to include the value of the benefits they could have selected in their wages. A plan is considered to have "favored" HCEs if over 25% of all the benefits are given to HCEs.

A benefit plan that covers union employees under a collective bargaining agreement is not included in this rule.

Interest Income

Interest is a passive form of income received from bank accounts and other sources. Interest income is reported to the taxpayer on IRS Form 1099-INT. If interest income exceeds $1,500, the taxpayer must report the interest on Schedule B (Form 1040). A taxpayer cannot file Form 1040EZ if his interest income exceeds $1,500. Tax-exempt interest is reported on page one of IRS Form 1040. The following are some other sources of taxable interest:

- Credit unions (which uses the term "dividends," but the IRS has ruled it should actually be considered interest)
- Domestic building and loan associations
- Domestic savings and loan associations
- Federal savings and loan associations
- Mutual savings banks
- Certificates of deposits (CDs) and other deferred interest accounts

Gift for Opening a Bank Account

If a taxpayer receives noncash gifts or services for making deposits or for opening an account in a savings institution, the value of the gift may have to be reported as interest. For deposits of less than $5,000, gifts or services valued at more than $10 must be reported as interest.

For deposits of $5,000 or more, gifts or services valued at more than $20 must be reported as interest. The value of the gift is determined by the financial institution.

A cash bonus for opening a new checking or credit card account is also taxable interest. However, the IRS has ruled that cash back and reward points earned on credit and debit card purchases are not taxable interest income.

Interest on Insurance Dividends

Interest on insurance dividends left on deposit with an insurance company that can be withdrawn annually is taxable in the year it is credited to the taxpayer's account. However, if the taxpayer cannot withdraw the income except on a certain date (the anniversary date of the policy or other specified date), the income is considered restricted and not taxable when it is earned. The interest is taxable in the year that the withdrawal is allowed.

Interest Earned on U.S. Treasury Bills, Notes, and Bonds

Interest on U.S. obligations, such as U.S. Treasury bills, notes, and bonds issued by any agency of the United States, is taxable for federal income tax purposes.

*Special note: The interest a taxpayer pays on loans borrowed from a bank to meet the minimum deposit required for a CD and the interest a taxpayer earns on the CD are two separate things. The taxpayer must include the total interest earned on the CD in income. If the taxpayer itemizes deductions, he can deduct the interest paid as investment interest paid, up to the amount of net investment income.

Example: Sienna wanted to invest in a $10,000 six-month CD. She deposited $5,000 in a CD with a credit union and borrowed $5,000 from another bank to make up the $10,000 minimum deposit required to buy the six-month CD. The certificate earned $575 at maturity in 2012, but Sienna actually received net $265 in interest income that year. This represented the $575 Sienna earned on the CD, minus $310 interest charged on the $5,000 loan. The credit union gives Sienna a Form 1099-INT for 2012 showing the $575 interest she earned. The other bank also gives Sienna a statement showing that she paid $310 interest for 2012. Sienna must include the total interest amount earned, $575, in her interest income for 2012. Only if Sienna itemizes can she deduct the interest expense of $310.

Wages and Employee Compensation

Wages, salaries, bonuses, and commissions are compensation received by employees for services performed. All income from wages, salaries, and tips is taxable to the employee and deductible by the employer. Employers are generally required to issue Form W-2s by January 31, which show the amount of wages paid to employees for the previous year. Wages are reported by the employee as taxable income on Form 1040.

Employers are required by law to withhold Social Security and Medicare taxes. If the employer fails to withhold Social Security and Medicare, the employee is required to file IRS Form 8919, *Uncollected Social Security and Medicare Tax on Wages.*

Advance commissions and other advance earnings are all taxable in the year they are received, whether or not the employee has earned the income. If the employee receives wages in advance, he must recognize the income in the year it is constructively received.

This is true even if the employee is forced to pay back some of the money at a later date. If the employee later pays back a portion of the earnings, that sum would be deducted from wages at that time.

Example: Maddox requests a salary advance of $1,000 on December 18, 2012 in order to go on a two-week vacation. Maddox must recognize the income on his 2012 tax return, even though he will not actually earn the money until 2013, when he returns from his vacation.

"Supplemental wages" is compensation that is paid to an employee in addition to his regular pay. These amounts are listed on the employee's Form W-2 and are taxable just like regular wages, even if the pay is not actually for work performed. Vacation pay is an example of supplemental wages that is taxable just like any other wage income, even though the employee has not technically "worked" for the income. Supplemental wages include:

- Bonuses, commissions, prizes
- Severance pay, back pay, and holiday pay
- Accumulated vacation pay and sick leave
- Payment for nondeductible moving expenses

Severance pay is taxable as ordinary income, just like wages. Even though severance pay is usually issued to employees who are being terminated and is not actually for work performed, it is still taxable to the employee and still subject to Social Security and Medicare tax. Unemployment benefits are taxable income. However, all forms of welfare benefits, such as food stamps and heating assistance programs, are exempt from federal taxation. Non-federal assistance benefits from a state or local agencies are also exempt.

Reporting Tip Income

Tips received by food servers, baggage handlers, hairdressers, and others for performing services are taxable as ordinary income. Individuals who receive $20 or more per month in tips must report their tip income to their employer. Employers must withhold Social Security, Medicare, and income taxes due on reported tips. The employer withholds FICA taxes due on tips from the employee's wages and pays both employer and employee portions of the tax in the same manner as the tax on the employee's regular wages.

Taxpayers who do not report all of their tips to their employer must report the Social Security and Medicare taxes on their Form 1040. Employees use Form 4137, *Social Security and Medicare Tax on Unreported Tip Income,* to compute and report the additional tax.

Taxpayers who are *self-employed* and receive tips must include their tips in gross receipts on Schedule C. Examples of this type of taxpayer include self-employed hair stylists and manicurists.

Example: Lydia works two jobs. She is an administrative assistant during the week and a bartender on the weekends. She reports all of her tip income ($3,000) to her employer. Her Forms W-2 show wage income of $21,000 (assistant) and $8,250 (bartender). Lydia must report $29,250 on her Form 1040, which is the total amount earned at both jobs. Lydia reported the tip income to her employer, so her bartending tips are already included on her Form W-2 for that job, so the amount she reports is $21,000 + $8,250.

Individuals who receive *less than* $20 per month in tips while working one job do not have to report their tip income to their employer. While all tips are subject to income tax, tips of less than $20 per month are:

- Exempt from Social Security and Medicare taxes
- Still subject to federal income tax and must be reported on Form 1040

Noncash tips (for example, concert tickets or other items) do not have to be reported to the employer, but they must be reported and included in the taxpayer's income at their fair market value.

Garnished Wages

An employee may have his wages garnished for many different reasons. Sometimes the employee owes child support, back taxes due, or other debts. Regardless of how much is actually garnished from the employee's paycheck, the full amount (the gross wages) is taxable to the employee and must be included in the employee's wages at year end.

Disability Retirement Benefits

Disability retirement benefits are taxable as wages if a taxpayer retired on disability before reaching the minimum retirement age. Once the taxpayer reaches retirement age, the payments are no longer taxable as wages. They are then taxable as pension income.

Disability Payments from an Insurance Policy

Disability income benefits from an insurance policy are excluded from income if the taxpayer pays the premiums for the policy. For health insurance paid for by the employer, the employer deducts the cost and the employee pays no tax on the premiums paid by the employer. The employee also does not pay any tax on the benefits received.

Sick pay is not the same thing as "disability pay." Sick pay is always taxable as wages, just like vacation pay.

Property In Lieu Of Wages

An employee who receives property instead of wages for services performed must generally recognize the FMV of the property when it is received. However, if an employee receives stock or other property that is restricted, the property is not included in income until it is available without restriction to the employee.

> **Example:** As part of his promotion, Barry's company gives him $5,000 worth of stock, a total of 500 shares. However, he cannot sell or exercise the shares for five years. If Barry quits his job, he forfeits the shares. He does not have to recognize this restricted stock as income in the year he received it. This is because the stock is subject to multiple restrictions. This stock will be taxable when Barry chooses to sell it or otherwise gains complete control over it.

Military Pay Exclusion-Combat Zone Wages

Wages earned by military personnel are generally taxable. However, there are special rules for military personnel regarding taxable income, including many exclusions for those on active duty.

Combat zone wages and hazardous duty pay are excludable for certain military personnel. Enlisted persons who serve in a combat zone for any part of a month may exclude their pay from tax. For officers, pay is excluded up to a certain amount, depending on the branch of service.

> **Example:** Lee is a Navy pilot who served in a combat zone from January 1, 2012 to November 3, 2012. He will only be required to report his income for December 2012, because all of the other income is excluded from taxation as combat zone pay. Even though Lee only served three days in November in a combat zone, his income for the entire month of November is excluded.

Substitute W-2 Form

If for some reason an employee does not receive his Form W-2 (perhaps the employer went out of business), the employee may file his tax return on paper using IRS Form 4852, *Substitute for Form W-2, Wage and Tax Statement*. An earnings statement or similar document may be used to re-create the data required in order to complete and file the taxpayer's return.

> **Example:** Manny worked for a plumbing company in 2012. In December 2012, the owner died, and final payroll returns were not filed. The business was closed and Manny never received a Form W-2 for the wages he earned in 2012. Manny may file a Form 4852 instead, explaining the circumstances why he could not obtain a W-2. Then Manny may use his earnings statement or other records to attempt to re-create his taxable income and withholding.

Barter Exchanges and Barter Income

Bartering is an exchange of property or services, usually without an exchange of cash. Barter may take place on an informal, one-on-one basis between individuals and businesses, or it may occur on a third party basis through a barter exchange company.

While our ancestors may have exchanged eggs for corn, today a person can barter a variety of services: computer tune-ups for auto repair, or dental work for carpet cleaning, for example. The FMV must be reported as income by both parties in the year the goods were exchanged or services sold.

If two people have agreed ahead of time as to the value of the services, the agreed-upon value will be accepted as the fair market value.

> **Example:** Brayden builds custom kitchen cabinets. Annemarie is a veterinarian. In 2012, Brayden builds new cabinets for Annemarie's kitchen, and she performs hip dysplasia surgery on Brayden's German shepherd. They agree in advance that the cost for the kitchen cabinets and the surgery is $2,500. They each must report $2,500 in income on their 2012 tax returns.

Alimony (as Income to the Recipient)

The concept of alimony needs to be understood in two ways: from the perspective of the payer and the payee. In this section, we will cover the concept of alimony as income to the recipient. Alimony is *taxable income* to the recipient and *deductible* by the payer.

> **Example:** Mark and Sibba are divorced. Their divorce decree calls for Mark to pay Sibba $200 a month as child support and $150 a month as alimony. Mark makes all of his child support and alimony payments on time. Therefore, in 2012, Mark may deduct $1,800 ($150 X 12 months) as alimony paid and Sibba must report $1,800 as alimony received. The amount paid as child support, $2,400 ($200 X 12), is not deductible by Mark and is not reported as income by Sibba.

Alimony paid is an adjustment to income for the payer, and is taxable to the receiving spouse as ordinary income. Spouses do not have to itemize in order to deduct their alimony payments. The alimony paid is listed on the first page of Form 1040; Form 1040A or Form 1040EZ cannot be used.

If a divorce agreement specifies payments of both alimony and child support and only partial payments are made by the payer, then the partial payments are considered to be child support until this obligation is fully paid. Any excess is then treated as alimony. Child support is not taxable income to the receiver and not deductible by the payer.

> **Example:** Sandra and Jessie are divorced. Their divorce decree calls for Jessie to pay Sandra $2,000 a month ($24,000 [$2,000 x 12] a year) as child support and $1,500 a month ($18,000 [$1,500 x 12] a year) as alimony. Jessie falls behind on his payments and only manages to pay $36,000. In this case, $24,000 is considered child support and only the remaining amount is considered alimony. Jessie can deduct only $12,000 ($36,000 - $24,000) as alimony paid. Sandra would report $12,000 as alimony income received.

If the payment amount is to be reduced based on a contingency *relating to a child* (e.g., attaining a certain age, marrying), the amount of the reduction will be treated as child support. It is important to remember that child support is not alimony, as the IRS treats the two very differently. Child support is never deductible because it is viewed as a payment that a parent is making simply for the support of his child.

Also, any alimony payments that continue after the receiving spouse has died will automatically be considered child support, not alimony.

Example: Under Cary's divorce decree, he must pay his ex-wife, Eugenia, $30,000 per year. The payments will stop after 15 years or upon Eugenia's death. The divorce decree provided that if Eugenia dies before the end of the 15-year period, Cary must still pay Eugenia's estate the difference between $450,000 ($30,000 annually × 15 years) and the total amount paid up to that time. Eugenia dies at the end of the tenth year, and Cary must pay her estate $150,000 ($450,000 − $300,000). Since the payment is required even after Eugenia's death, none of the annual payments are considered alimony for tax purposes. The payments are actually "disguised child support" and cannot be deducted by Cary as alimony.

Alimony payments made under a divorce agreement are deductible by the payer if all of the following requirements are met:

- The spouses may not file joint returns with each other.
- Payments are made in cash or a cash equivalent (such as checks or money orders). Payments made to a third party can be considered alimony. For example, if one spouse pays the medical bills of his ex-wife, the cash payment to the hospital can count as alimony.

Example: Ben is required to pay $1,000 per month in alimony to Karen, his former spouse. Karen has a medical bill of $1,500 that Ben agrees to pay in lieu of the regular alimony payment. The $1,500 would qualify as alimony payment to a third party, since it was made on Karen's behalf to her creditor.

In order for a payment to qualify as alimony:

- The divorce agreement may not include a clause indicating that the payment is something else (such as child support or repayment of a loan, etc.)
- If the spouses are legally separated, the spouses cannot live together when the payments are made.
- The payer must have no liability to make any payment (in cash or property) after the death of the former spouse.

Alimony does not include:

- Child support
- Payments that are community income
- Payments to keep up the payer's property
- Free use of the payer's property
- Noncash property settlements

Property settlements, which are simply a division of property, are not treated as alimony. Property transferred to a former spouse incident to a divorce is treated as a gift. "Incident to a divorce" means a transfer of property within one year after the date of the divorce, or a transfer of property related to the cessation of the marriage, as determined by the courts.

Securities Income (Dividends from Stocks & Bonds)

Investors typically buy and sell securities and then report income from dividends, interest, or capital appreciation. The income that is earned on these investments is reported on Schedule B. A taxpayer must file Schedule B, *Interest and Ordinary Dividends*, when any of the following apply:

- The taxpayer had over $1,500 of taxable interest or ordinary dividends.
- The taxpayer is claiming the education exclusion of interest from series EE savings bonds.
- The taxpayer received ordinary dividends as a nominee. "Nominee interest" occurs when a taxpayer receives a 1099-INT form, but the interest really belongs to another party. This is very common when taxpayers set up accounts for family members and minor children.
- The taxpayer had foreign accounts or received a distribution from a foreign trust.
- The taxpayer received interest as part of a seller-financed mortgage.

A. Ordinary Dividends

A "dividend" is a distribution of income made by a corporation to its shareholders, out of net earnings and profits. Ordinary dividends are corporate distributions in cash (as opposed to property or stock shares). Amounts received as dividends are taxed as ordinary income. Dividends are passive income, so they are not subject to self-employment tax.

Any distribution *in excess* of earnings and profits (both current and accumulated) is considered a recovery of capital and is therefore not taxable. Distributions in excess of earnings and profits reduce the taxpayer's basis. Once basis is reduced to zero, any additional distributions are capital gain and are taxed as such.

Ordinary dividends are reported to the taxpayer on Form 1099-DIV on Schedule B. If the total dividend income is $1,500 or less, all of the income can be reported directly on page one of IRS Form 1040.

B. Qualified Dividends

Qualified dividends are given preferred tax treatment. They must meet specific criteria in order to receive the lower maximum tax rate that applies to capital gains. Qualified dividends are reported to the taxpayer on Form 1099-DIV. Qualified dividends are subject to a 15% tax rate if the taxpayer's regular tax rate is 25% or higher. If the taxpayer's regular tax rate is under 25%, the qualified dividends are subject to a zero percent rate, which means they are essentially nontaxable. In order for the dividends to qualify for the lower rate, all of the following requirements must be met:

- The dividends must have been paid by a U.S. corporation or a qualified foreign corporation.
- The taxpayer must meet the holding period. The taxpayer must have held the stock for more than 60 days during the 121-day period that begins 60 days before the ex-dividend date. The ex-dividend date is the date *following* the declaration of a dividend.

When trying to figure the holding period for qualified dividends, the taxpayer may count the number of days he held the stock and include the day he disposed of the stock. The date the taxpayer *acquires* the stock is not included in the holding period.

Example: Israel bought 5,000 shares of Sundowner Corp. stock on July 9, 2012. Sundowner Corp. paid a cash dividend of 10 cents per share. The ex-dividend date was July 17, 2012. Israel's Form 1099-DIV from Sundowner Corp. shows $500 in dividends. However, Israel sold the 5,000 shares on August 12, 2012. Israel held his shares of Sundowner Corp. for only 34 days of the 121-day required holding period. The 121-day period began on May 18, 2012 (60 days before the ex-dividend date) and ended on September 15, 2012. Israel has no qualified dividends from Sundowner Corp. because he held the Sundowner stock for less than the required 61 days. He does not qualify for the preferred tax treatment that is given to qualified dividends.

C. Mutual Fund Distributions/Capital Gain Distributions

Taxpayers who receive mutual fund distributions during the year will also receive IRS Form 1099-DIV identifying the type of distribution received. A distribution may be an ordinary dividend, a qualified dividend, a capital gain distribution, an exempt-interest dividend, or a nondividend distribution. Mutual fund distributions can be reported on Form 1040 or Form 1040A, but not on Form 1040EZ.

Mutual fund distributions are reported depending upon the character of the income source. Capital gain distributions from a mutual fund are *always* treated as long-term *regardless* of the actual period the mutual fund investment is held.

Distributions from a mutual fund investing in tax-exempt securities will be tax-exempt interest. In some cases, a mutual fund may pay tax-exempt interest dividends, paid from tax-exempt interest earned by the fund. Since the exempt-interest dividends keep their tax-exempt character, they are not taxable. Even so, the taxpayer must report them on his tax return. This is an information reporting requirement only, and does not convert tax-exempt interest to taxable interest. However, this income is generally a "tax preference item" and may be subject to the alternative minimum tax. The mutual fund will supply the taxpayer with a Form 1099-INT showing the tax-exempt interest dividends.

If a mutual fund or Real Estate Investment Trust (REIT) declares a dividend in October, November, or December payable to shareholders but actually pays the dividend during January of the following year, the shareholder is still considered to have received the dividend on December 31 of the prior tax year. The taxpayer must report the dividend in the year it was declared.

D. Stock Dividends

A stock dividend is simply a distribution of stock by a corporation to its own shareholders. This happens when a corporation chooses to distribute stock rather than money. A stock dividend is also called a "stock grant" or a "stock distribution."

Generally, a stock dividend is not a taxable event. This is because the receiver of the stock (a shareholder) is not actually receiving any money. A nontaxable stock dividend does not affect a taxpayer's income in the year of distribution. A stock dividend will affect a shareholder's basis in his existing stock. The basis of the stockholder's existing shares is divided to include the new stock. So a stock dividend will essentially reduce basis.

> **Example:** Razor Ball Corporation agrees to a year-end stock dividend. Scarlett is a shareholder in Razor Ball. She currently owns 100 shares, and her basis in the shares is $50 each, for a total of $5,000. Scarlett is granted a stock dividend of 100 shares. After the dividend, Scarlett owns 200 shares. Her new basis in each individual share is $25 per share. However, her overall basis in the shares does not change (it is still $5,000). Scarlett would recognize income when she decided to sell the shares.

*Exception: If the taxpayer (shareholder) has the option to receive *cash instead of stock*, then the stock dividend becomes taxable. The recipient of the stock must include the FMV of the stock in his gross income. That amount then becomes the basis of the new shares received.

> **Example:** The Jausta Corporation agrees to issue a year-end stock dividend. Dale owns 1,000 shares in Jausta, and his current basis in the shares is $10 each, for a total of $10,000. In 2012, Dale is granted a stock dividend of 100 shares, but Jausta gives all the shareholders the option of receiving cash instead of stock. Therefore, the stock dividend becomes a taxable event. Dale decides to take the stock instead of the cash. The FMV of the stock at the time of the distribution is $15 per share. Dale must recognize $1,500 in income ($15 FMV X 100 shares=$1,500). After the dividend, Dale owns 1,100 shares and his basis in the new shares is $15 per share. Dale's basis in the old shares remains the same.

Social Security Benefits

Usually, if the taxpayer *only* has Social Security income, the income is not taxable, and a taxpayer is not required to file a tax return.

Social Security benefits *become* taxable once the taxpayer starts to receive other types of income, such as wages or interest income. The taxable portion of Social Security benefits is never more than 85%. In most cases, the taxable portion is less than 50%.[41]

To better understand the thresholds, if a taxpayer is filing single or HOH and combined income* is:

- Between $25,000 and $34,000 the taxpayer may have to pay income tax on up to 50% of Social Security benefits.
- More than $34,000, up to 85% of Social Security benefits may be taxable.

If a taxpayer filed jointly and combined income* is

- Between $32,000 and $44,000, the taxpayer may have to pay income tax on up to 50% of Social Security benefits.
- More than $44,000, up to 85% of Social Security benefits may be taxable.

If a taxpayer is filing MFS, he will probably pay taxes on his Social Security benefits.

> *Formula: The taxpayer's adjusted gross income
> + Nontaxable interest
> + ½ of Social Security benefits
> = **"combined income"**

---

[41] Social Security income is **not the same** as Supplemental Security Income (SSI). SSI is a federal income supplement program for the poor and the disabled, and is not taxable.

If the taxpayer also received other income in addition to Social Security, such as income from a job, the benefits will not be taxed unless modified adjusted gross income (MAGI) is more than the base amount for the taxpayer's filing status.

To figure the taxable portion of Social Security, first compare the BASE AMOUNT (shown below) for the taxpayer's filing status with the total of:

- One-half of the Social Security benefits, plus
- All other income, including tax-exempt interest.

When making this comparison, do not reduce other income by any exclusions for:

- Interest from qualified U.S. savings bonds,
- Employer-provided adoption benefits,
- Foreign earned income or foreign housing, or
- Income earned by bona fide residents of American Samoa or Puerto Rico.

BASE AMOUNTS: SOCIAL SECURITY

A taxpayer's BASE AMOUNT for figuring the taxability of Social Security is:

$25,000 for single, head of household, or qualifying widow(er),

$32,000 for married filing jointly, or

$25,000 for married filing separately (and lived *apart* from his spouse all year)

$-0- if the taxpayer is MFS (if lived with spouse at any time during the tax year)

How to Figure the Taxability of Social Security

To figure out what percentages of a taxpayer's Social Security benefits are taxable, the taxpayer must first determine the sum of modified AGI (MAGI) and add one-half of the Social Security benefits. After doing this calculation on a worksheet, if the amount is less than the base amount, then none of the Social Security is taxable.

Example: Bo and Yvonne are both over 65. They file jointly and they both received Social Security benefits during the year. At the end of the year, Bo received a Form SSA-1099 showing net benefits of $7,500. Yvonne received a Form SSA-1099 showing net benefits of $3,500. Bo also received wages of $20,000 and interest income of $500. He did not have any tax-exempt interest.

1. Total Social Security benefits:	$11,000
2. Enter one-half of SS	$5,500
3. Enter taxable interest and wages	$20,500
4. Add ($5,500 + $20,500)	$26,000

Bo and Yvonne's benefits are not taxable for 2012 because their income is not more than the base amount ($32,000) for married filing jointly.

Taxable State Income Tax Refunds

State income tax refunds are reportable as taxable income in the year received only if the taxpayer itemized deductions in the prior year. The state should send Form 1099-G, *Certain Government Payments*, by January 31. The IRS also will receive a copy of the Form 1099-G.

> **Example:** Wally claimed the standard deduction on last year's tax return and received a state tax refund of $600. The state tax refund is not taxable. Only taxpayers who itemize deductions and receive a state or local refund in the prior year are required to include the state tax refund in their taxable income.

Rents and Royalties

Income from rents and royalties must be included in gross income. Rental income is income from the use or occupation of property, such as a rental home. Income from royalties includes income from copyrights, trademarks, and franchises. Rental and royalty income is reported on **Schedule E**, and will be covered at length in Unit 13.

Nontaxable Income

Some types of income are nontaxable, some of which must be reported to the IRS, and others do not.

A. Veterans' Benefits

Veterans' benefits are nontaxable. Amounts paid by the Department of Veterans Affairs to a veteran or his family are nontaxable if they are for education, training, disability compensation, work therapy, dependent care assistance, or other benefits or pension payments given to the veteran because of disability.

B. Workers' Compensation

Workers' compensation is not taxable income if it is received because of an occupational injury. However, disability benefits paid by an employer (also called "sick pay") are taxable to the employee. Long-term disability income payments are included in gross income and are taxable to the employee.

C. Life Insurance Proceeds

Proceeds from life insurance are not taxable to the recipient. Consequently, life insurance premiums are not deductible by the payer, but an employer may choose to provide employees with life insurance as a fringe benefit and deduct the cost. However, a private individual, such as a sole proprietor purchasing life insurance for himself, may not deduct the premiums.

Sometimes, a taxpayer will choose to receive life insurance in installments, rather than a lump sum. In this case, part of the installment usually includes interest income. If a taxpayer receives life insurance proceeds in installments, he can exclude part of each installment from his income. To determine the excluded part, divide the amount held by the insurance company (generally the total lump sum payable at the death of the insured person) by the number of installments to be paid. Include anything over this excluded part as interest income.

> **Example:** Libby's brother died in 2012, and she is the beneficiary of his life insurance. The face amount of the policy is $75,000 and, as beneficiary, Libby chooses to receive 120 monthly installments of $1,000 each. The excluded part of each installment is $625 ($75,000 ÷ 120), or $7,500 for an entire year. The rest of each payment, $375 a month (or $4,500 for an entire year), is interest income to Libby.

D. Compensatory Damages and Court Settlements

Compensatory damages for personal physical injury or physical sickness are not taxable income, whether they are from a settlement or from an actual court award.

> **Example:** Felix was injured in a car accident in 2012. His legs were broken and he suffered other serious physical injuries. He received a settlement from the insurance company for his injuries totaling $950,000. This is nontaxable income, because it is payment for a physical injury.

Compensatory damages for "emotional distress" are usually taxable. Emotional distress itself is not a physical injury. If the emotional distress is due to unlawful discrimination or injury to reputation, the taxpayer must include the damages in taxable income, except for any damages received for medical care due to that emotional distress.

> **Example:** Kristina recently won a court award for emotional distress due to unlawful discrimination. The emotional distress resulted in a nervous breakdown and her hospitalization. The court awarded her damages of $100,000, including $20,000 to refund the cost of her medical care due to the nervous breakdown. In this case, $80,000 ($100,000 - $20,000) would be considered a taxable court award. The $20,000 of damages for reimbursement of her medical care would be nontaxable.

Punitive damages are taxable income. It does not matter if they relate to a physical injury or physical sickness.

Court awards for lost wages are always taxable as ordinary income.

Nontaxable Types of Interest Income

There are numerous examples of interest income that are not taxable to the recipient.

A. Municipal Bond Interest

A taxpayer may exclude interest income on municipal or "muni" bonds, which are debt obligations by state and local governments. Taxpayers must still report the interest on their income tax returns, but it is not taxable. Although a muni bond is generally exempt from federal income tax, it is often still taxable at the state level.

B. Frozen Deposits

A taxpayer may exclude interest income on frozen deposits. A deposit is considered frozen if, at the end of the year, the taxpayer cannot withdraw any part of the deposit because:

- The financial institution is bankrupt or insolvent, or
- The state where the institution is located has placed limits on withdrawals because other financial institutions in the state are bankrupt or insolvent.

> **Example:** Creed earned $2,500 in interest from his bank in 2012, but it became insolvent at the end of the year and all of Creed's money was frozen. He was unable to access any of his accounts until the following year. Creed does not have to recognize the income as taxable in 2012 because the interest qualified as a frozen deposit. He would recognize the income in 2013 when the funds finally became available for him to withdraw and use. Creed must still report the income on his 2012 tax return, but he may mark it as a "frozen deposit" and therefore not subject to income tax in the current tax year.

C. Mutual Funds Investing in Tax-Exempt Securities

Distributions from a fund investing in tax-exempt securities are tax-exempt interest. For 2012, tax-exempt interest paid by mutual funds is now shown on Form 1099-DIV, not Form 1099-INT as before.

D. Education Savings Bond Interest Exclusion

Taxpayers may choose to purchase and then eventually redeem Series EE bonds on a tax-free basis to pay college expenses. The expenses must be for the taxpayer, the taxpayer's spouse, or the taxpayer's dependents.

For 2012, the amount of the interest exclusion is phased out for married filing jointly taxpayers or qualifying widow(er)taxpayers whose modified AGI is between $109,250 and $139,250. If the modified AGI is $139,250 or more, no exclusion is allowed.

> **Caution:** Married taxpayers who file separately (MFS) do not qualify for the educational savings bond interest exclusion.

For single and head of household filing statuses, the interest exclusion is phased out for taxpayers whose modified AGI is between $72,850 and $87,850. If the modified AGI is $87,850 or more, no exclusion is allowed.

The exclusion is calculated and reported on IRS Form 8815, *Exclusion of Interest from Series EE and I U.S. Savings Bonds*. There are certain rules that must be followed in order for the educational exclusion to qualify:

- The bonds must be purchased by the owner. They cannot be a gift.
- The money received on redemption must be used for tuition and fees. The taxpayer cannot use tax-exempt bond proceeds for tuition and also attempt to take educational credits (such as the Lifetime Learning Credit) for the same amount. No "double dipping" is allowed.
- The total interest received may *only* be excluded if the combined amounts of the principal and the interest received *do not exceed* the taxpayer's qualified educational expenses.

> **Example:** In February 2012, Daniel and Blythe, a married couple, cash a qualified Series EE savings bond they bought ten years ago. They receive proceeds of $8,124, representing principal of $5,000 and interest of $3,124. In 2012, they paid $4,000 of their daughter's college tuition. They are not claiming an education credit for that amount, and their daughter does not have any tax-free educational assistance (scholarships or grants). Daniel and Blythe can exclude $1,538 ($3,124 × [$4,000 ÷ $8,124]) of interest in 2012. They must pay tax on the remaining $1,586 ($3,124 – $1,538) interest, since not all the interest was used for qualified tuition costs.

> **Example:** In 2012, Denise redeems her Series EE Bonds and receives a total of $4,000. Of that amount, $1,000 is interest income and the remainder is the return of principal ($3,000). Denise's qualified educational expenses (tuition and fees) are $5,800. Therefore, all of the interest earned on her Series EE Bonds qualifies for tax-exempt treatment.

If the taxpayer does not use the bonds for educational expenses, the interest income is taxable. Most taxpayers report the total interest when they cash the bonds. Some taxpayers choose instead to report savings bond interest as it accrues. Either method is acceptable.

Foreign Earned Income Exclusion

Generally, the income of U.S. citizens is taxed even if the income is earned outside the United States. Foreign earned income is income received for services performed in a foreign country while the taxpayer's tax home is also in a foreign country. The taxpayer must pass one of two tests in order to claim the foreign earned income exclusion. If eligible for this option, the taxpayer's income up to a certain threshold is not taxed.

- ## Test #1: "Bona Fide Residence Test," or
- ## Test #2: The "Physical Presence Test"

Bona Fide Residence Test: A U.S. citizen or U.S. resident alien who is a bona fide resident of a foreign country for an uninterrupted period that includes an entire tax year.

The Physical Presence Test: A U.S. citizen or U.S. resident alien who is physically present in a foreign country or countries for at least 330 full days during 12 consecutive months. A taxpayer may qualify under the physical presence test, and the income may span over a period of multiple tax years. If so, the taxpayer must prorate the foreign earned income exclusion based on the number of days spent in the foreign country.

For 2012, the maximum foreign earned income exclusion is $95,100. If the taxpayer is married filing jointly and both individuals live and work abroad, both taxpayers can choose to claim the foreign earned income exclusion.

Example: Brenda earned $80,000 while employed in Peru, and she qualifies for the foreign earned income exclusion. Brenda also has $6,000 in work-related expenses. She cannot deduct any of her expenses, because she is already excluding all of her income from taxation by taking the foreign earned income exclusion.

Example: Leila was a bona fide resident of China for all of 2012. She was paid $105,000 for her work in China. She can exclude $95,100 of the amount she was paid.

It does not matter whether the income is paid by a U.S. employer or a foreign employer. The foreign earned income exclusion is figured using Form 2555, *Foreign Earned Income,* which must be attached to Form 1040. Once the choice is made to exclude foreign earned income, that choice remains in effect for the year the election is made and all later years, unless revoked.

Nonresident aliens do not qualify for the foreign earned income exclusion. A taxpayer must be either a U.S. citizen or a legal resident alien of the United States who lives and works abroad and who meets certain other qualifications to exclude a specific amount of his foreign earned income.

The exclusion does not apply to the wages and salaries of members of the Armed Forces and civilian employees of the U.S. government.

Foreign Tax Credit: The Foreign Tax Credit can be used by U.S. taxpayers to avoid or reduce double taxation. A taxpayer cannot take the Foreign Tax Credit on income that has already been excluded from taxation by the foreign earned income exclusion. This credit is covered in detail in Unit 9, *Tax Credits.*

Clergy: Special Rules

There are special rules regarding the taxation of clergy members. "Ministers" or "clergy" are individuals who are ordained, commissioned, or licensed by a religious body or church denomination. They are given the authority to conduct religious worship, perform religious functions, and administer ordinances or sacraments according to the prescribed tenets and practices of that church.

Clergy members must include offerings and fees received for marriages, baptisms, and funerals as part of their income. A clergy member's salary is reported on IRS Form W-2. Additional payments for services are reported on the clergy member's Schedule C.

Minister's Housing Allowance

A minister's housing allowance (sometimes called a parsonage allowance) is excludable from gross income for income tax purposes, but not for self-employment tax purposes. A minister who receives a housing allowance may exclude the allowance from gross income to the extent it is used to pay expenses in providing a home.

The exclusion for minister's housing is limited to:
- The lesser of the fair market rental value (including utilities, etc.), or
- The actual amount used to provide a home.

The housing allowance cannot exceed reasonable pay and must be used for housing in the year they are received by the minister.

Example: William is an ordained minister who receives $32,000 in salary in 2012. He also receives an additional $4,000 for performing marriages and baptisms. His housing allowance was $500 per month, for a total of $6,000 per year. William must report the $32,000 as wages, $4,000 as self-employment income, and $6,000 as the housing allowance subject only to self-employment tax, not income tax.

Both salary and housing allowances must be included in income for purposes of determining self-employment tax.

Example: Abby is a full-time ordained minister at Waterfront Presbyterian Church. The church allows her to use a cottage that has a rental value of $5,000. The church also pays Abby a salary of $12,000. Her income for self-employment tax purposes is $17,000 ($5,000 + $12,000 salary). Ministers must include the FMV of a home on Schedule SE.

Example: Father Benicio is an ordained priest at the local Catholic Church. His annual income is $26,000, and he also receives a $10,000 housing allowance from the church. His housing costs for the year are $14,000. Therefore, Benicio's self-employment income is $36,000 ($26,000 salary + $10,000 housing allowance). But only his base salary ($26,000) is subject to income tax, because his actual housing expenses are more than his housing allowance.

Summary: Taxable vs. Nontaxable Income

TAXABLE INCOME	NONTAXABLE INCOME
Wages, salaries, tips, bonuses, vacation pay, severance pay, commissions	Gifts and inheritances
Interest	Life insurance proceeds
Unemployment compensation	Child support
Dividends	Certain veterans' benefits
Strike benefits	Interest on muni bonds (state and local bonds)
Bank "gifts" and cash bonuses for opening accounts	Employer-provided fringe benefits such as health insurance
Cancellation of debt (unless excludable)	Welfare payments, food stamps, other forms of public assistance
Alimony	Compensation or court awards for physical injury or illness
Gains from sales of property, stocks and bonds, stock options, etc.	Workers' compensation
Social Security benefits (above the base amount)	Combat pay
Most court awards or damages	Scholarships, employer-provided educational assistance,
Barter income	Canceled debt from a primary residence, bankruptcy, or insolvency
Prizes, awards, gambling winnings	Foreign earned income (if qualifying for the exclusion)

Earned Income	Unearned Income	Can be variable
Salaries	Dividends	Business profits
Wages	Interest	Partnership income
Commissions	Capital gains	Royalties
Bonuses	Gambling winnings	Rents
Professional fees	Annuities	Scholarships
Vacation pay	Alimony	Fellowships
Tips	Social Security	Fringe benefits
Self-employment income	Pensions	Court/lawsuit proceeds

Unit 5: Questions

1. Hank received Social Security in 2012 totaling $11,724. Also in 2012, Hank sold all of his stock and moved into senior housing. He received $31,896 of taxable income from the sale of the stock. What is the maximum taxable amount of Hank's Social Security benefits?

A. $31,896.
B. $20,172.
C. $9,965.
D. Not enough information provided.

The answer is C. The maximum amount that can ever be taxable on net Social Security benefits is 85%, which in Hank's case is $9,965. ###

2. Bruce and Ann are married and file jointly. They have three Forms 1099-INT:

1.   Epping National Bank, $62 (Bruce)
2.   Epping Credit Union, $178 (Ann)
3.   Breton Savings and Loan, $760 (Ann)

How much interest income should they report on Schedule B (Form 1040)?

A. None.
B. $760.
C. $240.
D. $1,000.

The answer is A. Schedule B is not used to report regular interest totaling $1,500 or less. Instead, these amounts can be reported directly on the taxpayer's Form 1040. ###

3. Which of the following types of income are exempt from federal tax?

A. Interest income.
B. Canceled debt.
C. Tips.
D. Inheritances.

The answer is D. Of the types of income listed here, only inheritances are exempt from federal taxes. ###

4. Under what circumstances must a person report taxable income?
A. Always.
B. Always, unless the income is only from interest.
C. Always, unless the income is so small that reporting it is not required by law.
D. Always, unless the person is identified as a dependent on someone else's tax return.

The answer is C. All taxable income must be reported on a tax return, unless the amount is so small that the individual is not legally required to file a return. Filing thresholds depend on a taxpayer's marital status, age, and dependency status. ###

5. Which of the following types of income are taxable?

A. Credit union dividends.
B. Veterans' life insurance dividends.
C. Workers' compensation.
D. Child support.

The answer is A. Credit union dividends are considered interest income and are subject to federal income tax. ###

6. Toni owns a savings bond, which she purchased as an investment to help pay for her daughter's education. She redeems the bond in 2012 and immediately uses all the funds to pay for her daughter Tyler's college tuition. The bond's interest is reported on _____.

A. Toni's tax return and is 100% taxable.
B. Tyler's tax return and is 100% taxable.
C. Toni's tax return and is 100% exempt from taxes.
D. Nothing. It is not taxable and not required to be reported, so long as Toni uses all the funds to pay for qualified higher education costs.

The answer is C. As the buyer and owner of the bond, Toni reports the interest on her tax return, but excludes the interest from her income because she paid for qualified higher education expenses the same year. ###

7. Joyce and Craig, a married couple, received $200 in interest from bonds issued by the state of Virginia. How should they report this on their Form 1040?

A. It must be reported as interest income, and it is 100% taxable.
B. It must be reported, but it is not taxable income on their Form 1040.
C. They do not have to report it.
D. None of the above.

The answer is B. The interest is tax-exempt municipal bond interest (state and local bonds). Although it is not taxable at the federal level, it must be reported on the taxpayer's return. ###

8. Which of the following tip income is exempt from federal income tax?

A. Tips of less than $20 per month.
B. Noncash tips.
C. Tips not reported to the employer.
D. All tips are taxable.

The answer is D. All tip income is subject to federal income tax, whether it is cash or noncash. Individuals who receive less than $20 per month in tips while working one job do not have to report their tip income to their employer, but the income is still subject to federal income tax and must be reported on the taxpayer's Form 1040. ###

9. Leona received the following income: wages, interest, child support, alimony, inheritance, workers' compensation, and lottery winnings. Determine what amount of her income is taxable.

Leona's Income:

SOURCE	Amounts
Wages	$13,000
Interest	$15
Child support	$6,000
Alimony	$2,000
Inheritance	$10,000
Workers' compensation	$1,000
Lottery winnings	$5,000

A. S13,015.
B. $16,015.
C. $20,015.
D. $30,015.

The answer is C. The wages, interest, alimony, and lottery winnings are taxable income and will appear on Leona's tax return ($13,000 + $15 + $2,000 + $5,000 = $20,015). Child support, inheritances, and workers' compensation are nontaxable income and will not appear on her tax return. ###

10. Salvador is in the U.S. Army and served in a combat zone from January 1 to September 2 of 2012. He returned to the United States and received his regular duty pay for the remainder of the year. How many months of income are taxable?

A. Zero. All the income is tax-free.
B. Three months are subject to tax.
C. Four months are subject to tax.
D. All twelve months are subject to income tax.

The answer is B. Since Salvador served for a few days in September, all the income in September is excluded as combat pay. If a taxpayer serves in a combat zone as an enlisted person for any part of a month, all of his pay received for military service that month is excluded from gross income. ###

11. A customer at a casino left a $10 poker chip as a tip for Steve, who is a hotel employee. Steve did not have any other tip income for the month. What is Steve's reporting requirement for this tip?

A. The poker chip is not legal tender, and is therefore not taxable.
B. Steve should report this tip income to his employer, and it will be taxed as wages on his Form W-2.
C. Steve must report the tip income on his return at its fair market value, which would be $10.
D. The tip is a gift, and therefore not taxable income.

The answer is C. Although this is not actual money, it is still taxable at its fair market value, which would be $10. The tip is not reportable to Steve's employer, since he earned less than $20 of tip income during the month. He should report the tip income on his return, subject to regular income tax. ###

12. Sven and Samantha file jointly in 2012 and received the following income for 2012. How much income should be reported on their 2012 joint tax return?
1. W-2 income for Samantha for wages of $40,000.
2. W-2 for Samantha for $2,000, the value of a trip she won to the Bahamas. She never went on the trip. But she is planning to take the trip in 2012.
3. Court settlement of $10,000 paid to Sven from a car accident for serious injuries he suffered.
4. $4,000 child support for Samantha's son from a previous marriage.

A. $40,000.
B. $42,000.
C. $46,000.
D. $52,000.

The answer is B. The wages earned and prize won by Samantha should be included on the joint return, and the accident settlement should be excluded from income. Samantha must recognize the prize, because even though she did not take the trip, she had constructive receipt of the winnings. Child support is not taxable. The answer is $42,000 ($40,000 wages + $2,000 prize). ###

13. Sandy received the following income in 2012:

1. Wages: $70,000.
2. Gambling winnings: $500 (Gambling losses, $1,000).
3. Dependent care benefits through her employer: $5,000.
4. Employer-provided parking pass: $240 per month.

Sandy had only $4,000 in qualified daycare expenses. How much gross income must she report on her tax return?

A. $70,500.
B. $71,500.
C. $71,740.
D. $73,400.

The answer is B. Dependent care assistance programs are not taxable, but only up to the amount of qualified expenses. Since Sandy received $5,000 but only had $4,000 in actual day care expenses, $1,000 is taxable to Sandy. The parking pass is an excluded benefit. Both the wages and gambling winnings must be included in the gross income total of $71,500 ($70,000 + $500 + $1,000). The gambling losses are not deductible from the net. Gambling losses are only allowable up to gambling winnings, and even then, only as an itemized deduction on Schedule A. ###

14. Ginny had the following income in 2012:

Social Security income:	$14,000
Interest income:	$125
Gambling winnings:	$1,000
Gambling losses:	$2,000
Settlement for a bodily injury:	$20,000
Child support payments:	$13,000
Food stamp benefits:	$5,000

How much taxable income must Ginny report on her tax return?

A. $14,000.
B. $14,125.
C. $15,125.
D. $30,000.
E. $48,000.

The answer is C. The Social Security income, gambling income, and interest income must all be reported. The accident settlement and the child support are not taxable. Food stamps and welfare payments also are not taxable income. The gambling losses do not affect the reporting of the gambling income. Gambling losses are a deduction on Schedule A, should Ginny choose to itemize. If Ginny does not itemize, the gambling losses are not deductible. ###

15. Brendan, a flight attendant, received wages of $30,000 in 2012. The airline provided transportation on a standby basis, at no charge, from his home in Little Rock to the airline's hub in Charlotte. The fair market value of the commuting flights was $5,000. Also in 2012, Brendan received reimbursements under an accountable plan of $10,000 for overnight travel, but only spent $6,000. He returned the excess to his employer. Brendan became injured on the job in November of 2012 and received workers' compensation of $4,000. What amount must he include in gross income on his 2012 tax return?

A. $30,000.
B. $34,000.
C. $35,000.
D. $37,000.

The answer is A. Brendan only has to include his wages in his 2012 return. The free flights offered on standby to airline personnel are considered a nontaxable fringe benefit. Reimbursements under an accountable plan and amounts paid for workers' compensation are nontaxable. Since Brendan returned the unspent amounts to his employer, the travel reimbursements qualify under an accountable plan, and the amounts spent are not taxable to him. ###

16. Debby broke her leg in a car accident in 2012 and was unable to work for three months. She received an accident settlement of $13,000 from the car insurance company. During this time she also received $7,500 in sick pay from her employer. In addition, she received $5,000 from her personally purchased accident policy. How much of this income is taxable income to Debby?

A. $5,000.
B. $7,500.
C. $12,500.
D. $18,000.

The answer is B. Only Debby's sick pay is taxable as wages. Sick pay from an employer is taxable like wages (similar to vacation pay), and is therefore includable in Debby's gross income. If a taxpayer pays the full cost of an accident insurance plan, the benefits for personal injury or illness are not includable in income. If the employer pays the cost of an accident insurance plan, then the amounts are taxable to an employee. ###

17. Jon and Li-hua filed a joint return for 2012. Jon received $10,000 in Social Security benefits and Li-hua received $16,000. They received no other income. What part of their Social Security benefits will be taxable for 2012?

A. $0.
B. $6,000.
C. $24,000.
D. $12,000.

The answer is A. If the only income received by the taxpayer is Social Security, the benefits generally are not taxable and the taxpayer probably does not have to file a return. If the taxpayer has additional income, he may have to file a return even if none of the Social Security benefits are taxable. ###

18. Income was "constructively received" in 2012 in each of the following situations except:

A. Wages were deposited in the taxpayer's bank account on December 26, 2012, but were not withdrawn by the taxpayer until January 3, 2013.
B. A taxpayer was informed his check for services rendered was available on December 15, 2012. The taxpayer did not pick up the check until January 30, 2013.
C. A taxpayer received a check by mail on December 31, 2012, but could not deposit the check until January 5, 2013.
D. A taxpayer's home was sold on December 28, 2012. The payment was not received by the taxpayer until January 2, 2013 when the escrow company completed the transaction and released the funds.

The answer is D. Constructive receipt does not require the taxpayer to have physical possession of the income. However, income is not considered constructively received if the taxpayer cannot access the funds because of restrictions. Since the taxpayer's control of the receipt of the funds in the escrow account was substantially limited until the transaction had closed, the taxpayer did not constructively receive the income until the closing of the transaction in the following year. ###

19. James is a self-employed attorney who performs legal services for a client, a small corporation. The corporation gives James 100 shares of its stock as payment for his services. The stock is valued at $2,000. Which of the following statements is true?

A. James does not have to include this transaction on his tax return.
B. James should report the income when he sells the stock.
C. The stock is taxable to James at its fair market value.
D. None of the above.

The answer is C. James must include the FMV of the shares in his gross income on Schedule C (Form 1040) in the year he receives them. The income would be considered payment for services he provided to his client, the corporation. ###

20. Rob owns a business that has a $10,000 profit in 2012. His wife, Cecilia, has a business loss of $12,000 for 2012. They both file Schedule C to report their self-employment income. Which of the following statements is true?

A. On their joint return, they will not have to pay self-employment tax because the losses from Cecilia's business offset Rob's income.
B. The spouses can file MFS and offset each other's self-employment tax.
C. Rob must pay self-employment tax on $10,000, regardless of his wife's losses.
D. If they choose to file separate returns, they may split the profits and losses equally between their two businesses.

The answer is C. Rob must pay self-employment tax on $10,000, regardless of how he and Cecilia choose to file. Taxpayers cannot combine a spouse's income or loss to determine their individual earnings subject to SE tax. However, if a taxpayer has more than one business, then he must combine the net profit or loss from each to determine the total earnings subject to SE tax. ###

21. Brent, a plastic surgeon, agreed to exchange services with a handyman. Brent removed a mole and the handyman fixed Brent's running toilet in his doctor's office. Mole removal is generally charged at $200, and the handyman generally charges $150 to fix a toilet. They agreed in advance that the fee would be $150. Neither exchanged actual cash. How much income must Brent recognize for this barter transaction?

A. $50.
B. $150.
C. $200.
D. $250.

The answer is B. Brent must include $150 in income. He may also deduct the cost of the repair ($150) if it qualifies as a business expense. If a taxpayer exchanges services with another person and both have agreed ahead of time on the value of those services, that value will be accepted as fair market value unless the value can be shown to be otherwise. ###

22. Ed received $32,000 in wages from his employer in 2012. He also won a prize from his employer because he helped develop a handbook for new employees. The prize was free lawn care service for a year, valued at $600. Ed also received $7,000 in child support and $2,000 in alimony from his ex-wife. Ed has full custody of his children. What is Ed's taxable income (before deductions and adjustments) for tax year 2012?

A. $32,000.
B. $32,600.
C. $34,600.
D. $39,600.

The answer is C. The wages and prize are both taxable income. Child support is not taxable to the receiver, nor deductible by the payer. The alimony is taxable to Ed and deductible by his ex-wife. The answer is figured as follows: ($32,000 + $600 + $2,000) = $34,600. ###

23. Scott opened a savings account at his local bank and deposited $800. The account earned $20 interest in 2012. Scott also received a $15 calculator as a gift for opening the account. On his credit card account, Scott received $100 worth of "reward points" for charging $10,000 in purchases, which he used to pay a portion of his credit card bill. How much interest income must Scott report on his IRS Form 1040?

A. $15.
B. $20.
C. $35.
D. $800.

The answer is C. If no other interest is credited to Scott during the year, the Form 1099-INT he receives will show $35 interest for the year. Scott must report the fair market value of the calculator on his return as interest income. A gift for opening a bank account is taxed as interest income. The IRS does not count reward points or cash back from a credit card as taxable interest income, so Scott neither has to report the $100 nor does he have to pay tax on it. ###

24. During the current year, Andrew received interest income of $300 from municipal bonds and $200 in interest from a certificate of deposit (CD). Which of the following statements is true?

A. Andrew is required to report the $500 in interest income on his income tax return, but none of the interest is taxable.
B. Andrew is not required to report any of the income on his tax return.
C. Andrew is required to report the $500 in interest income on his income tax return. The CD interest is taxable, but the muni bond interest is not.
D. Andrew is required to report only $200 of CD interest on his income tax return.

The answer is C. Under present federal income tax law, the interest income received from investing in municipal bonds is free from federal income taxes. However, the taxpayer is required to show any tax-exempt interest received on his tax return. This is an informational reporting requirement only. It does not change tax-exempt interest to taxable interest. The $200 interest from the CD is taxable and must be reported as interest income. ###

25. Kent invested in a mutual fund in 2012. The fund declared a dividend, and Kent earned $19. He did not get a Form 1099-DIV for the amount, and he did not withdraw the money from his mutual fund. Kent pulled the money out of his mutual fund on January 2, 2013. Which of the following statements is true?

A. The dividend is not reportable in 2012 because Kent did not receive the money yet.
B. The dividend is not reportable in 2012 because Kent did not receive a 1099-DIV.
C. The dividend must be reported in 2012.
D. The dividend is taxable and reportable in 2013.

The answer is C. Kent earned the money in 2012, and whether or not he received a 1099 for the income is irrelevant. Mutual fund dividends are taxable in the year declared regardless of whether the taxpayer withdraws the money or reinvests it. The money was constructively earned and available for withdrawal in 2012, so Kent must report the earnings in 2012. ###

26. Fran's bank became insolvent in 2012. One hundred dollars in interest was credited to her frozen bank account during the year. Fran withdrew $80, but could not withdraw any more as of the end of the year. Her 1099-INT showed $100 in interest income. Which of the following is true?

A. Fran's tax return must reflect the full amount of the interest.
B. Fran must include the $20 in her income for the year she is able to withdraw it.
C. None of the interest is taxable on a frozen deposit.
D. There is no such thing as a "frozen deposit."

The answer is B. Fran must include $80 in her income for 2012 but may exclude $20. She must include the $20 in her income in the year she is able to withdraw it. A deposit is considered frozen if, at the end of the year, the taxpayer cannot withdraw the deposit because the financial institution is bankrupt or insolvent. ###

27. Verla wanted to start investing. She deposited $4,000 of her own funds with a bank and also borrowed another $12,000 from the bank to make up the $16,000 minimum deposit required to buy a six-month certificate of deposit. The certificate earned $375 at maturity in 2012, but Verla only received $175 in interest income, which represented the $375 she earned minus $200 in interest charged on the $12,000 loan. The bank gives Verla a Form 1099-INT showing the $375 interest she earned. The bank also gives her a statement showing that she paid $200 in interest. How should Verla report all the interest amounts on her tax return?

A. Verla can choose to report only $175 of income.
B. Verla must report the $375 interest income. The $200 interest she paid to the bank is not deductible.
C. Verla must include the $375 in her income. Verla may deduct $200 on her Schedule A, subject to the net investment income limit.
D. Verla does not have to report any income from this transaction.

The answer is C. Verla must include the total amount of interest—$375—in her income. If she itemizes deductions on Schedule A (Form 1040), she can deduct $200 in interest expense, subject to the net investment income limit. To deduct investment expenses, the taxpayer must itemize. She may not "net" the investment income and expenses. ###

28. What is the maximum percentage of taxable Social Security benefits for a beneficiary?

A. 0%.
B. 50%.
C. 85%.
D. 100%.

The answer is C. Up to 85% of Social Security benefits may be taxable. No one pays federal income tax on more than 85% of his Social Security benefits. ###

29. Sheila and Ralph are married and both have life insurance. In December 2011, Ralph dies and Sheila, as the beneficiary, is awarded the life insurance. The face amount of the policy is $270,000. Instead of a lump sum, Sheila chooses to receive 180 monthly installments of $1,800 each over 15 years, starting January 1, 2012. How should Sheila treat these installments on her 2012 tax return?

A. All of the payments are excluded from income.
B. $18,000 is excluded from income per year, and $3,600 must be recognized as interest income.
C. $21,600 must be included in Sheila's income.
D. $18,000 will be excluded from income, and the remainder is taxed as a capital gain.

The answer is B. Life insurance proceeds are not taxable. However, the *interest* or investment gains earned on a life insurance installment contract are taxable. The face amount of the policy is $270,000. Therefore, the excluded part of each installment is $1,500 ($270,000 ÷ 180 months), or $18,000 for an entire year. The rest of each payment, $300 a month (or $3,600 for an entire year), is interest income to Sheila. ###

30. Randall is an ordained minister in the Evangelical Church of Chicago. He owns his own home and his monthly house payment is $900. His monthly utilities total $150. Fair rental value in his neighborhood is $1,000. Randall receives a housing allowance from his church in the amount of $950 per month. How much income must Randall include from his housing allowance amount?

A. $0.
B. $50 per month.
C. $150 per month.
D. $950 per month.

The answer is A. Ministers may exclude from gross income the rental value of a home or a rental allowance to the extent the allowance is used to provide a home, even if deductions are taken for home expenses paid with the allowance. A minister's housing allowance is excludable from gross income for income tax purposes, but not for self-employment tax purposes. ###

31. Alexander, age 64, is single and retired. He earned the following income in 2012. To determine if any of his Social Security is taxable, Alexander should compare how much of his income to the $25,000 base amount?

Part-time job	$8,000
Bank interest	$5,000
Social Security	$11,000
Taxable pension	$6,000
Total	**$30,000**

A. $30,000.
B. $11,000.
C. $24,500.
D. $25,000.

The answer is C. In order to figure out the taxable portion of Social Security, the taxpayer's modified adjusted gross income must be compared to the base amount.

Modified adjusted gross income equals adjusted gross income plus tax-exempt interest. To figure the amount of income that should be compared to the $25,000 base amount:

Part-time job	$8,000
Interest	$5,000
½ of Social Security	$5,500
Taxable pension	$6,000
Total	**$24,500**

Alexander does not have to pay tax on his Social Security. His provisional income plus Social Security is less than the base amount ($25,000). However, he is still required to file a tax return, because his overall income exceeds the minimum filing requirement. ###

32. Robert receives supplemental wages and a holiday bonus in 2012. Which items listed below are not considered taxable income to Robert?

A. Holiday bonus.
B. Overtime pay.
C. Vacation pay.
D. Travel reimbursements.

The answer is D. Travel reimbursements are considered part of an accountable plan and are not included in an employee's wages. ###

33. Tim is a priest at a Catholic church. He receives an annual salary of $18,000 and a housing allowance of $2,000 to pay for utilities. Tim lives rent-free in a small studio owned by the church. The fair rental value of the studio is $300 per month. Only the $18,000 salary was reported on the W-2. How much of Tim's income is subject to income tax?

A. $0.
B. $18,000.
C. $20,000.
D. $21,600.

The answer is B. Only $18,000, Tim's wages, is subject to income tax. The other amounts for the housing allowance and use of the studio are not subject to income tax, but they are subject to self-employment tax. ###

34. Jacob's personal car is repossessed. His auto loan was a recourse loan. He later receives a Form 1099-C, showing $3,000 in cancellation of debt income. How must this transaction be reported by Jacob?

A. The repossession is treated as a sale. Jacob must report the cancellation of debt income and any gain on the sale or repossession.
B. No reporting is required, because the loan was a recourse loan.
C. The amount must be reported as taxable interest income.
D. Not enough information to answer.

The answer is A. If a personal vehicle is repossessed, the repossession is treated as a sale, and the gain or loss must be computed. If the taxpayer is personally liable for a loan (a recourse loan), the canceled debt is taxable unless an exception applies. If a loan is "recourse," then the taxpayer must generally report two transactions: the cancellation of debt income and the gain or loss on the repossession. Since this was Jacob's personal car, any loss is not deductible.

35. Polly receives the following income and fringe benefits in 2012:

1. $30,000 in wages.
2. $2,000 Christmas bonus.
3. Parking pass at $90 per month.
4. Employer contributions to Polly's 401K plan in the amount of $900 for the year.
5. Free use of an indoor gym on the employer's premises, FMV valued at $500.

How much income must Polly report on her 2012 tax return?

A. $30,000.
B. $32,000.
C. $32,900.
D. $33,980.

The answer is B. Only the wages and the bonus are taxable. The parking pass is considered a nontaxable transportation benefit, and the employer contributions are not taxable until Polly withdraws the money from her retirement account. Polly does not have to report the use of the gym, because it is on the employer's premises and therefore not taxable. ###

36. Which of the following fringe benefits is taxable (or partially taxable) to the employee?

A. Health insurance covered 100% by the employer.
B. Employer-provided parking at $275 per month.
C. Group-term life insurance coverage of $50,000.
D. Employer contributions to an employee's 401K plan.

The answer is B. Employer-provided parking is an excludable benefit, but only up to $240 per month for qualified parking. Therefore, the amount above $240 ($275 - $240 = $35) becomes taxable to the employee. ###

37. Max owns a restaurant. He furnishes one of the waitresses, Caroline, two meals during each workday. Max encourages (but does not require) Caroline to have her breakfast on the business premises before starting work so she can help him answer phones. She is required to have her lunch on the premises. How should Max treat this fringe benefit to Caroline?

A. Caroline's meals are not taxable.
B. Caroline's meals are all taxable.
C. Caroline's lunch is not taxable, but her breakfast is.
D. Caroline's meals are taxed at a flat rate of 15%.

The answer is A. Meals furnished to Caroline are not taxable because they are for the convenience of the employer. Meals that employers furnish to a restaurant employee during, immediately before, or after the employee's working hours are considered furnished for the employer's convenience. Since Caroline is a waitress who works during the normal breakfast and lunch periods, Max can exclude from her wages the value of those meals. If Max were to allow Caroline to have meals without charge on her days off, the value of those meals would have to be included in her wages. ###

38. Sheng spends two years working overseas in Australia as a computer programmer for a private company. He has qualified foreign earned income, and makes $120,000 in 2012. What is the maximum amount Sheng can exclude from his income?

A. $0.
B. $92,400.
C. $95,100.
D. Sheng may exclude the full amount of his salary, with no income threshold.

The answer is C. For 2012, the maximum exclusion for the foreign earned income exclusion is $95,100. ###

39. Elaine is a cash-basis taxpayer and sells cosmetics on commission. She sells $200,000 in 2012, and her commission is 5% of sales. Elaine receives $10,000 in income from commissions, plus an advance of $1,000 in December 2012 for future commissions in 2013. She also receives $200 in expense reimbursements from her employer after turning in her receipts as part of an accountable plan. How much income should Elaine report on her 2012 tax return?

A. $0.
B. $11,000.
C. $11,200.
D. $10,200.

The answer is B. Elaine's commissions must be included in gross income, as well as advance payments in anticipation of future services, if the taxpayer is on a cash basis. The expense reimbursements from her employer would not be included in gross income. ###

40. Antonio is employed as an accountant by the Dawson and Enriquez firm. When Antonio travels for his audit work, he submits his travel receipts for reimbursement by his firm, which has an accountable plan for its employees. Which of the following statements is true?

A. Under an accountable plan, the reimbursed amounts are not taxable to Antonio.
B. Under an accountable plan, Antonio may still deduct his travel expenses on his tax return.
C. Under an accountable plan, Antonio's employer, Dawson and Enriquez, may not deduct the travel expenses, even though Antonio was reimbursed in full.
D. Under an accountable plan, reimbursed expenses are taxable to the employee, and the employer may also deduct the expenses as they would any other current expense.

The answer is A. Under an accountable plan, employee reimbursements are not included in the employee's income. The employer can deduct the expenses as current expenses on their tax return. The employee is not required to be taxed on any amounts received under a qualified accountable plan. ###

41. Bart had a $15,000 loan from his local credit union. He lost his job and was unable to make the payments on this loan. The credit union determined that the legal fees to collect might be higher than the amount Bart owed, so it canceled the $5,000 remaining amount due on the loan. Bart did not file bankruptcy nor is he insolvent. How much must he include in his income as a result of this occurrence?

A. $0.
B. $5,000.
C. $10,000.
D. $15,000.

The answer is B. Since Bart's inability to pay his debt is not a result of bankruptcy nor insolvency, the amount of the canceled debt ($5,000) should be included in gross income. ###

42. Which of the following fringe benefits provided by the employer will result in taxable income to the employee?

A. A cell phone used by a pharmaceutical salesperson who uses it to talk to clients while on the road.
B. Reimbursements paid by the employers for qualified business travel expenses.
C. Use of a company van for commuting.
D. Occasional coffee, doughnuts, and soft drinks.

The answer is C. Use of a company vehicle for commuting is not a qualified fringe benefit. Commuting expenses are not deductible. Use of a company van after normal working hours is a personal use and not a business use. This would result in taxable income to the employee. The parking permit, reimbursements for business travel, and the occasional coffee and doughnuts are considered noncash fringe benefits that are not taxable. ###

43. Carly was released from her obligation to pay a large credit card debt. She owed $10,000 to her credit card company, which agreed to accept $2,500 as payment in full. Carly was not insolvent and not in bankruptcy when the debt was canceled. What amount would be reported on Carly's Form 1040, line 21 (other income)?

A. $0.
B. $10,000.
C. $2,500.
D. $7,500.

The answer is D. Carly would report $7,500 on line 21 of her Form 1040 as cancellation of debt income. ###

44. Jan owns and operates a store in the downtown shopping mall. She reports her income and expenses as a sole proprietor on Schedule C. Jan is having financial difficulties and cannot pay all of her debts. In 2012, one of the banks that she borrowed money from in order to start her business cancels her debt. Jan is not insolvent. She had a loan balance of $5,000 when the debt was canceled. Which of the following statements is true?

A. Jan does not have to report the forgiveness of the debt as income.
B. Jan must report the $5,000 debt cancellation on Schedule A.
C. Jan must report the $5,000 debt cancellation as business income on Schedule C.
D. Jan must report the $5,000 debt cancellation as a long-term gain on Schedule D.

The answer is C. Canceled debt that is related to business income must be included on a taxpayer's Schedule C as business income. ###

45. Gene, a married taxpayer who files separately from his wife, bought his house in Florida in 2004 for $4.5 million, and financed the purchase with a mortgage loan of the same amount that required payments of interest only for the first five years. In 2006, the house appraised for $5.5 million, and he refinanced, this time with an interest-only mortgage loan of $5 million.

In 2012, the mortgage lender agrees to a short sale of the house for $3.2 million, and cancels the remaining $1.8 million (the amount in which the balance of the mortgage exceeded the sale proceeds.)

Based upon the information provided, what portion of the amount forgiven can Gene exclude from income?

A. $1.8 million.
B. $1.3 million.
C. $1 million.
D. Zero.

The answer is C. Absent an additional exclusion based upon insolvency, the excludable amount is $1 million. The additional amount of $500,000 that was borrowed when the property was refinanced in 2006 exceeds the purchase cost and therefore was not qualified personal residence indebtedness eligible for exclusion. The remaining portion of the debt forgiveness ($1.3 million) exceeds the limitation of $1 million for a MFS taxpayer.
Supporting calculations:

Balance of mortgage	$5,000,000
Proceeds of short sale	(3,200,000)
Amount of debt canceled	$1,800,000

Balance of mortgage	$5,000,000
Amount of QPRI	($4,500,000)
Portion that is not QPRI	$500,000

Amount of debt canceled	$1,800,000
Less portion that is not QPRI	($500,000)
Subtotal	**$1,300,000**
Less limit for MFS	($1,000,000)
Portion of QPRI not eligible for exclusion	$300,000

###

46. In 2012 Mina was discharged from her liability to repay $10,000 of credit card debt. The lender reported the discharged debt on Form 1099-C. Immediately prior to the debt cancellation, Mina had liabilities of $15,000 and the fair market value of her assets was $2,000.

What portion of the canceled debt must Mina include in income?

A. $10,000.
B. $3,000.
C. $5,000.
D. $0.

The answer is D. The amount of Mina's insolvency immediately prior to the debt cancellation exceeded the amount of debt that was discharged. Therefore, the entire amount of the debt cancellation can be excluded from income.

Supporting calculations:

Liabilities	$15,000
Fair market value of assets	($2,000)
Amount of insolvency	**$13,000**

Amount of debt cancellation	$10,000
Excess	**$3,000**

###

Unit 6: Adjustments to Gross Income

More Reading:
Publication 590, *Individual Retirement Arrangements*
Publication 521, *Moving Expenses*
Publication 970, *Tax Benefits for Education*

An *adjustment to income* directly reduces a taxpayer's income and thus the amount of tax he owes. Adjustments are deducted from gross income to arrive at adjusted gross income (AGI). An adjustment is not the same as a tax deduction. Rather, an adjustment is the best type of deduction—it occurs "above-the-line" on the tax form for adjusted gross income. Adjustments appear as direct subtractions from gross income in order to arrive at AGI.

Common Adjustments to Gross Income

There are many types of adjustments to gross income. Some are obscure, and some are very common. We will cover the most common ones in this unit, which are also the most common adjustments tested on the EA exam. These are the adjustments, listed in order, found on the 2012 Form 1040.

1. Educator expenses
2. Certain business expenses of reservists, performing artists, and fee-basis government officials
3. Health savings account deduction
4. Moving expenses
5. Deductible part of self-employment tax
6. Self-employed SEP, SIMPLE, and qualified plans
7. Self-employed health insurance deduction
8. Penalty for early withdrawal of savings
9. Alimony paid
10. IRA deduction
11. Student loan interest deduction
12. Tuition and fees
13. Domestic production activities deduction
14. Other adjustments (Line 36)
    - Archer MSA deduction
    - Jury duty pay remitted to an employer
    - Repayment of unemployment benefits
    - Other adjustments

Line 23: Educator Expense Deduction

Teachers are allowed to deduct up to $250 of unreimbursed expenses that they pay for books, supplies, computer equipment (including related software and services), other equipment, and supplementary materials used in the classroom. Since they are an adjustment to income, teachers can deduct these expenses even if they do not itemize deductions.[42]

For courses in health and physical education, expenses are deductible only if they are related to athletics. Nonathletic supplies for physical education and expenses related to health courses do not qualify. Materials used for home schooling also cannot be deducted.

Only certain teachers qualify. An eligible educator must work at least 900 hours a school year in a school that provides elementary or secondary education (K-12). College instructors do not qualify. The term "educator" includes:

- Teacher or instructor
- Counselor
- Principal
- Teacher's aide

Example: Devina is a third grade teacher who works full-time in a year-round school. She had 1,600 hours of employment during the tax year. She spent $262 on supplies for her students. Of that amount, $212 was for educational software. The other $50 was for supplies for a unit she teaches on health. Only the $212 is a qualified expense that she can deduct.

On a joint tax return, if both taxpayers are teachers, they both may take the credit, up to a maximum of $500. Any expenses that exceed the adjustment to income may still be deducted as "unreimbursed employee expenses" on Schedule A, subject to the 2% AGI limit.

Line 24: Certain Business Expenses of Reservists, Performing Artists, and Fee-Basis Government Officials

Certain employees are allowed to take their work-related expenses as an adjustment to income, rather than a deduction on Schedule A. The following individuals qualify for this tax treatment:

- **Reservist:** Members of the reserve component of the Armed Forces of the United States, National Guard, or the Reserve Corps of the Public Health Service. The adjustment is allowed for work-related expenses incurred while traveling more than 100 miles away from the taxpayer's home. The expense is limited to the regular federal per diem rate.
- **Qualified Performing Artist:** To qualify, the taxpayer must meet the following requirements for 2012:
  - Worked in the performing arts as an employee for at least two employers
  - Received at least $200 each from any two of these employers
  - Have related performing-arts business expenses that are more than 10% of gross income from the performance of those services
  - Have AGI of $16,000 *or less* before deducting expenses as a performing artist
- **Fee-Based Government Official:** A state or local government official who is compensated on a fee basis may deduct his employee business expenses whether or not he itemizes other deductions on Schedule A.

---

[42] This adjustment was scheduled to expire in 2012, but was retroactively reinstated for 2012 and extended through 2013 as part of the fiscal cliff legislation.

In the case of these special occupations, the workers' business expenses are deductible whether or not the taxpayer itemizes deductions.

Line 25: Health Savings Accounts

A health savings account (HSA) allows taxpayers to save and pay for health care expenses on a tax-preferred basis. The taxpayer can then take withdrawals from the HSA based on the amount of his qualifying medical expenses.

HSA contributions are 100% tax deductible from gross income. The amounts deposited in an HSA become an above-the-line deduction on Form 1040, and itemization of other deductions is not required.

An HSA must be set up exclusively for paying medical expenses for the taxpayer, his spouse, and his dependents. HSA accounts are usually set up with a bank, an insurance company, or by an employer.

To qualify, the taxpayer:

- Must not be enrolled in Medicare
- May not be claimed as a dependent on anyone else's 2012 tax return
- Must be covered under a high deductible health plan and have no other health coverage, other than that for a specific disease or illness; a fixed amount for a certain time period of hospitalization; or liabilities incurred under workers' compensation laws or tort liabilities.

Any eligible individual can contribute to an HSA. For example, an employee and his employer are both allowed to contribute to the employee's HSA in the same year. If an employer makes an HSA contribution on behalf of an employee, it is excluded from the employee's income and not subject to income tax or payroll tax.

In 2012, HSAs allow a taxpayer to avoid federal income tax on up to $3,100 for singles or $6,250 for joint filers. Taxpayers who are 55 and over may contribute an extra $1,000 to their HSAs.

2012 Health Savings Account Contribution Limits (HSA)

Taxpayer	Minimum Deductible	Maximum Out-of-Pocket	Contribution Limit	55 and Over
Single	$1,200	$6,050	$3,100	+$1,000
Family	$2,400	$12,100	$6,250	+$1,000

Excess contributions over these limits are subject to a 6% penalty.

Allowable medical expenses are those that would generally qualify for the medical and dental deduction. Qualified expenses include breast pumps, childbirth classes, dental treatment, hearing aids, Lasik eye surgery, long-term care premiums, weight loss and stop smoking programs, and nursing home care. As of 2011, over-the-counter medicines (other than insulin), unless prescribed by a doctor, are not considered qualified medical expenses.

A taxpayer generally pays medical expenses during the year without being reimbursed by his high deductible health plan, until he reaches the annual deductible for the plan. Withdrawals for nonmedical expenses from an HSA are allowed, but are subject to a 20% penalty, except in the following instances:

- When a taxpayer turns age 65 or older
- When a taxpayer becomes disabled
- When a taxpayer dies

Taxpayers will receive Form 5498-SA from the HSA trustee showing the amount of their contributions for the year. The deduction for an HSA is reported on Form 8889, *Health Savings Accounts.*

To claim the HSA deduction for a particular year, the HSA contributions must be made on or before that year's tax filing date. For 2012, HSA contributions must be made on or before the filing deadline, which is April 15, 2013.

Line 26: Moving Expenses

If a taxpayer moves due to a change in job or business location, he may deduct moving expenses that his employer has not reimbursed him for. The move must be work-related in order to qualify for this deduction.

A taxpayer who starts a first job or returns to full-time work after a long absence can also qualify for the deduction. Moving expenses incurred within one year from the date the taxpayer first reported to work at the new location can generally be deducted. Although the move must be work-related, there is no requirement that the job be in the same field or similar employment.

If a taxpayer does not move within one year of the date he begins the new job, the moving expenses are not deductible unless he can prove that circumstances existed that prevented the move within that time. Simply failing to sell one's former home, for example, would not be an adequate excuse.

Moving expenses are figured on Form 3903, *Moving Expenses.* The amount is then transferred to Form 1040 as an adjustment to income. To qualify for the moving expense deduction, the taxpayer must satisfy these tests:

- The move must be related to work or business, and
- The taxpayer must meet the **"Distance Test"** and the **"Time Test."**

The Time Test

The *time test* is different for employees than for people who are self-employed. For employees, moving costs are deductible only if the taxpayer works full-time at the new work location for at least 39 weeks in the first 12 months. For joint filers, only one spouse has to qualify for the time test in order to deduct moving expenses.

Self-employed taxpayers must work full-time 39 weeks in the first 12 months at the new location, and then at least 78 weeks within the first 24 months (two years) at the new location. For this test, any combination of full-time work as an employee or as a self-employed person qualifies. If the taxpayer fails to meet the time test, the taxpayer must report the moving expenses as "other income" on a later tax year, or amend the tax return on which the moving expenses was claimed.

Exceptions to the Time Test

There are certain times the time test does not need to be met, and the moving expenses will be deductible regardless.

Example: Randy quit his job and moved from California to Oregon to begin a full-time job as a mechanic for Motorcycle Customs, Inc. He worked at the motorcycle shop 40 hours each week. Shortly after his move, Randy also began operating a part-time motorcycle repair business from his home garage for several hours each afternoon and on weekends. Because Randy's principal place of business is Motorcycle Customs, he can satisfy the time test by meeting the 39-week test. However, if Randy is unable to satisfy the requirements of the 39-week test during the 12-month period, he can satisfy the 78-week test because he also works as a self-employed person.

A taxpayer does not have to meet the time test if any of the following applies:

- The taxpayer is in the armed forces and moved because of a permanent change of station.
- The taxpayer's main job location was outside the United States and he moved back to the United States because he retired from his position.
- A taxpayer is the surviving widow(er) of a person whose main job location at the time of death was outside the United States.
- The taxpayer's job at the new location ends because of death or disability.
- The taxpayer is transferred or laid off for a reason other than willful misconduct.

Example: Darrell's company transfers him from New York to Tennessee. He correctly deducts his moving expenses. Darrell expects to continue his full-time employment in Tennessee for many years and does not expect it to be a temporary move. A few months later, his employer is forced into bankruptcy and closes the entire Tennessee division. Darrell is laid off. He does not have to satisfy the time test.

Example: Shelby moves from Michigan to Ohio for a new job as a building manager. Six months after she starts the job, she dies. On Shelby's final tax return, her executor will be able to deduct Shelby's moving expenses, since her job ended at the new location due to death.

The Distance Test

Under the distance test, the new job must be at least 50 miles farther from the taxpayer's old home than the old job location was from the taxpayer's old home. If the taxpayer had no previous workplace, the new job must be at least 50 miles from the old home (see the diagram on the next page for clarification). This means that if a taxpayer starts a job for the first time, the place of work must be at least 50 miles from his former home to meet the distance test.

Example: Abe moved to a new city and took a job as an attorney in a different law firm. His old job was three miles from his former home. Therefore, in order to deduct his moving expenses, his new job location must be at least 53 miles from that former home. The distance test considers only the location of the former home, not the location of the former job.

For the EA exam, remember that members of the armed forces moving because of a permanent change of station or a military order are not required to meet the distance test or the time test.

> **Example:** Matt is enlisted in the Air Force, and has been transferred to another base 32 miles from his former home. Matt may still deduct his moving expenses without meeting the distance test or the time test, since he is a member of the armed forces and his move was due to a military order.

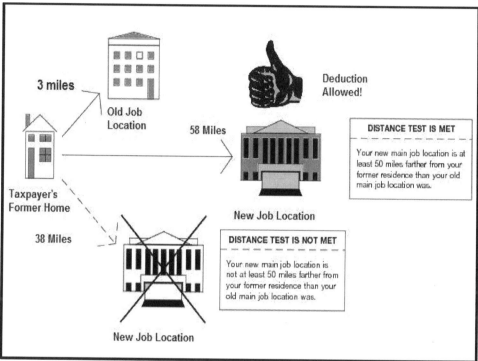

Qualifying Moving Expenses

Only certain expenses qualify for the moving expense deduction. Deductible moving expenses include:

- The cost of packing and moving household effects and family members.
- Storage costs (only while in transit and up to 30 days after the day of the move).
- Travel expenses (including lodging but not meals) for one trip per person. However, family members are not required to travel together. The taxpayer may choose to deduct actual costs or mileage.
- Any costs of connecting or disconnecting utilities required because a taxpayer is moving his household goods, appliances, or personal effects.
- The cost of shipping a car or pet to a new home.

Actual car expenses such as gas and oil are tax deductible if accurate records are kept, or a taxpayer can use the standard mileage rate instead. Parking fees and tolls are also tax deductible, but general car repairs, maintenance, insurance, or depreciation of a taxpayer's car are not tax deductible.

> **Example:** In February 2012, Ethan and Jackie moved from Minnesota to Washington, D.C. where Ethan was starting a new job. He drove the family car to Washington, D.C., a trip of 1,100 miles. His actual expenses were $281.50 for gas, plus $40 for tolls and $150 for lodging, for a total of $471.50. One week later, Jackie flew from Minnesota to Washington, D.C. Her only expense was a $400 plane ticket. The couple's moving expense deduction is $771.50 (Ethan's $471.50 + Jackie's $400).

For purposes of this rule, a taxpayer's home means his main residence. It does not include other homes owned by the taxpayer, such as vacation homes.

Employer-Reimbursed Moving Expenses

When an employer reimburses a taxpayer for moving expenses, the reimbursement is excluded from taxable income

However, if an employer reimburses an employee for "nondeductible" expenses (such as the expense incurred from breaking a lease), this reimbursement is taxable as wages. It must be treated as paid under a nonaccountable plan and be included as income on the employee's Form W-2. Expenses of buying or selling a home or breaking a lease (including closing costs, mortgage fees, and points) are never deductible as moving expenses.

Nondeductible Moving Expenses

Moving expenses that cannot be deducted for income tax purposes include:

- Pre-move house-hunting expenses
- Temporary living expenses
- Meals while traveling
- Expenses of buying or selling a home, home improvements to help sell a home, or loss on a home sale
- Real estate taxes
- Car tags, driver's license renewal fees
- Storage charges except those incurred in transit or for a foreign move

Seasonal Work and Temporary Absences: Exceptions

For purposes of the moving expense deduction, if a taxpayer's trade or business is seasonal, the off-season weeks when no work is available may still be counted as weeks during which he worked full time. In order to qualify, the off-season must be less than six months and the taxpayer must work full-time before *and* after the off-season.

Temporary absences from work are allowed. A taxpayer is still considered to be employed on a full-time basis during any week he is temporarily absent from work because of illness, labor strikes, natural disasters, or similar causes.

> **Example:** Marcus moves from Colorado to Jackson Hole, Wyoming to take a job as a manager of a ski resort. He works full-time during the ski season, and he is off for five months during the summer. Marcus may still count this time as full-time work, since his regular employment is expected to be seasonal.

Example: Xavier is an engineer who has been offered a job at XelCorp Engineering. He only agrees to accept the offer if XelCorp pays all his moving expenses. The cost of his professional movers was $9,600, which the company agrees to pay. This amount is deductible by XelCorp as a business expense and not taxable to Xavier, since it is a legitimate moving expense and allowable by the IRS. However, in order to entice him to move out of state, XelCorp also reimburses Xavier for a $7,500 loss on the sale of his home. Because this is a reimbursement of a nondeductible expense, it is treated as taxable to the employee and must be included in Xavier's Form W-2. Xavier has $7,500 added to his wages. The $7,500 is also deductible to XelCorp, but it is categorized as a wage expense and subject to payroll tax.

Extended Example: Nondeductible Moving Expenses

Ross and Claudia Kim are married and have two children. They owned a home in Charleston, South Carolina where Ross worked. On February 8, 2012, Ross's employer told him that he would be transferred to Albuquerque as of April 10, 2012. Claudia flew to Albuquerque on March 1 to look for a new home. She put a down payment of $25,000 on a house being built and returned to Charleston on March 4, 2012. The Kims sold their Charleston home for $1,500 less than they paid for it. They contracted to have their personal belongings moved to Albuquerque on April 3, 2012. The family drove to Albuquerque where they found that their new home was not finished. They stayed in a nearby motel until the house was ready on May 1. On April 10, 2012, Ross went to work at his new job in Albuquerque.

Pre-move house-hunting expenses	$524
Down payment on the Albuquerque home	$25,000
Real estate commission on the sale of the Charleston home	$3,500
Loss of on the sale of the Charleston home	$1,500
Meal expenses for the drive to Albuquerque	$320
Motel expenses while waiting for their home to be finished	$3,730
Moving truck expense	$8,000
Gas and hotel expenses while driving to Albuquerque	$980
Total expenses	**$43,554**

Out of all the expenses that the Kims incurred, only the cost of the moving truck and the actual trip to Albuquerque (the gas and hotel expense) can be deducted ($8,000 + $908 = $8,908). The rest of the expenses cannot be deducted. Meals are not deductible as moving expenses. Losses on the sale of a primary residence and pre-move house-hunting expenses are not deductible.

Example: Marlene moves to Florida from Missouri to take a job with a new employer. After working 25 weeks, her union votes to go on strike. She is off work for five weeks until the issue is resolved. Those five weeks count as a temporary absence and still may be counted as full-time work for purposes of satisfying the time test. Marlene still qualifies for the moving expenses deduction, because the time she spent on strike is considered a "temporary absence" for purposes of this test.

Line 27: One-Half of Self-Employment Tax

As detailed in Unit 5, self-employed taxpayers can subtract half of their self-employment tax from their income. This is equal to the amount of Social Security tax and Medicare tax that an employer normally pays for an employee, which is excluded from an employee's income.

SE tax must be paid if either of the following applies:

- The taxpayer had income as a church employee of $108.28 or more, or
- The taxpayer had self-employment income of $400 or more.

Line 28: Self-Employed SEP, SIMPLE, and Qualified Plans

Self-employed individuals are allowed to take a deduction for contributions to certain types of retirement plans. Line 28 of Form 1040 is used to report contributions to the following types of plans:

- Self-employed SEP (Simplified Employee Pension)
- Self-employed SIMPLE (Savings Incentive Match Plan for Employees)
- Self-employed qualified plans

Generally under these plans, contributions that are set aside for retirement may be currently deductible by the taxpayer, but are not taxable until later. Therefore, the contribution grows tax-free until the monies are distributed.

A taxpayer must have self-employment income in order to contribute to his own plan. However, a self-employed person with employees may still contribute to his employee's retirement plans, even if his business shows a loss for the year.

Line 29: Self-Employed Health Insurance Deduction

A self-employed taxpayer may also deduct 100% of his health insurance premiums as an adjustment to income. Premiums paid by the taxpayer for his spouse and dependents are also deductible as an adjustment to income. For the first time, health insurance premiums paid for coverage of an adult child under age 27 at the end of the year also qualify for this deduction, even if the child is not the taxpayer's dependent.

In addition, long-term care insurance is considered health insurance for purposes of this deduction. The policy can be in the name of the business or in the name of the business owner. A self-employed taxpayer must have a net profit for the year in order to take this deduction. So if the taxpayer is showing a loss on his Schedule C, he is not allowed to take this deduction. A self-employed taxpayer also may not take the deduction if either he or his spouse (if MFJ) is eligible to participate in an employer-sponsored and subsidized health insurance plan. This is true even if they decline coverage.

Line 30: Penalty on Early Withdrawal of Savings

If a taxpayer withdraws money from a certificate of deposit (CD) or other time-deposit savings account prior to maturing, he usually incurs a penalty for early withdrawal. This penalty is charged by the bank and withheld directly from a taxpayer's proceeds from the certificate.

Taxpayers can take an adjustment to income for early withdrawal penalties. The penalties are reported on a taxpayer's Form 1099-INT, *Interest Income*, or Form 1099-OID, *Original Issue Discount*. These forms will list the interest income, as well as the penalty amount.

Example: Earlier in 2012, Gloria invested in a certificate of deposit. However, in November, she had an unexpected medical expense and had to withdraw all the money early. Gloria made an early withdrawal of $15,000 from a one-year, deferred-interest CD in the current tax year. She had to pay a penalty of three months' interest, which totaled $150. Gloria can claim the penalty ($150) as an adjustment to income.

*Note: The penalty for early withdrawal of an IRA (retirement plan) is not tax-deductible.

Line 31: Alimony Paid as an Adjustment to Income

In Unit 5, we covered alimony as taxable income. Alimony is also a deductible expense by the individual who pays the alimony. Taxpayers may claim the deduction for "alimony paid" on Page 1 of Form 1040. They cannot use Form 1040A or Form 1040EZ.

By definition, alimony is a payment to a former spouse under a divorce or separation instrument. The payments do not have to be made directly to the ex-spouse. For example, payments made on behalf of the ex-spouse for expenses such as medical bills, housing costs, and other expenses can also qualify as alimony.

Example: Victoria divorced two years ago. Her divorce settlement agreement states that she must pay her ex-husband $16,000 a year. She is also required, per the divorce agreement, to pay his ongoing medical expenses. In 2012, the medical expenses were $9,500. She can deduct the full amount ($25,500) because it is all required by her divorce agreement.

Alimony does not include child support, which is never deductible. Alimony will be disallowed and reclassified as child support if the divorce decree states that the "alimony" will discontinue based on a contingency relating to the child.

Example: Neil pays child support and alimony to his ex-wife. They have one child together. The divorce decree states that he must pay $400 per month in child support and $500 per month in alimony. However, Neil's divorce agreement states that all payments will discontinue if the child gets married. This means that for tax purposes, all the payments must be treated as child support.

Requirements for Payments to Qualify as Alimony

Noncash property settlements, whether in a lump sum or installments, are not considered alimony. Voluntary payments (i.e., payments not required by a divorce decree or separation instrument) do not qualify as alimony. To qualify as alimony, all of these requirements must be met:

- The payments must be in cash or cash equivalents (checks or money orders).
- Payments must be required by the divorce decree.
- If only legally separated, spouses may not live in the same household.
- The payment may not be child support.
- The payer's liability for the alimony payments must stop upon the death of the recipient spouse.
- The parties may not file jointly.

Payments after Death and Voluntary Payments are not Alimony

If any alimony payments must continue after the ex-spouse's death, those payments are not considered alimony for tax purposes, even if they are made before death. These payments would normally be reclassified as child support, and therefore are not taxable to the recipient and nondeductible to the payer. Voluntary payments *outside* the divorce agreement do not count as alimony.

The person paying alimony can subtract it as an adjustment to income; the person receiving alimony claims it as taxable income.

> **Example:** Anthony has been divorced for three years. Under his divorce decree, he paid his ex-wife $12,600 in 2012. As a favor, he also made $2,400 in payments to cover part of her vehicle lease so she could keep steady employment. Anthony can take the $12,600 as an adjustment to income. He cannot count the lease payments because they were not required by the divorce agreement.

If a taxpayer's decree of divorce or separate maintenance provides for alimony and child support and the payer pays *less* than the total amount required, the payments apply first to child support. Any remaining amount is considered alimony.

> **Example:** Jeff must pay alimony and child support to his ex-wife, Liz. His monthly payment for alimony is $200, and his monthly payment for child support is $800. Jeff falls behind on his payments and is only able to pay $500 per month in 2012. The amount is calculated as follows: $200 x 12 = $2,400 (alimony due), $800 x 12 = $9,600 (child support due). Jeff can only pay $500 x 12 = $6,000; therefore he is short by $6,000 ($2,400 + $9,600 = $12,000 − $6,000). Since the amount he can pay falls short of the required child support payment by itself, all of his $6,000 will be reclassified as child support. Therefore, Jeff can deduct none of his payments as alimony. Also, Jeff's ex-wife does not have to claim any of the payments as alimony income. Child support is not taxable and not deductible by either party.

Line 32: Deduction for Traditional IRA Contributions

An IRA (Individual Retirement Arrangement) is a personal savings plan that offers tax advantages for setting aside money for retirement. Generally, amounts in an IRA, including earnings and gains, are not taxed until they are distributed.

The complex rules regarding contributions, withdrawals, and rollovers to IRAs will be covered extensively in Unit 14. Here, we will only discuss the adjustment to income that is allowed on Page 1 of Form 1040.

Only traditional IRAs qualify for tax-deductible contributions. Amounts that do not qualify for a deduction include:

- Roth IRA contributions
- Contributions that apply to the previous tax year
- Rollovers
- Nondeductible contributions due to the taxpayer's active participation in an employer-sponsored plan

To contribute to a traditional IRA, the taxpayer must:

- Be *under* the age of 70½ at the end of the tax year

- Have taxable compensation, such as wages income from self-employment (Taxable alimony and nontaxable combat pay are treated as compensation for IRA purposes)

For purposes of a contribution to a traditional IRA, compensation does not include passive income such as:

- Pension income
- Rental income
- Interest and dividend income

Contributions can be made to a traditional IRA at any time during the year or by the *due date* for filing the return, not including extensions.

> **Example:** Daniel wants to make a contribution to his traditional IRA for 2012, but he is unsure how much he should contribute. He sees his accountant on April 1, 2013, and Daniel decides that he wants to contribute the maximum amount. Daniel files his tax return on April 1 and takes the deduction for his contribution. Daniel now has until April 15, 2013 to make a tax deductible contribution to his traditional IRA for the 2012 tax year.

For 2012, the most a taxpayer can contribute to his traditional IRA generally is the *smaller* of the following amounts:

- 5,000 ($6,000 if age 50 or older), or
- The amount of taxable compensation.

> **Example:** Wes is 52 and self-employed. Normally, he would be able to contribute $6,000 to a traditional IRA. However, in 2012, he has $3,700 in self-employment income, and $23,000 in dividend income. Since only his self-employment income counts as "compensation" for purposes of an IRA contribution, the maximum he can contribute for the 2012 tax year is $3,700.

Line 33: Student Loan Interest Deduction

Generally, personal interest (other than mortgage interest) is not deductible on a tax return. However, there is a special deduction for interest paid on a student loan used for higher education.

Only student loan interest paid to an accredited college or university is eligible for this deduction. A "qualified student loan" is used solely to pay qualified education expenses for the taxpayer, his spouse, or dependents.

A taxpayer can claim the deduction if:

- He paid interest on a qualified loan in 2012
- He is legally obligated to pay interest on a qualified student loan
- His filing status is not married filing separately
- He (or his spouse if filing jointly) cannot be claimed as dependents on someone else's return

The maximum deduction for student loan interest in 2012 is $2,500. The loan begins to phase out for married taxpayers filing a joint return at $125,000 and phases out completely at $155,000. For single taxpayers the phase-out range is from $60,000 to $75,000.

Example: Veronica and her husband file jointly. Their modified adjusted gross income (MAGI) is $162,000. She completed her doctoral degree in 2012 and paid $3,400 in student loan interest in 2012. Due to their high MAGI, they may not deduct any of their student loan interest as an adjustment to income.

In order for the student loan interest to qualify, the student must have been enrolled at least half-time in a higher education program leading to a degree, certificate, or other recognized educational credential. A student who is taking classes for his own recreation does not qualify.

Example: Peter attends a local technical college where he is enrolled full-time in a certificate program for automotive repair. Peter may take the student loan interest deduction.

Qualified expenditures are the total cost of attending an eligible educational institution, including graduate school. Qualified expenses include:

- Tuition and fees
- Room and board
- Books, supplies, and equipment
- Other necessary school-related expenses, such as transportation

Before calculating "qualified expenses" on a tax return, the following tax-free income amounts must be subtracted:

1. Employer-provided educational assistance benefits
2. Tax-free withdrawals from a Coverdell Education Savings Account
3. U.S. savings bond interest already excluded from income
4. Tax-free scholarships and fellowships
5. Veterans' educational assistance benefits
6. Any other nontaxable payments (except gifts, bequests, or inheritances) received for educational expenses

Example: In 2012, Katelyn's educational expenses are $7,200. She also receives a gift of $1,000 from her aunt and $1,000 in veterans' educational assistance. Therefore, in 2012 Katelyn's qualified higher education expenses for purposes of the student loan interest deduction are $6,200. This is because veterans' assistance benefits must be subtracted from a taxpayer's educational expenses. The gift from her aunt does not have to be subtracted.

Under the terms of this deduction, a loan is not eligible if it was granted by a family member. This includes a spouse, brothers and sisters, half-brothers and half-sisters, ancestors (parents, grandparents, etc.), and lineal descendants (children, grandchildren, etc.). Loans from an employer plan also do not qualify.

The student loan interest deduction is "per return" not "per student." So, for example, if a taxpayer has three children in college and pays over $2,000 in student loan interest for each of them, the maximum deduction is still only $2,500.

Student Loan Interest Deduction: A Summary

Rules	Description
Maximum benefit	$2,500 per tax return, per year
Loan qualifications	The student loan: • Must have been taken out solely to pay qualified education expenses, and • Cannot be from a related person or made under a qualified employer plan.
Student qualifications	The student must be: • The taxpayer, a spouse, or a dependent, and • Enrolled at least half-time in a degree program.
Time limit	The taxpayer can deduct interest paid during the remaining period of the student loan.
Phase-out ranges	In 2012, the phase-out range is $60,000 to $75,000 of MAGI for single filers and $125,000 to $155,000 for MFJ. MFS filers do not qualify.

Line 34: Tuition and Fees Deduction

The tuition and fees deduction allows taxpayers to deduct qualified tuition and related expenses as an adjustment to income. The deduction is allowed for qualified higher education expenses paid for academic periods beginning in 2012 and the first three months of 2013.

In 2012, the maximum deduction is either $2,000 or $4,000, depending on MAGI. The deduction is calculated as follows:

- $4,000 if MAGI is $65,000 or less ($130,000 if MFJ)
- $2,000 if MAGI is $80,000 or less ($160,000 if MFJ)

The deduction is eliminated completely once a taxpayer's MAGI exceeds $80,000 for single filers and $160,000 if filing jointly.

A qualified student is:

- The taxpayer
- The taxpayer's spouse (if filing jointly)
- The taxpayer's dependent

Qualifying Educational Expenses: Tuition and Fees Deduction

The expenses that qualify for the tuition and fees deduction are very different than the expenses that qualify for the student loan interest deduction.

Generally, for the tuition and fees deduction, qualified education expenses are amounts paid for tuition expenses only at an eligible college or vocational institution. It does not matter whether the expenses are paid in cash, by check, by credit card, or with student loans. Qualified education expenses do not include amounts paid for:

- Room and board, medical expenses (including student health fees), transportation, or other personal expenses

- Course-related books, supplies, equipment, and nonacademic activities, unless they are required as a condition of enrollment
- Any course or other education involving sports, games, or hobbies, or any noncredit course

A taxpayer cannot claim the tuition and fees deduction based on expenses that have already been paid with a tax-free scholarship, fellowship, grant, or education savings account funds such as a Coverdell education savings account, tax-free savings bond interest, or employer-provided education assistance.

Tuition Received as a Gift (Special Rule)

Another individual may make a payment directly to an eligible educational institution to pay for a student's education expenses. In this case, the student is treated as receiving the payment as a gift from the other person and, in turn, paying the institution. In order for the taxpayer to claim the deduction for tuition received as a gift, the taxpayer may not be claimed on anyone else's tax return. If someone else can claim an exemption for the student, no one will be allowed a deduction for the tuition payment. In this case, there is also a special exemption in the law; the giver does not have to file a gift tax return.

Specifically, any tuition payments made by a grandparent (or anyone else) directly to a college to cover a student's tuition expenses are exempt from federal gift tax. The money will not qualify for a gift tax exemption if it is first given to the student, with instructions to pay the college.

Reporting Refunded Tuition After Claiming the Deduction

Sometimes a student will have his tuition refunded. If, after a tax return, a student receives a refund of amounts that were previously used to figure the tuition and fees deduction, the taxpayer must report the refund as income in the following year. The refunded amount is added to income by entering it on the "Other Income" line of Form 1040 in the following year—the year the refund of tuition is received. The taxpayer's current year tax return does not need to be amended.

Example: Keith has one daughter named Robin. He paid $8,000 in tuition and fees for Robin's college education in December 2012, and she began college in January 2013. Keith filed his 2012 tax return on March 1, 2013 and properly claimed a tuition and fees deduction of $4,000. After Keith filed his return, Robin dropped three classes and Keith received a refund of $5,600. Keith must refigure his tuition and fees deduction using $2,400 of qualified expenses instead of $8,000 ($8,000 - $5,600). He must include the difference of $1,600 ($4,000 - $2,400) on his 2013 Form 1040.

*Study Tip: On the EA exam, be prepared to understand the difference between the tuition and fees deduction and the student loan interest deduction; qualifying expenses, AGI limits, and deduction amounts are all different. A common "trick question" might be to verify a type of qualifying expense. Remember that in the case of the student loan interest deduction, qualifying expenses include housing, but they are not for the tuition and fees deduction.

A taxpayer filing MFS cannot take the tuition and fees deduction. Nonresident aliens also do not qualify for this deduction.

To prevent double-dipping, a taxpayer cannot claim the tuition and fees deduction and an education credit for the *same student*. A taxpayer who is eligible to claim the American Opportunity Credit or Lifetime Learning Credit[43] is allowed to figure his return both ways and choose the deduction that results in the lowest tax.

A taxpayer does not have to itemize in order to take the tuition and fees deduction.

Line 35: Domestic Production Activities Deduction

The Domestic Production Activities Deduction (DPAD) is a tax deduction that is given to businesses that have employees and also do manufacturing and other qualifying activities in the United States. The aim of this deduction is to stimulate domestic production.

This deduction is covered primarily in Part 2 of the exam, because it applies mainly to businesses. However, it is possible for a sole proprietor to qualify for this deduction, so long as the taxpayer has employees and pays wages to those employees.

Line 36: Other Adjustments

Line 36 of Form 1040 is reserved for more obscure deductions. There is a dotted line on the form that allows the taxpayer to indicate what type of adjustment is being taken, and most software programs will fill this in automatically. These are some of the miscellaneous adjustments that are entered on line 36:

1. **Archer MSA:** An Archer MSA[44] is a tax-exempt account that is set up with a U.S. financial institution in which a taxpayer can save money exclusively for future medical expenses. It is similar to a health savings account.

2. **Jury duty pay remitted to an employer:** Jury duty pay is reported as taxable income on Form 1040. However, some employees continue to receive their regular wages when they serve on jury duty even though they are not at work, and their jury pay is turned over to their employers. In that case, the amount is reported as a write-in adjustment.

3. **Repayment of unemployment benefits:** A taxpayer who repaid unemployment benefits may take the repaid amounts as an adjustment to income in the year the amount is repaid.[45]

---

[43] These education credits are discussed in Unit 9, Tax Credits.

[44] Although Archer MSAs still exist, they were superseded by HSAs, which were created in 2003 and are more widely available.

[45] Sometimes, a person will be forced to repay unemployment benefits back to the state. This happens most often when an individual continues to draw unemployment after he has started working again.

Unit 6: Questions

1. Jermaine and Anna have a MAGI of $45,000. They are married and file a joint return. Two years ago, they took out a loan so their daughter, Miranda, could earn her degree. Miranda is their dependent. In 2012, they paid $3,000 in student loan interest. How much student loan interest can Jermaine and Anna deduct on their tax return?

A. $0.
B. $1,000.
C. $2,500.
D. $3,000.

The answer is C. The maximum deduction for student loan interest is $2,500. The deduction is limited to the lesser of $2,500 or the amount of interest actually paid. ###

2. Contributions to a traditional IRA can be made:

A. Any time during the year or by the due date of the return, not including extensions.
B. Any time during the year or by the due date of the return, including extensions.
C. By December 31 (the end of the tax year).
D. Any time during the year, but only while the taxpayer is gainfully employed.

The answer is A. IRA contributions for tax year 2012 must be made by April 15, 2013. A taxpayer cannot make a contribution to an IRA after the due date of his tax return, even if he files for an extension. ###

3. All of the following statements are correct except:

A. A school counselor may qualify for the educator expense deduction.
B. A part-time teacher may qualify for the educator expense deduction.
C. A school principal may qualify for the educator expense deduction.
D. A college instructor may qualify for the educator expense deduction.

The answer is D. College instructors do not qualify. An eligible educator must work 900 hours a year in a school that provides elementary or secondary education (K-12). Part-time teachers qualify, so long as they meet the yearly requirement for hours worked. The term educator includes teachers, instructors, counselors, principals, and aides. ###

4. What is the maximum educator's expense deduction for two teachers who are married and file jointly?

A. $100.
B. $250.
C. $500.
D. $750.

The answer is C. On a jointly filed tax return, if both taxpayers are teachers, they both may take the deduction, up to a maximum of $500 ($250 each). ###

5. Which of the following statements is true?

A. Credit card interest can be deductible as student loan interest if qualifying educational expenses are paid.
B. On a married filing jointly return, a taxpayer may deduct student loan interest paid on behalf of his spouse.
C. The maximum deduction for student loan interest is $5,000 per student.
D. Taxpayers may deduct student loan interest even if they are not liable for the loan.

The answer is B. On a MFJ return, a taxpayer may deduct student loan interest paid on behalf of his spouse or dependents. This deduction is a maximum of $2,500 in 2012. Credit card interest does not qualify, and taxpayers must be liable for the loan in order to deduct the interest expense. ###

6. Drew borrowed $15,000 from his sister to pay for college. He signed a notarized loan statement and is paying regular payments of $500 per month at 10% interest. In 2012, he paid $3,200 in student loan interest. Which of the following is true?

A. Drew can deduct all the interest as qualified student loan interest.
B. Drew can deduct $2,500 of the interest as qualified student loan interest.
C. Drew cannot deduct the interest.
D. Drew can deduct $6,000 ($500 X 12 months).

The answer is C. Interest paid to a family member is not qualified interest for purposes of the student loan interest deduction. Related persons include a spouse, brothers and sisters, half-brothers and half-sisters, ancestors (parents, grandparents, etc.), and lineal descendants (children, grandchildren, etc.). ###

7. Years ago, Sammy took out a student loan for $90,000 to help pay the tuition at a university in the Ivy League. He graduated and began making payments on his student loan in 2012. Sammy made twelve payments in 2012, and he paid $1,600 in required interest on the loan. He also paid an additional $1,000 in principal payment voluntarily, attempting to get the debt paid off faster. How much is Sammy's student loan interest deduction?

A. $1,600.
B. $2,500.
C. $2,600.
D. $90,000

The answer is A. Only the interest is deductible. A payment toward the principal on the loan is not a deductible expense. Student loan interest is interest a taxpayer paid during the year on a qualified student loan. It includes both required and voluntary interest payments. ###

8. Which of the following expenses does not qualify for the student loan interest deduction?

A. Dorm housing.
B. Required books.
C. Required equipment.
D. Tuition for a non-degree candidate.

The answer is D. The student must be enrolled at least half-time in a program leading to a degree, certificate, or other recognized educational credential in order to qualify for the student loan interest deduction. Tuition for a non-degree candidate or someone who is taking classes just for fun or for general improvement does not qualify. ###

9. Which of the following qualifies as a deductible education expense for the tuition and fees deduction?

A. College club dues.
B. Student health fees.
C. Room and board.
D. Student activity fees required as a condition for enrollment.

The answer is D. Only the student activity fees qualify for the tuition and fees deduction. Deductions are not allowed for room and board and other basic expenses of going to college, other than required tuition and fees. Student activity fees, course-related books, supplies, and equipment may be deductible only if they are required by the institution as a condition of enrollment. ###

10. Addie paid $2,000 tuition and fees in December 2012, and she began college in January 2013. She filed her 2012 tax return on February 1, 2013, and correctly claimed a tuition and fees deduction of $2,000. But after Addie filed her return, she became ill and dropped two courses. She received a refund of tuition in the amount of $1,100 in April 2013. How must Addie report the refund of fees?

A. Addie may use the refund to pay qualified tuition in 2013 and not report the refund.
B. Addie may report the refund on her next year's tax return as "Other Income."
C. Addie is not required to report the refund.
D. Addie is required to amend her 2012 return and remove the deduction for tuition and fees.

The answer is B. Addie may include the difference of $1,100 on the "Other Income" line of her Form 1040 in 2013. Her 2012 return does not have to be amended. ###

11. Alimony does not include:

A. Noncash property settlements.
B. Payments to a third-party on behalf of an ex-spouse.
C. Medical expenses paid on behalf of an ex-spouse.
D. Cash alimony payments.

The answer is A. Noncash property settlements do not qualify as alimony. Alimony does not include child support, noncash property settlements, payments to keep up the payer's property, or use of the payer's property. Payments made to a third party or medical expenses paid on behalf of a former spouse may qualify as alimony. ###

12. In 2012, Patricia was offered a new job in a different state. She had the following moving expenses:

- $1,200 for transporting her household goods
- $550 in lodging for travel between her old home and her new home
- $250 in meals during the trip
- $250 to break the lease on her old home

Patricia moved to start a new job and met the distance and time tests. What are the total moving expenses that can be deducted on her tax return?

A. $2,150.
B. $1,900.
C. $1,750.
D. $2,000.

The answer is C. The answer is figured as follows:

Cost of moving goods:	$1,200
Lodging	$550
Deductible expenses	$1,750

A taxpayer cannot deduct any moving expenses for meals. The cost of breaking a lease to move to a new location is also not a deductible expense. ###

13. Dave and Bea file jointly. In March 2012, they move from Arizona to Connecticut, where Dave is starting a new job. Dave drives the car to Hartford. His expenses are $400 for gas, $40 for tolls, $150 for lodging, and $70 for meals. One week later, Bea drives to Hartford. Her expenses are $500 for gas, $40 for tolls, $35 for parking, $100 for lodging, and $25 for meals. A week later, they pay $600 to ship their pet, a miniature horse, to Connecticut. How much is their deduction for moving expenses?

A. $590.
B. $1,265.
C. $1,300.
D. $1,865.

The answer is D. The cost of meals is not deductible. The costs of travel, transportation, and lodging are all deductible. The costs of moving personal items and pets are deductible. The answer is figured as follows:

Dave's expenses $400 + $40 + $150 = $590
Bea's expenses $500+ $40 +$35 + $100 = $675
Cost of shipping horse = $600
Total deductible expenses: $590 + $675 + $600 = $1,865

If a married couple files jointly, *either* spouse can qualify for the full-time work test. Family members are not required to travel together. ###

14. Lynn was offered a position in another city. Her new employer reimburses her for the $9,500 loss on the sale of her home because of the move. How should this reimbursement be treated?

A. The employer can reimburse Lynn and make the payment nontaxable through an accountable plan, if properly documented.
B. Because this is a reimbursement of a nondeductible expense, it is treated as wages and must be included as pay on Lynn's Form W-2.
C. The reimbursement is tax-exempt because it is a qualified moving expense.
D. The expense is nontaxable so long as Lynn's employer makes the payment directly to her mortgage lender.

The answer is B. Because this is a reimbursement of a nondeductible expense, it is treated as paid under a nonaccountable plan and must be included as pay on Lynn's Form W-2. Expenses of buying or selling a home (including closing costs, mortgage fees, and points) are never deductible as moving expenses. If an employer offers to pay these "nondeductible" expenses as a condition of employment, then the amounts are treated like taxable compensation and must be reported and treated as such. ###

15. Ian and Pam are divorced. Pam has an auto accident and dies. Under their divorce decree, Ian must continue to pay his former spouse's estate $30,000 annually. The divorce decree states that upon Pam's death, the continued payments will be put into trust for their daughter, who is 12 years old. What is true about the $30,000 annual payment?

A. For tax purposes, it is alimony.
B. For tax purposes, it is child support.
C. For tax purposes, it is a gift.
D. Once Pam dies, the payments are taxable to the daughter.

The answer is B. The trust is to be used for the child's benefit and must continue after Pam's death. Therefore, the $30,000 annual payment is not alimony and is instead classified as child support for tax purposes. Any payment that is specifically designated as child support or treated as specifically designated as child support under a divorce agreement is not alimony. ###

16. Under his divorce decree, Rick must pay the medical expenses of his former spouse, Linda. In January 2012, Rick sends a check totaling $4,000 directly to General Medical Hospital in order to pay for Linda's emergency surgery. Which of the following statements is true?

A. This payment qualifies as alimony, and Linda must include the $4,000 as income on her return.
B. This payment does not qualify as alimony, but Rick can claim a deduction for the medical expenses on his return.
C. Linda must include the $4,000 as income on her return, but Rick cannot deduct the expense as alimony because it was paid to a third party.
D. None of the above.

The answer is A. The payment may be treated as alimony for tax purposes, because the medical payments are a condition of the divorce agreement. Payments to a third party on behalf of an ex-spouse under the terms of a divorce instrument can be alimony, if they qualify. These include payments for a spouse's medical expenses, housing costs (rent and utilities), taxes, and tuition. The payments are treated as received by the ex-spouse and included as income. ###

17. George paid $14,000 in alimony to his wife during the year. Which of the following is true?

A. George can only deduct alimony if he itemizes deductions on his tax return.
B. The deduction for alimony is entered on Schedule A as an itemized deduction.
C. George can deduct alimony paid, even if he does not itemize.
D. George can deduct alimony paid on Form 1040A.

The answer is C. George can deduct alimony paid, even if he does not itemize. He must file Form 1040 and enter the amount of alimony paid as an adjustment to income. An adjustment for alimony cannot be claimed on Form 1040EZ or Form 1040A. ###

18. Under the terms of a divorce decree, Blake transfers appreciated property to his ex-wife, Ming. The property has a fair market value of $75,000 and an adjusted basis of $50,000 to Blake. This transaction creates taxable alimony of _____ to Ming.

A. $0.
B. $25,000.
C. $75,000.
D. $50,000.

The answer is A. Transfers of property in the fulfillment of a divorce decree are not taxable events. Property settlements due to a divorce decree are not alimony; they are simply a division of assets and are treated as such. ###

19. If a taxpayer's decree of divorce provides for alimony and child support, and the payer pays less than the total amount required, the payments apply first to _____.

A. Alimony.
B. Child support.
C. Separate maintenance.
D. Tax delinquencies.

The answer is B. If a taxpayer's decree of divorce or separate maintenance provides for alimony and child support, and the payer pays less than the total amount required, the payments apply first to child support. Any remaining amount is considered alimony. ###

20. Kyle has an HSA, and he becomes permanently disabled in 2012. Which of the following statements is true?

A. Kyle may withdraw money from his HSA for nonmedical expenses, but the withdrawals will be subject to income tax and also an additional penalty.
B. Kyle may withdraw money from his HSA for nonmedical expenses. The withdrawals will be subject to income tax, but will not be subject to penalty.
C. Kyle may not take nonmedical distributions from his account.
D. Kyle must be at least 65 to take nonmedical distributions from an HSA.

The answer is B. Kyle is disabled, so his withdrawals are not subject to penalty. Withdrawals for nonmedical expenses from an HSA are allowed, but nonmedical distributions are subject to an additional penalty tax, except when the taxpayer turns 65, becomes disabled, or dies. ###

21. Seth makes an excess contribution to his HSA, by accidentally contributing over the maximum allowable amount. What is the penalty on excess contributions if Seth does not correct the problem?

A. No penalty.
B. 6% penalty.
C. 10% penalty.
D. 20% penalty.

The answer is B. The 6% penalty applies to excess contributions. Excess contributions made by an employer must be included in an employee's gross income. Excess contributions to an HSA are not deductible. ###

22. Emilio is a sophomore at California State University's degree program in Anthropology. This year, he paid $3,000 in tuition and $10,000 to live in optional on-campus housing. In addition to tuition, he is required to pay a fee of $300 to the university for the rental of the equipment he will use in this program. How much of these expenses qualify for the tuition and fees deduction?

A. $3,000.
B. $3,300.
C. $13,000.
D. $13,300.

The answer is B. The rental fee and the tuition costs qualify for the tuition and fees deduction, and Emilio may deduct the cost on his tax return. Because the equipment rental fee must be paid to the university and is a requirement for enrollment and attendance, it is a qualified expense. Student activity fees and expenses for course-related books, supplies, and equipment can be included in qualified educational expenses if the fees and expenses paid to the institution are required. The housing is not a qualified educational expense. ###

23. In 2012, Caylie had an HSA account set up with her employer. At the end of the year, she had $3,000 in the account. Then she quit her job and withdrew all the funds from her HSA. She did not use the $3,000 for qualifying medical expenses. What is the consequence of this action?

A. Nothing; taxpayers are allowed to withdraw from their HSA accounts at any time.
B. Nonmedical withdrawals from an HSA are prohibited and will result in a forfeiture of the funds.
C. Withdrawals from an HSA for non-eligible expenses are subject to a 20% penalty.
D. Withdrawals from an HSA for non-eligible expenses are subject to a 6% penalty.

The answer is C. Withdrawals from an HSA for non-eligible expenses are allowed, but the withdrawal will be subject to a 20% penalty, in addition to regular income tax. ###

24. During 2012, Deborah was self-employed. She had self-employment tax of $4,896. Which of the following statements is true?

A. Deborah may deduct 100% of the self-employment tax she paid on Schedule C.
B. Deborah may deduct 50% of the self-employment tax she paid on Schedule C.
C. Deborah may deduct 50% of the self-employment tax she paid as an adjustment to income on Form 1040.
D. Deborah may not deduct self-employment tax.

The answer is C. Deborah may deduct 50% of the self-employment tax she paid as an adjustment to income on page 1 of her Form 1040. A taxpayer can deduct one-half (not 100%) of self-employment tax paid as an adjustment on Form 1040. ###

25. Jasmine is a part-time art teacher at an elementary school. She spends $185 on qualified expenses for her art students and $75 on materials for a health course that she also teaches. She has 440 hours of documented employment as an educator during the tax year. How much can she deduct as a qualified educator expense as an adjustment to income?

A. $0.
B. $185.
C. $250.
D. $260.

The answer is A. Because she has only 440 hours of documented employment as an educator during the tax year, she cannot deduct her educator expenses as an adjustment to income. An educator must have at least 900 hours of qualified employment during the school year in order to take this deduction as an adjustment to income. ###

26. Marshall lost his job last year and withdrew money from a number of accounts. He paid the following penalties:

1. $100 penalty for early withdrawal from a certificate of deposit (CD).
2. $200 penalty from early withdrawal from a traditional IRA.
3. $50 late penalty for not paying his rent on time.

How much of these listed amounts can Marshall deduct as an adjustment to income on his Form 1040?

A. $0.
B. $100.
C. $200.
D. $250.

The answer is B. Early withdrawal penalties are tax-deductible if made from a time deposit account, such as a certificate of deposit. Taxpayers deduct any penalties on Form 1040 as an adjustment to income. ###

27. Chuck and Mallory are married and file jointly. Chuck is self-employed and his profit was $50,000 in 2012. They pay $500 per month for health insurance coverage. Mallory was a homemaker until March 1, 2012, when she got a job working for a local construction company. Mallory was eligible to participate in an employer health plan, but she and Chuck did not want to switch doctors, so she declined the coverage. Which of the following statements is true?

A. No deduction is allowed in 2012 for self-employed health insurance.
B. Chuck and Mallory may only deduct $1,000 in self-employed health insurance, which is for January and February, the two months they were not eligible to participate in an employer plan.
C. Chuck and Mallory may deduct 100% of their insurance premiums because they declined the employer coverage.
D. Chuck and Mallory may deduct 50% of their health insurance premiums on Chuck's Schedule C.

The answer is B. Chuck and Mallory may only deduct $1,000 in self-employed health insurance for the two months that they were ineligible to participate in an employer plan. No deduction is allowed for self-employed health insurance for any month that the taxpayer has the option to participate in an employer-sponsored and subsidized plan. This is true even if the taxpayer declines the coverage. Self-employed taxpayers may deduct 100% of health insurance premiums as an adjustment to income but only if neither they nor their spouses were able to participate in an employer health plan. ###

28. An adjustment to income is considered the most beneficial type of deduction because_____:

A. It favors taxpayers who choose to itemize their deductions.
B. It is simpler to figure out qualifying expenses for adjustments to income than it is other deductions.
C. It lowers a taxpayer's adjusted gross income, and thus his overall tax liability.
D. There is no significant difference between an adjustment to income and a regular tax deduction.

The answer is C. An adjustment to income directly reduces a taxpayer's income, and thus the amount of tax he owes. Adjustments are deducted from gross income to arrive at adjusted gross income. They are often referred to as "above-the-line" deductions.

29. Chase is moving for a new job. He has the following expenses:

cost of moving truck rental	$500
cost of moving family and pets	$300
cost for a storage unit while moving	$200
cost of breaking his existing apartment lease	$400
pre-move house-hunting.	$500

Assuming that Chase passes all the required tests, what is his moving expense deduction?

A. $500.
B. $800.
C. $1,000.
D. $1,900.

The answer is C. The cost of breaking a lease is not a deductible moving expense. House-hunting before a move is also not deductible. The cost of a storage unit while moving is deductible. Therefore, Chase may deduct the following: ($500 + $300 + $200 = $1,000). ###

30. Marina is a software specialist who works and lives in Boston. A company offers her a new job in Raleigh, North Carolina, more than 700 miles away. As part of the offer, she negotiates a deal to work part-time for the first six months. Marina's husband is a stay-at-home father to the couple's two young children. The family makes the move from Boston to Raleigh, and Marina begins work at her new job. Does she meet both the time and distance tests in order to deduct her moving expenses as an adjustment to income?

A. No, she does not meet the distance test.
B. No, she does not meet the time test or distance test.
C. She meets the distance test, but not the time test.
D. Marina meets both tests, and is able to deduct her moving expenses.

The answer is C. Marina is not able to deduct her moving expenses. She meets the distance test because her old home in Boston is more than 50 miles from her new office in Raleigh. However, to meet the time test, she must work full-time for a period of at least 39 weeks in the first 12 months. Since she is only working part-time for six months, this does not fulfill the requirements of the time test. A spouse does not to be employed for a MFJ couple to deduct moving expenses.

Unit 7: The Standard Deduction and Itemized Deductions

More Reading:
Publication 502, *Medical and Dental Expenses*
Publication 600, *State and Local General Sales Taxes*
Publication 936, *Home Mortgage Interest Deduction*
Publication 526, *Charitable Contributions*

Taxpayers may choose to take the standard deduction or itemize their deductions on their tax returns. If a taxpayer chooses to itemize, then he must file a Schedule A along with his Form 1040. Taxpayers should elect the type of deduction that results in the lower tax.

The standard deduction eliminates the need for taxpayers to itemize actual deductions, such as medical expenses, charitable contributions, and state and local taxes. It is available to U.S. citizens and resident aliens who are individuals, married persons, and heads of household. The standard deduction is adjusted every year for inflation. In some cases, the standard deduction can consist of two parts: the *basic* standard deduction and an *additional* standard deduction amount for age, blindness, or both.

The additional amount for blindness will be allowed if the taxpayer is blind on the last day of the tax year, even if he did not qualify as "blind" the rest of the year. A taxpayer must obtain a statement from an eye doctor that states:

- The taxpayer cannot see better than 20/200 even while corrected with eyeglasses, or
- The taxpayer's field of vision is not more than 20 degrees (the taxpayer has disabled peripheral vision).

The additional amount for age will be allowed if the taxpayer is at least age 65 at the end of the tax year.

2012 Standard Deduction Amounts

The standard deduction is a dollar amount that reduces the amount of income that is taxed. The amount is based on the taxpayer's filing status.

Standard Deduction Amounts	
Filing status	**2012**
Single or MFS	$5,950
Married filing jointly	$11,900
Head of household	$8,700
Qualifying widow(er)	$11,900

An *increased* standard deduction is available to taxpayers who are:

- 65 or older and/or
- Blind or partially blind

*Note: The "additional" standard deduction is not a credit or an itemized deduction. It is simply an increase over the regular standard deduction amount that Congress has decided to give taxpayers who are over 65 and/or blind.

The increased standard deduction amount in these cases is $1,150 per taxpayer for married filers and $1,450 for single and head of household.

Example: Joel, 46, and Christine, 33, are filing a joint return for 2012. Neither is blind. They decide not to itemize their deductions. Their standard deduction in 2012 is $11,900.

Example: Gilbert, 66, and Lisa, 59, are filing a joint return for 2012 and do not itemize deductions. Lisa is blind. Because they are married filing jointly, their base standard deduction is $11,900. Since Gilbert is over age 65, he can claim an additional standard deduction of $1,150. Since Lisa is blind, she can also claim an additional $1,150. Therefore, their total standard deduction is $14,200 ($11,900 + $1,150 +$1,150).

The standard deduction for a deceased taxpayer is the same as if the taxpayer had lived the entire year, with one exception: if the taxpayer died *before* his 65th birthday, the higher standard deduction for being 65 does not apply.

Example: Richard is single and died on November 1, 2012. He would have been 65 if he had reached his birthday on December 12, 2012. He does not qualify for a higher standard deduction for being 65, because he died before his 65th birthday. His standard deduction would be $5,950 on his final tax return, which should be filed by his executor.

Standard Deduction for Dependents (who file a return)

A dependent is also allowed a standard deduction. If a dependent is claimed on another person's return, his standard deduction amount is the greater of:

- $950, or
- The dependent's *earned* income (such as wages) plus $300, but not more than the regular standard deduction amount. For a single person, this is $5,950 in 2012.

Example: Georgia is single, 22, and a full-time student who has a part-time job on campus. Her parents supported her, so they claimed her as a dependent on their 2012 tax return. Georgia will also file a return, and she will take the standard deduction. In 2012, Georgia has interest income of $120, taxes withheld from her wages totaling $35, and total wages of $780 from her part-time job. Her standard deduction is $1,080 ($780 wages + $300).

The standard deduction will be higher if the dependent is 65 or older and/or blind.

Example: Amy is 19, single, and legally blind. She is claimed on her parents' 2012 return. Amy has interest income of $1,300 and wages from a part-time job of $2,900. She has no itemized deductions. Her base amount for the standard deduction is $3,200 ($2,900 + $300, which equals her wages plus $300). Because Amy is also blind, she is allowed an *additional* standard deduction amount of $1,450. So her standard deduction is figured as follows: ($2,900 + $300 + $1,450) = $4,650.

Itemized Deductions

Itemized deductions allow taxpayers to reduce their taxable income based on specific personal expenses. Itemized deductions are taken *instead* of the standard deduction. If the total itemized deductions are greater than the standard deduction, they will result in a lower taxable income and lower tax.

In general, taxpayers benefit from itemizing deductions if they have mortgage interest, significant unreimbursed medical expenses, or other expenses such as large charitable contributions. In most cases, the taxpayer may choose whether to take itemized deductions or the standard deduction, and may take whichever is more beneficial. However, taxpayers are *forced* to itemize in the following cases:

- Married filing separately when one spouse itemizes: the other spouse is also forced to itemize.
- A nonresident or dual-status alien during the year (who is not married to a U.S. citizen or resident).
- A taxpayer with a short year return.

Itemized deductions are claimed on Schedule A and include amounts paid for:

- Qualified medical and dental expenses
- Certain taxes (property tax and state income tax are the most common)
- Mortgage interest
- Gifts to charity
- Casualty and theft losses
- Certain miscellaneous deductions

We will review the specific requirements for these various itemized deductions over the course of the next two units.

Medical and Dental Expenses (Subject to the 7.5% Limit)

Medical and dental expenses are deductible only if taxpayers itemize their deductions. Further, taxpayers can deduct only the amount of unreimbursed medical expenses that exceeds 7.5% of their adjusted gross income (AGI).

Qualified medical expenses include expenses paid for:

- The taxpayer
- The taxpayer's spouse
- Dependents (the individual must have been a dependent at the time the medical services were provided or at the time the expenses were paid)

Exceptions: If a child of divorced or separated parents is claimed as a dependent on *either* parent's return, each parent may deduct the medical expenses he or she individually paid for the child. There is also an exception for medical expenses paid on behalf of former spouses pursuant to a divorce decree. In addition, a taxpayer may deduct medical expenses that were paid on behalf of an adopted child, even before the adoption is final. The child must qualify as a dependent and must be a member of the taxpayer's household during the year the medical expenses were paid.

Example: Raymond and Carmen are divorced. Their son, Colby, lives with Carmen, who claims him as a dependent. Carmen deducts Colby's annual medical and dental bills, including orthodontia expenses for his braces. However, in April, Colby falls on the playground and fractures his leg and arm. The out-of-pocket expenses are $5,500. Colby's father, Raymond, pays for the emergency room visit and the expenses related to the injury, and may deduct them even though he does not claim his son as a dependent on his return. This is based on the exception for divorced/separated parents.

A taxpayer can deduct medical expenses paid for a dependent parent. All the standard rules for a dependency exemption apply, so a dependent parent would not have to live with the taxpayer in order to qualify.

Example: Julie pays all the medical expenses for her mother, who is her dependent but does not live with Julie. The medical expenses are still deductible on Julie's tax return as an itemized deduction if the 7.5% limit is reached.

In this section, the term *7.5% limit* is used to refer to 7.5% of adjusted gross income. A taxpayer must subtract 7.5% (.075) of his AGI from gross medical and dental expenses to figure the medical expense deduction.

Example: Tracy's AGI is $40,000. She had actual medical expenses totaling $2,500. Tracy cannot deduct any of her medical expenses because they are not more than 7.5% of her AGI (7.5% of which is $3,000).

Example: Olivia's AGI is $100,000. In 2012, she paid for a knee operation. She had $10,000 of out-of-pocket medical expenses related to the surgery. In this case, $2,500 would be allowed as an itemized deduction, the amount in excess of the $7,500 base ($100,000 X .075 = $7,500).

Qualifying Medical Expenses

Qualifying medical expenses include the costs of diagnosis, cure, mitigation, treatment, or prevention of disease, and the costs for medical (not cosmetic) treatments. They include the costs of:

- Medically necessary equipment, supplies, and diagnostic devices
- Dental and vision care expenses, such as prescription eyeglasses and contact lenses
- Transportation costs to obtain medical care
- Qualified long-term care insurance

Deductible medical expenses may include but are not limited to:

- Fees paid to doctors, dentists, surgeons, chiropractors, psychiatrists, psychologists, and nontraditional medical practitioners
- In-patient hospital care or nursing home services, *including* the cost of meals and lodging charged by the hospital or nursing home
- Payments for acupuncture treatments
- Lactation supplies
- Treatment at a center for alcohol or drug addiction, for participation in a smoking-cessation program, and for prescription drugs to alleviate nicotine withdrawal
- A weight-loss program prescribed by a physician (but not payments for diet food items)

- Payments for insulin and payments for drugs that require a prescription
- Payments for admission and transportation to a medical conference relating to a chronic disease (but not the costs for meals and lodging while attending the conference)

Other examples of deductible medical expenses include the cost of false teeth, laser eye surgery, orthodontia, hearing aids, crutches, and wheelchairs. Even veterinary care can be deducted as a medical expense when it relates to the care of animals trained to assist persons who are visually-impaired, disabled, or hearing-impaired. Medical expenses must be primarily to alleviate or prevent a physical or mental defect or illness. Medical expenses do not include expenses that are merely beneficial to general health, such as vitamins, spa treatments, gym memberships, or vacations. In addition, over-the-counter medications cannot be deducted.

Medical Insurance and Long-term Care Premiums

Qualifying medical expenses include medical insurance premiums that the taxpayer has paid with after-tax dollars. A taxpayer may not deduct insurance premiums paid by an employer-sponsored plan unless the premiums are included in Box 1 of his Form W-2.[46]

A taxpayer may only include the medical expenses paid during the year, regardless of when the services were provided. Along with regular medical insurance, a taxpayer may also deduct the costs of qualified long-term care insurance premiums as a medical expense, assuming the 7.5% limit is met.

If a taxpayer or a dependent is in a nursing home and the primary reason for being there is medically related, the entire cost, including meals and lodging, is a medical expense.

Medically-related Legal Fees

A taxpayer can deduct legal fees that are necessary to authorize treatment for a mental illness. However, legal fees for the management of a guardianship estate or legal fees for conducting the affairs of a person being treated are not deductible as medical expenses.

Medical Expenses of Deceased Taxpayers

An election can be made to deduct medical expenses paid by a deceased taxpayer. This is legal for one year *after* the date of the taxpayer's death. The expenses may be treated as if paid when the medical services were provided (even if the medical expenses are not actually paid until after the taxpayer's death). In some cases the taxpayer's Form 1040 must be amended by filing a Form 1040X. The medical expenses of a deceased taxpayer are still subject to the 7.5% floor.

> **Example:** Anne had heart surgery in November 2012 and incurred $20,000 in medical bills. She died on January 2, 2013. The 2012 medical bills were still unpaid at the time of her death. The executor of Anne's estate may elect to deduct her medical expenses in 2012, even though the medical expenses are paid at a later date.

---

[46] New for 2012, the value of a taxpayer's annual health care coverage is now reported in Box 12 on Form W-2. The amount reported in the box should include both the portions paid by an employer and by the employee. It is a provision of the Affordable Health Care Act to try to show taxpayers the true cost of health care. However, while this amount is reported on a W-2, it does *not* mean the amount is taxable; it is for informational purposes only.

Cosmetic Surgery

Cosmetic surgery is only deductible if it is used to correct a defect or disease. A cosmetic procedure simply for the enhancement of someone's physical appearance is not a deductible medical expense.

Example: Adrienne undergoes surgery to remove a breast as part of treatment for cancer. She pays a surgeon to reconstruct her breast to correct a deformity that is directly related to the disease. The cost of the surgery is includable in her medical expenses.

Example: Miles, age one, was born with a cleft palate. His parents pay for cosmetic surgery to correct the deformity. The surgery is deductible as a medical expense because it corrects a defect.

Medically-related Meals, Lodging, and Transportation

Vehicle mileage may be deducted if the transportation is for medical reasons, such as trips to and from doctors' appointments. A taxpayer can choose to deduct the actual costs for taxis, buses, trains, planes, or ambulances, as well as tolls and parking fees.

If a taxpayer uses his own car for medical transportation, he can deduct actual out-of-pocket expenses for gas and other expenses, or he can deduct the standard mileage rate for medical expenses, which is 23 cents per mile in 2012.

A taxpayer can deduct the cost of meals and lodging at a hospital or similar institution if the principal reason for being there is to receive medical care. The care must be provided by a doctor, hospital, or a medical care facility, and there must not be any significant element of personal pleasure or recreation.

The IRS imposes a $50 limit, per person, per night, for lodging for medically-related issues. There is no deduction for meals.

Capital Improvements for Medical Reasons

Capital improvements such as home improvements are usually not deductible by the taxpayer. However, a home improvement may qualify as a deductible expense if its main purpose is to provide a medical benefit to the taxpayer or to dependent family members.

The deduction for capital improvements is limited to the excess of the actual cost of the improvements over the increase in the fair market value of the home. Home improvements that qualify as deductible medical expenses include:

- Wheelchair ramps
- Lowering of kitchen cabinets
- Railings and support bars
- Elevators

Tenants may deduct the entire cost of disability-related improvements, since they are not the owners of the property.

Example: Lonnie has a heart condition. He cannot easily climb stairs or get into a bathtub. On his doctor's advice, he installs a special sit-in bathtub and a stair lift on the first floor of his rented house. The landlord did not pay any of the cost of buying and installing the special equipment and did not lower the rent. Lonnie can deduct the entire amount as a medical expense, assuming he meets the 7.5% limit.

Medical Expenses: A Summary

1. In order to claim medical expenses, the taxpayer must itemize on Schedule A.

2. The deduction is limited. A taxpayer can only claim medical expenses that exceed 7.5% of adjusted gross income for the year.

3. The medical expenses must have been paid during the year, *regardless* of when the services were provided.

4. Taxpayers cannot deduct any reimbursed expenses. Therefore, total medical expenses for the year must be reduced by any insurance reimbursement.

5. A taxpayer may include qualified medical expenses paid for themselves, a spouse, and any dependents. Special rules apply to divorced or separated parents.

6. Medical expenses must be primarily to alleviate or prevent a physical or mental defect or illness. Taxpayers may deduct premiums for Medicare B; self-employed taxpayers may deduct premiums for health care coverage, if they had a net profit for the year and were not eligible to be covered by an employer-sponsored plan, including that of their spouses.[47] For drugs, taxpayers can only deduct prescription medication and insulin.

7. Medical-related transportation costs can be deducted.

8. Distributions from health savings accounts and withdrawals from flexible spending arrangements are generally tax free if used to pay qualified medical expenses.

9. Expenses that are not deductible as medical expenses include funeral or burial expenses, nonprescription medicines, toiletries, cosmetics, any program for the general improvement of health, maternity clothes, and cosmetic surgery unless it is to correct a defect.

Deductible Taxes

Taxpayers can deduct certain taxes if they itemize their deductions. To be deductible, the tax must have been imposed on the taxpayer and paid by the taxpayer during the tax year. Taxes that are deductible include:

- State, local, and foreign income taxes
- Real estate taxes
- Personal property taxes (such as DMV fees)
- State and local sales taxes

State and Local Taxes

Taxpayers are allowed to deduct state and local sales taxes in lieu of deducting state and local income taxes.[48] The taxpayer may choose whichever method gives them the larger deduction. Taxpayers can choose one of the following taxes, but not both:

- **Income taxes:** This includes withheld taxes, estimated tax payments, or other tax payments such as a prior year refund of a state or local income tax that taxpayers applied to their estimated state or local income taxes.
- **Sales taxes:** Taxpayers may deduct state and local sales taxes paid.

---

[47] An employee may not deduct health insurance premiums paid by an employer-sponsored health insurance plan unless the premiums are included in Box 1 of the employee's Form W-2.

[48] This deduction expired at the end of 2011. However, on January 1, 2013 Congress reinstated the deduction retroactively for 2012 and extended its provisions through 2013 as part of the American Taxpayer Relief Act of 2012, more commonly known as the "fiscal cliff" legislation.

Personal Property Taxes (DMV fees)

Personal property taxes are deductible if they are:

- Charged on personal property
- Based on the value of the property, and
- Charged on a yearly basis, even if collected more or less than once a year.

The most common type of personal property tax is a DMV fee. In order to be deductible, the tax must be based on the value of a property, such as a car or boat.

Real Estate Taxes

State, local, or foreign real estate taxes that are based on the assessed value of the taxpayer's real property (such as a house or land) are deductible. Real estate taxes are reported to the taxpayer on Form 1098, *Mortgage Interest Statement*. A taxpayer may deduct real estate taxes on any real estate property he owns, including foreign property. If a portion of a taxpayer's monthly mortgage payment goes into an escrow account, the taxpayer can only deduct the amount *actually paid* out of the escrow account during the year to the taxing authority. Some real estate taxes are not deductible, including taxes imposed for local benefits for improvements to property, such as assessments for streets, sidewalks, and sewer lines. In addition, itemized charges for services and homeowners' association fees are not deductible.

Example: Genevieve makes the following tax payments: state income tax, $2,000; real estate taxes, $900; local benefit tax for improving the sewer system, $75; homeowners' association fee, $250. Genevieve's total tax deduction is $2,900 ($2,000 + $900 = $2,900). The $75 local benefit tax and the $250 homeowners' association fee are not deductible.

If a property is sold, the real estate taxes must be prorated between the buyer and the seller according to the number of days that each owned the property. It does not matter who actually paid the real estate taxes. If, for example, the buyer paid all the taxes including delinquent taxes on a property, the amounts paid while the buyer was not the legal owner must be added to the property's basis[49], rather than deducted on the taxpayer's current year return.

Example: Mandy bought her home on September 1. The property tax was already overdue on the property when she decided to purchase it. The real estate taxes on the home were $1,275 for the year and were paid by Mandy as a condition of the sale. Since Mandy did not own the home during the time the property tax was due, then the amount paid must be added to the basis of the residence. Mandy cannot deduct the $1,275 on her Schedule A as an itemized deduction.

Foreign Income Taxes

Under the foreign earned income exclusion or the foreign housing exclusion, these taxes can be deducted on income that is not exempt from U.S. tax. Generally, income taxes paid to a foreign country can be deducted as:

- An itemized deduction on Schedule A, or
- A credit against U.S. income tax.

---

[49] A full discussion of how to calculate basis can be found in Unit 10, *Basis of Property*.

A taxpayer can choose between claiming the Foreign Tax Credit and claiming any foreign tax paid on Schedule A as an itemized deduction. The taxpayer may use whichever method results in the lowest tax.

Mortgage Interest and Other Deductible Interest

Certain types of interest are deductible as itemized deductions on Form 1040, Schedule A:

- Home mortgage interest (including points and mortgage insurance premiums) [50]
- Mortgage interest on a second home or vacation home, with a maximum of two homes
- Investment interest

Qualifying Home Mortgage Interest

Home mortgage interest is interest paid on a loan secured by a taxpayer's home. The loan may be a mortgage, a second mortgage, a home equity loan, or a line of credit. A taxpayer is allowed to deduct the interest on a primary residence and one second home. In order to qualify, the "home" can be a house, condominium, mobile home, house trailer, or houseboat. So long as a residence has sleeping, cooking, and toilet facilities, it may qualify for this deduction.

A second home can include any other residence a taxpayer owns and treats as a second home. A taxpayer does not have to actually use the home during the year in order to get a deduction of the mortgage interest paid on a second home. Home mortgage interest and points are reported to a taxpayer on Form 1098, *Mortgage Interest Statement,* by the financial institution to which the taxpayer made the payments.

Home mortgage interest is only deductible if the mortgage is secured debt, meaning the taxpayer must be legally liable for the debt.

An empty lot (bare land) does not qualify for the mortgage interest deduction. In order to be deductible as home mortgage interest, the loan must be secured by an actual home. If a taxpayer is planning to build a house, he can start deducting mortgage interest once construction begins.

> ***Note:** Although a taxpayer may deduct real estate taxes on *more than* two properties, a taxpayer may not deduct mortgage interest on more than two homes.

A taxpayer may deduct late charges on the loan as mortgage interest.

> **Example:** Reese owns his home and pays his mortgage on a monthly basis. During the year, he falls behind on his mortgage payments and sends in his payment late on two occasions. The mortgage company charges Reese a $35 late fee for each late payment. The late fees are deductible as mortgage interest.

Limits on the Mortgage Interest Deduction

If all of the taxpayer's mortgages fit into one or more of the following three categories, he can deduct the interest:

- Any mortgage the taxpayer obtained on or before 1987 (grandfathered debt.)

---

[50] Because of uncertainty about whether Congress would restore this deduction in 2012, the IRS eliminated the box for this item on Form 1098. Some mortgage companies have said they will not put the premiums paid on the 1098s. In that case, taxpayers will have to check their mortgage statements to figure what they paid. Since the write-off also applies for tax year 2013, the IRS will restore the box for mortgage interest premiums paid on 1098 forms for 2013.

- Any mortgage obtained after 1987 to buy or improve a home, but only if the mortgage debt totaled $1 million or less ($500,000 if MFS).
- A home equity mortgage, even if used for expenses other than to improve the home, but only if the home equity line is $100,000 or less. ($50,000 if MFS).

> **Example:** Shirley borrowed $800,000 against her primary residence and $500,000 against her secondary residence. Both loans were used solely to acquire the residences. The loan amounts add up to $1.3 million. Since the total loan amount exceeds the $1 million limit for home acquisition debt, Shirley's mortgage interest deduction is limited.

Qualified Mortgage Insurance Premiums (PMI)

Taxpayers can deduct private mortgage insurance (PMI)[51] premiums paid during the tax year on Schedule A, though the deduction is phased out at higher income levels. The deduction is phased-out ratably by 10% for each $1,000 by which the taxpayer's AGI exceeds $100,000. The deduction was scheduled to expire in 2012, but the fiscal cliff legislation extended it for tax years 2012 and 2013.

Home Mortgage Points

Points are the charges paid by a borrower to secure a loan. They are actually prepaid interest that a buyer pays at closing in order to secure a lower interest rate. They are also called:

- Loan origination fees (including VA and FHA fees)
- Maximum loan charges
- Premium charges
- Loan discount points
- Prepaid interest

Only points paid as a form of interest can be deducted. Points paid to refinance a mortgage are generally not deductible in full the year the taxpayer paid them, unless the points are paid in connection with the improvement of a main home.

Loan fees paid for specific services, such as home appraisal fees, document preparation fees, VA funding fees, or notary fees are not interest and are not deductible.

In order to deduct points in the year paid, the taxpayer must meet these requirements:

- The mortgage must be secured by the taxpayer's main home, and the mortgage must have been used to buy or build the home.
- The points must not be an excessive or unusual amount for the local area.
- The total points paid must not be more than the total amount of unborrowed funds.
- The points must be computed as a percentage of the loan principal, and they must be listed on the settlement statement.

Despite these restrictions, most homebuyers still qualify to take the deduction for points on the purchase of their primary residence.

---

[51] Lenders charge private mortgage insurance to protect themselves if a borrower defaults. It allows homebuyers to make smaller down payments than are ordinarily allowed.

Interest Paid on Home Equity Debt

The interest paid on a home equity line of credit is deductible by the taxpayer if certain rules are met. There is a $100,000 limit on the amount of debt that can be treated as home equity debt, and it is not deductible if it exceeds the property's fair market value.

Example: Carla bought her home for cash ten years ago. Its fair market value is now $80,000. She did not have a mortgage on her home until last year when she took out a $45,000 loan, secured by her home, to pay for her daughter's college tuition. This loan is home equity debt. Since the $45,000 loan is secured by her home and the loan amount is less than $100,000 in equity debt, the mortgage interest on the equity line is deductible.

The interest on home equity indebtedness is deductible by the taxpayer no matter how the proceeds are used.

Example: Jeremy and Ashley obtained two home equity loans totaling $90,000. They used the loans to pay off gambling debts, overdue credit card payments, and some nondeductible medical expenses. The couple can deduct the interest on their home equity loans because the total does not exceed $100,000.

Example: Chad bought his home five years ago. Its FMV now is $110,000, and the current balance on Chad's original mortgage is $95,000. His bank offers Chad a home mortgage loan of 125% of the FMV of the home. To consolidate some of his other debts, Chad agrees to take out a $42,500 home mortgage loan [(125% × $110,000) − $95,000] with his bank. Chad's home equity line exceeds the fair market value of the home. Therefore, his mortgage interest deduction relating to his equity line is limited. For tax purposes, Chad's qualified home equity debt is limited to $15,000. This is the amount that the FMV of $110,000 exceeds the amount of home acquisition debt of $95,000.

Deductible Investment Interest

If a taxpayer borrows money to buy property held for investment, the interest paid is investment interest. The deduction for investment interest expense is limited to the amount of net investment income. A taxpayer cannot deduct interest incurred to produce tax-exempt income, such as the purchase of municipal bonds. Investment interest expense is calculated on IRS Form 4952, *Investment Interest Expense Deduction.*

Example: Mariko borrows money from a bank in order to buy $3,000 worth of short-term bonds. The bonds mature during the year and Mariko makes $400 in investment interest income. She also has $210 in investment interest expense, which she paid on the loan originally taken out to buy the bonds. Mariko must report the full amount of $400 as investment interest income. The $210 in investment interest expense is a deduction on Schedule A.

A taxpayer can carry over to the next tax year the amount of investment interest that he could not deduct because of the passive activity rules. The interest carried over is treated as investment interest paid or accrued in that next year.

> **Example:** Jackson borrows money from a bank in order to buy $10,000 worth of U.S. gold coins. During the year, the coins lose value and he has no investment income. Jackson has $326 in investment interest expense, which he paid on the loan originally taken out to buy the coins. Jackson may not take a deduction for the investment interest expense, because he has no investment income to offset it. Jackson must carry over to the next tax year the amount of investment interest that he could not deduct because of this limit.

Investment income is any income that is produced by property that is held for investment. A taxpayer must first determine net investment income by subtracting his investment expenses (other than interest expense) from the investment income.

Nondeductible Interest and Investment Expenses

The following expenses cannot be deducted:

- Interest on personal car loans or other personal loans
- Annual fees for credit cards and finance charges for nonbusiness credit card purchases
- Loan fees for services needed to get a loan
- Interest on a debt the taxpayer is not legally obligated to pay
- Service charges
- Interest to purchase or carry tax-exempt securities
- Late payment charges paid to a public utility
- Expenses relating to stockholders' meetings or investment-related seminars
- Interest expenses from single-premium life insurance, endowment, and annuity contracts
- Interest incurred from borrowing on insurance
- Expenses incurred to produce tax-exempt income (this includes expenses incurred for both tax-exempt and taxable income that cannot be properly allocated)
- Short-sale expenses

A taxpayer cannot deduct fines and penalties paid to any government entity for violations of the law, regardless of their nature.

> **Example:** José and Blanca file a joint return. During the year, they paid:
>
> 1. $3,180 of home mortgage interest reported to them on Form 1098
> 2. $400 in credit card interest
> 2. $1,500 paid to a lender for an appraisal fee
> 3. $2,000 in interest on a car loan
>
> José and Blanca may report only their home mortgage interest ($3,180) as deductible interest. None of the other charges are deductible.

Charitable Contributions

Charities need funds to operate their tax-exempt programs, and most of the time these contributions come from taxpayers. A "charitable contribution" is a donation to a qualified organization. Taxpayers must itemize deductions to be able to deduct a charitable contribution.

Taxpayers can deduct contributions to qualifying organizations that:

- Operate exclusively for religious, charitable, educational, scientific, or literary purposes, or
- Work to prevent cruelty to children or animals, or
- Foster national or international amateur sports competition.

Other qualifying organizations include:

- War veterans' organizations, and
- Certain nonprofit cemetery companies or corporations.

Qualified donations also include donations for public purposes to the federal government of the United States, to any state, or to an Indian tribal government (example: a donation to the state capital's yearly toy drive).

To be deductible, contributions must be made to a qualifying organization, not to an individual. Taxpayers *must keep records* to prove the amounts of cash and noncash contributions they make during the year. Taxpayers can only deduct a contribution in the year it is actually made.

Nonqualifying Organizations

Even if an organization is a nonprofit, that does not automatically mean that it is a "charity" and contributions are deductible by donors. There are some organizations that still qualify as nonprofit groups for tax purposes, but they do not qualify as charitable organizations for purposes of deductible contributions. The following are examples of donations that do not qualify:

- Gifts to civic leagues, social clubs, labor unions, and Chambers of Commerce
- Gifts to groups run for personal profit
- Gifts to political groups, candidates, or political organizations
- Gifts to homeowners' associations
- Direct donations to needy individuals
- The cost of raffle, bingo, or lottery tickets, even if the raffle is part of a qualified organization's fundraiser
- Dues paid to country clubs or similar groups

Example: Renee ran a 10K race organized by the Chamber of Commerce, with the Chamber to donate proceeds to a cancer charity. She paid the race organizers a $30 entry fee and received a "free" T-shirt and pancake breakfast after the race. Renee did not make a contribution directly to the qualifying organization, the cancer charity. She paid the Chamber of Commerce, which is not a qualifying charitable organization. Therefore, none of her entry fee is tax deductible as a charitable expense. If the race had been organized by the qualifying organization itself, part of her entry fee may have been deductible.

Charitable Contributions: Substantiation Requirements

There are strict recordkeeping requirements for taxpayers who make charitable contributions. The IRS has different substantiation requirements for different types and amounts of contributions:

- Cash contributions of $250 or less
- Cash contributions of $250 or more

- Noncash contributions less than $500
- Noncash contributions more than $500
- Special rule for donated vehicles
- Volunteering expenses

Cash Donations of $250 or Less

Cash contributions include those paid by cash, check, debit card, credit card, or payroll deduction. For a contribution by cash or check, the taxpayer must maintain a record of the contribution. It must be either a bank record or a written receipt from the organization. If the value of the individual donation is *less than* $250, the taxpayer must keep at least a canceled check or credit card slip, a receipt, or some other reliable written record or evidence.

A taxpayer cannot deduct a cash contribution, regardless of the amount, unless he keeps one of the following:

- A bank record that shows the name of the qualified organization, the date of the contribution, and the amount of the contribution. Bank records may include:
  - A canceled check,
  - A bank or credit union statement, or
  - A credit card statement.
- A receipt (or a letter or other written communication) from the qualified organization showing the name of the organization, the date of the contribution, and the amount of the contribution.
- For payroll deductions, a pay stub or Form W-2, plus a pledge card or other document showing the name of the qualified organization.
- For text donations, a telephone bill, so long as it shows the name of the qualified organization, the date of the contribution, and the amount given.

Example: Gary donates $10 per week to the Humane Society. He always pays by check, and he keeps the canceled check as a record of his contribution. This is a valid method of recordkeeping for small donations under $250.

Cash Donations over $250

For cash donations over $250 dollars, the taxpayer must have a receipt or written acknowledgement from the organization that meets certain tests. It must include:

- The amount of cash the taxpayer contributed.
- The date of the contribution.
- Whether the qualified organization gave any goods or services as a result of the contribution (other than certain token items and membership benefits.) The absence of this simple statement by a charity has led to recent court cases in which major cash contributions have been challenged.
- A description and good faith estimate of the value of any goods or services provided in return by the organization (if applicable.)

The taxpayer must obtain the receipt on or before:

- The date the taxpayer files his tax return for the year he makes the contribution, or
- The due date, including extensions, for filing the return.

If the donation is via payroll deduction, any amount that exceeds $250 must be substantiated with a pay stub, W-2, and a statement about whether goods or services were given by the qualified organization.

Noncash Contributions: Substantiation Rules

In order to claim a deduction for noncash donations, the donated items must be in good condition. The taxpayer must get a receipt from the receiving organization and keep a list of the items donated. In most cases, the taxpayer will be able to claim a deduction for the fair market value of the contribution (generally what someone would be willing to pay at a garage sale or thrift store). No deduction is allowed for items that are in poor or unusable condition. Deductible items include:

- Fair market value of used clothing and furniture in good condition.
- Unreimbursed expenses that relate directly to the services the taxpayer provided for the organization. The value of time or services donated cannot be deducted.
- Part of a contribution above the fair market value for items received such as merchandise and tickets to charity balls or sporting events.
- Transportation expenses, including bus fare, parking fees, tolls, and either the actual cost of gas and oil or a standard mileage deduction of 14 cents per mile in 2012.

Example: Emily is an attorney who donates her time to her local church for their legal needs. In 2012, she spent 10 hours drafting documents for the church, which is a qualified organization. She also has $200 in out-of-pocket expenses because she purchased a new printer and office supplies for the church. The printer and office supplies were delivered directly to the church rectory for its use. Emily can take a charitable deduction for $200, the amount she spent on behalf of her church. She cannot take a deduction for the "value" of her time.

Noncash Contributions: Donations of Less Than $500

For each single contribution of at least $250 but not exceeding $500, the taxpayer must have all the documentation described for noncash contributions less than $250. In addition, the organization's written acknowledgement must state whether the taxpayer received any goods or services in return and a description and good faith estimate of any such items.

Noncash Contributions: Donations of More Than $500

If a taxpayer's total deduction for all noncash contributions for the year is over $500, he must also file Form 8283, *Noncash Charitable Contributions.* [52] If any single donation is valued at over $5,000, the taxpayer must also get an appraisal.

*Special $500 Rule for Donated Vehicles, Boats, and Airplanes

Special rules apply to any donation of a vehicle, boat, or airplane. If the taxpayer donates a vehicle to a charity and the taxpayer claims a deduction of more than $500, the taxpayer can only deduct the smaller of:

- The gross proceeds from the sale of the vehicle, or

---

[52] A Treasury Department audit report says that too many taxpayers are failing to comply with the requirements for noncash donations. The report says that hundreds of thousands of taxpayers claim noncash charitable donations of more than $500, but are not submitting a Form 8283 as required. The IRS is going to start flagging these returns and asking taxpayers to send in the missing forms before they can receive the charitable deduction.

- The vehicle's fair market value on the date of the contribution.

Form 1098-C shows the gross proceeds from the sale of the vehicle. If the taxpayer does not attach Form 1098-C, the maximum value that can be taken for a vehicle donation is $500. Vehicles that are not in working condition may have zero donation value.

> **Example:** Kevin donates his used motorcycle to his church fundraiser. The FMV ("Blue Book" value) of the motorcycle is $2,500. The church sells the motorcycle 60 days later; the organization sends Kevin a Form 1098-C showing the proceeds from the sale of the donated item. The church was only able to sell the motorcycle for $1,700. Therefore, Kevin may only deduct $1,700 on his Schedule A (the smaller of the FMV or the gross proceeds from the sale). He must attach a copy of Form 1098-C, *Contributions of Motor Vehicles, Boats, and Airplanes*, to his tax return.

*Exceptions to the $500 Rule for Donated Vehicles

There are two exceptions to the strict rules regarding vehicle donations:

- **Exception 1:** If the charity takes the vehicle for its own use, the taxpayer can deduct the vehicle's FMV.
- **Exception 2:** If the charity gives or sells the vehicle directly to a needy person, the taxpayer generally can deduct the vehicle's FMV at the time of the contribution.

Deductible Volunteering Expenses

A taxpayer may deduct expenses incurred while away from home performing services for a charitable organization only if there is no significant element of personal pleasure in the travel. However, a deduction will not be denied simply because the taxpayer enjoys providing services to a charitable organization. The taxpayer is still allowed to take a charitable contribution deduction for the expenses if he is on-duty in a genuine and substantial sense throughout the trip. The IRS does not allow a taxpayer to deduct a monetary "value" of the hours he spends volunteering.

> **Example:** Charles volunteered for the Boy Scouts in 2012. He was the den leader and regularly paid out-of-pocket expenses for travel, gas, and parking while performing duties and picking up supplies on behalf of the Scouts. Charles was not paid for his work. Charles may deduct his out-of-pocket costs related to the volunteer work, but he may not take a deduction for the value of his time.

> **Example:** Francine regularly volunteers at her local animal shelter. She uses her own car to travel back and forth to the shelter. She is not reimbursed for mileage. Francine also fosters kittens on behalf of the shelter. She pays for food and other supplies out-of-pocket while she is fostering the kittens. She is not reimbursed for these costs, either. Once the kittens are old enough for adoption, she returns them to the animal shelter so that they may be adopted by the public. Francine may deduct her mileage and her out-of-pocket costs as a charitable contribution.

Deductible Contributions and the 50% Limit

There are limits to the amounts that can be claimed as a deductible donation. A taxpayer may not take a deduction for charitable contributions that exceed 50% of his adjusted gross income. In other words, if a taxpayer had $40,000 in gross income in 2012, the maximum he could deduct as a charitable contribution in 2012 would be $20,000 (50% of AGI). Any amounts that are disallowed by this limit may be carried forward to a future year (explained later in this unit.)

There is a reduced limit of 30% or 20% that applies to certain organizations. This means that for certain nonprofit organizations, a taxpayer's contribution cannot exceed either 30% or 20% of his AGI.

Examples of 50% limit organizations include churches, hospitals, most schools, state or federal government units, and animal welfare organizations. Also included are corporations, trusts, or foundations organized solely for charitable, religious, educational, scientific, or literary purposes, or to prevent cruelty to children or animals, or to foster certain national or international amateur sports competition.

Organizations Subject to the 30% Limit

Certain organizations only qualify for the "30% limit." This means that the deductible amount of the contribution cannot exceed 30% of the taxpayer's AGI. A 30% limit applies to the following organizations:

- Veterans organizations
- Fraternal societies (such as Knights of Columbus or Elks)
- Nonprofit cemeteries

In addition, the 30% limit applies in the following cases:

- Gifts for the actual use of any organization (such as the donation of a table that the organization uses for itself)
- Any gift of appreciated property (such as stocks)

Appreciated property, also called capital gain property, may be given to an organization that is normally a 50% organization, such as a church. However, capital gain property is subject to either a 30% or 20% limit, regardless of the organization type that actually receives the donation.

> **Example:** Howard's adjusted gross income is $50,000. During the year, he gave appreciated stocks with an FMV of $15,000 to his synagogue, which is a 50% limit organization. Howard also gave $10,000 cash to a veteran's organization. The $15,000 gift of capital gain property is subject to the special 30% limit, even though it was given to a religious organization. The $10,000 gift is subject to the other 30% limit. However, both gifts are fully deductible by Howard because neither is more than the 30% limit that applies ($15,000 in each case), and together they are not more than the 50% limit of Howard's AGI ($50,000 x 50% = $25,000).

Appreciated Property and the 20% Limit

The 20% limit applies to all gifts of appreciated property to qualified organizations that are not 50% organizations. Any contributions made by the taxpayer and carried over to future years retain their original character. For example, contributions made to a 30% organization are always subject to the 30% limit of AGI.

A donor can choose to deduct gifts of long-term appreciated property under a 50% of AGI limit rather than the 30% or 20% limit. As a trade-off, however, the donor's deduction for the long-term appreciated property will be limited to its cost basis instead of its FMV.

Example: Vincent's adjusted gross income is $23,000. During the year, he gave appreciated stocks with an FMV of $10,000 to his fraternal society, Kiwanis, which is a 30% limit organization. Vincent makes no other donations during the year. The $10,000 donation of capital gain property (the stocks) is subject to the special 20% limit because it is capital gain property that was donated to a 30% limit organization. The donation is not fully deductible by Vincent, because it exceeds 20% of his AGI ($23,000 x 20% = $4,600). Therefore, the maximum deduction for charitable contributions that he can take is limited to $4,600, and he must carry over the remaining $5,400 to a future tax year.

Nonqualified Types of Donations

There are some expenses that do not qualify as charitable deductions, even if the amounts are given to a qualified charity or organization. Amounts that may not be deducted include contributions to political candidates; blood donated to a blood bank or the Red Cross; the cost of raffle, bingo, or lottery tickets, even if the amounts go to a qualified charity; and part of a contribution that benefits the taxpayer, such as the FMV of a meal eaten at a charity dinner.

Example: Bill goes to a local church fundraiser. His church is a qualified organization. The fundraiser includes a bingo game, with all the proceeds going to the church. Bill spends $200 on bingo cards, but does not win anything. Even though the $200 went to the church, the cost of the bingo game is not considered a charitable gift and is therefore not deductible.

Charitable Contribution Carryovers

A carryover is simply an amount that a taxpayer is unable to deduct in the current year. Charitable contributions are subject to a five-year carryover period. The taxpayer can deduct the unused contribution for the next five years until it is used up, but not beyond that time. In 2012, appreciated real property donated to charity for conservation purposes can be carried forward for 15 years.

Example: Louise owns 200 acres of wetlands. She decides to donate the property to the Wildlife Conservation Society, a 501(c)(3) organization. The property is then used for wildlife conservation and research only. This is a qualified conservation contribution eligible for a 15-year carryover.

The 30% of AGI limitation also has been increased to 50% for qualified conservation contributions (100% for farmers and ranchers.)

Unit 7: Questions

1. Which of the following taxes can taxpayers deduct on Schedule A?

A. Federal income tax.
B. Real estate tax.
C. Tax on alcohol and tobacco.
D. Foreign sales taxes.

The answer is B. Only the real estate tax is deductible. Taxpayers can deduct real estate tax on Schedule A as an itemized deduction. ###

2. Angie and Sheldon file a joint return and claim their two children as dependents. They have an adjusted gross income of $95,400. Last year the family accumulated $6,620 in unreimbursed medical and dental expenses that included the following:

1. Prescription eyeglasses for Angie $320
2. Prescription contacts for Sheldon $1,000
3. Sheldon's smoking-cessation program $5,300

The total of Sheldon and Angie's deductible medical expenses is _____.

A. $6,620.
B. $6,300.
C. $5,620.
D. $0.

The answer is D. Angie and Sheldon cannot deduct any of their medical expenses. Only the portion of total medical expenses that exceeds 7.5% of the taxpayer's AGI is deductible. The total of Angie and Sheldon's medical expenses, $6,620, is less than $95,400 x 7.5% = $7,155. ###

3. Which of the following is a deductible medical expense?

A. Liposuction.
B. Premiums for life insurance.
C. Prescription hearing aids.
D. Cost of child care while a parent is in the hospital.

The answer is C. Only the cost of the hearing aids is a deductible medical expense. Life insurance premiums, child care, and nonprescription medicines are not deductible. ###

4. All of the following are deductible medical expenses except _____.

A. Transportation for medical care.
B. Transportation to a medical conference related to the chronic disease of a dependent.
C. Smoking-cessation programs.
D. Nonprescription nicotine gum and patches.

The answer is D. Taxpayers may deduct transportation related to medical care. The cost of smoking programs and prescription drugs is also deductible. However, over-the-counter medicines are not deductible as medical expenses. ###

5. Max and Wendy are both 30 years old and file jointly for 2012. They decide not to itemize their deductions. Max is legally blind. What is their standard deduction amount in 2012?

A. $8,700.
B. $11,900.
C. $13,050.
D. $13,350.

The answer is C. The answer is figured as follows: ($11,900 + $1,150) on their Form 1040. Max is blind, so he and Wendy are allowed an additional $1,150 as a standard deduction amount. Their standard deduction is $13,050. ###

6. Which of the following taxpayers must either itemize deductions or claim zero as their deduction?

A. Mindy, who files a joint return with her husband.
B. Leslie, who claims two dependents and files Form 1040.
C. Pearl, whose itemized deductions are more than the standard deduction.
D. Gabe, whose wife files a separate return and itemizes her deductions.

The answer is D. Married taxpayers who file separately and whose spouses itemize deductions must either claim "0" as their deduction or itemize their deductions. ###

7. All of the following factors determine the amount of a taxpayer's standard deduction except _____.

A. The taxpayer's filing status.
B. The taxpayer's adjusted gross income.
C. Whether the taxpayer is 65 or older, or blind.
D. Whether the taxpayer can be claimed as a dependent.

The answer is B. The standard deduction amount depends on the taxpayer's filing and dependent status, and whether the taxpayer is blind or at least 65 years old. It is not based on the taxpayer's income. ###

8. Sara and James are both 25, and they have been married for two years. What is their standard deduction in 2012?

A. $11,900.
B. $8,700.
C. $5,950.
D. $950.

The answer is A. Sara and James may take the standard deduction for married couples who file jointly, which is $11,900 in 2012. ###

9. Brenda is 22, single, and recently graduated from college. She has no dependents. She provides all of her own support. What is her standard deduction in 2012?

A. $950.
B. $3,700.
C. $5,950.
D. $8,700.

The answer is C. Brenda is single, with no dependents. Her standard deduction is $5,950. ###

10. Which of the following taxpayers is *required* to itemize deductions?

A. Sophie, who has one dependent child.
B. Andrea, who wants to deduct the alimony she paid to her ex-husband.
C. Gabrielle, whose itemized deductions are more than the standard deduction.
D. Samir, who is a nonresident alien.

The answer is D. A nonresident or dual-status alien during the year (who is not married to a U.S. citizen or resident) must itemize deductions. He cannot choose the standard deduction. The other taxpayers listed are not required to itemize their deductions but may elect to do so. ###

11. All of the following are deductible medical expenses except _____.

A. Elective cosmetic surgery.
B. Lactation supplies.
C. Legal abortion.
D. Prescription birth control pills.

The answer is A. Elective cosmetic surgery is not a deductible medical expense. All the other expenses listed are acceptable as deductible medical expenses. ###

12. All of the following home improvements may be itemized and deducted as medical expenses except _____:

A. The cost of installing porch lifts and other forms of lifts.
B. The cost of lowering cabinets to accommodate a disability.
C. The cost of making doorways wider to accommodate a wheelchair.
D. The cost of an elevator costing $4,000 that adds $5,000 to the FMV of the home.

The answer is D. The deduction for capital improvements is limited to the excess of the actual cost of the improvements over the increase in the fair market value of the home. Since the elevator adds value to the home, it cannot be deducted as a medical expense. ###

13. Which of the following items is not a deductible medical expense?

A. Dental implants to replace broken or missing teeth.
B. Over-the-counter aspirin.
C. Guide dog expenses for a blind person.
D. Prescription contact lenses.

The answer is B. The cost of medical items such as false teeth, prescription eyeglasses or contact lenses, laser eye surgery, hearing aids, crutches, wheelchairs, and guide dogs for the blind or deaf are all deductible medical expenses. Over-the-counter medicines are not deductible. ###

14. Justin had the following medical expenses in 2012:

•$450 for contact lenses
•$800 for eyeglasses
•$9,000 for a broken leg, of which $8,000 was paid for by his insurance
•$200 for prescription drugs
•$1,900 for a doctor-prescribed back brace
•$200 for child care while in the hospital

What is his medical expense deduction before the imposition of the 7.5% income limit?

A. $1,900.
B. $4,350.
C. $4,550.
D. $12,350.

The answer is B. His medical expense deduction before limitations is $4,350 ($450 + $800 + $200 + $1,900 +$1,000). The babysitting is not deductible, even though it was incurred while Justin was obtaining medical care. The amount reimbursed by insurance is not deductible. ###

15. Jesse is in the process of adopting a child. In 2012, the child lived with Jesse, and he provided all of the child's support. However, the adoption is not final. Which of the following statements is true?

A. Jesse can include medical expenses that he paid before the adoption becomes final, if the child qualified as his dependent when the medical services were provided or paid.
B. Jesse cannot claim the medical expenses because the adoption is not final.
C. Jesse must save his receipts and, once the adoption becomes final, he may amend his tax return.
D. A taxpayer may only claim medical expenses for a biological child or a stepchild.

The answer is A. Jesse can include medical expenses that he paid before the adoption becomes final, so long as the child qualified as a dependent when the medical services were provided or paid. ###

16. Which of the following is a deductible medical expense?

A. Acupuncture for back pain.
B. Karate lessons for an overweight person.
C. Marriage counseling.
D. Teeth whitening.

The answer is A. In this instance, only acupuncture qualifies as an IRS-allowed medical expense. Medical care expenses must be primarily to alleviate or prevent a physical or mental defect or illness. They do not include expenses that are merely beneficial to general health, such as vitamins, gym classes, or vacations. ###

17. Dora's AGI is $40,000. She paid medical expenses of $3,500. Taking into account the AGI limit, how much can Dora deduct on her Schedule A?

A. $0.
B. $500.
C. $2,313.
D. $2,500.

The answer is B. Dora can deduct only $500 of her medical expenses because that is the amount that exceeds 7.5% of her AGI. Dora's AGI is $40,000, 7.5% of which is $3,000. ###

18. Which of the following taxes can taxpayers deduct on Schedule A?

A. Local sales taxes.
B. Fines for speeding.
C. Social Security taxes.
D. Homeowners' association fees.

The answer is A. In 2012, taxpayers have the option of claiming state and local sales taxes as an itemized deduction instead of claiming state and local income taxes (a taxpayer cannot claim both). Taxpayers may deduct sales taxes on Schedule A. The other expenses listed are not deductible as taxes on Schedule A. ###

19. Which of the following expenses are deductible on Schedule A?

A. Stamp taxes.
B. Parking ticket obtained while getting emergency medical care.
C. Drivers' license fees.
D. Personal property taxes paid on a speedboat.

The answer is D. Only the property taxes paid on the boat are deductible. These are also called "DMV fees." Parking tickets and fines are never deductible. Drivers' license fees and stamp taxes are not deductible. ###

20. Which of the following taxes is not deductible on Schedule A?

A. Property tax on a vacation home.
B. Special assessments to improve the sidewalks.
C. DMV fees based on the vehicle's value.
D. Property taxes paid on a home in Mexico.

The answer is B. The assessment to improve sidewalks is not deductible. Many states, cities, and counties also impose local benefit taxes for improvements to property, such as assessments for streets, sidewalks, and sewer lines. These taxes cannot be deducted, but they can be added to the property's basis. ###

21. Ryan is having money troubles and agrees to sell his home to Janie. Janie agrees to pay all the delinquent real estate taxes on the residence, totaling $2,000. How must Janie treat the property tax payment of $2,000?

A. Janie may deduct the taxes as an itemized deduction on her Schedule A.
B. Janie may not deduct the taxes. She must add the taxes paid to her basis in the property.
C. The taxes may be prorated and deducted over the life of her loan.
D. Janie may deduct the taxes paid as an adjustment to income.

The answer is B. Janie can only deduct the property taxes that are legally imposed on her. She cannot deduct property taxes because she was not the legal owner of the property when the taxes were imposed. Property taxes paid during a purchase may be added to the buyer's basis if the taxes are for the time period that the property was owned by the seller. ###

22. For a tax to be deductible, all of the following must be true except _____.

A. The tax must be imposed during the tax year.
B. The taxpayer must be legally liable for the tax.
C. The tax must be paid during the tax year.
D. The tax must be paid by the taxpayer.

The answer is A. Taxpayers can deduct tax imposed during a *prior* year, so long as the taxes were paid during the current tax year. ###

23. Christopher and Angie file a joint return. During the year, they paid:

- $5,000 in home mortgage interest
- $600 in credit card interest
- $4,000 interest on an auto loan
- $3,000 loan interest on an empty lot that was purchased for building a home

How much can Christopher and Angie report as deductible interest?

A. $0.
B. $5,000.
C. $8,000.
D. $8,600.

The answer is B. Only their home mortgage interest ($5,000) is deductible as interest on Schedule A. The other types of interest are all personal interest. Personal interest is not deductible. Interest paid on a plot of land is not deductible as mortgage interest, even if the taxpayer later decides to build a home on the property. Only the interest that is secured by an actual home (not land) would be deductible as mortgage interest. ###

24. Nathaniel owns a home, and he also has a cabin in the mountains that he maintains. The cabin sat empty all year. Which of the following statements is true?

A. Only the mortgage interest and property tax on his main home is deductible.
B. Both the mortgage interest and property tax on his main home and the cabin are deductible.
C. The mortgage interest on both homes is deductible, but the property tax on the cabin is not.
D. The mortgage interest and property tax on his main home is deductible, and the property tax on the cabin is deductible. Any mortgage interest on the second home is not deductible.

The answer is B. Both the mortgage interest and property tax on his main home and the second residence are deductible. The mortgage interest on a second home is deductible, even if the taxpayer did not use the home during the year. ###

25. For the mortgage interest deduction, which of the following choices would qualify as a home?

A. An empty lot where the taxpayer plans to build his main home.
B. A sailboat with a camp stove and no bathroom.
C. A vacation cabin without running water.
D. An RV with a small kitchen, bathroom, and sleeping area.

The answer is D. A qualified home includes a house, condominium, cooperative, mobile home, house trailer, boat, or similar property that has sleeping, cooking, and toilet facilities. ###

26. Harvey refinanced his home and paid closing costs in 2012. He used the proceeds from the refinance to put on a new roof and also to pay off one of his credit cards. He paid the following fees:

- $400 Loan origination fee (points)
- $500 Home appraisal fee
- $45 Document prep fee
- $60 Loan closing fee
- $70 Title insurance

How much of the fees Harvey paid to the bank for the loan is fully deductible in 2012?

A. $0.
B. $400.
C. $900.
D. $945.
E. $1,005.

The answer is A. Harvey may not fully deduct any of the expenses listed because the home loan is a refinance, not a purchase. Deductible fees are limited to home mortgage interest and certain real estate taxes. Points that represent interest on a refinancing are generally amortized over the life of the loan. Fees that are not associated with the acquisition of a loan (other than fees representing interest for tax purposes) generally only affect the basis of the home. Fees related to the acquisition of a loan, such as a credit report fee, are not deductible. ###

27. Ingrid is single with the following income and expenses:

- Wages $70,000
- Interest income $3,000
- Mortgage interest paid $24,000
- Investment interest expense $5,000
- Personal credit card interest $3,400
- Car loan interest $1,200
- Late fees on her mortgage $50

What is Ingrid's total allowable deduction for interest expense on her Schedule A?

A. $24,000.
B. $27,000.
C. $27,050.
D. $32,400.

The answer is C. The answer is: $24,000 + $3,000 + $50 = $27,050. The deduction for investment interest expense is limited to investment income. Late fees paid on a qualifying mortgage are deductible as interest. The remaining amount of interest expense must be carried over to the next tax year and may be used to offset income in future tax years. The credit card interest is not deductible. ###

28. Alexander and Melinda are married and file jointly. They have the following interest expenses in the current tax year. How much deductible interest do they have after limitations?

•$10,000 in mortgage interest on a main home
•$2,000 in mortgage interest on a second home
•$4,600 in interest on a car loan
•$600 in credit card interest
•$3,000 in margin interest expense
•$2,400 in investment income

A. $10,000.
B. $12,000.
C. $14,400.
D. $15,000.

The answer is C. The answer is figured as follows: $10,000 + $2,000 + $2,400 = $14,400. The mortgage interest on both homes is deductible. The interest on the auto loan and credit cards is not deductible. The margin interest expense is deductible, but limited to the amount of investment income, which is $2,400. Investment interest is deductible by individuals only to the extent of investment income. The remaining investment interest expense may be carried over to a future tax year. ###

29. All of the following are deductible charitable contributions that Larissa made to a qualifying battered women's shelter except _____.

A. Fair market value of the used kitchen appliances, in good condition, she donated to the shelter.
B. $35 of the $50 admission Larissa paid for a shelter fundraising dinner. (The fair market value was $15.)
C. Fair market value of the hours Larissa spent staffing the shelter.
D. Larissa's transportation costs for driving to and from her shift at the shelter.

The answer is C. Larissa cannot deduct the value of her volunteer hours. The value of a person's time and service is never deductible. ###

193

30. Which taxpayer is required to fill out Form 8283 and attach it to his or her return?

A. Abu, who made a single cash contribution of $650 to a qualified organization.
B. Hunter, whose deductible cash contributions totaled $550.
C. Marilyn, whose noncash contributions totaled $250.
D. Debra, whose noncash contributions totaled $600.

The answer is D. Debra would be required to fill out Form 8283, *Noncash Charitable Contributions*, and attach it to her return. That is because any noncash donation over $500 must be described on Form 8283. ###

31. Julia made the following contributions last year:

•$600 to St. Martin's Church (The church gave her a receipt)
•$32 to the SPCA
•$40 to a family whose house burned
•$50 for lottery tickets at a fundraiser
•$100 for playing bingo at her church
•Furniture with an FMV of $200 to Goodwill

The amount that Julia can claim as deductible cash contributions is _____.

A. $672.
B. $632.
C. $72.
D. $32.

The answer is B. Julia's donations to her church and to the SPCA are her only deductible cash contributions. Lottery tickets and bingo (or any type of gambling) are not charitable contributions, even if the proceeds go to a qualifying organization. The donation of furniture to Goodwill is not a cash contribution, and therefore would not be included in the calculation. Noncash contributions are reported separately from cash contributions. ###

32. Amelia donates $430 in cash to her church. What is required on the receipt to substantiate the donation correctly for IRS recordkeeping requirements?

A. The reason for the contribution.
B. Amelia's home address.
C. The amount of the donation.
D. Amelia's method of payment.

The answer is C. A taxpayer can claim a deduction for a contribution of $250 or more only if he has a receipt or acknowledgment from the qualified organization. The receipt must include:
- The amount of cash contributed
- Whether the qualified organization gave the taxpayer any goods or services in return
- A description and good faith estimate of the value of any goods or services provided in return by the organization (if applicable)

A receipt for the donation must also show the amount, the date, and the name of the organization that was paid. ###

33. Lindy donates her used car to a qualified charity. She bought it three years ago for $15,000. A used car guide shows the FMV for this type of car is $5,000. Lindy's friend, Buck, offered her $4,500 for the car a week ago. Lindy gets a Form 1098-C from the organization showing the car was sold for $1,900. How much is Lindy's charitable deduction?

A. $15,000.
B. $5,000.
C. $4,500.
D. $1,900.

The answer is D. Lindy can only deduct $1,900 for her donation. This is because she is only allowed to take the lesser of the car's FMV or the amount for which the charity was able to sell the car. Since the car only sold for $1,900, that is the amount of the donation, regardless of its Blue Book value. ###

34. Oscar donated a nice leather coat to a thrift store operated by his church. He paid $450 for the coat three years ago. Similar coats in the thrift store sell for $50. What is Oscar's charitable deduction?

A. $0.
B. $50.
C. $400.
D. $450.

The answer is B. Oscar's donation is limited to $50. Generally, the FMV of used clothing and household goods is far less than their original cost. For used clothing, a taxpayer should claim as the value the price that buyers actually pay in used clothing stores, such as consignment or thrift shops, or at garage sales. ###

35. Laney pays $105 for a ticket to a church dinner. All the proceeds go to the church. The ticket to the dinner has an FMV of $20, the cost of the dinner. At the dinner, Laney buys $35 worth of raffle tickets, which the church is selling as a fundraiser. She does not win any raffle prizes. What is Laney's deductible charitable contribution to her church?

A. $85.
B. $120.
C. $140.
D. $195.

The answer is A. To figure the amount of Laney's charitable contribution, she must subtract the value of the benefit received ($20) from the total payment ($105). Therefore, Laney can deduct $85 as a charitable contribution to the church. The cost of raffle tickets or other wagering activity is never deductible as a charitable contribution. ###

36. Deductions to the following organizations are subject to the 50% limitation on deductible contributions:

A. Churches.
B. Hospitals.
C. Fraternal societies such as the Kiwanis and the Lions Club.
D. Both A and B.

The answer is D. The 50% limit applies to the total of all charitable contributions made during the year. This means that the deduction for charitable contributions cannot exceed 50% of a taxpayer's AGI. A 30% limit applies to veterans' organizations, fraternal societies, nonprofit cemeteries, and certain private non-operating foundations. ###

37. Nancy donates $300 in cash to her local food bank. What type of documentation is required for her donation?

A. No documentation.
B. A canceled check.
C. A self-prepared statement.
D. A receipt for the donation showing the amount, date, and who was paid.

The answer is D. A taxpayer can claim a deduction for a contribution of $250 or more only if he has an acknowledgment or receipt of the contribution from the charity. The receipt must reflect the amount, date, and the name of the organization that was paid, plus a statement regarding whether any goods or services were given to the taxpayer. ###

38. Vera and Jack are married and file jointly. They contributed $15,000 in cash from their savings to their synagogue during 2012. They also donated $3,000 to a private foundation that is a nonprofit cemetery organization. A 30% limit applies to the cemetery organization. Their adjusted gross income for 2012 was $30,000. Vera and Jack's deductible contribution for 2012 and any carryover to next year is:

A. $18,000 with zero carryover to next year.
B. $15,000 with $2,100 carryover to next year.
C. $7,500 with $2,100 carryover to next year.
D. $15,000 with $3,000 carryover to next year.

The answer is D. Vera and Jack cannot deduct more than $15,000, which is 50% of their income of $30,000. The remaining amount must be carried forward to a future tax year (five years for most charitable deductions.) ###

39. During a fundraising auction at his local church, Lyle pays $600 for a week's stay at a beachfront hotel, where he stays during a vacation in August. He intends to make the payment as a contribution, and all the proceeds go to help the church. The FMV of the stay is $590. What is Lyle's charitable contribution?

A. $0.
B. $10.
C. $590.
D. $600.

The answer is B. Lyle can only deduct $10, because he received the benefit of staying at the property. Only the excess contribution over the FMV of the item qualifies as a charitable contribution. ###

40. Summer is a youth group leader who supervises teens on a weekend retreat. She is responsible for overseeing the setup of the trip and enjoys the activities she supervises during the retreat. She also oversees breaking down the campsite and helps transport the group home. Which of the following statements is true?

A. Summer may not deduct her travel expenses because she enjoyed the retreat. Therefore, it is a vacation and is not deductible.
B. Summer may deduct her out-of-pocket expenses, including travel expenses.
C. Summer may deduct only the travel expense to and from the campsite.
D. None of the above.

The answer is B. A taxpayer may claim a charitable contribution deduction for out-of-pocket expenses incurred while away from home performing services for a charitable organization only if there is no significant element of personal pleasure in the travel. However, a deduction will not be denied simply because the taxpayer enjoys providing services to a charitable organization. The taxpayer is still allowed to take a charitable contribution deduction for the expenses if he is on-duty in a genuine and substantial sense throughout the trip. Since Summer had substantial supervisory and leadership duties throughout the trip, her out-of-pocket expenses, including travel costs, are deductible. ###

41. Julio spent the entire day attending his human rights organization's regional meeting as a chosen delegate. He spent $50 on travel to the meeting and $25 on materials for the meeting. In the evening, Julio went to the theater with two other meeting attendees. He spent $50 on movie tickets. The charity did not reimburse Julio for any of his costs. How much can Julio deduct as a charitable expense?

A. $25.
B. $50.
C. $75.
D. $150.

The answer is C. Julio's charitable contribution is $75 ($50 + $25 = $75). He can claim his travel and meeting expenses as charitable contributions, because they are directly related to his charitable activities. However, he cannot claim the cost of the evening at the theater, as those are personal entertainment costs. ###

42. Ted pays a babysitter $100 to watch his children while he does volunteer work at the Red Cross. He also has $50 in transportation expenses, of which $10 was reimbursed by the organization. What is Ted's deductible expense?

A. $0.
B. $40.
C. $50.
D. $150.

The answer is B. Only Ted's transportation costs are deductible ($50 - $10 reimbursement = $40). A taxpayer cannot deduct payments for child care expenses as a charitable contribution, even if they are necessary so he can do the volunteer work. ###

43. In March 2012, Sonia volunteers for 15 hours in the office of a local homeless shelter. The full-time receptionist is paid $10 an hour to do the same work Sonia does. Sonia makes $15 per hour as a cashier at her regular job. She also has $16 in out-of-pocket expenses for bus fare to the shelter. How much can Sonia deduct on her taxes as a charitable contribution?

A. $16.
B. $150.
C. $225.
D. $241.

The answer is A. A taxpayer cannot deduct the "value" of his time or services as a charitable deduction. However, a volunteer may deduct out-of-pocket expenses and the costs of gas and oil or transportation costs for getting to and from the place where he volunteers. Sonia cannot use the standard mileage rate because she did not use her own car for transportation. ###

44. All of the following are nonprofit organizations. However, not all of them qualify for deductible contributions. Sam donated to each nonprofit listed. What is his total qualified deduction for 2012?

Amount	Organization
$100	Methodist church
$120	County animal shelter
$75	Salvation Army
$25	Red Cross
$50	Political contribution
$300	Chamber of Commerce
$670	Total Contributions

A. $320.
B. $370.
C. $220.
D. $670.

The answer is A. The contributions to the political organization and the Chamber of Commerce are not deductible on Schedule A. The deduction is figured as follows:
($100 + $120 + $75 + $25 = $320). ###

45. Ali participated in a fundraising raffle event for his local mosque. All the money collected by the mosque, a qualified organization, went to feed the homeless. Ali purchased $300 in bingo cards and won movie tickets valued at $60. What is Ali's charitable deduction?

A. $0.
B. $60.
C. $240.
D. $300.

The answer is A. Ali may not deduct any amount as a contribution. Deducting the cost of raffle, bingo, or lottery tickets is specifically prohibited by IRS Publication 17, even if the money goes to a qualified charity. The cost of raffle, bingo, or lottery tickets is never deductible as a charitable contribution. ###

46. Martin contributes to many organizations. In 2012, he donates $5,000 in cash to his church and $4,000 to his local Chamber of Commerce. He also contributes land with a fair market value of $16,000 to his church. Martin has a basis of $5,000 in the land. His taxable income for the year is $45,000. What is the maximum amount he can deduct for charitable contributions?

A. $9,000.
B. $18,500.
C. $22,500.
D. $25,000.

The answer is B. The contribution to the Chamber of Commerce is not a deductible contribution. The $5,000 contribution in cash is fully deductible, but gifts of appreciated property are subject to a maximum deduction of 30% of the taxpayer's adjusted gross income. However, charitable gifts of appreciated property held long-term are subject to a lower deductibility ceiling: 30% of AGI, with a five-year carryover of any excess deduction. So, Martin figures his charitable contribution as follows:

($45,000 x 30%) = $13,500
($5,000 + $13,500) = $18,500
Carryover = $2,500
($16,000 - $13,500 = $2,500) ###

47. All of the following statements regarding home equity debt are correct except:

A. There is a $150,000 limit on the amount of debt that can be treated as home equity debt for purposes of the mortgage interest deduction.
B. The taxpayer does not have to use the home equity loan on improvements to the home for it to be eligible as deductible interest.
C. The debt must not exceed the property's fair market value.
D. Both B and C.

The answer is A. The limit on the amount of debt that can be treated as home equity debt for purposes of the mortgage interest deduction is $100,000, not $150,000. ###

48. In 2012 Henry experienced numerous health problems. As a result, Henry and his wife Marie incurred the following medical expenses:

Physician and hospital fees	$10,000
Dental and orthodontic fees	$5,000
Medical and dental insurance premiums	$12,000
Eyeglasses and contact lenses	$1,000
Health club dues	$1,000
Prescription medications	$3,000
Nonprescription drugs and medicines	$1,000

They also drove 3,000 miles in connection with medical visits, and incurred parking and toll charges of $100. The insurance premiums were paid through Henry's employer-sponsored health insurance plan and were not reported as income in box 1 of his Form W-2. Henry and Marie had adjusted gross income of $100,000 in 2012. What is the amount of their medical expense deduction for the year on Schedule A?

A. $33,000.
B. $19,790.
C. $12,290.
D. $33,790.

The answer is C. The insurance premiums are not deductible because they were paid through an employer-sponsored health insurance plan and were not reported in box 1 of Form W-2. Neither health club dues nor nonprescription medicines (except for insulin) are deductible.

The deductible costs listed total $19,100, and the 3,000 miles driven in connection with medical visits can be deducted at a standard mileage rate of $.23, or $690. Deductibility of the resulting total of $19,790 is limited to the amount in excess of 7.5% of adjusted gross income, or $7,500, so the amount of their medical expense deduction calculated on Schedule A would be $12,290. ###

Supporting calculations:

Deductible expenses:

Physician and hospital fees	$10,000
Dental and orthodontic fees	$5,000
Eyeglasses and contact lenses	$1,000
Prescription medications	$3,000
Parking and tolls	$100
Mileage at standard mileage rate of $.23	$690
Total deductible expenses	**$19,790**

Adjusted gross income	$100,000
7.5% limit	($7,500)
Limitation ($19,750-$7,500)	
Medical expense deduction on Schedule A	$12,290

Unit 8: Other Itemized Deductions

More Reading:
Publication 561, *Determining the Value of Donated Property*
Publication 587, *Business Use of Your Home*
Publication 547, *Casualties, Disasters, and Thefts*
Publication 529, *Miscellaneous Deductions*

In this unit, we continue our look at deductions that taxpayers can take on their 1040 tax returns. We start with deductible nonbusiness casualty losses, which are reported on Schedule A. Casualty losses related to a business (including self-employed businesses that are reported on Schedule C and Schedule F) are treated differently.

Casualty Losses

A casualty is the damage, destruction, or loss of property resulting from an identifiable event that is sudden, unexpected, or unusual. Examples include a car accident, fire, earthquake, flood, vandalism, or theft.

Losses that do not meet this definition and are thus not deductible include:

- Damage done by pets
- Slow insect damage to trees, clothing, or household items, such as termite or moth damage
- Arson
- Lost property
- Progressive deterioration ("normal wear and tear")
- Losses in real estate value from market fluctuations
- Accidental breakage of china, dishes, or other items during regular use

A taxpayer must have proof of the casualty or theft in order to deduct it. The taxpayer must also prove that the loss was actually caused by the event. Specifically, the taxpayer must be able to prove:

- The type of casualty loss (car accident, fire, storm, etc.) and the date of occurrence
- That the taxpayer was the legal owner of the property, or at least legally liable for the damage (such as leased property where the lessee was responsible for damage)
- Whether insurance reimbursement exists

Example: Gregory rents a car from Reliable Rentals, Inc. He declines renter's insurance and signs a contract stating he will be responsible for any damage. The rental car is stolen and now Gregory is responsible for paying back Reliable Rentals. Gregory's car insurance does not have rental car coverage, so he is liable for the full amount. Gregory may deduct the loss as a casualty loss, subject to the applicable rules.

Personal casualty losses are subject to the "Single Event Rule." This means that events closely related in origin are considered a single event. For example, it is a single casualty when the damage comes from two or more closely related causes, such as wind and flood damage from the same storm. A single casualty may also damage two or more pieces of property, such as a hailstorm that damages both a taxpayer's home and his car parked in the driveway.

Nonbusiness Casualty Loss Limits ($100 & 10% Rule)

Each personal casualty or theft loss is limited to the excess of the loss over $100. In addition, a 10%-of-AGI limit applies to the net loss. The "$100 Rule" and "10% Rule" only apply to nonbusiness casualty losses, not to business property losses.

1. The $100 Rule

After a taxpayer has figured the casualty loss on personal-use property, he must reduce that loss by $100. This reduction applies to each total casualty or theft loss. It does not matter how many pieces of property are involved in a single event; the taxpayer only has to reduce the losses for each event by $100.

> **Example:** A fire damaged Dick's house in January, causing $3,000 in damage. In September, storm damaged his house again, causing $5,000 in damage. Dick must reduce each loss by $100.

> ***Note:** If a taxpayer has *more than one* casualty loss during the year, he must reduce each loss by $100 separately. Then the taxpayer must reduce the total of all losses by 10% of adjusted gross income.

2. The 10% Rule

The taxpayer must reduce the total of all personal casualty losses on personal-use property by 10% of his AGI. This rule does not apply to a net disaster loss within a federally declared disaster area.

Married couples filing jointly with a loss from the same event are treated as if they were one person, with the $100 Rule and 10% Rule being applied only one time.

Reporting a Casualty Loss or Gain

Taxpayers use Form 4684, *Casualties and Thefts*, to report a gain or loss from a personal casualty. The taxpayer may claim a deductible loss on personal-use property only if he itemizes deductions.

Sometimes taxpayers will have a gain from casualty losses because the insurance reimbursement will exceed their basis. However, if a taxpayer has a gain on damaged property, he can postpone reporting the gain if the insurance reimbursement is spent to restore the property.

Gain may also be postponed by buying replacement property within a specified period of time. The replacement period begins on the date the property was damaged, destroyed, or stolen, and ends two years after the close of the first tax year in which any part of the gain is realized. For a main home or its contents located in a federally declared disaster area, the replacement period is generally four years, rather than two. [53] For victims of Hurricane Katrina and certain other extreme disaster areas, the replacement period has been extended to five years, assuming the property is purchased in the same area.

---

[53] More detailed information about replacement property can be found in Unit 12, *Nonrecognition Property Transfers*.

For disaster area losses, taxpayers may choose to deduct the loss on the previous year's tax return, rather than in the year the disaster loss occurred. This may result in a lower tax for that year, often producing or increasing a cash refund.

For casualty losses in general, this is how the taxpayer determines his deduction:

1. Calculate the *lesser* of the FMV or adjusted basis of the item prior to the loss.
2. Subtract any payments/reimbursements from insurance.
3. Subtract $100 for each event (2012 limit).
4. Subtract 10% of the taxpayer's AGI.

Example: Many years ago, Al bought a vacation cottage for $18,000. A storm destroyed the cottage, now valued at $250,000. Al received $146,000 from his insurance company. He had a gain of $128,000 ($146,000 – $18,000 basis). Al spent the full $146,000 to rebuild his cottage. Since he used the insurance proceeds to rebuild his cottage, he can postpone reporting or recognizing the gain until the cottage is sold.

Decrease in FMV from a Casualty Loss

Casualty losses are deductible only for actual damage caused to a property. The cost of cleaning up or making repairs after a casualty is not included. Nor is a decline in market value of property in or near a casualty area.

Example: In 2012, Nicole purchased a condo for $200,000. Two months after the purchase, a hurricane destroyed five other properties on her block. A resulting appraisal showed that all of the properties within a five-mile radius had declined in fair market value by 15% because people were afraid to purchase homes in "hurricane territory." The reduction in the home's FMV is not a deductible casualty loss.

Insurance Reimbursements

Taxpayers can deduct qualified casualty losses to their homes, household items, and vehicles. A taxpayer may not deduct casualty and theft losses that are covered by insurance unless he files a claim for reimbursement. The taxpayer must reduce his casualty loss by the amount of the insurance reimbursement. If the taxpayer decides not to file an insurance claim but has a deductible, he may still claim the amount of the insurance deductible, since that amount would not have been covered by the policy anyway.

Example: Sonny has a $750 deductible on his car insurance. He has a car accident in 2012, incurring $6,000 of damage. The insurance company pays Sonny for the damage minus the $750 deductible. The amount of Sonny's casualty loss is based solely on his deductible. Sonny's actual casualty loss is only $650 ($750 – $100).

Example: Caitlyn has homeowners' insurance. In 2012, a small fire causes $8,000 in damage to her home. She does not want her insurance premium to go up, so she declines to file a claim and pays for the damage out-of-pocket. Her insurance policy carries a $1,500 deductible. Caitlyn cannot deduct the loss because she declined to file an insurance claim. However, she is allowed to deduct $1,500, the amount of the deductible, because her insurance would not have covered that amount in any case.

A taxpayer does not have to reduce his casualty loss by insurance payments received to cover living expenses in the following two situations:

- When a taxpayer loses use of his main home because of a casualty.

- When government authorities do not allow a taxpayer access to his main home because of a casualty or a threat of one.

However, if these insurance payments are more than the temporary increase in his living expenses, a taxpayer must include the excess in his income. This is not required if the casualty occurs in a federally declared disaster area. None of those insurance payments are taxable.

The taxable part of the insurance payment should be included in income for the year the taxpayer gains use of his main home, or, if later, for the year the taxable part of the insurance payment is received.

> **Example:** Olivia's main home was damaged by a tornado in August 2010. After repairs were made, she moved back into her home in November 2011. She received insurance payments in 2010 and 2011 that were $1,500 more than the temporary increase in her living expenses during those years. Olivia includes this amount in income on her 2011 Form 1040. In 2012, she receives another $500 to cover her living expenses in 2010 and 2011. She must include that payment on her 2012 tax return.

Rules for Determining Fair Market Value and Adjusted Basis

A casualty loss is limited to the lesser of the FMV of the property, or the property's adjusted basis right before the loss. The cost of replacement property is not part of a casualty or theft loss.

> **Example:** Don purchased an antique vase at a garage sale for $600. Later, he discovered that the vase was actually a rare collectible and its FMV was $20,000. The vase was stolen two months later during a robbery. Don's casualty loss is limited to the $600 he paid for it, which is his basis in the property. Don cannot claim a casualty loss deduction for $20,000, the value of the item.

> **Example:** Raquel bought a new leather sofa four years ago for $3,000. In April, a fire destroyed the sofa. Raquel estimates that it would now cost $5,000 to replace it. However, if she had sold the sofa before the fire, she probably would have received only $900 for it because the sofa was already four years old. Raquel's casualty loss is $900 (still subject to the $100 and 10% rules), the FMV of the sofa before the fire. Her loss is not $3,000 (her basis) and it is not $5,000 (the replacement cost).

Theft Losses

A theft loss may be deducted in the year that the theft is discovered. It does not matter when the theft actually occurred. Qualifying theft losses include:

- Blackmail
- Burglary
- Embezzlement, extortion
- Kidnapping for ransom
- Larceny, robbery
- Mail fraud

The taking of property must be illegal under the law of the state where it occurred, and it must have been done with criminal intent. However, a taxpayer does not have to show a conviction for theft.

If a taxpayer takes a deduction for stolen property and the property is later recovered by the police, he must report the recovery as income in the year the property is recovered. However, he must only report the amounts that actually reduced tax in an earlier year.

Nondeductible Losses

Decline in value of stock: A taxpayer may not deduct the decline in value of stock as a casualty loss, even if it is related to accounting fraud. There is an exception for Ponzi scheme losses, which may be deducted as capital losses.

The cost of insurance: The cost of insurance or other protection is not deductible as a casualty loss. This rule applies to nonbusiness assets only.

> **Example:** Jordan pays for renter's insurance to cover the furniture and appliances in his home from theft or other disaster losses. Jordan may not deduct the cost of the renter's insurance as a casualty loss.

> **Example:** Sydney is self-employed and owns a clothing boutique. She pays for hazard insurance on the boutique. Sydney may deduct the cost of the insurance on her shop as a regular business expense.

Business Casualty Losses

A business-related casualty loss is treated very differently than a personal casualty loss. Business casualty losses may be tested on either Part 1 or Part 2 of the exam. This is because a business loss may affect a self-employed taxpayer, as well as an investor who owns rental units. If income-producing property (such as rental property) is subject to a casualty loss, the amount of the taxpayer's loss is the adjusted basis in the property minus any salvage value and minus any insurance or other reimbursement received. The loss is figured as follows:

The taxpayer's adjusted basis in the property
MINUS
Any salvage value
MINUS
Any insurance reimbursement

> **Example:** Mario is a self-employed florist who owns his own shop. A utility van he uses for floral deliveries was involved in an accident. Mario had purchased the van for $70,000. The accumulated depreciation on the van prior to the accident was $40,000. He disposed of the van for $500 (salvage value of the scrap metal.) Mario's insurance company reimbursed him $20,000. His casualty loss is determined as follows:
>
> | | |
> | :--- | :---: |
> | Acquisition cost | $70,000 |
> | Less accumulated depreciation | ($40,000) |
> | Adjusted basis of van | $30,000 |
> | Minus salvage value | ($500) |
> | Initial loss from accident | $29,500 |
> | Minus insurance reimbursement | ($20,000) |
> | **Amount of casualty loss** | **$9,500** |

Miscellaneous Itemized Deductible Expenses

There are numerous other deductions taxpayers may take on their tax returns, with these miscellaneous expenses divided into two important categories:

- **Miscellaneous expenses subject to the 2% of AGI limit, and**
- **Miscellaneous expenses deductible in full (not subject to the 2% AGI limit).**

Miscellaneous Expenses Subject to the 2% Limit

A taxpayer may deduct certain expenses as miscellaneous itemized deductions on Schedule A. The taxpayer may only claim the amount that exceeds 2% of his AGI. There are many common types of these miscellaneous expenses subject to the 2% limit, including many expenses an employee may incur.

> **Example:** Andy's AGI is $45,000, and he has $1,100 in miscellaneous deductible work-related expenses. He must first figure out the 2% limit before he can start deducting these expenses (2% X $45,000 = $900). He can therefore deduct only $200 of those expenses ($1,100 - $900 = $200). Andy adds this amount to his Schedule A as an itemized deduction.

Investment expenses are allowed as a deduction if the expenses are directly connected with the production of investment income. Examples include investment counseling fees and the rental of a safe deposit box to keep investment documents. Investment expenses are included as a miscellaneous itemized deduction on Schedule A and are allowable only after applying the 2% limit.

Expenses related to a hobby are deductible, but only up to the amount of hobby income. A "hobby" is not considered a business because it is not carried on to make a profit.

Legal Fees

Many legal expenses are not deductible for individual taxpayers, such as the cost of attorney fees for drafting a will. But certain legal expenses are deductible, if they are incurred when a taxpayer is attempting to produce or collect taxable income, such as advice related to collecting alimony.

A taxpayer cannot deduct legal fees and court costs for getting a divorce. But he may deduct legal fees paid for tax advice in connection with a divorce and legal fees to obtain alimony. In order to be deductible, the tax advice fees must be separately stated on the attorney's bill. In addition, a taxpayer may deduct fees paid to appraisers, actuaries, and accountants for services in determining the correct tax or in helping to get alimony. A taxpayer can deduct fees for legal advice on federal, state, and local taxes of all types, including income, estate, gift, inheritance, and property taxes, even if the advice is related to a divorce. If an attorney's legal fee includes amounts for tax advice and other tax services, the taxpayer must be able to prove the expense was incurred for tax advice and not for some other legal issue.

> **Example:** The lawyer handling Jenna's divorce consults another law firm, which handles only tax matters, to obtain information on how the divorce will affect her taxes. Since Jenna consulted with the second law firm specifically to discuss tax matters, she can deduct the part of the fee paid to the second firm and separately stated on her bill, as an itemized deduction on Schedule A, subject to the 2% limit.

Example: The lawyer handling Mack's divorce uses the firm's tax department for tax matters related to his divorce. Mack's statement from the firm shows the part of the total fee for tax matters. This is based on the time required, the difficulty of the tax questions, and the amount of tax involved. Mack can deduct this part of his bill as an itemized deduction on Schedule A, subject to a 2% limit.

A taxpayer can claim deductible legal fees by claiming them as miscellaneous itemized deductions subject to the 2%-of-AGI limit.

Example: Betty pays an attorney $4,500 for handling her divorce. She also pays an additional $1,500 fee for services in collecting alimony that her former husband refuses to pay. Betty can deduct the fee for collecting alimony ($1,500), subject to a 2% limit, if it is separately stated on the attorney's bill. The $4,500 divorce fee is not deductible.

Unreimbursed Employee Business Expenses

An employee may deduct certain work-related expenses as itemized deductions. These expenses are first reported on Form 2106, *Employee Business Expenses*, and the amount is transferred to Schedule A. The taxpayer can deduct only unreimbursed employee expenses that are:

- Paid or incurred during the tax year,
- For carrying on the business of being an employee, and
- Ordinary and necessary.

An expense does not have to be required to be deductible. However, it must be a common expense that would be accepted in the taxpayer's trade or profession.

The following are examples of unreimbursed employee expenses that may be deductible:

- Business liability insurance premiums
- Malpractice insurance
- Depreciation on an asset the employer requires for work
- Dues to professional societies
- Subscriptions to professional journals
- Expenses of looking for a new job in the taxpayer's present occupation
- Legal fees related directly to a job
- Licenses and regulatory fees
- Tax counseling, preparation, and assistance
- Union dues
- Work clothes and uniforms (if required and not suitable for everyday use)
- Tools and supplies used for work
- Educator expenses
- Work-related education
- Home office or part of a home used regularly and exclusively in the taxpayer's work
- Travel, transportation, meals, and lodging related to the taxpayer's work
- Employee meals and entertainment

An employee may deduct unreimbursed business-related meals and entertainment expenses he has for entertaining a client, customer, or another employee. The limit on deductible meals and entertainment is 50% (the same for self-employed taxpayers and businesses). The taxpayer must apply the "50% limit" *before* applying the 2% of AGI limit. The taxpayer can deduct meals and entertainment expenses only if they meet the following tests:

- The main purpose of the meal or entertainment was the active conduct of business,
- The taxpayer conducted business during the entertainment period, and
- The taxpayer had more than a general expectation of some other specific business benefit at a future time.

Deductible Employee Travel Expenses

An employee may not deduct commuting expenses, which are the expenses incurred when going from a taxpayer's home to his main workplace. However, there are numerous instances where an employee may deduct mileage or other travel expenses relating to his employment. Deductible employee travel expenses include:

- Getting from one work location to another in the course of business
- Visiting clients or customers
- Going to a business meeting away from the regular workplace
- Traveling from a first job to a second job in the same day
- Getting from a taxpayer's home to a temporary workplace

Any amounts reimbursed by the employer are not deductible by the employee.

Conventions: Special Rules

A taxpayer may deduct the cost of travel and attendance to conventions in the U.S. or the "North American area," including Canada and Mexico[54]. For cruises, there is a $2,000 annual cap on deductions, or $4,000 if filing jointly and both spouses went on qualifying cruise ship conventions. The IRS imposes strict substantiation requirements for taxpayers attempting to use this deduction.

A deduction is not allowed for conventions focused exclusively on investments or financial planning.

Tax Home and Work Location

A taxpayer's "tax home" is his principal place of work, *regardless of where he actually lives*. A taxpayer's tax home is used to determine if travel expenses are deductible.

Travel and meal expenses are considered deductible if the taxpayer is traveling away from his *tax home*, which is determined based on the following two factors:

- The travel is away from the general area or vicinity of the taxpayer's tax home.
- The trip is long enough or far away enough that a taxpayer cannot reasonably be expected to complete the roundtrip without sleep or rest.

This does not necessarily mean that a taxpayer needs to stay overnight at the destination in order to deduct the expense. For example, it may mean that an individual has an all-day meeting and needs to get a few hours of sleep in a hotel before driving home.

---

[54] The IRS maintains a list of these countries, many of which are tourist meccas and may not normally be associated with being in the "North American area." Examples include Aruba, Jamaica, Costa Rica, Barbados, Bermuda, Panama, the Marshall Islands, and the Netherlands Antilles. (Revenue Ruling 2011-26).

Once a taxpayer has determined that he is traveling away from his *tax home*, he can deduct "ordinary and necessary" expenses incurred while traveling on business Examples of deductible travel expenses while a taxpayer is away from home include:

- The cost of getting to a business destination (air, rail, bus, car, ferry, etc.)
- Meals and lodging while away from home
- Taxi fares
- Dry cleaning and laundry
- Use of a car while at the business location
- Computer rental fees
- Baggage charges, including shipping samples and display materials to the destination
- Tips on eligible expenses

Multiple Work Locations

If a taxpayer has *more than one* place of business or work, the "tax home" must be determined using several factors. The following facts should be used to determine which one is the main place of business or work:

- The total time ordinarily spent in each place
- The level of business activity in each place
- Whether income from each place is significant

The most important consideration is the length of time spent at each location. If a taxpayer regularly works in more than one place, his tax home is the general area where the main place of business or work is located. If a taxpayer has more than one place of business, then his tax home is his main place of business.

Example: Gary is a marketing consultant who lives with his family in Chicago, but works full-time in Milwaukee where he stays in a hotel and eats in restaurants. Gary returns to Chicago every weekend. He may not deduct any of his travel, meals, or lodging expenses in Milwaukee because that is his tax home. Gary's travel on weekends to his family home in Chicago is not for work, so these expenses are also not deductible.

If a person does not have a regular place of business because of the nature of his work, then his tax home can be the place where he lives.

Example: Seville is a truck driver who lives in Tucson, Arizona with his family. Seville is employed by a trucking firm that has its main terminal in Phoenix. At the end of his long trucking runs, Seville returns to his home terminal in Phoenix and spends one night there before returning home. Seville cannot deduct any expenses he has for meals and lodging in Phoenix or the cost of traveling from Phoenix to Tucson. This is because Phoenix is Seville's "tax home" (Publication 463).

There are special rules for temporary work assignments. When a taxpayer is working away from his main place of business and the job assignment is temporary, his *tax home* does not change. The taxpayer can deduct his travel expenses because the job assignment is of a temporary nature, and therefore, the travel is considered business-related.

Note: A temporary work assignment is any work assignment that is expected to last for *one year or less*. Travel expenses paid or incurred in connection with a temporary work assignment away from home are deductible. However, travel expenses paid in connection with an *indefinite* work assignment are *not deductible*. Any work assignment over one year in duration is considered *indefinite*. A taxpayer cannot deduct travel expenses at a work location if it is realistically expected that he will work there for more than one year.

Example: Terry is a construction worker who lives and works primarily in Los Angeles. He is also a member of a trade union that helps him get work. Because of a shortage of jobs, Terry agrees to work at a construction site in Fresno. The Fresno job lasts ten months. Since the job lasts less than one year, the Fresno job is considered *temporary* and Terry's tax home is still in Los Angeles. Therefore, Terry's travel expenses are deductible since he was traveling away from his tax home for business or work. Terry can deduct travel expenses, including meals and lodging, while traveling between his temporary place of work and his tax home in Los Angeles.

There is a special rule for military personnel. Members of the armed forces on a permanent duty assignment overseas are not considered to be "traveling away from home."

Therefore, members of the military cannot deduct their travel expenses for meals and lodging while on permanent duty assignment. However, military personnel that are permanently transferred from one duty station to another may be able to deduct their moving expenses as an adjustment to income.

Office in the Home

If a taxpayer has an office in his home that qualifies as a principal place of business, he can deduct daily transportation costs between the home office and another work location in the same trade or business. These are not commuting expenses, because commuting expenses are never deductible. However, the travel between a home office to a business location would be considered deductible travel.

In order to qualify as a home office, the space must be used exclusively and regularly:

- As the taxpayer's principal place of business, or
- As a place to meet with patients or clients in the normal course of your business, or
- In any connection with a business where the business portion of the home is a separate structure not attached to the home.

Example: Vince is a self-employed bookkeeper who works exclusively out of his home office. He has many clients. Vince travels from his home office directly to his clients' locations and performs his bookkeeping services on-site. Vince does not have any other office. In this case, the travel from his home office to his clients' locations is deductible as business mileage.

Example: Martha is a part-time tax preparer. During tax season, she uses her study to prepare tax returns. She also uses the study to exercise on her treadmill. The room is not used exclusively in Martha's profession, so she cannot claim a deduction for the business use. Also, since the space does not qualify as a bona-fide home office, then the travel from her home office to another business location (such as a client's office or home) would not be deductible.

Calculating the Home Office Percentage

The home office deduction depends on the percentage of the home that is used for business. A taxpayer can use any reasonable method to compute business percentage, but the most common methods are to:

- Divide the area of the home used for business by the total area of the home, or
- Divide the number of rooms used for business by the total number of rooms in the home if all rooms in the home are about the same size.

Taxpayers may not deduct expenses for any portion of the year during which there was no business use of the home.

Example: Lillian is a self-employed bookkeeper, and she has a qualified home office. The entire square footage of her home is 1,200 square feet. Her home office is 240 square feet, so her home office percentage is 20% (240 ÷ 1,200) of the total area of her home. Her business percentage is 20%.

Example: Glenn is a tool salesman who is on the road most of the time, and his home is the only fixed location for selling tools. Glenn regularly uses the right half of his basement for storage of inventory and product samples. The expenses for the space are deductible as an employee-related home office expense.

Job Search Expenses

A taxpayer may deduct job search expenses, subject to the 2% of AGI limit, if the expenses relate to the same profession. Expenses incurred can be deducted even if the taxpayer does not find a new job.

If the job search qualifies, the taxpayer can deduct costs for using an employment agency or career counselor, and for traveling to interviews. The taxpayer may also deduct the cost of printing, preparing, and mailing resumes.

The following expenses are not deductible:

- Job search expenses for a new occupation
- Living expenses incurred during a period of unemployment between the ending of the last job and a new period of employment
- A taxpayer looking for a new job the first time

Job-Related Education

The cost of courses designed to maintain or improve the skills needed for a present job (or required by an employer or the law) is deductible as an employee business expense. The taxpayer may also choose to take an education credit. The education must meet at least one of the following tests:

- The education must maintain or improve skills that are required for the taxpayer's current line of work
- The education must be required by law or by the taxpayer's employer as a condition of his employment

If a taxpayer has a regular job and then enrolls in work-related education courses on a temporary basis, he can also deduct the round-trip costs of transportation between his home and school. This is true regardless of the location of the school, the distance traveled, or whether the taxpayer attends school on non-work days.

In some cases, a taxpayer may be able to take an education credit for his education expenses, so may choose between the credit and the miscellaneous itemized deduction, whichever produces a lower tax.

Deductible Uniforms

The cost of uniforms and other special work clothes required by an employer can be deducted as work-related expenses. The uniforms must not be suitable for everyday use. The taxpayer may also deduct the cost of upkeep, including laundry and dry cleaning bills.

Examples of employees who may deduct their uniforms include delivery workers, firefighters, health care workers, law enforcement officers, letter carriers, professional athletes, and transportation workers (air, rail, bus, etc.) Musicians and entertainers can deduct the cost of theatrical clothing and accessories that are not suitable for everyday wear. An employee can deduct the cost of protective clothing, such as safety shoes or boots, safety glasses, hard hats, and work gloves.

Full-time active-duty military personnel cannot deduct the cost of their uniforms. However, they may be able to deduct the cost of insignia, shoulder boards, and related items.

Nondeductible Expenses

The IRS has a lengthy list of expenses that cannot be deducted. These are just a sample of expenses that are not allowed:

- Lunch with coworkers, or meals while working late
- Club dues
- Lost or misplaced cash or property
- Hobby losses
- Residential telephone line
- Home security system
- Home repairs, insurance, and rent
- Personal legal expenses
- Losses from the sale of a home, furniture, or personal car
- Brokers' commissions
- Burial or funeral expenses, including the cost of a cemetery lot
- Check-writing fees
- Fees and licenses, such as car licenses, marriage licenses, and dog tags
- Fines and penalties, such as parking tickets
- Investment-related seminars
- Life insurance premiums
- Personal disability insurance premiums

Miscellaneous Deductions (Not Subject to the 2% Limit)

There are also some expenses that are not subject to the 2% limit. A taxpayer can fully deduct on Schedule A the expenses that fall under this category, without regard to any percentage of income limits. The expenses that are **not** subject to the 2% rule are:

1. Gambling losses to the extent of gambling winnings. The full amount of a taxpayer's gambling winnings is reported on line 21 of his Form 1040. Gambling losses are deducted on

Schedule A, up to the total amount of gambling winnings. Taxpayers must have kept a written record of their losses.

> ***Note:** Gambling losses in excess of winnings are not deductible. The full amount of winnings must be reported as income, and the losses (up to the amount of winnings) may be claimed as an itemized deduction.

2. Work-related expenses for individuals with a disability that enable them to work, such as attendant care services at their workplace.

> **Example:** Erin has a visual disability. She requires a large screen magnifier at work in order to see well enough so she can perform her work. Erin purchased her screen magnifier for $550. She may deduct the cost of the screen magnifier as an itemized deduction not subject to the 2% floor.

3. Amortizable premium on taxable bonds: If the amount a taxpayer pays for a bond is greater than its stated principal amount, the excess is called a "bond premium." If this occurs, the excess is treated as a miscellaneous itemized deduction that is not subject to the 2% limit.

4. Casualty or theft losses from *income-producing* property: A taxpayer can deduct a casualty or theft loss as a miscellaneous itemized deduction not subject to the 2% limit if the damaged or stolen property was income-producing property (property held for investment, such as stocks, bonds, gold, silver, vacant lots, and works of art).

5. A taxpayer can deduct the federal estate tax attributable to income "in respect of a decedent" that the taxpayer includes in gross income. Income in respect of a decedent is income that a deceased taxpayer would have received had the death not occurred and which was not properly includable in the decedent's final income tax return.

Unit 8: Questions

1. Alfred lives in Baltimore where he has a seasonal job for eight months each year and earns $25,000. He works the other four months in Miami, also at a seasonal job, and earns $9,000. Where is Alfred's tax home?

A. Miami.
B. Baltimore.
C. Alfred is a transient for tax purposes.
D. Alfred has no tax home.

The answer is B. Baltimore is Alfred's main place of work because he spends most of his time there and earns most of his income there. Therefore, Baltimore is Alfred's tax home for IRS purposes. ###

2. Brad is working on a temporary work assignment in another city. He is not sure how long the assignment will last. He travels overnight every week. So far, the work assignment has lasted 11 months in 2012, and Brad has incurred $800 in travel expenses and $300 in meal expenses. What is his deductible expense for this activity in 2012?

A. $0.
B. $800.
C. $950.
D. $1,100.

The answer is A. Brad cannot deduct any of the expenses, because travel expenses paid in connection with an indefinite work assignment are not deductible. ###

3. All of the following may be claimed as miscellaneous itemized deductions except _____.

A. Unreimbursed commuting expenses to and from work.
B. Professional society or union dues.
C. Expenses of looking for a new job.
D. Work-related expenses for individuals with a disability.

The answer is A. The expenses of commuting to and from work are not deductible expenses. ###

4. Patrice's antique Persian rug was damaged by a new kitten before it was housebroken. Patrice estimates the loss at $4,500. Her AGI for the year is $50,000. How much of the casualty loss may she deduct?

A. $0.
B. $4,500.
C. $3,000.
C. $2,900.

The answer is A. A casualty loss is not deductible if the damage is caused by a family pet. Because the damage was neither unexpected nor unusual, the loss is not deductible as a casualty loss. ###

5. Felicity is a self-employed midwife who has a home office. Felicity's principal place of business is in her home, although she does not meet with clients in her home. Instead, she goes out to her clients' homes and performs her duties on-site. Which of the following statements is true?

A. Felicity can deduct the cost of round-trip transportation between her home office and her clients' place of business.
B. Felicity cannot deduct the cost of round-trip transportation between her home office and her clients' homes, but she may deduct the transportation costs from her clients' homes to other business locations.
C. Felicity does not have a qualified home office, because she does not meet clients in her home.
D. None of the above.

The answer is A. Felicity can deduct daily transportation costs between her home office and a client's location. Felicity does not have to meet with clients in her home in order for her home office to qualify as her principal place of business. The transportation costs between two work locations are considered a deductible travel expense. ###

6. Eli purchased a used car for $11,000 in 2012. He forgot to purchase auto insurance, and three months later he totaled his car in an auto accident. The car's FMV on the date of the accident was $10,000. He was able to sell the car to a salvage yard for $300. Eli's AGI for 2012 was $50,000. What is Eli's deductible loss?

A. $0.
B. $4,200.
C. $4,600.
D. $9,700.

The answer is C. This is a nonbusiness casualty loss, so Eli must first reduce his loss by $100 and then 10% of his AGI. The answer is calculated as follows:

Basis:	$10,000
Insurance	$0
Salvage value	($300)
Statutory reduction	($100)
10% of AGI	($5,000)
Deductible Loss	$4,600

Eli's deductible casualty loss on Schedule A is $4,600. ###

7. Megan, an engineer, maintains a residence in Denver, Colorado where her employer has a permanent satellite office. In 2012, Megan's employer enrolls her in a ten-month executive training program at their corporate offices in Santa Clara, California. Megan will attend classroom training in Santa Clara and do temporary work assignments throughout the United States, but she does expect to return to work in Denver after she completes her training.

Every Monday she flies to Santa Clara and stays in the city the entire week. She maintains a small, one-bedroom apartment in Santa Clara and incurs all the ordinary and necessary expenses in the upkeep of the apartment. She returns to Denver on the weekends to spend time with family and attend to her personal affairs from her Denver residence. Where is Megan's "tax home" for 2012?

A. Santa Clara, California.
B. Denver, Colorado.
C. Neither, because Megan is a transient for tax purposes.
D. Both, because Megan spends time in both places.

The answer is B. Her tax home is still in Denver, because her work assignment is temporary. For IRS purposes, a work assignment is temporary if it is expected to last for one year or less. Since Megan is going to be away for only ten months, her tax home remains in Denver. Travel expenses paid or incurred in connection with a temporary work assignment away from home are deductible. ###

8. Isaac's home was damaged by a tornado. He had $90,000 worth of damage, but $80,000 was reimbursed by his insurance company. Isaac's employer had a disaster relief fund for its employees. Isaac received $4,000 from the fund and spent the entire amount on repairs to his home. What is Isaac's deductible casualty loss before applying the deduction limits?

A. $0.
B. $4,000.
C. $6,000.
D. $10,000.

The answer is C. Isaac's casualty loss before applying the deduction limits is $6,000. Isaac must reduce his unreimbursed loss ($90,000 - $80,000 = $10,000) by the $4,000 he received from his employer. Isaac's casualty loss before applying the deduction limits is $6,000 ($10,000 - $4,000). ###

9. Joshua's adjusted gross income is $20,000. Determine which expenses he would include in the total for his miscellaneous itemized deductions.

Expense Description:
Income tax preparation fee $100
Safe deposit box rental (to store bonds) $75
Life insurance premiums $600
Home security system $175
Loss on the sale of a personal vehicle $1,800
Investment journals and newsletters $250
Investment advisory fees $200
Attorney fees for preparation of a will $1,000

What is the total of Joshua's qualified miscellaneous itemized expenses (**before** the application of any AGI limits)?

A. $2,400.
B. $1,225.
C. $800.
D. $625.

The answer is D. The deductible expenses are the income tax preparation fee ($100); the safe deposit box rental ($75); the investment journals and newsletters ($250); and the investment advisory fees ($200). Therefore, his total deduction before application of the 2% floor is $625. ###

10. Brady's garage caught fire in 2012. The garage is not attached to his primary residence. Brady estimates the property damage at $6,000. He declines to file an insurance claim because he fixes the damage himself. Brady pays $3,000 for the cost of the materials. He estimates the value of his labor to be approximately $2,800. His insurance company has a $1,000 deductible for any casualty loss claim filed. What is Brady's deductible casualty loss before any deductions or income limitations?

A. $0.
B. $1,000.
C. $3,000.
D. $6,000.

The answer is B. If a taxpayer's property is covered by insurance, he cannot deduct a loss unless he files an insurance claim for reimbursement. However, if the taxpayer declines to file an insurance claim, the IRS limits eligible casualty losses to the amount that is not normally covered by insurance, such as the amount of the insurance deductible. ###

11. All of the following may be claimed as miscellaneous itemized deductions except _____.

A. Funeral expenses.
B. Union dues.
C. Laundry costs for uniforms.
D. Investment expenses.

The answer is A. Funeral expenses are not deductible as a miscellaneous itemized deduction. All of the other expenses listed are deductible as itemized deductions on Schedule A. ###

12. All of the following miscellaneous itemized deductions are subject to the 2% of AGI limit except _____.

A. Tax preparation fees.
B. Union dues.
C. Investment expenses.
D. Gambling losses to the extent of gambling winnings.

The answer is D. Gambling losses to the extent of gambling winnings are not subject to the 2% AGI limit. ###

13. Kim uses her home office while she works as a translator for an online translating company. Kim meets the requirements for deducting expenses for the business use of her home. Her home office is 480 square feet and her home is 2,400 square feet. What is Kim's business use percentage in order to figure her allowable deduction?

A. 5%.
B. 10%.
C. 15%.
D. 20%.

The answer is D. Kim uses 20% of her home for business. Her office is 20% (480 ÷ 2,400) of the total area of her home. Therefore, her business percentage is 20%. ###

14. Simon's AGI is $75,000. Therefore, the first_____ of miscellaneous employee work-related expenses is not deductible.

A. $1,000.
B. $1,500.
C. $5,625.
D. Some other amount.

The answer is B. Simon's employee work-related expenses are subject to the 2% limit of adjusted gross income. Therefore, Simon must figure his deduction on Schedule A by first subtracting 2% of his AGI (75,000 x 2% = $1,500) from the total amount of these expenses. ###

15. Marissa works as a tax preparer for A+ Tax Services. She was hired as a preparer three years ago, but this year her employer changed his educational requirements. Now all the tax preparers are required to take three additional courses in order to keep their current positions. Marissa incurred the following expenses when she took these courses:

$100 Required supplies
$550 Tuition
$120 Required books
$50 Credit card interest from paying tuition
$65 Bus passes to and from school
$885 Total educational expenses

What is Marissa's deductible work-related educational expense on her Schedule A before the 2% limitation?

A. $550.
B. $670.
C. $835.
D. $885.

The answer is C. Marissa may deduct all the costs as work-related educational expenses, with the exception of the credit card interest, which is a personal expense and not deductible. ###

16. During the year, Leon paid $350 to have his tax return prepared. He also paid union dues of $450 and paid an attorney $3,000 to draft his will. What is Leon's miscellaneous itemized deduction on his Schedule A before the 2% limitation?

A. $350.
B. $450.
C. $800.
D. $3,800.

The answer is C. The attorney fees for drafting the will are not deductible. The tax preparation fees and union dues are deductible and subject to a 2% of AGI floor. ###

17. Which of the following expenses does not qualify as a deductible transportation expense?

A. Getting from one client to another in the course of a taxpayer's business or profession.
B. Commuting expenses.
C. Traveling overseas to sign a business contract with a foreign supplier.
D. Going to a business meeting out-of-state.

The answer is B. A taxpayer can include in business expenses amounts paid for transportation primarily for and essential to business or trade. A taxpayer cannot deduct personal commuting expenses, no matter how far his home is from his regular place of work. ###

18. Which of the following will qualify for a deduction on Schedule A as an employee business expense?

A. The employer reimburses expenses under a tuition reimbursement (nontaxable) program.
B. Taking classes that maintain or improve skills needed in the taxpayer's present work.
C. Taking classes that are required by a taxpayer's employer or the law to keep his present salary, status, or job. The required education must serve a bona fide business purpose to the taxpayer's employer.
D. Both B and C.

The answer is D. Both B and C are correct. A taxpayer can deduct the costs of qualifying work-related education as business expenses. Choice "A" is incorrect because any amounts that are reimbursed by an employer cannot be deducted by the taxpayer. ###

19. Connor is deaf. He purchased a special device to use at work so he can identify when his phone rings. He paid for the device out-of-pocket, and his employer did not reimburse him. How should Connor report this on his tax return?

A. Connor may deduct the purchase as an itemized deduction, not subject to the 2% floor.
B. Connor may deduct the purchase as an itemized deduction, subject to the 2% floor.
C. Connor may not deduct the purchase because he is not totally disabled.
D. Connor may not deduct the purchase because he is not self-employed.

The answer is A. Connor may deduct the expenses for the special device as an impairment-related work expense. The deduction is not limited. If a taxpayer has a physical or mental disability that limits employment, he can choose to deduct the expense as a miscellaneous itemized deduction, not subject to the 2%-of-income floor.###

20. Abby has the following income and losses in 2012:

1. $45,000 in wages
2. $10,000 in gambling winnings
3. $13,000 in gambling losses
4. $1,500 in attorney fees for a divorce

How should these transactions be treated on her tax return?

A. Report $55,000 in taxable income and $10,000 in miscellaneous itemized deductions on Schedule A, not subject to the 2% floor.
B. Report $53,000 in taxable income and $13,000 in miscellaneous itemized deductions, subject to the 2% floor.
C. Report $55,000 in taxable income and $13,000 in miscellaneous itemized deductions on Schedule A, subject to the 2% floor.
D. Report $45,000 in taxable income and $14,500 in miscellaneous itemized deductions on Schedule A, not subject to the 2% floor.

The answer is A. The full amount of income must be reported on Form 1040 ($45,000 + $10,000 = $55,000). The gambling losses are deductible only up to the amount of gambling winnings; a taxpayer must report the full amount of gambling winnings on Form 1040. The taxpayer then may deduct gambling losses on Schedule A (Form 1040). Gambling losses are not subject to the 2% of income limitation, but taxpayers cannot report more gambling losses than they do gambling winnings. Attorney fees for a divorce are not deductible, (but separate legal advice related to collecting alimony is). ###

21. Brooke had adjusted gross income of $20,000 in 2012. Her home sustained damage from a storm, and she incurred a loss of $3,000. Her home insurance policy had a deductible of $2,500 for this type of loss, so she elected not to file a claim.

Based upon the information provided, what is the amount of casualty loss Brooke can deduct for the year?

A. $900.
B. $3,000.
C. $2,000.
D. $400.

The answer is D. Because the property was covered by insurance and Brooke did not file a claim, the casualty loss deduction is limited to the amount of the insurance deductible, as this amount would have been her out-of-pocket cost if a claim had been filed. This amount is further subject to a reduction of $100 and limited to the net amount that exceeds 10% of adjusted gross income.

Supporting calculations:

Loss from storm	$3,000
Limited to amount of deductible	$2,500
Less $100 threshold	($100)
Loss after $100 limit	$2,400
Adjusted gross income	$20,000
Multiply by 10% limit	$2,000
Casualty loss deduction ($2,400-$2,000)	$400

22. If a taxpayer's home was destroyed in a flood and the area was later declared a federally declared disaster area, how long would the taxpayer typically have to purchase replacement property?

A. One year.
B. Two years.
C. Four years.
D. Five years.

The answer is C. In most casualty losses, taxpayers have two years to purchase a replacement for damaged or destroyed property. But in the case of most federally declared disaster areas, the period is usually four years. In certain extreme cases, including those taxpayers affected by Hurricane Katrina, the replacement period has been extended to five years. ###

23. Enrique and Crystal had adjusted gross income of $75,000 in 2012 and incurred the following miscellaneous expenses:

Homeowners' association dues	$1,000
Fine from homeowners' association for violation of bylaws	$100
Loss from burglary of their home	$9,000
Tax preparation fees	$250

Based upon the information provided, what is the amount of expenses they can deduct for 2012?

A. $1,750.
B. $10,250.
C. $1,350.
D. $1,400.

The answer is D. Neither the homeowners' association dues nor the fine are deductible. The tax preparation fees did not exceed 2% of adjusted gross income, and therefore are not deductible. The amount of the burglary loss, less $100, that exceeds 10% of adjusted gross income is deductible as a casualty loss.

Supporting calculations:

Loss from theft	$9,000
Less $100 threshold	($100)
Loss after $100 limit	$8,900
Adjusted gross income	$75,000
Multiply by 10% limit	$7,500
Casualty loss deduction ($8,900--$7,500)	$1,400

24. All of the following statements are true except:

A. A taxpayer may deduct job-related expenses, subject to the 2% of AGI limit.
B. Job search costs, such as the use of an employment agency, are deductible expenses.
C. The job search does not have to result in a new job for the taxpayer in order for his expenses to be deductible.
D. A taxpayer may deduct expenses related to the search for a job in a new occupation.

The answer is D. For job search expenses to be deductible, they must relate to the taxpayer's existing occupation. A taxpayer may not deduct expenses if they are connected with the search for a job in a brand new field. ###

25. Wes had a fire in his garage in 2012 that destroyed his car and two beautiful oriental rugs. He had recently bought the car for $30,000. The FMV of the car just before the fire was $27,500. Its FMV after the fire was $500 (scrap value.) He had purchased the rugs for $2,500, and their FMV just before the fire was $5,000. Wes's insurance company reimbursed him a total of $24,000. Wes's AGI in 2012 was $70,000. What is his casualty loss deduction?

A. $0.
B. $3,500.
C. $1,000.
D. $900.

The answer is A. Wes does not have a deductible casualty loss. Since the fair market value of the car was lower than its cost, it is used as the starting point to determine his loss. Net of the salvage value, he had a loss of $27,000 on the car. His loss on the rugs is limited to his original cost since it was lower than FMV. Thus he had total losses of $29,500 before the insurance reimbursement, and a net loss of $5,500. After subtracting the $100 deduction, he had potentially deductible losses of $5,400. However, his deduction is limited to the amount of the losses that exceeds 10% of his AGI, or $7,000. ###

Calculations	Car	Rugs
Basis for the casualty loss	$27,000	$2,500
Insurance reimbursement	$24,000	
Net loss after insurance reimbursement ($29,500 -$24,000)	$5,500	
Subtract $100	$5,400	
AGI X 10% ($70,000 X 10%)	$7,000	
Allowable casualty loss	$0	

Unit 9: Tax Credits

More Reading:
Publication 972, *Child Tax Credit*
Publication 503, *Child and Dependent Care Expenses*
Publication 596, *Earned Income Credit*
Publication 970, *Tax Benefits for Education*
Publication 514, *Foreign Tax Credit for Individuals*

A tax credit directly reduces tax liability, which means it is usually more valuable than a tax deduction of the same dollar amount. It is important to understand this distinction for the EA exam. A tax deduction will reduce income that is subject to tax, but a tax credit will actually reduce tax *liability*—the amount the taxpayer is required to pay the IRS.

In some cases, such as with the Earned Income Credit, a tax credit is refundable. This can create a tax refund—even if the taxpayer does not owe any tax. There are two types of tax credits:

- **Nonrefundable credits**
- **Refundable credits**

Nonrefundable Tax Credits

A nonrefundable tax credit reduces tax liability dollar-for-dollar. It can cut the amount a taxpayer owes to zero but not beyond that, which means that any remaining credit will not be refunded to the taxpayer.

Most tax credits are nonrefundable, and some of the most common are:
- Child and Dependent Care Credit
- Child Tax Credit
- American Opportunity Credit (partially refundable but very restricted, so is nonrefundable for most taxpayers)
- Lifetime Learning Credit
- Retirement Savings Contributions Credit
- Residential energy credits
- Adoption Credit (refundable in 2010 and 2011, but nonrefundable again for 2012)

Refundable Tax Credits

A refundable tax credit is a credit that can produce a tax refund even if the taxpayer does not owe any tax. Refundable tax credits that can reduce tax liability below zero include the following:
- Credit for Excess Social Security Tax or Railroad Retirement Tax Withheld
- Additional Child Tax Credit
- Earned Income Credit

Child and Dependent Care Credit

The Child and Dependent Care Credit allows a taxpayer a credit for a percentage of child care expenses for children under age 13 and disabled dependents of any age. This is a nonrefundable credit for child care expenses that allow taxpayers to work or to seek work. The credit offsets regular tax and the alternative minimum tax.

Under the American Taxpayer Relief Act of 2012, the credit has increased to $3,000 for one child and $6,000 for two or more children.

The credit ranges from 20% to 35% of qualifying expenses, depending on a taxpayer's income. Taxpayers with AGI of $43,000 or more are allowed a credit of only 20% of qualifying expenses. However, the credit is not phased out at higher income levels.

A taxpayer must pass five eligibility tests in order to qualify for this credit:

- Qualifying person test
- Earned income test
- Work-related expense test
- Joint return test
- Provider identification test

Qualifying Person Test

For purposes of this credit, a qualifying person is:

- A dependent child under the age of 13
- A spouse who is physically or mentally unable to care for himself or herself
- Any other dependents who are unable to care for themselves

Example: Samuel paid someone to care for his wife, Janet, so he could work. Janet is permanently disabled and requires an in-home care aide. Samuel also paid to have someone prepare meals for his 12-year-old daughter, Jill. Both Janet and Jill are qualifying persons for the credit.

Only a custodial parent may take the Child and Dependent Care Credit.

Earned Income Test

Both the taxpayer and his or her spouse if married must have earned income during the year in order to qualify for this credit. This generally means both spouses must work. The credit is not available to MFS filers.

The taxpayer's spouse is treated as having earned income for any month he or she is:

- A full-time student, or
- Disabled

Example: Jessica and Quincy are married. Quincy worked full-time as a custodian in 2012. Jessica attended school full-time from January 1 to June 30. She was unemployed during the summer months and did not attend school the rest of the year. Jessica should be treated as having earned income for the six months she attended school full-time.

Work-Related Expense Test

Child and dependent care expenses must be work-related to qualify for this credit, meaning a taxpayer must be working or searching for work. Expenses incurred so that a spouse may do volunteer work or take care of personal business, or for a married couple to go on a "date night" do not qualify.

> **Example:** Patsy is a stay-at-home mom who volunteers several hours a week at a local autism information hotline. Her husband works full-time as a school vice-principal. They pay a babysitter to stay with their young daughter during the hours Patsy volunteers. The couple does not qualify for the dependent care credit because the babysitting expense is not work-related. Since Patsy does not have a job, is not disabled, and is not a full-time student, the child care expenses are ineligible.

> **Example:** Darcy's four-year-old son attends a daycare center while she works three days a week. The daycare charges $150 for three days a week and $250 for five days a week. Sometimes Darcy pays the extra money so she can run errands on her days off. However, this extra charge is not a qualifying expense. Darcy's deductible expenses are limited to $150 a week, the amount of her work-related daycare expense.

The following kinds of expenses qualify for the Child and Dependent Care Credit:

- Education: Preschool or other programs below the level of kindergarten; before or after-school care of a child in kindergarten or above
- Care outside the home for a child under 13 or a care center for a disabled dependent
- Transportation for a care provider to take a qualifying person to or from a place where care is provided
- Fees and deposits paid to an agency or preschool to acquire child care
- Household services, if they are at least partly for the well-being and protection of a qualifying person

> **Example:** Roger's 10-year-old child attends a private school. In addition to paying for tuition, Roger pays an extra fee for before and after-school care so he can be at work during his scheduled hours. Roger can count the cost of the before and after-school program when figuring the credit, but not the cost of tuition.

> **Example:** Emily is single and her elderly mother, Lorraine, is her dependent. Lorraine is completely disabled and must be in an adult daycare so she does not injure herself. Emily pays $8,000 per year for Lorraine to be in the adult daycare. Emily may take the dependent care credit, because Lorraine is disabled and incapable of self-care.

Examples of child care expenses that do not qualify include:

- Tuition costs for children in kindergarten and above
- Summer school or tutoring programs
- The cost of sending a child to an overnight camp (but day camps generally do qualify)
- The cost of transportation not provided by a care provider
- A forfeited deposit to a daycare center (since it is not for care and so is not a work-related expense)

Example: Ellie is divorced and has custody of her 12-year-old daughter, Destiny, who takes care of herself after school. In August, Ellie spends $2,000 to send Destiny to an overnight camp for two weeks. She also sends Destiny to a Girl Scout day camp for a week in July while Ellie is working. The cost of the Girl Scout camp is $75. Ellie may only count the $75 toward the child care credit because the cost of sending a child to an overnight camp is not considered a work-related expense. Next summer, when Destiny turns 13, she will no longer be a qualifying child under the rules of this credit.

Care expenses do not include amounts paid for food, clothing, education, or entertainment. Small amounts paid for these items, however, can be included if they are incidental and cannot be separated from the cost of care.

Example: Krista takes her three-year-old child to a nursery school that provides lunch and educational activities as part of its program. The meals are included in the overall cost of care, and they are not itemized on her bill. Krista can count the total cost when she figures the credit.

Payments for child care will not qualify for the credit if made to a family member who is either:

- The taxpayer's own child under age 19
- Any other dependent listed on the taxpayer's tax return

Taxpayers may combine costs for multiple dependents. For example, if a taxpayer pays daycare for three qualifying children, the $6,000 limit does not need to be divided equally among them.

Example: Alec has three children. His qualifying daycare expenses for his first child are $2,300. His qualifying expenses for his second child are $2,800, and the expenses for his last child are $900. Alec is allowed to use the total amount, $6,000, when figuring his credit.

Example: Diego and Valeria both work and have three children. They have $2,000 in daycare expenses for their son, Miguel; $3,000 for their son, Marcelo; and $4,000 for their daughter, Cecilia. Although their total child care expenses are $9,000, they may only use the first $6,000 as their basis for the Child and Dependent Care Credit.

Example: Lori is a single mother with a dependent child, Noah, who is five years old. Lori takes Noah to daycare five days per week so she can work. Lori makes $46,000 in wages and spends $5,200 per year on daycare for Noah. The maximum that Lori can claim as a dependent care credit is $3,000 since she only has one qualifying child, even though her actual expenses exceed that amount.

Joint Return Test

The joint return test specifies that married couples who wish to take the credit for child and dependent care must file jointly. However, a married taxpayer can be "considered unmarried" for tax purposes if he qualifies for head of household filing status. Taxpayers who file separately are not eligible for this credit.

In the case of divorced or separated taxpayers, only the custodial parent is allowed to take the Child and Dependent Care Credit.

Provider Identification Test

This test requires that taxpayers provide the name, address, and Taxpayer Identification Number of the person or organization who provided the care for the child or dependent.

If a daycare provider refuses to supply identification information, the taxpayer may still claim the credit. He must report whatever information he has (such as the provider's name and address) and attach a statement to Form 2441, *Child and Dependent Care Expenses,* explaining the provider's refusal to supply the information.

Child Tax Credit and Additional Child Tax Credit

Taxpayers with income below certain threshold amounts may claim the Child Tax Credit to reduce income tax for each qualifying child under the age of 17.

- **Child Tax Credit:** This is a *nonrefundable* credit of up to $1,000 per qualifying child. Taxpayers whose tax liability is zero cannot take the Child Tax Credit because there is no tax to reduce. However, taxpayers may be able to take the additional Child Tax Credit, which is refundable, even if their tax liability is zero.
- **Additional Child Tax Credit:** This is a *refundable* credit that may result in a refund even if the taxpayer does not owe any tax. Taxpayers who claim the Additional Child Tax Credit must claim the Child Tax Credit as well, even if they do not qualify for the full amount.

The Child Tax Credit is reduced if the taxpayer's modified adjusted gross income is above the threshold amounts shown below:

- Married filing jointly: $110,000
- Single, head of household, or qualifying widow(er): $75,000
- Married filing separately: $55,000

The credit is phased out incrementally as the taxpayer's income increases. The credit is reduced by $50 for each $1,000 of MAGI that exceeds the threshold amounts listed above.

In addition, the Child Tax Credit is limited by the amount of income tax and any alternative minimum tax owed.

Example: Cordell and Roxana file jointly and have two children who qualify for the Child Tax Credit. Their MAGI is $86,000 and their tax liability is $954. Even though their AGI is less than the threshold limit of $110,000, they can only claim $954, reducing their tax to zero. Because Cordell and Roxana cannot claim the maximum Child Tax Credit of $1,000, they may still be eligible for the additional Child Tax Credit.

Example: Clint files as head of household and has three children who qualify for purposes of the Child Tax Credit. His MAGI is $54,000 and his tax liability is $4,680. Clint is eligible to take the full credit of $1,000 per child ($3,000) because his MAGI is less than $75,000 and his tax liability is greater than $3,000.

Definition of a Qualifying Child for the Child Tax Credit

To be eligible to claim the Child Tax Credit, the taxpayer must have at least one qualifying child. To qualify, the child must:

- Be claimed as the taxpayer's dependent.

- Meet the relationship test: must be the son, daughter, adopted child, stepchild, foster child, brother, sister, stepbrother, stepsister, or a descendant of any of them (for example, a grandchild, niece, or nephew).
- Meet the age criteria: *under* the age of 17 at the end of the year.
- Not have provided over half of his or her own support.
- Have lived with the taxpayer for more than six months of the tax year.[55]
- Be a U.S. citizen, U.S. national, or resident of the U.S. Foreign-born adopted children will qualify if they lived with the taxpayer all year, even if the adoption is not yet final.

Example: Ed's son, Jeff, turned 17 on December 31, 2012. He is a citizen of the United States and has a valid SSN. According to the Child Tax Credit rules, he is not a qualifying child because he was not under the age of 17 at the end of 2012.

Example: Laura's adopted son, Nash, is 12. He is a United States citizen and lived with Laura for the entire tax year. Laura provided all of her son's support. Nash is a qualifying child for the Child Tax Credit because he was under the age of 17 at the end of the tax year; he meets the relationship requirement; he lived with Laura for at least six months of the year; and Laura provided his complete support.

Additional Child Tax Credit

The Additional Child Tax Credit is for certain individuals who do not qualify for the full amount of the nonrefundable Child Tax Credit. Since the Additional Child Tax Credit is *refundable*, it can produce a refund even if the taxpayer does not owe any tax.

Like the Child Tax Credit, the Additional Child Tax Credit allows eligible taxpayers to claim up to $1,000 for each qualifying child after subtracting the allowable amount of Child Tax Credit. For taxpayers with earned income over $3,000, the credit is based on the lesser of:

- 15% of the taxpayer's taxable earned income that is more than $3,000, or
- The amount of unused Child Tax Credit (caused when tax liability is less than the allowed credit).

Example: May and Dmitri have two qualifying children, a MAGI of $66,000, and a tax liability of $850. Because their tax liability is less than the full amount of the Child Tax Credit, they may be able to take the additional Child Tax Credit of up to $1,150 ($2,000 - $850).

In 2012, the IRS changed Form 8812 for the Additional Child Tax Credit to Schedule 8812. The schedule is now used to report both the Child Tax Credit and the Additional Child Tax Credit.

Adoption Credit

In 2012, a maximum nonrefundable credit of up to $12,650 per child can be taken for qualified expenses paid to adopt a child. For a special needs child, the credit is allowed even if the taxpayer does not have any adoption expenses.

The Adoption Credit phases out ratably between $189,710 and $229,710. The phase-out ranges are the same for all taxpayers regardless of filing status.

---

[55] There are special rules for children of divorced or separated parents, as well as children of parents who never married. In some cases the noncustodial parent may be entitled to claim the dependency exemption for a child and thus the Child Tax Credit and additional Child Tax Credit.

If a taxpayer receives employer-provided adoption benefits that are excluded from income, he may still be able to take the Adoption Credit. However, the exclusion and the credit cannot be claimed for the same expense.

Since the Adoption Credit is nonrefundable, any unused credit may be carried forward for five years. Qualified adoption expenses are directly related to the adoption of a child. These include:

- Adoption fees
- Court costs
- Attorney fees
- Travel expenses related to the adoption
- Re-adoption expenses to adopt a foreign child

Qualified adoption expenses do not include:

- Illegal adoption expenses
- A surrogate parenting arrangement
- The adoption of a spouse's child
- Any amounts that were reimbursed by an employer or any other organization

An eligible child is:

- Under 18 years old, or
- Disabled (of any age).

Until the adoption becomes final, a taxpayer may take the credit in the year after expenses were paid. Once the adoption becomes final, a taxpayer can take the credit in the year the expenses were paid.

Special needs child: A taxpayer may claim the full credit regardless of actual expenses paid or incurred. A special needs child is defined in the following ways:

- A United States citizen or resident.
- A state has determined the child cannot or should not be returned to his or her parents' home.
- A state has determined that the child will not be adopted unless assistance is provided to the adoptive parents.

In making the determination about special needs, a state may take into account the following factors: a child's ethnic background and age; whether he is a member of a minority or sibling group; and whether he has a physical, mental, or emotional handicap.

Example: Noel and Cassie adopt a special needs child, and the adoption is finalized in 2012. Their actual adoption expenses are $7,500. They are still allowed to take the full $12,650 credit in 2012.

Unsuccessful adoptions: A taxpayer who has attempted to adopt a child but is unsuccessful is still eligible for the Adoption Credit. Expenses are combined when there are multiple attempts to adopt, or when another adoption attempt is successful and finalized.

Foreign child: If the eligible child is from a foreign country, the taxpayer cannot take the Adoption Credit unless the adoption becomes final. A foreign child is defined as a child who was not a citizen or resident of the United States at the time the adoption effort began.

Education Credits in General

There are two education credits available that are based on qualified expenses a taxpayer pays for postsecondary education (college):

- The American Opportunity Credit[56]
- The Lifetime Learning Credit

There are general rules that apply to these credits, as well as specific rules for each. For example, taxpayers may take education credits for themselves, their spouse, and their dependents who attended an eligible educational institution during the tax year. Eligible educational institutions include colleges, universities, vocational schools, or community colleges. Taxpayers can claim payments that were prepaid for the academic period that begins in the first three months of the next calendar year.

> **Example:** Tom paid $1,500 in December 2012 for college tuition for the spring semester that begins in January 2013. Tom can deduct the $1,500 education credit on his 2012 return, even though he will not start college until 2013.

A taxpayer cannot claim education credits if he:

- can be claimed as a dependent on someone else's tax return
- files as married filing separately
- has AGI above the limit for the taxpayer's filing status
- or his spouse was a nonresident alien for any part of the tax year[57]

To claim the credit for a dependent's education expenses, the taxpayer must claim the dependent on his return, but he does not necessarily have to pay for all of the dependent's qualified education expenses.

In some circumstances, eligible students may claim education credits for themselves even if their parents actually paid the qualified tuition and related expenses. This would be the same tax treatment as if the parent had given the student a gift.

If a taxpayer does not claim an exemption for a dependent who is an eligible student, the student may claim the American Opportunity or Lifetime Learning Credit on his own return, if the situation applies.[58]

> **Example:** Cathy has a 19-year-old son named Trent who is her dependent and a full-time college student. Trent's grandmother paid his tuition directly to the college. For purposes of claiming an education credit, Cathy is treated as receiving the money as a gift and paying for the qualified tuition and related expenses. Since Cathy claims Trent as a dependent, she may still claim an education credit. Alternatively, if Trent claims himself on his own return and his mother does not, he might be able to claim the expenses as if he paid them himself.

If a taxpayer has education expenses for more than one student, he can take the American Opportunity Credit and the Lifetime Learning Credit on a per student basis. This

---

[56] The American Opportunity Credit was scheduled to expire in 2012, but was retroactively extended by the American Taxpayer Relief Act of 2012.

[57] In a case when one spouse is a U.S. citizen or a resident alien and the other spouse is a nonresident alien, the taxpayers may elect to treat the nonresident spouse as a U.S. resident. If the taxpayers make this choice, both spouses are treated as residents for income tax purposes and for withholding purposes.

[58] This concept is covered in more detail in Publication 970, with various examples.

means that a taxpayer may claim the American Opportunity Credit for one student and the Lifetime Learning Credit for another student on the same tax return.

> **Example:** Reed pays college expenses for himself and his dependent daughter, who is 18. Reed goes to graduate school, and he qualifies for the Lifetime Learning Credit. His daughter is an undergraduate, and she qualifies for the American Opportunity Credit. He can choose to take both credits on his tax return because he has two eligible students, his daughter and himself.

Qualified Education Expenses

Qualified education expenses are tuition and required related expenses.

> **Example:** Elias is a college senior who is studying to be a dentist. This year, in addition to tuition, he pays a fee to the university for the rental of the dental equipment he is required to use in the program. Elias's equipment rental fee is a qualified education expense.

Expenses that do not qualify include:

- Room and board
- Medical expenses, including student health fees
- Insurance
- Transportation or personal, living, or family expenses

Any course of instruction or other education involving sports, games, or hobbies is not a qualifying expense *unless* the course is part of the student's degree program.

Tuition expenses are reported to the taxpayer on Form 1098-T, *Tuition Statement*, issued by the school. Qualified education expenses must be reduced by the amount of any tax-free educational assistance received, such as Pell grants, tax-free portions of scholarships, and employer-provided educational assistance.

> **Example:** Faith received Form 1098-T from the college she attends. It shows that her tuition was $9,500 and that she received a $1,500 tax-free scholarship. Her maximum qualifying expenses for the education credit would be $8,000 ($9,500 - $1,500).

> **Example:** In 2012, Jacqueline paid $3,000 for tuition and $5,000 for room and board at her university. She was also awarded a $2,000 tax-free scholarship and a $4,000 student loan. To qualify for the education credit, she must first subtract the tax-free scholarship from her tuition, her only qualified expense. A student loan is not considered tax-free educational assistance because it must be paid back, so it is not income. To calculate her education credit, Jacqueline only had $1,000 in qualified expenses ($3,000 tuition - $2,000 scholarship).

American Opportunity Credit (AOC)

The American Opportunity Credit (AOC) allows taxpayers to claim a credit of up to $2,500 based on qualified tuition and related expenses paid for each eligible student. The credit covers: 100% of the first $2,000, and 25% of the second $2,000 of eligible expenses. This credit applies *per student*, up to the amount of tax. In 2012, under certain conditions, 40% of the AOC is refundable, which means the taxpayer can receive up to $1,000 even if no taxes are owed.[59] Requirements for the AOC are as follows:

---

[59] Because of specific age restrictions, an American Opportunity Credit claimed on a college student's return generally will not be refundable if the student is under age 24. This means, for practical purposes, the credit is nonrefundable for the vast majority of taxpayers.

- **Degree requirement:** The student must be enrolled in a program that leads to a degree, certificate, or other recognized educational credential.
- **Workload:** The student must take at least one-half of the normal full-time workload for at least one academic period beginning during the tax year.
- **No felony drug conviction:** The student must be free of any felony conviction for possessing or distributing a controlled substance.
- **First four years of education:** Only undergraduate education is eligible. A student in graduate school does not qualify for this credit. The credit can only be claimed for four tax years for one student.

The credit phases out for joint filers with income between $160,000 and $180,000 and for single filers with income between $80,000 and $90,000. Couples with income above $180,000 and single filers with income above $90,000 do not qualify.

If a student does not meet all of the conditions for the American Opportunity Credit, he may still be able to take the Lifetime Learning Credit.

Lifetime Learning Credit

The Lifetime Learning Credit is a nonrefundable tax credit of 20% of up to $10,000 of qualified tuition and fees paid during the tax year. The maximum credit is $2,000 per taxpayer. This amount is per tax return, not student. A family's maximum credit is the same regardless of the number of qualified students.

Requirements for the Lifetime Learning Credit are as follows:

- **No workload requirement:** A student is eligible no matter how many or how few courses he takes.
- **Non-degree courses eligible:** A student qualifies if he is simply taking a course to acquire or improve job skills.
- **All levels of postsecondary education:** A student may be an undergraduate, graduate, or professional degree candidate.
- **Unlimited number of years:** There is no limit on the number of years for which the credit can be claimed for each student.

Example: Roland attends Creek Community College after spending six months in prison for a felony cocaine conviction. He paid $4,400 for the course of study, which included tuition, equipment, and books required for the course. The school requires that students pay for books and equipment when registering for courses. The entire $4,400 is an eligible educational expense under the Lifetime Learning Credit. Roland does not qualify for the American Opportunity Credit because he has a drug conviction.

Example: Lai works full-time and takes one course a month at night school. Some of the courses are not for credit, but she is taking them to advance her career. The education expenses qualify for the Lifetime Learning Credit, but not for the American Opportunity Credit.

For 2012, the phase-out for the Lifetime Learning Credit for single filers is between $52,000 and $62,000. For joint filers, the phase-out is between $104,000 to $124,000.

If a taxpayer does not qualify for either of these education credits, he may still qualify for the tuition and fees deduction (as an adjustment to income, covered in Unit 6), which can reduce the amount of taxable income by up to $4,000. However, a taxpayer cannot claim the tuition and fees deduction in the same year that he claims either of the education credits. A taxpayer must choose to take either the tax credit or the deduction, and should consider which provides the greatest tax benefit.

Earned Income Credit

The Earned Income Credit (EIC) is also known as the earned income tax credit (EITC)[60], and it is frequently tested on the EA exam. The EIC is a fully refundable federal income tax credit for lower income people who work and who have earned income under a certain threshold.[61]

Rules for Qualifying for the Earned Income Credit

There are very strict rules and income guidelines for the EIC. To claim the EIC, a taxpayer must meet all of the following tests:

- Must have a valid Social Security Number. Any qualifying child must also have a valid SSN.
- Must have earned income from wages or self-employment.
- Passive income must not exceed $3,200 in 2012.
- Filing status cannot be MFS.
- Must be a U.S. citizen or legal resident all year (or a nonresident alien married to a U.S. citizen or resident alien filing MFJ).
- Cannot be a dependent of another taxpayer.

Qualifying Income for the EIC

Only earned income such as wages qualifies for the EIC. Qualifying earned income also includes:

- Tips
- Union strike benefits
- Net earnings from self-employment

For purposes of the EIC, earned income does not include the following:

- Social Security benefits
- Workfare payments
- Alimony or child support
- Pensions or annuities
- Unemployment benefits

*Note: Inmate wages do not qualify as earned income when figuring the Earned Income Credit. This includes amounts for work performed while in a prison work release program or in a halfway house.

Income that is excluded from tax is generally not considered earned income for the EIC. However, nontaxable combat pay is an exception, if the taxpayer elects to treat it as earned income.

---

[60] The IRS uses both terms. For consistency's sake, we refer to this credit as the Earned Income Credit (EIC), but you should be familiar with the other terminology as well.

[61] Legislation in 2009 increased the EIC to 45% for families with three or more children, and increased the beginning point of the phase-out range for joint filers (regardless of the number of children) to lessen the marriage penalty. The American Taxpayer Relief Act of 2012 extended these provisions through 2017.

Passive income from investments does not qualify as earned income for the EIC. Investment income includes taxable interest and dividends, tax-exempt interest, capital gain net income, and income from residential rental property. In 2012, any amount of investment income above $3,200 disqualifies a taxpayer from claiming the EIC.

Taxpayers Without a Qualifying Child

Low-income taxpayers without children may still qualify for the EIC in certain cases, but the rules are stricter and the amount of the credit is less.

Any taxpayer with a qualifying child may claim the EIC without any age limitations, but a taxpayer *without* a child can only claim the EIC if all of the following tests are met:

- Must be at least age 25, but under 65, at the end of the year (if married, either spouse can meet the age test)
- Must live in the United States for more than half the year
- Must not qualify as a dependent of another person
- Cannot file Form 2555 (related to foreign earned income exclusions[62])

EIC Thresholds and Limitations
2012 Tax Year

Earned income and adjusted gross income must each be less than:

- $45,060 ($50,270 MFJ) with three or more qualifying children
- $41,952 ($47,162 MFJ) with two qualifying children
- $36,920 ($42,130 MFJ) with one qualifying child
- $13,980 ($19,190 MFJ) with no qualifying children

> **Example:** Graham is single and his AGI is $39,000. He has one qualifying child. Graham cannot claim the EIC because his AGI exceeds the income threshold for single filers.

The amount of the Earned Income Credit varies between a maximum of $475 for a taxpayer with no qualifying children up to a maximum of $5,891 for married taxpayers with three or more children.

Qualifying Child Tests for the EIC

The definition of a "qualifying child" for purposes of the EIC is stricter than it is for the dependency exemption. In order to qualify for the EIC, the taxpayer's qualifying child must meet the following four tests:

1. **Relationship Test**
2. **Age Test**
3. **Residency Test**
4. **Joint Return Test**

Relationship Test for EIC

The child must be related to the taxpayer in the following ways:

- Son, daughter, stepchild, eligible foster child, adopted child, or a descendant of any of them (for example, a grandchild), or

---

[62] Taxpayers who do not exclude their foreign income from their gross income (by filing Form 2555 or Form 2555-EZ) may still be eligible for the EIC.

- Brother, sister, half-brother, half-sister, stepbrother, stepsister, or a descendant of any of them (for example, a niece or nephew).

> **Example:** Rusty is 31 and takes care of his younger sister, Colleen, who is 16. He has taken care of her since their parents died five years ago. Colleen is Rusty's qualifying child for purposes of the EIC.

An adopted child is always treated as a taxpayer's own child. An eligible foster child must be placed in the taxpayer's home by an authorized placement agency or by court order.

In the case of a foreign adoption, special rules apply. To claim the EIC, the taxpayer must have a valid SSN. Any qualifying child listed on Schedule EIC also must have a valid SSN. An ATIN number is not sufficient. However, the taxpayer can elect to amend the tax return once an SSN is granted and the adoption is final.

Age Test for EIC

In order to qualify for the EIC, the child must be:

- Age 18 or younger, or
- A full-time student, age 23 or younger, or
- Any age, if permanently disabled.

In addition, the qualifying child must be younger than the taxpayer claiming him, unless the child or person is permanently disabled.

> **Example:** Garth, age 45, supports his older brother, Jeremiah, age 56. Jeremiah, who is mentally challenged and permanently disabled, lives with Garth. In this case, Jeremiah meets the criteria to be Garth's qualifying child for purposes of the EIC.

Residency Test and Joint Return Test

The qualifying child (dependent) may not file a joint return with a spouse, except to claim a refund.

> **Example:** Margaret's 18-year-old son and his 18-year-old wife had $800 of interest income and no other income. Neither is required to file a tax return. Taxes were taken out of their interest income due to backup withholding, so they file a joint return only to get a refund of the withheld taxes. The exception to the joint return test applies, so Margaret's son may still be her qualifying child if all the other tests are met.

For the residency test, the child must have lived with the taxpayer in the United States for more than half of 2012. U.S. military personnel stationed outside the United States are considered to meet the residency test for purposes of the EIC.

A child who was born or died in 2012 meets the residency test for the entire year if the child lived with the taxpayer the entire time he or she was alive in 2012.

> **Example:** Tawanda gave birth to a baby boy in March 2012. The infant died one month later. The child would still be a qualifying child for purposes of the EIC because he meets the other tests for age and relationship.

EIC Fraud and Penalties

Taxpayers who improperly claim the EIC with a reckless or intentional disregard of the rules cannot take the credit for the next two years. Those who fraudulently claim the EIC may be banned from taking the credit for ten years.

Tax professionals face significant due diligence requirements in preparing EIC claims for their clients. A $500 penalty per failure is imposed on any preparer who fails to meet these requirements. For a more detailed discussion of the EIC, see Part 3 (Representation) of the EA PassKey Review.

Retirement Savings Contributions Credit (Saver's Credit)

Qualified individuals are allowed a nonrefundable credit of up to $1,000 ($2,000 MFJ) for eligible contributions to an IRA or an employer-sponsored retirement plan. The amount of the credit is the eligible contribution multiplied by the credit rate, based on filing status and AGI.

To be eligible for this credit,[63] a taxpayer must be at least 18 years old, and must not be a full-time student or claimed as a dependent on another person's return. In 2012, modified AGI cannot be more than:

- $57,500 for married filing jointly
- $43,125 for head of household
- $28,750 for single, married filing separately, or qualifying widow(er)

Example: Truman is 24 and earns $32,000 during the year. He is single and contributes $3,000 to his 401(k) plan at work. Truman is not eligible for the credit because his income exceeds the threshold limit of $28,750.

The taxpayer must have made voluntary contributions to a qualified retirement plan, including traditional IRAs and Roth IRAs; tax-exempt employee-funded pension plans; elective deferrals to 401(k) plans; and voluntary after-tax contributions to any qualified retirement plan or IRA.

Most workers who contribute to traditional IRAs already deduct all or part of their contributions. The Saver's Credit is in addition to these other deductions.

When figuring the credit, a taxpayer generally must subtract the amount of distributions received from his retirement plans from the contributions he has made. This rule applies to distributions received in the two years before the year the credit is claimed; the year the credit is claimed; and the period after the end of the credit year but before the due date, including extensions, for filing the return for the credit year.

Example: Rashid and Angela filed joint returns in 2010 and 2011, and plan to do so in 2012 and 2013. Rashid received a taxable distribution from a qualified plan in 2010 and a taxable distribution from an eligible deferred compensation plan in 2011. Angela received taxable distributions from a Traditional IRA in 2012 and tax-free distributions from a Roth IRA in 2013 before April 15. Rashid contributes to an IRA in 2012, and he and Angela qualify for the credit. Their modified adjusted gross income in 2012 is $53,000, below the Saver's Credit income limit. Rashid and Angela must reduce the amount of their qualifying contributions in 2012 by the total of the distributions they receive in 2010, 2011, 2012, and 2013.

The Saver's Credit amount can be as low as 10% or as high as 50% of a maximum annual contribution of $2,000 per person, depending on filing status and AGI.

---

[63]The IRS also refers to this credit as the "Saver's Credit," so either term may be used on the EA exam.

Foreign Tax Credit

The nonrefundable Foreign Tax Credit is designed to relieve taxpayers of the double tax burden that occurs when their foreign source income is taxed by both the U.S. and the foreign country.

U.S. citizens and resident aliens are eligible for the Foreign Tax Credit. Nonresident aliens are not eligible. Foreign tax paid is usually reported to the taxpayer by the financial institution on Form 1099-INT or Form 1099-DIV.

Four tests must be met to qualify for the credit:

- The tax must be imposed on the taxpayer.
- The taxpayer must have paid (or accrued) the tax.
- The tax must be a legal and actual foreign tax liability.
- The tax must be an income tax.

Taxpayers may claim the credit on line 47 of Form 1040 if, among other conditions, all foreign income is passive income and total taxes paid do not exceed $300 ($600 MFJ). If the tax paid exceeds $300 ($600 MFJ), then taxpayers must file Form 1116, *Foreign Tax Credit*, in order to claim the credit.

> **Example:** Yusuf and Fatima are married and file jointly. They own a number of foreign stocks, and their Form 1099-DIV shows foreign tax paid of $590. The couple is not required to complete Form 1116, because their foreign taxes are less than $600.

> **Example:** Colette is a shareholder of a French corporation. She receives $300 in earnings from the corporation. The French government imposes a 10% tax ($30) on Colette's earnings. She must include the gross earnings ($300) in her income. The $30 of tax withheld is a qualified foreign tax for purposes of the Foreign Tax Credit.

In most cases, it is to the taxpayer's advantage to take the Foreign Tax Credit since a credit directly reduces tax liability. However, taxpayers have the option to itemize foreign taxes as "Other Taxes" on Schedule A. They may choose either the deduction or the credit, whichever gives them the lowest tax, for all foreign taxes paid. Taxpayers cannot claim both the deduction and the tax credit on the same return. However, a taxpayer may alternate years, taking a credit in one year and a deduction in the next year.

Taxpayers also may not claim the Foreign Tax Credit for taxes paid on any income that has already been excluded from income using the foreign earned income exclusion or the foreign housing exclusion.

> ***Note:** Do not confuse the **Foreign Tax Credit** and the **foreign earned income exclusion**. The foreign earned income exclusion allows a portion of foreign earned income to be completely excluded from income, so it is not taxed. The Foreign Tax Credit adds the taxpayer's foreign income to his taxable income and then *reduces* the U.S. tax by the credit amount. The foreign earned income exclusion only applies to income that is earned while a taxpayer is living and working overseas. The Foreign Tax Credit applies to any type of foreign income, including investments.

Certain taxes do not qualify for the Foreign Tax Credit, including interest or penalties paid to a foreign country, taxes imposed by countries involved with international terrorism, [64] and taxes on foreign oil or gas extraction income.

The Foreign Tax Credit is nonrefundable, and the taxpayer is allowed a one-year carryback and a ten-year carryforward of any unused credit.

The Foreign Tax Credit cannot be more than the taxpayer's total U.S. tax liability multiplied by a fraction. The limit on this credit is figured by calculating the total tax liability multiplied by a fraction made up of total foreign income divided by total income from foreign and U.S. sources.

> **Example:** Harold's total tax liability is $1,000. In 2012, he made $20,000 from foreign-based investments, along with another $60,000 from U.S. sources. To figure the limit on the Foreign Tax Credit, Harold must take his total foreign income ($20,000) and divide it by the total income from all sources ($20,000 + $60,000). This gives Harold a fraction of .25, which is multiplied by his total tax liability ($1,000 x .25 = $250). This is the limit on his Foreign Tax Credit.
>
> (Foreign Source Taxable Income ÷ Worldwide Taxable Income) X
> (U.S. Income Tax before Credit = FTC Limitation.)

Residential Energy Credits

Taxpayers who purchase certain qualified energy-efficient improvements for their main home may be allowed a nonrefundable tax credit. There are two types of residential energy credits:

- **Residential Energy Efficient Property Credit**
- **Nonbusiness Energy Property Credit**

Both are nonrefundable credits that are calculated and claimed on IRS Form 5695, *Residential Energy Credits.*

Nonbusiness Energy Property Credit: Taxpayers may claim this credit for energy efficient property placed in service in 2012. The credit is equal to 30% of the cost of the following property:

- Solar energy systems (water heating and electricity)
- Fuel cells
- Small wind energy systems
- Geothermal heat pumps

No credit is allowed for equipment used to heat swimming pools or hot tubs. The credit is allowed for new construction as well as improvements to existing homes located in the United States.

Residential Energy Efficient Property Credit: The credit is equal to 10% of the cost of qualified energy efficient improvements to existing homes, plus 100% of the cost of any residential energy property costs paid or incurred in 2012. [65] Various credit amounts are given

---

[64] The list of terrorist nations includes Cuba, the Sudan, and North Korea— a full list of excluded nations is published in Publication 514, *Foreign Tax Credit for Individuals.*
[65] The American Taxpayer Relief Act of 2012 retroactively reinstated this credit for 2012 and extended it through 2013.

for qualified fans; furnaces and hot water boilers; electric heat pumps; biomass fuel stoves; central air conditioners; and certain types of water heaters. The total combined amount of credit that can be claimed is $500 for all tax years after 2005, or a combined $200 limit for exterior windows after 2005.

Additional Individual Taxpayer Energy Credits

The IRS also allows credits for other energy-related expenses:

- **Plug-in Electric Motorcycles and 3-Wheeled Vehicles:** A 10% individual income tax credit. Under revisions to the credit, golf carts and other low-speed vehicles do not qualify.[66]
- **Alternative Fuel Vehicle Property:** A 30% credit for the cost of installing qualified clean-fuel vehicle refueling property at a taxpayer's principal residence. The credit is limited to $1,000 per taxable year for nonbusiness taxpayers.[67]

Other Credits

A number of other credits are not widely used (or widely tested on the EA exam) because they are limited to certain individuals, or for certain types of asset purchases.

- **Mortgage Interest Credit:** Provides a nonrefundable credit to low-income homeowners who hold qualified mortgage credit certificates issued by local or state governments.
- **Health Coverage Tax Credit:** Provides a refundable credit for certain taxpayers who receive pension benefits from the Pension Benefit Guaranty Corporation. The credit pays 72.5% of qualified health insurance premiums for eligible individuals and their families.
- **Credit for Excess Social Security Tax**: Refunds workers who overpay their tax for Social Security, which usually happens when an employee is working two jobs and both employers withhold Social Security tax. If the taxpayer's withholding for Social Security tax exceeds the annual maximum, he can request a refund of the excess amount. This also applies to overpaid Railroad Retirement taxes.
- **Credit for the Elderly or Disabled**: This credit applies only to taxpayers 65 or older or taxpayers under 65 who retired on permanent disability. This nonrefundable tax credit has such strict income limitations that few taxpayers qualify for it.
- **Credit for Prior Year Alternative Minimum Tax**: This credit is available if a taxpayer paid AMT generated by deferral items in a prior year. It can only be used to the extent that regular tax exceeds the tentative minimum tax.

---

[66] Retroactively reinstated and amended for 2012.
[67] Retroactively reinstated for 2012 and extended through 2013.

Unit 9: Questions

1. All of these taxpayers contributed to their employers' 401(k) plan. Which taxpayer qualifies for the Retirement Savings Contributions Credit based on his or her adjusted gross income?

A. Ed, who is single and has an adjusted gross income of $35,200.
B. Sybil, who is married filing jointly and has an adjusted gross income of $55,000.
C. Bert, who is married filing separately and has an adjusted gross income of $30,600.
D. Carl, who is a qualifying widower and has a modified AGI of $29,000.

The answer is B. Sybil qualifies for the credit because her AGI is under $57,500, which is the threshold limit for married filing jointly. Taxpayers who file as single, qualifying widow(er), or married filing separately (such as Ed, Carl, and Bert) cannot qualify if they have an AGI that exceeds the AGI limits. ###

2. Gail's earned income from wages is $7,000. She has interest income of $3,250. She is single and has a valid Social Security Number. She does not have any dependents. Which of the following statements is true?

A. Gail qualifies to claim the Earned Income Credit.
B. Gail does not qualify for the Earned Income Credit.
C. Gail qualifies for the Earned Income Credit and the Child Tax Credit.
D. None of the above.

The answer is B. Gail does not qualify for the EIC because her investment income exceeds $3,200 for 2012. ###

3. For purposes of the EIC, which of the following types of income are considered "earned income"?
A. Alimony.
B. Interest and dividends.
C. Workfare payments.
D. Household employee income reported on Form W-2.

The answer is D. Household employee income is considered earned income, because it is a type of wages. Alimony, workfare payments, and interest and dividends are not considered earned income for purposes of the EIC. ###

4. Orlando is a university senior who is studying to be an optometrist. Which of the following expenses is a qualifying expense for the American Opportunity Credit?

A. The rental of the vision equipment he is required to use in this program.
B. Student health fees.
C. Room and board.
D. A physical education course not related to his degree program.

The answer is A. Because Orlando's equipment rental fee must be paid to the university as a condition for enrollment, it is considered a qualified related expense. Qualified tuition and related expenses do not include insurance or medical expenses (student health fees), room and board, transportation, or similar personal, living, or family expenses even if the fees must be paid to the institution as a condition of enrollment or attendance, or any course of instruction or other education involving sports, games, or hobbies, *unless* the course is part of the student's degree program. ###

5. Which of the following would be a qualifying child for purposes of the Child Tax Credit?

A. An 18-year-old dependent who is a full-time student.
B. A six-year-old nephew who lived with the taxpayer for seven months.
C. A child actor who is 15 years old and provides over half of his own support.
D. A foster child who has lived with the taxpayer for four months.

The answer is B. A nephew that lived with the taxpayer for seven months may qualify. In order to qualify for the Child Tax Credit, the taxpayer must have a qualifying child who lived with him for more than six months and who is under the age of 17. The child cannot have provided more than half of his own support. ###

6. Beatrice has three dependent children, ages 2, 12, and 18, who live with her. Assuming she meets the other criteria, what is the maximum Child Tax Credit she can claim on her 2012 tax return?

A. $0.
B. $1,000.
C. $2,000.
D. $3,000.

The answer is C. Beatrice can claim $2,000 as a maximum credit, or $1,000 for each qualifying child. For purposes of this credit, she only has two qualifying children, because one of her dependents is already over 17 and therefore no longer eligible for the credit. ###

7. Scott is 43 and unmarried. Scott's half-brother, Hayden, turned 16 on December 30, 2012. Hayden lived with Scott all year, and he is a U.S. citizen. Scott claimed Hayden as a dependent on his return. Which of the following is true?

A. Hayden is a qualifying child for the Child Tax Credit.
B. Hayden is not a qualifying child for the Child Tax Credit.
C. Hayden is not a qualifying child for the Child Tax Credit because siblings do not qualify.
D. Hayden only qualifies for the Child Tax Credit if he is a full-time student.

The answer is A. Hayden is a qualifying child for the Child Tax Credit because he was under age 17 at the end of 2012. Siblings can be qualifying children for purposes of this credit. ###

8. Which of the following statements regarding the Foreign Tax Credit is correct?

A. The Foreign Tax Credit is a refundable credit.
B. The Foreign Tax Credit is available to U.S. citizens and nonresident aliens.
C. Taxpayers may choose to take a deduction for foreign taxes paid rather than the Foreign Tax Credit.
D. Taxpayers can choose to claim both a deduction and a tax credit for foreign taxes paid, so long as the taxes were paid to different countries.

The answer is C. Taxpayers have the option to itemize foreign taxes on Schedule A. They may choose either the deduction or the credit, whichever gives them the lowest tax, for all foreign taxes paid. Taxpayers cannot choose to claim both the deduction and a tax credit on the same return. ###

9. The Lifetime Learning Credit is different from the American Opportunity Credit. However, they do share some of the same requirements. Which of the following requirements is true for both education credits?

A. There is no limit to the number of years the credits can be claimed.
B. Expenses related to housing are allowed as qualified education expenses.
C. The credits are available for only the first two years of postsecondary education.
D. To be eligible for either of the education credits, taxpayers must use any filing status other than married filing separately.

The answer is D. Taxpayers who use the filing status of married filing separately are not eligible to claim either the American Opportunity or Lifetime Learning Credits. ###

10. All of the following items are deductible as education-related expenses for the Lifetime Learning Credit except:

A. Required books.
B. On-campus child care in order to attend class.
C. Tuition.
D. Required fees.

The answer is B. Daycare is not a qualifying education expense. For purposes of the Lifetime Learning Credit, qualified education expenses are tuition and certain related expenses required for enrollment or attendance at an eligible educational institution. ###

11. Which of the following individuals is eligible for the American Opportunity Credit?

A. Garrett, who is enrolled full-time as a postgraduate student pursuing a master's degree in biology.
B. Lucy, who is taking a ceramics class at a community college.
C. Doug, who was convicted of a felony for distributing a controlled substance.
D. Beth, who is taking three-quarters of the normal full-time course load required for a computer science associate's degree program and who attended classes the entire school year in 2012.

The answer is D. Beth is eligible for the American Opportunity Credit because she is taking at least one-half of the normal full-time workload for her course of study for at least one academic period beginning in 2012. Graduate courses do not qualify, and courses that do not lead to a degree, certificate, or other recognized credential also do not qualify for this educational credit. Persons with felony drug convictions are ineligible for this credit. ###

12. In 2012, what is the maximum amount of the American Opportunity Credit?

A. $2,500 per tax return.
B. $2,500 per student.
C. $2,000 per tax return.
D. $1,000 per student.

The answer is B. In 2012 the maximum credit is $2,500 per student. The credit is *per* student *per* year, and the taxpayer's family may have more than one eligible student per tax return. ###

13. What is the maximum amount of the Lifetime Learning Credit in 2012?

A. $2,000 per student.
B. $2,500 per student.
C. $1,000 per student.
D. $2,000 per tax return.

The answer is D. The maximum credit is $2,000 per tax return. The credit is allowed for 20% of the first $10,000 of qualified tuition and fees paid during the year. The credit is per tax return, not per student, so only a maximum of $2,000 can be claimed each year, no matter how many qualifying students a taxpayer may have. ###

14. Samira and Rishi are married and file jointly. Their daughter, Chetana, was enrolled full-time in college for all of 2012. Samira and Rishi obtained a loan in 2012 and used the proceeds to pay for Chetana's tuition and related fees. They repaid the loan in 2013. When will they be entitled to claim an education credit?

A. They cannot claim an education credit.
B. 2013.
C. 2012.
D. Both 2012 and 2013.

The answer is C. Samira and Rishi are eligible to claim an education credit for the year 2012. The credit should be calculated for the year in which the taxpayer paid the expenses, not the year in which the loan is repaid. ###

15. Edwin is a professional bookkeeper. He decides to take an accounting course at the local community college in order to improve his work-related skills. Edwin is not a degree candidate. Which educational credit does he qualify for?

A. The American Opportunity Credit.
B. The College Saver's Credit.
C. The Lifetime Learning Credit.
D. The Mortgage Interest Credit.

The answer is C. Edwin qualifies for the Lifetime Learning Credit. He does not qualify for the American Opportunity Credit because he is not a degree candidate and because his course work-load does not meet the requirements. The "College Saver's Credit" does not exist. The Mortgage Interest Credit is not an education credit. ###

16. In 2012, Tyrone paid $5,000 of his own funds to cover all of the cost of his college tuition. Tyrone also received a Pell grant for $3,000 and a student loan for $2,000, which he used for housing costs and books. For purposes of figuring an education credit, what are Tyrone's total qualified tuition and related expenses?

A. $10,000.
B. $7,000.
C. $5,000.
D. $2,000.

The answer is D. The total qualified tuition payments are the net of the $5,000 tuition minus the grant of $3,000, which equals $2,000. The $3,000 Pell grant is tax-free, so it is not a qualified tuition and related expense and must be deducted from his overall qualifying costs. ###

17. Based on the Child and Dependent Care Credit rules, which of the following individuals meets the eligibility test for a qualifying person?

A. Jeremy, 5, who is taken care of by his mother at home all day.
B. Virgil, 21, a full-time student supported by his parents.
C. Leroy, 80, who lives at home with his son but is not disabled.
D. Leanne, 52, who is unable to care for herself and is married to Jake, an employed construction worker.

The answer is D. Leanne meets the qualifying person test because she is the spouse of someone who works, and she is unable to care for herself. ###

18. What is the maximum amount of the adoption tax credit for 2012?

A. $10,150.
B. $11,650.
C. $12,550.
D. $12,650.

The answer is D. The maximum credit for 2012 is $12,650 *per child*. If a taxpayer adopts two children, he will be eligible for the full credit on each child. The credit phases out for taxpayers with MAGI between $189,710 and $229,710. ###

19. Geraldine placed a $250 deposit with a preschool to reserve a place for her three-year-old child. Later, she changed jobs and was unable to send her child to that particular preschool, so she forfeited the deposit. She later found another preschool and had $4,000 in qualifying daycare costs. Which of the following is true?

A. The forfeited deposit is not deductible.
B. The forfeited deposit is deductible.
C. The forfeited deposit is a deduction on Schedule A.
D. Geraldine may deduct the deposit because she took her child to another preschool.

The answer is A. The forfeited deposit is not for actual child care, and thus it is not a work-related expense. A forfeited deposit is not actually for the care of a qualifying person, so it cannot be deducted as a child care expense and does not qualify for the Child and Dependent Care Credit. ###

20. Brett and Amy paid daycare for their three-year-old son so they could work. Their child care expenses were $3,000 in 2012. Amy also paid a deposit of $100 to the daycare and an enrollment fee of $35. Brett was reimbursed for $1,200 by his flexible spending account at work. How much of the child care expenses can they use to figure their Child and Dependent Care Credit?

A. $1,800.
B. $1,900.
C. $1,935.
D. $3,135.

The answer is C. Their child care expenses are figured as follows: ($3,000 + $100 + $35) - $1,200 = $1,935. If a taxpayer has a reimbursement under a flexible spending account, those amounts are pre-tax. Taxpayers cannot use reimbursed amounts to figure this credit. Fees and deposits paid to an agency or a daycare provider are qualifying expenses if the taxpayer must pay them in order to receive care. Only a forfeited deposit would be disallowed. ###

21. Nina pays for daycare for each of the following individuals so she can work. All of the following are qualifying individuals for purposes of the Child and Dependent Care Credit except:

A. Nina's husband, who is totally disabled.
B. Nina's son, age 13, who is Nina's dependent.
C. Nina's nephew, age 12, who is also Nina's dependent.
D. Nina's niece, who is 35, lived with her all year, and is completely disabled.

The answer is B. Nina's son does not qualify, because he is over the age limit for the credit. To qualify for the Child and Dependent Care Credit, the qualifying person must be under the age of 13 or completely disabled. ###

22. All of the following are qualified expenses for purposes of the Child and Dependent Care Credit except_____:

A. $500 payment to a grandparent for child care while the taxpayer is gainfully employed.
B. $300 payment to a daycare while the taxpayer is looking for employment.
C. $500 child care expense while the taxpayer obtains medical care.
D. $600 in daycare expense for a disabled spouse while the taxpayer works.

The answer is C. Child care costs to obtain medical care are not a deductible expense. Deductible daycare costs must be work related and for a child under 13, a disabled dependent, or a disabled spouse of any age. Child care so that the taxpayer can volunteer, obtain medical care, run errands, or do other personal business is not qualifying child care. ###

23. Which of the following expenses is not a qualified expense for purposes of the Adoption Credit?

A. Court costs.
B. Re-adoption expenses to adopt a foreign child.
C. Attorney fees for a surrogate arrangement.
D. Travel expenses.

The answer is C. The cost of a surrogate is not a qualified adoption expense. Qualified adoption expenses are expenses directly related to the legal adoption of an eligible child. These expenses include adoption fees, court costs, attorney fees, travel expenses (including amounts spent for meals and lodging) while away from home, and re-adoption expenses to adopt a foreign child. ###

24. Austin is a U.S. citizen who is adopting a foreign child. His income in 2012 was $31,000. The adoption is almost final, and he has an ATIN for the child. The child lived with Austin all year. Which of the following is true?

A. Austin can claim the Earned Income Credit because his child is a qualifying child.
B. Austin's income is too high to claim the Earned Income Credit in 2012.
C. Austin cannot claim the Earned Income Credit in 2012, but he can elect to amend his tax return once an SSN is granted and the adoption is final.
D. The Earned Income Credit is not applicable to foreign-adopted children.

The answer is C. To claim the EIC, the taxpayer must have a valid SSN issued by the Social Security Administration. Any qualifying child listed on Schedule EIC also must have a valid SSN. An ATIN is not sufficient for purposes of the EIC. However, the taxpayer can elect to amend the tax return once an SSN is granted and the adoption is final. ###

25. To qualify for the Earned Income Credit, which of the following is true?

A. The taxpayer must have a dependent child.
B. The taxpayer must be a U.S. citizen or legal U.S. resident all year.
C. The taxpayer's filing status can be MFS if the taxpayer does not live with his or her spouse.
D. The taxpayer's only income may be from Social Security benefits.

The answer is B. The taxpayer must be a U.S. citizen or legal resident all year. Taxpayers do not need to have a dependent child in order to qualify for the Earned Income Credit; however, the EIC is greatly increased if the taxpayer has a qualifying child. Single taxpayers who are low-income may still qualify for the credit. A taxpayer cannot claim the EIC if his filing status is MFS. A taxpayer must have earned income to qualify for the EIC; Social Security benefits do not qualify. ###

26. For those claiming the Earned Income Credit in 2012, the taxpayer's interest or investment income must be _____ or less.

A. $2,950.
B. $3,100.
C. $3,200.
D. $4,000.

The answer is C. For purposes of the EIC, interest or investment income must be $3,200 or less. ###

27. Monty and Belinda are married and living together. Monty earned $12,000 and Belinda earned $9,000 in 2012. They have two minor children and have decided to file MFS tax returns, each claiming one child as a dependent. Which statement is true?

A. They can both qualify for the Earned Income Credit on their MFS tax returns.
B. Based on the information, they may qualify for the EIC on a joint tax return.
C. Monty can file single and qualify for the EIC.
D. Belinda can file as head of household and claim the credit.

The answer is B. Since Monty and Belinda are married and live together, they can choose to file a joint return or each may choose to file separately. A taxpayer cannot qualify for the EIC on a MFS return, so Monty and Belinda must file jointly in order to claim the credit. ####

28. Which of the following filing conditions would not prevent an individual from qualifying for the Earned Income Credit for the year 2012?

A. MFS filing status.
B. A taxpayer with a qualifying child who is 23 and a full-time student.
C. Investment income of $3,300.
D. A taxpayer who is 68 years old without a qualifying child.

The answer is B. All the other choices are disqualifying for purposes of the EIC. At the end of the tax year, the child must be under age 19, or under age 24 and a full-time student, or any age and disabled. ###

29. The Nonbusiness Energy Property Credit can be used for very specific energy systems or improvements to a taxpayer's main home or main home under construction. Which of the following items is not a qualifying item for purposes of the credit?

A. Solar energy systems.
B. Geothermal heat pumps.
C. Small wind energy systems.
D. Energy-efficient windows.

The answer is D. The Nonbusiness Energy Property Credit is a credit of 30% of the costs of solar energy systems, fuel cells, small wind energy systems, and geothermal heat pumps. There is no dollar limit on this credit. Energy-efficient windows do not qualify for this credit, but they may for the Residential Energy Property Credit, which applies to certain other energy-efficient improvements installed in a taxpayer's primary residence. ###

30. Couples who file jointly may be eligible to deduct up to _____ per year for contributions to an IRA under the Retirement Savings Contributions Credit?

A. $500.
B. $1,000.
C. $2,000.
D. $5,000.

The answer is C. MFJ taxpayers are allowed a nonrefundable credit of up to $2,000 for eligible contributions to an IRA or an employer-sponsored retirement plan. The credit is $1,000 per year for single filers. ###

31. Generally, which is more beneficial to taxpayers when it comes to reducing income tax liability: a nonrefundable credit, a refundable credit, or a deduction?

A. A nonrefundable credit.
B. A refundable credit.
C. A deduction.
D. All are equally beneficial in reducing income tax liability.

The answer is B. A refundable credit is not limited by an individual's tax liability. It can provide a taxpayer a refund even if he has zero tax liability. An example is the Earned Income Credit. ###

32. Arlene is single. She has a sixteen-year-old grandson who lived with her from May through December of 2012. She provided 90% of his support and he provided the other 10%. Arlene's MAGI was $85,000 in 2012. Calculate the amount of her Child Tax Credit.

A. $250.
B. $500.
C. $1,000.
D. She is not entitled to the credit because a grandson is not a qualifying child for purposes of the child care credit.

The answer is B. Arlene is entitled to claim the Child Tax Credit because her grandson is a qualifying child for purposes of the credit: she provided more than half of his support, he is under 17, and he lived with her for more than half the year. However, Arlene cannot take the full $1,000 credit for her grandson because her income is above $75,000, the threshold for single, head of household, and qualifying widow(er) filers. The credit is reduced by $50 for each $1,000 of MAGI that exceeds the threshold amount. Thus, Arlene's credit is reduced by $500 (10 X $50). ###

33. Zoe attends Valley Oaks College full-time, pursuing an undergraduate degree in business. Because she changed majors in her junior year, she is now in her fifth year of college. She has a $4,000 Pell grant for the 2012 school year. Her parents have taken the American Opportunity Credit for Zoe the past four years. Calculate the amount her parents can claim for the AOC in 2012 given the following expenses for Zoe's education:

- Tuition: $15,000
- Room and board: $12,000
- Medical insurance: $1,000

A. $0.
B. $2,000.
C. $2,500.
D. $4,800.

The answer is A. Zoe does not qualify for the AOC because she is in her fifth year of college and her parents have already claimed the credit the prior four years. If she had been eligible for the credit, she would have had $11,000 in eligible expenses. Room and board and medical insurance are not qualified expenses for the AOC, and tuition must be reduced by any tax-free scholarships, such as the Pell grant. The AOC is a maximum credit of $2,500 per student (100% of the first $2,000 of eligible expenses and 20% of the next $2,000). Zoe would qualify for the Lifetime Learning Credit. ###

Unit 10: Basis of Property

> **More Reading:**
> Publication 551, *Basis of Assets*
> Publication 544, *Sales and Other Dispositions of Assets*

Understanding Basis

Almost everything a taxpayer owns and uses for personal purposes, pleasure, or investment is a capital asset. Examples include:

- A main home or vacation home
- Furniture, antiques, collectibles
- A car or boat
- Stocks or bonds (except when held for sale by a professional securities dealer)
- Gold, silver, coins, etc. (except when they are held for sale by a professional dealer)

The tax treatment of these assets varies based on whether the asset is personal-use, business property, or investment property.

When capital assets are sold, the difference between the asset's basis and the selling price is a **capital GAIN** or a **capital LOSS**.

In order to correctly calculate capital gains and losses, you must first understand the concept of "basis" and "adjusted basis." The basis of the asset is usually its cost. "Cost basis" is the amount of money invested into a property for tax purposes. Usually this is the cost of the item when it is purchased. However, there are some instances in which basis is different than the cost of the item. Basis is figured in another way when property is acquired by gift or inheritance. The cost basis of an asset can include:

- Sales taxes charged during the purchase
- Freight-in charges
- Installation and testing fees
- Delinquent real estate taxes that are paid by the buyer of a property
- Legal and accounting fees

All of these costs are added to an asset's basis. They are not deductible as an expense, whether or not the asset is business-use or personal-use.

> **Example:** Raoul purchases a new car for $15,000. The sales tax on the vehicle is $1,200. He also pays a delivery charge to have the car shipped from another dealership to his home. The freight charge is $210. Therefore, Raoul's basis in the vehicle is $16,410 ($15,000 + $1,200 + $210).

> **Example:** Hilda is a self-employed writer. She purchases a new printer for her home office. The printer costs $540, with an additional $34 for sales tax. Therefore, Hilda's basis in the item is $574 ($540 + $34).

In order to correctly report a capital gain or loss, a taxpayer needs to identify:

- The asset's **basis** (or adjusted basis):
    - **Basis** is the original cost of the asset.

251

- **Adjusted basis** includes original cost plus any increases or decreases to that cost (such as commissions, fees, depreciation, casualty losses, and insurance reimbursements.)
- The asset's **holding period**:
  - Short-term property is held one year or less.
  - Long-term property is held more than one year.
- The proceeds from the sale.

Basis of Real Property (Real Estate)

The basis of real estate usually includes a number of costs in addition to the purchase price. If a taxpayer purchases real property (a house, a tract of land, a building), certain fees and other expenses automatically become part of the cost basis. This also includes real estate taxes the seller owed at the time of the purchase, if the real estate taxes were paid by the buyer.

> **Example:** Tara sells Lawrence a home for $100,000. She is unemployed and has fallen behind on her property tax payments. Lawrence agrees to pay the delinquent real estate taxes as a condition of the sale. The delinquent property tax at the time of purchase totaled $3,500. The IRS does not allow a taxpayer to deduct property taxes that are not his legal responsibility. Therefore, Lawrence must add the property tax to his basis. Lawrence's basis in the home is $103,500 ($100,000 + $3,500).

If a property is constructed rather than purchased, the basis of the property includes the expenses of construction. This includes the cost of the land, building permits, payments to contractors, lumber, and inspection fees. Demolition costs and other costs related to the preparation of land must be added to the basis of the land.

> **Example:** Wanda purchases an empty lot to build her home. The lot costs $50,000. She also pays $2,800 for the removal of tree stumps before construction can begin. There is also an existing concrete foundation on the lot that Wanda dislikes, so she has the foundation demolished and removed in order to build a new foundation. The demolition costs are $6,700. All of these costs must be added to the basis of the land (not the basis of the building). Therefore, Wanda's basis in the land is $59,500 ($50,000 + $2,800 + $6,700).

Adding Settlement Costs to Basis

Generally, a taxpayer must include settlement costs for the purchase of property in his basis. The following fees are some of the closing costs that can be included in a property's basis:

- Abstract fees
- Charges for installing utilities
- Legal fees (including title search and preparation of the deed)
- Recording fees
- Surveys
- Transfer taxes
- Owner's title insurance

Also included in a property's basis are any amounts the seller legally owes that the buyer agrees to pay, such as back taxes or interest, recording or mortgage fees, charges for improvements or repairs, and sales commissions. A taxpayer cannot include fees incidental to getting a loan.

How to Figure Adjusted Basis

Before figuring gain or loss on a sale or exchange, a taxpayer usually must make increases or decreases to the basis of the property. The result is the **adjusted basis**.

Example: Brian buys a house for $120,000. The following year, he paves the driveway, which costs him $6,000. Brian's *adjusted basis* in the home is now $126,000 ($120,000 original cost + $6,000 in improvements).

Example: Whitney purchases a commercial washing machine for her pet grooming business. The washer costs $1,230, with an additional $62 in sales tax and freight and installation charges of $96. Whitney receives a manufacturer's rebate check for $300 several weeks later. Her basis in the washer is figured as follows:

Cost:	$1,230
Sales tax:	$62
Installation:	$96
Rebate:	($300)
Basis:	**$1,088**

Basis "Other Than" Cost

There are times when a taxpayer cannot use *cost* as the basis for property. In these cases, the fair market value or the adjusted basis of the property can be used. Below are some examples of when an asset's basis will be something other than cost.

Property Received in Exchange for Services

If a taxpayer receives property in payment for services, he must include the property's FMV in income, and this becomes his basis in the property. If two people agree on a cost beforehand and it is deemed reasonable, the IRS will usually accept the agreed-upon cost as the asset's basis.

Example: Cassidy is an EA who prepares tax returns for a long-time client named Katie. Katie then loses her job and cannot pay Cassidy's bill, which totals $450. Katie offers Cassidy an antique vase in lieu of paying her invoice. The fair market value of the vase is approximately $520. Cassidy agrees to accept the vase as full payment on Katie's delinquent invoice. Cassidy's basis in the vase is $450, the amount of the invoice that was agreed upon by both parties.

Basis After Casualty and Theft Losses

If a taxpayer has a casualty loss, he must decrease the basis of the property by any insurance proceeds. A taxpayer may increase the basis in the property by the amount spent on repairs that restore the property to its pre-casualty condition.

Example: Ira paid $5,000 for a car several years ago. It was damaged in a flood, so he spends $3,000 to repair it. He does not have flood insurance on the car. Therefore, his new basis in the car is $8,000 ($5,000 + $3,000).

Remember, after a casualty loss, insurance reimbursements decrease basis, while out-of-pocket repairs increase basis.

Assumption of a Mortgage or Loan

If a taxpayer buys property and assumes an existing mortgage on it, the taxpayer's basis includes the amount paid for the property plus the amount owed on the mortgage. The basis also includes the settlement fees and closing costs paid for buying the property. Fees and costs for getting a loan on the property (points) are not included in a property's basis.

> **Example:** Sondra buys a building for $20,000 cash and assumes a mortgage of $80,000 on it. Therefore, her basis is $100,000.

Basis Adjustments after an Involuntary Conversion

An involuntary conversion occurs when a taxpayer *involuntarily* gives up, sells, or exchanges property. This might happen after a disaster, such as a house fire, drought, or a flood. Involuntary conversions may also occur after casualties, thefts, or the condemnation of property. If a taxpayer receives replacement property as a result of an involuntary conversion, the basis of the replacement property is figured using the basis of the converted property. A taxpayer may also have to figure gain if the amount of the insurance reimbursement exceeds his basis of the asset.

> **Example:** Joy receives insurance money of $8,000 for her shed, which was destroyed by an earthquake. Joy's basis in the shed was $6,000. She uses $6,000 to purchase a new shed. Joy needs to recognize a $2,000 gain, since she realized a gain of $2,000 from the conversion ($8,000 - $6,000) and only used $6,000 of the $8,000 insurance proceeds to replace the shed.

Basis of Securities

A taxpayer's basis in securities (stocks or bonds) is usually the purchase price, plus any additional costs, such as brokers' commissions. In order to compute gain or loss on a sale, taxpayers must provide their basis in the sold property. The basis of stock is usually its cost, but basis can also include other fees.

When a taxpayer sells securities, the investment company will send Form 1099-B, *Proceeds from Broker and Barter Exchange Transactions,* showing the gross proceeds of the sale. Form 1099-B does not usually include how much taxpayers paid; they must keep track of this information themselves. If taxpayers cannot provide their basis, the IRS will deem it to be zero. Many taxpayers own shares of stock they bought on different dates or for different prices. This means they own more than one block of stock. Each block may differ from the others in its holding period (long-term or short-term), its basis (amount paid for the stock), or both.

In directing a broker to sell stock, the taxpayer may specify which block, or part of a block, to sell; this is called *specific identification.* The specific identification method requires good recordkeeping; however, this method simplifies the determination of the holding period and the basis of the stock sold, giving the taxpayer better control and versatility in handling an investment. If the taxpayer cannot identify the specific block at the time of sale, shares sold are treated as coming from the earliest block purchased; this method is called First In, First Out (FIFO).[68]

---

[68] Specific identification and First In, First Out (FIFO) are also common inventory methods that are used by businesses. You will learn more about how these inventory methods are used by businesses in Part 2 of the EA exam course books.

Adjusted Basis of Securities

Events that occur after the purchase of the stock can require adjustments (increases or decreases) to the per share basis of stock. The original basis per share can be changed by events such as stock dividends, stock splits, and dividend reinvestment plan (DRIP) accounts.

- **Stock dividends** are additional shares that companies grant to their shareholders. These additional shares increase the taxpayer's ownership so the original basis is spread over more shares, which decreases the basis per share.
- **Stock splits** occur when a corporation distributes more stock to its existing stockholders as a way to bring down the market price of its stock. For example, in a "2-for-1" stock split, a corporation issues one share of stock for every share outstanding. This then decreases the basis per share by half. The original basis of $200 for 100 shares becomes $200 for 200 shares. (The total basis does not change; only the basis per share of stock changes.)

Basis after a Stock Split (Stock Dividend)

The way to figure basis after a stock split or a stock dividend is to divide the taxpayer's adjusted basis of the old stock between the shares of the old stock and the new stock. For example, this means that if the old stock was priced at $10 per share, after the split each share would be worth $5. This is because the corporation's assets did not increase, only the number of outstanding shares.

Stock acquired in a nontaxable stock dividend or stock split has the same holding period as the original stock. If the original stock has a long-term holding period, stock received in a nontaxable stock dividend also has a long-term holding period. For example, if the original stock has a holding period of three months, the new stock immediately has a three-month holding period

A stock dividend and a stock split usually are not taxable events.

But after a stock split, a taxpayer needs to recalculate his basis for the newly acquired shares. The new basis per share is the total cost of the shares divided by the new share count.

Example: Sean bought 100 shares of MaxiWin Corp. for $50 per share. Sean's cost basis is $50 x 100 shares or $5,000. In 2012, MaxiWin issues a stock dividend, and Sean receives 100 additional shares of stock. Therefore, his new basis in each individual stock is $25 = ($5,000 ÷ [100+100]).

In rare cases, a stock dividend may be taxable. A taxable stock dividend occurs most often when shareholders have the option to receive cash or other property *instead* of stock. The holding period for stock received as a *taxable* stock dividend begins on the date of distribution.

Restricted Stock

If stock is granted to a taxpayer but is subject to restrictions, then the taxpayer does not have to report any income until the stock is either granted or sold (when it is taxable depends on the circumstances).

Restricted stock is stock that has been granted to a taxpayer (usually an employee of a company) that is nontransferable and subject to certain conditions, such as termination of employment or failure to meet certain performance targets. Stock-based compensation generally consists of either transferring stock or issuing stock options to an employee (or independent contractor) as part of a compensation package. Stock is considered transferred only if the employee has the risks and benefits of an owner of the stock.

Generally, restricted stock is not eligible for capital gains treatment, and the entire amount of the vested stock must be reported as ordinary income in the year of vesting. The amount that must be reported as ordinary income is calculated by subtracting the exercise price of the stock from the fair market value of the stock on the date of vesting. The difference is then reported as ordinary income by the shareholder.

If the shareholder decides to hold the stock and sell at a later date, then the difference between the sale price and the fair market value on the date of vesting is then reported as a capital gain or loss.

> **Example:** Natasha is a sales executive working for Borgnini Corp. As part of her compensation package, she receives a restricted stock grant of 2,000 shares. The restriction on the stock is lifted once she reaches certain sales targets. At the end of the year, Natasha reaches her sales goals, and the stock is vested. On her grant date, Borgnini stock is trading at $15 per share. Natasha decides to declare the stock at vesting, so she must report $30,000 (2,000 shares X $15 per share) as ordinary income.

Stock Options

Companies often grant stock options to their employees as an incentive. Stock options are not stock but merely the option to purchase stock at a later date. There are two types of stock options, and they have very different tax treatment.

Incentive Stock Options (ISO)

An incentive stock option allows an employee to purchase stock at a pre-established price (exercise price) that may be below the actual market price on the date of exercise. The tax advantage with an ISO is that income is not reported when the option is granted or when the option is exercised. Income is only reported once the stock is ultimately sold. However, the bargain element, representing the difference between the exercise price and the market value of the stock on the exercise date, is considered a tax preference item for AMT purposes. The employee's basis in the stock is the actual amount paid at exercise plus any amount paid for the option itself.

Nonqualified Stock Options (NQSO)

A nonqualified stock option also allows an employee to purchase stock at a pre-established price (exercise price). However, the difference between the exercise price and the market value of the stock on the exercise date must be recognized as ordinary income in the year the option is exercised. The employee's basis in the stock is the market value of the stock at exercise (which was used to determine his tax liability) plus any amount paid for the option itself.

Basis of Property Transferred From a Spouse (or Former Spouse)

The basis of property transferred by a spouse (or former spouse if the transfer is incident to divorce) is the same as the spouse's adjusted basis. Generally, there is no gain or loss recognized on the transfer of property between spouses or former spouses if the transfer is because of divorce. This rule applies even if the transfer was in exchange for cash, the release of marital rights, the assumption of liabilities, or other considerations.

> **Example:** Before they divorced, Demi and Zachary jointly owned a home that had a basis of $50,000 and an FMV of $250,000. When they divorced last year, Demi transferred her entire interest in the home to Zachary as part of their property settlement. Zachary's basis in the interest received from Demi is her adjusted basis in the home. His total basis in the home is their joint adjusted basis ($50,000).

> **Example:** Margot and Thornton divorced in 2012. Thornton owns stocks with a fair market value of $350,000 and a basis of $200,000. Pursuant to the divorce decree, Thornton transfers all of the stocks to his former spouse. The stock transfer is treated as a nontaxable transfer; therefore, no gain or loss is recognized by either party. Margot's basis in the stock is $200,000.

Basis of a Nonbusiness Bad Debt

There are two kinds of bad debts—business and nonbusiness. If someone owes a taxpayer money that he cannot collect, he has a bad debt. To deduct a bad debt, the taxpayer must have a basis in it—that is, the taxpayer must have already included the amount in income or must have already loaned out the cash.

Taxpayers must prove that they have taken reasonable steps to collect the debt and that the debt is worthless. A debt becomes worthless when it is certain that the debt will never be paid. It is not necessary to go to court if the taxpayer can show that a judgment from the court would be uncollectible. A partially worthless debt is not deductible. The taxpayer may take a bad debt deduction only in the year the debt becomes worthless, but a taxpayer does not have to wait until the debt comes due, if there is proof that the debt is already worthless (for example, if the debtor dies or declares bankruptcy).

Example: In January 2012, Stephanie loans her friend Jed $14,000 to buy a car. Jed signs a note and promises to pay the entire debt back with interest by December 31, 2012. Jed has a bad car accident in June 2012 and cannot pay his debts so he files for bankruptcy. Stephanie does not have to wait until the debt comes due. The bankruptcy means the loan has become worthless, since there is no longer any chance the amount owed will be paid. Stephanie can take the deduction for nonbusiness bad debt.

For a legitimate bad debt to be deductible, the intent of the loan must be genuine. If a taxpayer lends money to a relative or friend with the understanding that it will not be repaid, it is considered a gift and not a loan. There must be a true creditor-debtor relationship between the taxpayer and the person or organization that owes the money.

Loan Guarantees

A *loan guarantee* is not a true debtor-creditor relationship. If a taxpayer simply guarantees a debt (by cosigning on the loan) and the debt becomes worthless, the taxpayer cannot take a bad debt deduction. There must be a profit motive in order for the loan to qualify as a true debtor-creditor relationship.

Example: Lucas and Jason are co-workers. Lucas, as a favor to Jason, co-signs on an auto loan at their local credit union. Jason does not pay the loan and declares bankruptcy. Lucas is forced to pay off the note in order to maintain his credit. However, since he did not enter into a formal guarantee agreement to protect an investment or to make a profit, Lucas cannot take a bad debt deduction.

When minor children borrow from their parents, there is no genuine debt, and bad debt cannot be deducted. A legitimate nonbusiness bad debt is reported as a short-term capital loss on Schedule D (Form 1040). It is subject to the capital loss limit of $3,000 per year, or $1,500 if a taxpayer files MFS.

Basis of Inherited Property

The basis of an asset is generally its cost. However, in the case of inherited assets, heirs typically use a "stepped up" basis. It does not matter what the deceased person actually paid for the asset. The basis of inherited property is generally the FMV of the property on the date of the decedent's death. This means that when the property is sold, the gain will be calculated based on the change in value from the date of death.

This typically results in a beneficial tax situation for anyone who inherits property because the taxpayer generally gets an increased basis. However, there are cases in which this rule can work against taxpayers. Although most property such as stocks, collectibles, and bonds increase in value over time, there are also instances in which the value of the property's value drops. This would create a "stepped-down" basis.

Example #1: Sasha's uncle bought 300 shares of Harrison Foods stock many years ago for $500. Sasha inherited the Harrison stock when her uncle died. On the date of her uncle's death, the value of the stock was $9,000. Therefore, Sasha's basis in the stock is $9,000. She later sells the stock for $11,000. She has a capital gain of $2,000 ($11,000 - $9,000).

Example #2: With the same facts as above, if Sasha were to sell the stock for $8,000, she would have a capital loss of $1,000.

Example #3: Sasha's aunt also bought 100 shares of stock many years ago for $10,000. Sasha inherited the stock when her aunt died. On the date of her aunt's death, the value of the stock was $150. Therefore, Sasha's basis in the stock is $150. She later sells the stock for $150. She cannot report a loss on the stock. That is because the basis of the stock was stepped-down for tax purposes.

Usually, the basis of an estate is determined on the date of death. However, there is a special rule that allows the personal representative of the estate to elect a different valuation date. If the executor makes this election, the valuation date is six months *after* the date of death. For assets disposed within six months after death, the value at the date of disposition is used. This election is made in order to reduce the amount of estate tax that must be paid. In order to elect the alternative valuation date, the estate value and related estate tax must be less than they would have been on the date of the taxpayer's death.

If a federal estate tax return (Form 706) does not have to be filed for the deceased taxpayer, the basis in the beneficiary's inherited property is the FMV value at the date of death,[69] and the alternate valuation date does not apply.

If a taxpayer inherits property, the capital gain or loss on any later disposition of that property is always treated as a long-term capital gain or loss. This is true regardless of how long the beneficiary actually held the property. The taxpayer is considered to have held the inherited property for more than one year even if he disposes of the property less than one year after the decedent's death.

Basis of Property Received as a Gift

The basis of property received as a gift is determined differently than property that is purchased. The taxpayer must know the adjusted basis of the property just before it was gifted, its fair market value, and the amount of gift tax paid on it, if any, by the giver (donor).

Generally, the basis of gifted property is the same in the hands of the donee as it was in the hands of the donor. This is called a "transferred basis." For example, if a taxpayer gives his son a car and the taxpayer's basis in the car is $2,000, the basis of the vehicle remains $2,000 for the son. However, in cases where the donor pays gift tax, the amount of gift tax paid

---

[69] Most estates are not subject to the estate tax and are not subject to the requirement to file an estate tax return. A filing is required for estates with combined gross assets and prior taxable gifts exceeding a basic exclusion amount ($5,120,000 in 2012.) Detailed information about estate and gift taxes may be found in Unit 15, *Estate and Gift Taxes*.

that is attributable to appreciation of the property's value while the donor held it is added to his basis.

> **Example:** Alicia's father gives her 50 shares of stock. The FMV of the stock is currently $1,000. Her father has an adjusted basis in the stock of $500. Alicia's basis in the stock, for purposes of determining gain on any future sale, is $500 (transferred basis).

Figuring Basis on a Gift

If the FMV of the gifted property is **less** than the donor's adjusted basis (including any gift tax paid on appreciation while the donor held the property), the donee's basis for gain is the same as the donor's adjusted basis. If the donee reports a loss on the sale of gifted property, his basis is the lower of the donor's adjusted basis or the fair market value of the property on the date of the gift. The sale of gifted property can also result in no gain or loss. This happens when the sale proceeds are *greater* than the gift's FMV but *below* the donor's basis.

> **Example:** Charlie's grandmother, Leslie, bought 20 shares of Ford stock many decades ago. Her basis in the stock is $1,000, and thus Charlie's transferred basis is also $1,000. At the time of the gift, the stock has an FMV of $7,500. During the year, Charlie sells the stock for $7,500. He must report a taxable gain of $6,500. The answer is determined as follows: ($7,500 sale price - $1,000 basis = $6,500 capital gain).

> **Example:** Hugh gives his nephew, Russell, a gift of 500 shares of stock. Hugh's basis in the stock is $1,000, meaning Russell's transferred basis is also $1,000. However, the FMV at the time of the gift is only $900 because the stock has lost some value. Russell sells the stock two months later for $940. Russell does not have any gain or loss for tax purposes. This is because Russell's basis for determining gain is $1,000. However, Russell's basis for determining loss is $900 (the FMV at the time of the gift). This is an example of a sale of gifted property resulting in no gain or loss. This happens when the sale ($940) is above the gift's FMV ($900) but below the donor's basis ($1,000).

> **Example:** Benny's Aunt Roberta bought 100 shares of IBM stock when it was at $92. Roberta's basis for the 100 shares is $9,200. Roberta then gives the stock to Benny when it is selling at $70 and has an FMV of $7,000. In this case, Benny has a "dual basis" in the stock. He has one basis for purposes of determining a gain, and a different basis for determining a loss. Here are three separate scenarios that help illustrate how the gain or loss would be calculated when Benny sells the gifted stock:

> **Scenario #1:** If Benny sells the stock for more than his aunt's basis, he will use Roberta's basis to determine his amount of gain. For example, if he sells the stock for $11,000, he will report a gain of $1,800 ($11,000 - $9,200).

> **Scenario #2:** If Benny sells the stock for less than the FMV of the stock at the time of the gift ($7,000 in the example), he must use that basis to determine the amount of his loss. For example, if the stock continues to decline and Benny eventually sells it for $4,500, he can report a loss of $2,500 ($7,000 - $4,500).

> **Scenario #3:** If Benny sells the stock for an amount between the FMV and the donor's basis, no gain or loss will be recognized. For example, if Benny sells the stock for $8,000, there will be no gain or loss on the transaction.

The holding period for a gift is treated differently than the holding period for inherited and purchased property. If a taxpayer receives a gift of property, then the holding period includes the donor's holding period. This concept is also known as "tacking on" the holding period.

> **Example:** Florence gives her niece, Marion, an acre of land. At the time of the gift, the land had an FMV of $23,000. Florence's adjusted basis in the land was $20,000. Florence held the property for six months. Marion holds the land for another seven months. Neither held the property for over a year. However, Marion may "tack on" her holding period to her aunt's holding period. Therefore, if Marion were to sell the property, she would have a long-term capital gain or loss, because jointly they held the property for thirteen months, which is over one year.

Holding Period (Short-Term or Long-Term)

When a taxpayer disposes of investment property, he must determine his holding period in order to figure gain or loss. Holding periods vary based on whether the property was purchased, inherited, or acquired as a gift.

The holding period determines whether any capital gain or loss was a short-term or long-term capital gain or loss. This is very important, because long-term capital gains rates are given more beneficial tax treatment.

If a taxpayer holds investment property for more than one year, any capital gain or loss is *long-term* capital gain or loss. If a taxpayer holds property for one year or less, any capital gain or loss is *short-term* capital gain or loss.

> **Long-term= More than one year**
> **Short-term= One year or less**

To determine how long a taxpayer has held an investment property, he should begin counting on the date *after* the day he acquires the property. The day the taxpayer disposes of the property is part of the holding period.

> **Example:** Nicky bought 50 shares of stock on February 5, 2011 for $10,000. She sells all the shares on February 5, 2012 for $20,500. Nicky's holding period is not more than one year, and so she has a short-term capital gain of $10,500. The short-term gain is taxed at ordinary income rates. A long-term gain is taxed at preferential tax rates. If Nicky had waited one more day, she would have received long-term capital gain treatment on her gains, and it would have saved her on income taxes.

> **Example:** Stuart bought 100 shares of Castlebarry Corp. stock on October 1, 2011 for $1,200. To determine his holding period, Stuart must start counting his holding period on October 2, 2011 (the day *after* the purchase). He sells all the stock on October 2, 2012 for $2,850. Stuart's holding period has been over one year, and therefore, he will recognize a long-term capital gain of $1,650 ($2,850 - $1,200).

Stock acquired as a stock dividend (also called a stock split) has the same holding period as the original stock owned.

Unit 10: Questions

1. On February 11, 2012, Henry bought 1,000 shares of Greenbrae Corporation stock for $4 each, plus paid an additional $70 for his broker's commission. What is Henry's basis in the stock?

A. $1,000.
B. $4,000.
C. $4,070.
D. None of the above.

The answer is C. Henry's basis in the stock is $4,070 ([1,000 X $4] = $4,000 + $70). ###

2. Brigit purchased 1,000 shares of Free Drive, Inc. on January 3, 2012. The original basis in the 1,000 shares of stock she purchased was $5,100, including the commission. On August 14, 2012, she sold 500 shares for $3,300. What is the adjusted basis of the stock she sold?

A. $5,100.
B. $2,550.
C. $3,300.
D. $3,255.

The answer is B. Brigit's original basis in the total stock was $5,100, which is $5.10 per share, so her basis in the 500 shares she sold is 500 X $5.10, or $2,550. ###

3. Tariq bought two blocks of 400 shares of stock. He purchased the first block in April 2008 for $1,200 and the second block in March 2012 for $1,600. In June of 2012, he sold 400 shares for $1,500 without specifying which block of shares he was selling. Tariq's sold stock represents a

_____.

A. Short-term loss of $100.
B. Short-term gain of $300.
C. Long-term loss of $100.
D. Long-term gain of $300.

The answer is D. The basis and holding period would automatically default to the original block of shares, so Tariq realized a long-term gain of $300. ###

4. Consuela bought 40 shares of Giant Corporation for a total purchase price $1,540. She also paid a $20 broker's commission on the purchase. What is her initial basis per share?

A. $39.
B. $38.50.
C. $1,560.
D. $77.

The answer is A. Consuela's initial basis for this stock is $1,560, or $39 per share ($1,560 ÷ 40 shares). Cost basis includes the amount paid for the stock and any commission paid on the purchase. ###

5. On March 10, 2009, Hans bought 500 shares of Merring Roadster stock for $1,500, including his broker's commission. On June 6, 2012, Merring distributed Hans a nontaxable stock dividend of 10 additional shares. Three days later, he sold all his stock for $2,030. What is the nature of his gain on all the shares sold?

A. Long-term capital gain of $530.
B. Long-term capital gain of $500, short-term gain of $30.
C. Short-term capital gain of $530.
D. None of the above.

The answer is A. Although Hans owned the 10 shares he received as a nontaxable stock dividend for only three days, all the stock has a long-term holding period. Because he bought the stock for $1,500 and then sold it for $2,030 more than a year later, Hans has a long-term capital gain of $530 on the sale of the 510 shares. ###

6. Deirdre bought 100 shares of stock of Around Pound Corporation in 2005 for $10 a share. In January 2006 Deirdre bought another 200 shares for $11 a share. In July 2006 she gave her son 50 shares. In December 2009 Deirdre bought 100 shares for $9 a share. In April 2012 she sold 130 shares. Deirdre cannot identify the shares she disposed of, so she must use the stock she acquired first to figure the basis. The shares Deirdre gave her son had a basis of $500 (50 × $10). What is the basis of the 130 shares of stock Deirdre sold in 2012?

A. $880.
B. $1,380.
C. $1,300.
D. $1,000.

The answer is B. If a taxpayer buys and sells securities at various times in varying quantities and she cannot adequately identify the shares sold, the basis of the securities sold is the basis of the securities acquired first (FIFO). Deirdre figures the basis of the 130 shares of stock she sold as follows:

50 shares (50 × $10)	
Balance of stock from 2005:	$500
80 shares (80 × $11)	
Stock bought in January 2006:	$880
Total basis of stock sold	**$1,380**

###

7. Julian owned one share of common stock that he bought for $45. The corporation distributed two new shares of common stock for each share held. Julian then had three shares of common stock. What is Julian's new basis for each share?

A. $5.
B. $45.
C. $15.
D. $135.

The answer is C. Julian's basis in each share is $15 ($45 ÷ 3). If a taxpayer receives a nontaxable stock dividend, divide the adjusted basis of the old stock by the number of shares of old and new stock. The result is the taxpayer's basis for each share of stock. ###

8. Claire owned two shares of common stock. She bought one for $30 in 2007 and the other for $45 in 2008. In 2012, the corporation distributed two new shares of common stock for each share held (a "2-for-1" stock split). Claire had six shares after the distribution. How is the basis allocated between these six shares?

A. All six shares now have a basis of $12.50.
B. Three shares have a basis of $10 each and three have a basis of $15 each.
C. The shares are valued at $45 each.
D. Some other amount.

The answer is B. The shares now are valued as follows: three with a basis of $10 each ($30 ÷ 3), and three with a basis of $15 each ($45 ÷ 3). If a taxpayer receives a nontaxable stock dividend, he must divide the adjusted basis of the old stock by the number of shares of old and new stock. The result is the taxpayer's basis for each share of stock. ###

9. On her one-year anniversary at her new job, Faith's employer gave her restricted stock with the condition that she would have to return it if she did not complete a full five years of service with her company. Her employer's basis in the stock was $16,000, and its FMV is $30,000. How much should she include in her income for the current year, and what would be her basis in the stock?

A. Income of $16,000; basis of $30,000.
B. Income of $10,000; basis of $30,000.
C. Income of $30,000; basis of $16,000.
D. Faith would not report any income or have any basis in the stock until she has completed five years of service.

The answer is D. The stock is restricted, so Faith does not have constructive receipt of it. She should not report any income until she receives the stock without restrictions. Constructive receipt does not require physical possession of the item of income. However, there are substantial restrictions on the stock's disposition because Faith must complete another four years of service before she can sell or otherwise dispose of the stock. ###

10. Stephen purchases a truck for $15,000 to use in his carpentry business. He puts $5,000 down in cash and finances the remaining $10,000 with a five-year loan. He then pays taxes and delivery costs of $1,300. He also pays $250 to install a protective bedliner. What is Stephen's basis for depreciation in the truck?

A. $6,550.
B. $10,000.
C. $16,550.
D. $16,300.

The answer is C. Stephen's basis in the truck is the cost of both acquiring the property and preparing the property for use. Therefore, his basis is figured as follows: ($15,000 + $1,300 + $250) = $16,550. Any funds that are borrowed to pay for an asset are also included in the basis. ###

11. Mackenzie purchases an empty lot for $50,000. She pays $15,000 in cash and finances the remaining $35,000 with a bank loan. The lot also has a $4,000 lien against it for unpaid property taxes, which she also agrees to pay. Which statement below is correct?

A. Mackenzie's basis in the property is $50,000, and she may deduct the property taxes on her Schedule A as property taxes paid.
B. Mackenzie's basis in the property is $19,000.
C. Mackenzie's basis in the property is $54,000.
D. Mackenzie's basis in the property is $46,000.

The answer is C. Her basis is figured as follows: ($50,000 + $4,000 = $54,000). Mackenzie may not deduct the delinquent property taxes on her Schedule A. This is because any obligations of the seller that are assumed by the buyer increase the basis of the asset, and are not currently deductible. Since Mackenzie did not legally owe the property taxes but she still agreed to pay them, she must add the property tax to the basis of the property. ###

12. Marilyn won the lottery and then made personal loans to several friends. The loans were a true debtor-creditor relationship but not business related. She could not collect on many of these loans. How does Marilyn report these transactions?

A. The losses from the uncollectible loans are not deductible, since they were personal loans.
B. The losses are deductible as nonbusiness bad debt on Schedule D.
C. The losses are deductible as a business expense on Schedule C.
D. The losses are deductible on Schedule A as casualty losses.

The answer is B. A nonbusiness bad debt is reported as a short-term capital loss on Schedule D. It is subject to the capital loss limit of $3,000 per year. ###

13. Conrad purchased Blue-Chip Corporation stock in 2009 and sold it in 2012. In 2012, he also traded in a copy machine that he had been using in his business since 2008 for a new model. On December 15, 2012, Conrad's mother gifted him 35 shares of Energy Corp. stock that she had held for five years. Conrad sold the gifted stock two weeks after he received it from his mother. What is the holding period for all these assets?

A. All short-term.
B. Blue-Chip stock and copy machine are long-term and Energy Corp. stock is short-term.
C. All the stocks are long-term; the copy machine is short-term.
D. All are long-term.

The answer is D. All the property is long-term property. If a taxpayer holds investment property for more than one year, any capital gain or loss is a long-term capital gain or loss. If a taxpayer holds a property for one year or less, any capital gain or loss is a short-term capital gain or loss. If a taxpayer receives a gift of property, then the holding period includes the donor's holding period. Since Conrad's mother had already held the stock for a few years, it would receive long-term treatment in Conrad's possession. ###

14. When trying to determine the holding period for investment property, which of the following is important?

A. The cost of the property.
B. In the case of gifted property, the amount of the gift.
C. The date of acquisition.
D. The amount realized in the transaction.

The answer is C. To determine the holding period, a taxpayer must begin counting on the day after the acquisition date. If a taxpayer's holding period is not more than one year, the taxpayer will have a short-term capital gain or loss. The amount realized in the transaction has no bearing on the holding period. ###

15. For Mother's Day on May 13, 2012, Jonathon gives his mother, Caryna, a classic 1963 Corvette. Jonathon had purchased the car for $50,000 on January 4, 2012 and then worked for several months restoring it. At the time of his gift, the car's FMV was $63,000.

Although Caryna enjoys driving the Corvette, she dislikes its poor gas mileage and decides she would rather have a new Prius. She sells the Corvette on March 15, 2013 for $65,000. What is the nature of Caryna's gain or loss?

A. Short-term loss.
B. Short-term capital gain.
C. Long-term loss.
D. Long-term capital gain.

The answer is D. Even though Caryna owned the Corvette for less than a year, she has a long-term capital gain. That is because the time Jonathon owned the car—three months—is "tacked on" to Caryna's holding period of ten months. If a taxpayer receives a gift of property, the holding period includes the donor's holding period. ###

16. Esteban installs artificial turf at a client's home at a cost of $1,500. After the installation, his client, Andie, receives a foreclosure notice and is unable to pay Esteban's bill. She has a golden-doodle show dog that just had puppies. The FMV of each puppy is $1,800. Esteban loves animals and decides to take one of the puppies as full payment on Andie's delinquent bill. What is Esteban's basis in his new dog?

A. $0.
B. $300.
C. $1,500.
D. $1,800.

The answer is C. If a taxpayer receives property in payment for services, he must include the property's FMV in income, and this becomes his basis. However, if two people agree on a cost beforehand and it is deemed reasonable, the IRS will usually accept the agreed-upon cost as the asset's basis. ###

17. On July 1, 2012 Miletech Corporation granted 1,000 non-qualified stock options to an executive with an option price of $23 per share. On December 31, 2012, the executive exercised all of his options when the market price per share was $43. What is the basis of his stock and what amount should be included on his Form W-2 as income in 2012?

A. Basis $23,000; income $0.
B. Basis $43,000; income $20,000.
C. Basis $0; income $0.
D. None of the above.

The answer is B. The basis of the stock would be the value on December 31, 2012 (1,000 x $43 = $43,000). The options were issued at an option price of $23 which means that $20,000 ($43 - $23 = $20 x 1,000 = $20,000), representing the difference between his exercise price and the stock's value at exercise, must be included in his W-2 for 2012. When the stock is later sold, the taxpayer would recognize gain or loss equal to the difference between his sales proceeds and the $43,000 basis in the stock. ###

18. On June 1, 2012, Pham Software Corporation granted 500 incentive stock options to an executive with an option price of $25. On December 31, 2012, the executive exercised all of his options when the market price per share was $50. What is the basis of his stock and how much should be included on his Form W-2 as income for 2012?

A. Basis $12,500; income $0.
B. Basis $0; income $0.
C. Basis $12,500; income $12,500.
D. Basis $12,500; income $25,000.

The answer is A. For incentive stock options, the basis in the stock is based on the actual price per share paid upon exercise of the options. Any increase in value attributable to the difference between the exercise price and the value at the date of exercise is not recognized until the stock is sold. However, the taxpayer may need to make an adjustment for alternative minimum tax (AMT) purposes of $12,500 (500 x $25 = $12,500) for the bargain element. When the stock is sold, income will be recognized for the difference between the option price and the value on the date of the sale. ###

Unit 11: Capital Gains and Losses

More Reading:
Publication 550, *Investment Income and Expenses*
Publication 544, *Sales and Other Dispositions of Assets*
Publication 537, *Installment Sales*

The sale of assets—whether they are securities, such as stocks, or personal property, such as a main home—will result in a capital gain or loss. Learning how to calculate capital gains and losses is essential to understanding how property transactions are taxed.

Losses from the sale of personal-use property, such as a main home, furniture, or jewelry, are not deductible.

Example: Liam owns a Subaru that he uses to commute to work, run errands, and take on weekend ski trips. He purchased the car four years ago for $20,500. In 2012, he sells the car for $12,000. Liam cannot claim a loss from the sale of the car since it is his personal-use vehicle.

Example: Mason sold his personal computer to his friend for $750. Mason paid $5,000 for the computer five years ago. Mason used the computer to play games, surf the Internet, and pay bills on-line. He did not use the computer for business. Mason cannot deduct a loss on the sale of his personal computer.

Property held for personal use only, rather than for investment, is a capital asset, and a taxpayer must report a gain from its sale as a capital gain.

Example: Priscilla collects antique coins as a hobby. She is not a professional dealer. Two years ago, Priscilla gets lucky and purchases an antique Roman coin for $50. In 2012, she is offered $1,000 for the coin, and she promptly sells it. Priscilla has a taxable capital gain and she must report it on her tax return.

The capital gains tax rate depends on the holding period, type of asset, and the taxpayer's ordinary income bracket. Capital gains and deductible capital losses are reported on Schedule D (Form 1040), *Capital Gains and Losses*. Additional detail on certain transactions is first reported on Form 8949, *Sales and Other Dispositions of Capital Assets*.

Noncapital Assets

Assets held for business-use or created by a taxpayer for purposes of earning revenue (author's writings, copyrights, inventory, etc.) are considered *noncapital* assets. Gains and losses from the sale of business property are reported on Form 4797, *Sales of Business Property*, and in the case of individual taxpayers, the amounts flow through to Form 1040, Schedule D. [70]

The following assets are noncapital assets:

- Inventory or any property held for sale to customers
- Depreciable property used in a business, even if it is fully depreciated

---

[70] See Publication 544, *Sales and Other Dispositions of Assets,* for additional information on the sale of business property. Gains and sales of business property are covered more in Book 2.

- Real property used in a trade or business, such as a commercial building or a residential rental
- Self-produced copyrights, transcripts, manuscripts, drawings, photographs, or artistic compositions
- Accounts receivable or notes receivable acquired by a business
- Stocks and bonds held by professional securities dealers
- Business supplies
- Commodities and derivative financial instruments

Unlike capital assets, many noncapital asset losses may be deducted as business expenses.

Example: Tony is a sole proprietor of a fitness club. He also owns stock in a few companies as an investment. In 2012, Tony sold used fitness equipment from his club in order to make room for new equipment. Since the fitness equipment was business property, the sale of these assets is reported on Form 4797, *Sales of Business Property*. Also during the year, Tony sold some Google stock at a substantial profit. He has a capital gain on the stock and must report the sale on Schedule D.

Example: Michael is a self-employed fisherman who reports his income and loss on Schedule F. In 2012, he sells some of his commercial fishing equipment, which was business-use only. The fishing equipment is a noncapital asset, and the sale must be reported on Form 4797, *Sales of Business Property*. Also during the year, Michael sells his vacation home and has a substantial loss on the sale. Unlike the fishing equipment, the vacation home is a capital asset, and since it is personal-use only, Michael cannot deduct the loss on the sale.

The $3,000 Loss Limit and Loss Carryovers

Capital losses are always netted against capital gains. However, there is an exception for stock losses. *Up to $3,000* in excess capital losses is deductible against ordinary income in a tax year ($1,500 for taxpayers filing MFS). The allowable loss is referred to as the capital loss deduction limit. Unused losses are carried over to later years.

The carryover losses are combined with the gains and losses that actually occur in the next year. Short-term and long-term capital loss carryovers are reported on Schedule D.

The carryover retains its character as either long-term or short-term. A long-term capital loss carried over to the next tax year will reduce that year's long-term capital gains before it reduces that year's short-term capital gains.

Example: Arthur purchased stock two years ago for $16,000. The stock declines in value, and he finally sells the stock in 2012 for $12,000. Arthur has a $4,000 long-term capital loss. He also has $30,000 in wages in 2012. He may claim $3,000 of his long-term capital loss against his ordinary income, thereby lowering his gross income to $27,000 ($30,000 - $3,000). The remainder of the long-term capital loss must be carried forward to a future year ($1,000 carryover).

Unused losses may be carried over year after year until they are all deducted. There is no limit on how many times a capital loss can be carried over during the taxpayer's life.

Determining Capital Gain or Loss

A taxpayer determines gain or loss on a sale or trade of stock or property by comparing the amount realized with the adjusted basis of the property.

- GAIN: If the taxpayer realizes more than the adjusted basis of the property, the difference is a gain.
- LOSS: If the taxpayer realizes less than the adjusted basis of the property, the difference is a loss.

Example: Nadine purchased 50 shares of Hammaker Corporation stock five years ago for $5,000. Then, two years ago, she purchased 750 shares of Shelby Ironworks stock for $8,200. In 2012, Nadine sells all her stock. Her Hammaker stock sold for $2,000, which means she had a loss. Her Shelby stock sold for $13,000, which means she had a gain. All of Nadine's gains and losses are long-term, because she held all her stock for more than one year. Her long-term loss and long-term gain are netted against each other to figure her net capital gain. Nadine's gains and losses are figured as follows:

Stock	Basis	Sale Price	Gain (or loss)
Hammaker	$5,000	$2,000	($3,000)
Shelby	$8,200	$13,000	$4,800
Net Capital Gain			**$1,800**

There are many instances in which a taxpayer may have a realized gain that is not a taxable event.

A "recognized" gain or loss is the actual amount that must be included in income (or deducted from income) for tax purposes.

If a taxpayer sells securities through a broker during the year, he should receive Form 1099-B, *Proceeds from Broker and Barter Exchange Transactions*, by January 31 following the end of the tax year. This statement shows the gross proceeds from the sale of securities. The IRS also receives a copy of Form 1099-B from the broker. If Form 1099-B does not include the basis, the taxpayer must provide this information; otherwise, the IRS will deem the basis to be zero. (Any broker fees should be added to the basis, not deducted from the proceeds.)

Example: Corbin receives Form 1099-B showing a net sales price of $1,200 on the sale of 600 shares of Kominski Corporation. He bought the stock six years ago and sold it on September 25, 2012. His basis in Kominski, including commission, is $1,455. He has an overall loss on the stock, which he will report on Schedule D.

The sale and income (or loss) must be reported in the year the security is sold, regardless of when the taxpayer receives the proceeds from the stock sale.

Worthless and Abandoned Securities

Taxpayers may choose to "abandon" securities. Stocks, stock rights, and bonds (other than those held for sale by a securities dealer) that became worthless during the tax year are treated as though they were sold on the last day of the tax year. The taxpayer reports the loss as if he sold the shares for zero dollars on the last day of the taxable year.

This rule is helpful for a taxpayer who has a security that has declined in value so much that he wishes to take a loss on it rather than retain ownership.

To abandon a worthless security, a taxpayer must permanently surrender all rights to it and receive no consideration in exchange.

> ***Note:** Worthless securities get special tax treatment. Unlike other losses, a taxpayer is allowed to amend a tax return up to seven years prior in order to claim a loss from worthless securities. This is more than double the usual three-year statute of limitations for amending returns.

> **Example:** Reginald owned 500 shares of WorldCom stock. The company files for bankruptcy and the bankruptcy court extinguishes all rights of the former shareholders. Reginald learns of the bankruptcy court's decision in December 2012. Rather than wait for a formal notice from the court, Reginald chooses to abandon his WorldCom securities, knowing that his shares are worthless. He takes a capital loss on his 2012 tax return, reflecting the value of his worthless shares as "zero."

Capital Gain Distributions and Mutual Funds

A mutual fund is a regulated investment company generally created by pooling funds of investors to allow them to take advantage of a diversity of investments and professional management. Mutual funds often sell profitable investments at certain times throughout the year.

Form 1099-DIV reports capital gain distributions from the mutual fund. Profits of these sales are reported to the shareholders as capital gain distributions. If taxpayers (shareholders) decide to sell any of their shares in the mutual fund itself, Form 1099-B will be issued. The taxable gain or loss from the sale or exchange of the taxpayer's shares in a mutual fund is reported on Form 1040, Schedule D.

What makes these types of distributions unusual, however, is that capital gain distributions are *always* taxed at long-term capital gains tax rates, *no matter how long* a taxpayer has personally owned shares in the mutual fund.

Qualified Small Business Stock (Section 1244)   QSBS

There is a special type of stock called section 1244 small business stock (also called qualified small business stock or QSBS). QSBS is stock in qualifying domestic corporations that is subject to special tax rules that are favorable to the shareholder. Congress allows special treatment for this type of stock in order to spur investment in domestic corporations.

Qualified small business stock must be from a C corporation with gross assets of $50 million or less.

Losses on small business stock are considered ordinary losses rather than capital losses and any gain on a 1244 stock is a capital gain. This means that the losses are not subject to the capital loss limit ($3,000 per year), but gains are still given favorable capital gains rates. The amount that can be deducted as an ordinary loss is $50,000 for single filers and $100,000 for joint filers. Ordinary losses are more favorable to the taxpayer because he can deduct this loss against his ordinary gross income.

In order to qualify, the shareholder must be an individual or partnership; other entities such as corporations do not qualify for this specialized treatment.

Only the *original purchaser* of the stock can claim an ordinary loss. So, if this stock is inherited or gifted to another person, the special treatment for losses also does not apply.

Losses from the sale of section 1244 stock are reported on Form 4797, *Sales of Business Property*.

*Special Rule: Excluded Gains on Small Business Stock

Gains on qualified small business stock are also given preferential treatment:

- A taxpayer generally can exclude up to 50% of the gain from the sale or trade of qualified small business stock held for more than five years.
- For stock acquired after September 27, 2010 and before January 1, 2014,[71] the exclusion is 100%. The amount of gain eligible for the exclusion is limited to the greater of 10 times the taxpayer's basis in the stock or $10 million of gain from stock in that corporation.

Example: On December 15, 2012, Lenore purchases 100 shares of Button Makers USA, a domestic corporation with $20 million in annual revenue. The stock is qualified small business stock. Lenore must wait until December 16, 2017 to sell the stock in order to receive the 100% exclusion from gain.

Gains from qualified small business stock are reported on Schedule D (Form 1040).

Related Party Transactions and Capital Losses

Special rules apply to related-party transactions, which are business deals between two parties who are joined by a special relationship. If a taxpayer sells capital assets to a close family member or to a business entity that the taxpayer controls, he may not receive all the benefits of the capital gains tax rates, and he may not be able to deduct his losses. The related party transactions were put into place to prevent related persons and entities from shuffling assets back and forth and taking improper losses.

50% Control Rule

If a taxpayer controls more than 50% of a corporation or partnership, then any property transactions between the taxpayer and the business would be subject to related party transaction rules. In general, a loss on the sale of property between related parties is not deductible. When the property is later sold to an unrelated party, gain is recognized only to the extent it is more than the disallowed loss. If the property is later sold at a loss, the loss that was disallowed to the related party cannot be recognized. If a taxpayer sells or trades property at a loss (other than in the complete liquidation of a corporation), the loss is not deductible if the transaction is between the taxpayer and the following related parties:

- Members of immediate family, including a spouse, siblings or half-siblings, ancestors, or descendants (children, grandchildren, etc.). *Note: For purposes of this rule, uncles, aunts, nephews, nieces, cousins, stepchildren, stepparents, in-laws, and ex-spouses are not considered related parties.
- A partnership or corporation that the taxpayer controls. A taxpayer "controls" an entity when he has more than 50% ownership in it. This also includes partial ownership by other family members.
- A tax-exempt or charitable organization controlled by the taxpayer or a member of his family.
- Losses on sales between certain closely related trusts or business entities controlled by the same owners.

---

[71] This time period was extended from January 1, 2012 to January 1, 2014 by the American Taxpayer Relief Act of 2012.

Example: Hillary buys stock from her brother, Clyde, for $7,600. Clyde's cost basis in the stock is $10,000. He cannot deduct the loss of $2,400 because of the related-party transaction rules. Later, Hillary sells the same stock on the open market for $10,500, realizing a gain of $2,900. Hillary's reportable gain is $500 (the $2,900 gain minus the $2,400 loss not allowed to her brother).

Example: Vicky purchases stock from her father for $8,600. Her father's basis in the stock is $11,000. Vicky later sells the stock on the open market for $6,900. Her recognized loss is $1,700 (her $8,600 basis minus $6,900). Vicky cannot deduct the loss that was disallowed to her father.

In the case of a related party transaction, if a taxpayer sells multiple pieces of property and some are at a gain while others are at a loss, the gains will generally be taxable while the losses cannot be used to offset the gains.

Installment Sales

An installment sale is a sale of property in which at least one payment is to be received after the tax year in which the sale occurs. If a taxpayer sells property and receives payments over a number of years, he is allowed to use the installment method in order to defer tax by only reporting gains as each installment is received. A taxpayer's total gain on an installment method is generally the amount the selling price of the property sold exceeds the adjusted basis in that property. Each payment on an installment sale typically consists of the following three parts:

- Interest income
- Return of the adjusted basis in the property
- Gain on the sale

In each year the taxpayer receives a payment, he must include both the interest part and the part that is his gain on the sale. The taxpayer does not include in income the part that is the return of basis in the property. Basis is the amount of the taxpayer's investment in the property for investment purposes. A certain percentage of each payment (after subtracting interest, which is reported as ordinary income) is reported as installment sale income. The percentage is called the gross profit percentage[72] and is figured by dividing the gross profit from the sale by the contract price.

The selling price is the FMV of the property, any existing mortgage or debt the buyer pays or assumes, and any selling expenses the buyer pays.

If the installment sale includes any income due to depreciation recapture, it is reported as ordinary income in the year of the sale.

Example: Ernesto sells property in an installment sale at a contract price of $6,000. His gross profit is $1,500. The gross profit percentage on the sale is 25% ($1,500 ÷ $6,000). After subtracting interest, Ernesto reports 25% of each payment, including the down payment, as installment sale income. The remainder (balance) of each payment is the tax-free return of the property's basis.

---

[72] You may be required to figure gross profit percentage for either Part 1 or Part 2 of the EA exam using a set of figures provided. Gross profit percentage is commonly used in business to measure a company's performance.

> **Example:** In 2011, Chloe sells an empty lot with a basis of $40,000 for $100,000. Her gross profit is $60,000. She receives a $20,000 down payment and the buyer's note for $80,000. The note provides for four annual payments of $20,000 each, plus 8% interest, beginning in 2012. Chloe's gross profit percentage is 60%. She must report a gain of $12,000 on each payment received.

If the taxpayer decides not to use the installment method, he must report all the gain in the year of the sale. Installment sale rules do not apply to property that is sold at a loss.

The installment method cannot be used for publicly traded securities, such as stocks and bonds. This means that a taxpayer is forced to report gain on the sale of securities in the year of the sale, regardless of whether the proceeds are received until the following year.

> **Example:** Dillon owns 500 shares of stock, which he sells at a gain on December 29, 2012. Dillon does not receive the proceeds until January 15, 2013. Dillon is required to report the capital gain on the sale of the stock on his 2012 tax return. He cannot delay reporting the gain, and the sale is not considered an installment sale.

Installment sales are allowed to related parties (covered next). However, if a taxpayer sells property to a relative and the relative later sells or disposes of the property within two years of the original sale, the taxpayer will lose the benefit of installment reporting.

> **Example:** Lou sells a plot of land to his daughter, Melanie. The sale price is $25,000, and Lou realizes a profit on the sale of $10,000. Melanie agrees to pay in five installments of $5,000. A year later, Melanie sells the property to another person. Lou must report the entire profit of $10,000 on the sale, even though he may not have received all the installment payments. The installment method is disallowed on this related party sale, because the property was disposed of before the two-year holding period.

No gain or loss is recognized on the transfer of an installment obligation between a husband and wife if the transfer is incident to a divorce.

Installment sales are reported on Form 6252, *Installment Sale Income*, which is attached to Form 1040. A taxpayer may also be required to complete Schedule D or Form 4797.

Wash Sales and Disallowed Losses

A wash sale occurs when an investor sells a losing security to claim a capital loss, only to repurchase it again for a bargain. This used to be a common investor strategy until the IRS implemented a 30-day wash sale rule in which a taxpayer cannot recognize a loss on an investment if that investment was purchased within 30 days of sale (before or after the sale.)

A taxpayer cannot deduct losses from sales of securities in a wash sale. A wash sale is when a taxpayer sells securities and then turns around and:

- Buys identical securities,
- Acquires substantially identical securities in a taxable trade, or
- Acquires a contract or option to buy identical securities.

> **Example:** Carlos sells 1,000 shares of Granger Corporation stock on December 4, 2011 and takes a loss of $3,200. Carlos has seller's remorse, and on January 2, 2012 he buys back 1,000 shares of Granger stock. Because of the IRS wash sale rules, all of the $3,200 loss is disallowed. He cannot take the loss until he finally sells those repurchased shares at some later time. He must add the disallowed loss to the basis of the newly-purchased shares, resulting in an increase to the basis.

The wash sale rule time period actually lasts a total of 61 calendar days: the 30 days before the sale is made, the 30 days after the sale is made, and the day of the sale. To claim a loss as a deduction, the taxpayer needs to avoid purchasing the same stock (or similar security) during the wash sale period. For a sale on July 31, for example, the wash sale period includes all of July and August.

If a taxpayer's loss was disallowed because of the wash sale rules, he must add the disallowed loss to the basis of the new stock or securities. The result is an increase in the taxpayer's basis in the new stock or securities. This adjustment postpones the loss deduction until the disposition of the new stock or securities.[73]

For purposes of the wash sale rules, securities of one corporation are not considered identical to securities of another corporation. This means that a person can sell shares in one corporation and then purchase shares in a different corporation, and this will not trigger a wash sale. In order for a wash sale to apply, the shares must be identical.

Similarly, "preferred" stock of a corporation is not considered identical to the common stock of the same corporation.

If the number of shares of identical securities a taxpayer buys within 30 days is either more or less than the number of shares sold, the taxpayer must determine the particular shares to which the wash sale rules apply. A taxpayer does this by matching the shares bought with an equal number of the shares sold. A taxpayer must match the shares bought in the same order that he bought them, beginning with the first shares purchased.

> **Example:** Chelsea bought 100 shares of Sarbella Pharmaceuticals stock on September 24, 2011. On February 3, 2012, she sold those shares at a $1,000 loss. On February 10, 2012, Chelsea bought 100 shares of identical Sarbella stock. Since she *repurchased* identical shares ten days after selling the stock, she cannot deduct her $1,000 loss. She must add the disallowed loss to the basis of the 100 shares she bought on February 10. This is a wash sale.

It is considered a wash sale if a taxpayer sells stock and his spouse then repurchases identical stock within 30 days. This is true even if the spouses file separate tax returns.

---

[73] Wash sale rules do not apply to trades of commodity futures contracts and foreign currencies. The rules also do not apply to dealers in stocks or securities.

Unit 11: Questions

1. Norma sells an empty lot with an adjusted basis of $20,000. Her buyer assumes an existing mortgage on the property of $15,000 and agrees to pay Norma $10,000, with a cash down payment of $2,000 and then $2,000 every year (plus 12% interest) in each of the next four years. The selling price is $25,000. What is Norma's gross profit and gross profit percentage on the installment sale?

A. The gross profit is $5,000, and the gross profit percentage is 50%.
B. The gross profit is $10,000, and the gross profit percentage is 100%.
C. The gross profit is $15,000, and the gross profit percentage is 20%.
D. The gross profit is $5,000, and the gross profit percentage is 100%.

The answer is A. Norma's gross profit is $5,000, and the gross profit percentage is 50%. Her selling price is $25,000 ($15,000 existing mortgage + $10,000 payment over four years). Therefore, Norma's gross profit is $5,000 ($25,000 − $20,000 installment sale basis). The contract price is $10,000 ($25,000 − $15,000 mortgage). Her gross profit percentage is 50% ($5,000 ÷ $10,000). Norma must report half of each $2,000 payment received as gain from the sale. She must also report all interest received as ordinary income. ###

2. What is the maximum number of years a taxpayer can carry over an unused capital loss?

A. One year.
B. Two years.
C. Five years.
D. As many times as required to receive the entire deduction.

The answer is D. Unused capital losses may be carried over year after year until they are all deducted. There is no limit on how many times a loss can be carried over during the taxpayer's life. ###

3. Five years ago, Marsha bought 100 shares of stock. Her sale date was March 10, 2012. Marsha's original cost for the stock was $10,110, plus an additional $35 in broker's fees. When she sold the stock, she received gross proceeds of $8,859. What is the net gain or loss from this transaction?

A. $1,286 in long-term capital loss.
B. $1,286 in short-term capital loss.
C. $1,251 in long-term capital loss.
D. $1,251 in long-term capital gain.

The answer is A. The answer is figured as follows: The original basis is increased by the broker's commission. Therefore, Marsha's adjusted basis is $10,145 ($10,110 + $35). The gross proceeds from the sale are $8,859, which is subtracted from the basis, resulting in a long-term capital loss of $1,286 ($10,145 - $8,859).

4. Gianna purchased 200 shares of stock on January 2, 2012 for $1,000. She sold all the shares on December 31, 2012 for $2,500. On January 3, 2013, the stocks were delivered and payment was submitted to Gianna's account. How should this sale be reported?

A. $1,500 long-term gain on her 2012 return.
B. $1,500 short-term gain on her 2012 return.
C. $1,500 long-term gain on her 2013 return.
D. $1,500 short-term gain on her 2013 return.

The answer is B. The sale and income must be reported in the year the security is sold, regardless of when the proceeds were received. She held the shares for less than one year, so her gain is short-term. Therefore, Gianna has a short-term gain that must be reported on her 2012 tax return. ###

5. Ruben bought 100 shares of stock on October 1, 2011 when the share price was $26. He then sold them for $20 a share on October 1, 2012. How should this trade be reported, and what is the nature of Ruben's gain or loss?

A. Ruben has a short-term capital loss of $600.
B. Ruben has a long-term capital loss of $500.
C. This is a wash sale.
D. This is a short-term loss of $500.

The answer is A. Ruben has a short-term capital loss of $600 = (100 shares X $26) - (100 shares X $20). Ruben's holding period was not more than one year, which means that the loss must be treated as a short-term capital loss. To determine holding period, begin counting on the date *after* the date the taxpayer acquires the property. ###

6. Tahir purchased 100 shares in Foresthill Mutual Fund in April 2012 for $750. He received a capital gain distribution of $120 in 2012. The $120 was reported to him on Form 1099-DIV. How should this be reported on his tax return?

A. Tahir must reduce his stock's basis by $120.
B. Tahir must report the $120 as interest income.
C. Tahir must report the $120 as a long-term capital gain.
D. Tahir must report the $120 as a short-term capital gain.

The answer is C. Mutual funds frequently distribute capital gains to shareholders. Capital gain distributions for mutual funds are always taxed at long-term capital gain tax rates, no matter how long a taxpayer has actually held the mutual fund shares. ###

7. Fred bought ten shares of Jixi Corporation stock on October 1, 2011. He sold them for a $7,000 loss on October 1, 2012. He has no other capital gains or losses. He also has $20,000 of wage income. How must Fred treat this transaction on his tax return?

A. Fred may deduct the $7,000 as a long-term capital loss on his 2012 return.
B. Fred may deduct the $7,000 as a short-term capital loss on his 2012 return.
C. Fred may deduct $3,000 as a short-term capital loss to offset his wage income on his 2012 return. The remaining amount, $4,000, must be carried over to future tax years.
D. Fred may not offset any of his wage income, so the entire loss must be carried over to future tax years.

The answer is C. Fred has a short-term loss because he did not hold the stock for over one year. He may deduct $3,000 of the loss in 2012, netting against his wage income. The remaining amount, $4,000, must be carried over to future tax years. The carryover retains its character as either long-term or short-term. ###

8. Melissa purchased 1,000 shares of Devil Foods Company stock in 2010 at $10 per share. She sold 900 shares on January 15, 2012 at $9 per share, resulting in a $900 loss. Melissa's husband, Alex, purchased 900 shares on February 10, 2012. Alex and Melissa keep their finances separate and will file MFS in 2012. Which of the following is true?

A. Melissa may deduct the $900 capital loss on her tax return.
B. Melissa has a wash sale and her loss is not deductible.
C. Alex may deduct the loss on his separate tax return.
D. None of the above.

The answer is B. The loss is disallowed. Melissa has a wash sale, because her spouse repurchased identical securities within 30 days. It does not matter if they file MFS. If a taxpayer sells stock and her spouse then repurchases identical stock within 30 days, the taxpayer has a wash sale. ###

9. Nikhil's adjusted basis in 500 shares of Edico Corporation was $2,550. If Nikhil sold 500 shares for $3,300, then what is his reported sales price for the shares and the resulting gain or loss?

A. $3,300 sales price and $750 gain.
B. $3,300 sales price and $700 gain.
C. $3,255 sales price and $750 gain.
D. $2,550 sales price and $750 loss.

The answer is A. The sales price is $3,300, which is $750 more than the adjusted basis of the shares. ###

10. Kevin paid $1,200 for 100 shares of stock last year. He also paid his broker a $75 fee on the purchase of his stock. A few months later, Kevin sold the stock. His Form 1099-B shows $925 as the gross proceeds from the sale. What is the amount Kevin will report as his sales price?

A. $850.
B. $925.
C. $1,000.
D. $1,275.

The answer is B. The sales price of the stock always remains the same. The sales price (or gross proceeds) is never adjusted. The broker's commission is instead added to the stock's basis. ###

11. Dorian purchased 1,000 shares of Hometown Mutual Fund on February 15, 2009 for $15 per share. On January 31, 2012, he sold all his shares for $3.75 per share. He also earned $45,000 in wages in 2012. He has no other transactions during the year. How should this transaction be reported on his tax return?

A. Dorian has a short-term capital loss of $11,250. He will be allowed to offset $11,250 of his wage income with the capital loss.
B. Dorian must carry over the entire loss to a future tax year and offset capital gains.
C. Dorian may take a $3,000 capital loss on his 2012 tax return and the remainder of the losses will carry forward to subsequent years.
D. Dorian may take a $5,000 capital loss on his 2012 tax return and the remainder of the losses will carry forward to subsequent years.

The answer is C. Dorian cannot deduct all his stock losses in the current year. Dorian may take a $3,000 capital loss on his 2012 tax return and the remainder of the losses will carry forward to subsequent years. ###

12. Kayla's cost basis was $2,400 for 600 shares of stock she purchased in December 2009 and then sold in September 2012. She sold the 600 shares for $4,400 and paid a $100 broker's commission. Her broker reported the gross proceeds of $4,400 on Form 1099-B. What was the sales price for the shares and the amount and type of capital gain or loss?

A. $4,400 sales price and $2,000 short-term gain.
B. $4,400 sales price and $1,900 long-term gain.
C. $4,500 sales price and $2,100 short-term gain.
D. $4,500 sales price and $1,900 long-term gain.

The answer is B. The sales price was $4,400, which was $1,900 more than the adjusted basis of $2,500 ($2,400 cost + $100 commission) of the shares. ###

13. Colin purchased 100 shares of Entertainment Digital Media stock for $1,000 on December 1, 2010. He sold these shares for $750 on December 22, 2011. Colin has seller's remorse, and on January 19, 2012 he repurchases 100 shares of Entertainment stock for $800. Which of the following statements is true?

A. Colin may report his capital losses from the first sale of stock.
B. Colin has a reportable loss in 2011, and a taxable gain in 2012.
C. Colin may not deduct his stock losses and must add the disallowed loss to his basis.
D. Colin may report a $250 capital loss in 2012.

The answer is C. Because Colin bought substantially identical stock, he cannot deduct his loss of $250 on the sale. However, he may add the disallowed loss to the cost of the new stock to obtain his adjusted basis in the new stock. This is called the "wash sale rule." ###

14. If taxpayers cannot provide their basis in a property and the property is later sold, the IRS will deem the basis to be _____.

A. Zero.
B. Fair market value.
C. Actual cost.
D. Average cost.

The answer is A. In order to compute gain or loss on a sale, taxpayers must provide their basis in the sold property. The basis on property is usually its cost. If taxpayers cannot provide their basis in the property, the IRS will deem the basis to be zero. ###

15. Gerardo has 100 shares of Wild Fishery stock, which he purchased five years ago for $1,500. In May 2012, Wild Fishery issues a nontaxable stock dividend of 50 additional shares. Gerardo sells 60 shares on December 25, 2012. What is his adjusted basis in these 60 shares?

A. $500.
B. $600.
C. $900.
D. $2,250.

The answer is B. Gerardo's basis in the original stock was $1,500 for 100 shares, so his original basis per share was $15 ($1,500/100). The addition of 50 shares means Gerardo's basis per share *decreased* to $10 per share ($1,500/150). Therefore, Gerardo's basis in the 60 shares he sold in December is $600 ($10 adjusted basis per share X 60). ###

16. Oliver operates an electronics repair business as a sole proprietorship. In 2012, Oliver sold property that was acquired for use in the business for $15,000. The purchase price of the property was $12,000, and Oliver had claimed depreciation of $3,000 related to the property. He accepted a down payment of $5,000 from the buyer, along with a note requiring additional payments of $2,500 plus interest in each of the next four years.

Based upon the information provided, what amount of taxable income will result from the installment sale of this property in 2012?

A. Capital gain of $1,000 and ordinary income of $3,000.
B. Capital gain of $5,000 and ordinary income of $1,000.
C. Capital gain of $2,000.
D. Capital gain of $1,000 and ordinary income of $1,000.

The answer is A. The amount of depreciation deducted for the property ($3,000) is recaptured and reported in 2012 as ordinary income. This amount is added back to the adjusted basis of $9,000 to determine the adjusted basis for the installment sale ($12,000). This amount is subtracted from the total proceeds of the sale ($15,000) to determine the gross profit of $3,000, which derives a gross profit percentage of 20%. This percentage is applied to the portion of proceeds received in 2012 ($5,000) to determine the amount of capital gain recognizable this year. ###

Supporting calculations:

Original purchase price	$12,000
Less depreciation deductions	($3,000)
Adjusted basis at date of sale	$9,000
Depreciation recapture	$3,000
Adjusted basis for installment sale	$12,000
Proceeds of sale	$15,000
Gross profit	**$3,000**
Gross profit percentage 20%	
Proceeds in 2012	$5,000
Capital gain to be recognized	$1,000

Unit 12: Nonrecognition Property Transactions

More Reading:
Publication 523, *Selling Your Home*
Publication 544, *Sales and Other Dispositions of Assets*

Nonrecognition property transactions are transactions in which a taxpayer sells or exchanges property without any tax consequences. Some of these transactions are nontaxable, some are tax deferred, and some are considered nontaxable exchanges.

The three most common transactions that result in nonrecognition treatment are:

- Sale of a primary residence (section 121, excluded gain)
- Like-kind exchanges (section 1031 exchange)
- Involuntary conversions (section 1033 exchange)

In some cases, these transactions are partially taxable.

Sale of Primary Residence (Section 121)

In many cases, a taxpayer may exclude the gain from the sale of a primary residence. Up to $250,000 of gain may be excluded for single filers and up to $500,000 for joint filers. Generally, if the taxpayer can exclude all of the gain, it is not even necessary to report the sale. If all or part of the gain is taxable, then the sale must be reported on Schedule D.

A loss on the sale of a primary residence cannot be deducted.

The section 121 exclusion only applies to a "main home" and not to rental properties, vacation homes, or second homes. A taxpayer's main home is the residence where he lives most of the time. It does not have to be a traditional house. The main home can be a:

- House
- Houseboat, mobile home
- Cooperative apartment
- Condominium

In order to qualify as a "home," it must have sleeping, kitchen, and bathroom facilities.

Example: Wayne owns and lives in a house in the city. He also owns a beach house, which he uses only during the summer. The house in the city is his main home; the beach house is not. Wayne sells the beach house and has $100,000 in gain. The gain cannot be excluded, because the beach house is not his primary residence.

Eligibility Requirements for the Section 121 Exclusion

To be eligible for the exclusion, taxpayers must:

- Have sold the home that has been their main home
- Meet "ownership" and "use" tests
- Not have excluded gain in the two years prior to the current sale of their home

The Ownership Test and Use Test

To meet the *ownership* and *use tests,* during the five-year period ending on the date of the sale the taxpayer must have:

- Owned the home for at least two years (the ownership test), and
- Lived in the home as his main home for at least two years (the use test).

Example: For the past six years, Lindsay lived with her parents in the home her parents owned. On September 1, 2011, she bought the house from her parents. She continued to live there until December 14, 2012 when she sold it because she wanted a bigger house. Lindsay does not meet the requirements for exclusion. Although she *lived* in the property as her main home for more than two years, she did not *own* it for the required two years. Therefore, she does not meet both the ownership and use tests.

The required two years of ownership and use do not have to be continuous. Taxpayers meet the tests if they can show that they owned and lived in the property as their main home for either 24 full months or 730 days (365 x 2) during the five-year period.

Example: In 2004, Carter lived in a rented apartment. The apartment building was later changed to a condominium, which he bought on December 1, 2009. In 2010, Carter became ill, and on April 14 of that year he moved into his daughter's home. On July 10, 2012, while still living in his daughter's home, Carter sold his condo. He can exclude all the gain on the sale because he meets the ownership and use tests. His five-year period is from July 11, 2007 to July 10, 2012 (the date he sold the condo). He owned the condo from December 1, 2009 to July 10, 2012 (over two years). He lived there from July 11, 2007 (the beginning of the five-year period) to April 14, 2010 (over two years).

Ownership and use tests can be met during different two-year periods. However, a taxpayer must meet both tests during the five-year period ending on the date of the sale.

Example: Irene bought and moved into a house in July 2008. She lived there for 13 months and then moved in with her boyfriend and kept her house vacant. They broke up in January 2011. She moved back into her own house in 2011 and lived there for 12 months until she sold it in July 2012. Irene meets the ownership and use tests because during the five-year period ending on the date of sale, she owned the house for four years and lived in the house for a total of 25 months.

Short, temporary absences, even if the property is rented during those absences, are still counted as periods of use. Short absences include vacations and trips. Longer breaks, such as a one-year sabbatical, do not.

Example: Katarina bought her home on February 1, 2009. Each year, she left her home for a four-month summer vacation. Katarina sold the house on March 1, 2012. She may exclude up to $250,000 of gain. The vacations are short temporary absences and are still counted toward her periods of use.

Married Homeowners

The ownership and use tests are applied somewhat differently to married homeowners. Married homeowners can exclude gain of up to $500,000 if they meet all of the following conditions:

- They file a joint return.
- *Either* spouse must meet the ownership test (only one is required to own the home).
- Both spouses must meet the use test.
- Neither spouse must have excluded gain in the two years before the current sale of the home.

If either spouse does not satisfy all these requirements, the couple cannot claim the maximum $500,000 exclusion.

> **Example:** Leigh sells her main home in June 2012, and she has $350,000 of gain. She marries Kelly in September 2012. Leigh meets the ownership and use tests, but Kelly does not. Leigh can exclude up to $250,000 of gain on her 2012 tax return, whether she files MFJ or MFS. The $500,000 exclusion for joint returns does not apply in this case because Kelly does not meet the use test.

> **Example:** Robert owns a home that he has lived in continuously for eight years. In June 2009, he marries Annabel. She moves in with her husband and they both live in the house until December 1, 2012 when the house is sold. Robert meets the ownership test and the use test. Annabel meets the use test, because only Robert is listed as the owner of the property. On a jointly filed return, they may still claim the maximum $500,000 exclusion because they both meet the use test, and Robert meets the ownership test.

An unmarried couple who own a home and live together may take the $250,000 exclusion individually on their separate returns if they qualify for the use and ownership tests. Sometimes this exclusion also applies to family members who own a home and live together.

> **Example:** Greta and Sydney are twin sisters. They are both widowed and decide to purchase a home and live together. If they were to later sell the home, then the ownership and use tests would apply to them as well. Each sister would be able to claim an exclusion of up to $250,000 for their portion of the sale on their individual returns.

Deceased Spouses and Home Sales

There are special rules regarding the section 121 gain when a taxpayer's spouse dies. A taxpayer is considered to have owned and lived in a home during any period of time when the spouse owned and lived in it as a main home (provided that the taxpayer did not remarry before the date of sale). In effect, the holding period is "tacked on" for surviving spouses.

An unmarried surviving spouse may exclude up to $500,000 of gain if he or she sells the home within two years of the spouse's death.

> **Example:** Alice has owned and lived in her home for the last seven years. She marries William in April 2012, and he moves into the home with her. Alice dies six months later, and William inherits the property. He does not remarry. William sells the home on December 1, 2012. Even though William did not own or live in the house for two years, he meets the test requirements because his period of ownership and use includes the period that Alice owned and used the property before her death. William may qualify to exclude up to $500,000 of the gain because of the special rule that applies to surviving spouses.

This exclusion also applies to a home that is transferred by a spouse if the transfer is part of a divorce. In the case of a divorce, the receiving spouse is considered to have owned the home during any period of time that the transferor owned it.

Five-Year Test Period Suspension for Military Personnel

Taxpayers can choose to have the five-year test period for ownership and use suspended during any period the homeowner (or spouse if married) served on "qualified official extended duty" as a member of the armed services or Foreign Service of the United States, as an employee of the intelligence community, or as a member of the Peace Corps. This means that the taxpayer may be able to meet the two-year use test even if he and/or his spouse did not actually live in the home during the normal five-year period required of other taxpayers.

Taxpayers qualify if they serve at a duty station at least 50 miles from their main home or live in government quarters under government order. Taxpayers are considered to be on extended duty when they are called to active duty for more than 90 days or for an indefinite period.

> **Example**: Luis bought a home in 2001 and lived in it for two-and-a-half years. Beginning in 2005, he was on qualified official extended duty in the U.S. Army, and left the home vacant. He sold his home in 2012 and had a $12,000 gain. Luis would not normally meet the use test in the five-year period before the sale. However, he can disregard those six years, because of the special exclusion for military taxpayers.

This extension of time can also apply to taxpayers who have recently left the military.

Exception to the "Use Test" for the Disabled

There is an exception to the use test if, during the five-year period before the sale of the home, the taxpayer becomes physically or mentally unable to care for himself. The taxpayer must have owned and lived in the home for at least one year.

Under this exception, the taxpayer is still considered to have lived in the home during any time that he is forced to live in a medical facility, including a nursing home, because of medical reasons.

Qualifying for a Reduced Exclusion

Taxpayers who owned and used a home for less than two years (meaning they do not meet the ownership and use tests) may be able to claim a reduced exclusion under certain conditions. These include selling the home due to a change in place of employment, health, or unforeseen circumstances.

Unforeseen Circumstances

The IRS will accept that a home sale has occurred primarily because of unforeseen circumstances if any of the following events occur during the taxpayer's period of use and ownership of the residence:

- Death or divorce.
- Health reasons (for a spouse, child, or other related person, such as a father, sibling, etc. The related person does not have to be a dependent in order for the special circumstances to qualify for the exclusion.)
- Unemployment or a job change. (The "job related" exclusion qualifies if the new job is at least 50 miles farther than the old home was from the former place of employment. If there was no former place of employment, the distance between the new place of employment and the old home must be at least 50 miles.)
- Multiple births resulting from the same pregnancy.
- Damage to the residence resulting from a disaster, or an act of war or terrorism.
- Involuntary conversion of the property.

The circumstances may involve the taxpayer, his spouse, a co-owner, or a member of the taxpayer's household. The regulations also give the IRS the discretion to determine other circumstances as unforeseen. For example, the IRS Commissioner determined that the September 11, 2001 terrorist attacks were an "unforeseen circumstance."

> **Example:** Justin purchased his new home in Mississippi in June 2011, but shortly after he moved in he lost his job. He found a new job in North Carolina and sold his house in April 2012. Because the distance between Justin's new place of employment and his former home is at least 50 miles, the sale satisfies the conditions of the distance safe harbor. Justin's sale of his home is due to a change in place of employment, and he is entitled to claim a reduced exclusion of gain from the sale.

How to Figure the Reduced Exclusion

The reduced exclusion amount equals the full $250,000 or $500,000 (for married couples filing jointly) multiplied by a fraction. The numerator is the shorter of:

- The period of ownership that the taxpayer owned and used the home as a principal residence during the five-year period ending on the sale date, or
- The period between the last sale for which the taxpayer claimed the exclusion and the sale date for the home currently being sold.

The denominator is two years, or the equivalent in months or days. The amount of the reduced exclusion is figured by determining the number of days the taxpayer actually owned and used the property, divided by either 730 days (two years) or 24 months (two years).

> **Example:** Carrie purchases her home on January 1, 2012 for $350,000. Her mother is diagnosed with terminal cancer, and Carrie must move to care for her. Even though Carrie does not claim her mother as a dependent, the move still qualifies as an unforeseen circumstance. Carrie sells her home on May 1, 2012 for $430,000, realizing a gain of $80,000. She qualifies for the reduced maximum exclusion, and part of her gain is nontaxable. She owned and occupied the home for 121 days (January 1 to May 1). She may exclude $41,438 ($250,000 X [121 ÷ 730]). Therefore, Carrie's taxable gain is $38,562 ($80,000 - $41,438). This amount would be a short-term capital gain since she owned the house for less than one year.

> **Example:** Sabrina, a single taxpayer, lived in her principal residence for one full year (365 days) before selling it at a $400,000 gain in 2012. She qualifies for the reduced exclusion because she is pregnant with triplets (multiple births exclusion). Sabrina can exclude $125,000 of gain ($250,000 X [365 ÷ 730]).

Land Sale Only and Adjacent Lots

If a taxpayer sells the land on which his main home is located but not the house itself, he cannot exclude the gain. Similarly, the sale of a vacant plot of land with no house on it does not qualify for the Section 121 exclusion.

> **Example:** Theresa purchases an empty lot in 2008 for $90,000, intending to build her dream home. The construction was delayed and her house was never completed. In December 2012, Theresa sells the land for $150,000. She owned the property for more than a year, so she has $60,000 of long-term capital gain. None of the gain can be excluded from income, because there is no residence on the property.

If a taxpayer sells a vacant lot that is *adjacent to his main home*, he may be able to exclude the gain from the sale under certain circumstances. Gain from the sale of vacant land that was used as part of the principal residence may be excluded if the land sale occurs within two years before or after the sale of the home.

The sale of the land and the sale of the home are treated as one sale for purposes of the exclusion.

Figuring the Gain or Loss on a Home Sale

The following are used to figure the gain or loss on the sale of a home:

- Selling price
- Amount realized
- Basis
- Adjusted basis

Selling Price: The selling price is the total amount the taxpayer received for his main home. It includes money, all notes, mortgages, or other debts taken over by the buyer as part of the sale, and the fair market value of any other property or services that the seller received. Real estate sales proceeds are reported on Form 1099-S, *Proceeds From Real Estate Transactions*. If a taxpayer does not receive a Form 1099-S, he must figure basis by using sale documents and other records.

Amount Realized: The amount realized is the selling price minus selling expenses, which include commissions, advertising fees, legal fees, and loan charges paid by the seller, such as points.

Basis: The basis in a home is determined by how the taxpayer *obtained* the home. For example, if a taxpayer purchases a home, the basis is the cost of the home. If a taxpayer builds a home, then the basis is the building cost plus the cost of land. If a taxpayer receives a home through an inheritance or gift, the basis is either its FMV or the adjusted basis of the home.

Example: Eve is single. She sells her home for $350,000 in 2012. She purchased the home twenty years ago for $50,000 and has lived in it continuously since then. She pays $4,000 in seller's fees to sell the home. Her amount realized in the sale is $346,000 ($350,000 - $4,000 = $346,000). Her basis is subtracted from her amount realized in order to figure her gain: ($346,000 - $50,000 basis) = $296,000. Eve's gain is $296,000, but she qualifies for a section 121 exclusion because she meets the ownership and use tests. Therefore, she may exclude up to $250,000 of her gain from tax. Her taxable gain is figured as follows: ($296,000 gain - $250,000 section 121 exclusion) = $46,000 in long-term capital gain. If the selling price or amount realized is $250,000 or less ($500,000 or less if filing jointly), there is no need to figure the realized gain, assuming the ownership and use tests are met.

If the taxpayer inherited the home, the basis is its FMV on the date of the decedent's death, or the later alternate valuation date chosen by the representative for the estate.

Adjusted Basis: The *adjusted basis* is the taxpayer's basis in the home increased or decreased by certain amounts. Increases include additions or improvements to the home. In order to be considered a basis *increase*, an addition or improvement must have a useful life of more than one year (example: putting on a new roof or an additional bedroom). Repairs that simply maintain a home in good condition are not considered improvements and should not be added to the basis of the property. Decreases to basis include deductible casualty losses, credits, and product rebates.

> **Formula for figuring adjusted basis:**
>
> **Basis + Increases - Decreases = Adjusted Basis**

Example: Immanuel purchased his home years ago for $125,000. In 2012, Immanuel added another bedroom to the property. The cost of the addition was $25,000. This *increased* the house's basis. Immanuel's adjusted basis is therefore $150,000.

If the *amount realized* is more than the adjusted basis of the property, the difference is a gain, and the taxpayer may be able to exclude all or part of it. If the amount realized is less than the adjusted basis, the difference is a nondeductible loss.

Example: Pete sold his main home for $275,000. His selling expenses were $10,000. The amount realized on Pete's sale is $265,000 (selling price minus selling expenses). He purchased his home ten years ago for $180,000. Therefore, his gain on the sale of the house is $85,000 ($265,000 - $180,000). If Pete meets the ownership and use tests, he can exclude all the gain from the sale of his home, and the sale does not have to be reported on his tax return.

Proceeds from the sale of a main home that meets the ownership and use tests must be reported *only* if the taxpayer has a gain on the sale that is not fully covered by the exclusion. Gain from the sale of a home that is not the taxpayer's main home will generally have to be reported as income.

In both cases, the nonexcludable gain is taxable gain and must be reported on Schedule D. If the home was used for business purposes or as rental property, the gain is reported on Form 4797, *Sales of Business Property.*

If the taxpayer owns a home for one year or less, the gain is reported as a short-term capital gain. If the taxpayer owns the home for more than one year, the gain is reported as a long-term capital gain.

The fees and costs for obtaining a mortgage are not deductible and cannot be included in a home's basis. These costs include items such as termite inspections or title fees that would be required regardless of whether a taxpayer was financing the purchase. Points may be deducted as mortgage interest on Schedule A. The IRS defines points as prepaid interest paid by a home buyer at closing in order to obtain a mortgage or a lower interest rate.

If a taxpayer took depreciation deductions because he used his home as a rental or for other business purposes, he cannot exclude the part of the gain equal to any deductible depreciation. Section 121 applies only to the *nonbusiness* portion of a home.

Example: Erica lives in one side of a duplex she owns and rents out the other side. Both units are the same size. She purchased the duplex in 2004 for $200,000. In 2012, Erica sells the duplex for $340,000 for a total gain of $140,000. Since only half of the duplex counts as her primary residence, she would have to split the gain based on the portion of the property that qualifies as her main home. Under section 121, Erica may exclude one half of the gain ($70,000). The other $70,000 is long-term capital gain that she has to report. Erica also has the option to reinvest the proceeds from her rental property sale into a new property by executing a section 1031 exchange.

Like-Kind Exchanges (Section 1031 exchange)

A section 1031 "like-kind" exchange occurs when similar business property is exchanged. If a taxpayer trades business or investment property for similar property, he does not have to pay tax on the gain or deduct any loss until he disposes of the property he received. To qualify for nonrecognition treatment, the exchange must meet all of the following conditions:

- The property must be business or investment property. A personal residence does not qualify.
- The property must not be "held primarily for sale" (such as inventory).
- Securities such as stocks and bonds do not qualify for like-kind exchange treatment.
- Partnership interests do not qualify for like-kind exchange treatment.
- There must be an *actual exchange* of property (the exchange for cash is treated as a sale, not an exchange).
- The property to be received must be identified in writing within 45 days after the date of transfer of the property given up.

The replacement property must be received by the earlier of:

- The 180th day after the date on which the original property was given up in the trade, or
- The due date, including extensions, for the tax return for the year in which the transfer of the property relinquished occurs.

Taxpayers report like-kind exchanges to the IRS on Form 8824, *Like-Kind Exchanges*.

Rules Regarding Acceptable Like-Kind Exchanges

To qualify as a section 1031 exchange, the property must be "like-kind" property, such as the trade of real estate for real estate or personal property for personal property.

Real properties are generally acceptable as like-kind exchanges regardless of whether the properties are improved or unimproved. For instance, the exchange of a store building for farmland would be an acceptable trade.

The property also must be the same "class" of property. For example, the exchanges of an apartment building for an office building and a panel truck for a pickup truck qualify as trades of "like" property. However, the exchange of a semi-truck for a plot of land would not qualify as a section 1031 exchange, even if both properties were business properties.

> **Example:** Casey exchanges a private jet with an adjusted basis of $400,000 for an office building valued at $375,000. Private property (the jet) cannot be exchanged with real property (the building). Casey would not qualify for section 1031 treatment.

The trade of a piece of factory machinery for a factory building is not a qualifying exchange; nor is the trade of equipment or business property that is used within the United States with that used outside the United States, as the two are not considered "like" property.

Under the same rule, real estate located *inside* the United States and real estate located *outside* the United States is not "like property" and does not qualify for section 1031 treatment.

A taxpayer cannot deduct a loss in a section 1031 transaction.

Unacceptable and Disallowed Trades

The following types of property will not qualify for section 1031 treatment:

- Livestock of different sexes
- Securities, bonds, stocks, or notes
- Currency exchanges
- The exchange of partnership interests

What is "Boot"?

Although the Internal Revenue Code itself does not use the term "boot," the term is frequently used to describe property that is not "like-kind" property. The receipt of "boot" will cause a realized gain on an otherwise nontaxable exchange.

Usually this occurs when two people exchange property that is unequal in value, so one party pays cash, or "boot," to make up the difference.

The exchange is still valid, but the taxpayer who receives boot may have to recognize a taxable gain. Boot received can be offset by qualified costs paid during the transaction.

Example: Sloan wishes to exchange his rental property in a 1031 exchange. His relinquished rental property has an FMV of $60,000 and an adjusted basis of $30,000. Sloan's replacement property has an FMV of $50,000, and he also receives $10,000 in cash as part of the exchange. Sloan, therefore, has a realized gain of $30,000 on the actual exchange, but he is required to pay tax on only $10,000—the cash (boot) received in the exchange. The rest of his gain is deferred until he sells or disposes of the property at a later date.

The fair market value of the boot is recognized as taxable gain.

Sometimes boot is recognized when two people exchange property that is subject to a liability. Liabilities on property are "netted" against each other. The taxpayer is treated as having received boot only if he is relieved of a greater liability than the liability he assumes.

This is also called "debt reduction boot," and it occurs when a taxpayer's debt on the replacement property is less than the debt on the relinquished property. "Debt reduction boot" most often occurs when a taxpayer is acquiring a less valuable or expensive property.

Basis of Property Received in a Like-Kind Exchange

The basis of the property received is generally the adjusted basis of the property transferred.

Example: Judy has a rental house with an adjusted basis of $70,000. In 2012, she trades the rental house for an empty lot with an FMV of $150,000. Judy's basis in the lot is $70,000, which is the adjusted basis of her previous property.

Example: Adrian exchanges rental real estate (adjusted basis $50,000, FMV $80,000) for another rental property (FMV $80,000). No cash was exchanged in the transaction. Adrian's basis in the new property is the same as the basis of his old property ($50,000). Basis is increased by any amount that is treated as a dividend, plus any gain recognized on the trade. Basis is decreased by any cash received and the FMV of any other (additional) property received.

> **Example:** Peyton bought a new diesel truck for use in her catering business. She paid $43,000 cash, plus she traded in her old truck for $13,600. The old truck cost $50,000 two years ago. Peyton took depreciation deductions of $39,500 on the old vehicle. Even though she deducted depreciation of $39,500, the $3,100 gain on the exchange ($13,600 trade-in allowance minus her $10,500 adjusted basis) is not reported because the gain is postponed under the rules for like-kind exchanges.

The basis of any other or additional property received is its fair market value on the date of the trade. The taxpayer is taxed on any gain realized, but only up to the amount of the money and the fair market value of the "unlike" (or boot) nonqualified property received.

Property Plus Cash

If a taxpayer trades property and also pays money for it, the basis of the property received is the basis of the property given up, increased by any additional money paid. This is considered a "partially taxable exchange."

> **Example:** Jorge trades a plot of land (adjusted basis $30,000) for a different plot of land in another town (FMV $70,500). He also pays an additional $4,000 in cash. Jorge's basis in the new land is $34,000: his $30,000 basis in the old land plus the $4,000 additional money he paid.

Section 1031 Exchanges Between Related Parties

Like-kind exchanges are allowed between related parties and family members. However, if *either* party disposes or sells the property within two years after a 1031 exchange, the exchange is usually disqualified; any gain or loss that was deferred in the original transaction must be recognized in the year the disposition occurs.

For purposes of this rule, a "related person" includes close family members (spouses, siblings, parents, and children). There are some exceptions to this two-year rule:

- If one of the parties originally involved in the exchange dies, the two-year rule does not apply.
- If the property is subsequently converted in an involuntary exchange (such as a fire or a flood), the two-year rule does not apply.
- If the exchange is genuinely not for tax avoidance purposes, the subsequent disposition will generally be allowed.

Exchanges between related parties get close scrutiny by the IRS because they are often used by taxpayers to evade taxes on gains.

Involuntary Conversions (Section 1033)

An involuntary conversion occurs when a taxpayer's property is damaged, destroyed, or condemned, and the taxpayer then receives an award, insurance money, or some other type of payment. The property must be converted, beyond the taxpayer's control, as a result of:

- Theft, destruction, or other disaster,
- Condemnation, or
- Threat of condemnation.

Gain or loss from an involuntary conversion of property is usually recognized for tax purposes unless the property is a main home. A taxpayer reports the gain or deducts the loss in the year the gain or loss is realized. A taxpayer cannot deduct a loss from an involuntary conversion on personal-use property unless the loss resulted from a casualty or theft.

However, under section 1033, a taxpayer can avoid reporting gain on an involuntary conversion by receiving or investing in property that is similar to the converted property. If insurance proceeds or some other source produces a gain on the exchange, tax can be deferred by reinvesting the proceeds in property similar to the property that was subject to the involuntary conversion.

> **Example:** Denise owns a residential rental with an adjusted basis of $50,000. It is destroyed by a hurricane in 2012. Her property is insured, so the insurance company gives Denise a check for $100,000, which is the FMV of the home. Denise buys a replacement rental property six months later for $100,000. Her realized gain on the involuntary conversion is $50,000 ($100,000 insurance settlement minus her $50,000 basis). However, Denise does not have to recognize any taxable gain because she reinvested all the insurance proceeds in another, similar property. This is an example of a qualified 1033 exchange.

The Replacement Period

The replacement period for an involuntary conversion generally ends two years after the end of the first tax year in which any part of the gain is realized.

> **Example:** Barney owns a dog grooming business. On September 1, 2012, a flood destroys a storage shed filled with his grooming supplies. Barney's insurance company reimburses him for the entire loss. Barney has until December 31, 2014 to replace the shed and supplies using the insurance proceeds. Barney is not required to report the insurance proceeds on his 2012 tax return. So long as Barney reinvests all the insurance proceeds in the replacement property, he will not have any gain.

Real property that is held for investment or used in a trade or business is allowed a three-year replacement period. The replacement period is four years for livestock that is involuntarily converted because of weather-related conditions.

If a main home is damaged or destroyed and is in a federally-declared disaster area, the replacement period is extended to four years. Certain other extreme disaster areas, including Hurricane Katrina, the May 2007 Kansas storms and tornadoes, and the Midwestern area disasters of 2008, have a five-year replacement period, but only if the replacement property is purchased in the same area.

Property type	Replacement period
Most property except those noted below.	Two years
Real property that is held for investment or business use. This includes residential rentals, office buildings, etc.	Three years
Sale of livestock due to weather-related conditions.	Four years
Property in federally-declared disaster area	Four to five years

If a taxpayer reinvests in replacement property similar to the converted property, the replacement property's basis is the same as the converted property's basis on the date of the conversion. The taxpayer will have a carryover basis in the new property. Essentially, the taxpayer's basis in the new property will be its cost, reduced by any gain realized on the old property that was not recognized.

The basis may be *decreased* by the following:

- Any loss a taxpayer recognizes on the involuntary conversion

292

- Any money a taxpayer receives that he does not spend on similar property

The basis is *increased* by the following:

- Any gain a taxpayer recognizes on the involuntary conversion
- Any cost of acquiring the replacement property

Example: Paula paid $100,000 for a rental property five years ago. After factoring in her depreciation deductions, her adjusted basis in the property is $75,000 at the beginning of 2012. The property is insured for $300,000 and is destroyed by fire in June 2012. On December 15, 2012, Paula receives a $300,000 payment from her insurance company. She reinvests all the insurance proceeds, plus $5,000 more of her own savings, into a new rental apartment building. She qualifies to defer all of her gain. Her basis in the new rental property is $80,000 ($75,000 + $5,000 of her additional investment).

Example: Franco owns an apartment building in Oklahoma with a basis of $250,000. Franco receives an insurance settlement of $400,000 after the building is destroyed by a tornado. A year later, Franco decides to purchase another apartment building in Wisconsin for $380,000. Franco's realized gain on the involuntary conversion is $150,000 ($400,000 - $250,000 basis). Franco must recognize $20,000 of gain, because he received an insurance payment of $400,000, but only spent $380,000 on the replacement property ($400,000 - $380,000). His basis in the new property is $250,000, which is calculated as the cost of the new property in Wisconsin minus the deferred gain ($380,000 - $130,000 = $250,000). If Franco had used all the insurance proceeds and invested it in the new property, he would not have to report any taxable gain.

Condemnations

A condemnation is a type of involuntary conversion. Condemnation is the process by which private property is seized from its original owner for public use. The property may be taken by the government or by a private organization that has the legal power to seize it.

The owner generally receives a condemnation award (money or property) in exchange for the property that is taken. A condemnation is like a forced sale, the owner being the seller and the government being the buyer.

Example: The federal government informs Trevor that his farmland is being condemned to make it into a public park. Trevor goes to court to try to keep his property. The court decides in favor of the government, which takes Trevor's property and pays him $400,000 in exchange. Trevor's basis in the farmland was $80,000. He decides not to purchase replacement farmland. Therefore, he has a taxable event, and $320,000 would need to be recognized as income ($400,000 - $80,000 = $320,000). If Trevor were to purchase replacement property with the condemnation award, he would have a nontaxable section 1033 exchange.

A condemnation award is the money that is paid for the condemned property. Amounts taken out of the award to pay debts on the property are considered paid to the taxpayer and are included in the amount of the award.

Example: The state condemned Gabriel's property in order to build a light rail system. The court award was set at $200,000. The state paid Gabriel only $148,000 because it paid $50,000 to his mortgage company and $2,000 in accrued real estate taxes. Gabriel is considered to have received the entire $200,000 as a condemnation award.

The time period for replacing condemned property is the same as other qualified section 1033 exchanges—two years after the end of the first tax year in which any part of the gain on the condemnation is realized. For business-use property, the replacement period is three years instead of two.

> **Example:** Joel owns a pool hall. In February 2012, the building is condemned by the city because of the discovery of asbestos in the building. He receives his condemnation award in May 2012. He has until December 31, 2015 to replace the condemned pool hall with a similar building.

Condemnation of a Primary Residence

If a taxpayer has a gain because his main home is condemned, he can generally exclude the gain as if he had sold the home under the section 121 exclusion. Single filers can exclude up to $250,000 of the gain and joint filers up to $500,000.

> **Example:** Lane and Candace are married and file jointly. They paid $100,000 for their home ten years ago. The house is insured for $700,000. Their home is destroyed by a mudslide in 2012, so they receive an insurance payment of $700,000. They have a realized gain on the conversion of $600,000 ($700,000 - $100,000). But $500,000 of the gain is excluded under section 121, leaving $100,000 as taxable long-term capital gain. They may also choose to reinvest the insurance proceeds under the rules for involuntary conversions and defer all the gain.

Summary:
Nonrecognition Property Transactions
Section 121: Sale of Primary Residence
To be eligible for the exclusion, taxpayers must meet the following conditions during the five-year period ending on the date of the sale:
- The home sold had to be their main home where they lived most of the time.
- They had to own the home for at least two years (the ownership test)
- They had to live in the home as their principal residence for at least two years (the use test)
- They must not have excluded gain in the two years before the current sale of the home

The required two years of ownership/use do not have to be continuous. The maximum that can be excluded is $250,000 or $500,000 for MFJ.

Section 1031: Like-Kind Exchanges
Section 1031 exchanges only apply to business properties such as real estate, but not to exchanges of inventory, stocks, bonds, or partnership interests. The replacement property must be received by the earlier of:
- The 180th day after the date on which the original property was given up in the trade, or
- The due date, including extensions, for the tax return for the year in which the transfer of the property relinquished occurs.

Section 1033: Involuntary Conversions
An involuntary conversion occurs when a taxpayer's property is destroyed, stolen, condemned, or disposed of under the threat of condemnation, and the taxpayer receives property or money in payment, such as insurance or a condemnation award.

Unit 12: Questions

1. Erik sold his home for $275,000. His selling expenses were $10,000. What is the amount realized on this sale?

A. $265,000.
B. $275,000.
C. $285,000.
D. Some other amount.

The answer is A. The amount realized on Erik's sale is $265,000, the selling price minus selling expenses. ###

2. Isaiah lived in and owned his home for fifteen months. In 2012, he decides to move in with his new girlfriend, so he sells his home for $285,000. His adjusted basis in the home is $160,000. What is the amount and nature of his taxable gain on the sale?

A. $0 (the gain is excluded under section 121).
B. $160,000 short-term capital gain.
C. $125,000 long-term capital gain.
D. $125,000 short-term capital gain.

The answer is C. Since he does not meet the ownership or use tests, he cannot exclude any of his gain under section 121. The correct answer is $125,000, which is the result of subtracting the adjusted basis in the home from the amount realized ($285,000- $160,000 = $125,000). Since he owned the property for more than a year, his gain is taxed as a long-term capital gain. ###

21. In 2012 Annalise sold her primary residence in Utah and moved to Iowa. She had purchased the house in 2000 for $200,000, and she sold it in 2012 for $550,000, net of selling expenses. During the time she lived in the house, she paid $25,000 for improvements and $15,000 for repairs.

Assuming that Annalise utilizes the maximum available exclusion, what amount would she report as taxable gain?

A. $100,000.
B. $60,000.
C. $75,000.
D. $0.

The answer is C. Annalise's adjusted basis in the house would be the total of her original purchase price of $200,000 and the $25,000 cost of improvements. The cost of repairs would not be considered in determining her adjusted basis. Therefore, her gain on the sale would be $325,000, or the excess of her net proceeds over her adjusted basis. As she met the requirements for ownership and use of the house as her primary residence, she would qualify for the maximum exclusion of $250,000 available to a single taxpayer, and the taxable portion of her gain would be $75,000. ###

Purchase price of house	$200,000
Cost of improvements	$25,000
Adjusted basis	$225,000
Net proceeds of sale	**$550,000**
Gain on sale	$325,000
Exclusion for single taxpayer	($250,000)
Taxable gain	**$75,000**

4. Lucille owns a home in the Vail ski area (the "ski home"). She stays at the ski home most weekends and spends the entire months of December, January, and February there. When she is not at the ski home, she lives in a four-room apartment that she rents in Denver. For over half the year, she lives in Denver. What is Lucille's primary residence for purposes of the section 121 exclusion?

A. Her ski home in Vail.
B. Her apartment in Denver.
C. She is considered a transient for tax purposes.
D. None of the above.

The answer is B. Lucille's main home is her rental apartment in Denver because she lives there most of the time. If she were to sell the ski home, she would not qualify for the section 121 exclusion on the sale because it is a vacation home and not her primary residence. ###

5. Heather, a single woman, bought her first home in June 2002 for $350,000. She lived continuously in the house until she sold it in July 2012 for $620,000. Which of the following is true?

A. Heather may exclude up to $250,000 in gain. The remaining amount must be reported and will be taxed as a long-term capital gain.
B. Heather may exclude all the gain. There is no amount that needs to be reported.
C. Heather may not exclude any of the gain.
D. Heather may exclude $250,000 in gain. The remaining amount must be reported as a short-term capital gain.

The answer is A. Heather may exclude the maximum amount of gain ($250,000) from the sale of her home. Her gain is $270,000 ($620,000 - $350,000). Her taxable gain is $20,000 ($270,000 gain - $250,000 exclusion). The $20,000 taxable gain must be reported as a long-term capital gain. ###

6. Mitchell purchased his primary residence for $350,000 on January 1, 2009. On January 3, 2012, he sells the home for $320,000, incurring a loss of $30,000. How is this transaction reported?

A. Mitchell has a short-term capital loss that can be reported on Schedule D.
B. Mitchell cannot deduct any loss from the sale of his home.
C. Mitchell has a long-term capital loss that can be reported on Schedule D.
D. Mitchell has a deductible casualty loss.

The answer is B. If a taxpayer has a loss on the sale of a primary residence, he cannot deduct it on his return. Losses from the sale of a main home are never tax-deductible. ###

7. All of the following would generally be acceptable as "unforeseen circumstances" for a taxpayer to take a reduced exclusion on the sale of his primary residence except _____:

A. The home is condemned by the city.
B. A legal separation.
C. The birth of twin girls.
D. Moving to another state to be closer to grown children.

The answer is D. The move to be closer to grown children would not qualify. All of the following events would be qualifying events in order to claim a reduced exclusion from a premature sale:

•A divorce or legal separation.
•A pregnancy resulting in multiple births.
•Serious health reasons. (The person who is sick does not need to be the taxpayer's dependent).
•The home is sold after being seized or condemned (such as by a government agency).
•A move due to a new job or new employment.

If any of these exceptions apply, the taxpayer may figure a reduced exclusion based on the number of days he owned and lived in the residence. ###

8. Geoff sold his main home in 2012 at a $29,000 gain. He meets the ownership and use tests to exclude the gain from his income. However, he used one room of the home for business in 2010 and 2011. His records show he claimed $3,000 in depreciation for a home office. What is Geoff's taxable gain on the sale, if any?

A. $0.
B. $1,000.
C. $2,000.
D. $3,000.

The answer is D. Geoff can exclude $26,000 ($29,000 - $3,000) of his gain. He has a taxable gain of $3,000. He must report the gain from depreciation recapture. If a taxpayer took depreciation deductions because he used his home for business purposes or as a rental property, he cannot exclude the part of the gain equal to any depreciation allowed as a deduction. ###

9. Alfred and Kay are married and file jointly. They owned and used a home as their principal residence for 15 months. Alfred got a new job in another state and they sold their home in order to move for the new employment opportunity. What is the maximum amount that can be excluded from income under the rules regarding a reduced exclusion?

A. $22,727.
B. $250,000.
C. $312,500.
E. $500,000.

The answer is C. In this case, a reduced exclusion is available, even though the taxpayers did not live in the home for two full years. They qualify for a reduced exclusion because Alfred is moving for a change in employment. In this case, their maximum reduced exclusion is $312,500 [$500,000 x (15 months/24 months)]. The reduced exclusion applies when the premature sale is primarily due to a move for employment in a new location. ###

10. Bob and Grace were married in January 2008. They purchased their first home in March 2008 for $150,000. In February 2012, Bob and Grace legally separated, and the court granted Grace total ownership of the home as part of the divorce settlement. The divorce became final in June 2012, and the fair market value of the home at the time of the transfer was $370,000. Grace sells the house on December 23, 2012 for $480,000. What is Grace's taxable gain in the transaction?

A. $0.
B. $80,000.
C. $120,000.
D. $210,000.

The answer is B. Special rules apply to divorced taxpayers. Grace meets the ownership and use tests, and the basis in the property remains the same. Transfers related to a divorce are generally nontaxable, and the fair market value of the property at the time of the divorce has no bearing on the taxable outcome. The gain is figured as follows:

Original cost	$150,000
Sale price	$480,000
Total realized gain	$330,000
Sec. 121 exclusion	($250,000)
Taxable gain	$80,000

Since she owned the property for longer than one year, the taxable portion of Grace's gain would be reported as a long-term capital gain. ###

11. Shane and Phyllis move after living in their home for 292 days, because Phyllis became pregnant with triplets and they needed a larger home. The gain on the sale of the home is $260,000. Since they have lived there for less than two years but meet one of the exceptions, what is the actual amount of their reduced exclusion? (Two years=730 days)

A. $60,000.
B. $200,000.
C. $260,000.
D. $500,000.

The answer is B. The couple has an exclusion of $200,000 (292/730 multiplied by the $500,000 exclusion available for married taxpayers). The remaining $60,000 would be considered taxable capital gain income and would be reported on Schedule D. This move qualifies for the reduced exclusion, because multiple births from the same pregnancy are considered a health-related move. ###

12. Regina bought a house for $189,000 in July 2008. She lived there continuously for 13 months and then moved in with her boyfriend. They later separated, and Regina moved back into her own house in 2011 and lived there for 12 months until she sold it in July 2012 for $220,000. What is the amount and nature of her gain?

A. Regina has no taxable gain, because the sale qualifies for a section 121 exclusion.
B. $31,000 long-term capital gain.
C. $31,000 short-term capital gain.
D. $30,000 long-term capital gain.

The answer is A. This sale qualifies for section 121 treatment. Regina meets the ownership and use tests because during the five-year period ending on the date of sale, she owned the house for four years and lived in it for a total of 25 months. The gain is not taxable and does not need to be reported. ###

13. Jonah exchanged a rental building for another rental building. He had a basis of $16,000, plus he had made $10,000 in improvements prior to the exchange. He exchanged it for a building worth $36,000. Jonah did not recognize any gain from the exchange on his individual tax return. What is his basis in the new property?

A. $26,000.
B. $36,000.
C. $10,000.
D. $16,000.

The answer is A. The basis in the new building is the same as his basis in the old building, which was $16,000. The $10,000 in improvements is added to the $16,000, so the adjusted basis is $26,000. ###

14. Which of the following transactions do not qualify for a section 1031 like-kind exchange?

A. An exchange of a boutique in Manhattan for acres of farmland.
B. An exchange of an apartment building in New Mexico for an office building in Alaska.
C. An exchange of a business desk for a business printer.
D. An exchange of inventory for different inventory.

The answer is D. Inventory never qualifies for like-kind exchange treatment. The property must not be held "primarily for sale," such as merchandise, retail stock, or inventory. Generally, real property exchanges will qualify for like-kind treatment, even though the properties themselves might be dissimilar. ###

15. Allen is a flight instructor. He trades in a small plane (adjusted basis $300,000) for another, larger plane (FMV $750,000) and pays $60,000 in an additional down payment. He uses the plane 100% in his flight instruction business. What is his basis in the new plane?

A. $300,000.
B. $360,000.
C. $690,000.
D. $750,000.

The answer is B. Allen's basis is $360,000: the $300,000 basis of the old plane plus the $60,000 cash paid. The fair market value of the property has no bearing on Allen's basis in the new property. ###

16. Bailey exchanges his residential rental property (adjusted basis $50,000, FMV $80,000) for a different rental property (FMV $70,000). What is Bailey's basis in the new property?

A. $50,000.
B. $70,000.
C. $80,000.
D. $100,000.

The answer is A. His basis in the new property is the same as the basis of the old ($50,000). The basis of the property received is the same as the basis of the property given up. ###

17. Katherine owns a yacht that she uses for personal use. Her purchase price was $150,000. The yacht is destroyed in a storm in 2012. Katherine collects $175,000 from her insurance company and promptly reinvests all the proceeds in a larger, new yacht, which costs her $201,000. What is her basis in the new yacht?

A. $175,000.
B. $176,000.
C. $201,000.
D. $226,000.

The answer is B. The answer is figured as follows: ($175,000-$150,000) = $25,000: deferred gain; ($201,000-$25,000) = $176,000: new basis in the asset. Since Katherine purchased replacement property, the basis of the replacement property is the cost of the new yacht ($201,000) minus her deferred gain ($25,000). ###

18. A tornado destroyed Bryant's primary residence home on July 15, 2010. He wants to replace the home using a section 1033 exchange for involuntary conversions. What is the latest year that Bryant can replace the property in order to defer any gain from the insurance reimbursement?

A. Bryant must make the election by December 31, 2012.
B. Bryant must make the election by July 15, 2013.
C. Bryant must make the election by July 15, 2012.
D. Bryant must make the election by December 31, 2014.

The answer is A. Bryant must acquire qualifying replacement property by December 31, 2012 (two years from the end of the gain year) in order for the involuntary conversion to be a qualified section 1033 exchange. If Bryant's home were in a federally declared disaster area, he could have four years to replace the property, assuming he purchases the replacement in the same area. ###

19. Christian owns an office building with a $400,000 basis. The building was destroyed by a fire in 2012, and Christian receives insurance money totaling $600,000. He purchases a new office building for $450,000 and then invests the rest of the insurance proceeds in stocks. Which of the following statements is true?

A. Christian has $200,000 in taxable gain he must recognize on his tax return.
B. Christian has $150,000 in taxable gain he must recognize on his tax return.
C. Christian does not have a taxable gain, because he reinvested all the proceeds in qualifying investment property.
D. Christian has $50,000 in taxable gain he must recognize on his tax return.

The answer is B. Christian's realized gain is $200,000 ($600,000 - $400,000) and his taxable gain is $150,000. He purchased another building for $450,000, so he may defer $50,000 of the gain under section 1033 for involuntary conversions. The remainder of the gain, $150,000 ($600,000 - $450,000), must be recognized because he did not reinvest all of the remaining proceeds into "like-kind" property. If Christian had reinvested all the proceeds in the new building, then his entire gain would have been deferred, and he would not have to pay taxes on any of the amount. ###

20. Aiden exchanges a residential rental in Las Vegas with a basis of $100,000 for an investment property in Miami Beach valued at $220,000 plus $15,000 in cash. What is Aiden's taxable gain on the exchange, and what is the basis of the new property in Miami Beach?

A. Taxable gain: $15,000; basis: $100,000.
B. Taxable gain: $0; basis: $235,000.
C. Taxable gain: $15,000; basis: $135,000.
D. Taxable gain: $15,000; basis: $220,000.

The answer is A. Aiden's total realized gain on the exchange is $135,000 [$220,000 + $15,000] - $100,000 basis in the old property). Only the cash boot is taxable ($15,000). Aiden's basis in the new building is $100,000 (the original basis in the property he gave up.)

Unit 13: Rental and Royalty Income

> **More Reading:**
> Publication 527, *Residential Rental Property*
> Publication 550, *Investment Income and Expenses*
> Publication 946, *How to Depreciate Property*

Rental Income

Rental income is income from the use or occupation of property, whether for residential or commercial use. Rental income is generally subject to income tax, but not to self-employment tax, except in the case of bona fide real estate professionals.

Property owners can deduct the expenses of managing, conserving, and maintaining their rental properties. Common expenses include:

- Mortgage interest and property taxes
- Advertising
- Expenses incurred from the time a property is made available for rent to when it actually rented
- Maintenance, repairs, utilities, and insurance

Losses from Rental Real Estate: *Special $25,000 Rule*

Most rental income is passive income, meaning the taxpayer does not actively or materially participate in earning the income. "Nonpassive" activities are businesses or activities in which the taxpayer works on a regular, continuous, and substantial basis. Usually, taxpayers cannot deduct losses from passive activities from their active income. However, there is an exception in the IRC for losses relating to rental real estate activities. If a taxpayer *actively participates* in a rental real estate activity, he can deduct up to $25,000 of losses against nonpassive income.

The full $25,000 allowance is available for taxpayers whose MAGI is less than $100,000. For every $2 a taxpayer's MAGI exceeds $100,000, the allowance is reduced by $1. Once MAGI exceeds $150,000, the special allowance is no longer available. Suspended passive losses can be carried forward indefinitely and used in subsequent years against passive activity income. Suspended losses are also released when a property is eventually sold or disposed of.

If a taxpayer is married and files a separate return, but lived apart from his spouse for the entire tax year, the taxpayer's special allowance for rental losses cannot exceed $12,500 (one-half of the $25,000 special limit).

If the taxpayer *lived with* his spouse at any time during the year and is filing MFS, the taxpayer cannot offset any active income with passive rental losses.

Example: Philip and Susanne have wages of $98,000 and a rental loss of $26,800 in 2012. They manage the rental property themselves. Because they meet both the active participation and the gross income tests, they are allowed to deduct $25,000 of the rental loss. The loss offsets their active income (wages). The remaining amount over the $25,000 limit ($1,800) that cannot be deducted is carried over to the next year.

Example: Hal and Sally file MFJ and have AGI of $140,000. They have $25,000 in losses from their home rental that they actively manage. Because they actively manage the rental property, they qualify for the deduction of up to $25,000 in losses against nonpassive income. Therefore, Hal and Sally's deduction is reduced by $20,000 (0.5 x ($140,000 - $100,000). They will be able to deduct $5,000 ($25,000 - $20,000) against nonpassive income. The additional $20,000 in losses is carried forward to the following year.

Example: In March 2012, Campbell and Michelle legally separate and Campbell moves out of their home into an apartment. They jointly own a residential rental. Campbell earned $40,000 in wages in 2012, and Michelle earned $33,000 in wages. Their jointly-owned rental generated a loss of $6,000 for the year. Michelle and Campbell both filed MFS and reported $3,000 ($6,000 ÷ 2) of rental loss on their returns. Although Campbell and Michelle meet the active participation rules and the gross income test, neither is allowed to deduct any of the rental losses because they did not live apart for the entire year, and they are filing MFS. The loss is considered a "suspended passive activity loss" and must be carried over for use in a future year.

The Definition of "Active Participation"

To "actively participate," a taxpayer must own at least 10% of the rental property and make management decisions in a significant and bona fide way, such as approving new tenants and improvements to the property and establishing the lease and rental terms.

The concept of "active participation" is frequently litigated by the IRS.[74] The IRS expects taxpayers to be able to prove that they actively participated in the management of the rental. If the taxpayer is deemed to not have "actively participated," then rental losses are disallowed, and the taxpayer is not eligible for the special $25,000 loss allowance.

Reporting Rental Income and Losses

If a taxpayer is a cash-basis taxpayer, as are most individual taxpayers, he must report rental income when it is constructively received, i.e. available without restrictions.

If a property is strictly a rental property, the income and loss should be reported on Schedule E, *Supplemental Income and Loss*, which is filed along with IRS Form 1040.

Treatment of Advance Rent

"Advance rent" is any amount received before the period that it covers. Advance rent must be included in income in the year it is received, regardless of the period covered.

Example: Earl signs a ten-year lease to rent his commercial office building. In 2012, the first year of the lease, Earl receives $5,000 for the first year's rent in a lump sum (in advance) and $5,000 as rent for the last year of the lease. It does not matter that the advance rent covers the last year of the rental agreement. Earl cannot postpone recognition of the payment. He must recognize the full $10,000 on his 2012 tax return.

If a tenant pays the taxpayer to cancel a lease, the amount received for the cancellation is rental income. The payment is included in the year received regardless of the taxpayer's accounting method or the period for which the rental income is covered.

---

[74] Rules regarding active participation: Ref. IRC § 469(i), Reg. § 1.469-1T(e)(3).

Security Deposits

Security deposits are not considered taxable income, if the deposit is refundable to the tenant at the end of the lease. If the taxpayer (landlord) keeps the security deposit because the tenant did not live up to the terms of the lease or damages property, the retained deposit amount is recognized in the year the deposit is retained. If the security deposit is to be used as a final payment of rent, it is actually advance rent and not a security deposit.

Property or Services In Lieu Of Rent

If a taxpayer (landlord) receives property or services instead of cash rents, the fair market value of the property or services must be recognized as rental income. Just like other barter exchanges, if the tenant and landlord agree in advance to a price, the agreed upon price is the fair market value unless there is evidence to the contrary.

> **Example:** Beth's tenant, Chris, is a professional chimneysweep. Chris offers to clean all of Beth's chimneys in her apartment building instead of paying three months' rent. Beth accepts Chris's offer. Beth must recognize income for the amount Chris would have paid for three months' rent. Then Beth may include that same amount as a business expense for repairing the rental property. This is the correct procedure for recognizing rental income from an exchange of services.

If a tenant pays any expenses, those payments are rental income and the landlord must recognize them as such. The landlord can then deduct the expenses as deductible rental expenses.

> **Example:** Rosetta owns an apartment building. While she is out of town, the furnace in the apartment building breaks down. Kerry, Rosetta's tenant, pays for the emergency repairs out-of-pocket. Kerry then deducts the furnace repair bill from his rent payment. Rosetta must recognize both the rent income and the amount Kerry paid for the repairs. Rosetta can then deduct the cost of the furnace repair as a rental expense.

Partial Rental Use

Different rules apply to a property that is used partially for rental purposes and partially for personal use. "Minimal rental use" is when a taxpayer rents his actual home as a rental unit for a limited time.

If a taxpayer has a net profit from rental activity, he generally may deduct all of his rental expenses, including depreciation. However, if the taxpayer uses a rental property for personal use and later has a net loss on the rental activity, the deduction for rental expenses is limited, which means that the taxpayer cannot take a loss.

Taxpayers who use a property for both personal and rental purposes must divide their expenses properly. If an expense applies to both rental use and personal use, such as the heating bill for the entire house, the taxpayer must prorate the expense between the two. The taxpayer is allowed to use any reasonable method for dividing the expense, so long as it is applied consistently. The two most common methods for dividing expenses are:

- The number of rooms in the home, and
- The square footage of the home.

It may also be reasonable to divide the cost of some items (for example, the water bill) based on the number of people using the unit.

Another common situation is a duplex in which the landlord lives in one unit and rents out the other side. Certain expenses apply to the entire property, such as mortgage interest and real estate taxes, and must be split to determine rental and personal expenses.

Example #1: Pablo rents a granny cottage attached to his house. The granny cottage is 12 × 15 feet, or 180 square feet. Pablo's entire house, including the attachment, is 1,800 square feet. Pablo can deduct as a rental expense 10% of any expense that must be divided between rental use and personal use. Pablo's 2012 heating bill for the entire house is $600, and therefore $60 ($600 × .10) is considered a rental expense. The balance, $540, is a personal expense that Pablo cannot deduct.

Example #2: Gillian owns a duplex. She lives in one half and rents the other half. Both units are the same size. Last year, Gillian paid a total of $10,000 mortgage interest and $2,000 real estate taxes for the entire property. Gillian can deduct $5,000 mortgage interest and $1,000 real estate taxes on Schedule E. Gillian can claim the other $5,000 mortgage interest and $1,000 real estate taxes attributable to her personal use on Schedule A as itemized deductions.

Limit on Deductions for Personal-Use Property

Some property is rented out at certain times and used for personal use other times, such as a beach house rented for the summer. In this case, expenses must be allocated based on the number of days the property is used for each purpose.

When a taxpayer uses a dwelling both as a home and a rental unit, expenses must be divided between rental use and personal use. On personal-use property, if rental expenses exceed rental income, the taxpayer cannot use the excess expenses to offset income from other sources. The excess deductions can be carried forward to the next year and treated as rental expenses for the same property. Any expenses carried forward to the next year will be subject to any limits that apply for that year.

Example: Jack owns a vacation condo on Hilton Head Island. He uses it as a personal residence four months out of the year and rents it out to tenants the rest of the year. Since Jack uses the condo more than 15 days for personal use, the condo is considered a personal use dwelling. Jack's rental income is $5,000 in 2012, and his rental expenses are $7,000 because he had a tenant who damaged the property. Jack cannot deduct the full amount of rental expenses because the condo is still considered primarily a personal-use property for tax purposes. Jack may carry over the unused expenses and deduct them from future rental income.

How to Figure Days of Personal Use

A taxpayer must figure the number of days he uses a rental for his personal use. It is considered usage "as a personal home" if he uses the rental unit for personal purposes greater than:

- Fourteen days, or
- 10% of the total days it is rented at a fair rental price.

A day of personal use is any day that the unit/home is used by any of the following persons:

- The taxpayer or any person who has ownership interest in the property.

- A member of the taxpayer's family (unless the family member pays a fair rental price and uses the property as a "main home.")[75]
- Anyone under an arrangement that allows for the use of some other dwelling unit (such as a housing swap).
- Anyone at less than a fair rental price.

Days Used for Repairs and Maintenance

Any day that the taxpayer or other owners spend working on repairs and maintaining the property is not counted as a day of personal use. The main purpose of the stay must be to complete the repairs or maintenance. A day is not counted as personal use even if family members use the property for recreational purposes on the same day.

Example: Corey owns a mountain cabin that he normally rents out to tenants. He spends a week there with his family, working on maintenance each day. His family members spend their time fishing and swimming. Corey's main purpose of being at the cabin that week is to do maintenance work. Therefore, he does not have to count the days as personal use.
Example: Steve owns a rental condo in Hawaii. In March, Steve visits the unit to re-paint, replace the carpet, and repair damage done by the former tenant. He has records to prove all of the purchases and repairs. He is at the condo performing repairs for three weeks and stays at the condo during that time. None of his time at the condo is considered "personal use" time.

Donated Rental Property

A taxpayer also "personally uses" a dwelling unit if:
- He donates the use of the unit to a charitable organization, and
- The organization sells the use of the unit at a fundraising event, and the purchaser of the unit uses the unit.

*Exception: Minimal Rental Use, or the "15 Day Rule"

If a taxpayer rents his main home for *fewer* than 15 days (14 days or less), he does not have to recognize any of the income as taxable. This is called the "15 day rule." He also cannot deduct any rental expenses.

Example: Brynn owns a condo on the Gulf Coast. It is her main home. While she was away on vacation, she rented her condo for 14 days and charged $100 per day, for a total of $1,400. She also had $320 in expenses during that time. Brynn does not report any of the income or expenses since the rental qualifies under the exception for minimal rental use.

Rental Expenses and the "Placed in Service" Date

Rental property is "placed in service" when it is ready and available for rent. A taxpayer can begin to depreciate property and deduct expenses as soon as he places the property in service for the production of income.

A taxpayer cannot deduct any loss of rental income for the period a property is vacant. But if a taxpayer is actively trying to rent the property, he can deduct ordinary and necessary expenses as soon as the property is *made available* for rent.

---

[75] For this rental rule, "family" includes only spouses, children, parents, grandparents, grandchildren, siblings, and half-brothers and half-sisters.

Example: Rodrigo purchased a rental property in 2012. He made the property available for rent on March 1, 2012 by advertising the property in the local newspaper. Rodrigo finally found a tenant on June 1, 2012. Even though the rental was unoccupied from March to June, Rodrigo may still deduct the mortgage interest and other expenses related to the property. Expenses incurred while a property is vacant but available for rent are generally deductible.

Expenses for a Rental Property That is Later Sold

If a taxpayer sells property originally held for rental purposes, he can deduct the ordinary and necessary expenses for managing, conserving, or maintaining the property until it is sold.

Example: Gerry owns a rental property and wants to sell it. It is currently vacant, and Gerry still must pay the utility bills and landscaping costs. Gerry is also paying mortgage interest and property taxes. Gerry can deduct these expenses from his rental income.

Converting a Primary Residence to Rental Use

If a taxpayer changes a primary residence to rental use at any time other than the beginning of a tax year, he must divide yearly expenses, such as taxes and insurance, between rental use and personal use. A taxpayer can deduct as rental expenses only the portion that is for the part of the year the property was used or held for rental purposes. For depreciation purposes, the property is treated as being "placed in service" on the conversion date.

The taxpayer cannot deduct depreciation or insurance for the part of the year the property was held for personal use. However, the taxpayer can include the home mortgage interest, qualified mortgage insurance premiums, and real estate tax expenses for the part of the year the property was held for personal use as an itemized deduction on Schedule A (Form 1040).

Figuring the Basis of a Converted Property

When a taxpayer converts a property from personal use to rental use, he figures the basis for depreciation using the *lesser* of:

- Fair market value (the price the property would sell for on the open market), or
- The home's adjusted basis on the date of the conversion.

Depreciation Rules for Rental Property

Rental properties must be depreciated. Depreciation is an income tax deduction that allows a taxpayer to recover the cost of business-use property. It is an annual allowance for the wear and tear, deterioration, and/or obsolescence of the property. Most types of tangible property (except land and land improvements), such as buildings, machinery, vehicles, furniture, and equipment, are depreciable.

A taxpayer may only deduct a certain amount of depreciation expense each year, and must claim the correct amount. If a taxpayer does not claim all the depreciation he was entitled to deduct, he must still *reduce his basis* in the property by the full amount of depreciation that he could have deducted. Regardless of whether the taxpayer chooses to deduct the depreciation on his current return, he will still be treated as if he had taken the allowable deduction, and the basis in the property must be reduced.

Three basic factors determine how much depreciation a taxpayer can deduct:

- Basis

- Recovery period for the property
- Depreciation method used

Raw land is never depreciated because land does not wear out, become obsolete, or get used up. The costs of clearing, grading, planting, and landscaping are generally all part of the cost of land and cannot be depreciated. **Example:** In 2007, Lance purchased a home for $180,000. On the date of purchase, the assessed value of the land was $30,000. After living in the home for five years, Lance converted it to a rental property on April 1, 2012. Since land is not depreciated, Lance will include only the cost of the house when figuring the basis for depreciation. The basis of the house is $150,000 ($180,000 - $30,000). In 2012, the county assessor's office assigned the home an FMV of $185,000, of which $40,000 was for land and $145,000 for the house. The basis for depreciation on the house is the FMV on the date of change ($145,000), because it is less than Lance's adjusted basis ($150,000). Lance must use $145,000 as his basis for figuring depreciation on Schedule E.

Example: Diane owns an empty lot she purchased for $50,000, and she plans to build an apartment complex on it. Diane pays an additional $15,000 to clear the property of trees and debris so she can begin construction. Diane's basis in the land is therefore $65,000 ($50,000 + $15,000). The cost of clearing the brush must be added to the basis of the land, and is not deductible or depreciable.

Repairs vs. Improvements

A taxpayer can deduct the cost of repairs to rental property, but cannot deduct the cost of "improvements." A taxpayer recovers the cost of improvements by taking depreciation.

The taxpayer must separate the costs of repairs and improvements, and keep accurate records. The taxpayer will need to know the cost of improvements when the property is later sold, because improvements increase a property's basis.

A "repair" keeps a property in operating condition. It does not add to the value of a property or substantially prolong its life. Repainting a property inside or out, fixing gutters or floors, fixing leaks, plastering, and replacing broken windows are examples of repairs.

Example: Keith owns a rental home. A baseball broke a window, so he replaced it with an upgraded model—an insulated double-pane window that helps control heating and cooling costs. Even though this window is a substantial upgrade from the previous one, it is still considered a repair, because the old window was broken and needed to be replaced. If Keith had decided to replace all the windows, the upgrade would have been considered an "improvement," and Keith would have been required to depreciate the cost.

When a taxpayer makes an improvement to a rental property, the cost must be capitalized and depreciated. It cannot be deducted on the tax return as an expense. The capitalized cost is usually depreciated as if the improvement were separate property from the dwelling unit.

Example: Keith's rental property also has a bad roof leak, so he replaces the entire roof at a cost of $7,000. This is considered a substantial improvement and must be depreciated over time. Keith cannot expense the cost of the roof against current income.

Examples of Improvements

An *improvement* adds to the value of property, prolongs its useful life, or adapts it to new uses. Improvements include the following items:

- Putting a recreation room in an unfinished basement
- Paneling a den, putting in a fireplace, or other major construction
- Adding another bathroom or bedroom
- Putting decorative grillwork on a balcony
- Erecting a fence
- Installing new plumbing or wiring
- Putting in new cabinets
- Putting on a new roof
- Paving a driveway or adding a garage

Example: Glenna owns a rental home. In 2012, she spent $7,000 replacing the carpet, $2,540 to pave the driveway, and $350 to repair a cracked window. Only the window repair ($350) can be expensed on her 2012 tax return. The cost of the new carpet and the new driveway must be capitalized and depreciated over time.

Repair vs. Capitalization Rule Changes

In December 2011,[76] the IRS released temporary regulations that will mean major changes in determining whether certain costs are repairs or improvements, and thus whether they need to be expensed or capitalized. Under the changes, an improvement is redefined as a cost involving:

- A betterment of the unit of property,
- A restoration of the unit of property, or
- An adaptation of the unit of property to a new or different use.

The new IRS improvement standards apply to the building structure and each of the building's major component systems separately. The guidelines divide a building into nine different structural components called "building systems," such as those for plumbing, heating and air conditioning, and electrical. The effects of a repair on a specific building system, rather than the building as a whole, must be evaluated under the new, narrower definition of an improvement. The result will be to make costs more difficult to classify as repairs, meaning the taxpayer will not be able to deduct them as expenses but will have to capitalize them instead.

For example, under current guidelines significant repairs to an elevator may "better" the elevator but would not be significant to the building as a whole, so the repair could be expensed. Under the new guidelines, the costs would be significant to the *elevator system* and would have to be capitalized.

The final regulations are still being revised, and the IRS announced in December 2012 that it was delaying full implementation until 2014.[77] For 2012, the IRS is giving taxpayers the choice of whether to use the current rules or to adopt the new ones.

---

[76] Federal Register, Dec. 27, 2011.
[77] IRS Notice 2012-73.

Other Rental Property Expenses

There are many types of expenses that rental property owners may legitimately deduct. Examples include advertising, cleaning, maintenance, utilities, fire and liability insurance, taxes, interest, and commissions for the collection of rent. If a taxpayer buys a leasehold for rental purposes, he can deduct an equal part of the cost each year over the term of the lease.

Travel Expenses Related to Rental Property

A taxpayer can deduct the ordinary and necessary expenses of traveling away from home if the primary purpose of the trip is to collect rental income or to manage, conserve, or maintain his rental property.

> **Example:** Walt owns a rental property 200 miles from his home. Part of the rental home was damaged by fire. Walt travels to the property to inspect the damage and hire someone to do the repairs. His travel expenses are deductible as ordinary and necessary costs.

Cannot Deduct Prepaid Insurance Premiums: If a taxpayer pays an insurance premium on rental property for more than one year in advance, each year he can deduct the part of the premium payment that applies to that year. He cannot deduct the total premium in the year paid.

> **Example:** Connie owns a rental home. She receives a substantial discount from her insurance agent if she agrees to pay her hazard insurance two years in advance. Connie cannot deduct the full payment of the insurance in the year that she pays. She must prorate the insurance expense, even though she is a cash-basis taxpayer.

Cannot Deduct Local Benefit Taxes: Generally, a taxpayer cannot deduct charges for local benefits that increase the value of a property, such as charges for putting in streets, sidewalks, or water and sewer systems. These charges are non-depreciable capital expenditures that must be added to the basis of a property. A taxpayer can deduct local benefit taxes if they are for maintaining, repairing, or paying interest charges for the benefits.

Not Rented for Profit

If a taxpayer is not renting a property to make a profit, he can deduct his rental expenses only up to the amount of his rental income. Losses cannot be deducted or carried forward to the next year if the expenses are more than the rental income for the year.

If a taxpayer's rental income is more than his rental expenses for at least three out of five consecutive years, he is presumed to be renting the property to make a profit. A taxpayer who is starting rental activity and does not have three years showing a profit may elect to have the presumption made after five years of rental experience.

Depreciation Periods

The depreciation periods for business and rental property vary from three years to 20 years. Land improvements such as fences, bridges, and shrubbery must be depreciated over 15 or 20 years.

For property used in rental activities, a taxpayer must use the Modified Accelerated Cost Recovery System (MACRS), which is the required method of accelerated asset depreciation in the United States. Under MACRS, all assets are divided into classes that dictate the number of years over which an asset's cost will be recovered.

Buildings are depreciated using the straight-line method. Residential real estate is recovered over 27.5 years, and commercial buildings are depreciated over 39 years. Residential real estate is any structure that at least 80% of the gross rental income of the building is derived from dwelling units (such as an apartment complex), or a common residential rental home. All other real property is classified as "commercial nonresidential property" and must be depreciated over 39 years. An example is a factory building.

Only the building portion of the rental can be depreciated, so the value of the land must be separated from the value of the building. If a taxpayer is uncertain of the FMV of the land and the buildings, he may calculate the basis using the assessed values for real estate tax purposes.

> **Example:** In 2012, Shannon buys a rental property for $200,000. It has an assessed value of $160,000, of which $136,000 is for the house and $24,000 is for the land. Shannon can allocate 85% ($136,000 ÷ $160,000) of the purchase price to the house and 15% ($24,000 ÷ $160,000) of the purchase price to the land. Therefore, her basis in the house is $170,000 (85% of $200,000) and her basis in the land is $30,000 (15% of $200,000). Shannon may use $170,000 as her basis for depreciation on the property.

> **Example:** A residential rental building with a cost basis of $137,500 would generate depreciation of $5,000 per year ($137,500 / 27.5 years).

MACRS Recovery Periods
Depreciable Property Used in Rental Activities

Class of Property	Items Included
3-year property	Most computer software, tractor units, some manufacturing tools, and some livestock.
5-year property	Automobiles, computers and peripheral equipment, office machinery (faxes, copiers, calculators, etc.), appliances, stoves, refrigerators.
7-year property	Office furniture and fixtures, and any property that has not been designated as belonging to another class.
15-year property	Depreciable improvements to land such as shrubbery, fences, roads, and bridges.
20-year property	Farm buildings that are not agricultural or horticultural structures.
27.5-year property	Residential rental property (residential rental homes, condos, etc.)
39-year property	Nonresidential real estate, such as factory buildings.

Exception for Real Estate Professionals

Real estate professionals are *exempt* from the passive activity rules if certain conditions are met. Rental activities in which real estate professionals materially participate during the year are not passive activities. A real estate professional may elect to treat his rental income as non-passive income. If the real estate professional elects this treatment, the rental income is subject to self-employment tax, and the taxpayer must file a Schedule C, rather than a Schedule E.

Real estate "dealers" are defined as those who are engaged in the business of selling real estate to customers with purposes of making a profit from those sales. The benefit of being classified as a "real estate professional" is that the taxpayer is treated like a Schedule C business and there is no limit on the amount of losses the taxpayer can claim on the activity. A taxpayer will qualify as a real estate professional for the tax year if he meets both of the following requirements:

- More than half of the services performed during the tax year are performed in real estate or real property businesses in which the taxpayer materially participates.
- The taxpayer performs more than 750 hours of services during the tax year in real property trades or businesses in which he materially participates.

Rental income received from the use of or occupancy of hotels, boarding houses, or apartment houses is included in self-employment income *if* the real estate professional provided services to the occupants. Services are considered "provided to the occupants" if they are for the convenience of the occupants and not normally provided with the rental of rooms or space for occupancy only. Daily maid service, for example, is a service provided for the convenience of occupants, while heating, exterior lights, and the collection of trash are not.

Royalty Income

Royalties from copyrights, patents, and oil, gas, and mineral properties are taxable as ordinary income. Royalty income is generally considered passive income and subject to the passive activity rules.

Royalties are payments that are received for the use of property. The most common types of royalties are for the use of copyrights, trademarks, and patents. Royalties are also paid by companies that extract minerals and other substances from the earth, such as oil or gas. Mineral property includes oil and gas wells, mines, and other natural deposits, such as geothermal deposits. Royalty income and expenses are reported on Schedule E, *Supplemental Income and Loss.*

*Exception: There are special rules for taxpayers who are self-employed writers, artists, photographers, or inventors. In this case, the royalties are generated by a *self-created* copyright, trademark, or patent. Therefore, the royalties are reported as business income on Schedule C and are subject to self-employment tax.

Royalties from copyrights on literary, musical, or artistic works, and similar property, or from patents on inventions, are amounts paid for the right to use the property over a specified period of time. Royalties generally are based on the number of units sold, such as the number of books, tickets to a performance, or machines sold.

Example: In 2012, Don's brother died. Don inherited a copyright from his brother who had written an instruction manual for woodworking. Don then leased the copyrighted material to schools and colleges for their use in the classroom. Since this was not a self-created copyright, the income is considered passive income. Don must report the income from this copyright on Schedule E.

Unit 13: Questions

1. Thomas, who is single, owns a rental apartment building property. He actively participates in the rental activity by collecting rent and performing repairs. In 2012, Thomas had an overall loss of $29,000 on this rental activity and had no other passive income. His total income from wages is $60,000. How much of the rental loss may Thomas deduct on his 2012 return?

A. $0.
B. $6,000.
C. $25,000.
D. $29,000.

The answer is C. Thomas may deduct $25,000 in rental losses. The remaining amount, $4,000 ($29,000 - $25,000), must be carried over to the following year. ####

2. In 2012, Jane is single and has $40,000 in wages, $2,000 of passive income from a limited partnership, and $3,500 of passive losses from a rental real estate activity in which she actively participated. Which of the following statements is true?

A. $2,000 of Jane's $3,500 loss offsets her passive income. Jane may deduct the remaining $1,500 loss from her $40,000 wages.
B. Jane may not deduct the passive losses from her $40,000 in wages.
C. Jane may deduct any other losses.
D. Jane must carry over her losses to the subsequent tax year.

The answer is A. Jane may deduct the remaining $1,500 loss from her $40,000 wages. A taxpayer may deduct up to $25,000 per year of losses for rental real estate activities in which she actively participates. This special allowance is an exception to the general rule disallowing losses in excess of income from passive activities. ###

3. Which of the following costs incurred on rental property should be classified as a capital improvement and must be depreciated rather than expensed?

A. Replacing an entire deck.
B. Repairing a broken toilet.
C. Refinishing the existing wood floors.
D. Replacing a broken window pane.

The answer is A. The replacement of the deck would be considered a depreciable improvement. The other choices are repairs and may be deducted as current expenses. ###

4. Mike, a single taxpayer, had the following income and loss during the tax year:

- Salary $52,300
- Dividends $300
- Bank interest $1,400
- Rental losses ($4,000)

The loss came from a rental property that Mike owned. He advertised and rented the house to the current tenant himself. He also collected the rents and did the repairs or hired someone to do them. Which of the following statements is true?

A. Mike can claim the entire rental loss against his active income.
B. Mike cannot claim the rental loss because his income exceeds $50,000.
C. Mike cannot claim the rental loss because he is not a real estate professional.
D. Mike can claim $1,700 in rental losses and the remaining amount ($2,300) will be carried over to the following year.

The answer is A. Even though the rental loss is from a passive activity, Mike can use the entire $4,000 loss to offset his other income because he actively participated. If a taxpayer *actively participates* in a rental real estate activity, he can deduct up to $25,000 of losses against nonpassive income. This special allowance for rental activity is *an exception* to the general rule disallowing losses in excess of income from passive activities. ###

5. Gene signs a three-year lease to rent his business property. In December 2012, he receives $12,000 for the first year's rent and $12,000 as rent for the last year of the lease. He also receives $1,500 in 2012 as a refundable security deposit. How much of this income must Gene include in his 2012 tax return?

A. $1,500.
B. $12,000.
C. $24,000.
D. $25,500.

The answer is C. Gene must include $24,000 in his income in the first year. He must recognize all the advance rent as income immediately. The security deposit does not have to be recognized as income as it is refundable to the tenant. ###

6. Eric incurred the following expenditures in connection with his rental property. Which of them should be capitalized and depreciated?

A. New roof.
B. New kitchen cabinets.
C. New carpeting for all the bedrooms.
D. All of the above.

The answer is D. All of the property listed must be capitalized and depreciated. A taxpayer can deduct only the cost of repairs to his rental property. He cannot deduct the cost of improvements, but can recover the cost of improvements by taking depreciation over the life of the asset. ###

7. Rosemary's home is used exclusively as her residence all year except for 13 days. During this time, Rosemary rents her home to alumni while the local college has its homecoming celebration. She made $3,000 in rental income and had $500 in rental expenses. Which of the following statements is true?

A. All of the rental income may be excluded.
B. Rosemary may exclude only $2,500 of the rental income.
C. Rosemary may deduct her rental expenses when she reports her rental income on Schedule E.
D. Rosemary must recognize $3,000 in rental income.

The answer is A. All the rental income may be excluded under the "15 day rule." This home is primarily personal use, and the rental period is disregarded, which means the IRS does not consider it a rental. The rental income is not taxable, and any of the rental expenses (such as utilities or maintenance costs) are considered nondeductible personal expenses. ###

8. Terry purchased a heating, ventilating, and air conditioning (HVAC) unit for her rental property on December 15, 2012. It was delivered on December 28, 2012, and was installed and ready for use on January 2, 2012. When should the HVAC unit be considered "placed in service" for depreciation purposes?

A. December 15, 2012.
B. December 28, 2012.
C. January 1, 2012.
D. January 2, 2012.

The answer is D. The placed-in-service date is the date when an asset becomes available for use. In most cases, the placed-in-service date and the purchase date are the same, but that is not necessarily the case. Depreciation begins on the placed-in-service date. Since Terry did not actually have the HVAC unit in use until January 2, 2012, she must wait until 2012 to begin depreciating the unit. ###

9. Passive rental income and losses are reported on which IRS form?

A. Schedule E.
B. Schedule A.
C. Schedule C.
D. Schedule D.

The answer is A. Rental income and loss is reported on Schedule E, which is then attached to the taxpayer's Form 1040. Rental income is any payment received for the use or occupation of property, and is generally passive income. An exception exists for real estate professionals, who may report rental income on Schedule C. ###

10. Brian has a house in Arizona that is rented out for eight months each year. How many days can he use the house without losing income tax deductions?

A. As many days as he wants.
B. 14 days.
C. Zero days.
D. 24 days.

The answer is D. Brian can personally use his rental home the longer of 14 days or 10% of the time the rental was in use. The rental home was used for 240 days (30 x 8). Brian can use his rental home for 24 days (240 x 10%) with no impact in deducting expenses from his rental property. ###

11. In January 2012, Kimberly purchases a commercial office building and used office furnishings. The furnishings consist of chairs, desks, and file cabinets. The purchase price allocates $900,000 to the office building and $50,000 to the used office furnishings. According to the guidelines for MACRS depreciation, what recovery period must she use for the purchased items?

A. 27.5 years for the entire purchase (building and furnishings).
B. 39 years for the building and 5 years for the used office furnishings.
C. 15 years for the building and 5 years for the used office furnishings.
D. 39 years for the building and 7 years for the used office furnishings.

The answer is D. Commercial real estate is depreciated as 39-year property. The recovery period under MACRS for furniture is seven years. ###

12. Nick decides to convert his residence into rental property. He moves out of his home in May and starts renting it on June 1. He has $12,000 in mortgage interest on the home. How should Nick report his mortgage interest expense?

A. Nick can report $7,000 on Schedule E as interest expense and $5,000 on Schedule A as mortgage interest.
B. Nick should report the entire $12,000 on Schedule A.
C. Nick should report the entire $12,000 on Schedule E.
D. Nick can report $8,000 on Schedule E as interest expense and $4,000 on Schedule A as mortgage interest.

The answer is A. Nick must allocate his expenses between personal use and rental use. He can deduct as rental expenses seven-twelfths (7/12) of his yearly expenses, such as taxes and insurance. Starting with June, he can deduct as rental expenses the amounts he paid for items generally billed monthly, such as utilities. When figuring depreciation, he should treat the property as placed in service on June 1. ###

13. In 2012 Mimi has modified adjusted gross income of $120,000. She owns a rental house that has losses of $22,000 for the year. How much of the rental loss may she deduct on her tax return?

A. $0.
B. $11,000.
C. $15,000.
D. $22,000.

The answer is C. Mimi may only deduct $15,000 of the loss. The rental loss allowance is phased out when a taxpayer's MAGI is over $100,000. For every two dollars of income over $100,000, the rental loss allowance is reduced one dollar. The answer is figured as follows:

Mimi's income-MAGI threshold: ($120,000 - $100,000 = $20,000)
$20,000 X 50% = $10,000
$25,000 (normal rental allowance) - $10,000 = $15,000

$15,000 is the maximum in rental losses that Mimi can claim as a deduction. The remaining unused losses ($7,000) must be carried over to the following year. ###

14. Jake is a full-time freelance writer. He earns $23,000 in royalty income from one of his copyrighted books in 2012. He also has $4,000 in travel expenses related to the promotion of the book. How should this income be reported?

A. Jake must report $23,000 in taxable income on Schedule C.
B. Jake must report $23,000 in taxable income on Schedule E.
C. Jake must report $19,000 in taxable income on Schedule E.
D. Jake must report $19,000 in taxable income on Schedule C.

The answer is D. As a full-time writer, his royalty income is not considered passive income and therefore is subject to self-employment tax. Jake must report $19,000 in taxable income on Schedule C ($23,000 - $4,000 in expenses). ###

15. In general, income from a residential rental property is subject to what kind of tax?

A. Income tax.
B. Income tax, Social Security tax, and Medicare tax.
C. Income tax and Social Security tax, but not Medicare tax.
D. Income tax and Medicare tax, but not Social Security tax.

The answer is A. In general, income from rental real estate is subject to income tax, but not to self-employment tax, with a rare exception for bona fide real estate dealers/brokers. ###

16. Aaron converts his basement level into a separate apartment with a bedroom, a bathroom, and a small kitchen. He rents the basement apartment at a fair rental price to college students on a 9-month lease (273 days). He figures that 10% of the total days rented at a fair rental price is 27 days (273 days X 10%). In June, Aaron's brothers stay with him and live in the basement apartment rent-free for 30 days. Which is the true statement?

A. Aaron may deduct all of his expenses for the converted basement apartment, as it is 100% rental use.
B. Aaron may not deduct any of his rental losses because the converted basement apartment is considered personal use.
C. Aaron must recognize imputed rental income from his brothers' use of the property, even if he did not actually receive it.
D. Aaron must divide his expenses between personal use and rental use, but he is still allowed to deduct losses from the property.

The answer is B. Since Aaron's family members use the basement apartment for free, this usage counts as personal use for Aaron. Therefore, the basement apartment is no longer considered a 100% rental unit. Aaron's personal use (the 30 days his family used it for free) exceeds the greater of 14 days or 10% of the total days it was rented (27 days). When a taxpayer uses a dwelling unit both as a home and a rental unit, expenses must be divided between rental use and personal use, and the taxpayer may not deduct rental expenses that exceed the rental income for that dwelling unit. Aaron's losses, if he has any, are not deductible. ###

17. What is the depreciation period for residential rental property?

A. 20 years.
B. 22.5 years.
C. 27.5 years.
D. 39 years.

The answer is C. Residential rental property is depreciable over 27.5 years. ###

18. In 2012 Travis and Brittany moved to Canada. They decided to rent their house in California instead of selling it. They had purchased the home in 2006 for $500,000 and had paid $80,000 for various improvements through 2011. The purchase price of $500,000 was attributable to fair market values of $100,000 for the land and $400,000 for the house. Their new tenant paid a security deposit of $6,000 and moved in on July 1, 2012. The FMV of the property on July 1 was $525,000, comprised of $105,000 for the land and $420,000 for the house. The tenant then paid rent of $3,000 each month from July through December. Travis and Brittany incurred the following expenses in 2012 related to the house:

Mortgage interest $10,000
Property taxes $10,000
Casualty insurance $1,000

In addition, they paid $500 for repairs during December. Exclusive of depreciation expense, what was Travis and Brittany's taxable rental income for 2012?

A. $13,000.
B. $7,000.
C. $1,500.
D. $7,250.

The answer is B. Travis and Brittany must report six months of rental income at $3,000 per month, or $18,000, but the security deposit of $6,000 is refundable and therefore not recognized as income in 2012. They can deduct 6/12 of the amounts incurred for mortgage interest, property taxes, and casualty insurance, or $10,500, plus the $500 cost of repairs while the house was rented. Thus, their reportable net rental income before considering depreciation would be $7,000. ###

Supporting calculations:
Taxable income:
Six months of rent (at $3,000) 18,000

Less deductible expenses:
Mortgage interest (for six months)	$5,000
Property taxes (for six months)	$5,000
Casualty insurance (for six months)	$500
Repair cost	$500

Expenses **before** depreciation	$11,000
Rental income **before** depreciation	$7,000

19. Based upon the information in question 18, what is the amount of basis on which depreciation should be calculated for the rental period?

A. $400,000.
B. $480,000.
C. $580,000.
D. $420,000.

The answer is D. The basis for depreciation is the **lesser of** fair market value or the taxpayer's adjusted basis on the date the property was converted to rental use. The adjusted basis of the house on July 1, 2012 was $480,000 (original cost of $400,000 plus improvements of $80,000), but the FMV of $420,000 on the same date was lower. The basis of the land is not subject to depreciation. ###

Supporting calculations:

Adjusted basis of house:
Cost	$400,000
Improvements	$80,000
Total adjusted basis	$480,000

FMV on July 1, 2012	$420,000

20. Tae-hyun acquired a residential rental property in 2012 for $1 million, paid an additional $100,000 to replace the roof, and paid $50,000 for repairs. The purchase price of the property was determined to be allocable as follows: 90% to the building and 10% to land. The property was placed in service in March.

Based upon the information provided, on what amount can Tae-hyun calculate and claim a depreciation deduction for this property?

A. $1,050,000.
B. $500,000.
C. $1,150,000.
D. $1,000,000.

The answer is D. The depreciable basis for the property is the sum of the purchase price less the portion attributable to non-depreciable land, or $900,000, plus the cost of improvements ($100,000), or a total of $1,000,000. The cost of repairs ($50,000) is separately deductible as a current expense, and does not affect the depreciation calculation.

Supporting calculations:

Purchase price (less land cost)	$900,000
Improvements (roof repair)	$100,000
Depreciable basis	$1,000,000

21. Gabby owns a duplex. She lives in one half and rents the other. The property is condemned in order to add lanes to the interstate highway, and Gabby receives a condemnation settlement of $90,000. She originally paid $75,000 for the property and spent $15,000 for improvements prior to 2012. Through 2012, Gabby has claimed allowable depreciation deductions of $20,000 on the rental half of the property. She also incurred legal fees of $2,000 in connection with the condemnation settlement process. What amount of taxable gain or loss will Gabby report in 2012 as a result of the condemnation?

A. Taxable gain of $19,000.
B. Taxable gain of $18,000.
C. Taxable loss of $2,000.
D. Taxable loss of $22,000.

The answer is A. The gain and loss for the two portions of the property must be determined separately, as outlined in the following table. Gabby will have a taxable gain on the business portion of the property and the loss on the residential portion is not deductible. ###

	Residential Part	Business Part
Condemnation award received	$45,000	$45,000
Minus legal fees	($1,000)	($1,000)
Net condemnation award	$44,000	$44,000
Adjusted basis:		
Original cost, $75,000	$37,500	$37,500
Improvements, $15,000	$7,500	$7,500
Total	$45,000	$45,000
Minus depreciation	N/A	($20,000)
Adjusted basis, business part	$0	$25,000
Loss/Gain on property	**($1,000)**	**$19,000**

Unit 14: Individual Retirement Arrangements

More Reading:
Publication 590, *Individual Retirement Arrangements (IRAs)*
Publication 575, *Pension and Annuity Income*

There are several types of IRA accounts, but in this unit, we will only discuss traditional IRAs and Roth IRAs since these are the two most common types of retirement accounts and the ones most heavily tested on Part 1 of the EA exam. Each IRA has different eligibility requirements.

Traditional IRA: A traditional IRA is the most common type of retirement savings plan. In most cases, taxpayers can deduct their traditional IRA contributions as an adjustment to income. Generally, amounts in a traditional IRA, including earnings and gains, are not taxed until distributed. If a taxpayer's income is too high, the taxpayer's contributions to his traditional IRA might not be deductible.

Roth IRA: A Roth IRA is a retirement account that features nondeductible contributions and tax-free growth. In other words, a taxpayer funds his Roth IRA with after-tax income, and the income then grows tax-free. When a taxpayer withdraws money from a Roth IRA, the withdrawal will not be subject to income tax. Not everyone can participate in a Roth IRA. There are strict income limits, and higher wage earners may be prohibited from participating in a Roth IRA account because of their income threshold.

*NOTE: Only contributions to a traditional IRA are deductible as an adjustment to gross income. Roth IRA contributions are not deductible. Although contributions to a Roth IRA cannot be deducted, the taxpayer may still be eligible for the Retirement Savings Contributions Credit (the Saver's Credit), covered in Unit 9, *Tax Credits.*

Example: In 2012, Leo contributes $2,200 to a traditional IRA and $1,000 to a Roth IRA. The most Leo will be able to deduct as an adjustment to income is the $2,200 contribution to his traditional IRA. Roth IRA contributions are never deductible.

Traditional IRA Rules

Not everyone can contribute to a traditional IRA. In addition, not everyone who contributes to a traditional IRA is allowed to deduct the contribution.

In order to make contributions to a traditional IRA:
1. The taxpayer must be *under* age 70½ at the end of the year.
2. The taxpayer must have qualifying nonpassive income, such as wages, salaries, commissions, tips, bonuses, or self-employment income. Investment and pension income do not count.
3. If a taxpayer's income is too high (and if either he or his spouse is covered by an employer plan), his deductible IRA contribution will be phased out.

*Note: For purposes of making an IRA contribution, taxable alimony and nontaxable combat pay count as qualifying "nonpassive" income. This allows taxpayers to build retirement savings in IRAs even if they rely on alimony income for support. This applies only to taxable alimony income and does not include child support payments.

> **Example:** Stan is an Army medic serving in a combat zone for all of 2012. Although none of his pay is taxable, it is still considered qualifying compensation for purposes of an IRA contribution.

IRAs cannot be owned jointly. However, a married couple who files jointly may choose to contribute to each of their IRA accounts, even if only one taxpayer has qualifying compensation.

This means that one taxpayer may choose to make an IRA contribution on *behalf* of his or her spouse, even if only one spouse had compensation during the year. Each spouse must have a separate IRA account.

> **Example:** Joaquin, 48, and Meg, 52, are married and file jointly. Joaquin works as a paramedic and makes $46,000 per year. Meg is a homemaker and has no income. Even though Meg has no taxable compensation, Joaquin may still contribute to her IRA account. Their combined maximum contribution for 2012 is $11,000. Joaquin may deposit $5,000, and Meg may deposit $6,000 because she is over 50 years of age.

Contributions can be made to a traditional IRA at any time on or before the due date of the return (not including extensions). For the 2012 tax year, a person may make an IRA contribution up until April 15, 2013.

This makes an IRA contribution a rare opportunity for tax planning because it can occur after the tax year has already ended. A taxpayer can even file his return claiming a traditional IRA contribution *before* the contribution is actually made. However, if a contribution is reported on the taxpayer's 2012 return but is not made by the deadline, the taxpayer must file an amended return.

> **Example:** Paul files his 2012 tax return on March 5, 2013. He claims a $4,000 IRA contribution on his tax return. Paul may wait as late as April 15, 2013 (the due date of the return) to make the IRA contribution for tax year 2012.

A taxpayer must have taxable income in order to contribute to an IRA, so a person whose only income is from self-employment and who shows an overall loss for the year would not be able to contribute. However, if the taxpayer has wages *in addition* to self-employment income, a *loss* from self-employment would not be subtracted from the taxpayer's wages when figuring total compensation.

> **Example:** Marcy is 45 and works part-time as an employee for a local library. She earns $10,000 in wages during 2012. She also works part of the year as a self-employed photographer. In 2012, her photography business has a loss of $5,400. Even though the taxpayer's *net income* for 2012 is only $4,600 ($10,000 wages − $5,400 loss from self-employment), her qualifying income for purposes of an IRA contribution is still $10,000, the amount of her wages. This means that Marcy can make a full IRA contribution of $5,000 in 2012.

"Compensation" for purposes of contributing to an IRA does not include passive income such as:

- Rental income
- Interest income
- Dividend and portfolio income
- Pension or annuity income
- Deferred compensation

- Income from certain partnerships
- Prize winnings or gambling income
- Items (except for nontaxable combat pay) that are excluded from income, such as foreign earned income and housing costs

Taxpayers cannot make IRA contributions that are greater than their qualifying compensation for the year. This means that if a taxpayer only has passive income for the year, he cannot contribute to an IRA at all.

Example: Larry is 54 and wants to contribute to his traditional IRA. He is not a real estate professional, but he has $10,000 in passive rental income from residential rental properties. He also received $8,000 in interest income and has $3,000 in wages from a part-time job. The rental and interest income are passive income and are not considered "compensation" for purposes of funding his retirement account. Therefore, the maximum Larry can contribute to his traditional IRA is $3,000, the amount of his wage income.

2012 Traditional and Roth IRA Contribution Limits

Under 50 years of age:
- 2012 Contribution Limit: $5,000 per taxpayer
- Filing Jointly: $10,000

50 years and over:
- 2012 Contribution Limit: $6,000 per taxpayer
- Filing Jointly (Both 50 or older): $12,000

A taxpayer may choose to split his retirement plan contributions between a traditional IRA and a Roth IRA; however, the maximum contribution limits still apply. Although a person may have IRAs with several different financial institutions, for purposes of the contribution limits, tax law treats all of a taxpayer's IRAs as a single IRA.

Example: Alan is 32. He has a traditional IRA at his regular bank and a Roth IRA through his stockbroker. Alan can contribute to both of his retirement accounts this year, but the combined contributions for 2012 cannot exceed $5,000. Alan decides to contribute $3,000 to his Roth IRA and $2,000 to his traditional IRA.

Example: Naomi, 25, has only $3,000 in interest income in 2012. Naomi marries Carl during the year. In 2012, Carl has taxable wages of $34,000. He plans to contribute $5,000 to his traditional IRA. If he and Naomi file a joint return, each can contribute $5,000 to a traditional IRA. This is because Naomi, who has no qualifying compensation, can add Carl's compensation, reduced by the amount of his IRA contribution ($34,000 − $5,000 = $29,000), to her own compensation ($0) to determine her maximum contribution to a traditional IRA. Since they are filing a joint return, she can utilize Carl's qualifying compensation in order to contribute to her own traditional IRA. They both may contribute the maximum in 2012 ($5,000 each).

Even if they file a joint return, married taxpayers' combined IRA contributions cannot exceed their combined compensation, and neither spouse can contribute more than $5,000 (or $6,000 if 50 or older) to his or her own IRA.

Example: Elliott and June are both age 49 and married. Elliott has $23,000 in pension income for the year. June has $13,000 in pension income and $7,000 in wages. Only June's wages count as qualifying compensation for purposes of IRA contributions. June may contribute the maximum to her IRA ($5,000). If they file jointly, Elliott can contribute $2,000 (equal to the remaining amount of June's qualifying compensation, $7,000 – $5,000 = $2,000).

Once again, a married couple cannot set up a "joint" IRA account. Each individual must have his or her own IRA, but married spouses may choose to make contributions to a spouse's IRA, up to the legal limit, if they file jointly. If taxpayers choose to file separately, then they must consider only their own qualifying compensation for IRA purposes.

Example: Greg is 35, works full-time, and made $55,000 in 2012. His wife, Laverne, is 34, has a part-time job, and made $3,600 in 2012. They choose to file separately. Since they file MFS and Laverne only has $3,600 in compensation, she is limited to a $3,600 IRA contribution. Greg may contribute a full $5,000 to his own IRA account.

A taxpayer cannot claim the adjustment for an IRA contribution on Form 1040EZ; the taxpayer must use either Form 1040, Form 1040A, or Form 1040NR.

Traditional IRA Phase-outs

Phase-out Ranges for Deductibility

If the taxpayer (or his spouse) is not covered by an employer plan, he can take a deduction for traditional IRA contributions up to the smaller of:

- $5,000 ($6,000 if he is age 50 or older), or
- 100% of qualifying compensation.

However, the contribution will be phased out if either the taxpayer or his spouse (or both) are covered by a retirement plan at work.

Phase-out Ranges When Covered by an Employer Plan

If a taxpayer (or his spouse) is covered by an employer retirement plan, the tax-deductible contribution to a traditional IRA is phased out at the following modified adjusted gross income (AGI) limits:

Phase-outs for Taxpayers Covered by an Employer Plan	
Filing Status	**Income Range**
MFJ or QW	$92,000 - $112,000
MFS (living with spouse)	$0 - $10,000
Single, HOH, or MFS (living apart)	$58,000 - $68,000

Phase-outs for Taxpayers Not Covered By An Employer Plan:	
Filing Status	**Income Range**
MFJ (spouse covered by employer plan)	$173,000 - $183,000
MFS (spouse covered by employer plan)	$0 - $10,000
Single, QW, HOH, or MFS (spouse not covered)	No limit

If the taxpayer's modified AGI for the year is *below* the phase-out limits, the IRA contribution is fully tax-deductible. If modified AGI falls *within* the indicated income range, the

IRA contribution is partially deductible. If modified AGI is *above* the indicated range, none of the IRA contribution is deductible.

> **Example:** Tamara is single and earned $95,000 in 2012. She is covered by a retirement plan at work, but she still wants to contribute to a traditional IRA. She is phased out for the deduction because her income exceeds the threshold for single filers. If she contributes to a traditional IRA in 2012, she must file Form 8606 to report her nondeductible contribution.

Married taxpayers who file MFS have a much lower phase-out range than those with any other filing status. However, if a taxpayer files a separate return and did not live with his or her spouse at any time during the year, the taxpayer is not treated as married for purposes of these limits, and the applicable dollar limit is that of a single taxpayer.

> **Example:** Don, age 43, is separated from his wife, although they are not divorced. They have lived in separate residences for the past three years. In 2012, Don earns $40,000 and files MFS. He is allowed to deduct his full IRA contribution of $5,000. This is because he did not live with his spouse at any time during the year, and therefore he is not subject to the lower IRA phase-out limits that normally apply to MFS filers.

Rules for Deductibility of Traditional IRA Contributions

Separate limits apply to *contributions* to a traditional IRA and *the deductibility* of the contributions. Not everyone is allowed to deduct traditional IRA contributions. The deduction for contributions made to a traditional IRA depends on whether the taxpayer or his spouse is covered by an employer retirement plan and is also affected by income and filing status.

A taxpayer is permitted to have and contribute to a traditional IRA regardless of whether he or his spouse is covered by an employer retirement plan. However, if the taxpayer or his spouse is covered by an employer retirement plan, he may be entitled to only a partial deduction or no deduction at all.

If a taxpayer exceeds the income limits for making a fully tax-deductible contribution to a traditional IRA, the excess portion can still be made as a non-deductible or after-tax contribution. This means that, even though the full amount of the contribution may not be deductible, a taxpayer may still choose to contribute to his retirement on an after-tax basis. In either case, earnings will grow on a tax-deferred basis.

If a taxpayer makes nondeductible contributions to a traditional IRA, he must attach Form 8606, *Nondeductible IRAs*. Form 8606 reflects a taxpayer's cumulative nondeductible contributions, which is his tax basis in the IRA. If a taxpayer does not report nondeductible contributions properly, all future withdrawals from the IRA will be taxable unless the taxpayer can prove, with satisfactory evidence, that nondeductible contributions were made.

Required Minimum Distributions

A person cannot keep funds in a traditional IRA indefinitely. Eventually they must be distributed. Traditional IRAs are subject to required minimum distributions (RMDs). When a retirement plan account owner reaches 70½ years of age, he is required to take a minimum distribution from the IRA every year. The amount is based on IRS tables.[78] IRA owners are responsible for taking the correct amount of RMDs from their accounts on time every year.

---

[78] An RMD is calculated for each account by dividing the balance of the IRA account by a life expectancy factor that the IRS publishes in tables within Publication 590, *Individual Retirement Arrangements (IRAs)*.

Failure to take an RMD can result in a penalty tax equal to 50% of the amount the taxpayer *should* have withdrawn, but did not. If the taxpayer fails to take a required minimum distribution, he must file IRS Form 5329, *Additional Taxes on Qualified Plans*, to report the excise tax that applies as a result of the failure to take the RMD.

The first RMD must be taken by April 1 following the year the taxpayer turns 70½. The required minimum distribution for any subsequent year must be made by December 31.

A taxpayer must calculate the required minimum distribution for each year by dividing the IRA account balance at the end of the *preceding year* by the applicable distribution period per the IRS tables.

Example: Dinah was born on October 1, 1941. She reaches age 70½ in 2012. Her first RMD must be paid by April 1, 2013. As of December 31, 2012, her IRA account balance was $78,000. Using IRS tables, the applicable distribution period for someone her age (71) is 26 years. Her required minimum distribution for 2012 is $3,000 ($78,000 ÷ 26). That amount must be distributed to her by April 1, 2013, in order to avoid the 50% excise tax.

When the owner of an IRA dies, different RMD rules apply to the beneficiary of the IRA. Generally, these rules depend upon whether:

- The owner's death occurred before or after the required beginning date for distributions,
- The beneficiary is an individual, and
- The beneficiary is the owner's spouse.

If the beneficiary of a traditional IRA is the owner's spouse, he or she is granted special treatment. Surviving spouses may "roll over" their deceased spouse's IRA into their own.

Taxability of Distributions

Distributions from a traditional IRA are generally taxable in the year they are received, subject to the following exceptions:

- Rollovers
- Qualified charitable distributions
- Tax-free withdrawal of contributions
- Return on nondeductible contributions

Withdrawal Penalty on Early Distributions

A taxpayer may withdraw funds at any time from a traditional IRA account. However, early withdrawals from a traditional IRA before age 59½ will generally be subject to an additional 10% tax, in addition to normal income tax on the distributed amount.

There are some exceptions to the general rule for early distributions, however. An individual may not have to pay the additional 10% tax in the following situations:

- The taxpayer has unreimbursed medical expenses that exceed 7.5% of AGI
- The distributions do not exceed the cost of the taxpayer's medical insurance
- The taxpayer is disabled
- The distributions are not more than qualified higher education expenses
- The distributions are used to buy, build, or rebuild a first home
- The distributions are used to pay the IRS due to a levy

- The distributions are made to a qualified reservist (an individual called up to active duty)

Even though these distributions will not be subject to the additional 10% tax, they will be subject to income tax at the taxpayer's normal rates.

Distributions that are properly rolled over into another retirement plan or account (other than conversions to a Roth IRA, as discussed further below) are generally not subject to either income tax or the 10% additional penalty. Taxpayers must complete a rollover within 60 days after the day they receive the distribution.

> **Example:** Lauren, age 39, takes a $5,000 distribution from her traditional IRA account. She does not meet any of the exceptions to the 10% additional tax, so the $5,000 is an early distribution. Lauren must include the $5,000 in her gross income and pay income tax on it. She must also pay a 10% penalty tax on the early distribution. The penalty is $500 (10% × $5,000).

Qualified Charitable Distribution (QCD)

A taxpayer who is 70½ or older may choose to make a qualified charitable contribution (QCD) of up to $100,000 ($200,000 for MFJ taxpayers) from his IRA to qualified charitable organizations. The amount of the QCD may be excluded from taxable income and may also be counted toward the taxpayer's RMD. The 2012 American Taxpayer Relief Act extended this tax-free treatment of distributions for charitable purposes through December 31, 2013, with the following special rule: For QCDs made during January 2013, taxpayers can elect to have the distribution deemed to have been made during 2012.

Further, taxpayers who took IRA distributions during December 2012 and contributed all or a portion of the distributions to eligible charities during January 2013 can elect to have these amounts treated as QCDs for 2012. With the exception of the provision described above that applies to December 2012 and January 2013, the IRA trustee must make the distribution directly to the qualified charity (the taxpayer cannot request a distribution and then donate the money later). Likewise, any tax withholdings on behalf of the owner from an IRA distribution cannot qualify as QCDs.

Roth IRA Rules

Unlike a traditional IRA, none of the contributions to a Roth IRA are deductible, but the entire balance is generally tax-free at the time of withdrawal. However, distributions generally cannot be made until after a five-year holding period and after the taxpayer has reached age 59½. Further, income limits apply to Roth IRA contributions, which means high income earners may be prohibited from contributing to a Roth IRA. In 2012, the following income limit rules apply to Roth IRAs:

Anyone who earns income above the Roth threshold amount is not allowed to contribute or roll over into a Roth IRA.

The major differences between a Roth IRA and a traditional IRA are as follows:

- Contributions to a Roth IRA are not deductible by the taxpayer, and participation in an employer plan has no effect on the contribution limits.
- There are no required minimum distributions from a Roth IRA. A distribution is not required until a Roth IRA owner dies.
- Contributions to a Roth IRA can be made by persons who are over the age of 70½.

2012 Roth IRA Contribution Limits

Filing Status	Full Contribution	Phase-out Range	No Roth IRA Allowed
Single, HOH filers[79]	Less than $110,000	$110,000 - $125,000	$125,000 or more
MFJ and QW filers	Less than $173,000	$173,000 - $183,000	$183,000 or more
MFS (lived with spouse)	N/A	$0 - $10,000	$10,000 or more

IRA Rollovers in General

Generally, a "rollover" is a tax-free transfer from one retirement plan or account to *another* retirement plan or account. The contribution to the second retirement plan is called a "rollover contribution." If executed properly, *most* rollovers are nontaxable events. However, sometimes taxpayers will choose to convert a traditional IRA into a Roth IRA. In this case, the conversion will result in taxation of any previously untaxed amounts in the traditional IRA.

If a taxpayer receives an IRA distribution and wishes to make a rollover, he must complete the transaction by the 60th day after the day he receives the distribution from a traditional IRA account (or an employer's plan). The IRS may waive the 60-day requirement when the failure to do so would be inequitable, such as in the event of a casualty, disaster, or other event beyond the taxpayer's reasonable control.

If a taxpayer sells the distributed property (such as stocks distributed from an IRA) and rolls over *all the proceeds* into another traditional IRA or qualified retirement plan, no gain or loss is recognized. The sale proceeds (including any increase in value) are treated as part of the distribution and are not included in the taxpayer's gross income.

The IRS allows only one rollover per IRA account in a 12-month period. However, a trustee-to-trustee transfer (or "direct transfer") can be done more than once a year. A "trustee to trustee" transfer is when an IRA's current custodian (such as a bank) directly transfers the funds to a new custodian. The transfer is done between the two companies and the money never touches the taxpayer's hands.

Any taxable distribution paid from an employer-sponsored retirement plan is subject to a mandatory withholding of 20%, even if the taxpayer intends to roll it over later. If the taxpayer does roll it over and wants to defer tax on the entire taxable portion, he will be forced to add funds from other sources equal to the amount withheld. In order to avoid this, a taxpayer should always request a direct transfer—where the employer transfers the distribution directly to another eligible retirement plan. Under this option, the 20% mandatory withholding does not apply. It is called a "direct rollover" when a taxpayer has a check for his rollover funds made payable directly to his new retirement account.

Example: On September 4, 2012, Adam begins a new job. He decides to transfer the balance of his traditional IRA account to his new employer's plan. Adam receives a total distribution from his IRA of $50,000 in cash and $50,000 in stock. On October 4, he rolls over the entire amount totaling $100,000 into his new employer's plan.

---

[79] This phase-out range also applies to MFS taxpayers who did not live with their spouses at all during the year.

Rollover after the Death of an IRA Owner

After the death of a traditional IRA owner, a surviving spouse can elect to treat the IRA as being his or her own by changing the ownership designation, or to "roll over" the IRA balance to his or her own IRA account or certain types of qualified retirement plans. Only spouses are allowed either of these options.

An IRA may not be rolled over into the account of any other family member or beneficiary after death. However, any amounts remaining in an IRA upon a taxpayer's death would be payable to beneficiaries and subject to tax upon receipt. After an IRA owner dies, the beneficiary can generally take distributions over his remaining life expectancy. The beneficiary's "life expectancy" is calculated by using the age of the beneficiary in the year following the year of the IRA owner's death. The IRS has tables for making these calculations.

> **Example:** Allison, 42, and Lorenzo, 53, are married. Allison dies in 2012, and at the time of her death she has $50,000 in her traditional IRA account. Lorenzo chooses to roll over the entire $50,000 into his own IRA account, thereby avoiding taxation on the income until he retires and starts taking distributions.

If a Roth IRA owner dies, and the sole beneficiary is the spouse, he or she can delay distributions until the owner would have reached 70 ½ or treat the IRA as his or her own. For other beneficiaries, the account balance must generally be distributed by the end of the fifth calendar year after the owner's death, or be paid as an annuity over the beneficiary's life expectancy beginning the year following the year of death.

Conversion of a Traditional IRA to a Roth IRA

If a taxpayer wishes to convert his traditional IRA to a Roth IRA, he is required to pay federal income taxes on any pretax contributions, as well as any growth in the investment's value. Once the funds are converted to a Roth, all of the investment grows tax free, and funds can then be withdrawn on a tax-free basis.

> **Example:** Becky converted her traditional IRA to a Roth IRA in 2012. The traditional IRA had a balance of $100,000. The entire balance represents deductible contributions and earnings thereon that have not previously been taxed. She reports the amount of the balance that was converted as taxable income in 2012.

A Roth conversion is reported on Form 8606, *Nondeductible IRAs*.[80] Rules for Roth conversions are as follows:

- Taxpayers who decide to convert to a Roth must pay taxes on the amount they convert.
- Penalties apply if the taxpayer withdraws from the Roth within five years of the conversion
- Taxpayers can choose to do a partial conversion.

In the case of an inherited IRA, only an IRA inherited from a spouse may be converted to a Roth IRA. As a general rule, a taxpayer is allowed to treat an inherited IRA from his deceased spouse as his own IRA, which also includes the choice to do a Roth conversion. Non-

---

[80] Under a special rule that applied only to 2010 conversions to a Roth IRA, taxpayers must generally include half the taxable income in their income in 2011 and half in 2012, unless they chose to include all of it in income on their 2010 return. Taxpayers who also received Roth distributions in either 2010 or 2011 may be able to report a smaller taxable amount for 2012.

spousal beneficiaries (for example, a child who inherits an IRA from a deceased parent) are not allowed to roll over or convert a traditional IRA to a Roth IRA.

Excise Tax on Excess Contributions

If a taxpayer *accidentally* contributes more to his IRA than allowed, the excess contribution is subject to a 6% excise tax. The IRS will allow a taxpayer to *correct* an excess contribution if certain rules are followed. If he makes an excess contribution that exceeds his yearly maximum or his qualifying compensation, the excess contributions (and all related earnings) must be withdrawn from the IRA before the due date (including extensions) of the tax return for that year. If a taxpayer corrects the excess contribution in time, the 6% penalty will apply only to the interest earned on the excess contribution. Contributions made in the year a taxpayer reaches 70½ are also considered excess contributions.

Each year that the excess amounts remain in the traditional IRA the taxpayer must pay a 6% tax. However, this tax can never exceed more than 6% of the combined value of all the taxpayer's IRA at the end of the tax year. In order to correct an "improper contribution" to an IRA, the taxpayer must withdraw the contribution and any earnings on that amount. Relief from the 6% excise penalty is available only if the following are true:

- The taxpayer must withdraw the full amount of the excess contribution on or before the due date (including extensions) for filing the tax return for the year of the contribution.
- The withdrawal must include any income earned that is attributable to the excess contribution.

Taxpayers must include the earnings on the excess contribution as taxable income, and that income is reported on the return for the year in which the withdrawal was made.

Example: Betsy is 66, self-employed, and also owns rental properties. She contributes the maximum amount of $6,000 to her traditional IRA in December 2012. She is very busy and her records are poor, so she files for an extension to prepare her tax return. When Betsy finally gives her records to her accountant, he discovers that her taxable income from self-employment is only $3,000. Her passive rental income is $18,000. Only the self-employment income counts as "compensation" for purposes of contributing to a traditional IRA, so Betsy has inadvertently made an excess contribution of $3,000. She must withdraw the excess contribution and any interest earned on it by the extended due date of her return or face an excise tax of 6%.

Prohibited Transactions

Generally, a prohibited transaction is the improper use of a traditional IRA by the owner, a beneficiary, or a disqualified person (typically a fiduciary or family member). Types of prohibited transactions with a traditional IRA include:

- Borrowing money from it
- Selling property to it
- Using it as security for a loan
- Buying property for personal use with IRA funds

If a prohibited transaction occurs at any time during the year, the account ceases to be treated as an IRA and its assets are treated as if having been distributed as of the first day of the year. If the total fair market value as of that date is more than the basis in the IRA, the excess amount is reportable as taxable income. It may also be subject to the additional 10% tax on early distributions.

Traditional IRA vs. Roth IRA		
Issue	**Traditional IRA**	**Roth IRA**
Age limit	A person over 70½ cannot contribute.	No age limit.
2012 contribution limits	$5,000, or $6,000 if age 50 or older by the end of 2012.	$5,000, or $6,000 if age 50 or older by the end of 2012.
Are contributions deductible?	Usually, yes. Deductibility depends on AGI, filing status, and whether the person is covered by a retirement plan at work.	No. You can never deduct contributions to a Roth IRA.
Filing requirements	No filing requirement unless nondeductible contributions are made.	No filing requirement.
Mandatory distributions	A person must begin receiving required minimum distributions by April 1 of the year following the year he or she reaches age 70½.	No. There are no required distributions unless the IRA owner dies.
How distributions are taxed	Distributions from a traditional IRA are taxed as ordinary income.	Distributions from a Roth IRA are not taxed.
Income limits	No income limits.	There are income limits for contributions, but there are none that affect conversion of a traditional IRA to a Roth IRA. Taxes apply on the conversion.

Unit 14: Questions

1. Lucas, an unmarried college student working part-time, earns $3,500 in 2012. He also receives $500 in interest income and $4,000 from his parents to help pay tuition. What is his maximum IRA contribution in 2012?

A. $0.
B. $3,500.
C. $5,000.
D. $6,000.

The answer is B. His IRA contribution for 2012 is limited to $3,500, the total amount of his wages. The other income (the interest income and the gifted money from his parents) is not qualifying compensation for IRA purposes. ###

2. Vic, age 36 and single, is in the Marines. He has the following income in 2012:

$30,500 of nontaxable combat pay.
$2,100 of regular wages.
$4,600 of interest income.

What is the maximum amount of money that Vic can contribute to a traditional IRA?

A. $2,100.
B. $4,600.
C. $5,000.
D. $6,000.

The answer is C. Vic may contribute $5,000, the maximum contribution allowed for his age. That is because a taxpayer may elect to treat nontaxable combat pay as qualifying compensation for IRA purposes. The interest income is not considered compensation. ###

3. Celeste, who is 50 and single, worked for a telephone company in France and earned $48,500 for which she claimed the foreign earned income exclusion. In addition she earned $3,200 as an employee of an answering service while she was in the U.S. She also received alimony of $400 for the year. What is her maximum amount of allowable contribution to a traditional IRA for year 2012?

A. $3,200.
B. $3,600.
C. $5,000.
D. $6,000.

The answer is B. Foreign earned income and any other income that is excluded from tax (with the exception of nontaxable combat pay) is also excluded for IRA contribution purposes. Alimony of $400 and wages of $3,200 earned in the U.S. are considered compensation for purposes of an IRA contribution. ###

4. Rafael, 40, earns $26,000 in 2012. Although he is allowed to contribute up to $5,000 to his IRA, he only has enough cash to contribute $2,000. On May 15, 2013, Rafael expects to get a big bonus, and he wishes to make a "catch-up" contribution for 2012. Rafael filed a timely extension for his tax return. Which of the following statements is true?

A. Rafael can contribute an additional $3,000 in May 2013 for his 2012 tax year so long as he files his tax return by the extended due date.
B. Rafael cannot contribute an additional $3,000 after April 15, 2013.
C. Rafael can contribute an additional $3,000 in May 2013 for his 2012 tax year only if he files his return by April 15, 2013.
D. Rafael cannot make a 2012 contribution to his IRA after December 31, 2012.

The answer is B. Rafael cannot contribute an additional $3,000 after April 15, 2013, regardless of whether he files an extension. If contributions to a traditional IRA for the year were less than the limit, a taxpayer cannot contribute more after the original due date of the tax return to make up the difference. ###

5. Kristin, 42, is a full-time graduate student with $1,200 in wages. She marries Omar, 50, during the year. Omar has taxable compensation of $46,000 in 2012. What is the maximum they can contribute to their traditional IRA accounts in 2012 if they file jointly?

A. $1,200.
B. $6,200.
C. $10,000.
D. $11,000.

The answer is D. They can contribute $11,000 if they file jointly. Kristin can contribute $5,000, and Omar can contribute $6,000 because he is 50. Even though Kristin only has $1,200 in compensation, she can use Omar's compensation to determine her maximum contribution. ###

6. Jody is single, 51, and has the following compensation in 2012:

- $1,600 in annuity income
- $3,000 in wages
- $2,300 in alimony
- $3,000 in interest income
- $6,000 in rental income

What is the maximum amount that Jody can contribute to her traditional IRA in 2012?

A. $3,000.
B. $5,000.
C. $5,300.
D. $6,000.

The answer is C. Jody is over 50, so she can make up to $6,000 in IRA contributions during the year, but only if she has qualifying compensation. In this case, only Jody's wage income of $3,000 and the $2,300 in alimony qualify as compensation for purposes of an IRA contribution. The annuity income, rental income, and interest income are passive income and do not qualify. ###

7. Derek, age 62, is retired with $11,000 in interest income. He has no other taxable income in 2012. Derek marries Virginia, age 46, on March 26, 2012. Virginia has taxable compensation of $50,000 for the year. She plans to contribute $5,000 to a traditional IRA. How much can Derek contribute to an IRA?

A. $0.
B. $4,000.
C. $5,000.
D. $6,000.

The answer is D. Since Derek is over 50, if they file a joint return, he can choose to contribute $6,000 to an IRA. Even though Derek only has interest income, his wife has wage income. Each can contribute to a traditional IRA, even if only one spouse has qualifying compensation. ###

8. Colton, 49, and Molly, 52, are married and file jointly. They both work and each has a traditional IRA. In 2012, Molly earned $2,000 and Colton earned $50,000. If they file jointly, what is the maximum Molly can contribute to her IRA?

A. $2,000.
B. $5,000.
C. $6,000.
D. $12,000.

The answer is C. They can contribute up to $6,000 to Molly's IRA account because she is over 50 years old and can utilize Colton's earnings in order to make the maximum contribution. ###

9. An excess contribution to an IRA is subject to a tax. Which of the following is true?

A. The taxpayer will not have to pay the 6% tax on the excess contribution if he withdraws the excess contribution and any income earned on the excess contribution before the due date of the tax return for the applicable year, including extensions.
B. The 6% tax is due on both the excess contributions and any income earned on the excess contribution, even if the taxpayer withdraws the excess from the account.
C. A taxpayer will not have to pay the 6% tax if he withdraws the excess contribution and any income earned on the excess contribution before the due date of the tax return for the year, not including extensions.
D. A taxpayer will not have to pay the 6% on interest earned on the excess contributions so long as the taxpayer is disabled.

The answer is A. The taxpayer will not have to pay the 6% tax on the excess contribution if the excess contribution and any interest earned are withdrawn by the due date of his return, *including extensions*. If a taxpayer corrects the excess contribution in time, the 6% penalty will apply only to the interest earned on the excess contribution. ###

10. Elizabeth and Landon are 62 years old, married, and lived together all year. They both work and each has a traditional IRA. In 2012, Landon earned $4,000 in wages and $11,000 in annuity income. Elizabeth earned $52,000. They prefer to file separately. If they file separate returns, what is the maximum that Landon can contribute to his IRA?

A. $1,000.
B. $4,000.
C. $5,000.
D. $6,000.

The answer is B. As Landon is married and lived with his wife during the year but is filing separately, he can contribute no more than his $4,000 in wages, which is his only qualifying compensation for IRA purposes. ###

11. Preston and Ruby are 50 years old and married. They both work and each has a traditional IRA. In 2012, Preston earned $5,000 and Ruby earned $32,000. If they file jointly, what is the maximum they can contribute to their IRAs?

A. $5,000.
B. $6,000.
C. $10,000.
D. $12,000.

The answer is D. If married filing jointly, they can contribute up to $12,000 to all their IRAs. This is because they are over 50 and they each can make the maximum contribution of $6,000. ###

12. Frank, 72, and Sue, 61, are married and file jointly. In 2012, Frank earned $30,000 and Sue earned $5,000. If Frank and Sue file jointly, how much can they contribute to their traditional IRAs?

A. $5,000.
B. $6,000.
C. $11,000.
D. $12,000.

The answer is B. Only Sue can contribute to an IRA. Frank cannot contribute because he is over 70½ years old. However, Sue is over 50 and can utilize Frank's qualifying compensation in order to contribute the maximum of $6,000 to her IRA. ###

13. Miguel is 47. In 2012, he contributed $1,000 to a Roth IRA. He also wants to contribute to a traditional IRA account. What is the maximum he can contribute to a traditional IRA in 2012?

A. $0.
B. $3,000.
C. $4,000.
D. $5,000.

The answer is C. Assuming Miguel has sufficient qualifying compensation, he would be able to contribute $4,000; the 2012 maximum for contributions to all types of IRAs is $5,000 for taxpayers under 50. Taxpayers are allowed to have different types of IRA accounts, but the maximum contribution thresholds apply to their total contributions for the year. ###

14. Annette, age 40, and Gill, age 48, are married and file jointly. Annette is covered by a retirement plan at work, but Gill is not. In 2012, Annette contributed $2,000 to her traditional IRA and $3,000 to a traditional IRA for Gill. Annette has a modified AGI of $90,000; Gill has a modified AGI of $98,000. What is their allowable IRA deduction?

A. $5,000.
B. $3,000.
C. $2,000.
D. $0.

The answer is D. Annette and Gill's allowable IRA deduction is zero because their modified AGI is over the phase-out limit of $183,000 for 2012. However, they are still allowed to make nondeductible IRA contributions that would be reported on Form 8606. ###

15. Shari wants to roll over her retirement account to another bank. She received a distribution in 2012. How long does Shari have to complete the rollover in order to avoid income tax on the distribution?

A. 30 days.
B. 60 days.
C. Until the end of the year.
D. Until the due date of the return.

The answer is B. Shari has 60 days to complete the rollover. If she does not complete the rollover within 60 days, the distribution is treated as a taxable event and is subject to income tax in 2012. ###

16. Janelle plans to make a contribution to her traditional IRA. She files her 2012 tax return on March 1, 2013, claiming a deduction for her IRA contribution. However, she forgets to make the contribution in time and misses the deadline. What must Janelle do?

A. Janelle must file an amended return.
B. Janelle may claim the contribution as income in the following year.
C. Janelle must file an extension.
D. Janelle must pay an early withdrawal penalty.

The answer is A. If a contribution is reported on the 2012 return but is not made by the deadline, the taxpayer must file an amended return. IRA contributions must be made by the due date for filing the return, not including extensions. ###

17. David is 57 and he contributed $2,000 to his Roth IRA in 2012. What is the maximum he can contribute to a traditional IRA?

A. $0.
B. $3,000.
C. $4,000.
D. $5,000.

The answer is C. The 2012 maximum for contributions to all types of IRAs is $6,000 for taxpayers who are 50 or older. Since David is 57, and assuming he has sufficient qualifying compensation, he is allowed to contribute $4,000 to a traditional IRA in addition to the $2,000 contributed to the Roth IRA, for a combined total of $6,000. ###

18. Monica borrowed $100,000 and pledged the balance in her traditional IRA as security on the loan. At the beginning of 2012, the IRA had a balance of $70,000; at the time of the loan transaction, its balance was $80,000; and at the end of 2012, its balance was $75,000. Which of the following would result from this transaction?

A. Monica would have taxable income of $75,000.
B. Monica would have taxable income of $70,000.
C. Monica would have taxable income of $70,000.
D. Monica would have to pay an additional 10% penalty on her 2012 contribution to the IRA.

The answer is B. Pledging the IRA as security for a loan is considered a prohibited transaction that results in termination of the account's treatment as an IRA, and the FMV as of the beginning of the year is considered to be a taxable distribution. Assuming the entire balance of the account represented deductible contributions and earnings on them, Janelle would have had no basis in the account, and the entire $70,000 would be reportable as taxable income. ###

19. Which of the following is considered an excess contribution to an IRA?

A. A traditional IRA contribution made in the year a taxpayer reaches 70½.
B. A rollover to a Roth IRA.
C. A contribution made by a taxpayer who only has alimony income.
D. A Roth contribution made by a taxpayer who is 75.

The answer is A. Contributions to a traditional IRA made in the year a taxpayer reaches 70½ (and any later years) are considered excess contributions. In general, an excess contribution and any earnings on it are subject to an additional 6% tax if the taxpayer does not withdraw the contribution by the due date of the tax return, including extensions. ###

20. AJ was born on June 6, 1942. By what date must he take the first required minimum distribution from his traditional IRA?

A. April 1, 2012.
B. December 31, 2012.
C. December 31, 2013.
D. April 1, 2013.

The answer is D. The first required minimum distribution from a traditional IRA must be taken by April 1 of the year following the year in which the taxpayer turns 70½. AJ turned 70½ on December 6, 2012. ###

Unit 15: Estate and Gift Taxes

More Reading:
Publication 559, *Survivors, Executors, and Administrators*
Publication 950, *Introduction to Estate and Gift Taxes*

For Part 1 of the EA exam, you will be required to understand how estate and gift taxes affect individual taxpayers. For Part 2 of the exam, you will be tested on the treatment of estates as legal entities.

Estates in General

For federal tax purposes, an estate is a separate legal entity that is created when a taxpayer dies. The deceased taxpayer's property may consist of items such as cash and securities, real estate, insurance, trusts, annuities, business interests, and other assets. A person who inherits property from an estate is not taxed on the transfer. Instead, the estate itself is responsible for paying any applicable taxes before the property is distributed. However, if the estate's assets are distributed to beneficiaries before applicable taxes are paid, the beneficiaries can be held liable for the tax debt, up to the value of the assets distributed.

Requirements for the Personal Representative of an Estate

After a person dies, a personal representative, such as an executor named in his will or an administrator appointed by a court, will typically manage the estate and settle the decedent's financial affairs. If there is no executor or administrator, another person with possession of the decedent's property may act as the personal representative.

The personal representative is responsible for filing the final income tax return and the estate tax return, if required.

The personal representative is also responsible for determining any estate tax liability before the estate's assets are distributed to beneficiaries. The tax liability for an estate attaches to the assets of the estate itself, so if the assets are distributed to the beneficiaries before the taxes are paid, the beneficiaries may be held liable for the tax debt, up to the value of the assets distributed.

Either the personal representative or a paid preparer must sign the appropriate line of the return. Current IRS requirements require that the following tax returns be filed:

- The final income tax returns (Form 1040) for the decedent (for income received before death);
- Fiduciary income tax returns (Form 1041) for the estate for the period of its administration; (if necessary) and
- Estate Tax Return (Form 706), if the fair market value of the assets of the estate exceeds the applicable threshold for the year of death.

Example: James was unmarried when he died on April 20, 2012. His only daughter, Lillian, was named as the executor of his estate. James earned wages in 2012 before his death. Therefore, a final tax return is required for 2012. Lillian asks her accountant to help prepare her father's final Form 1040, which will include all the taxable income that James received in 2012 before his death. The accountant also helps Lillian with the valuation of her father's estate. After determining the fair market value of all her father's assets, they conclude that James's gross estate is valued at approximately $7 million. As this exceeds the threshold of $5,120,000 for 2012, an estate tax return (Form 706) is also required to be filed.

The Final Income Tax Return (Form 1040)

The taxpayer's final income tax return is filed on the same form that would have been used if the taxpayer were still alive, but "deceased" is written after the taxpayer's name. The filing deadline is April 15 of the year following the taxpayer's death, just like regular tax returns.

The personal representative must file the final individual income tax return of the decedent for the year of death and any returns not filed for preceding years. If an individual died after the close of the tax year but before the return for that year was filed, the return for that year will not be the final return. The return for that year will be a regular return and the personal representative must file it.

Example: Stephanie dies on March 2, 2012. At the time of her death, she had not yet filed her 2011 tax return. She earned $51,000 in wages in 2011. She also earned $18,000 in wages between January 1, 2012 and her death. Therefore, Stephanie's 2011 and 2012 tax return must be filed by her representative. The 2012 return would be her final individual tax return.

On a decedent's final tax return, the rules for personal exemptions and deductions are the same as for any taxpayer. The full amount of the applicable personal exemption may be claimed on the final tax return, regardless of how long the taxpayer was alive during the year.

Income In Respect of a Decedent

Income in respect of a decedent (IRD) is any taxable income that was earned but *not received* by the decedent by the time of death. IRD is not taxed on the final return of the deceased taxpayer. IRD is reported on the tax return of the person (or entity) that receives the income. This could be the estate, the surviving spouse, or another beneficiary, such as a child. Regardless of the decedent's accounting method, IRD is subject to income tax when the income is received. IRD retains the same tax nature after death as if the taxpayer were still alive. For example, if the income would have been short-term capital gain to the deceased, it is taxed the same way to the beneficiary. IRD can come from various sources, including:

- Unpaid salary, wages or bonuses
- Distributions from traditional IRAs and employer-provided retirement plans
- Deferred compensation benefits
- Accrued but unpaid interest, dividends, and rent
- Accounts receivable of a sole proprietor

> **Example:** Carlos was owed $15,000 in wages when he died. The check for these wages was not remitted by his employer until three weeks later and was received by his daughter and sole beneficiary, Rosalie. The wages are considered IRD, and Rosalie must recognize the $15,000 as ordinary income, the same tax treatment that would have applied for Carlos.

> **Example:** Beverly died on April 30. At the time of her death, she was owed (but had not yet received) $1,500 in interest on bonds and $2,000 in rental income. Beverly's beneficiary will include $3,500 in IRD in gross income when the interest and rent are received. The income retains its character as passive interest income and passive rental income.

IRD is includible in the decedent's estate and subject to estate tax, and may also be subject to income tax if received by a beneficiary. Therefore, the beneficiary may take a deduction for estate tax paid on the IRD. This deduction is taken as a miscellaneous itemized deduction on Schedule A, and is not subject to the 2% floor, as are most other miscellaneous itemized deductions.

IRS Form 1041, U.S. Income Tax Return for Estates and Trusts

An estate is a taxable legal entity that exists from the time of an individual's death until all assets have been distributed to the decedent's beneficiaries. Form 1041 is a fiduciary return used to report the following items for a domestic decedent's estate, trust, or bankruptcy estate:

- Current income and deductions, including gains and losses from disposition of the entity's property;
- A deduction for income that is either accumulated or held for future distribution or distributed currently to the beneficiaries; and
- Any income tax liability.

Current income would include IRD, if it was received by the estate rather than specific beneficiaries. As investment assets will usually continue to earn income after a taxpayer has died, this income, such as rents, dividends and interest, must be reported. Expenses of administering the estate can be deducted either from the estate's income on Form 1041 in determining its income tax, or from the gross estate on Form 706 in determining the estate tax liability, but cannot be claimed for both purposes. Schedule K-1 is used to report any income that is distributed to each beneficiary and is filed with Form 1041, with a copy also given to the beneficiary.

The due date for Form 1041 is the fifteenth day of the fourth month following the end of the entity's tax year, but is subject to an automatic extension of five months if Form 7004 is filed. The tax year may be either a calendar or fiscal year, subject to the election made at the time the first return is filed. An election will also be made on the first return as to method (cash, accrual, or other) to report the estate's income.

Form 1041 must be filed for any domestic estate that has gross income for the tax year of $600 or more, or a beneficiary who is a nonresident alien (with any amount of income).

Gross Estate

The estate tax is a tax on the transfer of property from an individual's estate after his death. It applies to the taxable estate, which is the gross estate less certain deductions. The gross estate is based upon the fair market value of the taxpayer's property, which is not necessarily equal to his cost, and includes:

- The FMV of all tangible and intangible property owned by the decedent at the time of death.
- The full value of property held as joint tenants with the right of survivorship (unless the decedent and spouse were the only joint tenants)
- Life insurance proceeds payable to the estate, or for policies owned by the decedent, payable to the heirs.
- The value of certain annuities or survivor benefits payable to the heirs.
- The value of certain property that was transferred within three years before the decedent's death.

The gross estate does not include property owned solely by the decedent's spouse or other individuals. Lifetime gifts that are complete (so that no control over the gifts was retained) are not included in the gross estate.

Deductions from the Gross Estate

Once the gross estate has been calculated, certain deductions (and in special circumstances, reductions to value) are allowed to determine the taxable estate. Deductions from the gross estate may include:

- Funeral expenses paid out of the estate.
- Administration expenses for the estate, including attorney's fees.
- Debts owed at the time of death.
- The marital deduction (generally, the value of the property that passes from the estate to a surviving spouse).
- The charitable deduction (generally, the value of the property that passes from the estate to a qualifying charity).
- The state death tax deduction (generally, any inheritance or estate taxes paid to any state).

The following items are not deductible from the gross estate:

- Federal estate taxes paid.
- Alimony paid after the taxpayer's death. These payments would be treated as distributions to a beneficiary.

Property taxes are deductible only if they accrue under state law prior to the decedent's death.

Marital Deduction

There are special rules and exceptions for transfers between spouses. The marital deduction allows spouses to transfer an unlimited amount of property to one another during their lifetimes or at death without being subject to estate or gift taxes.

To receive an unlimited deduction, the spouse receiving the assets must be a U.S. citizen, a legal spouse, and have outright ownership of the assets. The unlimited marital deduction is generally not allowed if the transferee spouse is not a U.S. citizen (even if the spouse is a legal resident of the United States). If the receiving spouse is not a U.S. citizen, assets transferred are subject to an annual exclusion, which is $139,000 in 2012.

Basis of Estate Property

The basis of property inherited from a decedent is generally one of the following:

- The FMV of the property on the date of death.
- The FMV on an alternate valuation date, if elected by the personal representative.
- The value under a special-use valuation method for real property used in farming or another closely-held business, if elected by the personal representative.
- The decedent's adjusted basis in land to the extent of the value excluded from the taxable estate as a qualified conservation easement.

Property that is jointly owned by a decedent and another person will be included in full in the decedent's gross estate unless it can be shown that the other person originally owned or otherwise contributed to the purchase price. The surviving owner's new basis of property that was jointly owned must be calculated. To do so, the surviving owner's original basis in the property is added to the value of the part of the property included in the decedent's estate. Any deductions for depreciation allowed to the surviving owner on that property are subtracted from the sum.

If property is jointly held between husband and wife as tenants by the entirety or as joint tenants with the right of survivorship (if they were the only joint tenants), one-half of the property's value is included in the gross estate and there is a step-up in basis for that one-half. If the decedent holds property in a community property state, half of the value of the community property will be included in the gross estate of the decedent, but the entire value of the community property will receive a step-up in basis.

Special Election for Decedent's Medical Expenses

Debts that were not paid before death, including medical expenses subsequently paid on behalf of the decedent, are liabilities of the estate and can be deducted from the gross estate on the estate tax return. However, if medical expenses for the decedent are paid out of the estate during the one-year period beginning with the day after death, the personal representative can alternatively elect to treat all or part of the expenses as paid by the decedent at the time they were incurred, and deduct them on the final tax return (1040) for the decedent.

Estates and Credits

Estates are allowed some of the same tax credits that are allowed to individuals. The credits are generally allocated between the estate and the beneficiaries. However, estates are not allowed the credit for the elderly or the disabled, the Child Tax Credit, or the Earned Income Credit.

Form 706: The Estate Tax Return

An estate tax return is filed using Form 706, *United States Estate (and Generation-Skipping Transfer) Tax Return*. After the taxable estate is computed, the value of lifetime taxable gifts is added to this number and the estate tax is computed. The tax is then reduced by the applicable credit amount. The applicable credit amount, formerly referred to as the unified credit, applies to both the gift tax and the estate tax applies to both the gift tax and the estate tax and it equals the tax on the basic exclusion amount.

For 2012, the basic exclusion amount is $5,120,000 and the related applicable credit amount is $1,772,800. Any portion of the applicable credit amount used against gift tax in a given year reduces the amount of credit that can be used against gift or estate taxes in later years. For estate tax purposes but not for gift taxes, the applicable credit amount may also include the tax applicable to the deceased spousal unused exclusion (DSUE). The DSUE is the unused portion of the decedent's predeceased spouse's estate that was not used against gift or estate tax liabilities. The predeceased spouse must have died on or after January 1, 2011 and the DSUE must have been reported on Form 706 filed on behalf of the first spouse's estate.

If required to be filed, the due date for Form 706 is nine months after the decedent's date of death. An automatic six- month extension may be requested by filing Form 4768. However, the tax is due by the due date and interest is accrued on any amounts owed that are not paid at that time.

The assessment period for tax is three years after the due date for a timely filed estate tax return. The assessment period is four years for transfers from an estate.

Generation-Skipping Transfer Tax (GST)

The generation skipping transfer tax (GST) may apply to gifts during a taxpayer's life or transfers occurring after his death, called bequests, made to "skip persons." A "skip person" is a person who belongs to a generation that is two or more generations *below* the generation of the donor. The most common scenario is when a taxpayer makes a gift or bequest to a grandchild.

The GST is assessed when a property transfer is made, including instances in which property is transferred from a trust. The GST tax is based on the amounts transferred to skip persons, after subtracting the allocated portions of the GST tax exemption. In 2012, the GST tax exemption is $5,120,000 and the GST tax rate is set at the maximum estate tax rate of 35%.

The GST is imposed separately and in addition to the estate and gift tax.

Example: Patrick sets up a trust that names his adult daughter, Helene, as the sole beneficiary of the trust. In January 2012, Patrick dies, and the trust passes to Helene. However, later in the year, Helene also dies, and now the trust passes to her children (Patrick's grandchildren). Patrick's grandchildren are "skip-persons" for purposes of the GST, and the trust fund property may be subject to the GST.

Any *direct* payments that are made toward tuition or medical expenses are exempt from gift tax or GST.

Example: Gordon wants to help support his grandchildren, but he wants to make sure that his gifts are not subject to gift tax, GST, or estate tax. So, in 2012, he offers to pay his grandchild's college tuition in full. Gordon writes a check directly to the college in the amount of $25,000. There is no tax consequence for this gift, and no reporting is required.

Gift Tax

The gift tax is imposed on the transfer of property by one individual to another and applies whether the donor intends the transfer to be a gift or not. Gift tax is always imposed on the donor, not the receiver, of the property. However, under special arrangements the donee may *agree* to pay the tax instead of the donor.

As discussed above, the estate tax and gift tax are subject to a combined basic exclusion amount ($5,120,000 in 2012) and use of any portion of this exclusion amount to reduce payment of gift taxes during a taxpayer's lifetime will reduce the amount available upon death to reduce applicable estate taxes. For 2012, the maximum gift tax rate is 35%.

Although any gift could potentially be a taxable gift, the following gifts are not taxable:

- Gifts that are not more than the annual exclusion. In 2012, the exclusion is $13,000 per person.
- Tuition or medical expenses paid for someone else, directly to the institution.
- Unlimited gifts to a spouse, so long as the spouse is a U.S. citizen.
- Gifts to a political organization for its use.
- Gifts to a qualifying charity.
- A parent's support for a minor child. This support is not considered a "gift" if it is required as part of a legal obligation, such as by a divorce decree.

Gift taxes are reported on Form 709, *United States Gift (and Generation-Skipping Transfer) Tax Return*. Form 709 is required for any of the following gifts:

- If the taxpayer gives more than the annual exclusion to at least one individual (except to a U. S. citizen spouse)
- If the taxpayer "splits gifts" with a spouse
- If a taxpayer gives a future interest[81] to anyone other than a U.S. citizen spouse

If the taxpayer's spouse is not a U.S. citizen, a gift tax return is required in the following instances:

- Any gifts totaling more than $139,000 (limit in 2012)
- A future interest of any value

If required, Form 709 is due by April 15, 2013. However, if the donor died during 2012, the filing deadline is the due date for his estate tax return (if earlier than April 15, 2013). Taxpayers who extend the filing of Form 1040 for six months using Form 4868 are deemed to have extended their gift tax return, if no gift tax is due with the extension. If gift tax is due, the tax payer must submit payment with a payment voucher. If the taxpayer does not extend Form 1040, the gift tax return can be extended separately.

Example: Earline gives her son, Dion, a gift of $13,000 in cash during the year. She also pays his college tuition, totaling $21,000. She writes the check directly to the college. Earline also pays for Dion's medical bills by issuing the check directly to his doctor's office. None of these gifts is taxable, and no gift tax return is required.

Example: Dave is single. In 2012, Dave gives his adult son, Noah, $15,000 to help start his first business. The money is not a loan, so Dave is required to file a gift tax return, since the amount exceeds the $13,000 annual exclusion amount.

---

[81] A "future interest" is a gift that cannot be immediately used, possessed, or enjoyed.

Gifts by Married Couples (Gift Splitting)

Both the basic exclusion amount and the annual exclusion for gifts to individuals apply separately to each spouse, and each spouse must separately file a gift tax return if he or she made reportable gifts during the year. However, if a married couple makes a gift to another person, the gift can be considered as being one-half from one spouse and one-half from the other spouse. This is known as gift splitting. Gift splitting allows married couples to give up to $26,000 to a person without making a taxable gift. Both spouses must consent to split the gift. Married couples who split gifts must file a gift tax return, even if one-half of the split gift is less than the annual exclusion.

Example: Harold and his wife, Margie, agree to split gifts of cash. Harold gives his nephew, Mark, $21,000, and Margie gives her niece, Nicole, $18,000. Although each gift is more than the annual exclusion ($13,000), by gift splitting they can make these gifts without making a taxable gift. In each case, because one-half of the split gift is not more than the annual exclusion, it is not a taxable gift. However, the couple must file a gift tax return.

Example: Felicia gives her cousin, Jessie, $24,000 to purchase a new car. Felicia elects to split the gift with her husband, Rafael, and Rafael is treated as if he gave Jessie half the amount, or $12,000. Assuming they make no other gifts to Jessie during the year, the entire $24,000 gift is tax free. Since they have decided to split the gift, Jessie and Rafael are required to file gift tax returns.

Basis of Property Received as a Gift

For purposes of determining gain or loss on a subsequent disposition of property received as a gift, the taxpayer must consider:

- The gift's adjusted basis to the donor just before it was given to the taxpayer,
- The gift's FMV at the time it was given to the taxpayer, and
- Any gift tax paid actually paid on appreciation of the property's value while held by the donor (as opposed to gift tax offset by the donor's applicable credit amount).

When a taxpayer sells property received as a gift, he calculates gain based upon the donor's adjusted basis plus any gift tax paid on the donor's appreciation. If the same property were sold at a loss, the taxpayer's basis would be the lower of the donor's adjusted basis or the FMV at the time of the gift.

Example: Darren's father gives him 20 shares of stock that are currently worth $900. Darren's father has an adjusted basis in the stock of $500. Darren's basis in the stock, for purposes of determining gain on any future sale of the stock, is $500. (This is the stock's transferred basis.)

Generally, the value of a gift is its fair market value on the date of the gift. However, the value of the gift may be less than its fair market value to the extent that the donee gives the donor something in return.

Example: Donald sells his son, Jared, a house for $10,000. At the time of the gift, the fair market value of the house is $90,000. Donald has made a gift to his son of $80,000 ($90,000 - $10,000 = $80,000).

Unit 15: Questions

1. Which of the following is not income in respect of a decedent?

A. Wages earned before death but still unpaid at the time of death.
B. Vacation time paid after death.
C. Taxable IRAs and retirement plans.
D. A royalty check that was received before death but not cashed.

The answer is D. Since the royalty check was received before the taxpayer died, it is not considered IRD income. Income in respect of a decedent is taxable income earned but not received by the decedent by the time of death. The fact that the royalty check was not cashed has no bearing on the nature of the income.

2. When is an estate tax return due?

A. Four months after the close of the taxable year.
B. Six months after the close of the calendar year.
C. Nine months after the date of death.
D. Twelve months after the date of death.

The answer is C. Estate tax returns are due nine months from the date of death, although the executor may request an extension of time to file.

3. Which of the following items is not an allowable deduction from the gross estate?

A. Debts owed at the time of death.
B. Medical expenses.
C. Funeral expenses.
D. Federal estate tax.

The answer is D. Federal estate tax is not deductible from the gross estate. All of the other items listed are allowable deductions from the gross estate.

4. The executor of Ophelia's estate is her sister, Elise. Elise decides to make a distribution of 100% of the estate's assets before paying the estate's income tax liability. Which of the following is true?

A. The beneficiaries of the estate can be held liable for the payment of the liability, even if the liability exceeds the value of the estate assets.
B. No one can be held liable for the tax if the assets have been distributed.
C. The beneficiaries can be held liable for the tax debt, up to the value of the assets distributed.
D. None of the above.

The answer is C. The tax liability for an estate attaches to the assets of the estate itself, so if the assets are distributed to the beneficiaries before the taxes are paid, the beneficiaries can be held liable for the tax debt, up to the value of the assets distributed.

5. Delia's estate has funeral expenses for the cost of her burial. How should the executor deduct these costs?

A. Funeral expenses are an itemized deduction on Form 1040.
B. Funeral expenses are deducted on Form 1041.
C. Funeral expenses are deducted on Form 706.
D. Funeral expenses cannot be deducted as an expense.

The answer is C. No deduction for funeral expenses can be taken on Form 1041 or Form 1040. Funeral expenses may only be claimed as a deduction from the gross estate on Form 706.

6. Duncan died in 2012. Following his death, the executor of his estate paid the following bills. Which of these is not an allowable deduction in determining Duncan's taxable estate?

A. Administration expenses.
B. State inheritance taxes.
C. Charitable contributions.
D. Alimony paid after the taxpayer's death.

The answer is D. Alimony paid after the taxpayer's death is not deductible from the gross estate. Deductions from the gross estate are allowed for:
• Funeral expenses paid out of the estate
• Administration expenses for the estate, including attorney's fees
• Debts owed at the time of death
• The marital deduction
• The charitable deduction
• The state death tax deduction

7. During December in each of the ten years prior to his death, Herman gave $30,000 to each of his two granddaughters. He also paid a total of $400,000 directly to Birchland College for their college tuition costs. When Herman died in June 2012, how much of his basic exclusive amount would he have used up as a result of these gifts to his granddaughters?

A. $600,000.
B. $1,000,000.
C. $340,000.
D. $400,000.

The answer is C. Each year's gift of $30,000 is reduced by the annual exclusion amount of $13,000, and a portion of Herman's basic exclusion amount must be used to avoid payment of gift tax on the excess amount of $17,000. Thus, over ten years, he uses a total of $170,000 for each granddaughter, or $340,000. Since the $400,000 was paid directly to Birchland College on behalf of the granddaughters, it is not subject to gift tax, and none of his basic exclusion amount must be used as a result of these additional gifts. It should be noted that his cash gifts to the granddaughters would also be subject to generation-skipping tax.

8. In general, who is responsible for paying the gift tax?

A. The estate.
B. The donor.
C. The receiver of the gift.
D. The executor.

The answer is B. The donor is generally responsible for paying the gift tax. ###

9. Donald's will provides that each of his ten grandchildren is to receive $1 million. Assuming that none of his GST exemption amount has previously been used in connection with gifts to the grandchildren or other skip persons, what portion of the total amount distributed to the grandchildren after his death in 2012 would be subject to GST?

A. $8,700,000.
B. $5,120,000.
C. $10,000,000.
D. $4,880,000.

The answer is D. The aggregate portion of his estate distributed to his grandchildren ($10 million) would be reduced by his exclusion amount for GST ($5,120,000) and the remainder of $4,880,000 would be subject to GST. ###

10. Dustin pays $15,000 in college tuition for his nephew, Rich, directly to Rich's college. Which of the following statements is correct?

A. The gift is taxable, and Rich must report the gift tax on his individual tax return (Form 1040).
B. The gift is not taxable, but Dustin must file a gift tax return.
C. The gift is taxable, and Dustin must file a gift tax return.
D. The gift is not taxable, and no gift tax return is required.

The answer is D. Tuition or medical expenses paid directly to a medical or educational institution for someone else are not included in the calculation of taxable gifts, and there is no reporting requirement. ###

11. In which case must a gift tax return be filed?

A. A married couple gives a gift of $13,000.
B. A married couple gives a gift of $15,000.
C. A single individual gives a gift of $4,000 to an unrelated person.
D. A wife gives a gift of $20,000 to her husband.

The answer is B. In order to make a gift to one individual in excess of the annual exclusion of $13,000 and avoid using any of their basic exclusion amounts, a married couple can use gift splitting. Gift splitting allows married couples to give up to $26,000 to a person without making a taxable gift ($13,000 from each spouse), but they are required to file a gift tax return. Gifts to a spouse generally do not require a tax return. ###

12. Shawn, a single taxpayer, has never been required to file a gift tax return. In 2012, Shawn gave the following gifts:

•$18,000 in tuition paid directly to a state university for an unrelated person.
•$13,500 paid to General Hospital for his brother's medical bills.
•$50,000 in cash donations paid to his city homeless shelter, a 501(c)(3).
•$15,000 as a political gift paid to the Libertarian Party (not a qualified charity).

Is Shawn required to file a gift tax return?

A. No.
B. Yes, because the donation to the political party is not an excludable gift.
C. Yes, because each of the gifts exceeded $13,000.
D. Yes, because the political gift is a reportable transaction.

The answer is A. None of the gifts is taxable, and no reporting is required. Tuition or medical expenses paid for someone directly to an educational or medical institution are not counted as taxable gifts. Nor are gifts to a political organization for its own use or gifts to a qualified charity. ###

13. In 2012, Jeffrey gives $25,000 to his girlfriend, Rachel. Which of the following statements is true?

A. The first $13,000 of the gift is not subject to the gift tax, but the remainder is subject to gift tax, and Rachel is responsible for paying it.
B. Rachel is required to file a gift tax return and pay tax on the entire gift.
C. Jeffrey is required to file a gift tax return, Form 709.
D. Jeffrey may choose to report the gift tax on Form 1040, Schedule A.

The answer is C. Jeffrey is required to file a gift tax return. Gift tax is paid by the donor, not the recipient, of the gift. The first $13,000 of the gift is not subject to gift tax because of the annual exclusion. The remaining $12,000 is a taxable gift. ###

14. All of the following gifts are excluded from the determination of the gift tax except:

A. A gift made to a political organization for its own use.
B. A cash gift given to a nonresident alien spouse of a U.S. citizen.
C. A medical bill paid directly to a hospital on behalf of a relative.
D. A gift made to a qualifying charity.

The answer is B. Although a full marital deduction is allowed for a spouse who is a U.S. citizen, a transfer of property to a noncitizen spouse is limited to $139,000 in 2012, and the excess amount would be subject to gift tax. ###

15. Alana had gifts totaling $28,000 in 2012 that were subject to gift tax. When is her gift tax return due?

A. March 15, 2013.
B. April 15, 2013.
C. June 15, 2013.
D. September 15, 2013.

The answer is B. Gift tax returns are typically due on April 15 of the following calendar year, and payment of the tax is also due then, although the filing may be subject to a six-month extension. If the donor died during 2012, the filing deadline is the due date for his estate tax return (if earlier than April 15, 2013). ###

16. Phil died in 2012. At the time of his death, he had assets of $4 million and liabilities of $500,000. He also had insurance policies in place that paid $1 million to his children.

Based upon the information provided, what is the taxable amount of Phil's estate that must be reported on Form 706?

A. $5 million.
B. $0.
C. $4 million.
D. $4.5 million.

The answer is B. The taxable amount of Phil's estate is $4.5 million. However, because this amount is less than the applicable exclusion amount of $5,120,000 for 2012, an estate tax return is not required to be filed.

Supporting calculations:

Assets	$4,000,000
Less liabilities	($500,000)
Life insurance proceeds	$1,000,000
Taxable estate	$4,500,000

###

Part 2: Businesses

Tammy the Tax Lady ®

Sorry, but that's not what I meant when I said you had to "pay the piper."

Unit 1: Business Entities in General

More Reading:
Publication 583, *Starting a Business and Keeping Records*
Publication 1635, *Understanding Your EIN*
Publication 334, *Tax Guide for Small Business*

Overview of EA Exam Part 2: Businesses

For Part 2 of the enrolled agent exam, you will be expected to know a broad range of information related to preparing tax returns for various types of businesses. You will need to understand the different types of business entities and the special tax laws that apply to each: sole proprietorships, partnerships, corporations, tax-exempt organizations; and farmers.

Part 2 of the exam also covers accounting methods and periods; business income; expenses, deductions, and credits; business assets and determining basis; trust and estate income tax; retirement plans; and much more. The material includes taxation issues that affect self-employed businesspersons, which are covered in both the Individual and Business parts of the EA exam, so there is a degree of overlap between the study guides.

We start with an overview of the different types of business entities. There are several types of business entities that are available for taxpayers to use in order to form and run their businesses. Each type has its own drawbacks, risks, and benefits. We briefly review each type below, and we will examine the more complex entities in depth in later units.

Sole Proprietorship

A sole proprietorship is an unincorporated business that is owned and controlled by one person. It may be a single-person business or it may have many employees, but there is only one owner who must accept all the risks and liabilities of the business. As the simplest business type, it is also the easiest to start. An estimated 70% of businesses in the United States are sole proprietorships.[82]

A sole proprietorship cannot be passed on to a new owner as the same business entity because, by definition, a sole proprietorship is owned and operated by a single, specific individual. If a business operated as a sole proprietorship is sold, it must be registered by the new owner as either a different sole proprietorship or as a different type of business entity.

A taxpayer does not have to conduct full-time business activities to be considered self-employed. Operating a part-time business in addition to having a regular job or business may also be self-employment, and may therefore constitute a sole proprietorship. An activity qualifies as a business if its primary purpose is for profit and if

---

[82] According to the U.S. Census Bureau, in 2008 there were more than 22 million tax returns filed by nonfarm sole proprietors; 3.1 million by partnerships; and 5.8 million for corporations.

the taxpayer is involved in the activity with continuity and regularity. That means a hobby[83] does not qualify as a business.

Sole proprietors will often receive Form 1099-MISC from their customers showing income they were paid. The amounts reported on Form 1099-MISC, along with any other business income, are reported and taxed on the taxpayer's personal income tax return. Income and expenses from the sole proprietorship are reported on Form 1040, Schedule C, *Profit or Loss from Business*.

			Form 1099-MISC	
		$		
		3 Other income	4 Federal income tax withheld	Copy B
		$	$	For Recipient
PAYER'S federal identification number	RECIPIENT'S identification number	5 Fishing boat proceeds	6 Medical and health care payments	
		$	$	
RECIPIENT'S name		7 Nonemployee compensation	8 Substitute payments in lieu of dividends or interest	This is important tax information and is being furnished to the Internal Revenue Service. If you are required to file a return, a negligence
		$	$	
Street address (including apt. no.)		9 Payer made direct sales of $5,000 or more of consumer	10 Crop insurance proceeds	

A taxpayer may use the simplified Schedule C-EZ if he or she:

- Had business expenses of $5,000 or less
- Did not claim any depreciation expense
- Used the cash method of accounting
- Did not have inventory at any time during the year
- Did not have a net loss from the business, and had no prior year passive activity losses
- Was the sole proprietor for only one business
- Had no employees during the year
- Did not deduct expenses for business use of his home, and had no depreciation or amortization to report for the year

If a sole proprietor has no employees, he is not required to obtain an Employer identification number (EIN).

Self-employed individuals who have net earnings of $400 or more from self-employment are required to pay self-employment tax by filing Schedule SE, *Self-Employment Tax* along with their Form 1040.

> **Example:** Darlene works as an independent contractor for Right Light Lighting Company. Right Light sends Darlene a Form 1099-MISC that shows she received $25,000 for contract work she did for them. She also receives cash payments of $7,000 from several different individuals for contract work she completed on their homes. Although she did not receive Forms 1099-MISC for the $7,000, Darlene must include the $7,000 cash payments as self-employment income along with the $25,000 on her Schedule C.

Husband and Wife Businesses

Many small businesses are operated jointly by a husband and wife, without incorporating or creating a formal partnership agreement. A husband and wife business

---

[83] A hobby is an activity typically undertaken for pleasure during leisure time. Income from a hobby is still taxable and reported on Form 1040, Line 21 as "other income." Hobby income is typically not subject to self-employment tax, and the use of losses from a hobby to offset income from other sources is limited.

may be considered a partnership whether or not a formal partnership agreement is made.

If a husband and wife each materially participates as the only members of a jointly owned and operated business, they may be treated as a *qualified joint venture*. This allows them to avoid the complexity of filing a partnership return, but still gives each spouse credit for Social Security earnings. Items of business income, gain, loss, deduction, and credit are split between the spouses in accordance with their respective interests in the business. The husband and wife then file separate Schedules C and separate Schedules SE. This option is available only to married taxpayers who file joint tax returns.

Partnerships

A partnership is a relationship that exists between two or more persons who join to carry on a trade or business. Each person contributes money, property, labor, or skill, and expects to share in the profits and losses of the business.

A partnership must file an annual information return to report the income, deductions, gains, and losses from its operations, but the partnership itself does not pay income tax. Instead, any profits or losses "pass through" to its partners, who are then responsible for reporting their share of the partnership's income or loss on their individual returns.

A partnership tax return is filed on IRS Form 1065, *U.S. Return of Partnership Income.* Since partners are not employees as such, they should not be issued a Form W-2. The partnership must furnish copies of Schedule K-1 to its partners, showing the income and losses that is allocated to each partner.

A partnership must always have at least one *general partner* whose actions legally bind the business and who is legally responsible for a partnership's debts and liabilities.

A *limited partner* is an investor whose liability is limited to his investment in the business. A limited partner has no obligation to contribute additional capital to the partnership, and therefore does not have an economic risk of loss for partnership liabilities. Income reported by the partnership to limited partners is considered passive income (and is not subject to self-employment tax), while income attributable to general partners is deemed to be active income.

Example: James and Madeline are father and daughter. Together they operate Hunnicutt Business Consulting. Each is active in the business, and each has an equal share in partnership interests and profits. In 2012, Hunnicutt had $80,000 in net profits. The partnership must file a Form 1065 reporting its income and loss for the year. The partnership must also issue two Schedules K-1—one to each partner, James and Madeline. Since they share profits and losses equally, James and Madeline will both have to report $40,000 in self-employment partnership income on their individual tax returns. Partnership income is reported on page 2 of Schedule E, *Supplemental Income and Loss (From rental real estate, royalties, partnerships, S corporations, estates, trusts, REMICs, etc.)*

A partnership can look very different depending on how it is structured—it can be anything from a small business run by a husband and wife to a complex business organization with hundreds of general partners and limited partners as investors. A partnership may have an unlimited number of partners.

> **Example:** Samuel and Jane are siblings who own Devil Dog Publishing, a monthly magazine for tattoo artists. Samuel writes most of the articles, and Jane takes care of the day-to-day operations of the magazine, including paying the bills and securing advertising. Samuel and Jane are in a partnership and must file Form 1065.

An unincorporated organization with two or more members is generally classified as a partnership for federal tax purposes if its members carry on a business and divide its profits. However, a joint undertaking merely to share expenses is not a partnership. For example, co-ownership of rental property is not considered a formal partnership unless the co-owners provide substantial services to the tenants.

> **Example:** Anderson and Sally are good friends who own a rental property together. Each owns a 50% interest. Anderson takes care of the repairs, and Sally collects and divides the rent. They do not have any other business with each other. The co-ownership of the rental property would not be considered a partnership for tax purposes. They would report their income and losses on Schedule E based on their ownership percentage, and then would divide the income and losses on their individual returns.

A partnership return must show the name and address of each partner and the partner's share of taxable income. The return must be signed by a general partner. A limited partner may not sign the return or represent a partnership before the IRS.

If a limited liability company (LLC) is treated as a partnership for federal tax purposes, it must file Form 1065 and one of its general partners or owners must sign the return.

Types of Partnerships Defined

Limited Partnership: A partnership that has at least one limited partner and at least one general partner. Limited partnerships allow investors to invest in businesses while reducing their own personal liability.

Limited Liability Partnership (LLP): An entity that is formed under state law by filing articles of organization as an LLP and is typically used for specific professional services, such as those offered by a law firm. Partners determine the structure of the organization and the distribution of profits and losses. Typically, an LLP allows each partner to actively participate in management affairs but still provides limited liability protection to each partner. A partner in an LLP generally would not be liable for the debt or malpractice of other partners and would only be at risk for the partnership's assets.

C Corporations

Most major companies are treated as C corporations for federal income tax purposes. In forming a corporation, prospective shareholders exchange money, property, or both for the corporation's capital stock.

A C corporation is considered an entity separate from its shareholders and must elect a board of directors who are responsible for running the company. A corporation conducts business, realizes net income or loss, pays taxes, and distributes profits to shareholders.

A C corporation may have an unlimited number of shareholders, both foreign and domestic. The profit of a C corporation is taxed to the corporation when earned, and it may also be taxed to the shareholders when distributed as dividends, resulting in double taxation.

The corporation does not get a tax deduction when it distributes dividends to shareholders, and shareholders cannot deduct any losses of the corporation. A corporation generally takes the same deductions as a sole proprietorship to figure its taxable income, but is also allowed certain special deductions. Corporations must file Form 1120, *U.S. Corporation Income Tax Return.*

S Corporations

S corporations are corporations that elect to pass corporate income, losses, deductions, and credit through to their shareholders for federal tax purposes, in a manner similar to partnerships. Shareholders of S corporations report the flow-through of income and losses on their personal tax returns and are assessed tax at their individual tax rates. This allows the shareholders of S corporations to avoid double taxation on their corporate income. However, the S corporation itself may be responsible for tax on certain built-in gains and passive income. S corporations are subject to the following requirements:

- Be a domestic corporation
- Have only allowable shareholders (partnerships, corporations, and nonresident aliens are not eligible)
- Have no more than 100 shareholders
- Have one class of stock
- Not be an ineligible type of corporation (certain financial institutions, insurance companies, and domestic international sales corporations are not eligible for S corporation status)

An S corporation is required to file a tax return every year, regardless of income or loss, by filing IRS Form 1120S, *U.S. Tax Return for an S Corporation*, and to report each shareholder's applicable share of income or losses to them on Schedules K-1.

Limited Liability Companies (LLC)

A limited liability company (LLC) is a corporation that is formed under state law. Depending upon whether it has a single member (owner) or multiple members, it may choose to be taxed for IRS purposes as a corporation, partnership, or sole proprietorship. Most often, LLCs elect to be taxed as partnerships. Thus, like the owners of S corporations and partnerships, the members of an LLC can avoid double taxation. An LLC can provide the liability protection of a corporation with the tax benefits of a partnership. Unlike a partnership, none of the members of an LLC are personally liable for its debts.

Personal Service Corporations (PSC)

A personal service corporation (PSC) is a corporation that performs services in the fields of health (including veterinary services), law, engineering, architecture, accounting, actuarial science, the performing arts, or consulting. In a PSC, the majority of the stock is owned by employees, retired employees, or their estates. Unlike other corporations, a qualified PSC is always taxed at a flat rate of 35% on taxable income.

A corporation is a personal service corporation if its principal activity during the prior tax year is performing personal services. Personal services include any activity performed in the fields of accounting, actuarial science, architecture, consulting, engineering, health (including veterinary services), law, and the performing arts. A corporation that provides these services will be considered a PSC if substantially all of its compensation is derived from providing personal services.

A person is considered an "employee-owner" of a personal service corporation if both of the following apply:

- He or she is an employee of the corporation or performs personal services for, or on behalf of, the corporation on any day of the testing period.
- He or she owns any stock in the corporation at any time during the testing period.

Unlike other corporations, personal service corporations are always taxed at a flat rate of 35%.

Farmers

The IRS defines the business of farming as someone who cultivates, operates, or manages a farm for profit. Types of farms include livestock, dairy, poultry, fish, and fruit.

Many self-employed farmers, just like Schedule C taxpayers, report income and expenses, and pay regular income tax and self-employment tax on their net profits from farming. However, they report their profit or loss on Schedule F. If the farming business is organized as a corporation or a partnership, the taxpayer files the appropriate tax return for the specific entity type.

Tax-Exempt Organizations (Nonprofit Entities)

The Internal Revenue Code outlines the requirements for tax-exempt organizations, commonly referred to as charitable organizations. They include nonprofit groups that are charitable, educational, and religious in purpose. An organization must be organized and operated exclusively for one of these purposes, and none of its earnings may go to any private shareholder or individual.

Nonprofit organizations may be created as corporations, trusts, or unincorporated associations, but never as partnerships or sole proprietorships. Most organizations must request tax-exempt status by filing Form 23, *Application for Recognition of Exemption*. However, churches, including synagogues, temples, and mosques, do not have to apply for formal exemption, because they are treated as tax-exempt by default.

Exempt organizations file Form 990 to report income and losses. Form 990 is usually an informational return only, but nonprofit organizations may in some instances be subject to tax on activities that are outside the scope of their tax-exempt status.

Employer Identification Number (EIN)

An employer identification number is used for reporting purposes. Unlike Social Security numbers that are assigned to individuals, EINs are assigned to business entities, including the following: sole proprietors, corporations, partnerships, nonprofit associations, trusts and estates.

A business must apply for an EIN if any of the following apply:

- The business pays employees
- The business operates as a corporation, exempt organization, trust, estate, or partnership
- The business files any of these tax returns:
  - Employment
  - Excise
  - Alcohol, Tobacco, and Firearms
- The business withholds taxes paid to a nonresident alien
- The business establishes a pension, profit sharing, or retirement plan

An EIN can also be requested by a sole proprietor who simply wishes to protect his Social Security number for privacy reasons. This way, a sole proprietor can give his EIN rather than his SSN to companies that need to issue him a Form 1099 for independent contractor payments.

If a sole proprietor decides to form a business entity such as a partnership or corporation, he will be required to request an EIN for each separate entity. A new EIN is required for any of the following changes:

- When a sole proprietor or partnership decides to incorporate
- When a sole proprietor takes on a partner and becomes a partnership
- When a partnership becomes a sole proprietorship (for example, when one partner dies)
- When a sole proprietor files for bankruptcy under Chapter 7 or Chapter 11
- When a taxpayer terminates one partnership and begins another partnership
- When a business establishes a pension, profit sharing, or retirement plan

A business does not need to apply for a new EIN in any of the following instances:

- To change the name of a business
- To change the location or add locations (stores, plants, enterprises, or branches of the same entity)
- If a sole proprietor operates multiple businesses (including stores, plants, enterprises, or branches of the same entity)

Further, a sole proprietor who conducts business as a limited liability company (LLC) does not need a separate EIN for the LLC, unless the business is required to file employment or excise tax returns.

Taxpayers can apply for an EIN online or use IRS Form SS-4, *Application for Employer Identification Number.*

Entity Classification Election Rules

Certain business entities may choose how they will be classified for tax purposes by filing Form 8832, *Entity Classification Election.*

An LLC with a single owner is classified as a sole proprietorship for income tax purposes, unless the owner files Form 8832 and chooses to be taxed as a corporation. A single-owner LLC is considered a "disregarded entity" for tax purposes, unless the owner elects to be treated as a corporation.

Similarly, the IRS will treat a domestic LLC with at least two members as a partnership by default unless it files Form 8832 and elects to be treated as a corporation.

An election to change an LLC's classification cannot take effect more than 75 days prior to the date the election is filed, nor can it take effect later than 12 months after the date the election is filed. Once a business entity chooses its classification, it cannot change the election again within five years (60 months).

Example: Kelly and Ned are married and own their own business. They decide to form an LLC for liability protection. Kelly files Form 8832, and she elects to classify their business as a partnership for tax purposes. A few months later, Kelly changes her mind and wants to change classifications and be taxed as a corporation. Kelly must wait at least 60 months in order to change the election.

Unit 1: Questions

1. A domestic LLC with at least two members that does not file Form 8832 is automatically classified as _____ for federal income tax purposes.

A. An S corporation.
B. A partnership.
C. A qualified joint venture.
D. A personal service corporation.

The answer is B. A domestic LLC with at least two members that does not file Form 8832 is classified as a partnership for federal income tax purposes. ###

2. Which of the following organizations does not require an EIN?

A. An estate.
B. A C corporation.
C. Nonprofit organizations.
D. A sole proprietorship with no employees.

The answer is D. A sole proprietorship without employees does not require an employer identification number. The other choices listed all require an EIN. ###

3. A sole proprietor will be required to obtain a new EIN in which of the following instances?

A. The sole proprietor is required to file excise tax returns.
B. The sole proprietor changes the name of his business.
C. The sole proprietor changes location.
D. The sole proprietor operates multiple locations.

The answer is A. A sole proprietor who is required to file excise tax returns (or employment tax returns) must obtain an EIN. A sole proprietorship is not required to obtain a new EIN when it changes location or its business name. A sole proprietor may operate many different businesses using the same EIN, so long as the businesses are also sole proprietorships. ###

4. In which of the following instances will a partnership not be required to obtain a new EIN?

A. The partners decide to incorporate.
B. The partnership is taken over by one of the partners and is subsequently operated as a sole proprietorship.
C. The general partner ends the old partnership and begins a new one.
D. The partnership adds other business locations.

The answer is D. A partnership is not required to obtain a new EIN simply to add business locations. In all of the other choices listed, the entity would need to obtain a new EIN. ###

5. Which of the following entities is considered separate from its shareholders or owners?

A. A partnership.
B. A C corporation.
C. A sole proprietorship.
D. An LLC.

The answer is B. A C corporation is considered an entity separate from its shareholders. ###

6. A sole proprietor may not be required to file Schedule SE if his net profit for 2012 was _____.

A. Less than $400.
B. $400 or more.
C. Less than $5,000 but more than $400.
D. More than $5,000.

The answer is A. If the net profit was less than $400, a taxpayer should enter the profit on line 12 of Form 1040 and attach Schedule C to the return. Schedule SE is not required unless it was a profit of $400 or more. ###

7. Don and Selma are married, and they run a small pet grooming business together. They would like to treat their business as a qualified joint venture. Which of the following is true?

A. Don and Selma may choose to report their qualified joint venture as a sole proprietorship on two separate Schedules C, so long as they file jointly.
B. Don and Selma may choose to report their qualified joint venture as a sole proprietorship on two separate Schedules C, so long as they file separate tax returns (MFS).
C. Don and Selma must file a partnership tax return for their business activity.
D. Don and Selma may file a single Schedule C, listing Don as the sole proprietor one year and Selma as the sole proprietor the next year.

The answer is A. Don and Selma may choose to report their qualified joint venture as a sole proprietorship on two separate Schedules C, so long as they file jointly. This option is only available to married taxpayers who file jointly. ###

8. Julian is self-employed and has a small business selling used books. The gross income from his business is $20,000 and his business expenses total $9,500. Which schedule must Julian complete to report his business income and expenses?

A. Schedule F.
B. Schedule C.
C. Schedule D.
D. Schedule A.

The answer is B. Julian must complete Schedule C to report his business income and expenses. ###

9. Mandy and her friend, Tammy, work together, making beaded necklaces and selling them at craft shows. They run their business professionally and jointly, always attempting to make a profit, but they do not have any type of formal business agreement. They share with each other the profits or losses of the business. They made $24,900 in 2012 from selling necklaces, and they had $1,900 in expenses. Where and how is the correct way for Mandy and Tammy to report their income?

A. Split the income and report the profits as "other income" on each taxpayer's individual Forms 1040.
B. Each must report her own income and expenses on Schedule C.
C. Mandy and Tammy should calculate income and subtract expenses, and then report the net amount as "other income" on each individual Form 1040.
D. Mandy and Tammy are working as a partnership and should report their income on Form 1065.

The answer is D. Mandy and Tammy are working as a partnership and should report their income on Form 1065, U.S. Return of Partnership Income. Related expenses are deductible, and they are reported as deductions. Each partner would then receive a Schedule K-1 to report their individual items of expenses and income on their Form 1040. ###

10. A personal service corporation is always taxed at a_____ rate.

A. 15%.
B. 28%.
C. 35%.
4. 39.6%.

The answer is C. A personal service corporation is created for the purpose of providing personal services to individuals or groups. Personal service corporations not eligible for graduated tax rates, like other C corporations. Personal service corporations pay a 35% flat rate on their taxable income. ###

11. Catherine is self-employed and would like to use the *simplest* form available to report her business income and loss. Which of the following expenses would **prevent** Catherine from using Schedule C-EZ?

A. Auto expenses related to his business activity.
B. Interest paid on business loans.
C. Legal and professional services and fees.
D. Expenses for business use of his home.

The answer is D. Taxpayers cannot use Schedule C-EZ if they deduct expenses for business use of their home. If the taxpayer plans to take a home office deduction, she must use Schedule C. ###

12. All of the statements are true about the following business entities except:

A. S and C corporations may have an unlimited number of shareholders.
B. An LLC typically provides the liability protection of a corporation but the tax benefits of a partnership.
C. "Pass through" entities include LLCs, LLPs, S corporations, and partnerships.
D. A sole proprietorship bears all the liabilities and risks of a business.

The answer is A. Only a C corporation may have an unlimited number of shareholders. An S corporation is limited to no more than 100 shareholders. ###

13. Which of the following is considered a drawback of the C corporation entity?

A. It may have many different shareholders.
B. It may have investors who are nonresident aliens.
C. Profits are subject to double taxation, once at the corporate level and again at the shareholder level when distributed as dividends.
D. It is run by a board of directors.

The answer is C. Corporations are subject to double taxation. The other statements are facts about C corporations but are not considered drawbacks. ###

Unit 2: IRS Business Requirements

> **More Reading:**
> Publication 583, *Starting a Business and Keeping Records*
> Publication 1779, *Independent Contractor or Employee*
> Publication 505, *Tax Withholding and Estimated Tax*

Recordkeeping Requirements for Businesses

Adequate records are important for a taxpayer to monitor business operations, verify his income and expenses, and to support expenses on his tax return. Except in a few cases, the law does not require a business to keep any specific kind of records or use a particular recordkeeping system, so long as the system clearly shows a business's income and expenses.

The taxpayer's recordkeeping system should include a summary of business transactions, which is usually made in the taxpayer's books, such as accounting journals and ledgers. The books must show the business's gross income, as well as the deductions and credits. Additional documents must be kept to support these entries. These include sales slips, paid bills, invoices, receipts, deposit slips, canceled checks, credit card charge slips, cash register tapes, Forms 1099-MISC, invoices, mileage logs, and cell phone records.

Electronic records are acceptable so long as they provide a complete and accurate record of data that is accessible to the IRS in a legible format. They are subject to the same controls and retention guidelines as those imposed on a taxpayer's original hard copy books and records.

Taxpayers must keep records as long as they are needed for the administration of any provision of the Internal Revenue Code. Usually this means that the business must keep records long enough to support income and deductions until the statute of limitations for the tax return has run out. [84]

Generally, a taxpayer must keep records for at least three years from when the tax return was filed or within two years of when the tax was paid, whichever is later. If a business has employees, it must keep all employment tax records for at least four years.

Taxpayers must keep records relating to property until the period of limitations expires for the year in which the property is disposed of in a taxable disposition. These records are needed to figure any depreciation, amortization, or depletion deduction, and to figure basis for computing gain or loss when the property is sold. A taxpayer may need to keep records relating to the basis of property even longer than the period of limitation since they are important in figuring the basis of the original or replacement property.

Business funds should be kept separate from personal funds. The IRS is more likely to audit a business and deny deductions and business losses if there is no clear

---

[84] The statute of limitations is the period of time in which taxpayers can amend a return to claim a credit or refund or the IRS can assess additional tax.

separation between business and personal expenses. A separate bank account for business-related transactions is advisable, with business-related bills paid from there rather than from a personal account.

Financial Statements

Financial statements are the formal records of a business's financial activities and are used to examine a business's financial health. There are many types of financial statements, but the two most common ones used for tax reporting purposes are the income statement and the balance sheet.

Income Statement

The income statement is also called the profit and loss statement. It is a financial statement that indicates how revenue is transformed into net income by showing the profit or loss during a certain period, such as a fiscal year or a calendar year. The income statement shows income and expenses, with the profit or loss shown at the bottom of the statement.

Balance Sheet

The balance sheet is a summary of a business's assets, liabilities, and equity on a specific date, such as at the end of its financial year. A balance sheet is often described as a snapshot of a company's financial condition and includes items of assets such as cash, petty cash, accounts receivable, inventory, prepaid insurance, land, buildings, equipment, and goodwill. On the liability side of the balance sheet are items such as accounts receivable, accrued benefits, payroll, and notes payable. Balances on a balance sheet are carried forward from year to year, unlike income statement accounts, which are closed out at year-end and only reflect business operations within a specified period.

Employer Reporting Requirements

Businesses with employees are subject to a number of reporting requirements, including the following:

Forms W-4: When a business hires an employee, it must have the employee complete a Form W-4, *Employee's Withholding Allowance Certificate*

Form W-4 tells the employer the worker's marital status, the number of withholding allowances, and any additional amount to use when deducting federal income tax from the employee's pay.

If an employee fails to complete a Form W-4, the employer must withhold federal income taxes from his wages as if he were single and claiming no withholding allowances.

Forms W-2: A business must complete, file with the Social Security Administration, and furnish to its employees Forms W-2, *Wage and Tax Statement,* showing the wages paid and taxes withheld for the year for each employee. Copies of W-2s must be given to both current and former employees no later than January 31 after the end of the tax year. Employers filing 250 or more Forms W-2 must file electronically unless granted a waiver by the IRS.

In 2012, employers with 250 or more workers have a new reporting requirement for health insurance.[85] *The Affordable Care Act* requires employers to report the cost of health care coverage under an employer-sponsored group health plan. The amount reported includes both the portion paid by the employer and the portion paid by the employee.

Forms 1099

A business must report nonemployee compensation paid during the tax year. It must provide a Form 1099-MISC to any independent contractor paid $600 or more by January 31, and send a copy to the IRS by February 28, or March 31 if the business files 1099s electronically. Specifically, the amounts that businesses are required to report on Forms 1099 include:

- Commissions, fees, and other compensation paid to a single individual when the total amount is $600 or more during the year
- Interest, rents, annuities, and income items paid to a single individual when the total amount is $600 or more

Under current law, most payments to corporations are exempt from Form 1099 reporting requirements. Also under current law, there is no requirement for payments issued in exchange for property, such as purchases of merchandise or equipment.

Forms 1099-MISC should only be used for payments that are made in the course of a trade or business. Personal payments are not reportable.

> **Example #1:** Brett hires a painter to paint his home. The job costs $2,500. Brett is not required to report the payment to the painter, because it is for his personal residence. Because it was a personal payment, Brett cannot deduct the cost on his tax return. However, the painter is still required to report the income on his personal return.

> **Example #2:** The following year, Brett calls the same painter to paint the interior of his business office, which he owns. The job costs $1,000. Since the cost is a business expense, Brett is required to issue a 1099-MISC to the contractor. The $1,000 is fully deductible on his business return as an expense.

Employment Taxes and Self-Employment Tax

Employers must withhold federal income tax from employees' wages. Businesses also withhold part of Social Security and Medicare taxes from employees' wages, and employers pay a matching amount. The IRS issues withholding tables each year so that employers can calculate out how much to withhold from each wage payment.

Employers must report federal income taxes withheld and employees' shares of employment taxes on Form 941, *Employer's Quarterly Federal Tax Return*, or Form 944, *Employer's Annual Federal Tax Return*. Businesses must also make federal tax deposits of employment taxes electronically, generally by using the Electronic Federal Tax Payment System (EFTPS).

In 2012, only the first $110,100 of wages and net earnings are subject to the Social Security portion of tax. There is no cap on the Medicare tax. Self-employed

---

[85] IRS Notice 2012-9.

taxpayers figure self-employment tax using Schedule SE (Form 1040). Self-employed taxpayers can deduct half of their SE tax in figuring their adjusted gross income. Wage earners cannot deduct Social Security and Medicare taxes as a tax deduction on their individual returns.

General partners in a partnership are also considered self-employed individuals, and their income is also subject to self-employment tax, just like sole proprietors. Partners in a partnership receive a Schedule K-1 reporting their share of the partnership's income, loss, deductions, and credits.

Social Security and Medicare Taxes	
Social Security tax rate	2012
Employer's portion	6.2%
Employee's portion	4.2%
Total for self-employed taxpayer	10.4%
Maximum earnings subject to Social Security taxes	$110,100

Medicare tax rate	2012
Employer's portion	1.45%
Employee's portion	1.45%
Total for self-employed individual	2.9%
Maximum earnings subject to Medicare taxes	No limit

Backup Withholding

If a business does not have a payee's Social Security Number or Taxpayer Identification Number, it must withhold federal income taxes at a 28% rate. This is called backup withholding.

Example: Tina is a dentist who hires a cleaning service for her office. The cleaning service refuses to provide a Taxpayer Identification Number, so Tina is required to automatically withhold income tax on her payment to the cleaning service. She must file a Form 1099-MISC for the cleaning service to report the backup withholding amounts.

Trust Fund Recovery Penalty (TFRP)

A trust fund tax is money withheld from an employee's wages (Social Security, Medicare, and income tax) by an employer and held in trust until paid to the Treasury. If a business does not deposit its trust fund taxes in a timely manner, the IRS may assess the trust fund recovery penalty (TFRP). The amount of the penalty is equal to the unpaid balance of the trust fund tax. The TFRP may be assessed against any person who:

- is **responsible** for collecting or paying withheld income and employment taxes, or for paying collected excise taxes, and
- **willfully fails** to collect or pay them.

Once the IRS asserts the penalty, it can take collection action against the personal assets of anyone who is deemed a "responsible person." It is not only the presidents of companies or top finance and accounting personnel who may be held responsible for the TFRP. A "responsible person" may also include the person who signs checks for the company or who otherwise has authority to spend business funds, such as a bookkeeper.

For the IRS to determine that an individual willfully failed to pay the required taxes, the responsible person:

- Must have been, or should have been, aware of the outstanding taxes, and
- Intentionally disregarded the law or was plainly indifferent to its requirements (no evil intent or bad motive is required).

> **Example:** Greta ran her own accounting business and also did the payroll for her local church. The church had four employees, including a choir director. Greta prepared and signed the payroll tax returns and all the checks and then gave them to the pastor to mail. The pastor did not mail the payroll tax reports or remit the payments to the IRS; instead, he took the money to purchase a new organ for the church. Greta knew the pastor was doing this, but did not report it. The IRS assessed the TFRP against the pastor, the church, and Greta. Even though Greta was just the bookkeeper, she knew that the pastor was improperly handling the payroll tax funds, and she did nothing about it, so the IRS can assess the TFRP against Greta.

Using available funds to pay other creditors when the business is unable to pay the employment taxes is an indication of willfulness.

Federal Unemployment (FUTA) Tax

A business reports and pays FUTA tax separately from federal income tax, and Social Security and Medicare taxes. FUTA tax is paid only by the employer—employees do not pay this tax or have it withheld from their pay. The standard FUTA tax rate is 6% on the first $7,000 of wages subject to FUTA. Employers may receive a credit of 5.4% when they file their Form 940, *Employers Annual Federal Unemployment (FUTA) Tax Return*, to result in a net FUTA tax rate of 0.6%.

Employee and Worker Classification

Because employers are responsible for withholding income, employment, and FUTA taxes, an employer must accurately determine whether a person is an independent contractor or an employee. An employer is not required to withhold or pay taxes on payments to independent contractors, which is why many employers will incorrectly classify a worker. An employer must understand the relationship that exists between himself and the person performing the services. A person performing services for business may be:

- An independent contractor
- An employee
- A statutory employee
- A statutory nonemployee

The IRS uses three characteristics to determine the relationship between a business and its workers:

- **Behavioral Control:** covers whether the business has a right to direct or control how the work is done.
- **Financial Control:** covers whether the business has a right to direct or control the financial and business aspects of the worker's job.
- **Type of Relationship:** relates to how the workers and the business owner perceive their relationship.

Examples of true independent contractors include web developers, mobile plumbers, freelance editors, and independent bookkeepers who follow an independent trade in which they offer their services to the public for a fee. However, whether such persons are truly employees or independent contractors depends on the facts in each case.

> **Example:** Roger, an electrician, submits a job estimate to a housing complex for electrical work at $16 per hour for 400 hours. He is to receive $1,280 every two weeks for the next ten weeks. Even if he works more or less than 400 hours to complete the work, Roger will receive $6,400. He also performs additional electrical installations under contracts with other companies that he obtains through advertisements placed in the local paper. Roger is an independent contractor.

> **Example:** Donna is a salesperson employed full-time by Supercargo Dealership, an auto dealer. She works six days a week and is on duty in the showroom on certain assigned days and times. Lists of prospective customers belong to the dealer. She has to develop leads and report results to the sales manager. Because of her experience, she requires only minimal assistance in closing and financing sales and in other phases of her work. She is paid a commission and is eligible for prizes and bonuses offered by the dealership. The business also pays the cost of health insurance and group-term life insurance for Donna. Donna is an employee of the dealership.

Employers who misclassify workers as independent contractors face substantial tax penalties. They are subject to additional penalties for failing to pay employment taxes and failing to file payroll tax forms.

Statutory Employees

Some workers are classified as statutory employees and are issued Forms W-2 by their employers. Statutory employees report their wages, income, and allowable expenses on Schedule C, just like self-employed taxpayers, but they are not required to pay self-employment tax, because their employers must treat them as employees for Social Security tax purposes.

Examples of statutory employees include full-time life insurance salespeople; traveling salespeople; certain commissioned truck drivers; officers of nonprofit organizations; and certain home workers who perform work on materials or goods furnished by the employer. If a person is a statutory employee, the "Statutory Employee" checkbox in box 13 of the taxpayer's Form W-2 should be checked.

Statutory Nonemployees Treated as Independent Contractors

There are two main categories of statutory nonemployees: direct sellers and licensed real estate agents. They are treated as self-employed for all federal tax purposes, including income and employment taxes if:

- Payments for their services are directly related to sales, rather than to the number of hours worked, and
- Services are performed under a written contract providing that they will not be treated as employees for federal tax purposes.

Compensation for a statutory nonemployee is reported on IRS Form 1099-MISC. The taxpayer then reports the income on Schedule C.

> **Example:** Adele works as a full-time real estate agent for Golden Gate Real Estate Company. She visits Golden Gate's offices at least once a day to check her mail and her messages. She manages dozens of listings and splits her real estate commissions with Golden Gate. She does not work for any other real estate company. Adele is a statutory nonemployee. Golden Gate properly issues Adele a Form 1099-MISC for commissions and she files a Schedule C to report her income and expenses.

Directors of a corporation (members of the governing board) are also treated as statutory nonemployees. If an exempt organization compensates board members for performing their duties as directors, the organization should treat them as independent contractors. This is the most common type of statutory nonemployee that may be involved in an exempt organization.

Employing Family Members

The tax requirements for family employees may differ from other employees. The rules vary depending on the family relationship and the business entity type.

1. **Child working for a parent in a sole proprietorship or partnership when each partner is the child's parent:** Payments for the child's services are subject to income tax withholding regardless of age. If the child is under 18, payments are not subject to Social Security and Medicare taxes. If the child is under 21, payments are not subject to FUTA tax. However, all taxes must be withheld if the parent's business is one of three types: a corporation, an estate, or a partnership if only one of the parents is a partner.

2. **Parent working for a child:** Income tax, Social Security, and Medicare taxes are withheld, but not FUTA tax, regardless of the business entity type.

3. **Spouse employed by a spouse:** Income tax, Social Security, and Medicare taxes are withheld, but not FUTA tax. However, FUTA tax is withheld if the spouse works for a corporation or a partnership, even if the individual's spouse is a partner.

Unit 2: Questions

1. U.S. tax law requires businesses to submit a Form 1099-MISC for every contractor paid at least _____ for services during a year.

A. $400.
B. $500.
C. $600.
D. $1,000.

The answer is C. U.S. tax law requires businesses to submit a Form 1099-MISC for every contractor paid at least $600 for services during a year. Each payer must complete a Form 1099-MISC for each individual or business. Corporations are exempt recipients, so if a business makes payments to a corporation, it is not required to issue a 1099-MISC to the corporation. ###

2. Dan is a full-time life insurance salesman and a statutory employee. He receives a Form W-2 for his earnings. How should he report his income?

A. On Form 1040 as regular wage income.
B. On Schedule C, not subject to self-employment.
C. On Schedule C, subject to self-employment tax.
D. On Schedule K.

The answer is B. Statutory employees are unique because they report their wages, income, and allowable expenses on Schedule C, just like self-employed taxpayers. However, statutory employees are not required to pay self-employment tax because their employers must treat them as employees for Social Security tax purposes. ###

3. What is the minimum amount of time an employer should keep employment tax records, such as copies of W-2s?

A. Indefinitely.
B. Three years.
C. Four years.
D. Five years.

The answer is C. The IRS advises employers to keep all employment tax records for at least four years. ###

4. In 2012, an employer with _____ employees or more must report the cost of health care coverage under employer-sponsored group health plans.

A. 50.
B. 100.
C. 200.
D. 250.

The answer is D. Under the Affordable Care Act, employers with 250 or more workers must provide this information on their employees' W-2s in 2012. ###

5. In 2012, what is the threshold for Social Security tax to be withheld from an employee's wages?

A. $106,800.
B. $110,100.
C. $113,700.
D. No cap.

The answer is B. The threshold for Social Security tax is $110,100 in 2012. In tax year 2013, the threshold is $113,700. Medicare taxes are withheld on an employee's wages without regard to income levels. ###

6. All of the following statements are true about the trust fund recovery penalty except:

A. Someone who is simply indifferent to the requirements for paying trust fund taxes will never be assessed the penalty.
B. The IRS can take collection against the personal assets of anyone deemed a "responsible person."
C. A trust fund tax is comprised of income tax and Social Security and Medicare tax that is withheld from an employee's wages and held in "trust" to be paid to the U.S. Treasury.
D. The amount of the TFRP is equal to the unpaid balance of the trust fund tax.

The answer is A. In assessing the trust fund recovery penalty, the IRS may hold someone responsible who intentionally disregarded the law or was "plainly indifferent" to its requirements. No evil intent or bad motive is required. ###

7. The IRS uses all of the following characteristics to assess the relationship between a business and its workers except:

A. Type of relationship.
B. Financial control.
C. Income level.
D. Behavioral control.

The answer is C. Income level is not a factor in determining a worker's status. The main issue involves whether the employer or the worker has the right to direct or control how the work is done, and to control the financial and business aspects of the job. This then helps determine whether a worker is an employee or an independent contractor. ###

8. Caden, age 16, works behind the counter of a juice bar owned by his mother, a sole proprietor. Which of the following taxes, if any, should be withheld from his paycheck?

A. Income tax.
B. Income tax, Social Security and Medicare taxes.
C. Income tax, Social Security and Medicare taxes, and FUTA tax.
D. None of the above.

The answer is A. Family members who work for other family members are subject to different tax requirements. Only income tax is taken out of the paycheck of a child under age 18, so long as he is working for a parent who is a sole proprietor. ####

Unit 3: Accounting Periods and Methods

> **More Reading:**
> Publication 334, *Tax Guide for Small Business*
> Publication 538, *Accounting Periods and Methods*

Tax Years

The tax year is an annual accounting period for reporting income and expenses. Individuals file their tax returns on a calendar year. Businesses have the option to file their tax returns on either a calendar year or a fiscal year basis.

Calendar tax year: Twelve consecutive months beginning January 1 and ending December 31.

Fiscal tax year: Twelve consecutive months ending on the last day of any month except December. A fiscal year-end does not have to fall on the same date each year. A "52/53-week" tax year is a fiscal tax year that varies from 52 to 53 weeks but does not have to end on the last day of the month. For example, some businesses choose to end their fiscal year on a particular day of the week, such as the last Friday in June.

> **Example:** Paula works for the state of California. The state follows a fiscal year budget that runs from July 1, 2012 through June 30, 2013. This is a 12-month period not ending in December. Most federal and state government organizations operate on a fiscal year basis, as do some corporations.

Short tax year: A tax year of less than 12 months. A short tax year may result in the first or last year of an entity's existence, or when an entity changes its accounting period (for example, from a fiscal year to a calendar year, or vice versa). Even if a business is not in existence for a full year, the requirements for filing the return and paying any tax liability are generally the same as if a full 12-month tax year had ended on the last day of the short tax year.

> **Example:** Eduardo and Jared started a business partnership in 2010. Eduardo died on November 1, 2012; therefore, the partnership is no longer in existence. Jared decides to continue the business as a sole proprietor. He must request a new employer identification number since his business structure has changed. The partnership is dissolved, and a final partnership tax return must be filed for the short tax year from January 1, 2012 to November 1, 2012.

> **Example:** Jillian formed Sorrento Rare Books, Inc. in February 2012. She immediately started having financial troubles and dissolved her corporation in October 2012. Jillian must file a short tax year corporate return for the period that Sorrento Rare Books was in existence.

A business adopts a tax year when it files its first income tax return. Any business may adopt the calendar year as its tax year. A new C corporation may generally elect to use a fiscal year instead. However, the IRS may require use of the calendar year in the following instances:

- The business keeps no books.
- There is no annual accounting period.
- The present tax year does not qualify as a fiscal year.
- The Internal Revenue Code or income tax regulations require use of a calendar year.

IRS Form 1128, *Application to Adopt, Change, or Retain a Tax Year*, is used to request a change in the tax year.

Required Tax Year

Partnerships, S corporations, and PSCs generally must use a required tax year. Unless it can establish a business purpose for a different tax year, a partnership's required tax year must generally conform to its partners' tax years. If a partner owns more than 50% interest in the partnership, this creates a majority interest in the capital and partnership profits. In this instance, the tax year of this partner is the required tax year for the partnership.

> **Example:** Busy Bee Partnership has two partners, both of which are C corporations. Corporation A owns a 30% partnership interest in Busy Bee and operates on a calendar year. Corporation B owns the remaining 70% of the partnership interest and operates on a fiscal year ending February 28. Since Corporation B owns a majority interest in Busy Bee, the partnership will file on the same tax year as Corporation B.

If there is no majority interest tax year, the partnership must use the tax year of all of the principal partners (those who have an interest of 5% or more in the capital and partnership profits). If there is no majority interest tax year and the principal partners do not have the same tax year, the partnership must use the tax year that would result in the *least aggregate* deferral of income to its partners.

> **Example:** Andrew and Bella each have a 50% interest in the Chef Supplies Partnership. Andrew uses the calendar year and Bella uses a fiscal year ending November 30. Chef Supplies must adopt a fiscal year ending November 30 because this results in the least aggregate deferral of income to the partners, as shown in the following table.

With Year End 12/31:	Year End	Interest	Months of Deferral	Interest Deferral	×
Andrew	12/31	50%	0	0	
Bella	11/30	50%	11	5.5	
Total Deferral				**5.5**	
With Year End 11/30:	Year End	Interest	Months of Deferral	Interest Deferral	×
Andrew	12/31	50%	1	0.5	
Bella	11/30	50%	0	0	
Total Deferral				**0.5**	

Unless it can establish a business purpose for using a fiscal year, an S corporation or PSC must generally use a calendar year. A partnership, an S corporation, or a PSC can file IRS Form 1128, *Application to Adopt, Change, or Retain a Tax Year* to support its business purpose for using a fiscal year. For example, a seasonal business (such as a ski resort) may elect a fiscal year based on a genuine business purpose. It is not considered a legitimate business purpose to elect a particular fiscal tax year so that partners or shareholders may defer income recognition.

Section 444 Election

A partnership, an S corporation, or a PSC can request to use a tax year *other than* its required tax year by filing Form 8716, *Election to Have a Tax Year Other Than a Required Tax Year*. This is known as a section 444 election and it *does not apply* to any business that establishes a genuine business purpose for a different accounting period.

A partnership or an S corporation that makes this election must make certain required payments based upon the value of the tax deferral the owners receive by using a tax year different from the required tax year. A PSC that makes the election must make certain distributions to its owner-employees by December 31 of each applicable year.

A business can request a section 444 election if it meets all of the following requirements:

- It is not a member of a tiered structure.
- It has not previously had a section 444 election in effect.
- It elects a year that meets the deferral period requirement.

The deferral period depends on whether the entity is using the election to retain its tax year or to adopt or change its tax year. If it intends to retain its tax year, it may only do so if the deferral period is three months or less. The deferral period is the number of months between the beginning of the retained year and the end of the first required tax year.

If the entity is requesting adoption or a change to a tax year other than the required tax year, the deferral period is the number of months from the end of the new tax year to the end of the required tax year. Generally, the IRS will allow a section 444 election only if the deferral period is less than the shorter of:

- Three months, or
- The deferral period of the tax year being changed

> **Example:** Davidson Partnership, a newly formed partnership owned by two calendar-year partners, begins operations on December 1, 2012. Davidson wants to make a section 444 election to adopt a September 30 tax year. Davidson's deferral period for the tax year beginning December 1, 2012 is three months, the number of months between September 30 and December 31.

The section 444 election remains in effect until it is terminated. If the election is terminated, another section 444 election cannot be made for any tax year. The election also ends automatically when any of the following occurs:

- The entity changes to its required tax year.

376

- The entity liquidates.
- The entity becomes a member of a tiered structure.
- The IRS determines that the entity willfully failed to comply with the required payments or distributions.
- The entity is an S corporation and the S election is terminated. However, if the S corporation immediately becomes a PSC, it can continue the prior section 444 election.
- A PSC ceases to be a PSC. Again, however, if a PSC becomes an S corporation, it can continue the prior election.

If a business files its first tax return using the calendar tax year and later changes its business structure (such as moving from a sole proprietorship to a partnership), the business must continue to use the calendar year unless it receives IRS approval or is otherwise forced to change in order to comply with the IRC. A taxpayer's death marks the end of his final tax year as an individual and the following day is the beginning of the first tax year for his estate. The executor or personal representative of the estate is responsible for filing the individual's final income tax return (Form 1040), income tax returns for the estate (Form 1041), and possibly an estate tax return (Form 706).

Example: Desmond is an unmarried physician. On July 1, 2012, he dies, and his son, Raleigh, is named the executor of his father's estate. Raleigh is responsible for filing Desmond's final individual tax return (Form 1040). The final Form 1040 covers the income earned between January 1 and July 1. In addition, he must file income tax returns for the estate for the period that begins on July 2 and ends when the estate's assets have been distributed. Raleigh must request an EIN for his father's estate, which is considered a separate legal entity for tax purposes. Desmond's assets are valued at approximately $15 million on the date of his death. Therefore, in addition to income tax returns, Raleigh is also required to file an estate tax return (Form 706).

The executor chooses the estate's tax period when he files its first income tax return. Generally, the estate's first tax year is any period of 12 months or less that ends on the last day of a month. If the executor selects the last day of any month other than December, the estate has adopted a fiscal tax year. The due date for Form 1041 is the fifteenth day of the fourth month following the end of the entity's tax year.[86]

Filing Due Dates for Entities

April 15th of each year is the normal due date for filing most individual and partnership returns. Any time a return due date falls on a Saturday, Sunday, or legal holiday, the due date is delayed until the next business day.

Corporate tax returns are due on March 15th, if the corporation is on a calendar year. If the corporation is on a fiscal year, the tax return is due on the fifteen day of the third month following the end of the tax year. Nonprofit organizations must file their information returns by May 15 if they are on a calendar-year reporting period.

---

[86] More detail on estates can be found in Unit 20, *Trusts and Estate Income Tax.*

If the exempt entity is on a fiscal year, the return is due on the fifteenth day of the fifth month following the end of the tax year.

> **Example:** A calendar year C corporation dissolved on July 22, 2012 and ceased all operations. Its final return is due by October 15, 2012 (the fifteenth day of the third month following the close of their short tax year). The return will cover the short period from January 1, 2012 through July 22, 2012.

Accounting Periods and Income Tax Return Due Dates

Entity Type	Accounting Period	Due Date of Return
Sole Proprietorship	Adopts the same tax year as the owner, typically a calendar year.	April 15 (same as individuals) . May request a 6 month extension.
Partnership	Adopts the same tax year as the partners who own more than 50% of the business, usually the calendar year.	April 15, or the 15th of the 4th month following the end of the tax year. May request a 5 month extension.
C Corporation	Fiscal year or calendar year.	March 15, or the 15th of the 3rd month following the end of the tax year. May request a 6 month extension.
S Corporation	Calendar year unless a valid section 444 election is made.	March 15, or the 15th of the 3rd month following the end of the tax year. May request a 6 month extension.
Exempt Entities	Fiscal year or calendar year.	May 15, or the 15th of the 5th month following the end of the tax year. May request a 3 month extension, and then a second 3 month extension.
Estates and Fiduciary returns (Form 1041 and Form 706)	Generally a fiscal year (the tax year begins on the day after the decedent's date of death and the executor then selects a tax year when the first return is filed.)	Form 1041 is due the 15th of the 4th month following the end of the tax year. Form 706 is due nine months after the date of death. A six month extension is available.

Extensions

Entities and individuals may request an extension of time to file their federal income tax returns. An extension does not grant the entity additional time to pay any tax due. It only provides additional time to file the return. Any estimated tax due must be paid by the filing deadline, or the entity will be subject to interest and penalties on the amount of unpaid tax.

Accounting Methods

An accounting method is a set of rules used to determine when and how income and expenses are reported. No single accounting method is required of all taxpayers. However, the taxpayer must use a system that reflects income and expenses, and it must be used consistently from year to year.

A business owner may use different accounting methods if he has two *separate and distinct* businesses. According to the IRS, two businesses will not be considered *separate and distinct,* however, unless a separate set of books and records is maintained for each business.

Example: Blake is a self-employed enrolled agent. He prepares tax returns from January through April every year. He is also a motivational speaker and does speaking engagements on martial arts because he is an accomplished martial artist. He decides to report his tax preparation business using the accrual method and his martial arts business using the cash method. He keeps separate books and records for each business. Blake may use different accounting methods because he has two separate and distinct businesses with separate sets of records.

Acceptable Accounting Methods

Businesses report taxable income under the following accounting methods:

- Cash method
- Accrual method
- Special methods of accounting for certain items of income and expenses
- Hybrid method using elements of the methods above

Different rules apply to each accounting method. The most common accounting method is the *cash method*, which is used by most individuals and small businesses. The *accrual method* is used by most large corporations and is a more accurate method of recognizing income and expenses, because it reflects when taxable income is actually earned.

Cash Method

The cash method of accounting is the simplest method to use, but the IRS restricts its use to certain types of businesses. The following types of businesses are required to use the accrual method:

- A corporation (other than an S corporation) with average annual gross receipts exceeding $5 million
- A partnership with a corporate partner (other than an S corporation) with average annual gross receipts exceeding $5 million
- Any business that carries or produces inventory, unless the business has average annual gross receipts of $1 million or less
- Any tax shelter, regardless of its size
- Any corporation with long-term contracts

> **Example:** Cameron and William Davis form the Davis and Davis Architectural Corporation, which is a C corporation. In 2012, the income for the corporation is $4.2 million. The Davis and Davis Corporation may still use the cash method because it has gross receipts under $5 million and does not have any inventory.

> **Example:** Corinne and her husband, Doug, run Bicycles-R-Us as a husband-and-wife partnership. Bicycles-R-Us designs and sells custom bicycles and carries a substantial inventory. In 2012, Bicycles-R-Us had gross receipts of $2.3 million. Bicycles-R-Us cannot use the cash method because it produces inventory and its average annual gross receipts exceed $1 million.

Exceptions: The following entities may use the cash method of accounting:

- A qualified family farming corporation with gross receipts of $25 million or less
- A qualified personal service corporation
- Artists, authors, and photographers who sell works that they have created by their own efforts

Gross Receipts Test

An entity (other than a tax shelter) that meets the gross receipts test can use the cash method. An entity generally meets the test if its average annual gross receipts are $5 million or less, determined by adding the gross receipts for that tax year and the two preceding tax years and dividing the total by three.

Gross receipts for a short tax year are annualized. An entity that fails to meet the gross receipts test for any tax year is prohibited from using the cash method and must change to the accrual method, effective for the tax year in which the entity fails to meet the test.

If a business produces or sells merchandise, it usually has inventory. Businesses that have inventory must use the accrual method unless their average annual gross receipts are $1 million or less.

> **Example:** Green Bay Corporation produces inventory and its gross receipts are $200,000 for 2010, $800,000 for 2011, and $1,100,000 for 2012. The company's average annual gross receipts are therefore $700,000 ([$200,000 + $800,000 + $1,100,000] ÷ 3 = $700,000). Green Bay Corporation is allowed to continue to use the cash method.

> **Example:** Crape Company makes golf car parts. The company carries inventory throughout the year. Crape's gross receipts have never exceeded $900,000. Therefore, Crape may continue to use the cash method.

The 12-Month Rule

Under the cash method, taxpayers generally deduct expenses when they are actually paid based upon the presumption that the expenses relate to the current tax year and are not deductible if paid in advance. This means that businesses generally may not attempt to lower their taxable income by paying expenses applicable to future years. The taxpayer would instead capitalize the costs paid in advance and deduct them in the years to which they apply. However, there is an exception called the 12-month rule. Under the 12-month rule, the cash-basis taxpayer is *not* required to capitalize amounts paid that do not extend beyond the earlier of the following:

- 12 months after the benefit begins, or
- The end of the tax year after the tax year in which payment is made.

> **Example:** Sherry is a calendar-year sole proprietor and pays $3,000 in 2012 for an insurance policy that is effective for three years (36 months), beginning on July 1, 2012. This payment does not qualify for the 12-month rule. Therefore, only $500 (6/36 x $3,000) is deductible in 2012, $1,000 (12/36 x $3,000) is deductible in 2013, $1,000 (12/36 x $3,000) is deductible in 2014, and the remaining $500 is deductible in 2015, when the policy expires.

> **Example:** Garrison Partnership is a calendar-year business. It pays $15,000 on July 1, 2012 for a business liability policy that is effective for one year beginning on July 1, 2012. The 12-month rule applies, and the full $15,000 is deductible in 2012.

> **Example:** Mikayla is a sole proprietor who rents retail space for her eyebrow threading business. She pays two years of rent in advance in order to receive a substantial discount from her landlord. She cannot use the 12-month rule because the benefit from her advance payment exceeds the 12-month time period. She must amortize the expense for rent over the time period to which the payment applies.

Constructive Receipt

Under the cash method, taxpayers report income when it is actually or "constructively" received during the tax year. Income is constructively received when the amount is credited to the taxpayer's account or made available without restriction so that the taxpayer or his agent has access to the funds. The taxpayer does not need to have physical possession of the payment.

> **Example:** Patel Brothers Partnership operates on the cash method. Interest income is credited to Patel's bank account in December 2012, but the partners do not withdraw it until January 2013. The partnership must include the interest income in its gross income for 2012, not 2013. The partnership had ownership and control of the income in 2012, so it is taxable in the year received.

Income is not considered to be constructively received if actual control of the income is restricted.

> **Example:** Better Jail Bonds LLP is a cash-basis partnership that bills a customer on December 10, 2012. The customer sends the company a check postdated to January 2, 2013. The check cannot be deposited until 2013 because it was postdated. Better Jail Bonds would include this income in gross income for 2013, since constructive receipt did not occur until then.

Accrual Method

Under the accrual method of accounting, an entity reports income in the year earned and deducts or capitalizes expenses as they are incurred. The purpose of the accrual method is to match income and expenses in the correct year. Under the accrual method, a business generally records income when a sale occurs or income is earned, regardless of when the business gets paid. Income is reported on the *earliest* of the following dates:

- When payment is received
- When the taxpayer earns the income
- When the income is due to the taxpayer
- When title has passed

A business that uses the accrual method must apply it to reporting expenses as well as income. Expenses are reported as soon as they are incurred. It does not matter when the business actually pays for the expenses.

The accrual method gives a more accurate assessment of a business's financial situation than the cash method. Income earned in one period is more accurately matched against the expenses that correspond to that period, so a business gets a better picture of net profits for each period.

Example: Ali's Computer Inc. is a calendar-year, accrual-basis corporation. The business sold a computer on December 28, 2012 for $2,500. Ali billed the customer in the first week of January 2013, but did not receive payment until February 2013. Ali must include the $2,500 in his 2012 income, the year the company actually *earned* the income.

Advance payments are generally included in income in the year they are received. However, an accrual basis taxpayer may postpone reporting the income for services to be performed in the next tax year. Advance payments for the sale of goods may be subject to an alternative method. The advance payment would be included in income in the earlier of:

- The tax year in which the business includes advance payments in gross receipts for its normal accounting method; or
- The tax year in which the business includes the income in financial reports, such as those provided to shareholders.

Hybrid Accounting Method

Businesses may also use a hybrid accounting method that is a combination of the cash, accrual, and other special methods if the hybrid method clearly reflects income and is used consistently. The following restrictions to the hybrid method apply:

- If an inventory is necessary to account for income, the business must use an accrual method for purchases and sales. The cash method can be used for other income and expense items.
- If an entity uses the cash method for reporting income, it must use the cash method for reporting expenses.
- If an entity uses the accrual method for reporting expenses, it must use the accrual method for reporting income.

Changing Accounting Methods

A business may choose any permitted accounting method when it files its first tax return. Subsequent changes, either in the overall accounting method or the treatment of a material item, generally require that the taxpayer obtain IRS approval. Prior approval is needed for:

- Changes from cash to accrual or vice versa, unless the change is required by tax law
- Changes in the method used to value inventory (such as switching from LIFO to FIFO)
- Changes in the accounting method to figure depreciation

The taxpayer must file Form 3115, *Application for Change in Accounting Method*, to request a change in either an overall accounting method or the accounting treatment of any item. However, IRS consent is not required for the following:

- Switching to straight-line depreciation from accelerated methods (once a taxpayer switches to straight-line for an asset, he cannot switch back)
- Making an adjustment in the useful life of a depreciable or amortizable asset (but a taxpayer cannot change the recovery period for MACRS or ACRS property)
- Correcting a math error or an error in figuring tax liability
- A change in accounting method when the change is required by tax law, such as when a business's average gross receipts exceed $5 million

Example: Gary is a general partner in Ultimate Consumer Goods, and discovers a major error in the useful life of a depreciable asset—the asset should have been depreciated over 15 years, rather than five. Ultimate Consumer Goods does not have to ask the IRS for permission in order to correct the depreciation error.

Inventory Tracking and Valuation

A business that produces or sells products must track its inventory in order to correctly calculate income. Businesses often make a full physical inventory count at the end of each tax year, as well as at other reasonable intervals. The recorded inventory balances are then adjusted to agree with the actual counts. Physical inventory counts may identify irregularities such as theft, as well as damaged goods and obsolete products.

Example: Wrightwood Grocery Store takes a physical inventory once a month. During the physical inventory, store employees are required to record any damaged goods such as dented cans and ripped packaging. When the physical inventory is completed, the manager does a reconciliation based to her records. She may also discover that a portion of the inventory is missing, apparently due to theft. She adjusts the books to record the theft losses and damaged merchandise.

A business's inventory should include all of the following, if applicable:

- Merchandise or stock in trade
- Raw materials
- Work in process
- Finished products
- Supplies that physically become a part of the item intended for sale (labels, packaging, etc.)

Merchandise that is included in inventory includes:

- Purchased merchandise if the title has passed to the taxpayer, even if the merchandise is still in transit or the business does not have physical possession of it for another reason.
- Goods under contract for sale that have not yet been segregated and applied to the contract.
- Goods out on consignment.
- Goods held for sale in display rooms or booths located away from the taxpayer's place of business

For mail order businesses, merchandise is generally included in the closing inventory until the buyer pays for it. The following merchandise is not included in inventory:

- Goods the business has sold, but only if legal title (ownership) has passed to the buyer.
- Goods consigned to the taxpayer.
- Goods ordered for future delivery if the business does not yet have title.

Land, buildings, and equipment used in a business are never included in inventory.

Shipping Terms and Transfer of Ownership

Certain shipping terms dictate when a taxpayer must recognize income or take an item out of inventory. The terms indicate the point at which ownership of goods transfers from shipper to buyer. The three most common terms are:

1. **FOB destination:** Title (ownership) of the goods passes to the buyer at the point of destination (when the goods arrive at the buyer's location).
2. **FOB shipping point:** Title (ownership) of the goods passes to the buyer at the point of shipment (when the goods leave the seller's premises). FOB shipping point is also called "FOB origin."
3. **C.O.D.** ("cash on delivery" or "collect on delivery"): Collection of the payment upon delivery. COD title does not pass until payment is remitted for the goods.

Example: Weitzman Furniture Company is a calendar-year, accrual-basis corporation that manufactures custom household furniture. For purposes of its financial reports, the company accrues income when it ships furniture. For tax purposes, it does not accrue income until the furniture has been delivered and accepted by the buyer. In 2012, the company receives an advance payment of $8,000 for an order of furniture to be custom manufactured for a total price of $20,000. Weitzman ships the furniture FOB destination to the customer on December 26, 2012, but it is not delivered and accepted by the customer until January 3, 2013. For tax purposes, Weitzman must include the $8,000 advance payment in gross income for 2012, and must include the remaining $12,000 of the contract price in gross income for 2013, after the furniture was accepted and the title passed to the buyer.

Acceptable Inventory Methods

There are several common inventory accounting methods, which identify the cost of items in inventory. They include the specific identification method, the weighted average cost method, FIFO, and LIFO.

Specific Identification Method

       This method is used when it is possible to identify and match the actual cost to specific items in inventory. It is most useful with an inventory that includes a limited number of highly specific and high-dollar items, such as custom goods or rare items like artwork or gemstones. The business simply accounts for each individual item as it is sold.

> **Example:** The Classic Custom dealership sells rare collectible and classic cars. Each car is inventoried and tracked individually by the license plate number. The cost of each car is tracked on a separate spreadsheet. When a car is sold, the vehicle is taken out of inventory. This is an example of specific identification inventory valuation.

Average Cost Method

       This method is commonly used when a company has large quantities of items that are largely interchangeable rather than individually unique. It allows the company to calculate an average cost per unit without tracking the individual units as they are purchased, manufactured, or sold. The formula for figuring average cost is:

> **Average Unit Cost = (Total Cost of Units Purchased or Manufactured)/ (Total Quantity of Units)**
>
> **Aggregate Inventory Cost = (Average Unit Cost) x (Units in Current Inventory)**

> ### Example: The Average Cost Method
>
> Anna owns a pet store. She purchases five dog leashes at $10 apiece. The following week, the price of the leashes goes up, and she purchases five more leashes at $20 apiece. Anna then sells five leashes the following week. The weighted average cost of Anna's inventory is calculated as follows:
>
> **Total cost of leashes:**
> (Five leashes at $10 each) = $50
> (Five leashes at $20 each) = $100
> Total number of units = 10 leashes
> Weighted average = $150 / 10 = $15
>
> $15 is the average cost per leash for the 10 leashes Anna has purchased. If she applies this average cost to the five leashes unsold at the end of the week, the calculated cost of the leashes on hand would be $75 ($15 times 5 leashes).

First-In, First-Out (FIFO)

       The first-in, first-out (FIFO) method is used by most major corporations to assign cost to their inventory.

       With FIFO, the assumption is that inventory is sold in the order that it is acquired or produced, with the oldest goods sold first and the newest goods sold last (such as rotating stock in a grocery store). The actual quantities in inventory at the end of the tax year are assigned costs based upon the cost of items of the same type that the business most recently purchased or produced.

The formula for figuring inventory based on the FIFO method is as follows:

> **Unit Cost per item = (Cost/Quantity) for the most recent lot of the item that was purchased or produced**
>
> **Aggregate Inventory Cost = (Unit Cost per item x Quantity) for each item**

In an economy with rising prices (inflation),[87] the use of FIFO will typically assign a higher value to ending inventory than other methods, and thus result in reporting higher taxable income.

Example: FIFO Method

Rabbata Electronics, a cash-basis, calendar-year taxpayer, sells car audio equipment. Beginning inventory on January 1 included 300 car stereos with cost of $20. On January 10 the business purchased 600 stereos at $20.10; on January 16 it purchased 400 stereos for $20.20; and on January 25 it purchased 500 stereos for $20.30. In January the business sold 1,200 car stereos. Under FIFO it is assumed that the oldest merchandise is sold first. Rabbata Electronics had a beginning inventory of 300 stereos—those units are assumed to leave inventory first, followed by the units purchased on January 10 and January 16. Thus, the cost assigned to the units on hand at the end of January is determined as follows:

Beginning inventory	**300**
January 10 purchases	600
January 16 purchases	400
January 25 purchases	500
Total units available	1,800
Units sold	(1,200)
Units in inventory at end of January	**600**

Composition based upon FIFO assumption:

January 25 purchases	500 @ 20.30 = 10,150
Unsold portion of January 16 purchases	100 @ 20.20 = 2,020
Total inventory at end of January	600 $12,170

Last-In, First-Out (LIFO)

The last-in, first-out (LIFO) method assumes that the newest inventory purchased or produced is sold first, and the oldest inventory is sold last. Since the prices of goods, labor, and materials generally rise over time, this method will typically result in assigning a lower aggregate cost to inventory on hand, higher amounts as the cost of sales, and thus lower taxable. As a result, use of the LIFO method is subject to close scrutiny by the IRS and highly complex rules governing its calculation. The formula for figuring inventory using the LIFO method is as follows:

> **Unit Cost per item = (Cost/Quantity) for the oldest lot of the item that was purchased or produced**
>
> **Aggregate Inventory Cost = (Unit Cost per item x Quantity) for each item**

---

[87] This concept of "rising prices" has been on numerous prior exams. Know the difference between LIFO and FIFO with regard to inventory valuation and how it affects income reporting.

Example: LIFO Method

Using the same background information for Rabbata Electronics outlined before, but using a LIFO assumption rather than FIFO, the 300 units on hand at January 1 are assumed to have a LIFO cost per unit of only $10 because Rabbata has been in business for twenty years and the unit costs of its purchases have approximately doubled in that period due to inflation. Therefore, the cost assigned to the units on hand at the end of January is determined as follows:

Beginning inventory	**300**
January 10 purchases	600
January 16 purchases	400
January 25 purchases	500
Total units available	1,800
Units sold	(1,200)
Units in inventory at end of January	**600**

Composition based upon LIFO assumption:

Beginning inventory	300 @ 10.00 =	3,000
Unsold portion of January 10 purchases	300 @ 20.10 =	6,030
Total inventory at end of January	600	$9,030

In comparison to the FIFO example above, the aggregate cost assigned to ending inventory using LIFO would be lower. Since the income generated by Rabbata in January from selling 1,200 would be the same using either accounting method for inventory, its taxable income would be higher using FIFO instead of LIFO.

Unless a business has used the LIFO method from its inception, it must obtain permission from the IRS to change to the LIFO from another method of inventory valuation. Permission is requested by filing Form 970, *Application To Use LIFO Inventory Method*.

Differences between FIFO and LIFO

Economic Climate	FIFO	LIFO
Periods of Rising Prices (Inflation)	(+) Higher value of inventory	(-) Lower value of inventory
	(-) Lower cost of goods sold	(+) Higher cost of goods sold
Periods of Falling Prices (Deflation)	(-) Lower value of inventory	(-) Higher value of inventory
	(+) Higher cost of goods sold	(+) Lower cost of goods sold

Valuing Inventory

The value of a business's inventory is a major factor in figuring taxable income. In addition to the inventory accounting methods described above, the following methods are commonly used to assign value to inventory: cost, lower of cost or market, and retail.

Cost Method: All direct and indirect costs are included.

- For merchandise on hand at the beginning of the tax year, cost means the ending inventory price of the goods.

- For merchandise purchased during the year, cost means the invoice price minus appropriate discounts, plus transportation or other charges incurred in acquiring the goods. It may also include other costs that must be capitalized under the uniform capitalization rules (covered later in this unit).
- For merchandise produced during the year, cost means all direct and indirect costs, including those that have to be capitalized under the uniform capitalization rules.

A trade discount is sometimes given for volume or quantity purchases. The cost of inventory must be reduced by trade discounts.

Lower of Cost or Market Method: The market value of each item on hand is compared with its cost and the lower amount is used as its inventory value. This is a good way to record the actual value of inventory when the inventory loses value quickly, such as happens with fashion clothing. This method applies to the following:

- Goods purchased and on hand
- The basic elements of cost (direct materials, direct labor, and certain indirect costs) of goods being manufactured and finished goods on hand

The lower of cost or market method cannot be used in conjunction with the LIFO method.

Example: Lower of Cost or Market

Graham makes leather motorcycle accessories at his factory. Under the lower of cost or market method, the following items would be valued at $600 in closing inventory.

Inventory Item	Cost	Market	Lower
Leather jacket	$300	$500	$300
Motorcycle helmets	$200	$100	$100
Leather motorcycle chaps	$450	$200	$200
Total	$950	$800	$600

Graham must value each item in the inventory separately. He cannot value the entire inventory at cost ($950) and at market ($800) and then use the lower of the two figures.

Retail Method: Under the retail method, the total retail selling price of goods on hand at the end of the tax year in each department or of each class of goods is reduced to approximate cost by using an average markup expressed as a percentage of the total retail selling price. For example, if a store marks up its merchandise by 35%, that percentage would be used as a basis for estimating the cost of its current inventory.

Cost of Goods Sold (COGS)

Part of the inventory equation consists of figuring cost of goods sold (COGS), which is deducted from a business's gross receipts to determine its gross profit. If an expense is included in COGS, it cannot be deducted again as a business expense. The following are types of expenses that go into figuring COGS:

- The cost of products or raw materials, including freight

- Storage
- Direct labor costs (including contributions to pensions or annuity plans) for workers who produce the products
- Factory overhead

Postage or shipping costs to deliver a finished product to a buyer are not included in inventory costs.

> **Example:** In calculating COGS, American Custom Shoes includes the cost of leather and thread in the shoes it manufactures, as well as wages for the workers that produce the shoes. The shipping cost of sending its finished shoes to customers is not included in COGS, and is deductible as a current expense.

> The equation for cost of goods sold is as follows:
> **Beginning Inventory + Inventory Purchases – Ending Inventory =**
> **Cost of Goods Sold**

COGS is recorded as an expense as the company sells its goods.

> **Example:** Doggie Delights Inc. is a cash-basis corporation that manufactures custom dog sweaters. In January, Doggie Delights has $20,000 in overall sales. In the same month, the corporation also has a number of expenses, including wages for the sweater designers ($5,000) and the cost of raw materials, including yarn, appliqué, rhinestones, and other raw materials ($3,000). The wages and the cost of the raw materials are directly related to the production of the inventory (the sweaters) and must be included in the cost of goods sold calculation. Other expenses not directly related to the manufacture of the sweaters, which might include items like a receptionist's salary ($1,500), telephone charges ($130), and advertising ($1,200) are also expensed, but are not part of COGS. The income statement for January would look like this:
>
> | | |
> |---|---|
> | Gross income from sales: | $20,000 |
> | COGS: ($5,000 + $3,000) | ($8,000) |
> | Gross profit | $12,000 |
> | Other expenses: ($1,500 + $130 + $1,200) | ($2,830) |
> | **Net income for January** | **$9,170** |

Other Inventory Requirements

Goods that cannot be sold at normal prices or are unusable because of damage, imperfections, shop wear, changes of style, odd or broken lots, or other similar causes should be valued at their actual selling price minus the direct cost of disposition, no matter which method is used to value the rest of the entity's inventory.

When a business incurs a casualty or theft loss of inventory, it increases the cost of goods sold by properly reporting opening and closing inventories. The business can also choose to take the loss separately as a casualty or theft loss. If the entity chooses to report a casualty loss, it must adjust opening inventory to eliminate the loss items and avoid counting the loss twice.

If a taxpayer removes items from inventory for personal use, he is required to subtract the cost of personal use items from total purchases.

Uniform Capitalization Rules (UNICAP)

The uniform capitalization rules (commonly referred to as UNICAP) provide detailed guidance regarding the direct costs and certain indirect costs related to the production of goods or the purchase of merchandise for resale that businesses must capitalize as the cost of inventory.

These costs cannot be expensed and deducted when incurred. They must be capitalized and deducted later, when the inventory is used or sold.

> **Example:** Creative Costumes manufactures Halloween and stage costumes. During August, Creative Costumes purchases raw materials to produce costumes for the upcoming holiday. All the materials and shipping costs associated with the inventory must be capitalized rather than expensed. As the Halloween costumes are sold, Creative Costumes expenses the costs associated with the inventory as cost of goods sold. At the end of each month, Creative Costumes does a physical inventory count and adjusts COGS for any damaged or stolen inventory.

> **Example:** MTG Studios produces movies for Hollywood. Film production is subject to the uniform capitalization rules, so MTG must capitalize all of its costs, including set design, costumes, special effects, film editing, and salaries for actors and production workers. When a film is finally completed and distributed, MTG Studios is allowed to deduct the production costs as COGS.

Most types of businesses are subject to the uniform capitalization rules, including the following:

- Retailers or wholesalers (if they produce or purchase merchandise for resale),
- Manufacturers who produce property for sale; and
- Taxpayers who construct assets for their own trade or business.

However, the uniform capitalization rules do not apply to the following:

- Resellers of personal property with average annual gross receipts of $10 million or less for the three prior tax years.
- Nonbusiness property (such as a hobby that produces occasional income).
- Research and experimental expenditures.
- Intangible drilling and development costs of oil and gas or geothermal wells.
- Property produced under a long-term contract.
- Timber raised, harvested, or grown, and the underlying land.
- Qualified creative expenses incurred as self-employed writers, photographers, or artists that are otherwise deductible on their tax returns.
- Loan originations.
- Property provided to customers in connection with providing services. It must be *de minimis* and not be included in inventory in the hands of the service provider.
- The costs of certain producers who use a simplified production method and whose total indirect costs are $200,000 or less.

Unit 3: Questions

1. Which of the following date ranges would be considered a fiscal tax year?

A. January 1, 2012 to December 31, 2012.
B. February 15, 2012 to February 15, 2013.
C. July 1, 2012 to June 30, 2013.
D. May 1, 2012 to May 31, 2013.

The answer is C. A fiscal tax year is any tax year that is 12 consecutive months and ends on the last day of any month except December. Answer A is incorrect because this is a calendar year, not a fiscal year. Answer B is incorrect because a fiscal year must end on the last day of the month. Answer D is incorrect because it is more than 12 consecutive months. ###

2. Which of the following dates would not be considered the end of an acceptable tax year?

A. January 31.
B. April 15.
C. December 31.
D. The last Friday in February.

The answer is B. April 15 is the IRS due date for individual tax returns, not the end of a tax year. Answer A is incorrect because January 31 is the last day of the month, which qualifies as a fiscal tax year-end. Answer C is incorrect because December 31 is a calendar year-end. Answer D is incorrect because a tax year that ends on the same day of the week every year is a 52/53-week tax year, which is a legitimate type of fiscal year. ###

3. What is the definition of the calendar year?

A. A calendar year is always from January 1 to December 31.
B. A calendar year is always a 12-month period ending on the last day of any month.
C. A calendar year can end on any day of the month, so long as the period spans 12 months.
D. A calendar year starts on April 15 and ends on April 15 the following year.

The answer is A. A calendar year is always the 12-month period from January 1 to December 31. ###

4. A business must adopt its first tax year by what date?

A. The due date (including extensions) for filing a return.
B. The due date (not including extensions) for filing a return.
C. The date the EIN is established.
D. The first time the business pays estimated payments.

The answer is B. A business must adopt its first tax year by the due date (not including extensions) for filing a return for that year. A business adopts a tax year when it files its first income tax return. ###

5. Vargas Cellular Corporation was organized on April 1, 2012. It elected the calendar year as its tax year. When is the first tax return due for Vargas Cellular for this short tax year?

A. April 15, 2013.
B. April 15, 2012.
C. March 15, 2013.
D. May 15, 2013.

The answer is C. Since the corporation chose a calendar year, its first tax return is due March 15, 2013. This short period return will cover April 1, 2012 through December 31, 2012. Corporate tax returns are due on the fifteenth day of the third month after the end of the corporation's taxable year. ###

6. Which of the following entities may use the cash method of accounting?

A. A family farming corporation with average gross receipts of $22 million.
B. A C corporation with average gross receipts of $50 million.
C. A tax shelter with $50,000 in average gross receipts.
D. A corporation with long-term contracts and average gross receipts of $900,000.

The answer is A. A family farming corporation may use the cash method of accounting if its average annual gross receipts are $25 million or less. A tax shelter must always use the accrual method, regardless of its gross receipts. A corporation with long-term contracts must always use the accrual method. A C corporation with gross receipts exceeding $5 million is required to use the accrual method. ###

7. Which of the following changes in accounting method does not require prior approval from the IRS?

A. A change from FIFO to LIFO inventory valuation.
B. A change from the cash method to the accrual method.
C. A change in the overall method of figuring depreciation.
D. A correction of a math error in depreciating an asset.

The answer is D. The correction of a math error does not require prior approval from the IRS. Consent from the IRS is not required for the following changes:
•Correction of a math error for computing tax liability or other mathematical error.
•A correction in depreciable life or correction of a depreciation error.
•An adjustment to an asset's useful life. ###

8. A company can choose to compute taxable income under which of the following methods?

A. Hybrid method.
B. Accrual method.
C. Cash method.
D. All of the above.

The answer is D. Unless specifically prohibited by the IRC or income tax regulations, a company can choose to compute its taxable income under any of the listed methods. Any accounting method may be acceptable if it clearly reflects income and is applied consistently from year to year. ###

9. Helen Banner is the owner of Banner's Custom Lamps, Inc., a calendar-year, accrual-basis S corporation. She sells five lamps to Sonny's Interior Design on December 21, 2012, billing Sonny's for $2,500. Sonny's Interior Design pays the invoice on January 15, 2013. Banner's Custom Lamps would include this income in which tax year?

A. 2012.
B. 2013.
C. 2014.
D. None of the above.

The answer is A. The income would be included in Banner's 2012 tax return, because Banner is using the accrual method of accounting for income and expenses. Under the accrual method, income is reported in the year earned and expenses are deducted in the year incurred. Since Banner sold the lamps in 2012, the income would be reported in 2012, regardless of when payment is actually received. ###

10. Ben owns a jewelry store. All of the following transactions are examples of constructive receipt of income in 2012 except?

A. Ben receives a check payment on December 31, 2012, but does not deposit the check in the bank until January 2, 2013.
B. Ben receives a direct deposit of funds to his bank account on December 15, 2012, but does not withdraw any of the funds until March 2013.
C. Ben receives a signed IOU from a delinquent account in November 2012. He receives payment on this account on January 10, 2013.
D. An escrow agent receives a payment on Ben's behalf that is restricted for his use. It is an advance payment for a custom ring, but he cannot access any of the funds until the ring is delivered and inspected. On December 25, 2012, the ring is delivered and the restriction is lifted. Ben picks up the cash on January 9, 2013.

The answer is C. According to the doctrine of constructive receipt, income is included in gross income when a person has an unqualified right to the funds. Constructive receipt must be more than just a billing, an offer, or a mere promise to pay. The amount promised to Ben as an IOU, therefore, does not have to be included in income for 2012. ###

11. Which of the following entities may not use the cash method of accounting?

A. A partnership that produces inventory for sale to customers and has $1.2 million in average annual gross receipts.
B. A C corporation without inventory that has $4.5 million in average annual gross receipts.
C. A qualified family farming corporation with $24 million in average annual gross receipts.
D. A sole proprietor with inventory and $500,000 in average annual gross receipts.

The answer is A. Generally, an entity cannot use the cash method if it has average annual gross receipts exceeding $5 million. However, if a company has inventory, the threshold for gross receipts is $1 million. A qualified family farming corporation may use the cash method if its average gross receipts do not exceed $25 million. ###

12. Ray operates a retail store using the accrual method of accounting and reports income on Schedule C, Net Profit or Loss from Business. He also runs a lawn care service that operates only in the summer months. Which of the following statements is true?

A. The lawn care business is required to use the accrual method of accounting because Ray has already elected this method for his other business, and all businesses operated by one individual must use the same method of accounting.
B. The lawn care business may use either the cash or accrual method of accounting, so long as both businesses have separate and distinct records.
C. Ray may keep one set of records for the two businesses and use different methods of accounting for each one.
D. Ray must combine the income for both businesses and keep one set of record books for both.

The answer is B. A taxpayer may use different methods of accounting for two distinct and separate businesses. Separate accounting books must be kept for each business. ###

13. The following are all acceptable methods of accounting for inventory except:

A. Specific identification.
B. Coupon method.
C. FIFO.
D. LIFO.

The answer is B. FIFO, LIFO, and specific identification are all acceptable inventory methods. The "coupon method" is not. ###

14. Jenny owns a small side business selling makeup door-to-door. She reports her income and loss on Schedule C. Occasionally, she takes items out of inventory for her own personal use. In 2012, she took $250 worth of makeup for her own use. What is the proper tax treatment of this action?

A. Jenny must reduce the amount of her total inventory purchases by $250.
B. Jenny may take an expense of $250 on Schedule C for the personal use items.
C. Jenny must increase the cost of her purchases by the value of her personal use items.
D. Jenny may deduct the $250 on Schedule A as an employee business expense.

The answer is A. Taxpayers are required to subtract the cost of personal use items from total purchases, if they remove items for personal use from business inventory. ###

15. Under the lower of cost or market method of valuing inventory, what is the value of the inventory as a whole, based on the table below?

Item	Cost	FMV
Shirts	$200	$500
Shoes	$300	$200
Shorts	$225	$150
Total	**$725**	**$850**

A. $725.
B. $850.
C. $750.
D. $550.

The answer is D. To value inventory using the "lower of cost or market" method, compare the cost and the fair market value of each of the items in inventory, and choose the lower of the two to obtain the inventory's value. The answer is calculated as follows:
(Shirts $200 + Shoes $200 + shorts $150) = $550 inventory valuation. ###

16. Which of the following activities would make a taxpayer subject to the uniform capitalization rules?

A. A taxpayer produces items as a hobby and occasionally sells them at a profit.
B. A taxpayer produces property for sale to wholesale retailers.
C. A taxpayer acquires raw land and holds it for investment.
D. A taxpayer refurbishes multiple automobiles for his own use.

The answer is B. A taxpayer is subject to the uniform capitalization rules if he produces real property or personal property for use in a trade or business. Producing items for personal use or as a hobby does not qualify. ###

17. Which of the following types of property are not exempt from the uniform capitalization rules?

A. Qualified expenses of a writer, photographer, or performing artist.
B. Timber and the underlying land.
C. Services provided to customers.
D. A corporation that produces audio recordings.

The answer is D. A corporation that produces audio recordings or films would be subject to UNICAP. Generally, the uniform capitalization rules apply to a taxpayer that produces property for use or resale in a business. A company that provides only services would not carry an inventory, so it is not subject to UNICAP. Independent (self-employed) authors, writers, and artists are exempt from the rules. ###

18. All of the following activities are exempt from the uniform capitalization rules except:

A. Resellers of personal property with average annual gross receipts of $25 million.
B. Intangible drilling and development costs of oil and gas or geothermal wells.
C. Research and experimental expenditures.
D. Property produced under a long-term contract.

The answer is A. Resellers of property with annual gross receipts of $10 million or less are exempt from UNICAP. A reseller with average annual gross receipts of $25 million would be subject to UNICAP. ###

19. Chris is the owner-shareholder of Chris's Clothing Company, an S corporation. He manufactures clothing items for resale to the general public and also sells them to wholesale distributors. Chris is trying to figure out his inventory calculations in order to file his 2012 tax return. Which of the following items should be included in his yearend inventory?

A. 2,000 t-shirts out on consignment for another retailer to sell.
B. The machinery used to manufacture the clothing.
C. An order of fabric that was in transit, FOB destination (the title had not yet passed to Chris).
D. 1,000 shirts that were shipped COD to a retailer that had not arrived at the buyer's warehouse.

The answer is A. Chris should include the consigned goods in his own inventory, since goods on consignment are not actually sold to the retailer, and title remains with Chris. Merchandise sent COD is included in inventory until it reaches the buyer, because title does not pass to the buyer until the item is delivered and paid for. Machinery and other fixed assets are not included in inventory. They are depreciated separately. ###

20. All of the following practices are acceptable methods of accounting for inventory except:

A. The taxpayer accounts for inventory and includes only direct costs associated with manufacturing the goods.
B. The taxpayer has a theft loss of inventory when a disgruntled employee steals substantial amounts of merchandise. The taxpayer chooses to increase his cost of goods sold to account for the stolen items, and properly reports his beginning and closing inventory.
C. The taxpayer values his inventory using the lower-of-cost or market method, using the lowest value for each item in his inventory valuations.
D. The taxpayer has two businesses, and chooses to use LIFO for the first business and FIFO for the second one. He keeps a separate set of books for each business.

The answer is A. Taxpayers must include direct and indirect costs in inventory. Taxpayers may claim a casualty or theft loss of inventory through the increase in the cost of goods sold by properly reporting opening and closing inventories. Taxpayers may choose to use different accounting methods for different businesses, so long as the businesses are kept separate and distinct accounting records are maintained for each. ###

21. Tuxedo House, a clothing retailer, had the following expenses in 2012. Based on the information below, what is Tuxedo House's cost of goods sold for the year?

Tuxedos purchased for resale: $20,000
Freight in $3,000
Freight out to customers $6,000
Beginning inventory $15,600
Ending inventory $12,000

A. $23,000.
B. $26,600.
C. $28,600.
D. $42,500.

The answer is B. The COGS is $26,600 ($15,600 beginning inventory + $20,000 purchases + $3,000 freight in, minus $12,000 ending inventory). Freight in and merchandise purchased for resale are part of the COGS, but freight out is not. ###

22. Thomas is a cash-basis sole proprietor who reports income and loss on Schedule C. He purchases a bulk order of watches for his mail order business. The watches cost $5,000, and the related shipping cost is $350. What is the correct treatment of the shipping cost he paid for delivery of the watches?

A. Thomas may elect to deduct the shipping cost on his tax return as a regular expense.
B. Shipping cost paid on the watches must be added to the basis of the inventory.
C. Thomas cannot deduct the shipping cost and cannot capitalize it.
D. Thomas may elect to deduct the shipping cost as an itemized deduction on Schedule A.

The answer is B. The shipping cost increases the asset's basis. If the property is merchandise bought for resale (such as inventory), the shipping cost is part of the cost of the merchandise and must be capitalized and later recovered as cost of goods sold when the watches are resold. ###

23. All of the following costs must be included in inventory except:

A. Shipping raw materials to the business's factory.
B. Shipping finished product orders to customers.
C. Raw materials.
D. Direct labor costs.

The answer is B. Shipping finished products to customers is not an expense that should be included in inventory. This cost is a current expense and would be deductible as postage, rather than capitalized as a cost of inventory. ###

Unit 4: Business Income

> **More Reading:**
> Publication 525, *Taxable and Nontaxable Income*
> Publication 538, *Accounting Periods and Methods*
> Publication 334, *Tax Guide for Small Business*

Gross income to a business includes all types of income, unless specifically exempt, in the form of money, property, or services. Sources of income for a business include all of the following:

- Income received for services
- Income received for manufacturing or selling merchandise
- Gains from the sale of business property or investment property
- Income from the discharge of indebtedness (debt forgiveness income)
- Income from an interest in an estate or trust
- Portfolio income from investments
- Fair market value of property or services received through bartering
- Rental activities and royalties

Just like individual taxpayers, businesses sometimes earn income that is exempt from tax. More often, businesses engage in transactions that *defer* income to a later date. An example is a section 1031 exchange, which allows for deferral of income on the exchange of business or investment property.

Sole proprietors report business income on Schedule C (Form 1040), or Schedule F (Form 1040) for farmers and fishermen. A partnership reports its income on Form 1065. Corporations file Form 1120, while S corporations use Form 1120S. In this unit, we will review the details of various types of business income.

Bartering Income

Bartering occurs when a taxpayer exchanges goods or services without exchanging actual money. An example of bartering is a plumber doing repair work for a dentist in exchange for dental services. The fair market value of goods and services received in exchange must be included in income in the year received.

> **Example:** Ethan is a self-employed social media marketer. He and Bryce, a house painter, are members of a barter club where members get in touch with one another directly and bargain. In return for Ethan's marketing services, Bryce paints Ethan's home. Ethan must report the exchange as income on Schedule C. Bryce must include in income the fair market value of the services Ethan provided.

Income from Canceled Debt

If a business-related debt is canceled or forgiven, other than as a gift or bequest, the business generally includes the canceled amount in income. However, a cash-basis business is not required to realize income from a canceled debt to the extent that the payment of the debt would have led to a business deduction.

> **Example:** Barbells Partnership is a cash-basis business. The company orders computer repair services on credit but later has trouble paying its debts. The computer repair company forgives the repair bill. The partnership is not required to recognize the canceled debt as income because payment of the repair bill would have been deductible as a business expense anyway.

In the above example, the canceled debt of an accrual-basis business would be considered income, because the deduction for the expense already would have been recorded.

If a taxpayer owes a debt to a seller for property he bought and the seller then reduces the amount owed, the taxpayer generally does not have income from the reduction. Unless the taxpayer is bankrupt or insolvent, the amount of the reduction is treated as a purchase price adjustment, and the basis in the property is reduced.

Real Estate Income

Businesses may have income from rental activity, which is any amount of money received or accrued as payment for the use of property. Types of rental income may also include rent payments and deposits from renters.

Generally, the IRS deems rental income as passive income, which is not subject to employment taxes. However, rental income is not passive income and is subject to employment taxes when the taxpayer is a professional real estate dealer. A taxpayer qualifies as a real estate dealer if he is primarily engaged in the business of selling real estate to customers. Rent received from real estate held for sale to customers is subject to self-employment tax, while income received from real estate held for investment is not subject to SE tax. Rental income is reported on the following forms:

- **Schedule C,** *Profit or Loss from Business* (used for professional real estate dealers)
- **Schedule E,** *Supplemental Income and Loss* (from rental real estate, royalties, partnerships, S corporations, estates, trusts, REMICs, etc.)

Self-employed real estate dealers or owners of a hotel, boarding house, or apartment building who provide services for guests must report their rental income and expenses on Schedule C, subject to self-employment tax. The services must be ones that are *not* normally provided with the rental of rooms for occupancy only, such as maid service, rather than services that *are* normally provided for the occupants' convenience, such as providing heat and light, cleaning stairways and lobbies, and collecting trash.

If a taxpayer is not a professional real estate dealer, he must report the rental income and expenses on Schedule E, Form 1040.

> **Example:** Joe owns two residential rental properties. He manages them and collects rents. He also has a full-time job as a restaurant manager. He is not a real estate dealer. Joe must report his rental income and losses on Schedule E. His rental income is considered passive income and is not subject to self-employment tax.

> **Example:** Evelyn is a licensed real estate agent. She sells properties and also maintains several rental properties. She works as a real estate agent full-time, and manages all the rental properties herself. Evelyn elects to treat her rental income on Schedule C, not Schedule E. Her losses are not limited, and the income is subject to self-employment tax.

Lease cancellation payments received from a tenant are reported as income in the year received. Advance rental payments received under a lease must be recognized in the year received, regardless of what accounting method or period is used. This means that a taxpayer who owns rental properties and receives rent in advance cannot delay recognizing the income, even if the taxpayer is on the accrual basis.

Personal Property Rents

A taxpayer in the business of renting personal property, such as equipment, vehicles, or formal wear, includes the rental income on Schedule C. Prepaid rent can also be received for renting personal property, and must be recognized in the year received.

Advance Payment for Services

Generally for accrual-based taxpayers, an advance payment for services to be performed in a later tax year is taxable in the year the payment is received. But if there is an agreement that the service will be completed by the end of the next tax year, the recognition of that income can be postponed and included in income the next year. The taxpayer cannot, however, postpone the recognition of income beyond the next year.

Service agreement: If a taxpayer receives an advance payment for a service agreement on property he sells, leases, builds, installs, or constructs, he can postpone reporting income. This applies only if the taxpayer offers the property without a service agreement in the normal course of business. Postponement is not allowed if:

- The taxpayer will perform any part of the service after the end of the tax year immediately following the year he receives the advance payment.
- The taxpayer will perform any part of the service at any unspecified future date that may be after the end of the tax year immediately following the year he receives the advance payment.

> **Example:** Ross is an accrual-based, calendar-year taxpayer who owns a television repair business. In 2012, he receives payments for one-year contracts that specify he will repair or replace certain TV components that break. Ross includes the payments in gross income as he earns them.

> **Example:** The Best Service Tennis Club is a calendar-year, accrual-based taxpayer that holds tennis clinics for new players. On November 1, the club receives payment for a one-year contract for 24 one-hour clinics beginning on that date. The club gives six clinics in 2012. Under this method of including advance payments, the club must include one-fourth (6/24) of the payment in income for 2012 and three-fourths (18/24) of the payment in 2013. This is true even if the club does not give all of the clinics by the end of 2013.

Guarantee or warranty: Generally, a taxpayer cannot postpone reporting income received under a guarantee or warranty contract.

Advance Payment for Sales

Special rules apply to including income from advance payments on agreements for the future sale of goods to customers, such as gift certificates or cards that can be redeemed later for goods. Under the accrual method, the advance payment is generally included in income in the year in which it is received.

However, there is an alternative method in which the advance payment can be included in gross receipts under the method of accounting the taxpayer uses for tax purposes or the method of accounting used for financial reports, whichever is earlier.

> **Example:** Tangerine Specialty Foods uses the accrual method of accounting for tax and financial reporting purposes and accounts for the sale of goods when it ships the goods. A customer purchases a $100 gift card from Tangerine's website on Dec. 28, 2012 using a credit card. Tangerine ships the gift card to the customer on January 3, 2013. Under the alternative method of reporting income for advance payment of sales, Tangerine may recognize the $100 in gross receipts in either 2012 (the tax year in which it received the payment) or 2013 (the tax year in which it shipped the gift card.)

Business Interest and Dividend Income

Businesses can earn interest just like individuals do. This is especially true if the business lends money to other businesses and individuals. In any business, interest received on notes receivable that have been accepted in the normal course of business is reported as business income.

A common example of this is when a C corporation owns stock in another corporation. The C corporation earns dividends and interest on its investments, just like an individual does.

For most sole proprietors, dividend income is nonbusiness income and reported on Form 1040. However, dividends are treated as business income to professional stockbrokers and securities dealers.

Business-Related Court Awards and Damages

The IRC excludes from taxation most types of court awards and settlements that grant compensation for physical injuries or illness.

Most other types of court awards and settlements are taxable income, which are included in business income, such as:

- Damages for:
    - Patent or copyright infringement,
    - Breach of contract, or
    - Interference with business operations.
- Compensation for lost profits
- Interest earned on any type of court award

- Punitive damages related to business income or business activity[88]

If a business owner or employee is injured by equipment and later receives a court settlement, the income is not taxable to the employee, but it is still deductible as a business expense by the company that issues the settlement.

Amounts Not Considered Business Income

Just as with individual taxpayers, there are types of business-related income and property transfers that are not taxable or reportable. Some of these transactions may be partially taxable, and some are transactions where the recognition of income is delayed until a later date. Examples include:

- Issuance of stock from the sale of Treasury stock
- Most business loans (these are debt, not income)
- State and local sales taxes that are collected and then remitted to state or local governments
- Like-kind exchanges of property
- Gain from an involuntary conversion, if the gain is reinvested properly
- Consignments (inventory that is owned by another business)
- A volunteer workforce for an exempt entity
- Workers' compensation for injuries or sickness
- A pension, annuity, or similar allowance for personal injuries or sickness resulting from active service in the armed forces
- Refundable security deposits (if returned to the renter after relinquishing the property)

---

[88] Punitive damages may be awarded in addition to compensatory damages for actual monetary losses. Punitive damages are subject to income tax, but not subject to self-employment tax (FICA).

Unit 4: Questions

1. Which of the following would not be considered income for tax purposes?

A. Interest earned on a court award.
B. Damages received in a suit or settlement for personal physical injuries.
C. Barter income from consulting services.
D. Legal damages awarded for copyright infringement.

The answer is B. Certain items of income are excluded from gross income by provisions in the Internal Revenue Code. Gross income does **not** include certain types of compensation for physical injuries. ###

2. Evelyn is a self-employed bookkeeper who performs services for a client, a small corporation. In exchange for her services, the corporation gives Evelyn 500 shares of stock with a fair market value of $4,000. How would the transaction be reported?

A. Evelyn must report the stock as a capital gain.
B. This is not a taxable event. Evelyn would not have to recognize the income until she sold the stock.
C. Evelyn must recognize the stock as interest income.
D. Evelyn must include the fair market value of the shares in her ordinary income.

The answer is D. Since the fair market value of the stock is $4,000, she must include that amount in her income. Bartering is an exchange of property or services. Evelyn must include the FMV of property or services received in her gross income. ###

3. When are advance rental payments taxable?

A. In the year they are received.
B. In the period in which they are accrued.
C. They are not taxable.
D. They are taxable when the checks are cashed.

The answer is A. Advance rental payments received under a lease must be recognized in the year received. This is true no matter what accounting method or period is used. This means that a taxpayer who owns rental properties and receives rent in advance cannot delay recognizing the income, even if the taxpayer is on the accrual basis. ###

4. Harley is a real estate professional who owns two duplexes and an office building, all of which he rents to tenants. He works on his rental activity full-time. How should Harley report his rental income?

A. On Schedule E.
B. On Schedule C.
C. On Schedule D.
D. Harley's rental income is not taxable because he is a real estate professional.

The answer is B. Normally, the IRS considers rental income as passive income, not subject to employment taxes, and it is reported on Schedule E, *Supplemental Income and Loss*. However, as a real estate professional, Harley's income is not passive and is subject to employment taxes. He must report his rental income on Schedule C, *Profit or Loss for Business*. ###

5. The Vitrano Tool Corporation rents large tools and machinery for use in construction projects. The company always charges a refundable security deposit and a nonrefundable cleaning deposit when someone rents a machine. Vitrano Tool Corporation received the following amounts in 2012:

Rental income	$50,000
Security deposits	$4,050
Cleaning deposits	$1,500

What amount should be included in the corporation's gross income?

A. $50,000.
B. $51,500.
C. $54,050.
D. $55,550.

The answer is B. The refundable security deposits are not taxable income, because those amounts are returned to the customer. The amounts included in gross income would be the rental income and the nonrefundable cleaning deposits ($50,000 + $1,500 = $51,500). ###

6. When is a business not required to realize income from a canceled debt?

A. Canceled debt is always taxable to a business.
B. A business does not have to realize canceled debt income to the extent that the payment of the debt would have led to a business deduction.
C. Canceled debt is never taxable income to a business.
D. Canceled debt is realized income to a sole proprietorship, but not to a C corporation or an S corporation.

The answer is B. Canceled debt is not realized income to a business to the extent that the payment of the debt would have led to a business deduction. All of the other answers are incorrect. ###

7. Camille, a calendar-year, accrual-based taxpayer, owns a studio that teaches ballroom dancing. On October 1, 2012, she receives payment for a one-year contract for 96 one-hour lessons beginning on that date. She gives eight lessons in 2012 and the rest in 2013. How and when must she recognize this payment as income?

A. All income must be recognized in 2012.
B. All income may be deferred until 2013 since that is when most of the lessons are given.
C. 8/96 of the income must be recognized in 2012 and the rest, 88/96, in 2013.
D. All of the income can be split equally between 2012 and 2012.

The answer is C. Under the rules of advance payment for services, Camille must recognize income from the eight lessons she gives in 2012 and recognize the rest in 2013, regardless of whether she actually has given all of the lessons by the end of 2013. ###

8. Assume the same facts as in the previous question, except the payment is for a two-year contract for 96 lessons. Camille gives eight lessons in 2012; 48 lessons in 2013; and 40 lessons in 2014. How and when must she recognize this payment as income?

A. All income must be recognized in 2012.
B. 8/96 of the income must be recognized in 2012; 48/96 in 2013; and 40/96 in 2014.
C. 8/96 of the income must be recognized in 2012 and 88/96 in 2013.
D. All of the income can be deferred and split equally between 2013 and 2014.

The answer is A. Camille must include the entire payment in income in 2012 since some of the services may be performed after the following year. ###

Unit 5: Business Expenses

> **More Reading:**
> Publication 535, *Business Expenses*
> Publication 538, *Accounting Periods and Methods*
> Publication 15-B, *Employer's Tax Guide to Fringe Benefits*
> Publication 587, *Business Use of Your Home*
> Publication 463, *Travel, Entertainment, Gift, and Car Expenses*

Business expenses are the costs of carrying on a trade or business, and are usually deductible if the business operates to make a profit. Some expenses must be treated differently than others, and some must be capitalized and depreciated.

Expenses under the Accrual Method

Under the accrual method of accounting, [89] a taxpayer generally deducts or capitalizes business expenses when both of the following apply:

- The **all-events test** has been met, which is defined as all events have occurred that fix the fact of liability, and the liability can be determined with reasonable accuracy.
- **Economic performance** has occurred.

Economic performance occurs as the property or services are provided or the property is used.

> **Example:** Tessa is an accrual-based, calendar-year taxpayer. She orders office supplies in December 2012 and receives them later in the month. She does not pay the bill for the supplies until January 2013. She can deduct the expense in 2012 because all events have occurred to fix the liability, the amount of the liability can be determined, and economic performance occurred in 2012.

Exception for recurring items

Expenses for certain recurring items may be treated as incurred during the tax year even though economic performance has not occurred. In the above example, office supplies may qualify as a recurring item. If so, the taxpayer can deduct them in 2012, even if the supplies are not delivered until 2013 when economic performance occurs. The exception for recurring items applies if all of the following requirements are met:

- The "all-events" test is met.
- Economic performance occurs by the earlier of the following dates:
  - 8½ months after the close of the year.
  - The date the taxpayer files a timely return, including extensions, for the year.
- The item is recurring in nature and the taxpayer consistently treats similar items as incurred in the tax year in which the all-events test is met.

---

[89] Under the cash method of accounting, a taxpayer generally deducts expenses in the tax year in which he actually pays them. There is an exception for certain payments under the 12-month rule, covered in Unit 3, *Accounting Methods*.

Either:

- The item is not material, or
- Accruing the item in the year in which the all-events test is met results in a better match against income than accruing the item in the year of economic performance.

To determine whether an item is recurring and consistently reported, the taxpayer must consider how frequently he has this same expense and how he reports it for tax purposes. A new expense or an expense that is not incurred every year can be treated as recurring if the taxpayer reasonably expects to incur it regularly in the future.

The exception does not apply to workers' compensation or tort liabilities.

Allowable Expenses

To be deductible, a business expense must be both "ordinary" and "necessary." An ordinary expense is one that is common and accepted in the taxpayer's industry. A necessary expense is one that is helpful and appropriate for the particular trade or business. However, an expense does not have to be "indispensable" to be considered necessary.

Before a business can deduct an item as an expense, it must first distinguish whether the expense is one used to figure cost of goods sold,[90] or whether it is a capital expense, or whether it is a personal expense. None of these are deductible as expenses. The following rules apply:

- If an expense is included in the cost of goods sold, it cannot be deducted again as a business expense. Some expenses must be capitalized rather than deducted.
- Personal, family, and living expenses generally cannot be deducted as business expenses.

In the remaining portion of this unit, we will review the types of business expenses that are allowable as deductions.

Employee Wages

An employer can deduct the pay it gives its employees if the pay is reasonable and for services performed by the employee. "Supplemental wages" refers to compensation paid in addition to an employee's regular wages. Supplemental wages include the following:

- Bonuses, commissions
- Overtime pay
- Accumulated sick leave
- Severance pay
- Taxable awards
- Prizes
- Back pay, retroactive pay increases
- Payments for nondeductible moving expenses

---

[90] A fuller explanation of cost of goods sold (COGS) can be found in Unit 3, *Accounting Methods*.

Supplemental wages are taxable to the employee just like regular wages and deductible as a wage expense by the employer. Businesses are responsible for federal income tax withholding, Social Security and Medicare taxes, and Federal Unemployment Tax Act (FUTA) taxes.

These taxes are withheld from an employee's paycheck, and the business owner remits them to the IRS. Most businesses are then required to deposit these taxes electronically using the Electronic Federal Tax Payment System (EFTPS), although some very small businesses may still opt to pay employment taxes with their payroll tax returns. In order for a business to deduct employee compensation, the expense must meet all of the following tests:

- The payments must be ordinary and necessary expenses directly related to the trade or business.
- The amounts must be reasonable. Reasonable pay is the amount that like businesses would normally pay for the same or similar services.
- There must be proof that services were actually performed (unless the compensation qualifies as supplemental wages, such as maternity leave, sick pay, or vacation pay).
- The expenses must have been paid or incurred during the tax year.

If the IRS determines pay is excessive, it can disallow the excess as a deduction.

Transfers of property to an employee can also be considered compensation, and the fair market value of the property on the date of transfer is deductible by the business and taxable to the employee as wages. A gain or loss is recognized on the transfer of the difference between the FMV and the basis of the property.

In addition to deducting employees' pay, a business may deduct expenses paid to independent contractors.

Employers are also able to deduct fringe benefits they provide to employees, which we cover in detail in Unit 6.

Business Gifts: the $25 Limit

Companies are allowed to spend up to $25 per year *per employee*, tax-free, for a business gift. This does not include cash gifts. Any amount in excess of $25 is disallowed as a business deduction. The $25 limit for business gifts does not include incidental costs — for example, packaging, insurance, and mailing costs, or the cost of engraving jewelry. Related costs are considered incidental only if they do not add substantial value to a gift.

Any additional costs for postage and wrapping paper, etc. may be deducted separately by the business.

> **Example:** Roggan Corporation gives each of its 75 employees a $25 fruit basket during the holidays. The company may deduct the cost of the gifts ($1,875 = $25 X 75). The gift is not taxable to the employee, and the fair market value of the gift is not included in the employee's wages.

A business may also deduct business-related gifts to clients and customers. The amount is still limited to $25 given to any person during the year. If a taxpayer and a spouse *both* give gifts, they are treated as one taxpayer for the purpose of the deduction, even if they both have separate businesses. A gift to the *spouse* of a business customer or client is generally considered an indirect gift to the customer or client.

> **Example:** Hawaii Fruit Corporation gives a large fruit and nut basket to its best customer, Dominic's Produce Company. The fruit basket costs $57, and the shipping and mailing of the basket costs $17. Hawaii Fruit Corporation can deduct $25 for the basket and $17 for the cost of mailing, for a total gift deduction of $42.

> **Example:** Miguel sells tools to Hammer's Hardware Store. He gives three fancy candy boxes to each of the store's owners to thank them for their patronage. Miguel pays $80 for each package, or $240 total. He can deduct a total of $75 ($25 limit × 3) for the packages. The remainder of the gift expense is disallowed.

Exceptions to the Gift Limit

Exceptions to the gift limit: The following items are considered promotional and not gifts for purposes of the $25 limit:

- An item that costs $4 or less with the business name clearly imprinted on it (examples include imprinted pens, desk sets, and plastic bags)
- Signs, display racks, or other promotional materials to be used on the business premises of the recipient

> **Example:** Betty's Beekeeper Company gives 150 imprinted pens to her customers and their employees. The pens cost $4 each and they are imprinted with Betty's business name, website, and phone number. She also gives ten of her best customers a beautiful wood rack to display her honeybee products in their stores. The display racks cost $100 each. None of these items is subject to the $25 gift limitation, since they are all promotional items and follow the IRS guidelines.

Business Travel, Meals, and Entertainment

To be deductible for tax purposes, business expenses for travel, meals, and entertainment must be incurred while carrying on a genuine business activity. Generally, the business must be able to prove that entertainment expenses, including meals, are directly related to the conduct of business.

Deductible Meal Expense: the 50% Limit

Travel and transportation costs are 100% deductible, but only 50% of the cost of meals and entertainment is deductible as a business expense. The 50% limit applies to business meals or entertainment incurred while:

- Traveling away from home (whether eating alone or with others) on business
- Entertaining customers at a restaurant or other location
- Attending a business convention or reception, business meeting, or business luncheon

Related expenses that are also subject to the 50% limit include:

- Taxes and tips on a business meal or entertainment activity
- Cost of a room in which the business holds a dinner or cocktail party

The 50% limit applies to meal and entertainment expenses incurred for the production of income, including rental or royalty income. It also applies to the cost of meals incurred while obtaining deductible educational expenses, such as meals during a continuing education seminar. The cost of transportation to a business meal or a business-related entertainment activity is not subject to the 50% limit.

Example: Karen is a business owner who takes a client to lunch. The total restaurant bill is $88. She also pays cab fare of $10 to get to the restaurant. Karen's deductible expense for this event is $54, figured as follows:		
Deductible meal expense	$88 X 50% =	$44
Deductible travel expense		$10
Total deductible expense		**$54**

Exceptions to the 50% Limit

There are some exceptions to the 50% limit. The following meals are 100% deductible by the employer:

- Meals that are included in employees' wages as taxable compensation
- Meals that qualify as a *de minimis* fringe benefit, such as occasional coffee and doughnuts
- Meals that are made available to the general public as part of a promotional activity, such as a real estate broker who provides dinner to potential investors at a sale presentation
- Meals furnished to employees when the employer operates a restaurant or catering service
- Meals furnished to employees as part of a teambuilding activity, such as a company picnic
- Meals that are required by federal law to be furnished to crew members of certain commercial vessels
- Meals furnished on an oil or gas platform or drilling rig located offshore or in Alaska

DOT Meals: Special 80% Allowance

There is also an exception for businesses subject to the U.S. Department of Transportation (DOT) "hours of service" limits. In 2012, the following qualified individuals can deduct 80% of meal expenses while traveling away from their tax home:

- Interstate truck operators and bus drivers who are under DOT regulations
- Air transportation workers (such as pilots, crew, dispatchers, mechanics, and control tower operators) who are under Federal Aviation Administration regulations
- Railroad employees (such as engineers, conductors, train crews, dispatchers, and control operations personnel) who are under Federal Railroad Administration regulations
- Merchant marines who are under Coast Guard regulations

Businesses are also allowed to deduct employees' meals at the 80% rate when DOT hours of service regulations apply.

Per Diem Rate for Business Travel

To ease recordkeeping requirements, a business may use the federal per diem rate as an alternative to keeping track of employees' actual expenses during business travel away from home.

Per diem is a daily allowance paid to a business's employees for lodging, meals, and incidental expenses incurred when traveling. The allowance is in lieu of paying their actual travel expenses. There is a per diem rate for combined lodging and meal costs, and a per diem rate for meal costs alone. An employer may use either per diem method for reimbursing employee travel expenses. A self-employed person can only use per diem for the meal costs. Per diem payments that are not in excess of the federal rate are not included in an employee's wages and are not taxable to the employee, if an employee submits an expense report to the employer. An expense report must show the time, place, and business purpose of the employee's travel.

The per diem rates differ based on domestic and foreign travel, and also vary by location. For example, the per diem rate in large cities like Los Angeles and New York is higher than for small cities. The IRS publishes the per diem rates every year in Publication 1542, *Per Diem Rates.* Taxpayers who choose to use the per diem rate still need to prove the time, place, and business purpose of the travel and meals.

In lieu of using the per diem rates for specific destinations, an employer may rely on simplified "high-low" rates established annually for travel within the continental United States. This method treats some cities as high-cost localities for all or part of the year, with a single per diem rate of $242 in 2012 and others as lower-cost cities with a per diem rate of $163 in 2012.[91]

Taxpayers that do not choose to use the per diem rate must keep adequate records of their travel expenses, including receipts, bills, or canceled checks. An exception is made for meals that cost under $75.

Regardless of whether the per diem rate is used or actual expenses are tracked, all travel expenses must be "ordinary and necessary" expenses incurred for business.

Entertainment Expenses: Business-Related

A business is allowed to deduct 50% of business-related entertainment expenses that are incurred for entertaining a client, customer, or employee. Once again, however, the expense must be both ordinary and necessary. It is not necessary to prove that the entertainment actually resulted in business income or other business benefit for the expense to be deductible.

Entertainment expenses that are generally not deductible are those that occur solely at a nightclub, theater, sporting event, cocktail party, or at a hunting lodge, on a fishing trip, or on a yacht.

The IRS looks at whether there is a "clear business setting" associated with the entertainment and whether there are "substantial distractions" at the location that

---

[91] The rate schedule is updated every October 1 for the start of the federal government's fiscal year. However, rates remained unchanged from January-September 2012 to October-December 2012 so the same high-low rates apply for the entire tax year.

prevent business from being conducted. If a taxpayer takes a client to a special event, he may not deduct more than the face value of the ticket, regardless of the amount paid. Then the taxpayer must apply the 50% limitation for entertainment expenses.

> **Example:** Following a day of business meetings, Erik wants to take his best two best clients to a basketball game, but the tickets are sold out. So Erik pays a scalper $390 for three tickets. The actual face value of each ticket is $52. Erik may only use the face value of the ticket as a basis for his deduction, and then he must further apply the 50% limit. Therefore, his deductible entertainment expense is $78, figured as follows:
>
> | | |
> |---|---|
> | Cost of three event tickets (face value only $52 X 3): | $156 |
> | Then, apply the 50% limit ($156 X 50%): | $78 |

There is an exception for tickets to sports events that benefit a charitable organization. A taxpayer can take into account the full cost paid for a ticket, even if it is more than the face value, if the entire net proceeds go to a qualified charity; its main purpose is to benefit the charity; and the event uses volunteers to do substantially all the event's work.

General Rules: Deductible Entertainment Expenses	
General rule	Expenses to entertain a client, customer, or employee are deductible.
Definitions	Entertainment includes any activity generally considered to provide entertainment, amusement, or recreation, and includes meals provided to a customer or client.
Tests	**Directly-related test**
	• Entertainment takes place in a clear business setting, or
	• The main purpose of entertainment is the active conduct of business, and
	• The taxpayer engages in business during the entertainment, and
	• The taxpayer has more than a general expectation of getting income or some other specific business benefit.
	Associated test
	• Entertainment is associated with the taxpayer's business, and
	• Entertainment occurs directly *before* or *after* a substantial business discussion.
Other rules	A business generally can deduct only 50% of entertainment expenses.
	A taxpayer cannot deduct expenses that are lavish or extravagant.

Recordkeeping for Travel, Entertainment & Gift Expenses

Expense	Amount	Time	Description	Business Purpose
Travel	Record of each expense for travel, lodging, and meals.	Dates for each trip and number of days spent on business.	Destination (name of city, town, etc.)	Business purpose for the expense.
Entertainment	Cost of each separate expense.	Date of entertainment.	Location of entertainment.	Business purpose for the expense.
Gifts	Cost of the gift.	Date of the gift.	Description of the gift.	Information about the recipients that shows the business relationship.
Transportation	Cost of each separate expense.	Date of the expense..	The business destination.	Business purpose for the expense.

Deductible Travel and Transportation Expenses

Taxpayers who travel away from home on business may deduct related expenses, including the cost of reaching their destination, the cost of lodging and meals, and other ordinary and necessary expenses.

Ordinarily, expenses related to use of a car, van, pickup, or panel truck for business can be deducted as transportation expenses. In order to claim a deduction for business use of a car or truck, a taxpayer must have incurred business-related costs related to one or more of the following:

- Traveling from one work location to another within the taxpayer's tax home area. (Generally, the tax home is the entire city or general area where the taxpayer's main place of business is located, regardless of where he actually lives.)[92]
- Visiting customers.
- Attending a business meeting away from the regular workplace.
- Getting from home to a temporary workplace. (A "temporary workplace" can be either within or outside the taxpayer's tax home area.)

Taxpayers are considered "traveling away from home" if their duties require them to be away from home substantially longer than an ordinary day's work and they need to sleep or rest to meet the demands of their work.

Travel business expenses incurred while away from home overnight are deductible expenses.[93] However, if a taxpayer uses his personal car while traveling away from home overnight on business, the rules for claiming car or truck expenses are the same as stated above.

---

[92] Costs related to travel between a taxpayer's home and regular place of work are commuting expenses and not deductible as business expenses.

If the travel includes some element of personal travel, the taxpayer must keep records showing how much is related to business and then figure the amount of personal travel because that portion is not deductible as a business expense.

Example: Paul flies to New Orleans on business and takes his wife with him so she can vacation there. Paul pays $190 for each airline ticket and $200 for a double hotel room. The cost of a single hotel room is $150. Paul can deduct the cost of his plane ticket and the cost of $150 for the hotel room. His wife's expenses are not deductible as a business expense.

Businesses must determine the nonbusiness portion of the expense by multiplying it by a fraction. The numerator of the fraction is the number of nonbusiness days during the travel and the denominator is the total number of days spent traveling.

Standard Mileage Rate

Most businesses may choose to use either the standard mileage rate or actual car expenses in order to figure the deduction for automobile expenses. A business owner is free to choose whichever method gives him a larger deduction.

In 2012, the standard mileage rate for business is 55.5 cents per mile. A taxpayer who chooses this standard rate may not deduct actual expenses of operating a vehicle, such as gas, oil, and insurance. Business-related parking fees and tolls may be deducted in *addition* to the standard mileage rate.

If a business chooses to use the standard mileage rate the first year an automobile is put into service, it will have to use the straight line method of depreciation if it later changes to using actual expenses.[94]

---

*Note: The standard mileage rate can now be used by cars for hire, such as a taxi. This law changed in 2011.

A business is prohibited from using the standard mileage rate if it:

- Operates five or more cars at the same time
- Claims a depreciation deduction using any method other than straight line
- Claims a section 179 deduction on a car
- Claims the special depreciation allowance on the car
- Claims actual car expenses for a car that was leased

The standard mileage rate cannot be used by C corporations. Only self-employed individuals, including partners in a partnership, can use the standard mileage rate. However, a C corporation can choose to reimburse an employee shareholder for mileage under an accountable plan.

Actual Vehicle Expenses

Actual vehicle expenses include the costs of the following items:

- Depreciation
- Lease payments
- Registration
- Garage rent

---

[94] Revenue procedure 2004-64.

- Repairs and maintenance
- Gas, oil, and tires
- Insurance, parking fees, and tolls

If business use of the vehicle is less than 100%, expenses must be allocated between business and personal use. Only the business use percentage of the automobile expense is deductible.

> **Example:** Brandon uses a delivery van in his landscaping business. He has no other car, so the van is used for personal travel on the weekends. Brandon chooses to deduct actual costs, rather than the standard mileage rate. Based on his records, Brandon's total automobile expenses in 2012 are $6,252, which includes the cost of diesel fuel, oil changes, tire replacement, and repairs. Brandon uses the vehicle 75% for business, so his allowable auto expense deduction using the actual expense method is $4,689 ($6,252 x 75%).

A business may also deduct the amounts reimbursed to employees for car and truck expenses.

Recordkeeping Requirements for Auto Expenses

To claim the standard mileage rate, a taxpayer needs to keep records that identify the vehicle and prove ownership or a lease, plus a daily log showing miles traveled, destination, and business purpose.

For actual expenses, a mileage log is also necessary, because it helps establish business use percentage.

For depreciation purposes, a taxpayer needs to show the original cost of the vehicle and any improvements as well as the date it was placed in service.

Business Rent Expense

Businesses may deduct expenses for renting property. Rented property includes real estate, machinery, and other items that an entity uses to conduct business. The cost of acquiring a lease is not considered rent and must be amortized.

Generally, rent paid in a trade or business is deductible in the year paid or accrued. If a taxpayer pays rent in advance, he can deduct only the amount that applies to his use of the rented property during the tax year. The rest of the payment can be deducted only over the period to which it applies.

Expenses applicable to a property that is used for multiple activities or purposes must be allocated among each activity.

> **Example:** The Barista Coffee Corporation owns a large building. It uses half of the building for its own manufacturing activity and rents the other half to tenants who run various unrelated businesses. One half of the corporation's building expenses (such as utilities, mortgage expense, and property tax) would be allocated to the rental activity, and the other portion of the building expenses would be allocated to Barista's regular business and manufacturing activity.

Partial Business Use of Property

If a taxpayer has both business and personal use of rented property, he may only deduct the amount actually used for business. To compute the business percentage, the taxpayer must compare the size of the property used for business to the entire size of the property. The resulting percentage is used to figure the business portion of the rent expense. Two commonly used methods for figuring the percentage are:

- Divide the area (length multiplied by width) used for business by the total area of the property.
- If rooms are approximately the same size, divide the number of rooms used for business by the total number of rooms.

> **Example:** Ainsley rents a business office to use as a studio for painting and also to run her tutoring business. Her total rental payments for the year are $11,000. The office is 1,000 square feet; she uses 800 square feet for the tutoring business and the remaining 200 square feet for her painting area. Therefore, she uses the office 80% for her business and 20% for personal purposes. The deductible portion of the rent expense is $8,800 (80% × $11,000).

Home Office Deduction

Taxpayers may be able to deduct certain expenses for the part of their home used for business, if the space is used regularly and exclusively as:

- The principal place of business, and/or
- Exclusively as the place to meet with patients, clients, or customers in the normal course of business; or
- In direct connection with the business, if the taxpayer uses a separate structure that is not attached to the home.

Because of the exclusive use rule, taxpayers are not allowed to deduct business expenses for any part of their home that is used for both personal and business purposes.

Self-employed people must fill out a special form to claim the home office deduction. Schedule C businesses must complete Form 8829, *Expenses for Business Use of Your Home,* and then transfer the total to their Schedule C when they file their income tax return (Form 1040).

Taxes as an Expense

Businesses deduct taxes in the year they pay them, regardless of what method of accounting the business uses. Under the accrual method, a business can deduct a tax before it pays it, if it meets the exception for recurring items discussed earlier in this unit.

Real Estate Taxes

In order for real estate taxes to be deductible, the taxing authority must calculate the property taxes on the assessed value of the real estate. If the property is sold, the deductible portion of the real estate taxes must be allocated between the buyer and the seller according to the number of days in the property tax year that each owned the property. The seller is treated as paying the taxes up to but not including the date of sale. The buyer is treated as paying the taxes beginning with the date of sale.

Not Deductible: Taxes for Local Improvements

Businesses cannot deduct taxes charged for local benefits and improvements that tend to increase the value of property. These include assessments for streets, sidewalks, water mains, sewer lines, and public parking facilities. A business must increase the basis of its property by the amount of the assessment.

A business may deduct taxes for local benefits if the taxes are for maintenance, repairs, or interest charges related to those benefits.

Example: Lawrence owns a business office on Main Street. In 2012, the city charges an assessment of $4,000 to each business on Main Street to improve the sidewalks. Lawrence cannot deduct this assessment as a current business expense. Instead, he must increase the basis of his property by the amount of the assessment.

Example: Waterfront City converts a downtown area into an enclosed pedestrian mall built to improve local businesses. The city assesses the full cost of construction, financed with 10-year bonds, against the affected properties. The city pays the principal and interest with the annual payments made by the property owners. The assessments for construction costs are not deductible as taxes or as business expenses, but are depreciable capital expenses. The part of the payment used to pay the interest charges on the bonds is deductible as taxes.

Taxes: Special Rules

Federal income taxes are never deductible. However, corporations and partnerships can deduct state and local income taxes imposed on them as business expenses. A self-employed individual who reports income on Schedule C may deduct state and local income taxes only as an itemized deduction on Schedule A (Form 1040).

Example: Reiner Company is a calendar-year C corporation incorporated in Iowa. Iowa imposes a 10% state tax on Reiner's corporate earnings. In 2012, Reiner pays $12,000 in state income tax to Iowa. This state tax would be deductible as a business expense on the corporation's federal tax return **(Form 1120).**

Interest charged on unpaid income tax assessed on individual income tax returns is not a business deduction, even when the tax due is related to income from a trade or business. This interest should be treated as a business deduction only in figuring a net operating loss deduction. Penalties on underpaid deficiencies and underpaid estimated tax are not deductible as interest.

Employment Taxes

A business's deduction for wages paid is not reduced by the Social Security, Medicare, and income taxes it is required to withhold from employees. Businesses can deduct the employment taxes they must pay from their own funds as taxes.

> **Example:** A partnership pays its secretary $18,000 a year. However, after withholding various taxes, the employee receives $14,500. The business pays an additional $1,500 in employment taxes. The full $18,000 should be deducted as wages. The business can also deduct the $1,500 (employer's portion of the FICA) paid as taxes.

Employers may also deduct any required state unemployment taxes or state disability fund taxes.

Self-Employment Tax

Self-employed individuals can deduct one-half of their self-employment tax as a business expense in figuring adjusted gross income. This deduction only affects income tax. It does not affect net earnings from self-employment or self-employment tax.

Other Deductible Taxes

1. **Franchise taxes:** Corporate franchise taxes are deductible as a business expense.
2. **Personal property tax:** Taxes imposed by a state or local government on personal property used in a taxpayer's trade or business are deductible.
3. **Occupational taxes:** A business may deduct any tax imposed by a state or local government on personal property used in its trade or business.
4. **Excise taxes:** Excise taxes that are ordinary and necessary expenses of carrying on a trade or business are deductible. Excise taxes are taxes paid when purchases are made on a specific good, such as gasoline, or activity, such as highway usage by trucks. Under the Affordable Care Act, indoor tanning salons are subject to a 10% excise tax, which is a deductible business expense.

Insurance Expenses

The following types of business-related insurance premiums are deductible as business expenses:

-   Insurance that covers fire, storm, theft, accident, or similar losses
-   Credit insurance that covers losses from business bad debts
-   Group hospitalization and medical insurance for employees, including long-term care insurance[95]
-   Liability insurance
-   Malpractice insurance
-   Workers' compensation insurance[96]
-   Contributions to a state unemployment insurance fund
-   Business interruption insurance that pays if a business is shut down due to a fire or other cause
-   Car insurance that covers vehicles used in a business (not deductible if a business uses the standard mileage rate to figure car expenses)

---

[95] If a partnership pays accident and health insurance premiums for its partners, it generally can deduct them as guaranteed payments to partners. If an S corporation pays accident and health insurance premiums for its more than-2% shareholder-employees, it generally can deduct them but must also include them in the shareholder's wages subject to federal income tax withholding.

[96] The same rules apply as detailed in the above footnote.

- Group-term life insurance for employees

If a cash-basis business pays an insurance premium for years in advance, it can only deduct the portion that applies to the current tax year, regardless of whether it prepaid the entire amount. The 12-month rule applies for cash-basis taxpayers.[97]

Example: Rick's Racing Bikes is a cash-basis business on a calendar year. On May 1, 2012, Rick's pays $2,000 for business insurance covering one year. The insurance policy begins May 1, 2012 and ends May 30, 2013. The 12-month rule applies. Rick's Racing Bikes may deduct the full $2,000 in 2012. The benefit does not extend beyond 12 months after the right to receive the benefit begins.

Example: Luxe Chocolate Corporation is a cash-basis business on a calendar year. On October 1, 2012, Luxe Chocolates pays $3,600 in advance for business insurance policy covering three years. The policy coverage begins October 1, 2012 and ends September 30, 2015. Since the advance payment covers more than 12 months (36 months), a portion of the $3,600 must be deducted ratably over the three-year period. To figure the monthly premium amount, the policy cost is divided by the coverage period: ($3,600 ÷ 36 = $100). The months of coverage in each tax year is then multiplied by the monthly premium:

     2012: deduction $300 ($3,600 ÷ 36 x 3).

     2013: deduction $1,200: ($3,600 ÷ 36 x 12).

     2014: deduction $1,200 ($3,600 ÷ 36 x 12).

     2015: deduction $900 ($3,600 ÷ 36 x 9).

Self-Employed Health Insurance Deduction

A self-employed individual may be able to deduct premiums paid for medical and dental insurance and qualified long-term care insurance for himself, his spouse, and his dependents. To qualify, a taxpayer must have a net profit reported on his Schedule C (Form 1040). He cannot take the deduction for any month he was eligible to participate in any employer-subsidized health plan (including one that his spouse was eligible for), even if he or his spouse did not actually participate in the plan.

As a result of the Affordable Care Act,[98] employees may now elect to include children under 27 years of age under their health coverage. The child does not have to be a dependent in order to qualify for this expanded benefit.

Interest Expense

Entities can deduct interest paid or accrued during the tax year on debts related to the business. If the interest relates to a business expense or purchase, it is deductible. It does not matter what type of property secures the loan. A business deducts interest as follows:

- **Cash method:** A business may deduct only the actual interest paid during the tax year, and cannot deduct a promissory note because it is a promise to pay and not an actual payment.

---

[97] Under the 12-month rule, a cash-based business is not required to capitalize amounts paid that do not extend beyond the earlier of the following: (1) 12 months after the benefit begins, or (2) The end of the tax year after the tax year in which payment is made.

[98] The *Affordable Care Act* was enacted on March 23, 2010.

- **Accrual method:** A business may deduct only interest that has accrued during the tax year.

A taxpayer cannot receive a tax deduction by paying interest early. Interest paid in advance can only be deducted in the tax year in which it is due. If a business uses the accrual method, it cannot deduct interest owed to a related person who uses the cash method until payment is made and the interest is includable in the gross income of that person.

Business Bad Debts

Most business bad debts are a result of credit sales to customers for goods or services that have been sold but not yet paid for. These are recorded in a business's books as either accounts receivable or notes receivable. If, after a reasonable amount of time a business has tried to collect the amount due but is unable to do so, the uncollectible part becomes a business bad debt.

A debt becomes worthless when there is no longer any chance the amount owed will be paid. A business does not have to wait for the debt to be due or to obtain a court judgment to show the debt is uncollectible.

A business bad debt is a loss from the worthlessness of a debt that was either:

- Created or acquired in the trade or business, or
- Closely related to a taxpayer's trade or business when it became partly or totally worthless.

To be considered closely related to a taxpayer's trade or business, the primary motive for incurring the debt must be business related.

A taxpayer may claim a business bad debt deduction only if the amount owed was previously included in his gross income. If a business loans money to a client, supplier, employee, or distributor for a business reason and the loan later becomes worthless, the business may deduct the loan as a bad debt. The loan must have a genuine business purpose in order for this treatment to qualify.

Example: Carol is an accrual-based taxpayer who owns an eyeglass manufacturing company. One of her salesmen, Bryson, loses all his samples and asks Carol for a loan to replace them. Carol loans Bryson $3,000 to replace his eyeglass samples and sample bags. Bryson later quits his job without repaying the debt. Carol has a business-related bad debt that she may deduct as a business expense.

If a taxpayer receives property in partial settlement of a debt, the debt should be reduced by the property's FMV, which becomes the property's basis. The remaining debt can be deducted as a bad debt when and if it becomes worthless.

Sometimes an entity will recover an old debt that was previously written off as worthless. If a business recovers a bad debt that was deducted in a prior year, the recovered portion must be included as income in the current year tax return. There is no need to amend prior year tax returns.

Business Start-up and Organizational Costs

Most of the costs associated with starting a business must be treated as capital expenditures. However, businesses are allowed to deduct a limited amount of start-up and organizational costs. In 2012, businesses may deduct $5,000 in start-up expenses. If expenses exceed $50,000, there is a dollar-for-dollar reduction until the deduction is eliminated.

Any remaining start-up expenses must be amortized ratably over 180 months (15 years) on Form 4562, *Depreciation and Amortization*. Start-up costs can be deducted in the tax year they are incurred, and the amortization period starts with the month the taxpayer begins operating the business.

Example: Bronco Corporation has start-up expenses of $51,000 in 2012. Bronco is $1,000 over the $50,000 threshold so it must reduce its deduction for start-up expenses by the amount that it is over the threshold. Bronco can deduct $4,000 of its start-up expenses: $5,000 allowable deduction, minus the excess $1,000. The remaining amount of start-up expenses, $47,000 ($51,000 - $4,000 allowable expense) must be amortized over 180 months.

Example: Clean Water Inc. opened for business on November 1, 2012. Prior to opening, the company incurred $21,200 in start-up expenses for advertising and manager training. Since Clean Water had less than $50,000 of start-up costs, the company is allowed to deduct the full $5,000, *plus* an additional $360 in amortization on its 2012 tax return [($21,200 - $5,000)/180 x 2 (two months, November and December)].

If a taxpayer completely disposes of a business before the end of the amortization period, he can deduct all the deferred start-up costs. However, the business can deduct these deferred start-up costs only to the extent they qualify as a loss.

Qualifying Start-up Costs

Business start-up costs are the expenses incurred before a business actually begins operations, and include any amounts paid in anticipation of the activity becoming an active trade or business.

Start-up costs are amounts paid or incurred for:
- Creating an active trade or business; or
- Investigating the creation or acquisition of an active trade or business.

Start-up costs may include:
- An analysis or survey of potential markets
- Advertisements for the opening of the business
- Salaries and wages for employees who are being trained and their instructors
- Travel and other necessary costs for securing prospective distributors, suppliers, or customers
- Salaries and fees for executives and consultants, or for similar professional services

For costs in excess of $5,000, the amortization period starts with the month the business begins operating its active trade or business.

> **Example:** Moonlight Corporation received its corporate charter on September 12, 2012. The company paid $15,500 in Internet and television advertising; $2,000 in training for employees; and $4,000 in consultant fees, all incurred before opening for business. Moonlight opens for business on January 8, 2013. The company can elect to expense $5,000 as a start-up cost in the 2012 tax year. It can then amortize the remaining $16,500 beginning in January 2013.

Start-up costs do not include deductible interest, taxes, or research and experimental costs.

Qualifying Organizational Costs

The costs of organizing a corporation or partnership are also deductible up to $5,000 in 2012, reduced by the excess of cost over $50,000. Just as with start-up costs, any remaining organizational costs must be amortized ratably over 180 months.

To qualify as an organizational cost it must be an expense:

- For the creation of the business
- Chargeable to a capital account
- For partnerships, the cost must be incurred by the due date of the tax return (excluding extensions) for the year business begins
- For corporations, the cost must be incurred before the end of the first tax year in which the corporation is in business

Examples of qualifying organizational costs include:

- The cost of temporary directors
- The cost of organizational meetings
- Filing fees for partnerships
- State incorporation fees for corporations
- Legal and accounting fees for setting up the business

Nonqualifying Organizational Costs

The following items are not qualifying organizational costs, and cannot be amortized:

- Costs for issuing and selling stock or securities, such as commissions, professional fees, and printing costs
- Costs associated with the acquisition of assets to the corporation or partnership
- The cost of admitting or removing partners, other than at the time the partnership is first organized
- The cost of making a contract concerning the operation of the partnership trade or business including a contract between a partner and the partnership
- The cost of issuing and marketing partnership interests such as brokerage, registration, and legal fees and printing costs

Start-up and organizational expenses are claimed as an "other deduction" on business returns (such as Form 1065 for partnerships or Form 1120 for corporations).

Self-employed taxpayers claim start-up expenses as an "other expense" on Schedule C or Schedule F.

If a business is completely dissolved, disposed of, or sold at a later date, the business may deduct any remaining deferred organizational or start-up costs on the final tax return.

Example: Rainbow Party Products formed five years ago. In 2012, the corporation experienced financial difficulties and eventually closed. At the time of dissolution, the corporation had $14,000 in remaining unamortized start-up and organizational costs. These costs are deductible immediately on the corporation's final tax return.

If a business never materializes after claiming start-up or organizational costs, the costs are treated differently depending on the entity type. In the case of a corporation, all investigatory costs are deductible as a business loss. In the case of an individual, the costs incurred before making a decision to acquire a business are considered personal costs and are generally not deductible.

Charitable Contributions by Businesses

Among business entities, only C corporations are permitted to deduct charitable deductions. The deduction is limited to 10% of taxable income, which is explained in detail in Unit 14, *Corporate Transactions*. Self-employed taxpayers may not deduct charitable contributions as business expenses, only as expenses on Schedule A if they itemize deductions.

Miscellaneous Business Expenses

There are many other types of expenses that are deductible for a business. Deductibility often depends on the facts and circumstances of the case. Some expenses that would be inappropriate in one line of business may be completely acceptable in another. The following are some common expenses businesses are allowed to deduct:

- Advertising
- Credit card convenience fees
- Certain franchise or trademark fees
- Education and training for employees
- Internet-related expenses, such as domain registration fees
- Interview expense allowances for job candidates
- Outplacement services provided to employees
- Legal and accounting fees directly related to operating a business
- Tax preparation fees for business returns
- License and regulatory fees paid annually to state or local governments
- Penalties paid for late performance or nonperformance of a contract
- Repairs to business property, including the cost of labor and supplies
- Subscriptions and memberships to trade magazines and professional organizations
- Supplies and materials consumed and used during year
- Utilities, including heat, lights, power, telephone service, and water and sewage

Costs That Can be Deducted or Capitalized

There are certain costs that businesses may choose to deduct or capitalize. There are specific rules about the special circumstances in which each may be deducted and how to amortize additional amounts. The following are costs that are generally capital expenses but that a business may elect to deduct:

- Research and experimental costs
- Carrying charges that a taxpayer pays to carry or develop real or personal property
- Certain intangible drilling costs
- Certain domestic exploration and development costs for mines or other natural deposits (other than oil or gas wells)
- Circulation costs for publishers of newspapers and magazines
- Certain environmental cleanup costs
- Qualified expenses in federally-declared disaster areas, such as control or abatement of hazardous substances; removal of debris or demolition of structures; or repair of business-related property damaged in a disaster area
- Reforestation costs up to $10,000
- Film and television production costs (only through 2012)

Nondeductible Expenses

The IRS does not allow the following types of expenses as business deductions:

- Political contributions, including indirect contributions such as advertising in a convention program of a political party. This includes lobbying expenses
- Dues for country clubs, golf and athletic clubs, and hotel and airline clubs, even if the club is used for business activity
- Penalties and fines paid to any governmental agency for breaking the law, such as parking tickets or fines for violating local zoning codes
- Legal and professional fees for work of a personal nature, such as drafting a will or damages arising from a personal injury; legal fees paid to acquire business assets (these are added to the basis of a property)

Unit 5: Questions

1. Alexa is a self-employed accountant who reports income and loss on Schedule C. She goes to a continuing education seminar out-of-state. She pays $400 for the seminar and $35 for a train ticket to the event. She also incurs $26 in restaurant meal expenses and $10 in taxi fare on the way to the restaurant. What is her deductible expense for this event?

A. $400.
B. $435.
C. $458.
D. $465.

The answer is C. The answer is $458 ($400 + $35 + $10 + [26 x 50%]). Her meal expenses are subject to the 50% rule, but the taxi fare is fully deductible. The cost of the train ticket and the seminar are also fully deductible. ###

2. In 2012, Helton Partnership, a cash-basis partnership, borrowed $50,000 to purchase machinery. $2,500 in interest on the loan was due in December 2012. Rather than pay the interest, the partnership refinanced the loan and the interest into a new loan amount totaling $53,800: the original loan amount plus interest and an additional $1,300 in loan origination fees. The first payment on the new loan was due January 29, 2013. How much interest is deductible?

A. $0.
B. $2,500.
C. $2,800.
D. $3,800.

The answer is A. The partnership is on the cash basis; therefore, it can only deduct interest actually paid during the year. Since the partnership did not actually pay any interest, it does not have a deductible expense. The fact that the loan was refinanced has no bearing on the deductibility of the interest in the current tax year. ###

3. Norman is the sole proprietor of McGowan Trucking Company. He is subject to the Department of Transportation rules for hours of service. In 2012, what percentage of his meals is he able to deduct while working as an interstate truck driver?

A. 50%.
B. 75%.
C. 80%.
D. 100%.

The answer is C. A taxpayer who is subject to the Department of Transportation's hours of service may deduct a larger percentage of his meal expenses when traveling away from his tax home. For the DOT hours of service limits, multiply meal expenses incurred while away from home on business by 80% in 2012. ###

4. Kimberly is a sole proprietor and files a Schedule C. How should she report the $2,000 in charitable contributions she made on behalf of her business in 2012?

A. The contributions may be deducted on Schedule A as an itemized deduction.
B. The contributions may be deducted on Schedule C as a business deduction.
C. The contributions may not be deducted.
D. Up to 10% of the taxpayer's charitable contributions may be deducted on Schedule C. The remaining amount must be carried over to the next taxable year.

The answer is A. Self-employed taxpayers may deduct these contributions on their Schedule A. The contributions cannot be deducted as a business expense on Schedule C. Only C corporations may deduct charitable contributions as a business expense. ###

5. Which of the following tests is not required in order for entertainment expenses to be deductible?

A. Business was engaged in during the entertainment event.
B. The main purpose of the entertainment was the conduct of business.
C. There was more than just the general expectation of business benefit.
D. The entertainment resulted in profit for the business.

The answer is D. The taxpayer is not required to prove that the entertainment event actually produced a profit. The taxpayer must meet all the following tests in order to deduct an entertainment expense:

• Business was engaged in during the entertainment event.
• The main purpose of the entertainment was the conduct of business.
• There was more than just the general expectation of business benefit. ###

6. Delia, a self-employed real estate agent, traveled to a business convention by train. The train ticket cost $100. At the convention, she purchased a new computer that cost $2,100 for use in her business. She also purchased a computer game for $50. Delia spent $80 on meals and $90 on her hotel room during the convention. How much is deductible as a current business expense?

A. $190.
B. $230.
C. $2,280.
D. $2,430.

The answer is B. Delia may deduct the cost of her hotel room, one-half of her meals expense, and her train ticket to attend the convention.

$100 + $90 + (80 X 50%) = $230

The cost of the computer game is a personal expense and not deductible. The cost of the computer is not a current expense, but instead must be capitalized and depreciated over its useful life. ###

7. Mountain Suppliers made a business loan to Sugarhill Corporation, a supplier, in the amount of $10,000. After paying $2,000, Sugarhill Corporation defaults, and the debt becomes worthless. How much may Mountain Suppliers deduct as a business bad debt?

A. $0.
B. $2,000.
C. $8,000.
D. $10,000.

The answer is C. Loans to a client, customer, employee, or distributor for a business reason can be deducted as a business bad debt. The amount of the loan, minus what was repaid, is the deduction on Mountain Supplier's tax return: $10,000-$2,000 = $8,000. ####

8. Marion owns a shoe repair shop. In 2012, she had the following income and expenses:

Repairs to shop floor	$1,000
City tax on her business assets	$2,000
Assessment for sidewalks	$5,800
Utilities for her store	$1,800

What is the tax treatment of the above expenditures?

A. Deduct repairs, property tax, and utilities as expenses. The assessment must be added to the basis of the property and depreciated.
B. All the above expenses are currently deductible.
C. The property tax must be deducted on Schedule A, and the rest of the expenses may be deducted as business expenses on Schedule C.
D. Only the utilities and repairs may be deducted.

The answer is A. The repairs, property tax, and utilities are all deductible as current expenses. The property tax is deductible as a business expense on Schedule C (rather than on Schedule A) because it is assessed on business property. Assessments for streets, sidewalks, sewer lines, and other public services generally add value to the property and must be added to the basis of the property rather than deducted as current expenses. ###

9. A corporation may deduct all the following taxes except:

A. Federal income taxes.
B. State income taxes.
C. Local income taxes.
D. Corporate franchise taxes.

The answer is A. Federal income taxes are never deductible as a business expense, no matter what the entity. Penalties assessed on delinquent taxes are also never deductible. ###

10. Bob owns Jackpot Pawn Shop. He makes a business loan to a client in the amount of $5,000. Bob also loans his brother $1,000 so he can buy a car. His brother, Keith, used to work sporadically at the shop as an employee. Both of the loans are now uncollectible. How much can Bob deduct as a business bad-debt expense?

A. $1,000.
B. $4,000.
C. $5,000.
D. $6,000.

The answer is C. Only the loan to the client would be deductible as a business bad-debt expense. A loan to a client, customer, employee, or distributor for a business reason can be deducted as a business bad debt. Since Keith is a related person and not a regular employee and the loan was for personal reasons, Bob may not deduct the loan to his brother as a business bad debt. ###

11. On January 1, 2012, Galveston Seafood Partnership, a calendar-year, cash-basis business, purchases a fire insurance policy for its business. The policy is for three years and is required to be paid in full the first year. Galveston Seafood pays $1,800 for the policy. How much of this policy is deductible in 2012?

A. $0.
B. $600.
C. $800.
D. $1,800.

The answer is B. If a cash-basis business pays an insurance premium in advance, it can only deduct the portion that applies to the current tax year, regardless of whether it prepaid the entire amount. Therefore, Galveston Seafood may only deduct the part of the policy that applies to the current year, figured as follows: $1,800 ÷ 36 (months) =$50 per month; $50 X 12 = $600, the current year insurance expense. The exception to this is the "12 month rule," in which the amounts paid do not create a benefit that does not exceed the earlier of:

•12 months after the first date on which the business receives the benefit; or
•The end of the tax year following the tax year in which payment is made. ###

12. Maddie rents a small storage unit for her business on February 1, 2012. She is given a discount if she pays the full amount of the lease upfront, which is $1,620 for a three-year lease. What is the amount of Maddie's 2012 deductible expense for leasing the storage unit?

A. $495.
B. $540.
C. $560.
D. $1,620.

The answer is A. If a taxpayer pays for rent or a lease in advance, only the amount that applies to the current year is deductible. The balance must be deducted over the period over which it applies. The answer is figured as follows:

Deductible lease expense for 2012:

$1,620 / 36 (months) = $45 per month
$45 X 11 months (February-December 2012) = $495. ###

13. Lily owns a dress shop. In 2009, she correctly deducted a $10,000 business bad debt after a fabric supplier defaulted on a loan. Then, in 2012, the fabric supplier wishes to do business with Lily again and repays $9,000 of the loan that was once in default. How must Lily report this payment?

A. Lily must amend her 2009 tax return to reflect the incorrect $10,000 bad debt deduction.
B. Lily must reflect this recovery of $9,000 as income in 2012.
C. Lily must reflect income of $9,000 in 2009 by going back and filing an amendment for that year.
D. Lily must amend her 2009 tax return, but she may still reflect $1,000 in bad debt deduction.

The answer is B. Lily is not required to amend her prior year return to report the recovery of the bad debt. Sometimes a business will recover an old debt that was previously written off as worthless. Since Lily recovers a bad debt that was deducted properly in a prior year, she must include only the recovered portion as income in her current year tax return. ###

14. Mike borrowed $100,000 to purchase a machine for his business. The machine cost $90,000. The rest of the money went into Mike's business account, and he purchased a jet ski with the money later in the year. However, the loan was secured entirely by his business assets. Which of the following statements is true?

A. Mike cannot purchase personal items with a business loan; therefore, none of the interest is deductible.
B. All of the interest is deductible, because it is secured by his business assets.
C. Only the amount of interest allocated to the business machine is deductible.
D. None of the answers is correct.

The answer is C. Generally, interest on a business loan is fully deductible. However, debt incurred for personal reasons is not deductible as a business expense. The amount of interest allocated to the business machine is deductible, but not the amount for the jet ski, which is a personal expense. ###

430

15. Brady owns Super Sweets Company. He gives business gifts to one of his best customers, as follows:

•Glass display for Super Sweets: $500
•Fruit basket: $50
•20 imprinted pens: $35
•Postage for the fruit basket: $20

How much can Brady deduct on his tax return as a business gift expense?

A. $25.
B. $525.
C. $580.
D. $605.

The answer is C. There is a $25 limit per person per tax year for business gifts; however, there are exceptions to this rule. Incidental costs, such as packaging, insuring, and mailing, are not included in determining the cost of a gift for purposes of the $25 limit. The following items are also not considered gifts for purposes of the $25 limit:

•An item that costs $4 or less with the business name imprinted on it
•Signs, display racks, or other promotional material to be used on the business premises of the recipient

Therefore, the business may deduct $580, figured as follows:

1. Glass display $500
2. Fruit basket $25 (only $25 is deductible as a gift expense)
3. 20 imprinted pens $35
4. Postage for basket $20
($500 + $25 + $35 + $20) = $580.

###

16. Garrett operates his printing business out of rented office space. He uses a truck to deliver completed jobs to customers. Which of the following statements is not correct?

A. Garrett can deduct the cost of round-trip transportation between customers and his print shop.
B. Garrett can deduct traveling costs between his home and his main workplace.
C. Garrett can deduct the cost of mileage to deliver completed jobs to the post office to mail.
D. Garrett can deduct the costs to travel to his customers who are disabled and cannot come to his shop.

The answer is B. A taxpayer cannot deduct the costs of driving a car between his home and his main workplace. These costs are personal commuting expenses. The costs of driving to meet with clients or do other business-related errands are deductible.
###

17. Carrie is the sole proprietor of a flower shop. She drove her van 20,000 miles during the year: 16,000 miles to deliver flowers to customers and 4,000 miles for personal use. Carrie wants to use actual costs instead of the standard mileage rate. What is Carrie's percentage of business use for the van?

A. 10%.
B. 20%.
C. 80%.
D. 90%.

The answer is C. Carrie can claim only 80% (16,000 ÷ 20,000) of the cost of operating her van as a business expense. She cannot count the personal miles and therefore must prorate the mileage to reflect her percentage of business use. ###

18. The Castellano Partnership paid the following penalties in 2012. Which are deductible?

A. A penalty paid to the county for violating construction regulations.
B. A penalty imposed by the IRS for late filing of a Form 1065 partnership return.
C. A penalty paid to the city for violating its sign ordinance.
D. A penalty for late performance of a contract.

The answer is D. Penalties paid for the late performance or non-performance of a contract are deductible. Penalties or fines paid to any government entity because of a violation of law are not deductible. ###

19. Which of the following costs qualify as business start-up costs?

A. State and local taxes.
B. Research and experimental costs.
C. A survey of potential markets.
D. Both B and C.

The answer is C. A business may deduct up to $5,000 in start-up costs in 2012. Start-up costs are costs incurred in creating an active trade or business or investigating the creation or acquisition of an active trade or business. Start-up costs include amounts paid for:
•An analysis or survey of potential markets, products, and labor supply
•Advertisements for the opening of the business
•Salaries and wages for training employees
•Salaries and fees for executives and consultants.
The other costs listed are not qualifying start-up costs. ###

20. Actual car expenses include the costs of the following items except:

A. Depreciation.
B. Lease payments.
C. Mileage.
D. Registration.

The answer is C. A taxpayer may choose to take the standard mileage rate or actual expenses. A taxpayer may not take both. If a taxpayer does not choose to use the standard mileage rate, he may deduct actual car or truck expenses. ###

21. Monique opens a bakery on October 16, 2012. Before the business opens, she had $53,000 in start-up expenses. How much may she deduct in start-up costs for 2012?

A. $0.
B. $3,000.
C. $5,000.
D. $2,850.

The answer is D. Because Monique's expenses exceed $50,000, she must reduce the initial year deduction by $1 for every $1 over $50,000. Thus, the $5,000 start-up costs deduction is reduced to $2,000. She figures the amortization on $51,000 ($53,000 - $2,000.) Her monthly amortization amount is $283 ($51,000 ÷ 180), so her first year amortization deduction is $850 ($283 X 3) for the three months her business is open. Her total start-up expense deduction for 2012 is $2,850. ###

22. Under the accrual method, a taxpayer generally deducts or capitalizes business expenses when the all-events test has been met and _____ has occurred.

A. The 12-month rule.
B. The recurring items exception.
C. Economic performance.
D. All of the above.

The answer is C. Economic performance occurs as the property or services are provided or the property is used. ###

23. All of the following statements are correct regarding the deductibility of business expenses except:

A. If an expense is included in the cost of goods sold, it must be deducted as a business expense.
B. Only some expenses may be deducted; others must be capitalized.
C. An expense does not have to be indispensable in order to be considered necessary.
D. Personal, family, and living expenses cannot be deducted as business expenses.

The answer is A. If an expense has already been included in the cost of goods sold, it cannot be deducted again as a business expense. All of the other statements are correct. ###

24. In December 2012, Nicholas travels to an industry meeting in San Francisco. His company uses the high-low method of per diem rates, and San Francisco is designated a high cost city with a rate of $242 a day. Which of the following statements is correct?

A. Nicholas does not need to submit an expense report if his company is using the per diem method for reimbursements.
B. Nicholas will be taxed on the $242 per diem reimbursement his company gives him.
C. The $242 rate only covers lodging and not meals.
D. Per diem rates are designed for the convenience of businesses, since employers do not have to keep track of and pay the actual travel expenses for their employees.

The answer is D. Per diem rates make reimbursing business travel easier for businesses. They are in lieu of employers paying the actual travel expenses of employees. Each of the other statements is incorrect. ###

25. For entertainment expenses to be deductible, the directly-related and _____ tests must be met.

A. Substantial.
B. Associated.
C. Profitability.
D. All of the above.

The answer is B. In addition to the directly-related test, deductible entertainment expenses must meet the associated test, meaning the entertainment is associated with the taxpayer's business and the entertainment occurs directly before or after a substantial business discussion. ###

26. Which of the following costs would qualify as business organizational costs?

A. Costs for issuing and selling stock in the new company.
B. State and local taxes.
C. Legal fees to draw up contracts for new partners.
D. State incorporation fees.

The answer is D. The costs of organizing a corporation or partnership are deductible up to $5,000 in 2012, reduced by the excess of cost over $50,000. Any remaining organizational costs must be amortized ratably over 180 months. Expenses must be for the creation of the business, and include the cost of temporary directors, organizational meetings, filing fees for partnerships, and state incorporation fees for corporations. Legal and accounting fees for setting up the business are allowable expenses, but costs of making partnership contracts are not. Printing expenses and other costs related to issuing stock or securities in the new company, also do not qualify as organizational costs. ###

27. In all of the following situations, a business is prohibited from using the standard mileage rate except:

A. If it is a C corporation.
B. If it deducts expenses for gas, oil, and insurance.
C. If it operates a fleet of four cars.
D. If it claims a section 179 deduction on a car.

The answer is C. A business is allowed to use the standard mileage if it operates a fleet of four cars. If it operates five or more cars at the same time, it is prohibited from using the standard mileage rate, which in 2012 is 55.5 cents per mile. ##

28. Leonora is a sole proprietor who is figuring her business deductions for 2012. What is the total amount she may deduct on her Schedule C?

• Bad debt from a bankrupt client: $350
• Business website charges: $240
• Electricity, gas, and water for her home office (400/1,600 square feet is business use): $1,200
• Continuing education seminars: $850
• Subscription to professional journals: $200
• Credit card convenience fees for her business: $150
• Health club dues: $600
• Bookkeeping for her business: $300
• Salvation Army donation: $150
• Health insurance for herself: $4,800
• Business interruption insurance: $300
• Trip to state capital to lobby for less regulation: $800

A. $2,690.
B. $7,490.
C. $8,290.
D. $8,390.

The answer is B. All the expenses are legitimate business deductions except for the health club dues, the charitable donation, and the lobbying trip to the state capital. Leonora must allocate the business portion of her utilities' expense, which is $300 (one-quarter business usage of $1,200.) Thus, the answer is figured as follows: $250 + $240 + $300 + $850 + $200 + $150 + $300 + $4,800 + $300 = $7,490. ###

Unit 6: Employer-Provided Fringe Benefits

> **More Reading:**
> Publication 15, *Employer's Tax Guide*
> Publication 15-A, *Employer's Supplemental Tax Guide*
> Publication 15-B, *Employer's Tax Guide to Fringe Benefits*

Fringe Benefits for Employees

A fringe benefit is a form of pay to employees for the performance of services. Some fringe benefits are taxable to the employee, and some are not. The IRS position is that any fringe benefit provided to employees is taxable and must be included in the recipient's pay *unless* the law specifically excludes it.

For Part 2 of the EA exam, you must understand how these benefits are treated from the employer's perspective. In this unit, we review the main types of fringe benefits employers offer their employees.

Taxable Fringe Benefits

An employer must include in a recipient's pay the amount by which the value of a fringe benefit is more than the sum of the following amounts:

- Any amount the law excludes from pay
- Any amount the recipient paid for the benefit

If the recipient of a taxable fringe benefit is an employee, the benefit is subject to employment taxes and must be reported on Form W-2. If the recipient of a taxable fringe benefit is not an employee, the benefit is not subject to employment taxes, but it may have to be reported on Form 1099-MISC for independent contractors or Schedule K-1 for partners.

Cafeteria Plans

A cafeteria plan, including a flexible spending arrangement, provides employees an opportunity to receive certain benefits on a pretax basis. The plan may make benefits available to employees, their spouses, and dependents. It may also include coverage of former employees. Participants in a cafeteria plan must be permitted to choose among at least one taxable benefit, such as cash, and one qualified benefit that is nontaxable. Generally, a cafeteria plan may not offer a benefit that defers pay. However, a cafeteria plan can include a qualified 401(k) plan as a benefit. Employee benefits may include:

- Accident, dental, vision, and medical benefits.
- Adoption assistance.
- Dependent care assistance
- Group term life insurance coverage
- Health savings accounts

Plans That Favor Highly Compensated Employees (HCEs)

If a cafeteria plan favors highly compensated employees, the value of their benefits become taxable. There cannot be special rules that favor eligibility for HCEs to participate, contribute, or benefit from a cafeteria plan. This is to discourage companies from offering spectacular tax-free benefits to their highly compensated executives, while ignoring the needs of lower-paid employees.

An HCE is any of the following:

- an officer
- a shareholder who owns more than 5% of the voting power or value of all classes of the employer's stock
- an employee who is highly compensated based on the facts and circumstances; or
- a spouse or dependent of a person described above.

Employer-provided benefits also cannot favor "key employees," defined as:

- An officer with annual pay of more than $165,000 in 2012, or
- An employee who is either a 5% owner of the business or a 1% owner of the business whose annual pay was more than $150,000 in 2012.

The law for highly compensated employees includes a "look-back provision," so employees who were previously considered HCEs are generally still considered HCEs for 2012 plan year testing.

If a plan favors HCE or key employees, the employer is required to include the value of the benefits they could have selected in their wages. A plan is considered to have "favored" HCEs if more than 25% of all the benefits are given to HCEs.

A benefits plan that covers union employees under a collective bargaining agreement is not included in this rule.

Simple Cafeteria Plans

Starting in 2011, eligible employers meeting certain requirements could establish a new type of "simple" cafeteria plan. A simple cafeteria plan is treated as automatically satisfying the nondiscrimination requirements that apply to cafeteria plans. The following rules apply:

- Employers must employ an average of 100 or fewer employees during either of the two preceding years.
- All employees who had at least 1,000 hours of service for the preceding plan year must be eligible to participate and able to select any benefit available under the plan. [99]
- Employers must make a contribution to provide qualified benefits on behalf of each qualified employee in an amount equal to:
  - A uniform percentage of not less than 2% of the employee's compensation for the plan year, or

---

[99] Employers may elect to exclude employees who are under age 21, have less than a year of service during the plan year, are covered under a collective bargaining agreement, and are nonresident aliens working outside the United States whose income did not come from a U.S. source.

- An amount which is at least 6% of the employee's compensation for the plan year or twice the amount of the salary reduction contributions of each employee, whichever is less.

Fringe Benefit Exclusion Rules

Certain fringe benefits exclude all or part of the value of certain benefits from the recipient's pay. In this next section, we provide an overview of the exclusion rules for these fringe benefits. Each of these benefits has its own definitions of who is considered a highly compensated employee and other exceptions as to who is covered or what income is taxable.

Accident and Health Benefits

An employer may exclude contributions it makes to an accident or health plan for an employee, including the following:

- Contributions to the cost of accident or health insurance, including long-term care insurance.
- Contributions to a separate trust or fund that directly or through insurance provides accident or health benefits
- Contributions to Archer MSAs or health savings accounts

Accident and health plans may provide benefits for employees, their spouses, their dependents, and their children.

Achievement Awards

Employers may generally exclude from an employee's wages the value of awards given for length of service or safety achievement.

An employer's deduction for employee achievement awards given to a single employee is limited to the following:

- $400 for awards that are not qualified plan awards
- $1,600 for all awards, whether or not they are qualified plan awards

A qualified plan award is one that does not discriminate in favor of highly compensated employees. The exclusion for employee awards does not apply to awards of cash, gift cards, or other intangible property such as vacations or tickets to sporting events.

Adoption Assistance

An adoption assistance program is a separate written plan that provides payments or reimbursements for qualifying employee expenses. The payments or reimbursements are not taxable to the employee.[100]

Athletic Facilities

The value of an employee's use of athletic facilities may be excluded from wages only if the facility is on premises that the employer owns or leases. Substantially

---

[100] An adoption program cannot favor HCEs, defined in this case as a 5% owner at any time during the year or preceding year, or who received more than $115,000 in pay for the preceding year, unless he was not also in the top 20% of employees when ranked by pay in the preceding year.

all the use of the gym or athletic facilities must be for a company's employees, their spouses, and their dependent children.

De Minimis (Minimal) Benefits

An employer may exclude the value of a de minimis benefit provided to an employee from the employee's wages. This is a property or service an employer provides that has so little value that accounting for it would be impractical. Examples of de minimis benefits include the following:

- Occasional personal use of a company copying machine
- Holiday gifts with a low fair market value
- Occasional parties for employees and their gifts

Cash and gift cards are never excludable as de minimis benefits, no matter how little the amount, except for occasional meal money or transportation fare.

Dependent Care Assistance

An employer can exclude the value of benefits provided to an employee for care of qualified dependents. The services must be provided to allow an employee to work.[101]

For 2012, an employee can generally exclude from gross income up to $5,000 of benefits ($2,500 if MFS) received under a dependent care assistance program each year. However, the exclusion cannot be more than the smaller of the earned income of either the employee or his or her spouse.

Educational Assistance

An employer can offer employees educational assistance for the cost of tuition, fees, books, supplies, and equipment. The payments may be for either undergraduate or graduate-level courses, and do not have to be work-related. In 2012, $5,250 may be excluded per year per employee. If an employer pays more than $5,250, the excess is taxed as wages to the employee. Not covered is the cost of courses involving sports, games, or hobbies, unless they are related to the business or are required as part of a degree program. The cost of lodging, meals, transportation is also not included in education expenses.

Tuition reduction: An educational organization can exclude the value of a qualified undergraduate tuition reduction to an employee, his or her spouse, or dependent child. Graduate education only qualifies if it is for the education of a graduate student who performs teaching or research activities for the educational organization.

Employee Discounts

Employers can exclude the value of employee discounts from wages up to the following limits:

- For a discount on services, 20% of the price charged nonemployee customers for the service.
- For a discount on merchandise, the company's gross profit percentage multiplied by the price nonemployee customers pay for the property.[102]

---

[101] The same HCE rules apply to dependent care assistance benefits.

Employer-Provided Cell Phones

The value of the business use of an employer-provided cell phone is excludable from an employee's income to the extent that, if the employee paid for its use, the payment would be deductible. The IRS has ruled that there must be substantial "noncompensatory" reasons for use of a phone which relate to the employer's business. Legitimate reasons include the employer's need to contact the employee at all times for work-related emergencies and the employee's need to be available to speak with clients away from the office.

However, a cell phone provided simply to promote an employee's morale or to attract a prospective employee is considered a form of compensation. In those cases, the value of a cell phone would no longer be a de minimis benefit and must be added to an employee's wages.

If an employer provides an employee with a cell phone primarily for noncompensatory business purposes, personal use of the phone also is excludable from an employee's income as a *de minimis* fringe benefit.[103]

Group-Term Life Insurance Coverage

An employer can exclude the cost of up to $50,000 of group-term life insurance from the wages of an insured employee. Any coverage above that amount must be included in the employee's wages, reduced by the amount the employee paid toward the insurance.

With some exceptions, life insurance is not group-term life insurance unless a business provides it to at least 10 full-time employees at some time during the year.[104]

Health Savings Accounts (HSAs)

An HSA is an account owned by a company's employee or former employee. Any contributions an employer makes become the employee's property and cannot be withdrawn by the employer. Contributions to the account are used to pay current or future medical expenses of the account owner, his or her spouse, and any qualified dependent. The medical expenses must not be reimbursable by insurance or other sources.

1. **Eligibility:** A qualified individual must be covered by a high deductible health plan with a deductible in 2012 of at least $1,200 for self-only coverage or $2,400 for family coverage. Annual out-of-pocket expenses to the beneficiary are limited to $6,050 for self-only coverage and $12,100 for family coverage. There are no income restrictions on an individual's eligibility to contribute to an HSA, nor is there a requirement the account owner have earned income to contribute.

---

[102] An HCE is defined in this case as a 5% owner at any time during the year or preceding year, or who received more than $115,000 in pay for the preceding year, unless he was not also in the top 20% of employees when ranked by pay in the preceding year.

[103] IRS Notice 2011-72.

[104] For this exclusion, a plan cannot favor key employees, defined as an officer having annual pay of more than $165,000; an individual who for 2012 was either a 5% owner of the business or a 1% owner of the business whose annual pay was more than $150,000. A plan does not favor key employees as to participation if it benefits at least 70% of the company's employees and at least 85% of the participating employees are not key employees.

2. **Employer contributions:** In 2012, an employer can contribute up to $3,100 for self-only coverage or $6,250 for family coverage to a qualified individual's HSA. The contribution amounts are increased by $1,000 for qualified individuals who are age 55 or older at any time during the year. No contributions can be made to an individual's HSA after he becomes enrolled in Medicare Part A or Part B.

3. **Nondiscrimination rules:** An employer's contribution amount to an employee's HSA must be comparable for all employees who have comparable coverage during the same period, or there will be an excise tax equal to 35% of the amount the employer contributed to all employees' HSAs. However, the Tax Relief and Health Care Act of 2006 allows employers to make larger HSA contributions for a non-highly compensated employee than for a highly compensated employee.[105]

Meals and Lodging Provided to Employees

An employer may exclude the value of meals and lodging it provides to employees if they are:

- On the employer's business premises, and
- For the employer's convenience.

For lodging, there is another rule: it must be required as a condition of employment. Lodging can be provided for the taxpayer, the spouse, and the taxpayer's dependents, and still not be taxable.

> **Example:** Henry is a project supervisor for Franklin Construction. He is provided free hotel lodging at remote job sites, where he is required to stay for many months while timber is cleared and the grounds are prepared for construction projects. The value of the lodging is excluded from income, because it is for his employer's convenience. The cost of the hotel is deductible by Franklin Construction as a business expense.

The exclusion from taxation does not apply if the employee can choose to receive additional pay instead of lodging.

Meals for the Convenience of the Employer

Meals provided to employees for the convenience of the employer are 100% deductible by the employer but are not taxable to the employees. Meals must be taken on the business premises, such as in the following instances:

- Workers such as police officers, firefighters, and other emergency personnel need to be on call for emergencies during the meal period
- The nature of the business requires short meal periods
- Eating facilities are not available in the area of work
- Meals are furnished to all employees on a regular basis, so long as meals are furnished to substantially all the employees for the convenience of the employer
- Meals are furnished immediately after working hours because the employee's duties prevented him or her from obtaining a meal during working hours

---

[105] An HCE is defined in this case as a 5% owner at any time during the year or preceding year, or who received more than $115,000 in pay for the preceding year, unless he was not also in the top 20% of employees when ranked by pay in the preceding year.

> **Example:** Paramedic Transport regularly provides meals to employees during working hours so that paramedics are available for emergency calls during the meal. The meals are therefore excludable from the employee's wages and still deductible by the employer.

> **Example:** An employer has pizza delivered to the office at a group meeting because the business requires the meeting be kept short, and there are no alternative restaurants in the immediate area.

If over half of a business's employees are furnished meals on the business premises for the *employer's* convenience, the business may treat all the meals furnished to the employees on the business premises as furnished for the "employer's convenience."

In the case of food service employees, meals furnished to restaurant employees before, during, or after work hours are considered furnished for the employer's convenience.

Moving Expense Reimbursements

An employer can generally exclude qualifying moving expense reimbursements from an employee's wages. The exclusion applies only to reimbursement of moving expenses that the employee could deduct if he or she had paid or incurred them without reimbursement. Deductible moving expenses include only the reasonable expenses of:

- Moving household goods and personal effects from the employee's former home to the new home, and
- Traveling, including lodging, from the former home to the new home.

Expenses for meals are not included, and the move must meet both the distance test and the time test. The distance test is met if the new job location is at least 50 miles farther from the employee's old home than the old job location was. The time test is met if the employee works at least 39 weeks during the first 12 months after arriving in the general area of the new job location.

No-Additional-Cost Services

An employer can exclude a service provided to an employee if it does not cause the business any substantial additional cost. The service must be offered to customers in the ordinary course of the line of business of the employer. Typically, no-additional-cost services are excess capacity services, such as airline, bus, or train tickets; hotel rooms; or telephone services provided free or at a reduced price to employees working in those lines of business.[106]

Retirement Planning Services

Employers with qualified retirement plans may exclude from an employee's wages the value of any retirement planning advice or information the business provides

---

[106] An HCE is defined in this case as a 5% owner at any time during the year or preceding year, or who received more than $115,000 in pay for the preceding year, unless he was not also in the top 20% of employees when ranked by pay in the preceding year.

to employees or spouses. The exclusion does not apply to services for tax preparation, accounting, legal, or brokerage services.

Transportation (Commuting) Services

Employers may provide transportation benefits to their employees up to certain amounts without having to include the benefit in the employee's income. Qualified transportation benefits include transit passes, paid parking, a ride in a commuter highway vehicle between the employee's home and workplace, and qualified bicycle commuting reimbursement.

In 2012, employees may exclude:

- $240 per month in combined commuter highway vehicle transportation and transit passes,[107] and
- $240 per month in parking benefits.

This nontaxable benefit is a combined maximum of $480 per month in 2012. Employees may receive transit passes and benefits for parking during the same month; they are not mutually exclusive.

An employer may also reimburse an employee for a bicycle that is used for commuting purposes. A qualified bicycle commuting reimbursement is a reimbursement of up to $20 per month for reasonable expenses incurred by the employee in conjunction with his commute to work by bike.

However, if an employer allows an employee to use a company vehicle for commuting, the value of the vehicle's use is taxable to the employee. Personal use of an employer's vehicle is also considered taxable wages to the employee.

Working Condition Benefits

This exclusion from wages applies to property and services an employer provides so that the employee can perform his or her job. A common example is an employee's use of a company car for business.

An employer who provides a car for an employee can exclude the amount that would be allowable as a deductible business expense if the employee paid for its use. Employers may instead choose to include the entire annual lease value of the car in the employee's wages. The employee can then claim any deductible business expense for the car as an itemized deduction on his personal income tax return.

A qualified nonpersonal-use vehicle is one that an employee is unlikely to use more than minimally for personal purposes because of its design. These include the following vehicles:

- Police, fire, and public safety vehicles; an ambulance or hearse
- Any vehicle designed to carry cargo with a loaded gross vehicle weight over 14,000 pounds

---

[107] Congress's fiscal cliff legislation of January 2, 2013 retroactively reinstated parity between the benefits for parking and transit benefits for 2012. The parity had expired at the end of 2011, so that for all of 2012 employers had expected the amount excluded for commuter highway vehicles or transit passes to be $125 a month, not $240. The IRS has issued guidance on FICA tax refunds and W-2 adjustments for businesses that gave transit benefits of more than $125 a month in 2012. Employers that treated the excess as wages can make adjustments, but they will have to reimburse their employees for the over-collected FICA tax before doing so.

- Delivery trucks with seating for the driver only
- A 20-person or more passenger bus
- School buses
- Tractors and other farm vehicles
- Vehicles such as cement mixers, garbage trucks, forklifts, and moving vans

Pickup trucks and vans of 14,000 pounds or less are qualified nonpersonal vehicles if they have been specially modified for business purposes, such as painted with advertising or marked with permanent decals, and have been fitted with certain special equipment specific to the business.

Accountable Plans

A business can reimburse employees for business-related expenses. Depending upon the type of plan the employer has, the reimbursement for business travel may or may not be taxable to the employee. There are two types of reimbursement plans:

- **Accountable Plans** - An accountable plan is not taxable to the employee and has strict substantiation requirements. Amounts paid under an accountable plan are not wages and are not subject to income tax withholding and payment of Social Security, Medicare, and Federal Unemployment (FUTA) taxes.
- **Nonaccountable Plans** - A nonaccountable plan is taxable to the employees as wages and is subject to all employment taxes and withholding. Generally, there are no substantiation requirements for a nonaccountable plan.

Example: Dana is a saleswoman for Sunshine Cosmetics. She takes two potential clients out to dinner and pays for the meal. She also keeps track of her business mileage on a spreadsheet. The following week, she submits her receipts and the spreadsheet to Sunshine Cosmetics for reimbursement. Dana's employer reimburses her for the out-of-pocket expenses she incurred. This arrangement is considered an accountable plan. The reimbursement is not taxable to Dana and is deductible by the employer as a regular business expense.

For expenses to qualify under an accountable plan, the employee must follow guidelines in order to have the expenses reimbursed. An accountable plan requires employees to meet all of the following requirements:

- Have incurred the expenses while performing services as employees
- Adequately account for the expenses within a reasonable period of time
- Adequately account for their travel, meals, and entertainment expenses
- Provide documentary evidence of their travel, mileage, and other employee business expenses
- Return any excess reimbursement or allowance within a reasonable period of time if paid in advance

Under an accountable plan, a business owner may *advance* money to employees in anticipation of an expense; however, certain conditions must be met. The cash advance must be reasonably calculated to equal the anticipated expense, and the business owner must make the advance within a reasonable period of time.

Unit 6: Questions

1. Evermore Inc. reimburses employees for their business travel. Which of the following is taxable to the employee?

A. Travel reimbursements made under an accountable plan.
B. Travel reimbursements made under a nonaccountable plan.
C. Parking passes at a cost of $240 per month.
D. A qualified bicycle commuting reimbursement.

The answer is B. Travel reimbursements made under a nonaccountable plan are taxable to the employee as wages. ###

2. All of the following are excludable from wages except:

A. An outstanding employee achievement award valued at $300.
B. Occasional snacks provided by the employer in the employee break room.
C. Employer-provided vehicles that employees may also use for personal purposes.
D. Meals furnished during work hours for the benefit of the employer.

The answer is C. The value of a vehicle for personal use by an employee is a taxable benefit. If an employer provides a car for an employee's use, the amount that can be excluded as a working condition benefit is the amount that would be allowable as a deductible business expense if the employee paid for its use. There are exceptions for emergency personnel such as police officers who are required to use their emergency vehicles. Employee achievement awards are exempt up to $1,600. Meals are exempt if either furnished for the employer's convenience or if de minimis. Snacks would usually be considered a de minimis benefit. ###

3. The Pancake House has a qualified benefit plan for its employees. The following benefits were offered to the employees. Which of these is fully taxable to the employee?

A. Qualified group term life insurance of $50,000.
B. Qualified dependent care of up to $5,000.
C. A membership to the local athletic club.
D. Free transit passes.

The answer is C. Memberships to athletic facilities are a taxable benefit. A workout area on the employer's premises is the exception. The other benefits are not taxable as part of a fringe benefit plan to employees. ###

4. Heart-Wise Ambulance Services provides meals and lodging for ten employees at the workplace as a condition of employment because the paramedics are not allowed to leave the premises when they are on a shift. The employees eat and sleep for free. Which of the following is true?

A. All the costs of meals and lodging can be excluded from the employees' wages and deducted as an expense by the employer.
B. The meals and lodging are not taxable to the employee, but the employer can only deduct 50% of the meal expense.
C. The meals and lodging are taxable to the employee and deductible by the employer. The employee may then deduct the cost as an employee-business expense.
D. None of the above.

The answer is A. Employers may exclude the value of meals and on-site lodging from an employee's wages. Lodging provided for the convenience of the employer is also excludable from an employee's wages. Since the employees are required to remain on the employer's premises, the value of the meals and lodging is a nontaxable benefit to the employees. Meals provided to employees for the convenience of the employer are 100% deductible by the employer, but are not taxable to the employees. To be considered "for the convenience of the employer," they must be taken on the business premises, and there are also other restrictions. ###

5. Which of the following benefits must be included in an employee's income?

A. Child care reimbursed under a qualified flexible spending plan.
B. Employee discounts on products.
C. A holiday gift of $50 in gas cards.
D. A holiday gift of a $25 canned ham.

The answer is C. Gifts in cash or cash equivalents such as gift cards must always be included in income. Fringe benefits that may be excluded from income include employee discounts, qualified transportation passes, parking, and de minimis holiday gifts. ###

6. Which of the following is not a fringe benefit that may be excluded from an employee's pay?

A. Dependent care assistance of up to $5,000 a year.
B. A cell phone given to an employee for excellent job performance.
C. Moving expense reimbursements.
D. Retirement planning services.

The answer is B. The value of an employer-provided cell phone is only excludable from an employee's wages if it is given for a noncompensatory business purpose. A cell phone used to boost morale or, in this case, as a type of financial bonus would be taxable to the employee. ###

7. Right Angles Engineering offers its employees an education reimbursement. Renee is a full-time employee working for Right Angles. In 2012, she takes graduate accounting courses and has $5,900 in tuition expenses and $300 in expenses for required books. Right Angles reimburses Renee for all the expenses. How should this reimbursement be treated?

A. All of the amounts are excluded from the employee's income, and the amounts are deductible by the employer as a qualified fringe benefit.
B. The first $5,250 of the educational expenses is excluded from the employee's wages as a qualified fringe benefit, and the remaining amount is taxable as wage income to Renee.
C. Only $5,900 (the tuition costs) of the educational expenses are excluded from the employee's wages as a qualified fringe benefit, and the remaining amount is taxable as wage income to Renee. The cost of the books is not a qualified educational expense.
D. All of the reimbursement is taxable as wages, because graduate courses do not qualify for reimbursement under a fringe benefit plan.

The answer is B. Although all of the expenses are qualified educational expenses, only the first $5,250 of the educational expenses is excluded from the employee's wages as a qualified fringe benefit, and the remaining amount is taxable as wage income to Renee. $5,250 is the maximum excluded benefit in 2012. If an employer pays more than $5,250 for educational benefits for an employee during the year, the excess is taxed as wages. ###

8. A simple cafeteria plan is _____:

A. A type of plan that makes all fringe benefits a company wants to offer nontaxable to employers and employees.
B. A plan that only offers benefits which defer pay.
C. A flexible spending arrangement.
D. A type of plan that allows employers with 100 or fewer employees to meet the nondiscriminatory requirements and offer certain benefits under a cafeteria plan.

The answer is D. A simple cafeteria plan is a newer form of cafeteria plan established under health care reform. It is designed for employers with 100 or fewer employees and gives employers a way to bypass some of the complicated nondiscriminatory requirements of regular cafeteria plans while offering similar benefits. ###

9. Antonio is employed by the GR Accounting Firm. When he travels for his audit work, he submits his meal and travel receipts for reimbursement by the firm, which has an accountable plan for its employees. Which of the following statements is true?

A. Under an accountable plan, the reimbursed amounts are taxable to Antonio and will be clearly listed on his Form W-2.
B. Under an accountable plan, Antonio may deduct his travel and meal expenses on his tax return, even though they have already been reimbursed by his employer.
C. Under an accountable plan, Antonio's employer may only deduct 50% of Antonio's meal expenses, even though Antonio was reimbursed in full for the expense.
D. Under an accountable plan, reimbursed expenses are usually taxable to the employee as wages, and the employer should deduct the expenses as wage expense.

The answer is C. The expenses for entertainment and meals must be reduced by 50%, regardless of whether the employer reimburses the employee for the full amount of the meals. Under an accountable plan, employee reimbursements are not included in the employee's income. The employer can deduct the expenses as current expenses on his tax return. ###

10. For cafeteria plans, a "key" employee in 2012 is defined as all of the following except:

A. An officer with annual pay of more than $165,000.
B. A 1% owner of the business with annual pay of more than $150,000.
C. A 10% owner of the business.
D. Both A and B.

The answer is C. Under the rules for cafeteria plans, a key employee is a 5% owner of the business, not a 10% owner. Both A and B are correct in describing key employees. ###

11. Certain types of fringe benefits cannot favor highly compensated employees. In 2012, how is an HCE defined for the following types of fringe benefits: adoption, dependent care, and educational assistance; employee discounts; lodging and meals on premises; and no-additional-cost services?

A. An employee with annual pay of more than $150,000 the preceding year.
B. An officer with annual pay of more than $165,000 the preceding year.
C. A 5% owner of the company, or one with annual pay of more than $150,000 the preceding year.
D. A 5% owner of the company, or one with annual pay of more than $115,000 the preceding year.

The answer is D. For the fringe benefits listed, an HCE is a 5% owner of the company or one with annual pay of more than $115,000 the preceding year. The second test can be disregarded if the employee was not also among the top 20% of employees when ranked by pay for the preceding year. Benefit plans cannot favor highly compensated employees to the detriment of other employees. ###

12. Which of the following statements is not correct about health savings accounts?

A. Contributions cannot be made to an individual's HSA after he becomes enrolled in Medicare.
B. Only taxpayers with gross income below $200,000 may contribute to an HSA.
C. Qualified individuals must be covered by high deductible insurance plans.
D. Contributions to an HSA are used to pay current or future medical owners of the account owner, his or her spouse, and qualified dependents.

The answer is B. There are no income restrictions on who may contribute to an HSA. ###

449

Unit 7: Business Credits & Deductions

More Reading:
Instructions for Form 3800, *General Business Credit*
Publication 334, *Tax Guide for Small Business*
Publication 536, *Net Operating Losses for Individuals, Estates, and Trusts*
Instructions for Form 8903, *Domestic Productions Activities Deduction*
Instructions for Form 4626, *Alternative Minimum Tax-Corporations*

Net Operating Losses (NOLs)

A net operating loss (NOL) is when a business has tax deductions that exceed its current income, resulting in negative taxable income. This happens when a business has more expenses than revenues during a given tax year. A loss from operating a business is the most common reason for an NOL.

By applying a net operating loss to preceding tax years, a business can receive a refund of previously paid taxes. The NOL can also be used to reduce future tax payments. A business may choose whether or not to "carry back" or "carry forward" an NOL.

The default election, called the carryback period, is to carry back a net operating loss two years. Then the business can carry forward any remaining NOL for up to 20 years. A business may also elect not to carry back an NOL and only carry it forward.

A valid election must be made in order to forgo the carryback period and only carry forward an NOL. If a taxpayer fails to file a return on time and does not make the proper election, he is forced to carryback the NOL.

Note: Any net operating loss that is not absorbed in the carryback (generally two years) and carryforward (20 years) periods is lost. It cannot be deducted in any other tax year.

In order for a sole proprietor to have an NOL, the loss must be caused by the following expenses:

- Deductions from a trade or business that result in an overall loss
- Deductions from work as an employee
- Casualty or theft losses (personal or business-related)
- Losses from rental property
- Moving expenses
- Losses from a farming business

An individual taxpayer may have a net operating loss if his adjusted gross income minus the standard deduction (or itemized deductions) is a negative number; this is most commonly caused by losses from a Schedule C business.

Longer Carryback Periods

There are certain instances in which a business qualifies for a longer NOL carryback period. The following are exceptions to the two-year carryback rule:

- If the NOL is due to a farming loss, qualified farmers are eligible for a five-year carryback period.
- "Qualified small businesses"[108] may carry back a loss three years if the loss is due to a federally declared disaster.
- Net operating losses due to a casualty or theft may be carried back three years.
- Product liability losses have a ten-year carryback period. An example would be when a business sells an item that is later subject to a recall and lawsuits.

Reporting Net Operating Losses

In order to claim a refund from an NOL, an individual taxpayer may choose to amend a prior year tax return, or may use IRS Form 1045, *Application for Tentative Refund*, to apply for a quick tax refund resulting from the carryback of an NOL.

If the taxpayer is self-employed, the net operating loss does not change the amount of self-employment tax to any of the years to which it is carried forward or back. Also, if a business or individual owes interest and penalties in a prior year, the NOL carryback will not abate them.

> **Example:** Gregory operates a farming business and files his return on Schedule F. In 2012, he has a net operating loss of $35,000. He had income of $25,000 in the prior year, so he elects to carry back his NOL in order to receive a refund of the income tax he paid. Gregory also owed self-employment taxes in 2011, but the NOL will not abate them. The NOL only offsets income tax.

The following items are not allowed when a business figures an NOL:
- Any deduction for personal exemptions
- Capital losses in excess of capital gains
- The exclusion of gain from the sale of qualified small business stock
- Nonbusiness deductions in excess of nonbusiness income (hobby losses)
- A net operating loss from *another* year (a carryback or a carryforward)
- The domestic production activities deduction (DPAD) cannot create or increase an NOL carryback or carryforward
- A self-employed taxpayer's contribution to a Keogh plan (a type of retirement plan for sole proprietors)

Income from other sources may eliminate or reduce a net operating loss for the year. For example, if a taxpayer has income from wages, as well as a net operating loss from a small business, then the wage income will offset the amount of the NOL.

> **Example:** Jim runs an auto detailing business as a sole proprietor. In 2012, he had an $8,000 NOL from his Schedule C business. Jim files jointly with his wife, Elaine. She has $23,000 in taxable income from wages. On their jointly filed return, Jim's net operating loss is absorbed by Elaine's $23,000 in wages, making their joint AGI $15,000 ($23,000 - $8,000 NOL).

---

[108] A "qualified small business" for purposes of this rule is a sole proprietorship or a partnership that has average annual gross receipts of $5 million or less during the three-year period ending with the tax year of the NOL.

Business Credits

There are a variety of tax credits for business. Credits are generally more valuable than deductions because they are subtracted directly from a business's tax liability. However, most tax credits are available in limited situations, applying only to certain industries or to very specific activities.

General Business Credit

Many business credits fall under the umbrella of the General Business Credit (GBC). The GBC is not a single credit but is instead a combination of 32 business credits. [109] Each business credit is claimed on a separate form, and then the credits are added in aggregate on Form 3800, *General Business Credit.*

The GBC is a nonrefundable credit that is subtracted directly from tax, reducing an entity's tax liability dollar for dollar. Generally, credits cannot be claimed to the extent that they would reduce a business's tax bill below its tentative minimum tax. The General Business Credit may not offset any of a business's employment tax liabilities.

Carryback and Carryforward

A business's GBC for the year consists of its carryforward of business credits from prior years plus the total of its current year business credits. If dollar limitations on the GBC prevent a business from claiming all of it in the year that it was earned, it can generally be carried back to the prior year and forward to the following 20 years.

List of Business Credits

The following are some of the more widely-used general business credits. The starred credits (marked like this: ***) are those most likely to be tested on the EA exam, according to the exam specifications on the Prometric website.

***Investment Credit (Form 3468)

The Investment Credit is the sum of the following five credits: Rehabilitation and Energy Credits, and the Advanced Coal, Advanced Energy, and Gasification projects.

- **Rehabilitation Credit:** This credit is given to businesses that rehabilitate pre-1936 buildings (10%) or certified historic structures (20%) of qualified expenditures. For 2012, the credit is temporarily increased to 13% for pre-1936 buildings and 26% for historic structures that are located in certain disaster zones.
- **Energy Credit:** This credit is given to businesses that use solar energy to generate electricity or that use geothermal deposits to power their equipment. The credit is between 10% and 30% for qualified fuel cell and other solar energy property,
- **Advanced Coal, Gasification, and Advanced Energy Project Credits:** These credits are designed to reduce greenhouse emissions by retrofitting existing technology to make it cleaner or spurring investment in alternative energy. In

---

[109] The number of general business credits for the 2012 tax year. Specific credits and their requirements vary from year to year.

the case of the Advanced Energy Credit, qualifying projects must re-equip, expand, or establish a manufacturing facility for the production of solar, wind, or geothermal energy, or electric cars.

The Investment Credit allows businesses to take a deduction for a percentage of certain investment costs from their tax liability *in addition* to the normal allowances for depreciation. In general, a business cannot claim the Investment Credit for property that is:

- Used mainly outside the United States
- Used by a governmental unit or foreign person or entity
- Used by a tax-exempt organization
- Used for lodging or in the furnishing of lodging ; or
- Any property that has already been expensed under section 179 (accelerated depreciation)

***Disabled Access Credit (Form 8826)

This is a nonrefundable tax credit for an eligible small business that incurs expenses to provide access to persons who have disabilities. The expenses must be incurred in order to allow the business to comply with the Americans with Disabilities Act. The amount of the Disabled Access Credit is 50% of qualified expenses, with a maximum credit per year of $5,000. To be eligible, a business must have earned $1 million or less or had no more than 30 full-time employees during the year.

***Work Opportunity Tax Credit (Form 5884)

The WOTC provides a credit to for-profit employers of as much as $9,600 per veteran who was hired and began work before the end of 2012. The credit for qualified tax-exempt organizations is a maximum of $6,240. The amount of this credit varies depending on factors such as the length of the veteran's unemployment before being hired.

Prior to 2012, businesses could take a Work Opportunity Credit equal to 40% of the first $6,000 of wages paid to new hires of one of eight targeted groups. These groups include welfare and food stamp recipients, ex-felons, summer youth employees, and SSI recipients. For 2012, the credit was amended to allow only the hiring of certain qualified veterans.

However, the *American Taxpayer Relief Act of 2012* extended all of these credits retroactively to cover workers hired in 2012. Since employers claiming the WOTC are required to have a state agency certify workers as credit eligible within a month of hiring, it is not clear how the retroactive reinstatement of the credit will be implemented.

Alternative Motor Vehicle Credit (Form 8910)

This credit consists of the following credits for certain alternative motor vehicles placed in service during the year:

- Qualified fuel cell motor vehicle credit
- Advanced lean burn technology motor vehicle credit
- Qualified hybrid motor vehicle credit

- Qualified alternative fuel motor vehicle credit
- Qualified plug-in electric drive motor vehicle conversion credit.

This credit is unusual because it is allowed for both personal and business-use vehicles. If the credit is claimed for a personal vehicle, the credit is a nonrefundable personal credit and will reduce the taxpayer's regular tax as well as the alternative minimum tax.

If the credit is claimed for a business-use vehicle, the credit becomes part of the General Business Credit, so it is available for carryback and carryforward treatment.

Other Credits

Qualified Plug-in Electric Drive Motor Vehicle Credit (Form 8936): This is a $2,500 to $7,500 credit for each new qualifying plug-in electric vehicle purchased or leased during the year.

Credit for Alternative Fuel Vehicle Refueling Property: This credit allows a 30% credit for the cost of installing clean-fuel vehicle refueling property to be used in a business, up to $30,000 a year.[110]

Energy Efficient Appliance Credit (Form 8909): This credit is available for manufacturers of eligible dishwashers, clothes washers, refrigerators. The amount of the credit is based on how little energy a particular appliance uses[111].

Energy Efficient Home Credit (Form 8908): This credit ranges from $1,000 to $2,000, and is available for eligible contractors of certain energy-efficient homes sold for use as residences. [112]

Credit for Employer Social Security and Medicare Taxes Paid on Certain Employee Tips (Form 8846): This credit is generally equal to the employer's portion of Social Security and Medicare taxes paid on tips received by employees of restaurants and other food service establishments where tipping is customary. An employer must meet both of the following requirements to qualify for the credit:

- The business has employees who received tips from customers for serving food or beverages.
- The business paid employer Social Security and Medicare taxes on these tips.

The credit does not apply to other tipped employees, such as hairdressers or bellhops.

Credit for Employer Differential Wage Payments (Form 8932): This credit provides certain small businesses with an incentive to continue to pay wages to an employee performing services on active duty in the uniformed services of the United States for a period of more than 30 days.[113]

Credit for Employer-Provided Childcare Facilities and Services (Form 8882): This credit applies to the qualified expenses a business incurs for employee childcare,

---

[110] Expired at the end of 2011, but retroactively extended through 2013 by the American Taxpayer Relief Act of 2012.
[111] Also retroactively extended through 2013.
[112] Also retroactively extended through 2013.
[113] Also retroactively extended through 2013.

childcare resources, and childcare referral services. The credit is up to 25% of the cost of the childcare facility plus 10% of resource and referral costs. A business is limited to a credit of $150,000 per tax year.

Credit for Small Employer Health Insurance Premiums (Form 8941): This credit applies to the cost of health insurance premiums that an eligible small business provides certain employees. For tax-exempt small businesses, the credit is generally limited to 25% of premiums paid. For all other small employers, the credit is generally 35% of premiums paid. For purposes of this credit, an eligible business must have had fewer than 25 full-time equivalent employees for the tax year, with average annual wages of less than $50,000.

Credit for Small Employer Pension Plan Start-up Costs (Form 8881): This credit applies to pension plan start-up costs of a new qualified defined benefit or defined contribution plan (including a 401(k) plan), SIMPLE plan, or simplified employee pension plans. In order to qualify, the business must not have employed more than 100 employees in the preceding year. The credit is 50% of eligible costs up to a maximum credit of $500 per year for the first three years of the retirement plan.

Credit for Increasing Research Activities: A credit for expenses related to qualified research intended for use in developing new or improved technology that would be used in a taxpayer's business.[114]

Other, more obscure, general business credits include ones for everything from maintaining railroad tracks and training mine rescue teams to makers of orphan drugs and distilled spirits. EA exam-takers do not need to know specifics of these narrowly-based credits.

In addition to credits designed to spur specific economic investment, Congress frequently passes other specific incentives for businesses to engage in certain types of business activity. In 2012, section 181 allows film and television producers to expense the first $15 million of production costs incurred in the United States ($20 million if in economically depressed areas), rather than capitalizing the costs under normal uniform capitalization rules.[115]

Domestic Production Activities Deduction (DPAD)

The domestic production activities deduction, authorized by IRC section 199, is designed to stimulate domestic manufacturing and farming. In 2012, the DPAD is equal to 9% of the *lesser* of:

- The business's qualified production activities income, or
- Taxable income determined without regard to the DPAD.

The deduction is limited to 50% of wages paid on Form W-2 by the company for the year. Therefore, if a company does not have any employees, it is not eligible for this deduction. This provision is to encourage domestic employment and to discourage outsourcing.

---

[114] Expired at the end of 2011, but retroactively extended through 2013 by the American Taxpayer Relief Act of 2012.

[115] Also retroactively extended through 2013.

*Note: Payments made to independent contractors and reported on Form 1099 are not wages and do not qualify for purposes of the DPAD.

Example: Brent Wise Corporation manufactures building components in the United States that it wholesales to building contractors. All of Brent Wise's manufacturing activity is in the U.S., and therefore qualifies for the DPAD. In 2012, Brent Wise had gross sales of $650,000 from its manufacturing activity and paid $225,000 in wages to its employees. Brent Wise's DPAD deduction would therefore be the lesser of:

•9% of the $650,000 in sales, or

•50% of the $225,000 wages.

Thus, Brent Wise's DPAD would be $58,500 (.09 x $650,000).

Eligible Activities for the DPAD

The following activities are qualified production activities eligible for claiming the DPAD:

- Manufacturing goods in the United States
- Selling, leasing, or licensing items that have been manufactured in the United States
- Selling, leasing, or licensing motion pictures that have been produced in the United States (except for pornography)
- Construction of real property in the United States
- Engineering and architectural services relating to a U.S.-based construction project
- Software development in the United States
- The production of water, natural gas, and electricity in the United States (simply transmitting or distributing these goods does not qualify)
- The growth and processing of agricultural products and timber

In order to figure the deduction, a business must correctly calculate its domestic production gross receipts (DPGR).

Example: Raiser Ranch Inc. is a slaughtering plant that has various locations in the United States as well as two locations in Brazil. Although the type of production activity is qualified for the DPAD, Raiser Ranch must track how much of its production occurs in the United States, because only the U.S. production qualifies for the DPAD. Raiser Ranch must allocate its gross receipts between the factory production in the United States and Brazil to calculate DPGR.

Reporting the DPAD Deduction

The DPAD is reported on IRS Form 8903, *Domestic Production Activities Deduction*. The deduction is available to individuals, trusts and estates, C corporations, partnerships, and other pass-through entities such as S corporations and LLCs.

Individual taxpayers (Schedule C and Schedule F) claim the deduction as an adjustment to income on Form 1040. Individual partners or shareholders include their share of the DPAD from pass-through entities, such as partnerships, LLCs taxed as partnerships, and S corporations. C corporations claim the deduction directly on Form 1120.

In 2012, the deduction may not exceed 9% of a C corporation's taxable income or 9% of AGI for sole proprietors, partners in a partnership, and owner-shareholders of S corporations. Estates and trusts are also eligible for the DPAD, but only if the income is not passed through to beneficiaries.

Not Qualified DPAD Activities

The following types of business are specifically excluded from claiming the DPAD:

- Construction services that are cosmetic in nature, such as drywall and painting.
- Leasing or licensing items to a related party.
- Selling food or beverages prepared at restaurants or dining establishments.
- The *transmission* or distribution of electricity, natural gas, or water (although the *production* of electricity, natural gas, or potable water in the United States is a qualified activity).
- Any advertising, product placement, customer service businesses, and other telecommunications services.
- Most service type businesses.

Alternative Minimum Tax

Federal tax law gives special treatment to certain types of income and allows deductions and credits for certain types of expenses. Business taxpayers who benefit from this special treatment may have to pay at least a minimum amount of tax through an additional alternative minimum tax (ATM).

First enacted by Congress in 1969, the AMT is an effort to ensure that individuals and corporations pay at least a minimum amount of tax.[116]

The AMT is the excess of the tentative minimum tax over the regular tax. Thus, the AMT is owed only if the tentative minimum tax is greater than the regular tax. The tentative minimum tax is calculated separately from the regular tax. In general, the tentative minimum tax is computed by:

1. Starting with AGI less itemized deductions, or with AGI for taxpayers who are not claiming itemized deductions, for regular tax purposes,
2. Eliminating or reducing certain exclusions, deductions, and credits that are allowed in computing the regular tax, to derive alternative minimum taxable income (AMTI),
3. Subtracting the AMT exemption amount,
4. Multiplying the amount computed in (3) by the AMT rate, and
5. Subtracting the AMT Foreign Tax Credit.

When calculating the AMT using this formula, businesses must include a number of "tax preference items." After AMT adjustments, these tax preference items are added

---

[116] The American Taxpayer Relief Act retroactively increased the AMT exemption amounts for 2012. Lawmakers also created a permanent fix to the AMT, which has been modified 19 times since 1969. Going forward, the AMT will be indexed to inflation, meaning the income threshold for being subject to the AMT will rise automatically each year.

back into taxable income to determine the AMTI (see step two). For business taxpayers, tax preference items include depletion, excess intangible drilling costs, tax-exempt interest on private activity municipal bonds; accelerated depreciation on property placed in service before 1987; and exclusion of gain on qualified small business stock.[117]

For sole proprietors and partners of a partnership, the AMT is calculated on Form 6251, *Alternative Minimum Tax-Individuals.* For corporations, the AMT is calculated on Form 4626, *Alternative Minimum Tax-Corporations.* A corporation is treated as a small corporation exempt from the AMT if its gross receipts for the last three years are less than $7.5 million, or $5 million for the company's first three-year testing period.

---

[117] For the EA exam, test-takers should not have to calculate the AMT, but should be able to recognize specific tax preference items for business.

Unit 7: Questions

1. The General Business Credit is defined as:

A. A single business credit for small businesses.
B. A set of various credits available to businesses.
C. The credit for dependent care.
D. A collection of charitable deductions for businesses.

The answer is B. The General Business Credit consists of various credits available to businesses. The GBC is also the total of the carryforward of business credits from prior years plus the total current year business credits. ###

2. Farwell Corporation is a qualified small business for purposes of the General Business Credit. The corporation could not use all of its credits in 2012. What is the carryover period for the GBC?

A. The GBC may be carried back two years and carried forward 5 years.
B. The GBC may be carried back five years and carried forward 10 years.
C. The unused GBC cannot be carried over to another tax year.
D. The GBC may be carried back one year and carried forward for 20 years.

The answer is D. Normally, businesses can carry back unused business credits one year and carry them forward 20 years. ###

3. Stacy owns the Peach Pit Cannery. In 2012, she renovated her cannery to come into compliance with the Americans with Disabilities Act. The Peach Pit Cannery had gross receipts of $750,000 and spent $15,000 on disabled access upgrades. What is Stacy's current year Disabled Access Credit?

A. $2,500.
B. $5,000.
C. $7,500.
D. $15,000.

The answer is B. The amount of the Disabled Access Credit is 50% of the qualified expenses, but the maximum credit per year is $5,000. ###

4. The standards of the Disabled Access Credit conform to the _____?

A. Architectural Standards Act.
B. U.S. Department of Labor.
C. Americans with Disabilities Act.
D. National Organization on Disability.

The answer is C. The Disabled Access Credit is a nonrefundable tax credit for an eligible small business that pays expenses to provide access to disabled persons. The taxpayer must pay or incur the expenses to enable the business to comply with the Americans with Disabilities Act. ###

5. In 2012, the Work Opportunity Tax Credit provides a credit for businesses that do which of the following?

A. Provide job training for out-of-work individuals.
B. Give severance to laid-off workers.
C. Invest in federal empowerment zones.
D. Hire unemployed veterans and other individuals in targeted groups.

The answer is D. The WTOC offers credits to businesses who hire out-of-work veterans, as well as other individuals in eight different targeted groups. ###

6. Which of the following is not part of the Investment Credit in 2012?

A. Gasification Project Credit.
B. Hydroelectric Power Credit.
C. Rehabilitation Credit.
D. Energy Credit.

The answer is B. The Investment Credit is the sum of five credits that are designed to spur investment in activity that reduces greenhouse emissions and rehabilitates historic property. In 2012, the Investment Credit consists of the Rehabilitation and Energy Credits, and the Advanced Coal, Advanced Energy, and Gasification Projects. There is no credit for hydroelectric power. ###

7. Bettina owns her own photography business, and she has an NOL in the current year. She elects to carry back her losses to a previous period. How long may she carry back and carry forward her NOL?

A. Back 5 years, forward 20 years.
B. Back 2 years, forward 20 years.
C. Back 3 years, forward 25 years.
D. Back 2 years, forward 5 years.

The answer is B. In general, a net operating loss may be carried back two previous years, and the remaining loss may be carried forward to each of the subsequent 20 years. ###

8. Which event would create a genuine NOL?

A. Selling a personal used car for a loss.
B. Selling a primary residence for a loss.
C. Casualty loss from a fire on a business location.
D. Large losses from the sale of corporate stock.

The answer is C. Only the casualty loss is potentially deductible for purposes of the net operating loss. Losses from the sale of stock are capital losses and cannot be used to create an NOL. Losses from the sale of personal-use property or a primary residence are not deductible. ###

9. Gabriel is a small business owner who reports income and loss on Schedule C. He had an NOL in 2012 due to a business casualty loss. His losses occurred in a presidentially declared disaster area. What is the earliest year that Gabriel can carryback his losses?

A. 2008.
B. 2009.
C. 2010.
D. 2011.

The answer is B. In the case of a loss due to a federally declared disaster area, qualified small businesses may carry back a loss three years instead of the normal two-year carryback period. ###

10. Which of the following items is allowed when figuring a net operating loss?

A. Capital losses in excess of capital gains.
B. A net operating loss from another year (a carryback or a carryforward).
C. The domestic production activities deduction.
D. The loss from the theft of business property.

The answer is D. Only the losses due to the theft of business property would be allowed in figuring a net operating loss. ###

11. Which of the following does not qualify for the domestic production activities deduction (section 199)?

A. Manufacturing goods in the United States.
B. Construction of buildings in the United States.
C. Selling food or beverages prepared at restaurants.
D. Software development in the United States.

The answer is C. Selling food or beverages prepared at restaurants is **specifically disallowed** for purposes of the DPAD. Most U.S.-based manufacturing qualifies for the DPAD. ###

Unit 8: Basis of Business Assets

More Reading:

Publication 551, *Basis of Assets*

Publication 547, *Casualties, Disasters, and Thefts*

A business asset is any type of property used in the conduct of a trade or business: land, buildings, machinery, furniture, trucks, patents, and franchise rights are all examples. Some assets are tangible, and others are intangible. Taxpayers must capitalize the cost of business assets, rather than deduct them in the year the cost is incurred.

Basis is the amount of a taxpayer's investment in property for tax purposes. In order to compute gain or loss on the sale of an asset, a business must be able to determine its basis in the property sold. The basis of property is also used to determine depreciation, amortization, depletion, and casualty losses. If a business cannot determine the basis of an asset, the IRS will deem it to be zero.

Cost Basis of Business Assets

The basis of property is usually its cost—the amount a business pays for an asset. The basis of an asset also includes amounts paid for the following items:

- Sales tax on the purchase
- Freight to obtain the property
- Installation and testing
- Excise taxes
- Legal and accounting fees to obtain property
- Revenue stamps
- Recording fees
- Real estate taxes (if assumed by the buyer)
- Settlement costs for the purchase of real estate
- The assumption of any liabilities on the property

Example: Naomi pays $4,000 for a commercial dryer for her laundromat. Naomi also pays $500 for shipping and sales tax. The installation cost for the dryer is $250. These costs are added to the purchase price, resulting in a basis of $4,750.

Certain events that occur during the period of ownership may increase or decrease the basis, resulting in an *adjusted basis*. The basis of property is *increased* by the cost of improvements that add to the value of the property. The basis of property is *decreased* by depreciation, insurance reimbursements for casualty and theft losses, and certain other items such as rebates.

Basis of Real Property

Real property, often called real estate, is land and anything built on or attached to it. When a taxpayer buys real property, certain fees and other expenses become part of the cost basis in the property.

Real estate taxes: If a taxpayer pays real estate taxes on property he buys that the seller owed, those taxes are added to the basis and cannot be deducted.

Settlement costs: Settlement fees and closing costs for buying a property are added to its basis. These include abstract fees; charges for installing utility services; legal fees, including title search and preparation of the sales contract and deed; recording fees; surveys; transfers; owner's title insurance; and any amounts the seller owes that the taxpayer agrees to pay, such as charges for improvements or repairs and sales commissions.

Assumption of mortgage: If a taxpayer buys property with an existing mortgage, the basis includes the amount he pays for the property plus the amount of the mortgage that he assumes.

> **Example:** The Oceanside Partnership purchases a commercial building for $200,000 in cash and assumes a related mortgage of $800,000. The partnership also pays $5,500 in legal fees to a real estate attorney to handle the purchase. Oceanside's basis in the building is $1,005,500 ($200,000 + $800,000 + $5,500).

Constructing assets: If a taxpayer builds property or has assets built for him, the expenses of construction are added to the basis. These expenses include land; labor and materials; architect's fees; building permit charges; payments to contractors; payment for rental equipment; inspections; employee wages paid for the construction work; and the cost of building supplies and materials used in the construction. The value of the taxpayer's own labor or any other labor he did not pay for are not included in the basis.

Demolition Costs: Demolition costs *increase* an asset's basis rather than decrease it because they are necessary expenses in order to prepare a property for use. Costs incurred to demolish a building are added to the basis of the land on which the demolished building was located. The costs associated with clearing land for construction also must be added to the basis of the land. For example, if a business pays to demolish an existing building and clear the lot of debris so new construction can begin, all of the costs associated with the preparation of the land are added to the land's basis.

> **Example:** Tony buys a lot with a badly damaged building on it for $25,000. He demolishes the building and prepares the land for a new structure. The demolition costs $13,000. Tony's new basis in the land is $38,000 ($25,000 + $13,000).

Rehabilitation Costs: Rehabilitation costs increase basis. However, any rehabilitation credits allowed for the expenses must first be subtracted.

Not Included in the Basis of Real Property

The following settlement fees and closing costs cannot be included in the basis of a property:

- Casualty insurance premiums
- Rent or utility costs related to occupancy of the property before closing

- Any charges for acquiring a loan, such as mortgage insurance premiums, loan assumption fees, cost of a credit report, fees for appraisal reports, fees for refinancing a mortgage, and points.

Points are prepaid interest on a loan and are deducted as interest over the life of the loan, rather than added to an asset's basis.

Improvements to Business Property

There are many costs that will increase an asset's basis, such as making additions or improvements to business property. The costs of making improvements to an asset are capitalized if the improvements:

- Add to the value of the asset,
- Appreciably lengthen the time a business can use it, or
- Adapt it to a different use.

Any cost that is added to the basis of an asset cannot be deducted currently. Examples of improvements include installation of new electric wiring, a new roof, adding central air conditioning, or renovation of a kitchen.

In contrast, a repair keeps a property in operating condition but does not add to its value or substantially prolong its life. Examples include repainting a property or replacing broken windows.

> **Example:** Douglas repairs a leaky toilet in a rental duplex. The repair may be deducted as a current expense. The following year, Douglas replaces the entire plumbing system in the duplex with new pipes and bathroom fixtures. This is an improvement that increases the value of the property. Douglas must capitalize the cost of the new plumbing, and thus increase the property's basis, and depreciate the cost of this improvement over its useful life.

Since improvements increase a property's basis, a taxpayer must keep accurate records to distinguish between the costs of repairs and improvements.

Repair vs. Improvements (Capitalization Rule Changes)

In December 2011,[118] the IRS released temporary regulations that will require major changes in determining whether certain costs are repairs or improvements, and thus whether they need to be expensed or capitalized. Under the changes, an improvement is redefined as a cost involving:

- The **betterment** of a **unit** of property,
- The **restoration** of a **unit** of property, or
- The **adaptation** of a **unit** of property to a new or different use.

The new IRS improvement standards apply to the building structure and to each of the building's major component systems separately. The guidelines divide a building into nine different structural components called "building systems," such as those for plumbing, heating and air conditioning, and electrical.

The effects of a repair on a specific building system, rather than the building as a whole, must be evaluated under the new, narrower definition of an improvement. The

---

[118] Federal Register, Dec. 27, 2011.

result will be to make costs more difficult to classify as repairs, meaning the taxpayer will be less likely to deduct them as expenses and more likely to capitalize them.

For example, under current guidelines significant repairs to an elevator may "better" the elevator but would not be significant to the building as a whole, so the repair could be expensed. Under the new guidelines, the costs would be significant to the *elevator system* and would have to be capitalized.

> **Example:** A landlord purchases an apartment building in 2010 for $750,000. In 2012 he spends $8,000 to fix wiring in the electrical system. Under the old IRS rules, the $8,000 likely would be considered a repair because it is relatively small compared to the overall cost of the building. Under the new rules, the electrical system is a separate structural component. This means that the $8,000 must be compared with the cost of the electrical system alone, not the cost of the whole building. This makes the expense more significant and more likely to constitute an improvement.

The final regulations are still being revised, and the IRS announced in December 2012 that it was delaying full implementation until 2014.[119] For the 2012 tax year, taxpayers have the choice to use the current rules or adopt the new ones.

Other Increases to Basis of Business Property

Among the items that increase the basis of property are the following:

- The cost of extending service lines to the property
- Impact fees
- Legal fees, such as the cost of defending and perfecting title
- Zoning costs

Government assessments for items such as paving roads and sidewalks increase the value of an asset, and therefore must be added to an asset's basis. A business cannot deduct assessments as taxes, but may deduct charges for maintenance, repairs, or interest charges related to the improvements.

Decreases to Basis

A business must decrease the basis of property by items that represent a return of capital for the period during which the business holds the property. For example, rebates and casualty losses are among the items that decrease an asset's basis.

> **Example:** Kristin buys a copier that costs $1,200 to use in her business. She sends in a rebate receipt and receives a $50 rebate from the manufacturer. The correct way to account for this rebate is to reduce the basis of the asset to $1,150 ($1,200 - $50).

Items that reduce the basis of property also include the following:

- Deductions for amortization, depreciation, section 179, and depletion (covered in Unit 9, *Depreciation of Business Assets*)
- Nontaxable corporate distributions
- Exclusion of subsidies for energy conservation measures

---

[119] IRS Notice 2012-73.

- Residential energy credits, vehicle credits, the Investment Credit, and the Credit for Employer-Provided Child Care
- Certain canceled debt excluded from income
- Easements

Casualty Losses

Deductible casualty losses and insurance reimbursements reduce the basis of property. A casualty is defined as the damage, destruction, or loss of property resulting from an identifiable event that is sudden, unexpected, or unusual.

Deductible casualty losses related to business and income-producing property (such as rental property)are reported on IRS Form 4684, *Casualties and Thefts*, and are deductible without regard to whether they exceed the $100 and 10% of AGI thresholds that apply for personal use property.

Example: Ramon has a fire at his home that destroys his couch and coffee table, which are personal-use property. The loss for his personal furniture is $5,000. This loss must be reduced by $100, and Ramon can deduct the portion that exceeds 10% of his AGI. The same fire also damages a business asset, an expensive laptop that he had brought home that day in order to catch up on his work. The computer is destroyed and results in a business casualty loss of $3,000 that is fully deductible.

A casualty loss is not deductible if the damage or destruction is caused by progressive deterioration due to normal wear and tear from weather conditions or insect damage. If an entity has business property that is stolen or destroyed, the loss is figured as follows:

The taxpayer's adjusted basis in the property
MINUS
Any salvage value
MINUS
Any insurance or other reimbursement received

Theft Losses

Many businesses are victims of theft, which is defined as the taking of money or property by the following means: blackmail, burglary, embezzlement, extortion, kidnapping for ransom, larceny, and robbery. The taking of property must be illegal under the state law where it happened, and it must have been done with criminal intent.

Example: Jeff owns a sports shop that sells memorabilia. Several years ago, Jeff purchased some signed football jerseys for display for $150, which is his adjusted basis in the property. Jeff's jerseys were stolen in 2012. The FMV of the jerseys was $1,000 just before they were stolen, and insurance did not cover them. Jeff's deductible theft loss is $150, which is his basis in the jerseys.

Casualty losses are generally deductible only in the tax year during which the casualty occurred, even if a business does not repair or replace the damaged property until a later year. Theft losses that are not reimbursable can be deducted only in the year the business discovers the property was stolen.

Insurance Reimbursements: If a business has property that is covered by insurance, it must file an insurance claim for reimbursement, or it will not be able to deduct the loss as a casualty or theft. The portion of the loss not covered by insurance, such as a deductible, is not subject to this rule.

Example: Howard and Gayle are partners and have a gourmet food truck that is used 100% for business purposes. Howard has an accident that causes $2,350 in damage to the truck. He and Gayle decide to pay the repair bill out-of-pocket so their business insurance costs will not increase. The insurance policy has a $500 deductible. Because the insurance would not cover the first $500 of a vehicle collision, only the $500 would be deductible as a casualty loss. This is true even when the business does not file an insurance claim, because the policy would not have reimbursed the deductible.

A business that has a casualty or theft loss must decrease its basis in the property by any insurance or reimbursement it receives and by any deductible loss. The result is the adjusted basis in the property.

A business must increase its basis in the property by the amount spent on repairs that restore the property to its pre-casualty condition. If a business's casualty or theft loss deduction causes deductions to be more than its income for the year, it has a net operating loss. The NOL could be carried back to an earlier year for tax the business already paid, resulting in a refund, or the NOL could be carried forward to lower tax in a later year.

Basis of Securities

The basis of stocks, bonds, and other securities is the purchase price plus any costs of purchase, such as commissions and recording or transfer fees. Stock is generally purchased in various quantities. A taxpayer must keep track of the basis per share of all stock bought and sold.

Example: In 2012, Yuen Corporation purchases 2,000 shares of Catalyst Corporation stock. The cost of the stock is $24,000, and Yuen pays a broker's fee of $550 on the purchase and transfer. Therefore, the basis of the stock is $24,550 ($24,000 + $550).

Events that occur after the purchase of the stock can require adjustments to the per share basis of stock. The original basis per share can be changed by events such as stock dividends, stock splits, and DRIP (dividend reinvestment plan) activity.

- Stock dividends involve the issuance of additional shares to current shareholders. The taxpayer's ownership total basis is unchanged but is spread over more shares, which decreases the basis per share.
- A stock split is similar to a stock dividend. For example, a two-for-one stock split increases the number of outstanding shares two-fold and decreases the value and the basis per share by half.

The total basis remains the same in a stock split. For example, if a taxpayer has 100 shares at $50 per share, his basis is $5,000. Assuming a 2 for 1 stock split, the taxpayer now has 200 shares at $25, which still equals $5,000.

> **Example:** In 2012, Zollinger Partnership purchases 100 shares of Better Electronics for $11,000. There is an additional $200 in broker's commissions, so the original basis per share is $112 ([$11,000 + $200] ÷ 100). Later in 2012, Zollinger receives 40 additional shares of Better Electronics' stock as a nontaxable stock dividend. The $11,200 basis must now be spread over 140 shares (100 original shares plus the 40-share stock dividend). The adjusted stock basis is $80 per share ([$11,200 ÷ 140).

Basis Other Than Cost

There are many times when a taxpayer cannot use cost as basis. In these cases, the fair market value or the adjusted basis of the property can be used.

Property received for services: If a taxpayer receives property for his services, he must include its FMV in income. The amount included in income becomes the basis. If the services were performed for a price agreed on beforehand, it will be accepted as the FMV of the property if there is no evidence to the contrary.

When property is transferred in lieu of wages, the employer is entitled to deduct its fair market value at the time of the transfer. A gain or loss is realized if there is a difference between the fair market value and the adjusted basis of the property.

Bargain purchases: A bargain purchase is a purchase of an item for less than its FMV. If, as compensation for services, a taxpayer buys goods or other property at less than the FMV, the difference between the purchase price and the property's FMV must be included in his income. His basis in the property is its FMV (the purchase price plus the amount included in income.)

Unit 8: Questions

1. Jade purchases a condemned warehouse for her business, but it is in such bad condition that she decides to demolish it and build a new one. The demolition costs $15,600. How must Jade report these costs on her tax return?

A. The cost for the demolition is added to the basis of the land where the original demolished structure was located.
B. The demolition may be expensed on her tax return on Schedule E.
C. The demolition cost is an itemized deduction on her Schedule A.
D. The demolition cost must be amortized over 180 months.

The answer is A. Demolition costs or other losses related to the demolition of any building are added to the basis of the land. ###

2. What item would not be included in an asset's basis?

A. Sales tax.
B. Installation charges.
C. Recording fees.
D. Interest paid on a loan to purchase the asset.

The answer is D. Interest charges are not added to an asset's basis. Interest is a currently deductible expense. ###

3. Ian buys a building. He makes a $15,000 down payment in cash. He also assumes a mortgage of $180,000 on it and pays $1,000 in title fees and $2,000 in points. What is Ian's basis in the building?

A. $15,000.
B. $195,000.
C. $196,000.
D. $198,000.

The answer is C. Ian's basis is $196,000. The title fees, mortgage amount, and the down payment are added together to figure the original cost basis of the building. The points are not included in the basis. ###

4. Irina owns a bookstore. In 2012, she has a business loss of $14,000 due to water damage from a storm. The loss is completely covered by insurance. However, Irina will not be reimbursed by her insurance company until 2013. How should she treat this loss?

A. She should claim the entire loss as a casualty loss in 2012 and then claim the income from the insurance company reimbursement in 2013.
B. She must reduce the amount of her inventory loss in 2012. For 2013, she must include the insurance reimbursement as income.
C. She does not need to make any adjustments to her tax return, since she knows she will receive a reimbursement within a short period of time.
D. She must reduce her cost of goods sold in 2012 to reflect the loss and then claim the reimbursement as income in 2013.

The answer is C. Irina expects to be fully reimbursed for her loss, so no adjustments are necessary. If Irina was reimbursed by her insurance company and her reimbursement either exceeded her losses or was less than her losses, then an adjustment would be necessary. ###

5. Under new IRS rules, what are the categories for determining what constitutes an improvement to property?

A. Betterment, restoration, or adaptation.
B. Prolonging life and creating value.
C. Renovation, amelioration, or restoration.
D. Enhancement and repair.

The answer is A. Under the new rules, an improvement is redefined as a cost involving a betterment of the unit of property, a restoration of the unit of property, or an adaptation of the unit of property to a new or different use. ###

6. How does a stock split affect basis?

A. There is no effect.
B. It increases the basis of stock.
C. It decreases the basis of stock.
D. It decreases the basis of a share of stock but does not affect the total basis of the stock.

The answer is D. A stock split increases the number of outstanding shares, which decreases the per-share value, but it does not change the basis of the stock as a whole. ###

7. Priscilla's Pastries, a sole proprietorship, bought a building for $250,000 in cash in March 2012. Priscilla paid the title company $13,000 in settlement fees to purchase the property. She also assumed an existing mortgage of $35,000 on the property. Legal fees of $9,500 were incurred in a title dispute with the former owner in April 2012. The title was finally transferred to Priscilla in May 2012. Property taxes in the amount of $2,600 were incurred on the property after ownership was transferred. What is Priscilla's basis in the building in December 2012?

A: $250,000.
B: $285,000.
C: $307,500.
D: $310,100.

The answer is C. The basis is $307,500 ($250,000 + $13,000 + $35,000 + $9,500). The settlement fees, mortgage assumed by the buyer, and the legal fees for defending a title are all included in the basis of the property. Priscilla cannot deduct the cost of the legal fees on her tax return as an expense. Instead, the amount must be added to the basis and depreciated. The property taxes are not included in the basis of the building because they were incurred when Priscilla was already the legal owner. Instead, the property taxes may be deducted as a current expense. ###

8. Which is not a correct statement regarding repairs vs. improvements under IRS rules?

A. A repair generally may be deducted as a current business expense.
B. A repair keeps a property in operating condition but does not add to its value or substantially prolong its life.
C. An improvement adds value to an asset, or appreciably lengthens the time a business can use it.
D. A taxpayer may choose whether to expense or capitalize improvements.

The answer is D. Improvements to a property cannot be deducted as expenses; they must be capitalized. ###

9. Arrowhead Model Builders is constructing a custom home. Calculate the basis of the property from the following information:

•$125,000 land purchase price
•$40,000 construction loan
•$3,000 points on construction loan
•$12,000 real estate taxes
•$20,000 tear-down of existing home
•$10,000 clearing brush
•$50,000 construction workers' wages
•$25,000 value of owner's labor
•$300,000 construction materials

A. $227,000.
B. $557,000.
C. $560,000.
D. $582,000.

The answer is B. All items are added to the property's basis except for the points on the loan (this is an expense that is deducted over the life of the loan) and the value of the owner's labor. ###

10. Franco purchases 50 shares of Canine Country stock for $3,500. He pays a broker's fee of $100. He later receives 40 additional shares of Canine Country stock. The following year, the company does a two-for-one stock split. Calculate the total basis of Franco's Canine Country stock and his per share basis:

A. Stock basis: $3,500; per share basis: $38.88.
B. Stock basis: $3,500; per share basis: $19.44.
C. Stock basis: $3,600; per share basis: $20.
D. Stock basis: $3,600; per share basis: $40.

The answer is C. The basis is the stock's purchase price plus the broker's fee ($3,500 + $100 = $3,600). After the stock split, Franco has 180 shares of stock (50 shares + 40 shares X 2 = 180). The stock split reduces his per share basis by half to $20 ($3,600 ÷ 180 shares of stock = $20). ###

Unit 9: Depreciation of Business Assets

More Reading:
Publication 946, *How to Depreciate Property*

Capital Expenditures

Under the Internal Revenue Code, certain costs and purchases must be capitalized, including the following:

- The expenses of going into business (start-up costs),
- The cost of business assets, and
- The cost of business improvements.

Capital expenditures are generally not currently deductible, but many of these costs may instead be recognized as depreciation or amortization expense over lives assigned to individual assets.

Example: Better Produce, Inc. is a canning company that processes fruits and vegetables. In 2012, it has an older canning machine that ceases to function. Better Produce has the option to purchase a new machine for $500,000, or completely rebuild its old machine, which will extend its useful life for another five years. Better Produce chooses to rebuild the machine at a cost of $125,000. The $125,000 cost must be capitalized and depreciated over its useful life, which in this case is five years.

Depreciation Overview

A depreciable asset usually has value well beyond the year in which it is purchased. Depreciation is an income tax deduction that allows a business to recover the cost or other basis of property. It is an annual allowance for the wear and tear, deterioration, or obsolescence of an asset. The amount allowed as an annual depreciation deduction is intended to roughly approximate the reduction in the value of a capital asset as it ages. Tax depreciation is based on the original, historical cost of the asset and is not indexed for inflation.

The cost of land and many land improvements cannot be depreciated. Most other types of tangible property, such as buildings, machinery, vehicles, furniture, and equipment, are depreciable. Likewise, certain intangible property, such as patents, copyrights, and computer software, is amortizable.

In order to be depreciated or amortized, an asset must meet all the following requirements:

- The taxpayer generally must own the property. However, taxpayers may also depreciate capital improvements for property they lease (for example, a fence that is built on property that the business leases from another party).
- A taxpayer must use the property in business or in an income-producing activity. If a taxpayer uses the property for *both* business and personal use,

he can only deduct an amount of depreciation based on the business-use percentage.

- The property must have a useful life of more than one year.

The property ceases to be depreciable when the business has fully recovered the property's cost or when the taxpayer sells or retires it from service, whichever happens first. In order to properly depreciate an asset, a taxpayer must identify the following:

- The depreciable basis of the property
- Whether the taxpayer elects to expense any portion of the asset
- The depreciation method for the property
- The class life of the asset (which is representative of the asset's useful life)
- Whether the property is listed property
- Whether the taxpayer qualifies for any bonus first year depreciation

The following assets are not depreciable:

- Property with a useful life of one year or less.
- Property placed in service and disposed of in the same year.
- Equipment that is used to build capital improvements.
- Section 197 intangibles such as copyrights and patents, which must be amortized, not depreciated.

Example: Natalie is a self-employed bookkeeper who is required to purchase new income tax return preparation software every year. She cannot depreciate the software but may instead deduct its cost as a business expense since the item only has a useful life of one year.

Taxpayers must use Form 4562, *Depreciation and Amortization* to:

- Claim deductions for depreciation and amortization,
- Make an election under section 179 to currently expense certain depreciable property, and
- Provide information on the business/investment use of automobiles and other listed property.

Example: Ron's Business Rentals made a down payment on a rental property and assumed the previous owner's mortgage. Ron owns the property and now may depreciate it.

Example: Harris's Doughnut Shop bought a new van that will be used only for business. Harris will be making payments on the van for the next five years. Harris owns the van and can depreciate it.

Modified Accelerated Cost Recovery System (MACRS)

The modified accelerated cost recovery system (MACRS) is the depreciation method generally used for most *tangible* property, such as machinery, buildings, and automobiles. Under MACRS, all assets are divided into nine separate classes that dictate the number of years over which their cost will be recovered. Each MACRS class has a schedule that specifies the percentage of the asset's cost that is depreciated each year.

For example, trucks are depreciated over five years, and fruit trees are depreciated over ten years.

MACRS Class Life Table

Property Class	Asset Type
3-year property	Certain tractor units; race horses over two years old; qualified rent-to-own property.
5-year property	Computers; office machinery; automobiles, taxis, buses, and trucks; breeding cattle and dairy cattle; appliances, carpets, and furniture used in residential retail activity; certain geothermal, solar, and wind property.
7-year property	Office furniture and fixtures; agricultural machinery and equipment; any other property that does not have a designated class life.
10-year property	Vessels and water transportation equipment; trees or vines bearing fruit or nuts; single purpose agricultural or horticultural structures.
15-year property	Improvements to land such as fences, roads, and bridges; municipal wastewater treatment plants; qualified restaurant and retail improvement property; qualified leasehold improvement property.
20-year property	Certain municipal sewers; farm buildings (other than single purpose agricultural or horticultural structures).
25-year property	Certain municipal sewers; water utility property.
27.5-year property	Residential rental property, if more than 80% of its gross rental income is from dwelling units.
39-year property	Section 1250 nonresidential real property, such as office buildings, stores, and warehouses.

The depreciation calculations spread out deduction of the asset's cost over a recovery period roughly consistent with the asset's estimated useful economic life. Certain assets, such as computers, office furniture, and cars, are assigned the same recovery period in all industries.

Real property is depreciated using the straight-line method, with an equal amount of expense each year. The recovery periods for buildings vary depending upon the property's use. For example, nonresidential buildings, such as office buildings, shopping malls, and factories, are depreciated over a 39-year recovery period. Residential buildings, such as apartment complexes and residential rentals, are depreciated over a 27.5-year period.

Placed-in-Service Date

Depreciation begins when a taxpayer places property in service for the production of income. This is called the placed-in-service date.

> **Example:** Donald buys a machine for his business that is delivered on December 20, 2012. However, the machine is not installed and operational until January 12, 2013. It is considered placed in service in 2013, and the first depreciation expense deduction can be claimed in 2013.

If the machine had been ready and available for use when it was delivered, it would have been considered placed in service in 2012 even if it were not actually used until 2013.

> **Example:** On June 23, 2012, Sue bought a house to use as residential rental property. She made several repairs and had it ready for rent on September 5, 2012. At that time, she began to advertise the home for rent in the local newspaper. Sue can begin to depreciate the rental property in September because it is considered placed in service when it is ready and available for rent.

Salvage Value (Scrap Value)

An asset cannot be depreciated below its salvage (or scrap) value. Salvage value is the asset's estimated FMV at the end of its useful life. Salvage value is affected both by *how* a business uses the property and *how long* it uses it. If it is the business's policy to dispose of property that is still in good operating condition, the salvage value can be relatively large. If the business's policy is to use property until it is no longer usable, its salvage value can be zero.

> **Example:** Cooper Trucking operates a trucking fleet that delivers produce. Cooper Trucking purchases a new delivery truck in 2012 for $125,000. The MACRS class life of the truck is five years. At the end of five years, Cooper Trucking estimates it will sell the used delivery truck at auction for $30,000, so it uses this amount as salvage value. The basis of the truck is $125,000, but the *basis for depreciation* is $95,000 ($125,000-$30,000), since the business expects to recover $30,000 at the end of the asset's useful life.

Common Depreciation Methods

A business generally may use any accepted depreciation method. However, once it chooses a depreciation method for an asset, the business must generally use the same method for the life of the asset.

Straight-Line Depreciation

> **Straight-line Depreciation = (Cost - Salvage Value) ÷ Useful Life**

This is the simplest depreciation method. To use the straight-line method, a business must first determine the asset's basis, salvage value, and class life. If the asset has a salvage value, it is subtracted from the basis. The balance is the total depreciation expense deduction the business can take over the useful life of the property. For an asset that originally cost $200, has an estimated salvage value of zero, and a five-year recovery period, the straight-line depreciation allowance would be $40 ($200 ÷ 5) each year for five years.

A business may switch to the straight-line method at any time during the useful life of the property without IRS consent. However, after a business changes to straight-line, it cannot change back to any other method for a period of ten years without written permission from the IRS.

> **Example:** On April 1, 2012, the Redstone Granite Corporation purchases a computer system for $40,000. The system has a five-year class life under MACRS. There is no salvage value. Depreciation is figured as follows:
>
> Depreciation for 2012 = ($40,000 ÷ 5 years) x (9 months ÷ 12) = **$6,000.**
> Depreciation for 2013 = ($40,000 ÷ 5 years) x (12 ÷ 12) = **$8,000.**

The Double-Declining Balance Method

This method uses a flat percentage depreciation rate over the class life of the asset. For example, if five years is the asset's cost recovery period, the double-declining balance method has a depreciation rate of [2 ÷ 5], or twice the straight-line depreciation rate. Instead of spreading the cost of the asset evenly over its life, this method expenses the asset by applying a constant rate to the declining balance of the asset, which results in declining depreciation expense each successive period.

The logic for the double-declining balance method is that there should be a greater deduction in the earlier years when the asset is more productive.

> **Example:** For an asset that originally cost $200 and has a five-year recovery period, double-declining balance depreciation is $80 = ([2 ÷ 5]x $200) in the first year; $48 = ([2 ÷ 5]x[$200 - $80]) in the second year; $28.80 = ([2 ÷ 5]x[$200 - $80 - $48]) in the third year; and so on.

Although assets are usually depreciated according to the MACRS tables, there are other depreciation methods that are not based on a term of years. This is common in manufacturing businesses, where the useful life of machinery can vary based on production.

A business can elect to exclude certain property from MACRS by making an election on Form 4562.

Unit-of-Production Method

This method allocates depreciation based on the asset's units of activity, rather than on a set number of years. For example, airplanes may be depreciated based on air miles, delivery trucks based on miles driven, and machinery based on the number of units produced.

Depreciation is computed by dividing the total cost of the asset (minus salvage value) by its projected units-of-production capacity. Then, to determine depreciation expense each period, the business multiplies the depreciation per unit of production (or activity) by the number of units during the period.

Example: The Kumar Company owns a machine that produces computer components. It was purchased for $500,000 and the machine is expected to produce 240,000 units over its useful life. The salvage value of the machine is estimated at $20,000. Using the units of production method, the machine's depreciable basis is $480,000 ($500,000 - $20,000 salvage value). The depreciable basis is divided by the number of units that the machine is expected to produce ($480,000 ÷ 240,000). This equals depreciation of $2 per unit produced. If the machine produces 30,000 components in 2012, depreciation for the year will be $60,000 ($2 x 30,000 units). If the machine produces 25,000 parts in 2013, its depreciation will be $50,000 ($2 x 25,000 units). The depreciation will be calculated similarly each year until the asset's accumulated depreciation reaches $480,000. At that point, even if the machine is still in use, it will be considered fully depreciated, and the depreciation will stop.

Section 179 Deduction

The section 179 deduction is a special allowance that allows certain small businesses to elect to take a full deduction for the cost of new or used property in the first year they place it in service, rather than depreciating it over its useful life. However, a business may choose to use standard depreciation methods for its assets instead of electing to use the section 179 deduction.

To qualify for the section 179 deduction, the property must meet all the following requirements:

- It must be tangible property, with the exception of off-the-shelf computer software
- It must be acquired for business use (and used more than 50% for business in the year placed in service)
- It must have been acquired by purchase (not as a gift)
- It must not have been purchased from a related party, including a spouse, ancestors, or lineal descendants

Eligible property generally includes the following:

- Machinery and equipment.
- Property contained in or attached to a building (other than structural components), such as refrigerators, grocery store counters, office equipment, printing presses, testing equipment, and signs.
- Gasoline storage tanks and pumps at retail service stations.
- Livestock, including horses, cattle, hogs, sheep, goats, and mink and other furbearing animals.
- Computer software ("off-the-shelf" computer software is one of the few *intangible* assets that is eligible for section 179)
- Business vehicles with a gross vehicle weight in excess of 6,000 pounds

Section 179 Limits and Phase-Outs

The section 179 deduction may not exceed taxable income for the year. For example, if a business's taxable income is $150,000, the section 179 deduction cannot exceed $150,000. However, an amount disallowed due to this limitation may be carried over for an unlimited number of years.

The deduction can be elected for individual qualifying assets, up to a maximum of $500,000 for 2012. The deduction amount may be increased by up to $35,000 for businesses in qualifying enterprise zones and up to $100,000 for businesses in federally declared disaster areas. However, to the extent the cost of qualifying section 179 property placed in service by the taxpayer exceeds $2 million, the maximum is reduced on a dollar-for-dollar basis, and eliminated if the total cost of qualifying property is at least $2.5 million.[120]

Qualified Real Property (QRP)

Businesses generally may not deduct the costs of real property under section 179. However, a special provision presently allows businesses to use up to $250,000 of the $500,000 limit described above for costs of qualified real property (QRP).[121]

This provision applies only to the following:

- Qualified leasehold improvement property
- Qualified restaurant property (such as renovation of a restaurant building)
- Qualified retail improvement property (such as an interior upgrade of a retail clothing store)

Example: Armando owns an Italian restaurant. In 2012, he renovates the interior by upgrading the booths and remodeling the kitchen at a cost of $260,000. He also purchases a computer for use in his business at a cost of $5,000. Therefore, Armando has the following qualifying expenses for the section 179 deduction:

Computer:	$5,000
Qualified real property :	$260,000
Total asset purchases in 2012:	**$265,000**

Since the limit for expensing QRP under section 179 is $250,000, Armando may only expense $250,000 of the renovation costs. However, he may still take the section 179 deduction for the full cost of the computer, since the limit for other qualifying property is $500,000 in 2012. Armando's allowable section 179 deduction is therefore limited to $255,000 ($5,000 computer + $250,000 of QRP). The excess amount of $10,000 may be depreciated over the useful life applicable for this type of real property.

---

[120] The section 179 deduction limits were increased in 2010 and 2011, but were scheduled to decrease in 2012. However, the American Taxpayer Relief Act of 2012 retroactively reinstated the $500,000 deduction and $2 million dollar phase-out for tax year 2012 and extended these levels through 2013.
[121] Congress also retroactively reinstated the QRP provision for 2012 and extended it through 2013.

> **Example:** In 2012, Ashby Corporation purchases refurbished manufacturing equipment costing $2.1 million. The cost of the equipment is $100,000 more than $2 million limit, so Ashby Corporation must reduce its section 179 dollar limit to $400,000 ($500,000 – $100,000). The remaining cost basis of $1.7 million ($2.1 million - $400,000 deducted under section 179) may be recovered using regular depreciation methods. ***Note:** the equipment in this scenario is not eligible for bonus depreciation because it is used.

Trade-in Property: If a business buys qualifying property with cash and a trade-in, its depreciable basis for purposes of the section 179 deduction includes *only* the cash the business paid.

> **Example:** Soccer Time, a retail sports shop, traded two wood displays with a total adjusted basis of $680 for a new glass display that cost $1,320. Soccer Time received an $800 trade-in allowance for the old displays and paid an additional $520 in cash for the new glass display. The shop also traded a used van with an adjusted basis of $4,500 for a new van costing $9,000. Soccer Time received a $4,800 trade-in allowance on the used van and paid $4,200 in cash for the new van. Only the portion of the new property's basis paid by cash qualifies for the section 179 deduction. Therefore, Soccer Time's qualifying costs for the section 179 deduction are $4,720 ($520 + $4,200).

Bonus Depreciation

If the cost of business property cannot immediately be deducted as a section 179 expense, a business may elect to take bonus depreciation for certain types of new property (***Note:** Unlike section 179, bonus depreciation does **not** apply to used property). This provision allows a business to write off 50% of certain property costs in the first year, with the remaining cost depreciated over the asset's useful life. Applicable section 179 deductions are generally used first, followed by bonus depreciation, unless the business has an insufficient level of taxable income.

The bonus depreciation allowance generally applies to tangible personal property with a recovery period of 20 years or less, as well as to certain buildings and leasehold improvements, office equipment, and purchased computer software. The property must be new and in original use condition (unlike the requirement for section 179 deduction, which is allowed for both new and used property.)

Bonus depreciation is useful to businesses that spend large amounts on equipment during the year because it is not subject to the same $2 million phase-out as the section 179 deduction.

Listed Property

Special rules apply to listed property, which includes cars and other vehicles used for transportation; property used for entertainment, recreation, or amusement such as photographic or video-recording equipment; and certain computers. If an item is used for both business and personal purposes, deductions for depreciation and section 179 are based on the percentage of business use. Further, if business use is not more than 50%, section 179 deductions and bonus depreciation allowances are not allowed, and depreciation must be calculated using the straight-line method.

> **Example:** In 2012, Eleanor buys and places into service a new computer that costs $4,000. She uses the computer 80% for her business and 20% for personal purposes. The business part of the cost of the property is $3,200 (80% × $4,000), which she may deduct under section 179.

Property that is 100% business-use, such as a desktop computer and printer used exclusively at a business location (including a qualified home office), is not considered listed property. Further, the IRS no longer categorizes cellular telephones as listed property.

Heavy Sports Utility Vehicle Exception:[122] A taxpayer cannot elect to expense under section 179 more than $25,000 of the cost of any heavy sport utility vehicle (SUV) and certain other vehicles placed in service during the tax year. This rule applies to vehicles weighing between 6,000 and 14,000 pounds. Ambulances, hearses, taxis, transport vans, clearly marked emergency vehicles, and other qualified non-personal use vehicles are excluded from the $25,000 limit.

Section 280F "Luxury Automobile" Depreciation Limits: For certain other passenger vehicles weighing less than 6,000 pounds and used more than 50% for business purposes, the total depreciation deduction is also limited, as outlined under section 280F. Although the term "luxury" automobile is used in section 280F's caption, it does not appear in the general rule, and the depreciation limits affect most new cars. The IRS releases guidance regarding tax treatment for specific makes and models of vehicles each year, adjusted for inflation. In 2012, bonus depreciation is capped at $11,160 for cars and $11,360 for trucks and vans during the first year they are placed into service.[123]

Depletion

Depletion is similar in concept to depreciation, and is the method of cost recovery for mining and agricultural activities. Depletion refers to the exhaustion of a natural resource as a result of production, such as using up of natural resources by mining, quarrying, or felling (of timber).

Mineral property, timber, and natural gas are all examples of natural resources that are subject to the deduction for depletion. There are two ways of figuring depletion:

- Cost depletion
- Percentage depletion

Cost Depletion

This method allocates the cost of a natural resource over the total anticipated volume to yield cost depletion per unit (expressed in tons, barrels, etc.) A depletion deduction is then allowed each year based on the units exploited.

---

[122] This use of the section 179 deduction became known as the "Hummer Tax Loophole" because it allowed businesses to buy large SUVs and write them off. The IRS has since modified the tax code with the limits described above. EA exam-takers should be familiar with the limits on vehicle depreciation.
[123] Revenue Procedure 2012-14.

After a business determines the property's basis, estimates the total recoverable units, and knows the number of units sold during the tax year, it can calculate the cost depletion deduction as follows:

> Divide the property's basis for depletion by estimated total recoverable units
>
> **= Rate per unit**
>
> Multiply the rate per unit by actual units sold = **Cost depletion deduction**
>
> **Example:** In 2012, Brian buys a timber farm, and he estimates the timber can produce 300,000 units when cut. At the time of purchase, the adjusted basis of the timber is $24,000. Brian then cuts and sells 27,000 units. Brian's depletion rate for each unit is $.08 ($24,000 ÷ 300,000). His deduction for depletion in 2012 is $2,160 (27,000 × $.08).

Percentage Depletion

This is an alternative method of computing depletion. Under this method, a flat percentage of gross income from the property is taken as the depletion deduction. Percentage depletion may not be used for timber and its use for oil and gas properties is subject to strict limits.

To figure percentage depletion, businesses multiply a certain percentage, specified for each mineral, by gross income from the property during the year. The percentage depletion deduction generally cannot be more than 50% (100% for oil and gas property) of taxable income from the property, before the depletion deduction and the domestic production activities deduction (DPAD).

Some businesses employ cost depletion at the outset of operations when a large number of units of the deposit are extracted and sold, and then convert to percentage depletion later when percentage depletion yields a more sizable deduction.

Amortization

Intangible assets include goodwill, patents, copyrights, trademarks, trade names, and franchises. Amortization is used to deduct the cost of an intangible asset over the projected life of the asset, in a manner similar to the straight-line method of depreciation.

The basis of an intangible asset is usually the cost to buy or create it and must be determined before the asset can be amortized. Businesses determine yearly amortization by dividing the cost of the intangible asset by the useful life of the intangible asset.

> **Example:** Sean spent $125,000 to purchase a copyright. The copyright has a remaining life of 15 years; the amount amortized each year is $8,333.
>
> **Initial Cost ÷ Useful Life = Amortization per Year**
>
> ($125,000 ÷ 15 = $8,333 per year)

> **Example:** Charlotte purchases a trademark from another company. The trademark costs $28,880. The trademark has 16 years remaining before expiration. She must amortize the asset over 16 years (192 months). Therefore, the monthly amortization expense is $150 ($28,880 ÷ 192).

> **Example:** On April 1, 2012, Frank buys a patent for $5,100. The patent will expire in 17 years. He amortizes the patent using the straight-line method over its useful life of 17 years. He divides the $5,100 basis by 17 years to get his $300 yearly deduction. He only owned the patent for nine months during 2012, so he multiplies $300 by 9/12 to get his deduction of $225 for the first year. In 2013, Frank can deduct $300 for the full year.

Patents: The basis of a patent is generally the cost of its development, such as research and experimental expenditures, drawings, working models, and legal and governmental fees. If the business is allowed to deduct research and experimental expenditures as current business expenses, it cannot include these same costs in the basis of the patent. The value of an inventor's time is not considered part of the basis, unless compensation cost is incurred (as in the case where the inventor is an employee of a business).

Copyrights: The basis of a copyright will usually be the costs of obtaining the copyright, including copyright fees, attorney fees, and clerical assistance.

The useful life of a patent or copyright is the lesser of the life granted by the government or the remaining life when the business acquires it (if it is purchased or acquired from the original owner).

> **Example:** Jackson purchases a patent for an electrical power strip. He plans to manufacture the power strip and sell it to customers. The patent has nine years left before expiration, so Jackson may depreciate the cost over nine years.

However, if the patent or copyright becomes valueless before the end of its useful life, the remaining cost can be deducted as an expense in the year that happens.

> **Example:** Harriet purchases a patent for a popular toy design that has a useful life of 10 years. However, two years after the purchase, the toy design is deemed hazardous to children, and all the toys are recalled. The patent is now considered worthless, and the remaining cost can be expensed.

Patents and copyrights are not eligible for section 179 deductions or any other accelerated depreciation method.

A business may amortize the capitalized costs of section 197 intangibles over a 15-year period (180 months). Section 197 intangibles are assets that are created in connection with the acquisition of a business, and include goodwill, formulas and trademarks, franchise licenses, and intangibles such as favorable relationships with customers or suppliers that are carried over from the business being purchased. These intangible assets are not eligible for accelerated or bonus depreciation.

Unit 9: Questions

1. The maximum section 179 expense a business can elect to deduct for qualified real property placed in service in 2012 is:

A: $179,000.
B: $250,000.
C: $500,000.
D: $2 million.

The answer is B. In 2012, there is a special provision that allows taxpayers to deduct up to $250,000 of qualified real property (QRP) under section 179. This special allowance for QRP is included within the maximum $500,000 section 179 limit. For example, a taxpayer can have $250,000 of QRP and $250,000 of other business property to make up the $500,000 section 179 depreciation allowance. ###

2. The Friendship Spirit Partnership bought the Andrews Brothers Partnership. The goodwill and covenant not to compete associated with the purchase was valued at $100,000. Per section 197, what is the number of years over which goodwill can be amortized?

A. 5 years.
B. 10 years.
C. 15 years.
D. 25 years.

The answer is C. Goodwill is a section 197 intangible. A business must amortize over 15 years (180 months) the capitalized costs of section 197 intangibles. ###

3. Which of the following would not qualify for a depletion deduction?

A. Oil well.
B. Timber.
C. Diamond mine.
D. Gasoline refinery factory.

The answer is D. A gasoline refinery would not qualify since it is not the depletion of a natural resource but is instead a factory that refines the product. Depletion is the exhaustion of natural resources, such as mines, wells, and timber, as a result of production. ###

4. Which of the following types of business property qualifies for the section 179 accelerated depreciation deduction?

A. A delivery truck.
B. A business building.
C. A residential rental property.
D. A patent.

The answer is A. To qualify for the section 179 deduction, the property must be tangible personal property. Buildings, houses, and other real property generally do not qualify for section 179 treatment. Intangible assets, such as patents and copyrights, must be amortized over their useful life. ###

5. Tom owns a construction business. He would like to switch his assets to straight-line depreciation for easier accounting and tracking of the assets. All of the following statements are correct except:

A. A business may switch to the straight-line method at any time during the useful life of the property without IRS consent.
B. A business must always request permission from the IRS to switch to the straight-line method.
C. When the change to straight-line is made, depreciation is figured based on the taxpayer's adjusted basis in the property at that time.
D. Tom can choose to switch all of his assets to straight-line no matter what type of depreciation method he has been using previously.

The answer is B. A business does not need to request IRS permission to switch to the straight-line method of depreciation. No special consent is required. ###

6. Levi owns a convenience store. He purchases two computers from his grandfather and places both in service in 2012 as part of a bona fide business transaction. The computers cost $750 each. Which of the following is true?

A. Levi can take a section 179 deduction for the computers.
B. Levi can take regular MACRS depreciation on the computers.
C. Levi is not allowed to depreciate the computers since they were purchased from a related party. But he may take bonus depreciation on the computers.
D. Levi may take either section 179 or bonus depreciation on the computers.

The answer is B. The computers do not qualify as section 179 property because Levi and his grandfather are related persons, meaning Levi cannot claim a section 179 deduction. However, Levi may still depreciate the computers using the MACRS depreciation schedule. ###

7. Mary purchases a new computer that costs $1,100. She uses the property 75% for her business and 25% for personal purposes. What is Mary's section 179 depreciation deduction?

A. $0.
B. $275.
C. $825.
D. $1,100.

The answer is C. The business part of the cost of the property is $825 (75% × $1,100). ###

8. Camarillo Mexican Cantinas bought a restaurant for $500,000 on January 15, 2012. Included in the purchase price were business assets as follows:

•Certificate of deposit: $100,000
•Accounts receivable of $50,000
•Truck with FMV of $80,000 and adjusted basis of $68,000
•Industrial oven with FMV of $20,000 and adjusted basis of $18,000

For depreciation purposes, what portion of the $500,000 lump-sum payment is allocated to the combination oven?

A. $18,000.
B. $53,320.
C. $20,000.
D. $50,000.

The answer is C. Absent any information indicating the seller was a related party, their adjusted basis would not be relevant to how Camarillo Mexican Cantinas allocates the total purchase price among the individual assets acquired. Instead, since the total paid ($500,000) to acquire the business exceeds the total FMV of the assets acquired ($250,000), they would allocate value based in proportion to (but not more than) the FMV of each individual asset, and the remainder would be allocated to goodwill. ###

9. Lou is a sole proprietor who buys a cellular phone for $720 in 2012. Based on his phone records, Lou uses the cell phone 45% for business use and 55% for personal use. What is Lou's section 179 deduction for 2012?

A. $0.
B. $324.
C. $396.
D. $720.

The answer is A. When a taxpayer uses property for both business and nonbusiness purposes, he can elect the section 179 deduction only if he uses the property more than 50% for business in the year the asset is placed into service. Lou may still choose to use another depreciation method for the business portion of the phone. ###

10. Which of the following property is a business not able to depreciate?

A. Property placed in service and disposed of in the same year.
B. Intangible assets.
C. Machinery.
D. Buildings.

The answer is A. Property placed in service and disposed of in the same year is not depreciated. Business property ceases to be depreciable when the taxpayer has fully recovered the property's cost or when the taxpayer disposes of it. If a business buys and then disposes of an asset in the same year, it would not be depreciated. ###

11. Using MACRS, what is the recovery period for depreciating a commercial office building?

A. 20 years.
B. 25 years.
C. 27.5 years.
D. 39 years.

The answer is D. Commercial real property is depreciated over a 39-year recovery period. ###

12. Kerman Corporation is a calendar-year, cash-basis corporation that specializes in constructing office buildings. Kerman bought a truck on December 1, 2012 that had to be modified to lift materials to second-story levels. The truck is 100% business-use. After the lifting equipment was installed, Kerman accepted delivery of the modified truck on January 10, 2013. The truck was placed in service on January 23, 2012, the date it was ready and available to perform the function for which it was bought. When can Kerman start depreciating the truck?

A. 2012.
B. 2013.
C. 2014.
D. Never.

The answer is B. Kerman may not depreciate the truck until it is placed in service for business use, which was in 2013. ###

13. Which of the following vehicles is considered listed property for tax purposes?

A. An ambulance.
B. A passenger automobile weighing 6,000 pounds or less.
C. A taxi.
D. A marked police car.

The answer is B. The IRS considers regular passenger automobiles weighing 6,000 pounds or less as listed property. ###

14. In 2012, Vanner Partnership placed in service section 179 property with a total cost of $2,025,000. The partnership's taxable income in 2012 was $600,000. What is Vanner's allowable section 179 deduction for 2012?

A. $0.
B. $475,000.
C. $500,000.
D. $600,000.

The answer is B. The partnership must reduce its section 179 dollar limit by $25,000, the amount of its qualifying purchases that exceeds the $2 million limit ($2,025,000 – $2,000,000). Its maximum section 179 deduction is $475,000 ($500,000 – $25,000). The partnership's taxable income from the active conduct of all its trades or businesses for the year was $600,000, so it can deduct the full $475,000. ###

15. Alex is having financial difficulties, so he sells his office building to Cheryl, a real estate investor, who plans to use it as a business rental property. Alex was liable for $5,000 in delinquent real estate taxes on the property, which Cheryl agrees to pay. How should Cheryl treat this transaction?

A. Cheryl cannot deduct these taxes as a current expense; she must add the amount to the basis of the property.
B. Cheryl can deduct these taxes as a current expense on her Schedule A.
C. Cheryl can deduct these taxes as a current expense on her Schedule E.
D. Cheryl can deduct these taxes as a current expense on her Schedule C.

The answer is A. Cheryl may not deduct the taxes as a current expense, since they are delinquent real estate taxes and the person who is legally liable for the debt is Alex. However, the taxes may be added to the property's basis and depreciated as part of the purchase price, since Cheryl intends to use the property as a rental. ###

16. TJ buys and places in service professional video-recording equipment in 2012. He pays $15,000 cash and receives a $3,000 trade-in allowance for used video equipment. He used both the old and new video-recording equipment 90% for business and 10% for personal purposes. His allowable section 179 deduction is:

A. $16,200.
B. $13,500.
C. $12,600.
D. $15,000.

The answer is B. The section 179 deduction applies only to the amount actually paid in cash and not to the value of his trade-in allowance, and further applies only to the portion used for business purposes. Thus, the deduction is limited to 90% of $15,000, or $13,500. ###

17. Lucy and Jessica are equal partners in a restaurant. In 2012, they purchase a new $30,000 pizza oven for the restaurant and want to take the section 179 deduction for the full cost of the oven. The partnership's ordinary income before the section 179 deduction is $25,000. There were no other qualifying section 179 purchases during the year. What is the amount of section 179 deduction that Lucy can deduct on her individual tax return?

A. $0.
B. $6,000.
C. $12,500.
D. $15,000.

The answer is C. The section 179 deduction for the $30,000 oven is limited by the partnership income. The section 179 deduction cannot exceed overall income for the year, so it is limited to $25,000. Then the deduction is split between the two partners ($25,000 X 50%) = $12,500. Section 179 is a separately stated item on a partnership tax return. ###

Unit 10: Disposition of Business Assets

> **More Reading:**
> **Publication 544, *Sales and Other Dispositions of Assets***

Business assets may be sold, traded, exchanged, abandoned, or destroyed. A business may recognize a gain or loss if it:

- Sells property for cash
- Exchanges property for other property
- Receives payment from a tenant for the cancellation of a lease
- Receives payment for granting the exclusive use of a copyright
- Receives property to satisfy a debt
- Abandons property
- Receives insurance reimbursement for damaged property

A taxpayer may fully depreciate an asset until its adjusted basis is zero, but continue to use the asset thereafter until it is no longer useful. If an asset is sold, the amount received is compared to the asset's adjusted basis to determine whether a gain or loss should be recognized.

To properly report the disposition of an asset, a taxpayer must first determine whether it is a *capital asset*, a *noncapital asset,* or a *section 1231 asset.*

Capital Assets

Capital assets include personal-use assets; collectibles; and investment property such as stocks, bonds, and other securities (unless held by a professional securities dealer). A personal residence and personal-use car are both examples of capital assets. A gain from the disposition of personal-use property is a capital gain, but a loss is generally not deductible, except for certain casualty losses.

> **Example:** Jim collects toy mechanical banks as a hobby, and he owns 15 of them, which have appreciated in value. He is not a professional dealer. Jim's mechanical banks are considered capital assets.

Noncapital Assets

Noncapital assets include inventory, accounts receivable, and other assets used in a trade or business, as residential rental property, or to produce royalties. The definition of a "capital asset" varies based on the type of asset, and for how long the asset is held.

> **Example:** In February 2012, Ines purchases a black-and-white copy machine for use in her business. The machine cost $6,000, but by July she realizes she needs a color copier instead. It is too late to return it to the store, so Ines sells the used black-and-white copier for $3,000. The copier is a business asset held for less than a year, so it is treated as a noncapital asset. She recognizes an ordinary loss that may be deducted on her business's income tax return.

Section 1231 Assets

Section 1231 assets include business (noncapital) assets that have been held for more than one year, as well as certain business and investment property disposed of in involuntary conversions.

The tax code gives special treatment to transactions involving disposition of section 1231 assets. If the taxpayer has a net loss from all section 1231 transactions, the loss is treated as ordinary loss. If the section 1231 transactions result in a net gain, the gain is generally treated as capital gain (except for depreciation recapture, which is taxed as ordinary income, as discussed below).

Example: Philip owns an antique vase that he purchased at auction two years ago. He also owns a residential rental property that he purchased three years ago, as well as two vehicles. One is a pizza delivery van he bought five years ago that he uses exclusively in his restaurant business. The other vehicle is his personal-use SUV that he uses for commuting and everyday errands. Phillip's assets are categorized as follows:

1. Antique vase: A capital asset, because it is a collectible

2. Residential rental property: Section 1231 rental property (held over one year and business-use)

3. Pizza delivery van: Section 1231 business property (held over one year and business-use)

4. SUV: A capital asset, because it is a personal-use vehicle

Section 1231 Transactions

Section 1231 assets include depreciable business property such as buildings, machinery, timber, unharvested crops, livestock, and leaseholds. Section 1231 assets can also include nondepreciable real property (such as land that is purchased for business use) and property that is held for the production of income but that is involuntarily converted due to theft, casualty, or condemnation. Other examples of section 1231 assets include the following:

- Machinery used in business
- A patent, copyright, or other intangible asset used in a business
- Hotels, office buildings, warehouses, residential apartment complexes, and other residential rental property
- Any asset held for more than one year that is used for the production of income and has been involuntarily converted

In order to qualify as section 1231 property, the property must have been held for more than one year. Gain or loss on the following transactions is subject to section 1231 treatment:

1. **Sale or exchange of cattle and horses:** They must be held for draft, breeding, dairy, or sporting purposes and held for 24 months or longer.

2. **Sale or exchange of other livestock:** Other livestock includes hogs, mules, sheep, goats, donkeys, and other fur-bearing animals. They must be held for draft, breeding, dairy, or sporting purposes and held for 12 months or longer.

3. **Sale or exchange of depreciable (or amortizable) property:** Business property that is held for more than one year. Examples include machinery and trucks, as well as amortizable section 197 intangibles such as patents or copyrights.
4. **Sale or exchange of business real estate:** The property must be used in a business activity and held for more than one year. Examples include barns and office buildings.
5. **Sale or exchange of unharvested crops:** The crops and land must be sold, exchanged, or involuntarily converted at the same time and to the same person, and the land must have been held longer than one year. Growing crops sold with a leasehold on the land, even if sold to the same person in a single transaction, are not included.

Example: Harwell Inc. manufactures shipping containers. Harwell has owned the land and the building that houses its manufacturing operations for many years. The land and the building are therefore section 1231 assets, because they are used in a business and have been held for more than one year. Harwell also has unsold shipping containers in inventory. Inventory is generally not a section 1231 and its sale in the ordinary course of business results in ordinary income or loss.

Example: Six years ago, Superior Design Inc. purchased a computer for $10,000. The company sells it this year for $700. Superior Design had depreciated the computer down to its salvage value, which was estimated at $1,000. The company has a loss of $300 on the sale of the computer ($1,000 salvage value minus $700 sale price). The computer is a section 1231 asset and the loss is an ordinary loss.

Section 1231 and Involuntary Conversions

The sale, exchange, or involuntary conversion of inventory is not a section 1231 transaction. This applies to business property or a capital asset held in connection with a trade or business or a transaction entered into for profit, such as investment property, but not to property held for personal use, such as a personal residence. The business property in these transactions must have been held for more than a year.

The sale of a copyright, literary, musical, or artistic composition is not a section 1231 transaction if a taxpayer's personal efforts created the property, or if it was received as a gift from a previous owner whose personal efforts created it. The sale of such property results in ordinary income and generally is reported on Form 4797, *Sales of Business Property.*

Example: Debbie is a self-employed writer who reports her income on Schedule C. She writes a popular crockpot cookbook and publishes it. A few years later, Debbie sells the copyright of the manuscript to a publisher. The sale is ordinary income and must be reported on Form 4797. This is not a section 1231 transaction, because the copyright was self-created.

Depreciation Recapture

Depreciation recapture is required when a business sells previously depreciated or amortized property at a gain. In this instance, the business may have to recapture the portion of the gain attributable to depreciation and treat this amount (even if otherwise nontaxable) as ordinary income. The balance of the gain in excess of the recaptured depreciation is treated as capital gain.

Example: Jeff runs Hammerton Dairy Farm, which is a calendar-year sole proprietorship. In February 2010, Jeff buys a tractor (5-year property) that costs $10,000. MACRS depreciation deductions for the tractor are $1,500 in 2010 and $2,550 in 2011 (based upon MACRS table A-14 for 150% declining balance depreciation using a half-year convention). Jeff sells the tractor in May 2012 for $7,000. The MACRS deduction in 2012 is $893 (½ of $1,785). The gain on the sale of the tractor that must be treated as ordinary income is figured as follows:

Amount received in the sale	$7,000
Original purchase price	$10,000
MACRS depreciation deductions ($1,500 + $2,550 + $893)	($4,943)
Adjusted basis	$5,057
Gain realized ($7,000 - $5,057)	**$1,943**

The realized gain is less than the amount of depreciation subject to recapture, so the entire amount is treated as ordinary income.

In determining depreciable recapture for property sold at a gain, there is a critical distinction between two types of property: section 1245 and section 1250. For section 1245 property, any gain attributable to previously deducted depreciation allowance is taxed as ordinary income. For section 1250 property, the depreciation recapture is limited to the portion of previously deducted depreciation allowances in excess of deductions that would have been taken if computed using the straight-line method.

Example: The Drake Partnership owns a $20,000 business machine that has been depreciated $12,000 over the years, so the partnership's adjusted basis in it is $8,000. In 2012, the partnership sells the machine for $25,000. The total gain on the sale is $17,000 ($25,000 - $8,000). The partnership must recognize ordinary income of $12,000 (to recapture depreciation deductions taken on the machine) and the remaining $5,000 ($17,000 - $12,000) is treated as a capital gain.

Example: Years ago, Mabel purchased a painting for her corporate office for $125,000. Mabel has taken depreciation deductions of $39,000 and her adjusted basis in the painting in 2012 is $86,000. The painting has appreciated in value, and, Mabel sells it in December 2012 for $180,000 and realizes a gain of $94,000 ($39,000 of ordinary income from depreciation recapture and $55,000 in long-term capital gain).

Section 1245 Property

Section 1245 property is defined by either:

1.   Personal (tangible or intangible) property[124], or
2.   Other tangible property (not including buildings) that is depreciable and that is:

---

[124] Personal property is **not the same** as "personal-use" property. In its most general definition, personal property includes any asset other than real estate. The distinguishing factor between personal property and real estate is that personal property is movable and real property is fixed permanently to one location, such as land or buildings.

a. Used as an integral part of certain specified activities (manufacturing, production, extraction, or furnishing transportation, communications, electrical energy, gas, water, or sewage disposal services), or

b. A facility used for the bulk storage of fungible[125] commodities (examples of highly fungible commodities are crude oil, wheat, etc.)

For example, a grain silo would be considered section 1245 property rather than section 1250 property, even if it was attached permanently to the land. Storage structures for oil and gas and other minerals would be considered section 1245 property.

Example: Several years ago, Crystal purchased a used binding machine at auction for her business. The cost of the machine was $1,000. Crystal has claimed $400 in depreciation on the machine. In 2012, Crystal sells the machine for $1,100. Her gain is as follows:

Sale price of the machine:	$1,100
Minus adjusted basis ($1,000 - $400):	$600
Crystal's gain on the sale of the machine:	$500

A portion of the gain is ordinary income ($400 of depreciation recapture for section 1245 property), and the remainder of $100 is long-term capital gain.

Section 1250 Property

Section 1250 property generally consists of buildings (including their structural components), other inherently permanent structures, and land improvements of general use and purpose. Examples of section 1250 property include residential rental property, factory buildings, and office buildings. Since buildings are generally depreciated using the straight-line method, taxpayers usually get more favorable treatment of depreciation recapture for section 1250 property.

Example: Maeve has owned an apartment building for almost twenty years. She originally purchased the building for $2.5 million. After taking straight-line depreciation deductions, her adjusted basis in 2012 is $800,000 and she sells the property for $4.5 million. Her gain is as follows:

Sale price	$4,500,000
Minus adjusted basis	$800,000
Gain on sale	**$3,700,000**

Because the building is section 1250 property and Maeve has only taken straight-line depreciation, there is no depreciation recapture, and the entire amount of the gain is treated as long-term capital gain.

Installment Sales

An installment sale involves a disposition of property in which the seller receives at least a portion of the sales proceeds during a year subsequent to the year of the sale. The resulting gain is typically reported using the installment method. If a business elects

---

[125] A fungible good or asset is one that is essentially interchangeable with other goods or assets of the same type, such as a specific grade of a particular commodity. Another example is a dollar bill—it does not matter where or when the dollar bill was produced, because there is no difference between one dollar and another dollar.

out of using the installment method, it must report the entire gain in the year of the sale, even though it may not receive the remaining proceeds until later years. Each payment received on an installment sale transaction may include the following components:

- Return of the seller's adjusted basis in the property
- Gain on the sale
- Interest income (attributable to financing the sales over a period of time)

The taxpayer must calculate a gross profit percentage, representing the ratio of the gain on the sale (numerator) to the total proceeds to be paid less any interest portion (denominator). The denominator will also equal the total of the gain and the return of the seller's adjusted basis in the property. Each year, including the year of sale, the total payments received less the portion attributable to interest is multiplied by the gross profit percentage to determine the portion of the gain that must be recognized. The gain is reported on Form 6252, *Installment Sale Income*. In certain circumstances, the business may be treated as having received a payment, even though it has not received cash. For example, the receipt of property or the assumption of a mortgage on property sold may be treated as a payment.

Example: A business sells a machine for a price of $6,000, with a gross profit of $1,500, and it will receive payments totaling $6,000 plus interest over four years. The gross profit percentage is 25% ($1,500 ÷ $6,000). After subtracting the applicable interest portion from each payment, the business will apply the gross profit percentage to each installment, including the down payment, and report the resulting amount as installment sale income for each tax year in which it receives payments. The remainder of each payment is the tax-free return of the machine's adjusted basis.

Example: In 2012, the Greenbelt Partnership sells land to a buyer under an installment sale. The land has a basis of $40,000, and the sale price is $100,000. Therefore, the gross profit is $60,000. Greenbelt receives a $20,000 down payment and the buyer's note for $80,000. The note provides for four annual payments of $20,000 each, plus 8% interest, beginning in 2013. Greenbelt's gross profit percentage is 60%. Greenbelt reports capital gain of $12,000 for each payment of $20,000 received in 2012 and 2013. In 2014, Greenbelt and the buyer agree to reduce the purchase price to $85,000, and payments during 2014, 2015, and 2016 are reduced to $15,000 for each year. The new gross profit percentage is 46.67%. Greenbelt will report capital gain of $7,000 (46.67% of $15,000) for each of the $15,000 installments paid in 2014, 2015, and 2016.

If the arrangement is modified at a later date or the full amount of the sale price is not paid, the resulting gross profit on the sale may also change.

An installment sale may trigger depreciation recapture. If a business reports the sale of property under the installment method, any applicable depreciation recapture under section 1245 is taxable as ordinary income in the year of sale, even if no payments are received in that year. If the gain is more than the depreciation recapture amount, the remainder of the gain would be recognized using the installment method rules.

An installment sale does not apply to:

- The sale of inventory, even if the business receives a payment after the year of sale
- A sale that results in a loss
- The sale of publicly traded property (such as stocks or bonds)
- The sale of depreciable property between related parties

Like-Kind Exchanges (Section 1031)

A like-kind exchange occurs when a business or individual exchanges business or investment property for similar property. IRC section 1031 provides that income from the exchange is not taxable currently, but is deferred until the acquired property is later sold or otherwise disposed.

The simplest form of 1031 exchange is a simultaneous swap of one property for another. However, it may also be arranged as a deferred exchange, in which the disposition of one property and the later acquisition of a replacement property are mutually dependent parts of an integrated transaction. In contrast, simply selling a property and using the proceeds to purchase another similar property is a taxable transaction.

A common type of 1031 exchange is an exchange of real property (real estate). Generally, real property can be exchanged even if the properties are substantially different. For example, an exchange of farmland for a commercial building will still qualify for nonrecognition treatment. However, entities may exchange other types of business property, such as machinery and vehicles, and intangible assets, such as patents and copyrights. To qualify as a like-kind exchange, the property traded and the property received must be similar, with both either business property or investment property.

All of the following can be exchanged as like-kind property:

- Condos, raw land, apartment buildings, duplexes, commercial buildings, residential rentals, and retail buildings
- A single business property exchanged for two or more properties and vice versa
- Water rights, mineral rights, oil and gas interests, copyrights, trademarks, and other intangible assets (but not partnership interests or securities)
- Livestock (but not livestock of different sexes)

Certain property does not qualify for section 1031 exchange treatment, including the following:

- Inventory, or any property purchased for resale
- Stocks, bonds, notes, or other securities
- Livestock of different sexes
- Real property within the United States and real property outside the United States
- Exchanges of shares of corporate stock in different companies

- Exchanges of partnership interests or LLC membership interests
- A personal residence, or personal-use property, such as a personal car
- Land under development for resale
- Corporation common stock

Strict rules and timetables apply to a section 1031 exchange if it does not entail a simultaneous exchange of properties. The exchanger has a maximum of 45 days after the sale to identify a list of potential replacement properties and 180 days after the sale to acquire one of those properties.

> **Example:** A corporation purchases a medical office building for $300,000. After four years, the fair market value of the property is $350,000. If the corporation were to sell the property, it would recognize a gain of $50,000, of which a portion attributable to recapture of any accelerated depreciation would be treated as ordinary income. If the corporation instead arranges a like-kind exchange through which it would either receive a similar property in exchange, or invest the proceeds from the sale of the building in a similar property, the taxable gain would be deferred.

Section 1031 requires that a qualified intermediary be used to facilitate tax-deferred exchanges. This is an independent party who acquires the relinquished property and transfers it to the buyer. The intermediary holds the sales proceeds to prevent the taxpayer from having actual or constructive receipt of the funds. The intermediary then acquires the replacement property and transfers it to the taxpayer to complete the exchange within the allowable time limits. If a qualified intermediary is not used, the exchange will not be allowed.

> **Example:** Otis owns a piece of raw land in Texas he wants to exchange, and he arranges a 1031 exchange transaction. When the land sale closes, his escrow company holds the proceeds. Within 45 days Otis identifies an apartment building he wants to buy in Arkansas and successfully negotiates a contract to buy the building. Within the required 180 days, the escrow company releases the funds he needs to close the purchase, and the exchange transaction is complete. The escrow company is considered a qualified intermediary, and Otis has successfully postponed recognition of any gain related to disposition of the original property.

Boot in an Exchange

Boot is a term used to describe cash or other property that is included in an exchange or other transaction that might otherwise qualify for nonrecognition of gain. The party that receives boot will typically be required to recognize taxable gain to the extent of the amount received.

A typical transaction involves one party exchanging property to another party for like-kind property and either additional cash or property that does not qualify as like-kind. The taxpayer who receives the boot may have to recognize a taxable gain to the extent of the fair market value of the boot received. However, this gain cannot exceed the amount of gain that would have been recognized if the property had been sold in a taxable transaction. Boot received can be offset by qualified costs paid during the transaction.

> **Example:** Stephen and Tricia decide they will exchange rental properties. Stephen's rental property is more valuable, so Tricia agrees to exchange her rental property and an additional $10,000 in cash. Therefore, Stephen will be required to recognize $10,000 of gain on the transaction.

> **Example:** Andrew wishes to exchange his rental property in a 1031 exchange. His relinquished rental property has an FMV of $60,000 and an adjusted basis of $30,000. Andrew's replacement property has an FMV of $50,000, and he also receives $10,000 in cash (boot) as part of the exchange. Andrew, therefore, has a realized gain of $30,000 on the actual exchange, and he has a taxable gain of $10,000— equal to the cash (boot) received in the exchange. The rest of his gain is deferred until he sells or disposes of the new property at a later date.

Sometimes, boot is recognized when two people exchange properties that are subject to liabilities. Liabilities on property are netted against each other. The taxpayer is treated as having received boot only if he is relieved of a greater liability than the liability he assumes. This is called debt reduction boot, and it occurs when a taxpayer's debt on the replacement property is less than the debt on the relinquished property. This occurs most often when a taxpayer is acquiring a less expensive or valuable property.

A business or individual may have to recognize gain on a partially taxable like-kind exchange, but would never recognize a loss. However, a loss on a like-kind exchange would affect the taxpayer's basis in the property received, and the tax treatment when it is ultimately sold or disposed.

Basis of Property Received in a Like-Kind Exchange

The basis of the property received is generally the adjusted basis of the property transferred.

> **Example:** Judy has a rental house with an adjusted basis of $70,000. In 2012, she trades the rental house for an empty lot with a FMV of $150,000. Judy's basis in the empty lot is $70,000, equal to the adjusted basis of her previous property.

If a taxpayer trades property and also pays money, the basis of the property received is the basis of the property given up, increased by any additional money paid.

> **Example:** Peyton buys a new diesel truck for use in her delivery business. She pays $43,000 cash, and she trades in her old truck for a trade-in allowance of $13,600. The old truck cost $50,000 two years ago. Peyton has taken depreciation deductions of $39,500 on the old vehicle. Even though she deducted depreciation of $39,500, the $3,100 gain on the exchange ($13,600 trade-in allowance minus her $10,500 adjusted basis) is not reported because the gain is postponed under the rules for like-kind exchanges. Her basis in the new truck is $53,500, the total of the cash paid ($43,000) and her adjusted basis of $10,500 in the old truck.

Example: Jorge trades a plot of land (adjusted basis $30,000) for a different plot of land in another town (FMV $70,500). He also pays an additional $4,000 in cash. Jorge's basis in the new land is $34,000 (his $30,000 basis in the old land plus the $4,000 additional money he paid).

The basis of any additional property received is its fair market value on the date of the trade. The taxpayer is taxed on any gain realized, but only up to the amount of the boot received (any cash and the fair market value of nonqualified property).

Like-Kind Exchanges Between Related Parties

Like-kind exchanges are allowed between related parties, which for purposes of a section 1031 exchanges are defined as:

- Family members (siblings, spouses, ancestors, and lineal descendants.)
- An individual and an entity (corporation or partnership) in which the individual owns either directly or indirectly more than 50% in value of the entity. This includes ownership by a spouse or close family member.
- Two entities in which the same individual owns directly or indirectly more than 50% of each.
- An estate in which the taxpayer is either the executor or beneficiary of the estate.
- A trust in which the taxpayer is the fiduciary and the related party is a beneficiary either of that same trust or a related trust or a fiduciary of a related trust.

Exchanges between related parties get close scrutiny by the Internal Revenue Service, because they are often used by taxpayers to evade taxes on gains.

Although section 1031 does not prohibit related-party exchanges, it requires a longer holding period to deter taxpayers from exchanging assets with family members or related businesses in order to dispose of them immediately and shift the gain.

For exchanges between related parties, the nonrecognition treatment will not apply if either property in the exchange is disposed of within two years. Exceptions to this rule include:

- If one of the parties originally involved in the exchange dies, the two-year rule does not apply.
- If the property is subsequently converted in an involuntary exchange (such as a fire or a flood), the two-year rule does not apply.
- If the exchange is genuinely not for tax avoidance purposes, the subsequent disposition generally will be allowed.

Example: Tim and John are brothers. Tim owns a residential rental property and John owns a tract of land. In 2012, they exchange the properties. Since they are related parties, they each must hold the properties for at least two years or the exchange will be disallowed and treated as a sale. In early 2013, John dies. In this case, the 1031 exchange is still valid, because the holding period rule does not apply if one of the parties in a related exchange dies before the two-year period expires.

Involuntary Conversions/Section 1033

An involuntary conversion occurs when a taxpayer's property is destroyed, stolen, condemned, or disposed of under the threat of condemnation, and he receives other property or money in payment, such as insurance or a condemnation award. In order to qualify as an involuntary conversion, the destruction or condemnation must be beyond the taxpayer's control.

Gain or loss from an involuntary conversion of property is usually recognized for tax purposes unless the property is a main home. A taxpayer cannot deduct a loss from an involuntary conversion of property held for personal use unless the loss resulted from a casualty or theft. However, a taxpayer may be able to avoid reporting gain on an involuntary conversion if he receives or invests in property similar to the converted property. This is called a section 1033 conversion. The gain on the involuntary conversion is then deferred until a taxable sale or exchange occurs at a later date.

> **Example:** Denise owns a residential rental property with an adjusted basis of $50,000. It is destroyed by a hurricane in 2012. Her property is insured, so Denise receives insurance reimbursement for $100,000, the fair market value of the property. Denise buys a replacement rental property six months later for $100,000. Her gain on the involuntary conversion is $50,000 ($100,000 insurance settlement minus her $50,000 basis). However, Denise does not have to recognize any taxable gain in 2012 because she reinvested all the insurance proceeds in another, similar property.

The replacement period for an involuntary conversion generally ends two years after the end of the first tax year in which any part of the gain on the condemnation is realized.

> **Example:** Anders owns a trophy business. On May 30, 2012, a tornado destroys a garage with Anders's trophies and other business supplies. His insurance company reimburses him for the entire loss. Anders has until December 31, 2014 to replace the garage and supplies using the insurance proceeds. He is not required to report the insurance proceeds on his 2012 tax return. So long as he reinvests all the insurance proceeds in replacement property, he will not have taxable gain until he disposes of the replacement property.

A three-year replacement period is allowed for real property that is held for investment, such as office buildings or residential rentals. The replacement period is four years for livestock that is involuntarily converted because of weather-related conditions. If the property is subject to an involuntary conversion in certain federally declared disaster areas, the replacement period can be up to five years.

Property Type	Replacement Period
Most property except those noted below.	Two years.
Real property held for investment or business use. This includes residential rentals, office buildings, etc.	Three years.
Livestock, due to weather-related conditions.	Four years.

The replacement property must be purchased before the end of the tax year in which the replacement *deadline* applies. If the involuntary conversion property is not replaced within the allowed time period, an amended tax return would have to be filed for the year the involuntary conversion occurred, reporting a taxable transaction.

If a taxpayer reinvests in replacement property similar to the converted property, the replacement property's basis is the same as the converted property's basis on the date of the conversion.

Usually, the taxpayer's basis in the new property will be its cost, reduced by any gain realized on the old property that was not recognized. However, the basis may be increased by any gain the taxpayer recognizes on the involuntary conversion and decreased by the following:

- Any loss the taxpayer recognizes on the involuntary conversion
- Any reimbursement he receives and does not reinvest in similar property

---

Example: Cody is a general contractor who uses a truck for his business. The truck is destroyed in an accident. It had been partially depreciated, and its adjusted basis was $40,000. The insurance company sends a check for $55,000 to replace the truck. Two months later, Cody uses all the insurance money to purchase a replacement truck, and he pays an additional $2,000 out-of-pocket in order to purchase the new vehicle. The basis in the new truck is $42,000 ($40,000 basis of the old truck + $2,000 additional out-of-pocket cost). Another way of reaching the same answer is as follows: Cody paid a total of $57,000 for the new truck, including the insurance proceeds of $55,000 plus an additional $2,000. This cost is reduced by the amount of gain that he has not recognized on the involuntary conversion, $15,000 (replacement proceeds of $55,000 less adjusted basis of $40,000), to derive the basis of the new truck: $42,000. This does not have to be reported as a taxable transaction because it is a qualified involuntary conversion of business property.

Example: Paula owns a rental condo in Virginia with a basis of $125,000. The building was destroyed by flooding, and Paula receives an insurance settlement of $200,000. A year later, she decides to purchase another condo in Maryland for $175,000. Paula's realized gain on the involuntary conversion is $75,000 ($200,000 - $125,000 basis). Paula must recognize $25,000 of gain, because she received an insurance payment of $200,000, but only spent $175,000 on the replacement property. Her basis in the new property will be $150,000, which is calculated as the cost of the new property in Maryland minus the deferred gain ($175,000 - $25,000 = $150,000), or alternatively, as the basis of the old property plus the recognized gain ($125,000 + $25,000 = $150,000). If Paula had used all the insurance proceeds and invested it in the new property, she would not have to report any taxable gain.

Condemnations

An involuntary conversion may result from a condemnation, when the government or another organization with legal authority seizes private property from its original owner for public use. The owner generally receives a condemnation award (money or property) in exchange for the property that is taken. A condemnation is like a forced sale, the owner being the seller and the government being the buyer.

Example: The state government informs Troy that it is condemning his motel in order to widen a highway. Troy goes to court to try to keep his property. The court decides in favor of the government, which takes his property and pays him $400,000 in exchange. Troy's basis in the motel was $80,000. He decides not to purchase replacement property. Therefore, he has a taxable gain, and $320,000 must be recognized as income ($400,000 - $80,000 = $320,000). If Troy were to purchase replacement property with the condemnation award, he would have a nontaxable section 1033 exchange.

Amounts taken out of the condemnation award to pay debts on the property are considered paid to the taxpayer and included in the amount of the award.

Example: The city awarded Katie $200,000 after condemning her land to build a conference center. However, she was paid only $148,000 because the city paid $50,000 to her mortgage company and $2,000 for accrued real estate taxes. Katie is considered to have received the entire $200,000 as a condemnation award.

Unit 10: Questions

1. Which of the following dispositions of depreciable property can trigger depreciation recapture?

A. Installment sale.
B. Gift.
C. Transfer at death.
D. Section 1031 exchange where no money or unlike property is received.

The answer is A. An installment sale can trigger recapture. If a business reports the sale of previously depreciated property using the installment method, any applicable depreciation recapture under section 1245 or 1250 is taxable as ordinary income in the year of sale. ###

2. Arbordale Acres is a farming corporation. In 2012, Arbordale sells a used tractor for $25,000. The original cost of the tractor was $20,000, and it is fully depreciated. What is the tax treatment for Arbordale's sale of the tractor?

A. There is no gain or loss on the sale of the tractor.
B. Arbordale has a gain of $25,000. The first $20,000 is considered section 1245 recapture and is taxed as ordinary income. The remaining $5,000 is considered section 1231 capital gain.
C. Arbordale has a gain of $25,000. The first $15,000 is considered section 1245 recapture and is taxed as ordinary income. The remaining $10,000 is considered section 1231 capital gain.
D. The entire gain is a section 1245 gain and will be taxed as depreciation recapture as ordinary income.

The answer is B. The first $20,000 is considered section 1245 recapture and is taxed as ordinary income. The remaining $5,000 is considered section 1231 capital gain. ###

3. Which of the following is not section 1245 property?

A. Computer.
B. Office building.
C. Display shelving.
D. Grain silo.

The answer is B. Section 1245 property does not include real estate such as buildings and structural components; therefore, the office building would not be included. Storage structures such as oil and gas storage tanks, grain storage bins, and silos are not treated as buildings but as section 1245 property. ###

4. Which of the following assets is not section 1231 property?

A. An office building.
B. Unharvested crops.
C. A business asset held for less than one year.
D. A patent.

The answer is C. In order to qualify as section 1231 property, the property must have been held by the business for over one year. ###

5. Caraway Carwash paid $200,000 for business equipment in January 2012. Caraway sells the equipment for $180,000 in October 2012. Caraway had not taken any depreciation on the equipment. How will this transaction be reported?

A. Caraway has a section 1231 loss of $20,000 on the sale of the equipment. This is treated as an ordinary loss.
B. Caraway has a section 1231 loss of $20,000 on the sale of the equipment. This is treated as a capital loss.
C. This is an installment sale, with a loss of $20,000. This is treated as an ordinary loss.
D. Caraway has an ordinary loss.

The answer is D. Because the business asset was held for less than one year, the business has an ordinary loss. The loss will therefore offset ordinary income and is immediately deductible. ###

6. Jennifer operates Right Hair Salon, a sole proprietorship. In 2012, she sells all of her salon chairs for $3,500 in order to buy new ones. She had purchased the chairs seven years ago for $15,000, and they were fully depreciated. Therefore, her basis in the chairs is zero. How should she report this section 1231 transaction?

A. She reports a gain of $3,500 on Form 4797 and Schedule C. The entire $3,500 is treated as depreciation recapture, which is subject to ordinary income tax rates, as well as self-employment tax.
B. She reports a gain of $3,500 on Form 4797 and Schedule C. The entire $3,500 is treated as depreciation recapture, which is subject to ordinary income tax rates but not self-employment tax.
C. She reports a gain of $3,500 on Form 4797 and Schedule C. The entire $3,500 is taxed as a long-term capital gain.
D. She is not required to report this sale.

The answer is B. Since the amount realized from the sale is less than Jennifer's original cost for the chairs, the entire gain is treated as depreciation recapture, which is subject to ordinary income tax rates but not self-employment tax. She reports the sale on Form 4797 and Schedule C. ###

7. Which of the following property types qualifies for section 1031 like-kind exchange?

A. A personal residence.
B. Inventory property.
C. Corporation common stock.
D. An empty lot held for investment.

The answer is D. Real property held for investment qualifies for like-kind exchange treatment. A personal residence, inventory, and common stock do not qualify for section 1031 treatment. ####

8. On January 10, 2012, a rental office building owned by Clovis Investments Corporation burns down. The property had an adjusted basis of $260,000, and Clovis receives an insurance reimbursement of $310,000. Clovis buys another rental office property for $290,000 in March 2012. What is Clovis's recognized gain as a result of this transaction?

A. $0.
B. $20,000.
C. $30,000.
D. $50,000.

The answer is B. This transaction is treated as an involuntary conversion. Clovis recognizes a taxable gain of $20,000 ($310,000 - $290,000), equal to the portion of the insurance reimbursement that was not reinvested in replacement property. Clovis's unrecognized gain is $30,000, the difference between the $50,000 realized gain and the $20,000 recognized gain. The basis of the new property is as follows:

Cost of replacement property	$290,000
Minus gain not recognized	($30,000)
Basis of replacement property	**$260,000**

If Clovis had reinvested all the insurance proceeds into a new property, the entire gain would have been deferred, and the involuntary conversion would have been completely nontaxable. ###

9. Barbara exchanges an apartment building with an adjusted basis of $125,000 for a business office building. The fair market value of Barbara's property is $500,000. The fair market value of the business office building, the property Barbara receives, has an FMV of $475,000. What is Barbara's basis in the new building?

A. $125,000.
B. $475,000.
C. $500,000.
D. $525,000.

The answer is A. Generally, an exchange of real property qualifies as a nontaxable exchange under section 1031. In a nontaxable exchange situation, the FMV of the buildings has no bearing on the basis. In this case, the basis of the new property is the same as the basis of the old property ($125,000). ####

10. Scott has a plane that he used in his business for two years. Its adjusted basis is $35,000, and its trade-in value is $45,000. He trades his old plane for a new plane that costs $200,000 and pays the dealer an additional $155,000 in cash. What is Scott's basis of the new plane?

A. $35,000.
B. $155,000.
C. $190,000.
D. $200,000.

The answer is C. Scott's basis is $190,000 ($155,000 of cash paid plus the $35,000 adjusted basis of the old plane). ###

11. The Karabell Company trades a delivery truck with an adjusted basis of $11,000 and cash of $6,000 for a new truck with a fair market value of $25,000. How much gain must Karabell recognize in this exchange, and what is its basis in the new truck?

Gain	Basis of New Truck
A. $0	$17,000
B. $0	$25,000
C. $8,000	$17,000
D. $8,000	$25,000

The answer is A. This exchange qualifies as a nontaxable exchange. Any gain on the exchange is deferred until the new asset is later sold or exchanged again. The $6,000 of cash is added to the basis of the old truck to determine the basis of the new truck. ###

12. Which of the following property exchanges does not qualify as a like-kind exchange?

A: Exchange of an apartment building for an office building.
B. Exchange of livestock of different sexes.
C: Exchange of improved property for unimproved property.
D: Exchange of farm machinery for factory machinery.

The answer is B. The exchange of livestock of different sexes does not qualify. The exchange of real estate for real estate and the exchange of business property for similar business property are exchanges of like-kind property. ###

13. Fran and Zachary are mother and son who complete a section 1031 exchange in March 2012. On January 29, 2013, Fran dies, and her property is inherited by her husband, who promptly sells it. Which of the following statements is true?

A. Since one of the properties in the exchange has been sold before the two-year time limit for related parties, the section 1031 exchange is disallowed, and both parties must pay tax on the transaction.
B. The exchange is still valid.
C. Since this was a related party exchange, the section 1031 exchange is still valid for Zachary, but Fran's estate must pay tax on the exchange, since her husband disposed of the property before the two-year waiting period.
D. The nonrecognition treatment is lost for both parties, but Fran's husband is liable for the tax on the exchange, since he was the owner of the property when it was sold.

The answer is B. In a related-party exchange, the nonrecognition treatment will be lost if either property in the exchange is disposed of within two years. However, there are exceptions to this rule. The section 1031 exchange will still be valid if either party in the transaction dies, or if the property is subject to an involuntary conversion. ###

14. Which of the following trades qualifies as a nontaxable like-kind exchange?

A. The exchange of a vacant lot in the city with farmland in the country.
B. The exchange of a Toyota Prius owned by one car dealer for a Ford C-Max Hybrid owned by another car dealer.
C. The exchange of shares of stocks for units of bonds.
D. The exchange of an apartment building in New York City for an apartment building in Mexico City.

The answer is A. The exchange of a vacant lot for a tract of farmland qualifies for like-kind exchange treatment. Section 1031 specifically excludes exchanges of inventory; stocks, bonds, notes, other securities, or evidence of indebtedness; partnership interests; livestock of different sexes; and property used predominantly in the United States and property used predominantly outside the United States. Properties are like-kind if they are of the same nature or character, even if they differ in grade or quality. ###

15. Special rules apply to like-kind exchanges between related persons. For purposes of a section 1031 exchange, what qualifies as a related person?

A: The taxpayer and the taxpayer's spouse.
B: The taxpayer and a corporation in which the taxpayer has a 51% ownership.
C: A partnership in which the taxpayer owns a 53% interest, and a partnership in which the taxpayer's spouse owns a 52% interest.
D: All of the above.

The answer is D. The taxpayer and a member of his immediate family are related persons for purposes of like-kind exchanges. Any business where the taxpayer has beneficial ownership (over 50%) is also considered a related party. ###

16. Caliper Corporation purchases a machine to use in its business operations in July 2012. The cost of the machine is $250,000, not including $18,500 in sales tax. The entire purchase of the machine is financed with a small business loan. During 2012, Caliper Corporation pays interest of $10,500 on the loan. What is the proper treatment of this transaction?

A. Caliper Corporation must capitalize $279,000 as the total cost of the machine, and record depreciation expense each year.
B. Caliper Corporation may take a deduction for the interest paid on the loan ($10,500). The other costs, including sales tax, should be capitalized and depreciated.
C. Caliper Corporation may deduct all the costs, including the machine purchase, as a current business expense in 2012.
D. Caliper Corporation may deduct the sales tax and the loan interest as business expenses.

The answer is B. Caliper Corporation can take a deduction for the interest paid on the loan. However, the sales tax is not deductible. It must be added to the cost of the depreciable asset and depreciated over the useful life. The interest on a business loan, however, is a current expense and should be treated separately from the basis of the asset. ###

17. Sergio is a self-employed carpenter who owns a compressor for use in his business. He trades the compressor (adjusted basis $3,000) for a large table saw (FMV $7,500) and pays an additional $4,000 cash to the seller in a qualified exchange. What is Sergio's basis in the saw?

A. $7,000.
B. $7,500.
C. $4,000.
D. $3,000.

The answer is A. The basis of the saw is $7,000 (the $3,000 basis of the old asset plus the $4,000 paid). ###

18. Angelina trades a laser printer used in her tax practice for a new color model. The cost of the original printer was $5,000 and she had taken $1,000 of depreciation. She exchanged her old printer as a trade-in and paid an additional $2,000 in cash to complete the exchange. What is Angelina's basis in the new printer?

A. $1,000.
B. $2,000.
C. $6,000.
D. $7,000.

The answer is C. The adjusted basis of the old printer was $4,000 ($5,000 - $1,000 depreciation). Then she paid an additional $2,000 to acquire the new printer. Therefore, the basis of the new model is:

Original model adj. basis	$4,000
Cash paid	$2,000
Basis of new model	**$6,000**

###

19. Sadie owns a gym. She sells some used fitness equipment in 2012 for $65,000. She had purchased the equipment in 2008 for $90,000. She has taken $60,000 of depreciation, which includes a section 179 deduction of $10,000. Which of the following will Sadie report on the sale of the equipment?

A. Ordinary loss of $25,000.
B. Long-term capital gain of $35,000.
C. Ordinary income of $35,000.
D. Ordinary income of $10,000 and long-term capital gain of $25,000.

The answer is C. Sadie has a gain of $35,000, equal to the difference between her sales proceeds of $65,000 and her adjusted basis of $30,000 (cost of $90,000 less accumulated depreciation of $60,000). Although she has had the property for more than one year, it is personal property classified as section 1245 property and therefore is subject to depreciation recapture to the extent of the entire amount of depreciation (and section 179 deductions) taken. Since this amount exceeds her gain, the entire amount of the gain is treated as ordinary income. ###

20. Cecil operates an electronics repair business as a sole proprietorship. During 2012, Cecil sold property that was acquired for use in the business for $10,000. The purchase price of the property was $20,000 and Cecil had claimed the following deductions: section 179 deduction of $5,000 and depreciation of $8,000.

Based upon the information provided, what amount of taxable income will result from the sale of this property?

A. Capital gain of $3,000.
B. Ordinary income of $3,000.
C. $0.
D. Ordinary income of $10,000.

The answer is B. The disposition of the property results in a gain of $3,000 (equal to the proceeds of $10,000 less adjusted basis of $7,000 representing the purchase price of $20,000 less depreciation and section 179 deductions of $13,000). The gain is characterized as ordinary income to the lesser of the actual gain or the amount of depreciation and section 179 expenses recaptured ($13,000). ###
Supporting calculations:

Purchase price	$20,000
Less depreciation and section 179 deductions	($13,000)
Adjusted basis at date of sale	**$7,000**

Proceeds	$10,000
Gain on sale	$3,000
Depreciation recapture (as ordinary income)	**$13,000**

####

Unit 11: Partnerships in General

More Reading:
Publication 541, *Partnerships*

Partnership Basics

An unincorporated business with two or more members is generally classified as a partnership for federal tax purposes. A partnership is a pass-through entity. Its major advantage is that it is not directly taxed on its income. Instead, income and loss are determined at the partnership level and are only taxable to the individual partners. In this respect, a partnership is similar to a sole proprietorship.

Unlike a corporation, a partnership does not require any formal legal documents. A partnership must have at least two partners and at least one of them must be a general partner. A joint undertaking merely to share expenses is not a partnership. For example, co-ownership of rental property is not a partnership unless the co-owners provide services to the tenants.

> **Example:** Will and Todd are brothers, and they co-own a single residential rental that they inherited from their mother. They use a management company to run the property. Will and Todd are not partners, and their co-ownership of the property does not automatically create a partnership.

As described in Unit 1, certain entities with different legal structures may be classified as partnerships for tax purposes, either based upon their election by filing Form 8832, *Entity Classification Election,* or by default (as in the case of a domestic LLC with at least two members that is classified as a partnership unless it files Form 8832 and elects to be treated as a corporation). However, the following organizations are prohibited from being classified as partnerships:

- A corporation (although a corporation can be a partner in a partnership)
- Any joint-stock company or joint-stock association
- An insurance company
- Certain banks
- A government entity
- An organization required to be taxed as a corporation by the IRS
- Certain foreign organizations
- Any tax-exempt (nonprofit) organization
- Any real estate investment trust (REIT)
- Any organization classified as a trust or estate
- Any other organization that elects to be classified as a corporation by filing Form 8832

The Partnership Agreement

The term "partnership agreement" refers to any written document or oral agreement that bears on the underlying economic arrangement of the partners, including allocations of income, gain, loss, deductions, and credits. Examples of such documents include:

- Loan and credit agreements
- Assumption agreements
- Indemnification agreements
- Subordination agreements
- Correspondence with a lender concerning terms of a loan
- Loan guarantees

A partnership agreement may be modified during the tax year and even after the tax year has closed. However, the partnership agreement cannot be modified after the due date for filing the partnership return for the year, not including extensions.

Example: Terry and Dawn run a cash-basis, calendar-year partnership. They split the proceeds 50-50. In 2012, they decide to alter the partnership agreement. They have until the due date of the partnership return to change the partnership agreement. Filing for an extension does not give them additional time.

A Partnership's Tax Year

A partnership generally must conform to the tax year of the partners. This means that partnerships typically report income on a calendar year basis. However, a partnership may request a fiscal year based on a legitimate business purpose. In order to qualify as a legitimate business purpose, the partnership must be able to prove that the decision to adopt a different tax year is not simply to defer income recognition by the partners.

A partnership may request a fiscal tax year based on a natural business year so that it closes its books after its busiest or most profitable period. A natural business year is a 12-month period where at least 25% of total gross receipts are received in the last two months of the year.

Example: John and Kate run a seasonal business making pool equipment. Their busiest time of the year is during the summer months, and more than 60% of their income is received during June and July. John and Kate may request a fiscal year based on a legitimate business purpose—that is, the natural tax year of their seasonal business.

In the absence of a legitimate business purpose, a partnership may still request a fiscal year that does not conform to the tax year of its partners by making a section 444 election (explained previously in Unit 3).

Partnership Filing Requirements

Every partnership must file a tax return unless it has no activity whatsoever, (with no income or losses during the year). A partnership reports its income and loss on Form 1065, which is due on the 15th day of the fourth month following the close of the tax year. Since most partnerships are calendar-year partnerships, their tax returns are due on the same day as individual returns. A partnership may request a five-month extension to file (unlike individuals and corporations that may request a six-month extension). Therefore, a calendar-year partnership can request an extension until September 15 to file its tax return. The extension is requested on Form 7004, *Automatic Extension of Time to File Certain Business Income Tax, Information, and Other Returns.*

The partnership return must show the name and address of each partner and the partner's distributive share of taxable income (or loss) on Schedule K-1. The partnership is also required to furnish a copy of each partner's Schedule K-1 to every partner by the due date (including extensions) of the partnership tax return. The individual partner then reports his share of partnership income on Schedule E of Form 1040.

Example: Lovett Partnership is a calendar-year, cash-basis partnership that is required to file a Form 1065 every year. The partnership has five partners and each partner receives a Schedule K-1 for his share of partnership income and losses, which are then reportable on the partners' individual tax returns. Each partner must receive his Schedule K-1 by the due date of the partnership return (or the extended due date, if the partnership requests an extension).

The IRS requires partnerships with more than 100 partners (Schedules K-1) to file their returns electronically. If a partnership fails to do so, it may be subject to penalty unless it was unable to file electronically (because the e-filing was rejected, the return required paper attachments, etc.)

The partnership return must be signed by a general partner.

The penalty for late filing is $195 per month, per partner, for up to 12 months. For example, if a partnership has four partners and files its tax return two months late, it would be liable for a late filing penalty of $1,560 ($195 × 2 months × 4 partners). Additional penalties may apply if the partnership fails to furnish Schedules K-1 to its partners, fails to supply a tax identification number, or fails to furnish information on tax shelters. These penalties may not be imposed if the partnership can show reasonable cause for its failure.

Partners who work in the business are not employees and do not receive a Form W-2. No withholding is taken out of their distributions to pay the income and self-employment taxes that they report on their Forms 1040. General partners are considered to be self-employed and therefore must pay estimated payments just like other self-employed individuals. Limited partners are subject to self-employment tax only on guaranteed payments, such as salary and professional fees for services rendered.

General Partnership vs. Limited Partnership

A partnership can either be a general partnership or a limited partnership. In a general partnership, all the partners have unlimited liability for partnership debts. In a limited partnership, at least one partner is a limited partner who is only liable for partnership liabilities up to his investment in the partnership. Limited partners generally cannot participate in the management or the day-to-day administration of the partnership.

A limited partner has no obligation to contribute additional capital to the partnership and therefore does not have an economic risk of loss in partnership liabilities. In this respect, a limited partner is like an investor in a corporation. A limited partner is not subject to self-employment tax on his distributive share of income.

A limited partnership (LP or LLP) is formed under state limited liability law. A limited partnership can have an unlimited number of investors, but there must always be at least one general partner. Usually, the owners of limited liability partnerships offer professional services (attorneys, doctors, etc.) This entity type protects individual partners from liability for the malpractice of other partners. However, all the partners remain liable for the general debts of the partnership.

Capital Interests

A capital interest in a partnership is an interest in its assets that is distributable to the owner of the interest in either of the following situations:

- The owner withdraws from the partnership
- The partnership liquidates

The right to share in earnings and profits is not itself a capital interest in the partnership.

Example: Rasheda and Aaron form a partnership in order to open a restaurant. Aaron is an experienced restaurant manager, but he has no money to invest. Rasheda owns the building and the restaurant equipment. Her basis in the assets is $100,000. Therefore, Rasheda has a capital interest in the partnership. Aaron does not.

Family Partnerships

Members of a family can be legitimate partners and form a partnership together. However, family members will be recognized as partners only if one of the following requirements is met:

- If capital is a material income-producing factor, the family members must have acquired their capital interest in a bona fide transaction (even if by gift or purchase from another family member); actually own the partnership interest; and actually control the interest. This means that a family member who acquires a partnership interest from another family member needs to treat the activity as a bona fide business activity.
- If capital is not a material income-producing factor, the family members must have joined together in good faith to conduct a business. They must have agreed that contributions of each entitle them to a share in the profits and that some capital or service is provided by each partner.

Capital (investment) is a material income-producing factor if a substantial part of the gross income of the business comes from the use of capital. For example, this would apply if the operation of the business requires substantial inventories or investment in a plant, machinery, or equipment. In general, capital is not a material income-producing factor if the income of the business consists principally of fees, commissions, or other compensation for personal services performed by members or employees of the partnership.

Related Persons and Partnership Losses

For purposes of determining a partner's distributive share, an interest purchased by one family member from another family member is considered a gift from the seller. The fair market value of the purchased interest is considered donated capital. For this purpose, members of a family include only spouses, ancestors, and lineal descendants (grandson, daughter, son, stepson, etc.)

A loss on the sale or exchange of property between related persons is not deductible. Under the related party transaction rules, an individual is considered as also owning the partnership interest directly or indirectly owned by his family. Members of a family, for this purpose, include only brothers, sisters, half-brothers, half-sisters, spouses, ancestors, parents, and lineal descendants (children, grandchildren).

Husband and Wife Businesses

An unincorporated business jointly owned by a husband and wife is generally classified as a partnership for federal tax purposes. However, a married couple can elect instead to be treated as a "qualified joint venture." In order to make this election, both spouses must materially participate in the business, they must be the only members in the venture, and they must file a joint tax return. If this election is made, they do not file Form 1065. Instead, all items of income and loss are divided between the spouses based on their respective interests in the venture.

Each spouse reports his or her respective share of these items as a sole proprietor on Schedule C or Schedule F (Form 1040) and reports self-employment income on Schedule SE.

Costs of Organizing and Starting a Partnership

The costs to organize a partnership and to start up a business are treated much like similar costs incurred by other types of businesses. Limited amounts of organizational and start-up costs can be deducted in the year the partnership's active trade or business begins. Amounts not deducted can be amortized ratably over a period of 180 months. The election to either amortize or capitalize these costs is irrevocable and applies to all organizational and start-up costs related to the trade or business. The partnership must complete and attach Form 4562, *Depreciation and Amortization*, to its tax return.

A partnership can amortize an organizational cost only if it meets all the following tests:

- It is for the creation of the partnership itself and not for starting or operating the partnership trade or business.
- It is chargeable to a capital account.
- It is incurred by the due date of the partnership return (excluding extensions) for the first tax year in which the partnership is in business.

- It is for a type of item normally expected to benefit the partnership throughout its entire life.

Qualifying partnership organizational costs include the following fees:

- Legal fees for services related to the organization of the partnership, such as negotiation and preparation of the partnership agreement.
- Accounting fees for services related to the organization of the partnership.
- Filing fees.

The following costs cannot be deducted or amortized:

- The cost of acquiring assets for the partnership or transferring assets to the partnership
- The cost of admitting or removing partners, other than at the time the partnership is first organized
- The cost of making a contract concerning the operation of the partnership trade or business including a contract between a partner and the partnership
- Syndication costs for issuing and marketing interests in the partnership, such as brokerage, registration, and printing costs

If a partnership is liquidated (ceases operations) before the end of the amortization period, the unamortized amount of qualifying organizational costs can be deducted in the partnership's final tax year, but only to the extent they qualify as a loss from a business. Start-up costs include amounts paid or incurred in connection with an existing activity engaged in for profit and for the production of income in anticipation of the activity becoming an active trade or business. Start-up costs include amounts paid for the following:

- An analysis or survey of potential markets, products, labor supply, transportation facilities, etc.
- Advertisements for the opening of the business.
- Salaries and wages for employees who are being trained and their instructors.
- Travel and other necessary costs for securing prospective distributors, suppliers, or customers.
- Salaries and fees for executives and consultants, or for similar professional services.

Special Partnership Allocations

Unlike S corporations, which must report all income and expenses in proportion to stock ownership, partnerships allow more flexibility. Special allocations of income, gain, loss, or deductions can be made between the partners based on their partnership agreement.

Partnership agreements can be written to reflect whatever economic sharing and risk sharing arrangements the parties wish. Special allocations permit partners to assume different levels of risk and to set the timing of income in accordance with their preferences.

For example, the partnership agreement may allocate all of the depreciation deductions to one partner or specify that the partners share capital, profits, and losses in different ratios. Further, the sharing of profits does not have to coincide with the sharing of losses.

Example: Pandora, who has design and sewing skills, forms a partnership with Jayne, who has the money to invest in developing a clothing line. Jayne contributes $100,000 in cash to the partnership. Pandora and Jayne agree to split the business profits 20/80 until Jayne recovers her entire investment; thereafter, profits will be split 50/50. These special allocations are written into their partnership agreement.

Example: Nico and Rhoda form a partnership. Nico contributes $1,000 and Rhoda contributes $99,000. Due to Nico's expertise in management and his daily participation in the partnership's business, the partnership agreement provides that he will be allocated 20% of the partnership taxable income and 2% of the partnership loss. Thus, although Nico owns only 1% in partnership capital, his profit sharing ratio is 20%. This tax allocation between Nico and Rhoda is allowable so long as the distribution of economic benefits between the two is also in the same ratio (i.e., 20% to Nico and 80% to Rhoda).

Example: Alicia and Danni form a partnership to run a cupcake bakery. The bakery is opened during the year, and the partnership has ordinary income of $10,000. The partnership agreement states that they will share income and loss equally (50/50). Alicia and Danni agree that the $10,000 income will be distributed equally between them. However, for tax purposes, they want the income to be specially allocated as $7,500 to Alexia and $2,500 to Danni. The tax allocation (75/25) is not consistent with the underlying economic agreement on their partnership agreement (50/50). Unless the partnership agreement contains other provisions that justify this allocation, it has no economic effect and must be reallocated to the partners based on their true economic sharing ratio (50/50).

Separately Stated Items

Many of the individual components of a partnership's income are calculated similarly to those of an individual. However, some deductions are not allowed at the partnership level, and certain items of income and loss must be separately stated on the tax return. These separately stated items flow through to the partners with a specific character. For example, if a partnership makes charitable contributions, it must list the charitable contributions as a separately stated item. The individual partners then report their share of the charitable contributions on their individual Schedule A.

In order to determine taxable income, all partnership income must first be divided into:

- **Separately stated items, and**
- **Ordinary income or loss.**

The following items must be separately stated:

- Net short-term capital gains and losses
- Net long-term capital gains and losses

- Charitable contributions
- Dividends eligible for a dividends-received deduction
- Taxes paid to a foreign country
- Taxes paid to a U.S. possession (Guam, Puerto Rico, etc.)
- Section 1231 gains and losses
- Section 179 deductions and bonus depreciation
- Any tax-exempt income and expenses related to the tax-exempt income
- Investment income and related investment expenses
- Rental income, portfolio income, and related expenses
- Any recovery items, such as bad debts

Any item of income that is not a separately stated item is a component of ordinary income.

Taxable income includes ordinary income, all the separately stated items, and any other adjustments, such as business expenses and cost of goods sold.

Example: The Stevenson Partnership operates as an accrual-based business. Its gross receipts for 2012 were $250,000. In addition to those gross receipts, the company also had the following items of income and expenses:

•Liability insurance	($5,000)
•Charitable contributions	($2,000)
•Continuing education	($9,000)
•Rental income	$25,000
•Guaranteed payments to partners	($15,000)

The ordinary income for the Stevenson partnership is figured as follows:

Gross income	$250,000
Liability insurance	($5,000)
Continuing education	($9,000)
Guaranteed payments to partners	($15,000)
The ordinary income of the partnership is therefore:	**$221,000**

The rental income and charitable contributions are not considered in determining ordinary income of the partnership. Instead, these are separately stated items that pass through to the partners and retain their character, just as they would for a sole proprietorship. The separately stated items are reported on each individual partner's return (Form 1040). Guaranteed payments are deductible to the partnership because they are treated like wages and are taxable to the partners.

Guaranteed Payments

A partnership may be required by the terms of the partnership agreement to make guaranteed payments to one or more partners without regard to whether the partnership has income or loss for the year.

Guaranteed payments are not the same as partnership distributions. They may compensate the partner for services or for the use of capital, as if they were made to a person who is not a partner. Guaranteed payments are generally deducted by the partnership on Form 1065 as a business expense and reported on Schedule K-1.

The partner who receives a guaranteed payment reports the full amount of the payment as ordinary income on Schedule E (Form 1040) of his individual tax return for the tax year in which the partnership's tax year ends, and also reports his distributive share of the partnership's ordinary income or loss. Guaranteed payments are not subject to income tax withholding.

> **Example:** Erica is a partner in the Bookertown Partnership. Under the terms of her partnership agreement, she is entitled to a guaranteed payment of $10,000 per year, regardless of how profitable the partnership is. In 2012, Erica's distributive share of partnership income is 10%. Bookertown Partnership has $50,000 of ordinary income after deducting Erica's guaranteed payment. She must include ordinary income of $15,000 ($10,000 guaranteed payment + $5,000 [$50,000 × 10%] for her distributive share) on her individual income tax return (Form 1040).

Cash and Property Contributions to a Partnership

When a partnership is formed, the partners contribute property or cash in exchange for their partnership interests. Generally, neither the partner nor the partnership recognizes gain or loss in connection with contributions, whether made in connection with the partnership's formation or after it is operating. However, a partner's contribution can result in gain or loss recognition in the following situations:

- When property is contributed to a partnership that would be treated as an investment company if it were incorporated. A partnership is treated as an investment company if over 80% of the value of its assets is held for investment in cash or readily marketable items.

- When contributed property is distributed to a different partner within seven years of the original contribution date. The contributing partner would recognize gain on the difference between the fair market value and the adjusted basis of the property as of the contribution date. The character of the gain or loss will be the same as would have resulted if the partnership had sold the property to the distributee partner. This rule is designed to prevent partners from shifting assets around in order to mask revenue.

- When a partner contributes cash or property to a partnership and then receives a distribution of different property. In this case, the transaction may be considered a disguised sale. A disguised sale is not treated as a contribution and a subsequent distribution, but as a sale of property, if:
  - The distribution would not have been made if the initial contribution had not occurred; and
  - The partner's right to the distribution does not depend on the success of partnership operations.

When a partner contributes property to a partnership, the partnership's basis is generally the same as the adjusted basis of the partner, including any gain recognized by the partner in connection with the contribution. The partner's holding period for the property is also carried over. For example, if a partner contributes a building with an FMV of $100,000 and a basis of $50,000, the basis of the building in the hands of the partnership would generally be $50,000.

Contribution of Services to a Partnership

A partner can acquire an interest in a partnership as compensation for services performed or to be performed. The tax treatment depends upon whether the partner receives a capital interest or a profits interest. If a partner receives a capital interest as compensation for services, the partner must recognize ordinary income equal to the fair market value of a partnership interest that is transferred in exchange for services. The amount is treated as a guaranteed payment and is included in the partner's gross income in the first tax year during which the partner can transfer the interest. If a partner receives a profits interest as compensation for services, the receipt may not be taxable to the partner or the partnership, except in certain circumstances.

Example: Greer is an attorney who contributes her services to a partnership in exchange for a 10% partnership interest. It is deemed a capital interest, as the partnership agreement provides for distribution of assets to Greer in the event she withdraws from the partnership or the partnership liquidates. The fair market value of the partnership interest is $3,000. Greer is required to recognize $3,000 in ordinary income, and her basis in the partnership is $3,000. The payment is deducted by the partnership as a guaranteed payment and is taxable to Greer as ordinary income.

Basis of a Partner's Interest

A partner's basis in his partnership interest may be referred to as **outside basis**. This is in contrast to the partnership's basis in its assets, which is known as **inside basis**.[126]

The initial basis of a partnership interest is generally equal to the cash plus the adjusted basis of any property the partner contributed. The adjusted basis of a partner's partnership interest is ordinarily determined at the end of the partnership's tax year. However, if there is a sale or exchange of all or part of a partner's interest or a liquidation of his entire interest in a partnership, the adjusted basis must also be determined on the date of liquidation.

The following items increase a partner's basis in the partnership:
- The partner's additional cash contributions to the partnership
- The partner's increased liabilities
- The partner's increased share (or assumption of) partnership liabilities
- The partner's distributive share of partnership income
- The partner's distributive share of the excess of the deductions for depletion over the basis of the depletable property

---

[126] On the EA exam, these two terms may be used in questions in which you must determine partnership or partner basis.

Sometimes a partner will be required to recognize a gain when he contributes an asset to the partnership that is subject to liability (such as the contribution of a building that is subject to a mortgage). If the partner must recognize a gain as a result of his partnership contribution, this gain is added to the basis of his partnership interest.

Any increase in a partner's individual liabilities because of his assumption of partnership liabilities is treated as if it were a contribution to the partnership by the partner. If a partner's share of partnership liabilities increases, this increase is treated as if the partner contributed cash or property to the partnership.

Example: Sam and Abdul have a partnership. Sam contributes a machine to his partnership that has an adjusted basis of $400 and an FMV of $1,000. Abdul contributes $1,000 cash. Each partner has increased his capital account by $1,000, which will be reflected in the partnership books. However, the adjusted basis of Sam's interest is only $400 and Abdul's partnership interest is $1,000.

A partner's basis in the partnership is *decreased* by the following items:

- The money and adjusted basis of property distributed to the partner by the partnership.
- The partner's distributive share of the partnership losses.
- The partner's distributive share of nondeductible partnership expenses that are not capital expenditures. This includes the partner's share of any section 179 expenses, even if the partner cannot deduct the entire amount on his individual income tax return.
- The partner's deduction for depletion for any partnership oil and gas wells, up to the proportionate share of the adjusted basis of the wells allocated to the partner.

If a partner's share of partnership liabilities decreases or the partnership assumes any of the individual partner's liabilities, the amounts are treated as distributions to the partner by the partnership.

If contributed property is subject to a debt and the debt is assumed by the partnership, the basis of the contributing partner's interest is reduced (but not below zero) by the portion of the liability assumed by the other partners. The partner must reduce his basis because the assumption of the liability is treated as a distribution to him. The other partners' assumption of the liability is treated as a contribution by them to the partnership.

Example: Al acquired a 20% interest in a partnership by contributing a moving van that had an adjusted basis to him of $8,000 and a related $4,000 loan balance. The partnership assumed the loan. The basis of Al's interest is:

Adjusted basis of contributed property	$8,000
Minus: Auto loan assumed by other partners (80% × $4,000)	($3,200)
Basis of Al's partnership interest	**$4,800**

A partner's basis can never go below zero. So, in order to prevent a negative basis, a partner must recognize gain equal to the amount that the decrease in a partner's share of liability exceeds his basis.

Example: Raymond acquired a 20% interest in a partnership by contributing an asset that had an adjusted basis to him of $8,000 and a related $12,000 loan. Since the value of the asset is less than the amount of the loan, Raymond's partnership basis is zero. The $1,600 difference between the loan assumed by the other partners, $9,600 (80% × $12,000), and his basis of $8,000 is treated as capital gain from the sale or exchange of a partnership interest. However, this gain would not increase the basis of his partnership interest. His partnership basis would remain zero.

Partnership Loss Limitations

The amount of a partnership's loss that a partner is allowed to deduct on his individual tax return is dependent on the partner's basis in the partnership. In general, a partner cannot deduct losses that exceed his partnership basis. Losses disallowed due to insufficient basis are carried forward until the partner can deduct them in a later year.

However, debts on behalf of the partnership can *increase* a partner's individual basis. So, for example, if a partner takes out a $50,000 loan in order to finance partnership operations and he personally guarantees the debt, the partner is allowed to take losses due to his debt basis.

Example: Rebecca invests $1,000 in the Andrews Partnership in return for a 10% partnership interest. The Andrews Partnership takes out a $500,000 loan and incurs $100,000 in losses during the first year. Rebecca's share of partnership liabilities would increase her basis to $51,000 [$1,000 cash investment + ($500,000 × 10%). Rebecca's share of the loss is $10,000 ($100,000 × 10%). Rebecca is allowed to deduct the entire loss, because her partnership basis was increased by debt basis.

This only applies if the partner is at risk for the loss. If the partner does not have any personal liability to satisfy the debt, deductible losses are limited by the at-risk rules. The at-risk rules limit the deductibility of losses to the partner's basis *reduced* by his share of any nonrecourse debt. This means that a partner is prohibited from taking losses based on partnership liabilities unless the partner would be forced to satisfy the debt with his personal assets. This is intended to prevent abusive deductions from real estate and other tax shelter activities.

Partnership Liabilities

If a partner's share of partnership liabilities increases, or a partner's individual liabilities increase because he assumes partnership liabilities, this increase is treated as a contribution of money by the partner to the partnership. A partner (or related person) is considered to assume a partnership liability when:

- He is personally liable for it,
- The creditor knows that the liability was assumed by the partner or related person,
- The creditor can demand payment from the partner or related person, and
- No other partner or person related to another partner will bear the economic risk of loss on that liability immediately after the assumption.

The effect of liabilities on the individual partner's basis depends mainly on two factors:

- Whether or not the liability is recourse or nonrecourse
- Whether or not the partner is a general or limited partner

A nonrecourse liability is usually secured by an asset or property, and its terms provide that the creditor has no claim against the owner of the property. At most, the creditor may have a claim against the property. An example of this would be a home loan where the bank's only recourse in case of default is to repossess the house. A partnership liability is considered a nonrecourse liability if no partner has an economic risk of loss for that liability.

> **Example:** Reuben purchases a used van for his business but he is unable to make the payments. The loan is a nonrecourse loan because the only action the lender can take is to repossess the vehicle. The lender cannot seek payment from Reuben for the balance of the loan.

> **Example:** Gary and Stanton form a general partnership, with cash contributions of $2,000 from each. Under the partnership agreement, they share all partnership profits and losses equally. The partnership also borrows an additional $10,000 and purchases equipment. Both partners are liable for the debt. This debt is included in the partners' basis in the partnership. Each partner's basis would include his allocated share of the liability of $5,000. Therefore, each partner's basis is now $7,000 (the initial $2,000 contribution + $5,000 share of the liability).

A partner's share of nonrecourse liabilities is proportionate to his share of partnership profits. A partner's basis in a partnership interest includes the partner's share of a partnership liability only if, and to the extent, the liability:

- Creates or increases the partnership's basis in any of its assets,
- Gives rise to a current deduction to the partnership, or
- Is a nondeductible, noncapital expense of the partnership.

In a cash-basis partnership, any liabilities that are accrued but unpaid are not included in the basis calculation for each individual partner. A partnership liability is a recourse liability when the individual partners have an economic risk of loss. A partner has an economic risk of loss to the extent that partner or a related person would be obligated to make payments to a creditor in the event of a constructive liquidation. Generally, in a constructive liquidation, the following events are treated as occurring at the same time:

1. All partnership liabilities become payable in full
2. All of the partnership's assets have a value of zero, except for property contributed to secure a liability
3. All property is disposed of by the partnership in a fully taxable transaction for no consideration
4. All items of income, gain, loss, or deduction are allocated to the partners
5. The partnership liquidates

Partners generally share recourse liabilities based on their ratios for sharing losses. A limited partner has no obligation to contribute additional capital to the partnership, and therefore does not have an economic risk of loss in partnership recourse liabilities. Therefore, unless a limited partner guarantees a partnership liability or makes a loan to the partnership, his basis will generally not be affected by the partnership's recourse liabilities.

Unit 11: Questions

1. In 2012 Raj and Ellie formed Spring Lawn, a calendar-year partnership, to provide yard maintenance to residential customers. Before they began operations in November 2012, they incurred legal fees of $2,000 and consulting expenses of $1,000 to draft the partnership agreement and file the required forms. They also paid a commission of $600 to a broker to market partnership interests. How much of these expenses may be deducted or amortized?

A. $0.
B. $600.
C. $3,000.
D. $3,600.

The answer is C. The partnership may choose to deduct the amounts for legal fees and consulting expenses ($2,000 + $1,000 = $3,000). However, the amount paid in commissions to a broker to market partnership interests must be capitalized and cannot be amortized or deducted. The costs for marketing and issuing interests in the partnership such as brokerage, registration, legal fees, and printing costs are syndication costs that are not deductible or amortizable. ###

2. Which of the following statements is true?

A. The IRS requires partnerships with more than 100 partners to file their returns electronically.
B. The IRS requires all partnerships to file electronically.
C. The IRS requires limited partnerships with more than 10 partners to file their returns electronically.
D. The IRS requires partnerships with 100 or more partners to file electronically.

The answer is A. The IRS requires partnerships with more than 100 partners (Schedules K-1) to file their returns electronically. Partnerships with 100 or fewer partners are not required to electronically file their returns. ###

3. Polly and Diane form P&D Partnership in 2012. Polly contributes $16,000 cash and Diane contributes equipment with a fair market value of $15,000 and an adjusted basis of $5,000. What amount should Diane report as a gain as a result of this transaction?

A. $0.
B. $3,000.
C. $5,000.
D. $8,000.

The answer is A. Usually, neither the partner nor the partnership recognizes a gain or loss when property is contributed to the partnership in exchange for a partnership interest. This applies whether a partnership is being formed or is already operating. However, if an asset is encumbered by a liability, such as a mortgage, there is a possibility that the partner will recognize a gain in connection with the contribution. ###

4. Which of the following statements regarding limited partnerships is correct?

A. A limited partner has an economic liability for damages and an economic risk of loss.
B. A limited partner does not have an economic risk of loss in partnership recourse liabilities.
C. A limited partner does not have an economic risk of loss in partnership recourse liabilities; however, a limited partner is required to contribute additional capital.
D. A limited partner is treated just like a general partner when it comes to recourse liability.

The answer is B. A limited partner generally has no obligation to contribute additional capital to the partnership and therefore does not have an economic risk of loss in partnership recourse liabilities. Thus, absent some other factor such as the guarantee of a partnership liability by the limited partner or the limited partner making a loan to the partnership, a limited partner generally does not have an economic risk of loss from the partnership recourse liabilities. ###

5. Otto and Janelle form a cash-basis general partnership with cash contributions of $20,000 each. Under the partnership agreement, they share all partnership profits and losses equally. They borrow $60,000 and purchase depreciable business equipment. However, Otto has poor credit, so Janelle is the only signer on the loan. Janelle is required to pay the creditor if the partnership defaults, so she has an economic risk of loss related to the loan. The payments on the loan are made out of the partnership bank account. What is Janelle's basis in the partnership, and what is Otto's basis?

A. Janelle: $80,000, Otto: $20,000.
B. Janelle: $60,000, Otto: $20,000.
C. Janelle: $20,000, Otto: $20,000.
D. Janelle: $60,000, Otto: $60,000.

The answer is A. This loan amount is included in Janelle's basis in the partnership because she has an economic risk of loss related to this liability. An additional $60,000 of basis in the partnership's depreciable property was created as a result of incurring this debt. Her basis in the partnership would be $80,000 ($20,000 + $60,000), while Otto's basis would be only $20,000. ###

6. When payments are made by a partnership to partners that are without regard to partnership income, these payments are called:

A. Capital gains.
B. Ordinary distributions.
C. Passive income.
D. Guaranteed payments.

The answer is D. Guaranteed payments are those made by a partnership to a partner that are determined without regard to the partnership's income. A partnership treats guaranteed payments for services, or for the use of capital, as a business expense, just as if they were made to a person who is not a partner. ###

7. Daniel is a general partner in the Vrettos Partnership. During the year, Daniel personally assumes $100,000 of the partnership's liabilities. Which of the following statements regarding partnership liabilities is true?

A. The assumption of partnership debt by Daniel is treated as a distribution of cash to Daniel, and it decreases Daniel's partnership basis.
B. The assumption of partnership debt by Daniel increases his basis.
C. Daniel cannot assume partnership liabilities.
D. Only limited partners are allowed to assume partnership liabilities.

The answer is B. The assumption of partnership debt by Daniel increases his basis. If a partner's share of partnership liabilities increases, or a partner's individual liabilities increase because he assumes partnership liabilities, this increase is treated as if the partner made a contribution to the partnership.###

8. If a partnership requests additional time to file its return, for how long will the filing deadline be extended?

A. Three months.
B. Five months.
C. Six months.
D. Nine months.

The answer is B. Form 7004, Automatic Extension of Time to File Certain Business Income Tax, Information, and Other Returns, is used by partnerships to extend their filing deadline for five months. ###

9. The G&H Partnership has two partners, Gil and Hassid. They share profits and losses equally (50/50). The partnership has the following activity during the year.

Gross income from operations:	$200,000
Business expenses:	$30,000
Tax-exempt interest income:	$10,000
Rental income:	$120,000
Charitable contributions:	$4,000

What is Hassid's share of the partnership ordinary income?

A. $85,000.
B. $91,000.
C. $100,000.
D. $105,000.

The answer is A. The rental income, tax exempt income, and charitable contributions are all separately stated items. They do not affect the calculation of ordinary income. Instead, each partner's share of the separately stated items is passed through to the individual partners. Hassid's share of the partnership's ordinary income is split evenly with Gil, so his portion is figured as follows:

($200,000 - $30,000) = $170,000
$170,000 X 50% =$85,000 ###

10. Roadhouse Partnership forms in 2012. Roadhouse decides to amortize its organizational costs. Which of the following costs would not be considered an organizational or start-up cost qualified for amortization?

A. The costs of transferring a building to the partnership.
B. Legal fees to draft the partnership agreement.
C. Accounting fees for services related to the organization of the partnership.
D. The cost of training employees before the business opens.

The answer is A. The expenses for acquiring or transferring assets to a partnership cannot be amortized. They must instead be included in the basis of a partnership interest. The other choices are all costs that may be amortized or deducted as qualifying start-up or organizational costs. ###

11. Which of the following increases the basis of a partner's interest in a partnership?

A. A partner's share of tax-exempt interest from municipal bonds owned by the partnership.
B. A decrease in the partner's share of liabilities.
C. A distribution of $2,000 in cash to the partner.
D. A property distribution with an FMV of $5,000.

The answer is A. Partnership income, including tax-exempt interest, increases a partner's basis in his partnership interest. ####

12. José and Carlos form a partnership. Each contributes $20,000 during the initial formation of the partnership. Their partnership agreement states that José will receive 35% of the distributive income, and Carlos will receive 65%. In 2012, the partnership has a net profit of $200,000. What is each partner's distributive share of the partnership profits?

A. José: $70,000, Carlos: $130,000.
B. José: $100,000, Carlos: $100,000.
C. José: $35,000, Carlos $65,000.
D. Some other amount.

The answer is A. The profits are allocated according to the partnership agreement. Jose's distributive share is calculated as follows: 35% X $200,000 = $70,000. Carlos's share is figured as follows: 65% X $200,000 = $130,000. ###

13. John, Robin, Shanette, and Theresa form a partnership. Each partner contributes $10,000 and receives an equal interest in the partnership (25%). Under the partnership agreement, they share partnership profits and losses equally. The partnership borrows $135,000 and purchases business equipment. All the partners except for Theresa personally guarantee the liability. What is each partner's basis after this transaction?

A. Theresa's basis is zero, and the other partners each have a basis of $58,333.
B. Theresa's basis is $10,000, and the other partners each have a basis of $43,750.
C. Theresa's basis is $10,000, and the other partners each have a basis of $55,000.
D. Each partner has a basis of $43,750.

The answer is C. If a partner's share of partnership liabilities increases, this increase is treated as a contribution of money by the partner to the partnership. This debt is included in the partners' basis in the partnership because incurring it creates an additional $135,000 of basis in the partnership's depreciable property. However, since Theresa does not have an economic risk of loss for this liability, the liability does not increase her basis. The basis for each of the remaining partners would include his or her share of the liability ([$135,000 ÷ 3 partners] = $45,000 + $10,000 their original investment). ###

14. Racing Horses Partnership has seven partners. The partnership files its tax return three months late. What is the IRS penalty for late filing of the partnership return?
A. $0.
B. $585.
C. $780.
D. $4,095.

The answer is D. The penalty for late filing is $195 per month, for each partner, for up to 12 months. The penalty is calculated as follows: $195 X 3 months X 7 partners = $4,095. ###

15. Carolyn and Jerome form a partnership in 2012. Each contributes $5,000 for an equal partnership interest. Their partnership agreement states that they will share income and loss equally. However, because of her accounting expertise, Carolyn will receive a guaranteed payment each year of $21,000, regardless of the partnership's income or loss. In 2012, the partnership earns $50,000 before deducting the guaranteed payment. What is Jerome's distributive share of partnership profits for 2012?

A. $0.
B. $14,500.
C. $22,500.
D. $25,000.

The answer is B. The guaranteed payment must be deducted before figuring each partner's distributive share. The answer is figured as follows:
$50,000 - $21,000 = $29,000
$29,000 X 50% = $14,500
Guaranteed payments are deducted from partnership income before determining the distributive share of income or loss for each partner. ###

16. The D&D Healthy Pet Stores operates as an accrual-based partnership and files a Form 1065 for 2012. In addition to receipts from pet food sales of $250,000, the partnership has the following items of income and expenses for 2012:

•Salaries	$50,000
•Insurance	$5,000
•Charitable contributions	$5,000
•Licenses	$5,000
•Rental income	$25,000
•Guaranteed payments	$75,000

What is the correct ordinary income or loss that D&D Healthy Pet Stores should report on line 22 of their 2012 Form 1065?

A. $85,000.
B. $115,000.
C. $100,000.
D. $150,000.

The answer is B. All of the items listed are included in the calculation of ordinary income except the charitable contributions and the rental income, both of which must be separately stated on Form 1065. Thus, ordinary income will be $115,000 ($250,000 -$50,000 - $5,000 - $5,000 - $75,000). Like the other deductions listed, guaranteed payments to partners are treated as a deduction in determining ordinary income or loss. ###

17. Monica contributes property with a fair market value of $7,000, an adjusted basis of $4,000, and a related mortgage of $1,000 which the partnership assumes, to a partnership for a 40% interest in the partnership. What is Monica's basis in her partnership interest?

A. $4,000.
B. $3,000,
C. $6,000.
D. $3,400.

The answer is D. The basis of Monica's interest is the adjusted basis of the property she contributes ($4,000) less the portion of the related mortgage liability assumed by the other partners (60% x $1,000 = $600), or $3,400. ###

18. A partner is not considered at risk for which of the following amounts?

A. The money and adjusted basis of any property the partner contributed to activity.
B. The partner's share of net income retained by the partnership.
C. A partnership's nonrecourse liability.
D. Certain amounts borrowed by the partnership for use in the activity if the partner is personally liable for repayment.

The answer is C. The at-risk rules limit the deductibility of losses to the partner's basis reduced by his share of any of the partnership's nonrecourse debt. ###

19. Bea acquired a 30% interest in a partnership by contributing property that had an adjusted basis to her of $25,000, fair market value of $50,000, and a $40,000 mortgage. The partnership assumed the liability. What is Bea's gain or loss on the contribution of her property to the partnership?

A. $0.
B. $3,000 gain.
C. $12,000 gain.
D. $10,000 loss.

The answer is B. The basis of Bea's partnership interest should be the adjusted basis of the property contributed ($25,000) less the portion of the mortgage liability assumed by the other partners (30% x $40,000 = $28,000). However, this would result in a basis of negative $3,000, and a partner's basis can never go below zero. In order to prevent a negative basis, Bea must recognize a gain of $3,000. ###

20. Hatam Persian Restaurant operates as a calendar-year partnership. Hatam's two partners, Afsar and Ted, share profits and losses 60% and 40% respectively. For tax year 2012, Hatam Restaurant had the following income and expense:

- Gross sales $270,000
- Cost of goods sold $80,000
- Bank interest income $2,500
- Wages paid $50,000
- Short-term capital loss $5,000

Compute the partnership's ordinary income and flow-through amounts to the partners:

A. Afsar: ordinary income $85,500 and short-term capital loss $3,000; Ted: ordinary income $57,000 and short-term capital loss $2,000.
B. Afsar: ordinary income $82,500; Ted: ordinary income $55,000.
C. Afsar: ordinary income $81,000, interest income $1,500, and short-term capital loss $3,000; Ted: ordinary income $54,000, interest income $1,000, and short-term capital loss $2,000.
D. Afsar: ordinary income $84,000, interest income $1,500, and short-term capital loss $3,000. Ted: ordinary income $56,000, interest income $1,000, and short-term capital loss $2,000.'

The answer is D. Interest income and short-term capital losses are separately stated items that flow through to each partner, and retain their character. The other items listed are components of ordinary income, determined as follows: gross sales of $270,000, less cost of goods sold of $80,000 and wages of $50,000 = ordinary income of $140,000. Absent any provisions in the partnership agreement to the contrary, both ordinary income and the separately stated items would be allocated according to the 60%/40% profit-sharing arrangement. ###

21. The Bissinger Cosmetics Partnership generated income and expenses as stated below. What is the amount of ordinary income (loss) from trade or business activities that Bissinger should report for 2012?

•Employee wages: $15,000
•Rental real estate income: $20,000
•Charitable contributions: $500
•Cost of goods sold: $10,000
•Income from cosmetics sales: $75,000

A. $65,000.
B. $69,500.
C. $50,000.
D. $30,000.

The answer is C. Bissinger's ordinary income for 2012 is equal to its sales income less cost of goods sold and wages ($75,000 - $10,000 - $15,000 = $50,000). The income from rental real estate and the charitable contributions must be separately stated on the partnership's tax return. ###

22. Davisville Partnership sold a capital asset to Winters Partnership at a loss of $50,000. Davisville had held the property for five months. Davisville is owned 30% by Marvin, 30% by LaTroy, and 40% by Geoff, Marvin's brother. Winters Partnership is owned 80% by Dixon Corporation. Marvin owns 25% of the stock of Dixon Corporation and Geoff's daughter owns 60% of Dixon Corporation. How much of the loss should Davisville Partnership recognize for tax purposes on their tax return for the year of the sale?

A. $0.
B. $3,000.
C. $35,000.
D. $50,000.

The answer is A. A loss is not allowed from a sale or exchange of property directly or indirectly between a partnership and a person whose direct or indirect interest in the capital or profits of the partnership is more than 50%. In this case, Marvin and Geoff own a combined interest of 70% in the Davisville Partnership, and they indirectly own over 50% in Winters Partnership. (Since Marvin and Geoff's daughter own a combined interest of 85% in Dixon Corporation, their indirect interest in Winters Partnership is 85% times 80%, or 68%.) ###

Unit 12: Partnership Distributions & Liquidations

More Reading:
Publication 541, *Partnerships*

Partnership Distributions

Partnership distributions include the following:

- Distributions of the partnership's earnings for the current or prior years
- A withdrawal by a partner in anticipation of the current year's earnings
- A complete or partial liquidation of a partner's interest
- A distribution to all partners in a complete liquidation of the partnership

A partnership is not a taxable entity, and its income and loss flow through and are reported on the partners' individual tax returns. Each partner is taxed on his distributive share of income, whether or not it is actually distributed. Therefore, when distributions are made to the partners in connection with these earnings, they are generally not taxable.

A partnership distribution is not taken into account in determining the partner's distributive share of the partnership income or loss. If any gain or loss from the distribution is recognized by the partner, it must be reported on his return for the tax year in which the distribution is received. Cash or property withdrawn by a partner in anticipation of the current year's earnings is treated as a distribution received on the last day of the partnership's tax year. A partner's adjusted basis in his partnership interest is decreased (but not below zero) by the cash and adjusted basis of property distributed to the partner.

A partnership generally does not recognize any gain or loss because of distributions it makes to partners. The partnership may be able to elect to adjust the basis of its undistributed property.

Example: The adjusted basis of Angela's partnership interest is $14,000. She receives a distribution of $8,000 cash and land that has an adjusted basis of $2,000 and a fair market value of $3,000. The distribution decreases the basis of her partnership interest to $4,000 [$14,000 − ($8,000 + $2,000)]. Because the cash received does not exceed the basis of her partnership interest, Angela does not recognize any gain on the distribution. Any gain on the land will be recognized when she later sells it.

Unless there is a complete liquidation of a partner's interest, the basis of property (other than cash) distributed to the partner is its adjusted basis to the partnership immediately before the distribution. However, the basis of the property distributed to the partner cannot be more than the adjusted basis of his interest in the partnership, reduced by any cash received in the same transaction.

> **Example:** The basis of Mike's partnership interest is $10,000. He receives a distribution of $4,000 cash and a parcel of land that has an adjusted basis to the partnership of $8,000. His basis for the land is limited to $6,000 ($10,000 - $4,000, the cash he receives), since the total amount cannot exceed his partnership interest. After the distribution, his partnership basis would be zero.

When a partnership distributes the following items, the distribution may be treated as a sale or exchange of property rather than a distribution:

- Unrealized receivables or substantially appreciated inventory items distributed in exchange for any part of the partner's interest in other partnership property, including cash
- Other property, including cash, distributed in exchange for any part of a partner's interest in unrealized receivables or substantially appreciated inventory items

This treatment does not apply to the following distributions:

- A distribution of property to the partner who contributed the same property to the partnership
- Payments made to a retiring partner or successor in interest of a deceased partner that are the partner's distributive share of partnership income or guaranteed payments

Any gain or loss on a sale or exchange of unrealized receivables or inventory items a partner received in a distribution is treated as ordinary income or loss.

> **Example:** Marcia was a partner in Illuminated, a business that sold handmade candles. In 2010, the store closed and Marcia received, through dissolution of the partnership, inventory that has a basis of $19,000. She sells the entire inventory for $24,000. The $5,000 gain is taxed as ordinary income. If she had held the inventory for more than five years, her gain would have been capital gain, provided the inventory was a capital asset in her hands at the time of sale.

Distributions in Excess of Basis

A partner cannot have a negative partnership basis. If a partner has distributions that exceed his adjusted basis during any tax year, the excess is generally treated as a capital gain to the partner. This can occur, for example, when a partner's share of the decrease in partnership liabilities during the taxable year and the cash distributions received by the partner during the taxable year exceed the basis of the partner's partnership interest.

However, if a partner's losses for the year exceed his basis, the losses are limited to the basis of his partnership interest (with some exceptions to this rule in a partnership liquidation). Any partnership losses and deductions that exceed the partner's basis may be carried forward indefinitely until the partner's basis in the partnership increases.

If a partnership acquires a partner's debt and extinguishes the debt by distributing it to the partner, the partner will recognize capital gain or loss to the extent the fair market value of the debt differs from the basis of the debt. The partner is treated as having satisfied the debt for its fair market value. If the issue price of the debt exceeds its FMV when distributed, the partner may have to include the excess amount in income as canceled debt.

Sale of a Partnership Interest

A partnership interest is a capital asset. Typically that means any gain or loss on the sale or exchange of a partnership interest is treated as a capital gain or loss. Gain or loss is calculated as the difference between the amount realized and the adjusted basis of the partner's interest in the partnership. If the selling partner is relieved of any partnership liabilities, he must include the liability relief as part of the amount realized for his interest.

An exchange of partnership interests generally does not qualify as a nontaxable exchange of like-kind property. This applies regardless of whether they are general or limited partnership interests or interests in the same or different partnerships.

> **Example:** Selene became a partner in the Rincon Partnership by contributing cash to the formation of the partnership. The adjusted basis of her partnership interest at the end of 2012 is $20,000, which includes her $15,000 share of partnership liabilities. Selene sells her interest in the partnership for $10,000 in cash on December 31, 2012. At the time of the sale, she had been paid her share of the partnership income for the tax year. Selene realizes $25,000 from the sale of her partnership interest ($10,000 cash payment + $15,000 liability relief). She must report $5,000 ($25,000 realized – $20,000 basis) as a capital gain.

Liquidation of a Partnership

When a partnership dissolves or stops doing business, it is called a partnership liquidation. A partnership can dissolve when a partner dies, or when one partner drops out of the business.

The basis of property received in complete liquidation of a partner's interest is the adjusted basis of the partner's interest in the partnership reduced by any cash distributed to the partner in the same transaction. A partner's holding period for property distributed to him includes the period held by the partnership, and if contributed to the partnership by a partner, the period held by that partner also.

> **Example:** Tim's basis in his partnership interest is $20,000. In a distribution in liquidation of his entire interest, he receives a delivery truck and a utility trailer (neither of which is inventory or unrealized receivables). The truck has an adjusted basis to the partnership of $15,000 and an FMV of $15,000. The trailer has an adjusted basis to the partnership of $15,000 and an FMV of $5,000. To figure his basis in each property, Tim first assigns a basis of $15,000 to the truck and $15,000 to the trailer. This leaves a $10,000 basis decrease (the $30,000 total of the assigned basis minus the $20,000 allocable basis). He allocates the entire $10,000 to the trailer (its unrealized depreciation). Tim's basis in the truck is $15,000, and his basis in the trailer is $5,000 ($15,000 - $10,000).

Sometimes, a partnership will dissolve with unamortized organizational or start-up expenses. If a partnership is liquidated before the end of the amortization period, the unamortized amount of qualifying organizational costs and start-up expenses can be deducted in the partnership's final tax year.

Liquidation at Partner's Retirement or Death

Payments made by the partnership to a retiring partner or a deceased partner's estate or in liquidation of the interest of a retiring or deceased partner in exchange for his interest in partnership property are considered a distribution, not a distributive share or guaranteed payment that could give rise to a deduction for the partnership. A retiring partner or deceased partner is treated as a partner until his interest in the partnership has been completely liquidated.

Recognizing Loss on Liquidating Distribution

In a partnership liquidation, the liquidating distributions are similar to regular distributions except that the partner may recognize a loss if the total basis of the cash and property received is less than the partner's basis in the partnership. A partner cannot recognize a loss on a partnership distribution unless all of the following requirements are met:

- The adjusted basis of the partner's interest in the partnership exceeds the distribution.
- The partner's entire interest in the partnership is liquidated.
- The distribution is in cash, unrealized receivables, or inventory items.

Partnership Termination

A partnership generally terminates when one of the following events takes place:

- All its operations are discontinued and no part of any business, financial operation, or venture is continued by any of its partners in a partnership.
- At least 50% of the total interest in partnership capital and profits is sold or exchanged within a 12-month period, including a sale or exchange to another partner.

The partnership's tax year ends on the date of termination. If a partnership is terminated before the end of its regular tax year, Form 1065 must be filed for the short tax year from the beginning of the tax year through the date of termination. The return is due the fifteenth day of the fourth month following the date of termination.

If a partnership is converted into an LLC classified as a partnership, the conversion does not terminate the partnership, and there is no sale, exchange, or termination of partnership interests. The partnership's tax year does not close, and the LLC can continue to use the partnership's taxpayer identification number.

If a business partnership breaks up and one of the former partners is insolvent and cannot pay any of the partnership's debts, existing partners will sometimes be forced to pay more than their share of the liabilities. If a partner pays any part of the insolvent partner's share of the debts, he can take a bad debt deduction.

Related Party Transactions

A partnership cannot deduct a loss on the sale or trade of property if the transaction is directly or indirectly between related parties. Losses will not be allowed from a sale or exchange of property (other than an interest in the partnership) directly or indirectly between a partnership and a person whose direct or indirect interest in the capital or profits of the partnership is more than 50%.

If the sale or exchange is between two partnerships in which the same persons directly or indirectly own more than 50% of the capital or profits interests in each partnership, no deduction of a loss is allowed.

Example: George and Lynn are siblings. Lynn is a 60% partner in the Buildrite Machinery Partnership, and George is a 55% partner in the Schlutter Partnership. If the partnerships sell property to each other, no loss will be allowed in the transaction, because the partnerships are considered related parties. Losses will instead be suspended until the property is eventually disposed of in a non-related party transaction.

The basis of each partner's interest in the partnership is decreased (but not below zero) by the partner's share of the disallowed loss.

If the purchaser later sells the property, only the gain realized that is greater than the loss not allowed will be taxable. If any gain from the sale of the property is not recognized because of this rule, the basis of each partner's interest in the partnership is increased by the partner's share of that gain.

Unit 12: Questions

1. The adjusted basis of Tammy's partnership interest is $24,000. She receives a distribution of $9,000 cash and machinery that has an adjusted basis of $1,000 and a fair market value of $7,000. How much gain should Tammy recognize on this distribution?

A. $0.
B. $1,000.
C. $2,000.
D. $7,000.

The answer is A. No gain or loss is recognized in this transaction. Because the sum of cash received and adjusted basis does not exceed the basis of her partnership interest, Tammy does not recognize any gain on the distribution. Any gain on the machinery will be recognized when she sells it. ###

2. The adjusted basis of Steve's partnership interest is $10,000. He receives a distribution of $4,000 cash and a utility van that has an adjusted basis to the partnership of $9,000 and a fair market value of $12,000. This was not a liquidating distribution. What is Steve's basis in the van?

A. $5,000.
B. $6,000.
C. $12,000.
D. $16,000.

The answer is B. Steve's basis for the van is limited to $6,000 ($10,000 basis – $4,000, the cash he receives). His basis in the van is limited by Steve's basis in his partnership interest. ###

3. Marty is permanently retiring from Sunnyside Partnership this year. His adjusted basis in the partnership is $50,000. He receives a distribution of $65,000 in cash. How would Marty report this transaction?

A. $15,000 gain upon distribution.
B. $50,000 gain upon distribution.
C. $65,000 capital gain.
D. $65,000 ordinary income.

The answer is A. Marty must recognize $15,000 of gain. This is the difference between his adjusted basis in the partnership and the amount of his distribution ($65,000 - $50,000). Upon receipt of the distribution, a retiring partner or the successor in interest of a deceased partner recognizes gain to the extent that any cash (and marketable securities treated as cash) distributed is more than the partner's adjusted basis in the partnership. ###

4. Bart and Ellen are equal partners in B&E Partnership. In 2012, the partnership breaks up. Bart is insolvent, and Ellen becomes responsible for paying a portion of his partnership debt. Which of the following statements is true?

A. Ellen cannot take a bad debt deduction for any debt that the partnership incurred.
B. Bart is not responsible for paying any of his liabilities after dissolution.
C. Ellen can take a bad debt deduction for any amount that she must pay that is not her share of the partnership liability.
D. None of the above.

The answer is C. Ellen is allowed to take a bad debt deduction for the liabilities she must pay that are not her share of partnership liabilities. If a business partnership dissolves and one of the former partners is insolvent and cannot pay his share of the partnership's debts, other partners may have to pay more than their respective shares. If a partner pays any part of the insolvent partner's share of the debts, he can take a bad debt deduction for the amount paid. ###

5. The adjusted basis of Hugo's partnership interest is $150,000. He receives a nonliquidating distribution of $80,000 cash and land that has an adjusted basis to the partnership of $100,000. What is the basis of the land in Hugo's hands?

A. $70,000.
B. $100,000.
C. $120,000.
D. $150,000.

The answer is A. Hugo's basis for the distributed property is limited to $70,000 ($150,000 - $80,000, the cash received). In a nonliquidating distribution, the basis of property (other than cash) distributed to the partner by a partnership is the adjusted basis to the partnership immediately before the distribution. However, the basis of the property distributed to the partner cannot be more than the adjusted basis of his interest in the partnership. ###

6. Bill owns a 75% capital interest in the Shanahan Partnership. Bill's wife, Veronica, is a 65% owner in the Underdahl Partnership. Bill and Veronica file separate tax returns and keep all their books and records separate. Shanahan Partnership sells Underdahl Partnership a factory machine for $7,600. Shanahan's partnership basis in the machinery is $10,000. What is Shanahan Partnership's deductible loss?

A. $0.
B. $2,400.
C. $7,600.
D. $10,000.

The answer is A. Shanahan Partnership's loss of $2,400 is not deductible. A loss on the sale or exchange of property between related persons is not deductible. This applies to both direct and indirect transactions. The fact that Bill and Veronica file separate tax returns does not prevent them from being related parties for purposes of this transaction. ###

7. In 2012, Laney sold her partnership interest for $45,000. Her adjusted basis at the time of the sale was $29,500, which includes her $12,500 share of partnership liabilities. When she initially invested in the partnership, she contributed $10,000 worth of equipment. There was no profit or loss at the partnership level at the time she sold her interest. What is the amount and nature of her income or loss from the sale of her partnership interest in 2012?

A. $7,500 ordinary loss.
B. $10,000 capital gain.
C. $12,500 ordinary income.
D. $28,000 capital gain.

The answer is D. When Laney sold her partnership interest, she was relieved of her $12,500 share of the partnership's liabilities, so her adjusted basis for purposes of calculating her gain on sale of the interest is $17,000 ($29,500 - $12,500). Thus, her gain is $28,000 (proceeds of $45,000 less adjusted basis of $17,000). Approached differently, the amount of liability relieved from Laney upon sale of her interest might be viewed as additional proceeds, but her gain would still be $28,000 ($45,000 + $12,500 - $29,500). As a partnership interest is a capital asset, any gain or loss recognized on the sale of the interest is typically treated as a capital gain or loss. ###

8. The adjusted basis of Adrian's partnership interest is $17,500. He received a distribution of $9,000 cash and a piece of land with an adjusted basis of $2,500 to the partnership and a fair market value of $4,000. What is the gain to be recognized at the time of these distributions?

A. $0.
B. $1,500.
C. $4,500.
D. $6,000.

The answer is A. Because the total of cash and the basis of property distributed ($9,000 + $2,500 = $11,500) does not exceed Adrian's adjusted basis of $17,500 in his partnership interest, he will recognize no gain as a result of the distribution. He assumes the partnership's adjusted basis of $2,500 in the property received, and will recognize gain or loss if he later sells this property. ###

9. Alice's outside basis in Dogan Tiles Partnership on January 1, 2012 was $11,000. She is a 50% partner and shares profits and losses in the same ratio. For 2012, the partnership's ordinary business income was $40,000 and tax-exempt interest income was $700. If the partnership were to liquidate on December 31, 2012, what would be Alice's basis for determining gain or loss?

A. $24,900.
B. $30,750.
C. $31,350.
D. $30,300.

The answer is C. Alice's basis on December 31, 2012 would be determined as follows:

Basis at January 1, 2012	$11,000
50% share of ordinary business income	$20,000
50% share of tax-exempt interest income	$350
Basis at December 31, 2012	$31,350

Calculation:
($11,000 + $20,000 + $350 = $31,350) ###

10. Nora, a partner in the Maass Partnership, receives $1,000 cash and property worth $2,000, in which Maass has a basis of $1,500. Nora's outside basis at the time of the distribution is $20,000. The partnership has assets of $40,000 and no outstanding liabilities. This distribution is made at the end of the year after partnership income (loss) has been recorded. How much gain should Nora recognize on the distribution and what is her basis in the property received?

A. Nora recognizes a gain of $500 on the property received and her basis in the property is $2,000.
B. Nora recognizes gain of $1,500 on the property and cash received. Her basis in the property received is $3,500.
C. Nora recognizes no gain on the property received. Her basis in the property received is $1,500.
D. Nora recognizes a gain of $1,000. Her basis in the property received is $1,500.

The answer is C. Nora recognizes no gain because the total of cash and the basis of property received does not exceed her basis in the partnership. She assumes the partnership's basis of $1,500 in the property received, and may recognize gain or loss if she later sells the property. ###

Unit 13: C Corporations in General

More Reading:

Publication 542, *Corporations*

Publication 544, *Sales and Other Dispositions of Assets*

Instructions for Form 1120, *U.S. Corporation Income Tax Return*

Most major companies are C corporations, which are taxed under subchapter C of the Internal Revenue Code. A C corporation can own property in its own name and it can be sued directly. The shareholders who own stock in a corporation do not own its individual assets. Individual shareholders are protected from legal liability, except in very unusual circumstances.

The IRS requires certain businesses to be taxed as corporations. The following businesses formed after 1996 are automatically treated as corporations:

- A business formed under a federal or state law that refers to it as a corporation
- A business formed under a state law that refers to it as a joint-stock company or joint-stock association
- Insurance companies
- Certain banks
- A business owned by a state or local government
- A business specifically required to be taxed as a corporation by the IRC (for example, certain publicly-traded partnerships)
- Certain foreign businesses
- Any other business that elects to be taxed as a corporation and files Form 8832, *Entity Classification Election*

Basic Concepts

1. A C corporation enjoys perpetual life and limited liability.
2. Earnings of a C corporation may be taxed twice: first at the corporate level and again at the shareholder level if they are distributed as dividends. Shareholders of a C corporation cannot deduct corporate losses. A corporation must maintain a list of all its shareholders, and generally must conduct at least one shareholder meeting per year.
3. A C corporation must file a charter, issue stock, and be overseen by a board of directors. A C corporation may have a single owner-shareholder or millions of shareholders.
4. Corporate existence starts when the articles of incorporation are filed with the state office that handles incorporations (e.g., usually the Secretary of State), along with any required filing fees.
5. If a C corporation liquidates, it will recognize gain or loss on the sale or distribution of its assets. Corporate shareholders then recognize gain or loss on the surrender of their stock to the corporation.

6. A C corporation may sell common or preferred stock with different voting rights.
7. One of the major advantages of a C corporation is the ability for shareholder-employees to receive tax-free employee fringe benefits that are 100% deductible to the corporation as a business expense.

C Corporation Filing Requirements

All domestic corporations in existence for any part of a tax year (including corporations in bankruptcy) must file an income tax return, regardless of their taxable income. A C corporation typically files Form 1120, *U.S. Corporation Income Tax Return*, but it may file Form 1120-A if its gross receipts, total income, and total assets are each under $500,000.

A corporation must continue to file tax returns even if there is no business activity or profits. However, it does not have to file after it has formally dissolved. The only exception to this filing requirement is for tax-exempt organizations (which may be organized as corporations). Exempt organizations file Form 990 rather than Form 1120.

A corporation filing a short-period return (for example, a corporation that dissolves in the middle of the year) must generally file by the fifteenth day of the third month after the short period ends. This means that a calendar-year corporation must file its tax return by March 15 of the following year.

> **Example:** Greenbook Inc. is a domestic corporation with a fiscal year tax year-end of March 31. Greenbook must file Form 1120 by June 15.

> **Example:** Finman Design Corporation's tax year ends December 31. It must file its Form 1120 by March 15.

Electronic filing using the Electronic Federal Tax Payment System (EFTPS) is *mandatory* for C corporations that have $10 million or more in assets and at least 250 or more returns of any type, including information returns such as Forms W-2 or Forms 1099.

A corporation must file Form 7004, *Automatic Extension of Time to File Certain Business Income Tax, Information, and Other Returns,* to request a six-month extension of time to file its income tax return. Form 7004 does not extend the time for paying the tax due on the return. Interest, and possibly penalties, will be charged on any part of the tax due and not paid. The interest is figured from the original due date of the return to the date of payment.

A penalty for late filing is assessed at 5% of any unpaid tax for each month the return is late, up to a maximum of 25% of the unpaid tax on the return. The late filing penalty is reduced by any late payment penalty for the same period. The minimum penalty for any return that is over 60 days late is the *smaller* of the tax due on the return, or $135. The penalty for late payment of corporate income tax is one half of 1% of the unpaid tax for each month that the tax is not paid, up to a maximum of 25% of the unpaid tax.

These penalties will not be imposed if the corporation shows reasonable cause for not paying or filing on time.

Estimated Tax Payments

Corporations are required to make estimated tax payments if they expect their tax due to be $500 or more during the taxable year. Penalties apply if estimated tax payments are not made on time. Most business entities, including corporations, are now required to use EFTPS to make their estimated tax payments. Installments are due on a quarterly basis, on the fifteenth day of the fourth, sixth, ninth, and twelfth months of the corporation's taxable year. So, for example, a calendar year corporation is required to make estimated payments on April 15, June 15, September 15, and December 15.

> **Example:** Longinotti Textiles Corporation's tax year ends January 31. Estimated tax payments are due on May 15, July 15, October 15, and January 15 (of the following year).

There is no penalty for underpayment of estimated tax if the tax is less than $500, or if each quarterly estimated tax payment is *at least* 25% of the corporation's current-year tax. There is also no underpayment penalty if each estimated tax installment is at least 25% of the income tax on the prior year return. However, this provision will not apply in the following instances:

- If the prior tax year was a short year (less than 12 months)
- If the corporation did not file a return for the prior year
- If the prior year tax return showed zero tax liability
- If the corporation had at least $1 million of taxable income in any of the last three years

Corporate Refunds and Amended Returns

Corporations may use Form 1139, *Corporate Application for Tentative Refund,* or Form 1120X, *Amended U.S. Corporation Income Tax Return,* to apply for a refund. A corporation can get a refund faster by using Form 1139.

The corporation cannot file Form 1139 before filing the return for a corporation's capital loss year, but it must file Form 1139 no later than one year after the year it sustains the capital loss.

If the corporation does not file Form 1139, it must file Form 1120X (an amended return) to apply for a refund. The corporation must file Form 1120X within three years of the due date, including extensions, for filing the return for a year in which it sustains a loss.

If a corporation accidentally overpays its estimated tax, it may use Form 4466, *Corporation Application for Quick Refund of Overpayment of Estimated Tax,* to obtain a quick refund of its estimated tax payments. Form 4466 may be used if a corporation's overpayment is at least 10% of its anticipated tax liability and at least $500.

Corporate Taxation

Unlike a partnership or an S corporation, a C corporation is not a pass-through entity. This means that the earnings of a C corporation are taxed twice. Corporate income is taxed when it is earned and then taxed again when it is distributed to shareholders as dividends. A corporation does not receive a tax deduction for the distribution of dividends to its shareholders.

Income does not retain its character when it is distributed to the shareholders. A corporation can have revenue from many different sources, including sales of products, services, and investment income. If, for example, a C corporation has rental income, it pays tax on this and any other sources of income at the corporate level.

When its after-tax income is distributed to shareholders, the rental income does not retain its character as rental income. It is distributed merely as a dividend. This is true even if the income is tax-exempt income to the corporation. For example, a C corporation may earn tax-exempt income from investing in municipal bonds. However, if this income is used to make distributions to shareholders, the distributions will be taxed as dividends to the shareholders.

Example: In 2012, Riden Paper Products receives tax-exempt income from bonds. The C corporation subsequently distributes income to its shareholders as taxable dividends. Even though a portion of the income was originally tax-exempt, it does not retain its tax-exempt character when distributions are made to the shareholders. In contrast, in the case of an S corporation or a partnership, the income would have retained its character when it was passed through to the partners or S corporation shareholders.

Example: Super Sailing Inc. is a calendar-year C corporation with 20 shareholders. After deducting business expenses, Super Sailing has $150,000 in taxable net income in 2012. The corporation also earns $4,000 in interest from municipal bonds. The $4,000 of tax-exempt bond interest is excluded from the corporation's taxable income. In December 2012, Super Sailing also distributes $120,000 to its shareholders. The company cannot take a tax deduction for the distribution. Each shareholder has an equal stake in the company, so each one receives $6,000 in dividend income ($120,000 ÷ 20 = $6,000). Each shareholder is required to recognize $6,000 in dividend income for 2012.

Accumulated Earnings Tax

A corporation is allowed to accumulate its earnings for a possible expansion or other bona fide business reasons. However, a corporation may be subject to the accumulated earnings tax if it does not distribute enough of its profits to shareholders. This tax was instituted to prevent corporations from hoarding income in order to avoid income tax for its shareholders by permitting earnings to accumulate instead of being distributed.

The tax is levied at a rate of **15% of accumulated taxable income**. If the accumulated earnings tax applies, interest is also assessed from the date the corporate return was originally due, without extensions.

An accumulation of $250,000 or less is generally considered reasonable for most businesses. However, for PSCs, the limit is $150,000. Reasonable needs of the business include the following:

- Specific, definite, and feasible plans for use of the earnings accumulation in the business.

- The amount necessary to redeem the corporation's stock included in a deceased shareholder's gross estate, if the amount does not exceed the reasonably anticipated total estate and inheritance taxes and funeral and administration expenses incurred by the shareholder's estate.

The absence of a bona fide business reason for a corporation's accumulated earnings may be indicated by many different circumstances, such as a lack of regular distributions to its shareholders or withdrawals by the shareholders classified as personal loans. However, actual moves to expand the business generally qualify as a *bona fide* use of the accumulated income. Examples of qualified accumulations include:

- The expansion of the company to a new area or a new facility
- Acquiring another business through the purchase of stock or assets
- Providing for reasonable estimates of product liability losses

The fact that a corporation has an unreasonable accumulation of earnings is sufficient to establish liability for the accumulated earnings tax unless the corporation can show the earnings were not accumulated to allow its individual shareholders to avoid income tax.

Corporate Alternative Minimum Tax

The tax laws give special treatment to some types of income and allow special deductions and credits for some types of expenses. As these laws allow some corporations with substantial economic income to significantly reduce their regular tax liabilities, the corporate alternative minimum tax (AMT) is intended to ensure that corporations pay at least a minimum amount of tax on their income. A corporation owes AMT if its tentative minimum tax is more than its regular tax.

Small corporations are exempt from corporate AMT. Most corporations will automatically qualify for the exemption in their first year of existence. After its first year, a corporation is considered a small corporation if its average annual gross receipts for the prior three years (or portion thereof) do not exceed $7.5 million ($5 million for its first three-year period).

If the corporation fails the $7.5 million test for any year, the corporation will become ineligible for the AMT exemption for that year and all subsequent years. If a corporation fails to qualify under the first year's $5 million limit, it will never qualify for the AMT exemption even if its gross receipts remain under the $7.5 million exemption limit.

The starting point for the determination of income for AMT purposes is the corporation's regular taxable income. Regular taxable income is modified by a series of additional computations called adjustments and preferences. Adjustments can either increase or decrease taxable income, whereas preferences are calculated on a property-by-property basis and only apply to the extent that they are positive.

Adjustments include a portion of accelerated depreciation on buildings and equipment, amortization of pollution control facilities, mining exploration and development expenses, income reported under the completed contract method of accounting, and installment sales income.

Corporations use Form 4626, *Alternative Minimum Tax-Corporations*, to figure their minimum tax for AMT purposes. Corporations use Form 8827, *Credit for Prior Year Minimum Tax*, to figure the minimum tax credit, if any, for alternative minimum tax incurred in prior tax years and any minimum tax credit carry forward. A minimum AMT tax credit may be carried forward indefinitely.

Accounting Methods for C Corporations

Like other entity types, C corporations may use any permissible accounting method for keeping track of income and expenses. Permissible methods include:

- Cash
- Accrual
- Special methods of accounting for certain items of income and expenses
- Hybrid method using elements of the methods above

A corporation with more than $5 million in average annual gross receipts is required to use the accrual method. If a corporation produces inventory, then the accrual method is generally required for sales and purchases of merchandise, unless average gross receipts are $1 million or less.

Nonaccrual Experience Method for Bad Debts

The nonaccrual experience method is a method of accounting for bad debts. If a corporation uses the accrual method of accounting and qualifies to use the nonaccrual experience method for bad debts, it is not required to accrue service-related income that it expects to be uncollectible.

Accrual-method corporations are not required to maintain accruals for certain amounts from the performance of services that, on the basis of their experience, will not be collected, if:

- The services are in the fields of health, law, engineering, architecture, accounting, actuarial science, performing arts, or consulting (personal service corporations); or
- The corporation's average annual gross receipts for the three prior tax years do not exceed $5 million.

This provision does not apply if the corporation charges interest on late payments, or if the business charges customers any penalty for failure to pay an amount timely. A business is permitted to use the nonaccrual experience method only for amounts earned for performing services. It cannot use this method for amounts owed from activities such as lending money, selling goods, or acquiring receivables.

Corporate Formation

A corporation is formed initially by a transfer of money, property, or services by prospective shareholders in exchange for stock in the corporation. For example, when a business is created using a corporate structure or a business previously operated as a partnership or sole proprietorship opts to become a corporation, a transfer of assets to the corporation usually takes place. The transfers of property to corporations have tax consequences to both the corporation and the shareholders.

Contributions to the capital of a corporation are not taxable transactions to the corporation, whether or not they are made by the shareholders. A shareholder will not recognize gain when a cash contribution is made for stock. This is just like when a person purchases stock on the open market for cash. The shareholder's basis in the stock is the amount of cash contributed. However, if a shareholder contributes property to a corporation, he generally recognizes gain and the basis of the contributed property to the corporation is the same as the basis that the shareholder had in the property, after increases for any gain that the shareholder recognized in the exchange.

The basis of property contributed to capital by anyone other than a shareholder is zero.

Example: The city of Omaha, Nebraska gives Madera Corporation a plot of land as an enticement to locate its business operations there. Madera accounts for the property as a contribution to capital. The land has zero basis since the property was contributed by a non-shareholder.

If stock is exchanged for services, the recipient of the stock recognizes taxable income based upon fair market value of the services provided, and that amount is his basis in the stock.

Example: Justin is a web designer who provides web design services to a corporation. He agrees to accept stock as payment, rather than cash. The stock is valued at $5,000. Justin must recognize ordinary income of $5,000 as payment for services he rendered to the corporation. His basis in the stock is $5,000.

There is an exception, however, for situations when property is contributed and the shareholder controls the corporation immediately after the transfer. This is called a *Section 351 transfer,* and is explained next.

Nontaxable Corporate Transfers: Section 351

If a taxpayer transfers property to a corporation in exchange for stock and immediately afterward the taxpayer controls the corporation, the exchange may not be taxable. This rule applies both to individuals and to entities that transfer property to a corporation. The rule also applies whether the corporation is being formed or is already in operation. The effect is to allow the investing shareholder to contribute assets to a corporation without immediate tax consequences, and defer recognition of taxable gain until the stock received is later disposed. This nonrecognition rule does not apply in the following situations:

- The corporation is an investment company.
- The taxpayer transfers the property in a bankruptcy proceeding in exchange for stock that is used to pay creditors.
- The stock is received in exchange for the corporation's debt (other than a security, such as a bond) or for interest on the corporation's debt (including a security) that accrued while the taxpayer held the debt.

In order to be considered in control of a corporation immediately after the exchange, the transferors must own at least 80% of the total combined voting power of all classes of stock entitled to vote and at least 80% of the outstanding shares of each class of nonvoting stock.

> **Example:** Mandy owns an office building. Her basis in the building is $100,000. She organizes a corporation when the building has a fair market value of $300,000. Mandy transfers the building to the corporation for all its authorized capital stock. No gain is recognized by Mandy or the corporation on the transfer.

This nonrecognition rule does not apply when services are rendered in exchange for stock. The value of stock received for services is income to the recipient.

> **Example:** Wayne is an architect. In 2012, he transfers property worth $35,000 and renders services valued at $3,000 to a corporation in exchange for stock valued at $38,000. Right after the exchange, Wayne owns 85% of the outstanding stock. No gain is recognized on the exchange of property. However, Wayne must recognize ordinary income of $3,000 as payment for services he rendered to the corporation.

If, in addition to stock, the shareholder receives money or property in exchange for the contribution of property, he would recognize gain to the extent of any money received plus the fair market value of property received.

Both the corporation and certain stockholders involved in a nontaxable exchange of property for stock must attach to their income tax returns a complete statement of all facts pertinent to the exchange. Based upon revised regulations issued in 2012, the reporting requirement now applies to stockholders that own 5% or more of a public company or 1% or more of a privately held company.

Assumption of Shareholder Liabilities in a Section 351 Exchange

Generally, when an entity assumes a liability for a taxpayer, this is treated as if the taxpayer had received cash in the amount of the liability relief. However, in the case of a section 351 exchange, a corporation may assume a shareholder's liability without triggering any gain, so long as the liability is less than the shareholder's adjusted basis.

The shareholder's basis in his stock must be reduced by the amount of the liability assumed by the corporation. If the liability assumed exceeds the contributing shareholder's basis, the excess is treated as a gain to the shareholder.

> **Example:** Casey transfers machinery to a corporation in exchange for all of the corporation's outstanding stock. The machinery's FMV at the time of the transfer is $200,000. Casey's basis in the machinery is $80,000. The machinery is encumbered by an outstanding loan of $30,000, which the corporation assumes. In this example, the section 351 exchange is valid, and no gain or loss is recognized in the transaction. Casey's basis in the stock is $50,000 ($80,000 basis of property contributed minus the $30,000 loan that was assumed by the corporation.)

Exclusions from Nonrecognition Treatment

This nonrecognition rule does not apply when the property transferred is of a relatively small value when compared to the value of stock already owned, and the main purpose of the transfer is to qualify for the nonrecognition of gain or loss. Property transferred will not be considered to be of small value if its FMV is at least 10% of the FMV of the stock already owned or to be received by the transferor.

If a group of transferors exchanges property for corporate stock, each transferor does not have to receive stock in proportion to his interest in the property transferred. If a disproportionate transfer takes place, it will be treated for tax purposes in accordance with its true nature. It may be treated as if the stock were first received in proportion and then some of it used to make gifts, pay compensation for services, or to satisfy the transferor's obligations.

If there is no good business reason for the corporation to assume a shareholder's liabilities, or if the main purpose of the exchange is to avoid federal income tax, the assumption is taxable to the shareholder.

If a corporation transfers its stock in satisfaction of indebtedness and the fair market value of its stock is less than the indebtedness, the corporation has income to the extent of the difference from the cancellation of indebtedness. For example, if stock is given to an individual in order to pay for a debt, the transfer does not qualify for nonrecognition treatment.

Corporate Start-up and Organizational Costs

Capital expenditures are costs that cannot be deducted in the year in which they are paid or incurred, and must be capitalized. The general rule is that if the property acquired has a useful life longer than the taxable year, the cost must be capitalized. The cost is then amortized or depreciated over the life of the asset. The following items related to corporate equity transactions cannot be amortized or deducted:

- Costs associated with issuing and selling stock or securities, such as commissions, professional fees, and printing costs
- Costs associated with the transfer of assets to the corporation

For qualified start-up and organizational costs, a corporation may elect to take an immediate deduction for up to $5,000 of business start-up costs and up to $5,000 of organizational costs, rather than amortize the costs. Any remaining costs must be amortized ratably over a 180-month period. The amortization period starts with the month the corporation begins operating. The $5,000 deduction is reduced (but not below zero) by the amount the total start-up or organizational costs exceed $50,000. If the costs exceed $55,000 or more, the deduction is reduced to zero.

The election is generally made on the corporation's first income tax return, filed by the due date (including extensions) for the tax year in which business begins. However, if the corporation files its return on time without making an election, it can still make an election by filing an amended return within six months of the due date of the return (excluding extensions).

The election to either amortize or capitalize these costs is *irrevocable* and applies for the current tax year and all subsequent years. The corporation must complete and attach Form 4562, *Depreciation and Amortization,* to its corporate tax return. Start-up costs include expenses such as:

- Advertising the business before it actually opens

- Wages for training new employees
- Wages paid to employees during training, and the costs of the training itself

Start-up costs do not include research and development expenses.

To qualify as an organizational cost it must be:

- For the creation of the corporation
- Chargeable to a capital account
- Amortizable over the life of the corporation
- Incurred before the end of the first tax year in which the corporation is in business

Examples of qualifying organizational costs are:

- The cost of temporary directors
- The cost of organizational meetings
- State incorporation fees
- The cost of legal services for writing the corporate bylaws or the corporate charter

If a corporation dissolves or is disposed of before the amortization period is complete, the remaining unamortized costs can be deducted on the corporation's final return.

Reconciliation of Book Income vs. Tax Income

Differences in accounting rules for financial reporting (book income) and tax reporting can lead to differences in the amounts of income reported to shareholders and tax authorities. Preparation of a C corporation's income tax return includes a reconciliation of book income to taxable income. The differences in book and taxable income are reconciled in Schedule M-1 of Form 1120 by small corporations with less than $10 million in assets. Larger corporations with over $10 million in assets use Schedule M-3.[127] Schedule M-3 provides additional information and contains three main sections:

- Financial statement reconciliation
- Detail of income/loss items
- Detail of expenses/deductions

Some examples of items that would be included in the reconciliation on Schedule M-1 or Schedule M-3, if applicable, are:

- Charitable contribution carryover (the amount of charitable contributions that are disallowed for tax purposes and must be carried over to the next taxable year.)
- Travel and entertainment in excess of the allowable 50% limit.
- Income subject to tax that is not included in the books.
- Federal income taxes paid or accrued, which are deductible for accounting purposes but not for tax purposes.
- Advance rental income.

---

[127] A domestic corporation with total assets of $10 million or more is required to file Schedule M-3, *Net Income (Loss) Reconciliation for Corporations with Total Assets of $10 million or More,* along with its main return.

Unit 13: Questions

1. Carrera Italian Foods Corporation incurred $40,000 in start-up costs when it opened for business in 2012. Instead of deducting the costs, the corporation elected to amortize all of them. What is the minimum period over which these expenses can be recovered?

A. 12 months.
B. 36 months.
C. 60 months.
D. 180 months.

The answer is D. A corporation can choose to amortize start-up expenses over 180 months. ###

2. The accumulated earnings tax is imposed on C corporations that accumulate earnings beyond the reasonable needs of their businesses. Which of the following reasons would not be an example of a qualified accumulation?

A. The expansion of the company to a new area or a new facility.
B. Acquiring another business through the purchase of stock or other assets.
C. Allowing the shareholders to take bona fide loans from the corporation.
D. Providing for reasonable estimates of product liability losses.

The answer is C. Allowing shareholders to draw personal loans from a corporation is not a valid reason for a corporation to accumulate earnings. In fact, this is one of the items the IRS looks for that may lead to imposing the accumulated earnings tax upon a corporation. Making loans to shareholders would allow them to access the corporation's earnings without taking taxable distributions. The accumulated earnings tax is imposed when a corporation tries to avoid income tax by permitting earnings and profits to accumulate instead of being divided or distributed. ###

3. If a corporation's tentative minimum tax (AMT) exceeds the regular tax, the excess amount is:

A. Payable instead of the regular tax.
B. Carried back to abate losses from prior years.
C. Payable in addition to the regular tax, unless a corporation is insolvent.
D. Payable in addition to the regular tax.

The answer is D. If a corporation's tentative minimum tax exceeds the regular tax, the excess amount is payable in addition to the regular tax. ###

4. Which of the following types of domestic business entities will be automatically taxed as a corporation?

1. A joint stock company.
2. An insurance company.
3. Any business formed under a state law that refers to it as a corporation.
4. A single member limited liability company (LLC).

A. All of the above.
B. 1, 2, and 3 only.
C. 3 only.
D. 2 and 3 only.

The answer is B. A single member LLC will be taxed as a sole proprietorship unless an election is made by filing Form 8832, *Entity Classification Election.* The rest of the choices are automatically required to be taxed as corporations. ###

5. BRB Corporation's fiscal tax year ends June 30. Not counting extensions, what is the due date for its tax return?

A. September 15.
B. April 15.
C. October 15.
D. January 15.

The answer is A. The due date for BRB Corporation's income tax return is September 15. Generally, a corporation must file its income tax return by the fifteenth day of the third month after the end of its tax year. ###

6. The accumulated earnings tax is levied at a rate of _____ on accumulated taxable income.

A. 5%.
B. 10%.
C. 15%.
D. 50%.

The answer is C. The accumulated earnings tax is levied at a rate of 15% of accumulated taxable income. ###

7. What is the penalty for a corporation that fails to make estimated tax payments?

A. One-half of 1% per month, up to a maximum of 25%.
B. 5% per month, up to a maximum of 25%.
C. 5% per month, up to a maximum of 35%.
D. 5% per month, up to a maximum of 100%.

The answer is A. If a corporation fails to make estimated tax payments, there is a late payment penalty of one-half of one percent per month, up to a maximum of 25%. ###

8. Nell transfers property with a basis of $200,000 and an FMV of $350,000 to a corporation in exchange for stock with a fair market value of $300,000. This represents 65% of the stock of the corporation. How much gain is recognized by Nell on this transaction?

A. $0.
B. $50,000.
C. $100,000
D. $150,000.

The answer is C. Nell must recognize a taxable gain of $100,000 ($300,000 FMV of stock minus $200,000 basis) on the transaction. IRC section 351 provides that no gain or loss will be recognized if property is transferred to a corporation solely in exchange for stock and immediately after the exchange the shareholder is in control of the corporation. However, Nell did not control the corporation after the transfer. In order to be in control of a corporation, the transferor must own, immediately after the exchange, at least 80% of the total combined voting power of all classes of stock entitled to vote and at least 80% of the outstanding shares of each class of nonvoting stock. Since Nell only has control over 65% of the shares, the exchange is taxable. ###

9. Lisa transfers property worth $35,000 and renders services valued at $3,000 to a corporation in exchange for stock valued at $38,000. Right after the exchange, Lisa owns 85% of the outstanding stock. How much income, if any, must Lisa recognize in this transaction?

A. $0.
B. $3,000.
C. $35,000.
D. $38,000.

The answer is B. Lisa recognizes ordinary income of $3,000 as payment for services she rendered to the corporation. Normally, the exchange of money or property for a controlling interest in a corporation is treated as a nontaxable exchange. However, the exchange of services for stock does not qualify for this treatment. The value of stock received in exchange for services is taxed as income to the recipient. ###

10. Topcare Pet Products, a cash-basis corporation that operates on the calendar year, is required to make estimated tax payments. What are the due dates for the estimated payments?

A. April 15, June 15, September 15, and December 15.
B. January 15, March 15, June 15, September 15, and December 15.
C. March 1, June 1, September 1, and December 1.
D. None of the above.

The answer is A. Installments for corporations are due by the fifteenth day of the fourth, sixth, ninth, and twelfth months of the year. So, for example, a calendar-year corporation would have estimated tax due dates of April 15, June 15, September 15, and December 15. ###

11. Metro Street Cars Corporation had a profitable 2012 and was required to make estimated payments during the year totaling $19,000. However, because of serious economic difficulties, Metro expects to post a loss in 2013. Which statement is true about Metro's required estimated payments?

A. Metro must make a minimum estimated tax payment of $500.
B. Metro must make estimated payments of at least 90% of the prior year's tax liability.
C. Metro is required to pay 100% of the prior year tax liability.
D. Metro is not required to make estimated payments in 2013.

The answer is D. Metro Street Cars Corporation does not have to make estimated payments if it expects to post a loss during the year. A corporation must make installment payments of estimated tax only if it expects its estimated tax for the year to be $500 or more. However, it should be noted that payment of 100% of the prior year's liability, as is answer C, would provide a safe harbor in the event that the corporation's tax liability exceeds the amount estimated. ###

12. Multitasker Corporation realized net income of $300,000 for book purposes in 2012. Included in book net income are the following:

Federal income taxes	$4,000
Excess of capital losses over capital gains	$10,000
Tax exempt interest income	$5,000

What is Multitasker's taxable income?

A. $290,000.
B. $304,000.
C. $280,000.
D. $309,000.

The answer is D. Multitasker's taxable income is determined as follows:

Net income per books	$300,000
Plus federal income tax expense per books	$4,000
Plus excess of capital losses over capital gains	$10,000
Less tax exempt interest income	($5,000)
Taxable income	**$309,000**

###

13. Lori and Marcus each transfer property with a basis of $10,000 to a corporation in exchange for stock with a fair market value of $30,000. The total stock received by them represents 75% of the corporation's stock. The other 25% of the corporation's stock was issued earlier to Anne, an unrelated person. The taxable consequences are:

A. None, because it is a transfer of property for stock.
B. Lori and Marcus each recognize a gain of $20,000.
C. Lori and Marcus each recognize a gain of $30,000.
D. 80% of the transaction is recognized as a taxable gain.

The answer is B. If a shareholder contributes property to a corporation, he generally recognizes gain. The basis of the contributed property to the corporation is the same as the basis that the shareholder had in the property, after increase for any gain that the shareholder recognized in the exchange. There is an exception for situations in which property is contributed and the shareholder controls the corporation immediately after the transfer. In order to be considered in control of a corporation immediately after the exchange, the transferors must own at least 80% of the total combined voting power of all classes of stock entitled to vote and at least 80% of the outstanding shares of each class of nonvoting stock. In this case, Lori and Marcus do not own at least 80% of the corporation immediately afterward, so the exception does not apply. ###

14. Kathleen transferred a factory building with an adjusted basis of $70,000 and a fair market value of $110,000 to the Carpentaria Corporation in exchange for 100% of Carpenteria Corporation stock and $20,000 cash. The building was subject to a mortgage of $25,000, which Carpenteria Corporation assumed. The fair market value of the stock was $75,000. Which is the amount of Kathleen's realized gain and recognized gain?

A. $25,000 realized gain; $25,000 recognized gain.
B. $50,000 realized gain; $40,000 recognized gain.
C. $50,000 realized gain; $20,000 recognized gain.
D. $35,000 realized gain; $20,000 recognized gain.

The answer is C. In situations where a shareholder contributes property for stock in a corporation and then controls the corporation immediately after the transfer, she typically would not recognize gain. However, if the shareholder receives money or property in addition to the corporation's stock in exchange for her contribution of property, she would recognize gain to the extent of any money received plus the fair market value of property received. In this case, Kathleen's realized gain is calculated as follows:

Fair value of stock received	$75,000
Cash received	$20,000
Mortgage assumed by corporation	$25,000
Total fair value received	$120,000
Adjusted basis of property	($70,000)
Realized gain	**$50,000**

Kathleen recognizes gain only to the extent of the cash received ($20,000). ###

Unit 14: Corporate Transactions

More Reading:
Publication 542, *Corporations*

Unlike S corporations and partnerships, a C corporation is not a pass-through entity. For federal income tax purposes, a C corporation is recognized as a separate taxpaying entity. A corporation conducts business, realizes net income or loss, pays taxes, and distributes profits to its shareholders. Certain items are unique to C corporations, which we will review in this unit.

Capital Gains and Losses

C corporations are subject to their own tax rate schedules, which may vary from year to year as Congress adjusts the lowest and highest rates.

Unlike the capital gains of individuals, the capital gains of corporations are taxed at the same rate as ordinary income. A corporation figures its capital gains and losses much like an individual. However, in the case of a C corporation, capital losses are only deductible up to the amount of its capital gains. A C corporation is not allowed to offset capital losses against its other income the way individuals can (up to a limit).

If a corporation has an excess capital loss, it may carry the loss back or forward to other tax years and deduct it from any net capital gains that occurred in those years. The default election is for a corporation to carry back its capital losses to the earliest of three preceding years in which it had net capital gains; any remaining losses may be carried forward a maximum of five years.

A capital loss from another year cannot produce or increase a net operating loss in the year to which it is carried back. In other words, corporations can carry capital losses only to years that would otherwise have had a net capital gain.

Example: In 2012, a calendar-year corporation has a capital gain of $3,000 and a capital loss of $9,000. The capital gain offsets some of the capital loss, leaving a net capital loss of $6,000. The corporation treats this $6,000 as a short-term loss when carried back or forward. The corporation carries the $6,000 short-term loss back one year. In the prior year the corporation had a short-term capital gain of $8,000 and a long-term capital gain of $5,000 (a total of $13,000 in capital gains). It carries back the loss and subtracts the $6,000 short-term loss (carryback) first from the net short-term gain. This results in a net capital gain of $7,000. This consists of a net short-term capital gain of $2,000 ($8,000 - $6,000) and a net long-term capital gain of $5,000 for the prior year, which allows the corporation to receive a refund of income tax paid in the prior year.

There are some instances in which longer carryback and carryforward periods are allowed. Capital losses that are a result of foreign expropriation[128] may not be carried back, but may be carried forward for ten years. In the case of a regulated investment company (RIC), net capital losses may be carried forward eight years.

---

[128] This is when a foreign nation expropriates a corporation's assets for its own use.

When a corporation carries back or carries forward a capital loss, the loss does not retain its character as a long-term loss. All capital loss carryforwards and carrybacks are treated as short-term losses. A C corporation cannot carry back capital losses to any year when it was previously an S corporation.

Net Operating Losses (NOLs)

A corporation figures and deducts a net operating loss (NOL) the same way an individual, estate, or trust does. The same carryback (two years) and carryforward (up to 20 years) periods apply, and the same sequence applies when the corporation carries two or more NOLs to the same year. A corporation must carry back an NOL to the earliest of the two years prior to the year the NOL is generated that had taxable income. If the NOL is not fully used against taxable income from the prior two years, the remaining NOL can be carried forward for up to 20 years.

A corporation figures a net operating loss the same way it figures taxable income. It starts with gross income and subtracts its deductions. If its deductions are more than its gross income, the corporation has an NOL. However, the following rules apply for figuring NOL:

- A corporation cannot increase its current year NOL by carrybacks or carryovers from other years in which it has a loss.
- A corporation cannot use the domestic production activities deduction to create or increase a current year NOL.
- A corporation can take the deduction for dividends received, without regard to the aggregate limits that normally apply.
- A corporation can figure the deduction for dividends paid on certain preferred stock of public utilities without limiting it to its taxable income for the year.

An NOL will only reduce income tax. If the corporation owes other taxes or penalties from a prior year, a carryback will not reduce the penalties.

> **Example:** The Artisan Cheese Company has been in business for five years. In the prior year, the corporation had net income of $30,000. However, business slowed, and Artisan Cheese has a net operating loss of $20,000 in 2012. The company decides to carry back its net operating loss in order to recover all of the income taxes it paid in the prior year. In the prior year, the Artisan Cheese also incurred a $1,200 penalty for failing to remit estimated taxes on time. The corporation cannot recover the amount paid for the estimated tax penalty. An NOL carryback will not abate interest and penalties from a prior year. An NOL will only offset income tax.

A C corporation with a net operating loss can file for a refund by using Form 1139 or by amending its corporate tax return using Form 1120X. If a corporation elects to waive carryback and instead carry forward its NOL, it enters the carryover on Form 1120, Schedule K. If the corporation is filing a consolidated return, it must also attach a required statement or the election will not be valid.

If a corporation reasonably expects to have a net operating loss in its current year, it may automatically extend the time for paying income tax liability for the preceding year by filing IRS Form 1138, *Extension of Time For Payment of Taxes by a Corporation Expecting a Net Operating loss Carry Back.*

Charitable Contributions of a C Corporation

C corporations may deduct charitable contributions that are made to qualified organizations, up to 10% of taxable income. A corporation figures its taxable income for the purposes of this limit *without regard to* the following:

- The deduction for charitable contributions
- The dividends-received deduction
- The domestic production activities deduction
- Any net operating loss carryback to the tax year
- Any capital loss carryback to the tax year

The rules regarding what qualifies as a charitable organization are the same for corporations as they are for individuals. Generally, no deduction is allowed for any charitable contribution of $250 or more unless the corporation gets a receipt from the donee organization. The written receipt or acknowledgment should show the amount of cash contributed or a description of the property contributed. The receipt or acknowledgment should also give a description and a good faith estimate of the value of any goods or services provided in return for the contribution, or state that no goods or services were provided in return for the contribution.

If a corporation (other than a closely held or personal service corporation) claims a deduction of more than $500 for contributions of property other than cash, a schedule describing the property and the method used to determine its fair market value must be attached to the corporation's return. In addition the corporation should keep a record of:

- The approximate date and manner of acquisition of the donated property.
- The cost or other basis of the donated property held by the donor for less than 12 months prior to contribution.
- Any donation of a used vehicle, boat, or similar property if it takes a deduction larger than $500 for the donated vehicle.

If the deduction claimed for donated property exceeds $5,000, the corporation must complete Form 8283, *Noncash Charitable Contributions,* and attach it to its tax return. A corporation must obtain a qualified appraisal for all deductions of property claimed in excess of $5,000. A qualified appraisal is not required for the donation of cash, publicly traded securities, or inventory.

A corporation using the accrual method of accounting can deduct unpaid contributions if the board of directors authorized the contributions, and the corporation pays the contributions within 2.5 months after the close of the year. A declaration stating that the board of directors adopted the resolution during the tax year must accompany the return. The declaration must include the date the resolution was adopted.

Example: Ladera Corporation is a calendar-year, accrual-basis corporation. Ladera's board of directors approves a charitable contribution of $5,000 to the United Way on December 15, 2012. Ladera Corporation deducts the contribution on its 2012 corporate tax return. Ladera does not have to actually pay the contribution until March 15, 2013, 2.5 months after the close of its tax year.

A corporation using the cash method of accounting deducts contributions in the tax year they are paid.

Carryover of Excess Charitable Contributions

A corporation can carry over charitable contributions made during the current year that exceed the 10% limit to each of the subsequent five years, subject to the same 10% limitation in each year. A corporation loses any excess contributions not used within that five-year period. No carryback is allowed for charitable contributions. A corporation cannot deduct a carryover of excess contributions to the extent it increases a net operating loss carryover.

Example: Hernandez Sporting Goods has net income of $600,000 in 2012 before taking into account its charitable contribution. The corporation donated $80,000 to a qualified charity in 2012. It also has a net operating loss carryover of $100,000 from a prior year. Therefore, the corporation's charitable deduction is limited to $50,000. The allowable contribution deduction is figured as follows:

($600,000 - $100,000 = $500,000) × 10% = $50,000

The charitable contribution that is not allowed in the current tax year can be carried forward up to five years. If Hernandez Sporting Goods does not use the remainder at the end of five years, the deduction is lost.

Example: Gromwell Corporation, a calendar-year C corporation, makes a large charitable contribution in 2012. As a result, the corporation has a carryover of excess contributions paid in 2012 and it does not use all the excess on its return for 2013. Gromwell Corporation can carry the rest over to 2014, 2015, 2016, and 2017. After that time, it can no longer carry over the excess 2012 charitable contributions.

Dividends-Received Deduction

A corporation can deduct a percentage of certain dividends received from other corporations in which it has an ownership stake. The dividends-received deduction (DRD) is designed to reduce the consequences of double taxation. Without this deduction, corporate profits would be taxed to the corporation that earned them, then to its corporate shareholder, and then *again* to the individual shareholders of the corporation.

The DRD complements the consolidated return regulations, which allow affiliated corporations to file a single consolidated return for U.S. federal income tax purposes. It is only available to C corporations and not to LLCs, S corporations, partnerships, or individuals.

Generally, if a corporation receives dividends from another corporation, it is entitled to a deduction of 70% of the dividends it receives. If the corporation receiving the dividend owns 20% of the other corporation, the deduction increases to 80% of the dividends received.

If the corporation receiving the dividends owns more than 80% of the distributing corporation, it is allowed to deduct 100% of the dividends it receives, making the dividends essentially nontaxable to the receiving corporation.

To summarize, the deduction for dividends received is based on the percentage of stock ownership in the distributing corporation:

Percentage of ownership	Dividends-Received Deduction
Less than 20%	70%
20 - 80%	80%
Greater than 80%	100%

The percentage of stock ownership is determined without regard to preferred stock.

Example: The Quincy Corporation owns 25% of LightStar Corporation. The Quincy Corporation has taxable income of $70,000 *before* taking into account its dividend income. In 2012, Quincy received $100,000 in dividends from LightStar. Quincy receives an 80% dividends-received deduction, figured as follows: $80,000 = ($100,000 × 80%). Therefore, the Quincy Corporation only has to recognize $20,000 of the dividends received from LightStar Corporation. In 2012, the Quincy Corporation's taxable net income is $90,000 ($70,000 + $20,000).

If a corporation is entitled to a 100% DRD, there is no taxable income limitation, and the corporation may deduct the full amount of the dividends received. However, if a corporation is entitled to a 70% DRD, it can deduct amounts only up to 70% of its taxable income. If a corporation is entitled to an 80% DRD, it can deduct amounts only up to 80% of its taxable income. In each case, the corporation would determine taxable income *without* the following items:

- The DRD
- The net operating loss deduction
- The domestic production activities deduction
- Any adjustment due to the nontaxable part of an extraordinary dividend
- Any capital loss carryback to the tax year

Example: Jamestown Corporation owns 85% of the outstanding stock in Humboldt Corporation. In 2012, Jamestown Corporation receives $250,000 in dividends from Humboldt Corporation. Because Jamestown Corporation has over 80% ownership of Humboldt Corporation, the dividends are not taxable. Jamestown Corporation may claim the dividends-received deduction for the dividends received from Humboldt Corporation.

Corporations cannot take a deduction for dividends received from the following entities:

- A real estate investment trust (REIT)
- A tax-exempt corporation
- A corporation whose stock was held less than 46 days
- A corporation whose preferred stock was held less than 91 days
- Any corporation, if another corporation is under an obligation to make related payments for positions in substantially similar property

Dividends on deposits in domestic building and loan associations, mutual savings banks, cooperative banks, and similar organizations are taxed as interest income—not dividends. They do not qualify for the DRD.

Small business investment companies can deduct 100% of the dividends received from taxable domestic corporations.

Effect of NOL on the Dividends-Received Deduction

If a corporation has an NOL for a tax year, the DRD must be figured differently. The limit of 80% (or 70%) of taxable income does not apply if use of the unlimited DRD by the receiving corporation would result in a net operating loss.

Example: Verde Eco-Products Corporation loses $25,000 from its own business operations in 2012. Verde Eco-Products also receives $100,000 in dividend income from a 20%-owned corporation. Therefore, Verde Eco-Product's taxable income in 2012 is $75,000 ($100,000 - $25,000 loss) *before* the DRD. If Verde Eco-Products claims the full DRD of $80,000 ($100,000 × 80%) and combines it with a loss from operations of $25,000, it will create an NOL of ($5,000). Therefore, the 80% of taxable income limit does not apply. The corporation can deduct the full $80,000 DRD.

Example: Redwood Patio Corporation has a loss of $15,000 from business operations in 2012. However, it also has dividends of $100,000 from a corporation in which it holds an interest of 50%. Therefore, Redwood's taxable income is $85,000 *before* applying the DRD. After claiming the DRD of $80,000 ($100,000 × 80%), its taxable income is $5,000. Because Redwood will not have an NOL after applying a full DRD, its allowable DRD is limited to 80% of its taxable income, or $68,000 ($85,000 × 80%).

Related Party Transactions

Strict rules apply to related party transactions. A corporation that uses an accrual method of accounting cannot deduct business expenses and interest owed to a related person who uses the cash method until the corporation makes the related payment and the amount is included in the related person's income. These rules also deny the deduction of a loss on the sale or trade of property (other than in the complete liquidation of a corporation) between related persons.

For purposes of these rules, the following persons are considered related to a corporation:

- A corporation that is a member of the same controlled group.

- An individual who owns, directly or indirectly, more than 50% of the value of the outstanding stock of the corporation.
- A partnership, if the same persons own more than 50% of the value of the outstanding stock of the corporation and more than 50% of the partnership.
- An S corporation, if the same persons own more than 50% of the value of the outstanding stock of each corporation.
- A trust fiduciary, when the trust or its grantor owns, directly or indirectly, more than 50% of the value of the outstanding stock of the corporation.
- An employee-owner of a personal service corporation, regardless of the amount of stock owned.

In determining whether a person directly or indirectly owns any of the outstanding stock of a corporation, the following rules apply:

- Stock directly or indirectly owned by or for a corporation, partnership, estate, or trust is considered owned proportionately by or for its shareholders, partners, or beneficiaries.
- An individual is considered to own the stock that is directly or indirectly owned by or for his family. Family includes only brothers and sisters (including half-brothers and half-sisters), a spouse, ancestors, and lineal descendants.
- An individual owning any stock in a corporation is considered to own the stock that is directly or indirectly owned by his partner.

> **Example:** Robert is a 90% owner in Nampa Boots Corporation. His wife, Eileen, is a 55% owner of Terabyte Corporation. For tax purposes, Robert is considered a related person for the purposes of ownership in Terabyte Corporation. Therefore, for the related-party transaction rules, Robert is also considered a 55% owner in Terabyte Corporation and Eileen is considered a 90% owner in Nampa Boots Corporation.

Closely Held Corporations and the At-Risk Rules

A closely held corporation generally has a small number of shareholders (usually family) and no public market for its corporate stock. The corporate ownership and management often overlap. A corporation is considered to be closely held if all of the following apply:

- It is not a personal service corporation.
- At any time during the last half of the tax year, more than 50% of the value of its outstanding stock is, directly or indirectly, owned by or for five or fewer individuals. An individual in this case includes certain trusts and private foundations.

The reason why this issue is important to the IRS is because of the application of the at-risk rules. These rules dictate that losses are only allowed up to the amount at risk of financial loss. If the corporation does not have a risk of financial loss in an activity, the losses are not deductible. The amount at-risk generally equals:

- The money and the adjusted basis of property contributed by the taxpayer to the activity, and
- The money borrowed for the activity.

The at-risk amount also includes the FMV of any property (adjusted for any liens or encumbered mortgages) that is pledged as security or collateral for the debts of the activity.

Example: Allworth Corporation is a closely held C corporation with only two shareholders: a father and son. Allworth Corp. invests $50,000 in a business venture, and also pledges the value of a factory building as collateral for a $100,000 loan that is used in the business venture. Allworth's factory building has a fair market value of $150,000 but is also secured by a lien of $125,000. Allworth Corp.'s amount at-risk in the business venture is only $75,000 ($50,000 plus the $25,000 ($150,000 - $125,000) equity in the building).

The following items increase an entity's amount at-risk:

1. A contribution of additional cash (or property) to the venture.
2. Any recourse loan for which the corporation is liable for repayment.

The amount at-risk is decreased by the following items:

1. An investor's withdrawal of cash or property from the activity.
2. A nonrecourse loan where the corporation is not liable for repayment.

The amount at risk cannot be decreased below zero. If this occurs, suspended losses from prior years must be reduced.

Controlled Groups

A controlled group is a group of corporations that are related through common ownership, typically as either parent-subsidiary or brother-sister. A parent-subsidiary controlled group involves a parent corporation that owns at least 80% or more of the voting power of at least one other corporation (with possible additional corporations that are at least 80% owned by either the common parent or one of the subsidiary entities). A brother-sister controlled group involves situations in which five or fewer individuals, estates, or trusts own 80% or more of the combined voting power for multiple corporations, and have identical common ownership within the individual corporations of at least 50%.

A controlled group is allowed a single set of graduated income tax brackets, a single exemption amount for AMT purposes, and a single accumulated earnings credit of $250,000. In each case, these amounts must be allocated among the members of the group. Members of controlled groups are also subject to rules regarding related party transactions that may require deferral of recognition for losses or expenses incurred by one party.

Unit 14: Questions

1. The Farber Corporation owns 10% of the Lewisville Corporation. In 2012, Farber receives $10,000 in dividends on Lewisville stock. What is the amount of the dividends-received deduction that Farber Corporation can take?

A. 10%.
B. 50%.
C. 70%.
D. 80%.

The answer is C. The dividends deduction for less-than-20% owned stock is generally 70%. ###

2. The Surf's Up Corporation had an NOL of $110,000. Which of the following statements is true?

A. The corporation can forgo the carryback period and choose to carry the entire loss forward to the next 20 years.
B. The corporation is required to carry back losses for two years and then forward for 15 years.
C. The corporation can carry back losses five years and carry them forward for 25 years.
D. A corporation cannot carry back losses. It can only carry them forward.

The answer is A. A corporation is not required to carry back losses. It may elect to forgo the carryback period. Net operating losses can be carried back to the two years before the loss year and forward to the 20 years following the loss year. ###

3. BMD Corporation is a calendar-year corporation that uses the accrual method of accounting. What is the last day that the corporation can make a charitable contribution and still deduct it on its 2012 tax return?

A. December 31, 2012.
B. April 15, 2012.
C. January 15, 2013.
D. March 15, 2013.

The answer is D. The corporation has until March 15 of the following year to pay the contribution. A corporation using the accrual method can choose to deduct unpaid contributions for the tax year if the board of directors authorizes the contribution during the tax year, and the corporation pays the contribution within 2.5 months after the close of the year. ###

4. In 2012, Mansour Corporation has a $15,000 loss from its business operations. In addition, Mansour has received $100,000 in taxable dividends from a 30%-owned corporation. Therefore, its taxable income is $85,000 before applying the dividends-received deduction. What is the corporation's dividends-received deduction?

A. $15,000.
B. $68,000.
C. $80,000.
D. $100,000.

The answer is B. The corporation would not have an NOL after applying the full dividends-received deduction, so its allowable dividends-received deduction is limited to 80% of its taxable income (before applying the DRD), or $68,000 ($85,000 × 80%). ###

5. Davidson Corporation owns 50% of Nguyen Corporation's outstanding common stock. Davidson has taxable income of $8,000, which includes dividends received of $10,000 from its investment in Nguyen Corporation. What is Davidson Corporation's taxable income after applying the dividends-received deduction?

A. $0.
B. $1,600.
C. $6,400.
D. $8,000.

The answer is B. Davidson Corporation cannot deduct the full $8,000 (80% × $10,000) dividends-received deduction that would normally apply based upon its 50% ownership because doing so would not result in a net operating loss. The deduction is instead limited to 80% of taxable income (before applying the DRD), which is $6,400 (80% × $8,000).

Taxable Income:	$8,000
Minus DRD:	($6,400)
Income after DRD:	**$1,600**

###

6. In 2012 Real Time Corporation made contributions totaling $20,000 to qualified charitable organizations. Due to income limitations, Real Time Corporation could only deduct $15,000 of the contributions on its return. Which of the following statements regarding the excess contributions of $5,000 is correct?

A. Excess charitable contributions can be carried back two years and carried forward 20 years.
B. Excess charitable contributions can be carried forward 20 years
C. Excess charitable contributions can be carried back three years and carried forward ten years.
D. Excess charitable contributions can be carried forward five years. They cannot be carried back.

The answer is D. The corporation can carry over excess charitable contributions made during the year that result from the 10% limit on deductibility to each of the subsequent five years. Any excess charitable contributions that are not used in this five-year period are lost. A corporation cannot carry back excess charitable contributions. ###

7. Xena Corporation is a cash-basis, C corporation. In 2012, the corporation has a net short-term capital gain of $23,000 and a net long-term capital loss of $29,000. How should these capital gains and losses be treated?

A. The corporation may deduct a $6,000 long-term capital loss on its 2012 tax return.
B. The corporation may carry back the $29,000 long-term capital loss to a prior year, where it may only be deducted against long-term capital gains.
C. The corporation may carry back the $6,000 net capital loss to a prior year, where it may be deducted against short-term capital gains.
D. The corporation must carry forward the entire capital loss to the following tax year. Carryback of capital losses is not allowed.

The answer is C. The corporation may carry back the $6,000 capital loss to the earliest of the three preceding years, where it may be deducted against short-term capital gains. Any remaining losses can be carried forward for up to five years. The corporation treats this $6,000 as a short-term loss when carried back or forward, because capital loss carrybacks and carryforwards do not retain their original character. ###

8. The Capital Cross Corporation is a calendar-year C corporation. In 2012, Capital Cross has $4,000 in charitable contributions that it cannot use on the current year return because of income limitations. How should this unused contribution be treated?

A. The corporation can carry over unused charitable contributions for five years.
B. The corporation can carry over unused charitable contributions for 20 years.
C. The corporation can carry over unused charitable contributions for 10 years.
D. The corporation can carry back unused charitable contributions for three years, and carry them forward for five years.

The answer is A. A corporation can carry over charitable contributions for five years. It loses any unused amounts after that period. Corporate charitable contributions cannot be carried back. ###

9. Redd Beauty Products and Helena Mountain Coffee are domestic corporations. Redd Beauty owns 25% of Helena Mountain Coffee. Redd Beauty's income from its business operations in 2012 is $500,000. In addition to its business income, Redd Beauty received dividends from Helena Mountain Coffee of $100,000. What is Redd Beauty's dividends-received deduction?

A. $70,000.
B. $80,000.
C. $100,000.
D. $20,000.

The answer is B. Generally, if a corporation receives dividends from another corporation in which it owns an interest of 20% to 80%, it is entitled to a deduction of 80% of the dividends received, subject to limitation based upon its taxable income without regard to the DRD and certain other items. Since Redd owns 25% of Helena, its DRD is 80% of $100,000, or $80,000. ###

10. The Arbabi Plastics Corporation is a calendar-year C corporation. In 2012, it has $400,000 of taxable income before consideration of the following additional items:
•$50,000 of charitable contributions
•A dividends-received deduction of $70,000
•A domestic production activities deduction of $40,000

What portion of the charitable contributions is deductible in 2012?

A. $50,000.
B. $29,000.
C. $40,000.
D. $36,000.

The answer is C. Arbabi Plastics' deductible charitable contributions are limited to 10% of its taxable income, before consideration of the following items:

•The deduction for charitable contributions
•The dividends-received deduction
•The domestic production activities deduction
•Any net operating loss carryback to the tax year
•Any capital loss carryback to the tax year

Calculation: $400,000 X 10% = $40,000 ($10,000 would be carried over to the next year). Qualifying contributions in excess of this limitation can be carried over for five years. ###

11. McClimate Corporation owns 25% of Wilson Foods Corporation. In 2012, McClimate received $10,000 dividends from Wilson Foods stock. Assuming no other limitations apply, McClimate's dividends-received deduction is _____:

A. $7,000.
B. $8,000.
C. $2,000.
D. $0.

The answer is B. If a corporation receiving dividends owns 20% of the corporation issuing the dividends, it generally qualifies for a dividends-received deduction equal to 80% of the dividends received. It can deduct amounts up to 80% of its taxable income, calculated without regard to the DRD itself and certain other items. ###

12. Which of the following statements about a controlled group of corporations is true?

A. Members of a controlled group are entitled to only one accumulated earnings tax credit.
B. A parent corporation and its 80% owned subsidiary would be considered members of a controlled group.
C. Members of controlled groups are subject to rules regarding related party transactions that may require deferral of recognition for losses or expenses incurred by one party.
D. All of the above.

The answer is D. A parent-subsidiary controlled group involves a parent corporation that owns at least 80% or more of the voting power of at least one other corporation. A controlled group is allowed a single set of graduated income tax brackets, a single exemption amount for AMT purposes, and a single accumulated earnings credit of $250,000. ###

13. During 2012, Bernardino Jewelry, a domestic C corporation, had the following income, expenses, and deductions:

Gross receipts:	$95,000
Net capital gains:	$10,000
Business expenses, (**not** including charitable contributions):	$65,000
Charitable contribution:	$20,000
NOL carryover from 2011:	$30,000

What is the amount of Bernardino Jewelry's allowable charitable contribution deduction for 2012?

A. $1,000.
B. $20,000.
C. $4,000.
D. $3,000.

The answer is A. A C corporation may deduct charitable contributions made to qualified organizations, up to 10% of taxable income. Taxable income for this purpose is determined without regard to certain items, including the charitable contribution deduction itself and any net operating loss carryback (but not carryforward) to the tax year. Therefore, Bernardino Jewelry's charitable contribution deduction would be determined as follows:

Gross receipts	$95,000
Expenses	($65,000)
Net capital gains	$10,000
NOL from 2011	($30,000)
Taxable income before contribution deduction	$10,000
Deduction limit at 10%	$1,000

###

Unit 15: Corporate Distributions & Liquidations

More Reading:
Publication 542, *Corporations*

Corporate Distributions

Corporate distributions or dividends occur when cash, stock, or other property is distributed to shareholders based on the shareholders' ownership of stock. When a corporation earns profits, it can retain the profits in the business (as retained earnings), or it can pay all or a portion of the profits as dividends to shareholders. The amounts a corporation pays as dividends are not deductible expenses. Dividends are most commonly paid in cash. However, a dividend can take the form of stock or other property.

The most common kinds of corporate distributions are:

- Ordinary dividends (either in cash or in property)
- Capital gain distributions
- Nondividend distributions
- Distributions of stock or stock rights

A distribution is calculated by adding the amount of any cash paid to the shareholder plus the fair market value of any property transferred to the shareholder. The distribution amount is reduced by the following liabilities:

- Any liability of the corporation the shareholder assumes
- Any liability that the property is subject to upon distribution, such as mortgage debt the shareholder assumes in connection with distribution of ownership in a building

The amount of a distribution can never go below zero, no matter how much liability a shareholder assumes. The FMV of the distributed property becomes the shareholder's basis in the property.

Ordinary dividends are generally paid out of the earnings and profits of a corporation and are taxable as ordinary income to the shareholders rather than capital gains.

Distribution Reporting Requirements

A corporation must file Form 1099-DIV, *Dividends and Distributions,* with the IRS for each shareholder who receives a dividend of $10 or more during a calendar year. A corporation must send Forms 1099-DIV to the IRS along with Form 1096, *Annual Summary and Transmittal of U.S. Information Returns,* by February 28 (March 31 if filing electronically) of the year following the year of the distribution.

The corporation is also required to furnish Forms 1099-DIV to shareholders by January 31 of the year following the close of the calendar year during which the corporation made the distributions.

The corporation is allowed to furnish Forms 1099-DIV early to shareholders. A business may furnish Forms 1099-DIV to shareholders any time after April 30 of the year of the distributions if the corporation has made its final distributions for the calendar year.

Distributions from Earnings and Profits

The amount of corporate earnings and profits (E&P) determines the tax treatment of corporate distributions to shareholders. Distributions of a C corporation are deducted first from current E&P, and then from any accumulated E&P from prior years. Any part of a distribution from current-year earnings and profits or accumulated earnings and profits is reported as dividend income to the shareholder.

Corporate distributions in excess of E&P are nontaxable to the shareholder to the extent of the shareholder's stock basis. The starting point for determining corporate E&P is initially increased by the corporation's taxable income. The following transactions *increase* the amount of E&P:

- Long-term contracts reported on the completed contract method
- Intangible drilling costs deducted currently
- Mine exploration and development costs deducted currently
- Dividends-received deduction

The following transactions *reduce* the amount of E&P:

- Corporate federal income taxes
- Life insurance policy premiums on a corporate officer
- Excess charitable contribution (over 10% limit)
- Expenses relating to tax-exempt income
- Excess of capital losses over capital gains
- Corporate dividends and other distributions

Accumulated Earnings and Profits

Accumulated earnings and profits are earnings that the corporation accumulated before the current year and has not distributed to its shareholders. Sometimes a corporation will make a distribution that exceeds its current E&P. If a corporation's current E&P are less than the total distributions made during the year, part or all of each distribution is treated as a distribution of accumulated earnings and profits.

If accumulated earnings and profits are reduced to zero, the remaining part of each distribution reduces the adjusted basis of the shareholder's stock. This is referred to as a nondividend distribution and it is not taxable to the shareholder until his basis in the stock is fully recovered. This nontaxable portion is considered to be a return of capital that he had previously invested in the corporation. If the corporation makes nondividend distributions to a shareholder that exceed the adjusted basis of his stock, the excess distribution is treated as a gain from the sale or exchange of property and is taxable to the shareholder as capital gain.

If nondividend distributions are made to shareholders, the corporation must report these distributions to the IRS on Form 5452, *Corporate Report of Nondividend Distributions*.

Example: Tobias is the only shareholder of Seaside Corporation, a calendar-year corporation. During the year, Seaside makes four $1,000 distributions to Tobias. At the end of the year (before subtracting distributions made during the year), the corporation has $10,000 of current year profits. Since the corporation's current year earnings and profits ($10,000) were more than the amount of the distributions it made during the year ($4,000), all of the distributions are treated as distributions of current year earnings and profits. The corporation must issue Form 1099-DIV to Tobias by January 31 to report the $4,000 distributed to him as dividends. Seaside Corporation must use Form 1096, *Annual Summary and Transmittal of U.S. Information Returns*, to report this transaction to the IRS by February 28 (March 31 if filing electronically). The corporation does not deduct these dividends on its income tax return.

Stock Distributions

Stock distributions or stock dividends occur when a corporation issues additional shares of its own stock to shareholders, rather than paying a cash dividend or distributing property.

Stock rights, also known as stock options, may be distributed by a corporation to some or all of its shareholders to allow them to purchase additional shares at a set price.

Distributions by a corporation of its own stock or stock rights are generally tax-free to shareholders and not deductible by the corporation. However, they may be treated as property distributions in certain situations, including when:

- The shareholder has the choice to receive cash or other property instead of stock or stock rights.
- The distribution gives cash or other property to some shareholders and an increase in the percentage interest in the corporation's assets or earnings and profits to other shareholders.
- The distribution is in convertible preferred stock.
- The distribution gives preferred stock to some shareholders and common stock to other shareholders.
- The distribution is on preferred stock.

A corporation must capitalize, rather than deduct, the expenses of issuing a stock dividend, such as printing, postage, and any fees for listing on stock exchanges.

Constructive Distributions

A constructive distribution may occur when a corporation confers a benefit upon a shareholder. A transaction may initially be recorded by the corporation as an expense and the IRS may re-categorize it instead as a constructive distribution. This would make the transaction nondeductible to the corporation and in many instances taxable to the shareholder. Examples of constructive distributions include:

- **Unreasonable compensation:** If a corporation pays an employee-shareholder an unreasonably high salary considering the services actually performed, the excessive part of the salary may be treated as a distribution.

- **Unreasonable rents:** If a corporation rents property from a shareholder and the rent is unreasonably higher than the shareholder would charge a stranger for use of the same property, the excessive part of the rent may be treated as a distribution.
- **Cancellation of a shareholder's debt:** If a corporation cancels a shareholder's debt without repayment by the shareholder, the amount canceled may be treated as a distribution.
- **Property transfers for less than FMV:** If a corporation transfers or sells property to a shareholder for less than its FMV, the excess may be treated as a distribution.
- **Below market or interest-free loans**: If a corporation gives a shareholder an interest-free loan or at a rate below the applicable federal rate, the uncharged interest may be treated as a distribution.

Transfers of Property to Shareholders

A property distribution is treated as if the corporation had sold the property to the shareholder. A corporation (either a C corporation or an S corporation) recognizes gain on a distribution of property to a shareholder if the FMV of the property is more than its adjusted basis. For this purpose, the FMV is considered to be the greater of the property's actual FMV or the amount of liabilities the shareholder assumes in connection with the distribution. If the distributed property was depreciable or amortizable, the corporation may have to treat all or a portion of the gain as ordinary income from depreciation recapture.

The transaction is taxable to the shareholder at FMV and is reported on Form 1099-DIV and Form 5452, *Corporate Report of Nondividend Distributions*. A corporation generally cannot recognize a loss on a distribution of property (i.e., where the property's FMV is less than the adjusted cost basis). However, a corporation is allowed to recognize losses when depreciated property is distributed to shareholders in complete liquidation (when the corporation ceases operations).

Stock Redemptions

A stock redemption occurs when a corporation buys back its own stock from a shareholder in exchange for cash or property. The stock acquired may be canceled, retired, or held as treasury stock.

A shareholder is required to treat the amount realized on a stock redemption as either a dividend or a sale of stock. Stock redemptions are generally treated as dividends unless certain conditions are met, as follows:
- The redemption is not equivalent to a dividend, meaning that the shareholder's proportionate interest and voting power in the corporation has been substantially reduced.
- There was a substantially disproportionate redemption of stock, meaning that the amount received by the shareholder is not in proportion to his stock ownership.

- The redemption was due to a complete termination of a shareholder's interest in the corporation.
- The redemption is of stock held by a non-corporate shareholder and was part of a partial liquidation.
- The distribution is received by estate and does not exceed the sum of death taxes plus funeral and administration expenses to be paid by the estate.

The corporation must realize a gain from the redemption, as if the property were sold at its fair market value to the shareholder. The corporation must recognize income on the distribution of depreciated property to the extent of depreciation or the amount realized, whichever is less. The corporation may not recognize a loss on a stock redemption unless:

- The redemption occurs in a complete liquidation of the corporation, or
- The redemption occurs on stock held by an estate.

Corporate Liquidations and Dissolution

Liquidating distributions are distributions received by a shareholder during a complete or partial dissolution of a corporation. When a corporation dissolves, it redeems all of its stock in a series of distributions.

Complete liquidation occurs when the corporation ceases to be a going concern and its activities are merely for the purpose of winding up its affairs, paying its debts, and distributing any remaining balance to its shareholders. In certain cases in which the buyer is a corporation in control of the distributing corporation, the distribution may not be taxable. A corporate dissolution or liquidation must be reported on Form 966, *Corporate Dissolution or Liquidation*, within 30 days after the resolution or plan is adopted to dissolve the corporation or liquidate any of its stock. Exempt entities are not required to file Form 966, even if they are organized as corporations.

When property is distributed in a complete liquidation, the transaction is treated as if the corporation sold the assets to a buyer at fair market value. The corporation recognizes gain or loss on the liquidation in an amount equal to the difference between the FMV and the adjusted basis of the assets distributed. A corporation is allowed to recognize losses during the liquidation, except for losses resulting from transactions with related parties.

Amounts received by the shareholder in complete liquidation of a corporation are treated as full payment in exchange for the shareholder's stock. A liquidating distribution is considered a return of capital and is not taxable to the shareholder until the shareholder recovers all of his basis in the stock. After the basis of the stock has been reduced to zero, shareholders must report the liquidating distribution as a capital gain.

If a dissolving corporation distributes property that is subject to a liability, the gain or loss is adjusted to reflect assumption of the liability. If the liability is greater than the FMV of the property, the amount of the liability is treated as the FMV of the property. A corporation is required to provide each shareholder a Form 1099-DIV from the corporation showing the amount of the liquidating distribution.

A corporation must file an annual return for the year it goes out of business, even if it has no income or business activity in that year. The IRS ordinarily has three years from the date an income tax return is filed (or its due date, whichever is later) to charge any additional tax that is due.

If a dissolving corporation is filing a final return, the corporation can request a prompt assessment from the IRS after filing the return. In the case of a deceased taxpayer whose estate is a shareholder in a dissolving corporation, the fiduciary representing a dissolving corporation or a decedent's estate may request a prompt assessment of tax. In either instance, this reduces the time for making the assessment to 18 months from the date the written request for prompt assessment was received.

Example: The Maurer Farm Equipment Corporation is going through a complete liquidation. Saul, a shareholder, receives a liquidating distribution of property (a tractor). Maurer Corporation's basis in the tractor is $3,000. The fair market value of the tractor is $13,000. However, the tractor is encumbered by a liability of $15,000 (an unpaid loan), which Saul assumes. Because the remaining loan amount is more than the FMV of the tractor, the amount of the liability is treated as the FMV. The corporation must recognize a $12,000 gain on the distribution ($15,000 loan - $3,000 basis), and Saul is treated as having received a liquidating distribution of $15,000.

Unit 15: Questions

1. Which of the following statements about stock distributions is correct?

A. Stock distributions must be treated as a cash distribution that is taxable to the shareholder.
B. Stock distributions are usually taxable to the corporation when distributed to shareholders.
C. Stock distributions are deductible by a corporation as an expense.
D. Stock distributions are generally not taxable to shareholders and not deductible by the corporation.

The answer is D. Generally, distributions of stock and stock rights are not taxable to shareholders and not deductible by the corporation. ###

2. April bought corporate stock five years ago for $1,000. In 2011, she received a return of capital of $800. April did not include this amount in her income, but correctly reduced the basis of her stock to $200. She received another return of capital of $300 in 2012. The first $200 of this amount reduced April's stock basis to zero. How should she report the remaining $100 in distributions?

A. April must report $100 in long-term capital gain in 2012.
B. April does not have to report the additional return of capital.
C. April must report the $100 as ordinary income.
D. April must report any additional return of capital as a capital loss.

The answer is A. When the basis of a shareholder's stock has been reduced to zero, the shareholder must report any additional return of capital received as a capital gain. Since April has held the stock for more than one year, the gain is reported as a long-term capital gain. ###

3. Party Time Corporation distributes to a shareholder $75,000 in cash and a delivery truck with a $40,000 adjusted basis and a $60,000 FMV. What gain or loss, if any, must Party Time Corporation recognize?

A. No gain or loss is recognized in this transaction.
B. $20,000 gain.
C. $40,000 gain.
D. $20,000 loss.

The answer is B. A corporation will recognize a gain on the distribution of property to a shareholder if the FMV of the property is more than its adjusted basis ($60,000 FMV - $40,000 adjusted basis = $20,000). This is the same treatment the corporation would receive if the property were sold for its FMV. ###

574

4. Three years ago, Mark purchased 100 shares of Rock Star, Inc. for $10 per share. In 2012 Rock Star, Inc. completely liquidated and distributed $20,000 to Mark in exchange for all of his stock. Mark must report this distribution as:

A. A $20,000 long-term capital loss.
B. A $19,000 short-term capital gain.
C. A $19,000 long-term capital gain.
D. A $19,000 ordinary gain.

The answer is C. Mark has a $19,000 long-term capital gain. His basis in the stock was $1,000 [100 shares stock x $10]. So his gain is figured as follows: ($20,000 - $1,000). Gain or loss that is recognized to shareholders on distributions in a corporate liquidation is generally determined by the difference between the total of the cash and property received by the shareholders and the basis of the stock they surrendered. The gain or loss will be long-term or short-term depending on the length of time the stock was held. Since Mark purchased the shares several years ago, his holding period exceeds one year and is therefore recognized as long-term capital gain on his return. ###

5. Geraldine owns 1,000 shares of Kimball Software Corporation. Her shares were all acquired three years ago, and her basis in the stock is $20,000. Kimball Software completely liquidated in 2012 and distributed $56,000 in two payments to Geraldine. Geraldine received $16,000 in December 2012 and $40,000 in January 2013. How much gain or loss is recognized by Geraldine in 2012 and 2013?

A. $4,000 loss in 2012 and $40,000 gain in 2013.
B. $4,000 loss in 2012 and $44,000 gain in 2013.
C. No gain or loss in 2012 and $40,000 gain in 2013.
D. No gain or loss in 2012 and $36,000 gain in 2013.

The answer is D. The liquidating distribution is not taxable until the shareholder's stock basis ($20,000) has been recovered. Geraldine recovered $16,000 of her basis in 2012 and the remaining balance of $4,000 in 2013. Her recognized gain is $36,000 ($56,000 total distribution - $20,000 basis), and she will recognize no gain or loss in 2012. Geraldine will recognize $36,000 of capital gain in 2013. ###

6. All of the examples below are considered corporate distributions except?

A. Ordinary dividends to a shareholder.
B. Capital gain distributions to a shareholder.
C. Constructive distributions to an employee-shareholder.
D. Wage compensation to an employee-shareholder.

The answer is D. Salaries or wages to an employee-shareholder is not considered a distribution. Instead, the wages would be treated as a business expense just like wages for the corporation's other employees. The wages are deductible by the corporation and then taxable to the employee-shareholder. ###

7. Ryan is a shareholder in PRK Corporation with a basis of $20,000 in his stock. He also has an outstanding $10,000 loan that he owes to the corporation. In 2010, Ryan files for bankruptcy and defaults on the loan. PRK Corporation cancels Ryan's debt in 2012. How should this cancellation of debt be reported?

A. The debt cancellation is a $10,000 distribution to Ryan.
B. The debt cancellation is considered a return of capital to Ryan.
C. The debt cancellation is a charitable contribution to Ryan.
D. The debt cancellation is a $10,000 capital gain to Ryan.

The answer is A. If a corporation cancels a shareholder's debt without repayment by the shareholder, the amount canceled is treated as a distribution to the shareholder. In this instance, the distribution would likely be treated as ordinary income. ###

8. The Red Dog Corporation paid dividends to the following shareholders in 2012:

•Marie: $1,000 in dividends.
•Rose: $90 in dividends.
•Laura: $9.75 in dividends.
•Timothy: $100 in dividends.

The Red Dog Corporation is required to issue a Form 1099-DIV to which shareholders?

A. All shareholders must receive a Form 1099-DIV.
B. Marie and Timothy only.
C. Timothy, Marie, and Rose only.
D. Only Marie.

The answer is C. A C corporation is required to issue a Form 1099-DIV with the IRS for each shareholder who is paid dividends of $10 or more during a calendar year. Since Laura did not receive at least $10 in dividends, a Form 1099-DIV is not required. ###

9. Six years ago, Sabine purchased 100 shares of Vitality Nature Corporation stock for $50 per share. In 2012, the corporation liquidated. After paying all of its outstanding liabilities, Vitality Nature distributed $10,000 in cash and appreciated property worth $90,000 to all of its shareholders. Sabine's portion of the distributed assets and cash was $12,000. What must she report from this liquidating distribution in 2012?

A. $0 gain.
B. $3,000 capital gain.
C. $7,000 capital gain.
D. $10,000 capital gain.

The answer is C. The capital gain is figured as follows: Her basis is $5,000 ($50 x 100 shares). The excess of her portion of the distribution over her basis: ($12,000 distribution - $5,000 basis) results in a $7,000 capital gain. ###

10. Distributions of stock rights are generally tax-free to shareholders. Which of the following statements is not correct?

A. Even if a shareholder has a choice to receive cash instead of stock rights, so long as the shareholder chooses to receive stock rights, the distribution will be tax-free.
B. Stock rights are distributions by a corporation of rights to acquire its own stock.
C. Stock rights are sometimes called stock options.
D. Stock rights can be taxable in some circumstances.

The answer is A. If the shareholder has a choice to receive cash instead of stock rights, the distributions of stock and stock rights are taxable. ###

11. Buffalo Corporation displays a collection of fine artwork in its main office. When the 75% shareholder retires, he is presented with his choice from the art collection. He selects a painting with a fair market value of $250,000. Buffalo Corporation's basis in the painting is $100,000. How should the transaction be reported on the Buffalo Corporation's tax return?

A. $150,000 loss.
B. $150,000 distribution.
C. $150,000 taxable gain.
D. $250,000 taxable gain.

The answer is C. The corporation must recognize a gain for any property distributed that has an FMV higher than its adjusted basis. This is the same treatment the corporation would receive if the property were sold for its FMV. The answer is figured as follows:

FMV of distribution:	$250,000
Subtract adjusted basis:	($100,000)
Recognized gain:	$150,000

It should be noted that the FMV of $250,000 is also reported as a distribution to the shareholder, and will be his basis in the painting. ###

12. The Midwestern Grain Corporation distributes property with an adjusted basis of $1,000 and a fair market value of $4,000 subject to a liability of $6,000 to Joseph, a shareholder. What is the gain or loss, if any, Midwestern Grain must recognize as a result of the distribution?

A. $3,000 gain.
B. $1,000 loss.
C. $5,000 gain.
D. $0.

The answer is C. A distribution of property to a shareholder is treated as if the corporation had sold the property to the shareholder. The corporation recognizes gain on the distribution if the FMV of the property is more than its adjusted basis. The FMV is considered to be the greater of the property's actual FMV or the amount of liability the shareholder assumes in connection with the distribution. In this case, the FMV is considered to be the liability of $6,000 assumed by Joseph, so Midwestern Grain must recognize a gain of $5,000 ($6,000 − adjusted basis of $1,000). ###

13. Millerton Software is a C corporation that was formed in 2003. At the beginning of 2012, Millerton Software had accumulated earnings and profits of $100,000. The company makes a $5,000 distribution to its 100% shareholder in the first month of each quarter. In 2012, Millerton Software had $150,000 in gross income and $140,000 in expenses from ordinary business operations. Millerton also received $5,000 in fully tax-exempt interest from state bonds. What part of the second quarter distribution is treated as a distribution of accumulated earnings and profits?

A. $1,250.
B. $2,500.
C. $3,750.
D. $5,000.

The answer is A. Distributions from a C corporation are deducted first from current E&P, and then from any accumulated E&P from prior years. Any part of a distribution from current-year E&P or accumulated E&P is reported as dividend income to the shareholder. If a corporation's current earnings are less than the total distributions made during the year, part or all of each distribution is treated as a distribution of accumulated E&P. Since Millerton's distributions during the year ($20,000) were more than its current year E&P of $15,000 ($150,000 - $140,000 + $5,000), the amount of each distribution is treated as having been paid partially from current year E&P (in the ratio of current E&P for the year to total distributions for the year ($15,000/$20,000 x $5,000 = $3,750). The remainder of each distribution ($5,000 - $3,750 = $1,250) is treated as having been paid from accumulated E&P. ###

Unit 16: S Corporations

More Reading:
Form 1120S and Instructions

The rules governing S corporations are found in subchapter S of the Internal Revenue Code. An S corporation has similarities to both a C corporation and a partnership. Like a partnership, an S corporation is a pass-through entity and is generally not taxed on its earnings. Instead, earnings and losses pass through to shareholders. Like a C corporation, an S corporation enjoys liability protection that a partnership does not.

S corporations do have some drawbacks. They are less flexible than partnerships. There are some instances in which an S corporation is forced to pay tax on its earnings. There are restrictions on the number and type of shareholders an S corporation can have. For example, the number of S corporation shareholders is limited to 100, while a C corporation may have an unlimited number of shareholders and a partnership may have an unlimited number of partners.

Electing S Corporation Status

In order to become an S corporation, a business must file an S election on Form 2553, *Election by a Small Business Corporation.* The filing must be made within 2.5 months of the start of its tax year in order for the election to be effective at the beginning of the year. An election made after the first 2.5 months of the tax year becomes effective on the first day of the following tax year, unless the corporation receives IRS approval to make the election retroactive to the beginning of the tax year. The IRS will generally accept a late S election, so long as the following requirements are met:

- The entity must qualify for S corporation status, except for not having filed Form 2553 in a timely manner.
- The entity had intended to be classified as an S corporation as of the effective date of the S corporation election.
- The entity applies for relief no later than six months following the due date of the tax return.
- The corporation either had reasonable cause or inadvertently failed to file Form 2553 in a timely manner.
- The corporation has not yet filed tax returns for the first tax year for which it intends to file as an S corporation, or the corporation has filed its first tax return using Form 1120S and the shareholders properly reported their share of income in a manner consistent with the corporation's intention to be an S corporation.
- No shareholder has reported inconsistencies with the S election.

If the S election is made during the corporation's tax year for which it first takes effect, any individual stockholder who holds stock at any time during the part of that year before the election is made must also consent to the election, even though the person may have sold or transferred his stock before the election is made.

> **Example:** Ron, Tara, and William are all equal shareholders in a C corporation. In March 2012, William decides to retire and sells all his shares in the C corporation to Sandra, an unrelated person. In April, Ron, Tara, and Sandra vote to elect S corporation status. All the current shareholders must agree to the election. William must also agree, even though he sold his stock before the election was made.

An S corporation may choose to use the cash or accrual method of accounting if it meets the requirements. However, an S corporation may not use the cash method if it is a tax shelter.

S Corporation Requirements

The main requirements for S corporation status are:

- It cannot have more than 100 shareholders.
- Shareholders must be U.S. citizens or residents, if individuals, or certain kinds of trusts, banks, estates, or certain tax-exempt corporations. Corporate shareholders and partnerships are excluded. (In contrast, an S corporation is allowed to own a partnership interest or own stock in a C corporation).
- A business must meet the definition of a small business corporation, per IRC section 1361.
- An S corporation can only have one class of stock, but that stock can be voting or nonvoting. The difference in voting rights allows one group of shareholders to retain voting control, while still allowing other shareholders to benefit from corporate earnings. However, all the stock of an S corporation must possess identical rights to distribution and liquidation proceeds.
- Profits and losses must be allocated to shareholders in proportion to each one's interest in the business.
- Nonresident aliens cannot be shareholders in an S corporation.
- All shareholders of an S corporation must give written consent for the S election.

> **Example:** A husband and wife own 90% of an S corporation and their son owns the remaining 10% of the stock. The son announces his marriage to a nonresident alien, to whom he gifts one-half of his stock. The S corporation's status is revoked, because a nonresident alien cannot hold stock ownership in an S corporation.

For the purpose of the 100-shareholder limit, related persons are considered one shareholder. Spouses are automatically treated as a single shareholder. Families, defined as individuals descended from a common ancestor, plus spouses and former spouses of either the common ancestor or anyone lineally descended from that person, are considered a single shareholder so long as any family member elects such treatment.

When a shareholder dies, the deceased shareholder's spouse and the estate are still considered one shareholder for the purpose of the shareholder limit. A husband and wife cannot be considered a single shareholder if they divorce, or if the marriage is dissolved for any other reason than death. Therefore, a shareholder's divorce can potentially increase the number of shareholders to a number in excess of the 100-shareholder limit. When an S corporation fails to meet these restrictions, the S election is considered terminated, and the S corporation ceases to be an S corporation and is instead taxed as a C corporation. The following entities cannot elect S corporation status:

- A bank or thrift institution that uses the reserve method of accounting for bad debts
- An insurance company
- A domestic international sales corporation (DISC)
- Any foreign entity

Termination of an S election

Once the S election is made, it stays in effect until terminated. The election will terminate automatically in any of the following cases:

- The corporation no longer qualifies as a small business corporation.[129]
- For each of three consecutive tax years, the corporation
  - Has accumulated earnings and profits,[130] and
  - Derives more than 25% of its gross receipts from passive investment income. The election terminates on the first day of the first tax year beginning after the third consecutive tax year. In addition, the corporation must pay a tax for each year it has excess net passive income.
- The shareholders willingly revoke the S election.
- The corporation creates a second class of stock.

An S election can be revoked only with the consent of the *majority* shareholders. This means that, at the time the revocation is made, the revoking shareholders hold more than 50% of the corporation's stock (including nonvoting stock).

A shareholder revocation may specify an effective revocation date that is on or after the day the revocation is filed. If no date is specified, the revocation is effective at the start of a tax year if the revocation is made on or before the fifteenth day of the third month of that tax year.

If no date is specified and the revocation is made after the fifteenth day of the third month of the tax year, the revocation is effective at the start of the next tax year. To voluntarily revoke an S election, the corporation must file a statement of revocation with the IRS. The statement must be signed by each shareholder who consents. A revocation may also be rescinded before it takes effect.

---

[129] This termination of an election is effective as of the day the corporation no longer meets the definition of a small business corporation. A statement notifying the IRS of the termination and the date it occurred is attached to Form 1120S for the final year of the S corporation.

[130] This only applies to S corporations that were once C corporations. That is because an S corporation cannot accumulate earnings and profits as a C corporation can. However, it is possible for a C corporation to elect S corporation status and still have accumulated earnings and profits at the time of the election.

When an S corporation terminates its election, it creates two short tax years. The corporation must allocate income and loss on a pro rata basis between the period it operated as an S corporation and the period as a C corporation that was created when the S election was terminated. The entity must file Form 1120S for the S corporation's short year by the due date (including extensions) of the C corporation's short year return.

> **Example:** On May 1, 2012, Zander Corporation, a calendar-year S corporation, exceeded 100 shareholders. This will create two short tax years—one for the S corporation and one for the C corporation. Zander must file a Form 1120S and a Form 1120.

Inadvertent Termination of an S Election

An S corporation may unintentionally lose its S status and revert to a C corporation. If the IRS deems that the revocation was inadvertent (that the shareholders did not mean to revoke their S election or that the revocation was accidental), the corporation may be allowed to correct the error and retain its S election status.

> **Example:** In 2012, Morrison Window Blinds, a calendar-year S corporation, inadvertently terminates its S status. The S corporation shareholders immediately correct the problem. Therefore, the S corporation status is considered to have been continuously in effect, and no termination is deemed to have occurred. Only a single S corporation tax return will need to be filed for tax year 2012.

A terminating event will be considered inadvertent if the event was not within the control of the corporation, and the shareholders did not plan to terminate the election. In order to qualify after a terminating event, all of the following must occur:

- The S election must have involuntarily terminated either because:
  - The corporation no longer qualified as a small business corporation, or
  - It had accumulated earnings and profits from past C corporation activities.
- The IRS must agree that the termination was inadvertent.
- The corporation must take reasonable and immediate steps to correct the issue.
- The shareholders and the corporation must agree to any adjustments proposed by the IRS.
- The corporation must request a private letter ruling from the IRS for any inadvertent termination relief.

If the status of an S corporation is terminated, either because the shareholders elect to become a C corporation or because a terminating event has occurred, the S corporation cannot elect to become an S corporation again for at least five years. However, the IRS may waive the five-year restriction.

Filing Requirements

An S corporation files its tax return on IRS Form 1120S, *U.S. Income Tax Return for an S Corporation*. Individual items of income, deductions, and credits pass through to individual shareholders and are reported on Schedule K-1. The return must be signed and dated by an authorized corporate officer or, in certain instances, by a fiduciary such as a receiver, trustee, or assignee, on behalf of the corporation.

An S corporation is always required to file a tax return, regardless of income or loss. The filing requirement ends only when the corporation is totally dissolved. The IRS mandates electronic filing for S corporations with $10 million or more in assets that file 250 or more returns of any type (W-2, 1099, K-1) per year. The tax return is due on the fifteenth day of the third month following the tax year end. For a calendar-year corporation, the tax return is due March 15. A corporation that has dissolved must generally file by the fifteenth day of the third month after the date it dissolved.

A six-month extension of time to file can be requested using Form 7004, *Automatic Extension of Time to File Certain Business Income Tax, Information, and Other Returns.*

Shareholders are required to pay estimated tax for their individual returns. S corporations are only required to pay estimated tax if $500 or more of certain corporate-level taxes apply.

S Corporations: Required Tax Year

An S corporation must use one of the following as its tax year:

- A calendar year
- A natural business year
- A fiscal year duly elected and approved by the IRS under section 444
- An ownership tax year (the tax year that coincides with <50% ownership of the corporation)
- A 52-53 week year that ends with reference to a year listed above

An S corporation may always use a calendar year, or any other tax year for which it establishes a bona fide business purpose.

A new S corporation must use Form 2553, *Election by a Small Business Corporation,* to elect a tax year. An existing S corporation that wishes to change its existing tax year may use Form 1128, *Application to Adopt, Change, or Retain a Tax Year.*

However, Form 8716, *Election to Have a Tax Year Other Than a Required Tax Year,* is used to apply for a tax year change under section 444.

S Corporation Income and Expenses

As with a partnership, all the income of an S corporation must be allocated to the shareholders, even if it is not distributed. Income, gains, losses, deductions, and credits are allocated to a shareholder on a pro-rata basis, according to the number of shares of stock held by the shareholder on each day of the corporation's tax year, and retain their character when they are passed through. The shareholder then reports the items on his individual tax return (Form 1040).

Some of the items that pass through to shareholders on a pro rata basis and retain their character must be separately stated on an S corporation's tax return. These include:

- Net income or loss from rental real estate activity (rental income)
- Portfolio income or loss that includes:

- Interest income
- Dividend income
- Royalty income
- Capital gains or losses
- Section 1231 gain or loss
- Charitable contributions
- Section 179 expense deduction
- Foreign taxes paid or accrued
- Expenses related to portfolio income or loss
- Credits, including:
  - Low-income housing credit
  - Qualified rehabilitation expenses
- Investment interest expense
- Tax preference and adjustment items needed to figure a shareholder's AMT
- Nonbusiness bad debts

Unlike a C corporation, an S corporation is not eligible for a dividends-received deduction.

Limited Taxation of S Corporations

S corporations generally are not subject to taxation since they are primarily pass-through entities. However, in certain cases, S corporations are subject to taxes. A subchapter S corporation may have to pay income tax due to:

- Excess net passive investment income
- Built-in gains
- Investment credit recapture
- LIFO recapture

None of these taxes are deductible as business expenses by the S Corporation.

An S corporation may also be responsible for other taxes, such as payroll taxes if it has employees, and penalties, such as late filing penalties.

Excess Net Passive Investment Income: An S corporation that had been a C corporation previously and had accumulated earnings and profits (E&P) during that period may have to pay tax at the corporate level on excess net passive income (ENPI). Further, if the corporation has passive investment income for three consecutive tax years, it may lose its S status.

If an S corporation that was formerly a C corporation has accumulated E&P at the end of the tax year and has passive investment income in excess of 25% of its gross receipts for three consecutive taxable years, the S election is terminated as of the beginning of the fourth year.

Example: For 2010, 2011, and 2012, Herzing Corporation, a calendar-year S corporation, earned passive investment income in excess of 25% of its gross receipts. If Herzing Corporation has accumulated E&P from earlier years in which it was a C corporation, its S election would be terminated as of January 1, 2013, and the corporation would be taxed as a C corporation as of January 1, 2013.

The purpose of this requirement is to discourage a corporation with accumulated earnings and profits (E&P) from becoming or functioning as a holding company in order to obtain favorable tax treatment as an S corporation. For this purpose, passive investment income includes interest, dividends, and royalties. If income is generated in the ordinary course of business, it is non-passive, or active, income.

> **Example:** Trailblazer Inc. is an S corporation with accumulated E&P from earlier years when it was a C corporation. In 2012, Trailblazer's first taxable year as an S corporation, it has gross receipts of $75,000:
>
> - $5,000 is royalty payments from Trademark A
> - $8,000 is royalty payments from Trademark B
> - $62,000 is gross receipts from regular operations
>
> Trailblazer created Trademark A, but Trailblazer did not create Trademark B or perform significant services with respect to the development or marketing of Trademark B. Because Trailblazer created Trademark A, the royalty payments from Trademark A are derived in the ordinary course of business and are not considered passive income for purposes of determining Trailblazer's passive investment income. However, the royalty payments for Trademark B are included within the definition of royalties for purposes of determining Trailblazer's passive investment income. Trailblazer's passive investment income for the year is $8,000.

If the corporation has always been an S corporation, the ENPI tax would not apply. The tax rate on excess net passive income is 35%. This tax is applied on passive income from activities such as royalties, rents, dividends, and interest. The tax is applied against the lesser of:

- Excess net passive income, or
- Taxable income figured as though the corporation were a C corporation.

Built-in Gains (BIG) Tax

The built-in gains (BIG) tax may apply to the following S corporations:

- An S corporation that was a C corporation before it elected to be an S corporation.
- An S corporation that acquired an asset with a basis determined by reference to its basis (or the basis of any other property) in the hands of a C corporation (a transferred-basis acquisition).

The built-in gains tax requires an S corporation to measure the amount of unrecognized appreciation that existed at the time an S election is made or an asset was acquired. The amount of unrecognized gain is determined for each asset. The net of unrecognized built-in gains and built-in losses is the company's unrecognized built-in gain.

The S corporation then pays taxes at the highest corporate rate based on the recognized built-in gain. The tax is reported on Form 1120S. The amount of the tax is a deduction for the shareholders.

The built-in gains tax is imposed on assets sold by an S corporation that it held when it was converted from a C corporation, unless the assets are held by the S corporation for a certain period of time. The current statutory period is five years after conversion from a C corporation to an S corporation.

The built-in gains tax only applies to corporations that elected S status after 1986, and it only affects property dispositions during the recognition period.[131] The applicable recognition period is the five-year period beginning:

- On the first day of the first tax year for which the corporation is an S corporation, for an asset held when the S corporation was a C corporation, or
- On the date the asset was acquired by the S corporation, for an asset with a basis determined by reference to its basis in the hands of a C corporation.

Investment Credit Recapture: Business credit recapture is generally the responsibility of the entity that claims the credit. If the company is an S corporation when the credit originates, the credit passes through to the shareholders and they must report the recapture on IRS Form 4255, *Recapture of Investment Credit*. However, if a C corporation claims the General Business Credit and then converts to S status, the S corporation itself may be responsible for the recapture.

LIFO Recapture Tax: Corporations that account for inventory using the last in, first out (LIFO) method are subject to a LIFO recapture tax in the final year before making an S corporation election. This tax is intended to address built-in gains on inventory that might not otherwise be recognized during the normal recognition period. The taxable LIFO recapture amount is the amount by which the amount of inventory assets calculated under the first in, first out (FIFO) method exceeds the amount under the LIFO method.

"*Inventory assets*" refers to stock in trade of the corporation, or other property of a kind that would properly be included in the inventory of the corporation if on hand at the close of the taxable year.

The LIFO recapture tax is paid in four equal installments, beginning on the due date of the final C corporation return. The three subsequent installments are payable on the due date of the first three S corporation returns. If the LIFO value is higher than the FIFO value, no negative adjustment is allowed.

S Corporation Basis

In computing stock basis, the shareholder starts with his initial capital contribution to the S corporation or the initial cost of the stock purchased (the same as for a C corporation). The order in which stock basis is increased or decreased is important. Both the taxability of a distribution and the deductibility of a loss are dependent on stock basis, and there is an ordering rule for computing stock basis. Stock basis is adjusted annually, on the last day of the S corporation year, in the following order:

- Increased for income items and excess depletion

---

[131] The American Taxpayer Relief Act of 2012 extended this temporary five-year recognition period to sales occurring in 2012 and 2013.

- Decreased for distributions
- Decreased for nondeductible, noncapital expenses and depletion
- Decreased for items of loss and deductions

A shareholder's basis in his S corporation stock may vary based on how the stock was acquired (by purchase, gift, or inheritance). In general, a shareholder's basis in S corporation stock is determined as follows:

Stock Acquired	How Stock Basis is Determined
Stock Purchase	If the S corporation shares were purchased outright, initial basis is the cost of the shares.
S corporation capitalized	If the shares were received when the S corporation was formed under IRC §351, the basis in the stock is equal to the basis of the property transferred to the corporation, reduced by the amount of property received from the corporation, increased by gain recognized on the transfer, and decreased by any boot received (IRC §358).
Prior C corporation	Initial basis in S corporation stock is the basis in the C corporation stock at the time of conversion.
Gift	The recipient's basis in shares received by gift is generally the donor's basis (IRC §1015). Suspended passive activity losses can increase the basis of a gift (IRC §469).
Inheritance	The basis of inherited stock is its fair market value at the date of death or, if elected, the alternate valuation date (IRC §1014).
Services rendered to the S corporation	Basis in stock received in exchange for services is measured by the stock's fair market value, rather than by the value of the services (Treas. Reg. §1.61-2).

S corporation shareholders must pay taxes on their share of the corporation's current year income, whether or not the amounts are distributed. The shareholder's Schedule K-1 reflects the income, loss, and deductions that are allocated to him but does not state the taxable amount of a distribution. The taxable amount of distributions is contingent upon the shareholder's stock basis and it is the shareholder's responsibility to track his individual basis.

S corporation distributions are generally not treated as dividends, except in rare cases where a corporation has accumulated earnings and profits from years before it elected to become an S corporation. S corporation distributions (except dividend distributions) are considered a return of capital and reduce the shareholder's basis in the stock of the corporation.

If a shareholder receives a nondividend distribution from an S corporation, the distribution is tax-free to the extent it does not exceed his stock basis; his debt basis is not considered. If the amount distributed exceeds the shareholder's basis in the stock, the excess is treated as a capital gain from the sale or exchange of property.

A shareholder's deduction for his share of losses is limited to the adjusted basis of his stock and any debt the corporation owes the shareholder. Any loss or deduction not allowed because of basis limitations is carried over and treated as a loss or deduction in the next tax year. A shareholder's basis can never be reduced below zero.

The basis adjustment rules under IRC §1367 are similar to the partnership rules. However, while a partner has a unitary basis in his partnership interest, the adjustments to the basis of stock of an S corporation are applied on a separate share basis. A loss, deduction, or distribution will decrease stock basis. Here are the rules for figuring shareholder basis in an S corporation:

- Nondeductible expenses reduce a shareholder's stock and debt basis before loss and deduction items. If nondeductible expenses exceed basis, they do not get carried forward.
- If the current year has different types of losses and deductions that exceed the shareholder's basis, the allowable losses and deductions must be allocated pro rata based on the size of the particular loss and deduction items.
- A shareholder is not allowed to claim losses and deductions in excess of stock and debt basis. Losses and deductions not allowable in the current year are suspended due to basis limitations.
- Suspended losses and deductions due to basis limitations retain their character in subsequent years. Any suspended losses or deductions in excess of stock and debt basis are carried forward indefinitely until basis is increased in subsequent years or until the shareholder permanently disposes of the stock.
- In determining current year allowable losses, current year loss and deduction items are combined with the suspended losses and deductions carried over from the prior year, though the current year and suspended items should be separately stated.
- A shareholder is only allowed debt basis to the extent he has personally lent money to the S corporation. A "loan guarantee" is not sufficient to allow the shareholder debt basis.
- Part or all of the repayment of a reduced basis debt is taxable to the shareholder.
- If stock is sold, suspended losses due to basis limitations are lost forever. The sales price does not have an impact on the stock basis. A stock basis computation should be reviewed in the year stock is sold or disposed of.

S corporation shareholders are required to compute both stock basis and debt basis. For losses and deductions that exceed a shareholder's stock basis, the shareholder is allowed to deduct the excess up to his basis in loans he personally made to the S corporation. Debt basis is computed similarly to stock basis, but there are some differences.

If a shareholder has S corporation losses and deductions in excess of stock basis and those losses and deductions are claimed based on debt basis, the debt basis of the shareholder will be reduced by the claimed losses and deductions. If an S corporation repays reduced basis debt to the shareholder, part or all of the repayment is taxable to the shareholder. The amount of loss that is deductible on a shareholder's tax return is limited to the shareholder's at-risk basis. These limits (and the order in which they apply) are the adjusted basis of:

- Cash and the adjusted basis of property that the shareholder contributed to the S corporation, and
- Any loans the shareholder makes to the corporation or any amounts that are borrowed for use by the S corporation for which the shareholder is directly liable.

An S corporation that engages in rental activity or an S corporation with a shareholder who does not materially participate in S corporation activities is subject to passive activity loss rules.

These rules provide that losses and credits from passive activities can generally be applied only against income and tax from passive activities. Passive activity loss limitations do not apply to S corporations but to its individual shareholders. If the passive activity loss rules apply, the shareholders' at-risk amount must be reduced by the full amount allowable as a current deduction.

Reasonable Wages

An S corporation may wish to pay little or no wages to employees or officers who are also shareholders, as wages are subject to employment taxes while distributions to shareholders are not. However, if an S corporation is not paying a reasonable salary to a shareholder-employee, distributions to him may be reclassified as wages subject to employment taxes. Therefore, an S corporation will be at risk if it attempts to avoid paying employment taxes by having its officers treat their compensation as cash distributions, payments of personal expenses, or loans rather than as wages. There are no specific guidelines for reasonable compensation in the IRC or in IRS regulations. Factors considered by the courts in determining reasonable compensation for employees or officers of an S corporation include:

- Training, experience, duties and responsibilities
- Time and effort devoted to the business
- Dividend history
- Payments to non-shareholder employees
- Timing and manner of paying bonuses to key people
- Amounts that comparable businesses pay for similar services
- Compensation agreements
- The use of a formula to determine compensation

The regulations provide an exception for an officer of a corporation who does not perform any services or performs only minor services and receives no compensation. Such an officer would not be considered an employee for tax purposes.

Health Insurance Premiums for Shareholders

Fringe benefits paid to employees that are not shareholders or who have ownership of less than 2% are generally deductible by the S corporation and tax-free to the employee. However, for shareholder-employees that have at least 2% ownership, health and accident insurance premiums paid on their behalf are deductible by the S corporation as fringe benefits and are reportable as wages for income tax withholding purposes on the shareholder-employee's Form W-2. The S corporation can exclude the value of these health benefits from the employee's wages subject to Social Security, Medicare, and FUTA taxes.

A 2% shareholder-employee is eligible for an AGI deduction for amounts paid during the year for medical care premiums if the medical care coverage is established by the S corporation. If the medical coverage plan is in the name of the shareholder and not in the name of the S corporation, a medical care plan can still be considered to be established by the S corporation if:

- The S corporation either paid or reimbursed the shareholder for the premiums, and
- Reported the premium payment as wages on the shareholder's Form W-2.

Neither Schedule K-1 (Form 1120S) nor Form 1099 can be used as an alternative to Form W-2 to report this additional compensation.

> **Example:** Victory Sports Drinks, an S corporation, provides fringe benefits such as health insurance to its two owner-shareholders. Victory paid $5,000 in insurance premiums. The corporation treats the shareholders as having received the health insurance as additional compensation and includes the insurance expenditure as W-2 wage income. The shareholders report the health insurance as income.

The S corporation cannot take a deduction for amounts incurred during periods in which the owner-shareholder is eligible to participate in any subsidized health plan maintained by another employer (or the spouse's employer).

> **Example:** CJ is the single owner-shareholder in an S corporation. He pays the health insurance for himself and his wife. CJ's wife works full-time for an employer who has offered to provide family health coverage. Franklin and his wife declined the coverage because they do not want to switch doctors. Because Franklin has the option to participate in an employer plan (through his wife), he cannot deduct the health insurance premiums provided by his S corporation.

Corporate Distributions

The amount of an S corporation distribution is equal to the sum of all cash and the fair market value of the property received by a shareholder. If an S corporation distributes appreciated property (such as stocks), the S corporation and the shareholder must treat the distribution as a sale to the shareholder. To the extent the FMV of the property exceeds the shareholder's basis, he would recognize capital gain. Gain is determined when the final year-end reconciliations are made and the shareholder has adjusted his stock basis for any increases but before any decreases attributable to the current year are deducted. Distributions from an S corporation with no accumulated earnings and profits are generally treated as a nontaxable return of capital.

Distributions up to the shareholder's adjusted stock basis are treated as a nontaxable return of capital. Distributions that exceed the shareholder's adjusted stock basis are reported as a capital gain and must be reported on the individual shareholder's Schedule D. Distributions from an S corporation are not subject to payroll tax. Withdrawals from an S corporation in the form of dividends are subject to federal taxes at ordinary income tax rates. Wages are subject to employment taxes and income tax at the shareholder level. Distributions from an S corporation must be paid to all shareholders on the same date, as a pro rata distribution based on each shareholder's individual ownership percentage. This is one of the drawbacks of an S Corporation vs. a partnership. A partnership agreement can include income allocation that is not based on ownership percentage.

The Accumulated Adjustments Account (AAA)

If a C corporation elects to become an S corporation, it may have an accumulated adjustments account (AAA). The AAA is a corporate account and does not belong to any particular shareholder. The S corporation maintains the account to track undistributed income that has been taxed during the period its S election is in effect.

S corporations with accumulated E&P must maintain the AAA to determine the tax effect of distributions during S years and the post-termination transition period. It is not mandatory to track AAA if the S corporation does not have prior year C corporation earnings and profits (E&P) (IRC section 1368). Nevertheless, if an S corporation without accumulated E&P engages in certain transactions where an AAA account is required, such as a merger into an S corporation with accumulated E&P, the S corporation must be able to calculate its AAA at the time of the merger. Therefore, it is recommended that the AAA be maintained by all S corporations. The AAA may have a negative balance at year end.

Termination of a Shareholder's Interest

A shareholder may sell or liquidate his stock interest in an S corporation. The sale is treated the same way as the sale of stock in a C corporation. The shareholder reports the sale of the stock on Schedule D. The gain or loss that is recognized by the shareholder is the difference between the shareholder's basis and the sale price of the stock. If a shareholder in an S corporation terminates his interest in a corporation during the tax year, the corporation, with the consent of all affected shareholders (including those whose interest is terminated), may elect to allocate income and expenses as if the corporation's tax year consisted of two separate short tax years, the first of which ends on the date of the shareholder's termination. To make this election, the corporation must attach a statement to a timely filed original or amended Form 1120S for the tax year for which the election is made and state that it is electing to treat the tax year as if it consisted of two separate tax years. The statement must also explain how the shareholder's entire interest was terminated (e.g., sale or gift), and state that the corporation and each affected shareholder consent to the election. A single statement may be filed for all terminating elections made for the tax year. If this election is made, the taxpayer should write "Section 1377(a)(2) Election Made" at the top of each affected shareholder's Schedule K-1.

Unit 16: Questions

1. Danielle is a 50% owner in Goodpaster Software Corporation, an S corporation. Danielle's basis is $5,000 in the corporation. At the end of 2012, Goodpaster Corporation reports $10,000 in ordinary income. In December 2012, Goodpaster makes a distribution to Danielle of appreciated property. It is a rare motorcycle originally purchased for $1,000 but now worth $8,000. How much income does Danielle have to report on her individual return?

A. $0.
B. $1,000.
C. $2,000.
D. $8,000.

The answer is A. If an S corporation distributes appreciated property, the S corporation and the shareholder will treat the distribution as a sale to the shareholder. The distribution lowers Danielle's stock basis to $2,000.

Danielle's adjusted basis:	$5,000
S corp. income × 50%:	$5,000
Adjusted basis 12/31/12:	$10,000

Distribution

FMV of property:	$8,000
Less: Shareholder's basis:	$10,000
Capital gain	**$0**

####

2. Close family members can be treated as a single shareholder for S corporation purposes. A family member in this instance includes:

A. A nonresident alien spouse.
B. A first cousin.
C. The estate of a deceased shareholder's spouse.
D. A divorced spouse.

The answer is C. Spouses are automatically treated as a single shareholder, and when a shareholder dies, the deceased shareholder's spouse and the estate are still considered one shareholder for the purpose of the shareholder limit. A husband and wife cannot be considered a single shareholder if they divorce, or if the marriage is dissolved for any other reason than death. An S corporation cannot have a nonresident alien member, so a nonresident alien spouse would not qualify. ###

3. All of the following statements about S corporations are true except:

A. S corporations cannot have more than 100 shareholders.
B. S corporations can own stock in a C corporation.
C. S corporations have only one class of stock.
D. A C corporation can own stock in an S corporation.

The answer is D. An S corporation can own shares in a C corporation, but a C corporation cannot own shares in an S corporation. ###

4. A calendar-year S corporation operating on the accrual basis has the following income items and expenses. What is the income of this S corporation, not counting the separately stated items?

Gross receipts:	$300,000
Interest income:	$25,000
Royalty income:	$10,000
Salary paid to shareholder:	$20,000

A. $55,000.
B. $280,000.
C. $320,000.
D. $345,000.

The answer is B. Ordinary income would reflect the gross receipts of $300,000 less salary expense to the shareholder of $20,000, or $280,000. Interest income and royalty income would be separately stated items on Form 1120S, but would not be considered in determining ordinary income or loss. The amount is figured as follows: ($300,000 - $20,000 = $280,000). ###

5. In which circumstance is a C corporation unable to elect to become an S corporation?

A. The C corporation has 50 shareholders.
B. The C corporation is incorporated in Canada.
C. The C corporation has common stock with voting and nonvoting rights.
D. The C corporation is on a fiscal year with a legitimate business purpose.

The answer is B. A C corporation can elect to become an S corporation if it otherwise qualifies. Only domestic U.S. corporations are allowed to elect S status. An S corporation can only have one class of stock, but differences in voting rights are allowed. An S corporation can have a fiscal year if it has a legitimate business purpose for doing so. ###

6. All S corporations, regardless of when they became an S corporation, must use a permitted tax year. A permitted tax year is any of the following except:

A. The calendar year.
B. A tax year elected under section 444.
C. A fiscal tax year with a legitimate business purpose.
D. A short tax year.

The answer is D. A short tax year is only applicable when an S corporation is in its first year or its S status is terminated. ###

7. Which of the following items is not a separately stated item on an S corporation return?

A. Charitable contributions.
B. Net short-term capital gains or losses.
C. Interest income.
D. Interest expense on a business loan.

The answer is D. Charitable contributions, interest income, and short-term capital gains and losses are all separately stated items. The interest on a business loan is not a pass-through item; it is a business expense, as it would be for any other entity. ###

8. On January 15, 2012, Elliott decides to voluntarily terminate his corporation's S status, switching to a C corporation. The termination was approved by the IRS. A year later, he changes his mind and wishes to elect S corporation status again. How long does Elliott have to wait to elect S corporation status again?

A. 18 months.
B. Two years.
C. Four years.
D. Five years.

The answer is D. A corporation must generally wait five years to make another election. ###

9. On December 31, 2011, Adrienne had a $2,000 basis in Liaison Corporation, an S corporation. She owns 50% of Liaison's outstanding stock. At the beginning of 2012, Adrienne contributed a patent that she had acquired for $1,000 to Liaison Corp. During 2012 Liaison Corp received $5,000 in royalty income from that patent. Liaison also had $2,500 of ordinary income and $500 of section 179 deductions. At the end of 2012, Liaison returned ownership of the patent, which now had a fair market value of $5,000, to Adrienne. What is Adrienne's basis in Liaison Services at the end of 2012?

A. $1,000.
B. $1,500.
C. $2,500.
D. $5,000.

The answer is B. Adrienne's basis is calculated as follows:

Basis at December 31, 2011	$2,000
Contribution of patent	$1,000
50% share of 2012 income:	
• Royalty income	$2,500
• Ordinary income	$1,250
Basis prior to consideration of distribution	6,750
Distribution of patent, at FMV	($5,000)
Subtotal	**$1,750**
50% share of section 179 deduction	($250)
Basis at December 31, 2012	**$1,500**

###

10. Bettendorf River Company is a calendar-year C corporation that wishes to elect S corporation status in 2012. What is the latest date that Bettendorf River Company can elect S status for tax year 2012?

A. March 15, 2012.
B. March 15, 2013.
C. February 15, 2012.
D. December 31, 2012.

The answer is A. An eligible corporation must make an S election within two months and 15 days of its tax year (or within 2.5 months of its inception) to become an S corporation. Since Bettendorf is a calendar-year corporation, its tax year begins January 1. It must make the election on or before March 15. ###

11. S corporations are generally not subject to taxation and are primarily pass-through entities. But in certain cases, S corporations are subject to taxes. Which of the following taxes do not apply to S corporations?

A. Excess net passive investment income.
B. Built-in gains tax.
C. Self-employment tax.
D. LIFO recapture.

The answer is C. S corporations are not subject to self-employment tax. Self-employment tax only applies to individuals. The S corporation may have to pay tax due to:

•Excess net passive investment income
•Built-in gains
•Investment credit recapture
•LIFO recapture ###

12. A C corporation may not elect to become an S corporation if:

A. It is a domestic corporation.
B. It has voting and nonvoting stock.
C. It has two classes of stock.
D. It has common stock.

The answer is C. A corporation may not elect S corporation status if it has two classes of stock. A corporation may have both voting and nonvoting stock because they are not considered different classes of stock. A corporation must be a domestic corporation in order to qualify for S corporation status. ###

13. On January 1, 2012, Seth purchased 50% of the stock of Rancho Sendero, an S corporation, for $100,000, and also loaned the corporation $20,000. At the end of 2012, Rancho Sendero incurred an ordinary loss of $180,000. How much of the loss can Seth deduct on his personal income tax return for 2012?

A. $ 90,000.
B. $180,000.
C. $ 0.
D. $120,000.

The answer is A. An S corporation shareholder may deduct his share of the corporation's losses only to the extent of his stock and debt basis. Before consideration of Rancho Sendero's 2012 loss, Seth's stock basis and debt basis were $100,000 and $20,000, respectively. Therefore, he can deduct his entire 50% share of the company's ordinary loss. ###

14. How much is the tax on excess net passive income?

A. 10%.
B. 15%.
C. 25%
D. 35%.

The answer is D. Excess net passive income is taxed at a rate of 35% to S corporations. ###

15. In January 2012, Christopher and Eva are shareholders in Garabedian Company, a C corporation. Christopher owns 65% of the corporate stock and Eva owns the remainder. Christopher decides that he wants to convert to an S corporation. Which of the following statements is true regarding the conversion?

A. Christopher and Eva must both consent to the conversion to the S corporation.
B. The election to become an S corporation is taken on Form 1120S.
C. Christopher may choose, on his own, to convert the C corporation to an S corporation because he owns the majority interest (more than 50% of the stock).
D. Christopher and Eva cannot elect S corporation status, because a C corporation cannot elect to become an S corporation.

The answer is A. All the shareholders must consent to an S election. ###

16. Which of the following events would cause the termination of an S corporation's status?

A. An S corporation that has an estate as a shareholder.
B. An S corporation that has a nonprofit corporation 501(c)(3) shareholder.
C. An S corporation that issues one share of stock to a C corporation.
D. An S corporation that owns one share of stock in a C corporation.

The answer is C. An S corporation cannot issue stock to a C corporation. S corporation shareholders must be U.S. citizens or U.S. residents, and must be physical entities (persons), so corporate shareholders and partnerships are generally excluded. Certain estates and trusts can also be shareholders. Certain tax-exempt corporations, notably 501(c)(3) corporations, are permitted to be shareholders. An S corporation may own stock in a C corporation. ###

17. Given the following information, what is the total amount of separately stated income items of this S corporation?

Rental real estate income $ 300,000
Interest income $25,000
Royalty income $10,000
Section 1231 gain $20,000
Gross receipts $700,000

A. $355,000.
B. $345,000
C. $700,000.
D. $720,000.

The answer is A. All of the income, except for the gross receipts, must be separately stated on the S corporation's tax return. The total of the separately stated items is figured as follows:

Rental activities:	$300,000
Interest income	$25,000
Royalty income	$10,000
Section 1231 gain	$20,000
Total	**$355,000**

###

18. Which of the following will not terminate an S corporation's status?

A. The S corporation no longer qualifies as a small business corporation.
B. The S corporation, for each of three consecutive tax years, has accumulated earnings and profits, and derives more than 25% of its gross receipts from passive investment income.
C. The S corporation creates a second class of stock.
D. The S corporation earns the majority of its revenue from passive activities.

The answer is D. All of the following actions will terminate an S election:

• When the corporation no longer qualifies as a small business corporation.
• For each of three consecutive tax years, the corporation
• Has accumulated earnings and profits, and
• Derives more than 25% of its gross receipts from passive investment income.
• The S election may be willingly revoked by the shareholders.
• An S election will be terminated if the corporation creates a second class of stock (such as common and preferred stock). ###

19. On January 1, 2012, Gloria, Kristin, and Nancy are all equal shareholders in Fairview Heights Corporation, a calendar-year C corporation that has been in existence for four years. On March 1, 2012, Gloria sells her entire stock interest in the corporation to an unrelated party, Irving. Irving immediately wants to convert the corporation to an S corporation. What is required in order for the corporation to convert to S status?

A. Irving may convert the corporation into an S corporation so long as Kristin and Nancy consent.
B. Gloria must also consent to the election, along with Kristin and Nancy.
C. Irving may convert the corporation to an S corporation on his own.
D. The corporation cannot convert to S status until it has been in existence for five years.

The answer is B. In order for the election to be made, Gloria must also consent to the election, even though she has sold all of her shares to Irving. All the shareholders must consent to the election. If the S election is made during the corporation's tax year for which it first takes effect, any individual stockholder who holds stock at any time during the part of that year before the election is made must also consent to the election, even though the person may have sold or transferred his stock before the election is made. ###

20. Francisco is the single employee-shareholder in his S corporation. At the beginning of the year, his stock basis was $50,000. The corporation had zero income in 2012. The corporation distributed property to Francisco with an FMV of $75,000 and an adjusted basis of $62,000. What is the treatment of the distribution?

A. $50,000 as a return of capital and $25,000 taxable capital gain.
B. $50,000 as a return of capital and $12,000 taxable capital gain.
C. $60,000 as a return of capital and $15,000 taxable capital gain.
D. $62,000 as a return of capital and $0 taxable gain.

The answer is A. The distribution is figured as follows:

Francisco's adjusted basis:	$50,000
S corporation income	$0
Adjusted basis 12/31/12:	$50,000

Distribution

FMV of property:	$75,000
Less: shareholder's basis:	$50,000
Capital gain:	**$25,000**

Francisco must report $25,000 in capital gain income on his personal tax return. The distribution reduces the shareholder's basis in his stock, and the remaining amount exceeding the basis is treated as capital gain. ###

21. Fisherton Textiles, a qualified S corporation, has no accumulated earnings and profits. In 2012, Fisherton Textiles distributed property to Lydia, its sole shareholder, with a fair market value of $150,000 and an adjusted basis of $114,000. After recognizing her share of Fisherton's current year income, Lydia's adjusted basis in the company's stock at the end of the year was $100,000. How should Lydia handle the distribution?

A. $100,000 as return of capital and $50,000 as a nontaxable distribution.
B. $100,000 as return to capital and $36,000 as taxable capital gain.
C. $100,000 as return to capital and $50,000 as taxable capital gain.
D. $100,000 as a nontaxable distribution.

The answer is C. Distributions from an S corporation with no accumulated earnings and profits are generally treated as a nontaxable return of capital, up to the amount of the shareholder's adjusted stock basis. However, if an S corporation distributes appreciated property, the distribution is treated as a sale to the shareholder. To the extent the FMV of the property exceeds the shareholder's basis, she would recognize capital gain. Gain is determined when the final year-end reconciliations are made and the shareholder has adjusted her stock basis for any increases but before any decreases attributable to the current year are deducted. The gain is reported as a capital gain on the shareholder's Schedule D. ###

22. Sydney owns 50% of the Verrengia Company, a calendar-year S corporation. At the beginning of the year, Sydney's stock basis is $3,000. At the end of 2012, Verrengia has $2,000 in income and distributes a large machine with an FMV of $7,000 to Sydney. How much income must Sydney report on her individual tax return for this distribution?

A. $0.
B. $3,000.
C. $5,000.
D. $6,000.

The answer is B. After recognizing her 50% share of Verrengia's income for the year, the basis of Sydney's stock is $4,000. Since the FMV of the property distribution exceeds her basis, she recognizes capital gain to the extent of the excess amount ($3,000). The distribution is figured as follows:

Sydney's adjusted basis	$3,000
S Corp income X 50%	$1,000
Adjusted basis 12/31/2012	$4,000

Distribution

FMV of machine	$7,000
Less: shareholder's basis	($4,000)
Her capital gain	**$3,000**

###

23. Greenhouse Gardens is an S corporation. It has four shareholders: Jordan, Mai, Simon, and Nora. The corporation has 10,000 shares outstanding. The shareholders have the following ownership:

Shareholder	**Ownership**
Jordan	4,500 shares
Mai	2,000 shares
Simon	2,000 shares
Nora	1,500 shares
Total	**10,000 shares**

Nora and Jordan wish to terminate the S election, but Mai and Simon do not. What statement is true?

A. Jordan can elect to terminate the corporation's S status on his own.
B. All of the shareholders must agree to terminate the election.
C. Nora and Jordan have enough stock ownership to terminate the election.
D. At least 75% of the shareholders with active ownership must agree to the termination.

The answer is C. An S election may be revoked if shareholders holding more than 50% of the stock agree to the termination. Since Nora and Jordan own more than 50% of the outstanding stock, they can elect to revoke the S election. ###

Unit 17: Farmers and Farming Corporations

More Reading:

Publication 225, *Farmer's Tax Guide*

Congress has enacted many tax laws specific to farming that reflect the highly unpredictable nature of the business and that treat farming differently from other businesses. For example, farmers have a different schedule for paying estimated taxes; they may postpone gain or income in certain cases that other businesses cannot; they may deduct a higher percentage of mileage expenses than other businesses; and they are given special tax considerations when disaster strikes.

Farming businesses as sole proprietorships report income and loss on Schedule F, *Profit or Loss from Farming*. Farmers are generally considered self-employed and must pay self-employment tax on their earnings. Schedule F is also used by self-employed fishermen.

Self-employed farmers must complete Schedule SE (self-employment tax) to figure out how much they should pay in taxes for Social Security and Medicare. A farmer is usually self-employed if he operates his own farm or rents farmland from others to engage in the business of farming.

A farming business may also be organized as a partnership or a corporation. Farming businesses are primarily engaged in crop production, animal production, or forestry and logging. A farm includes stock, dairy, poultry, fish, fruit, and tree farms. It also includes plantations, ranches, timber farms, and orchards.

Certain associated businesses are not considered "farming businesses" and instead must file on Schedule C. Examples of businesses that are not considered farming businesses include:

- Veterinary businesses
- Businesses that only supply farm labor
- Businesses that raise or breed dogs, cats, or other household pets
- Businesses that are only in the business of breeding
- Businesses that provide agricultural services such as soil preparation and fertilization

Examples of true farming businesses include:

- Fruit and tree nut farming
- Crop farming
- Forest nurseries and timber tracts
- Aquaculture farms
- Beef cattle ranching
- Crop shares for use of the farmer's land

Farm income does not include any of the following:

- Wages received as a farm employee

- Income received under a contract for grain harvesting with workers and machines furnished by the taxpayer
- Gains received from the sale of farm land and depreciable farm equipment
- Gains from the sale of securities, regardless of who owns the securities

Rents from Farming, Including Crop Shares

If a farmer rents his farmland for someone else to use, it is generally rent income, not farm income. This is true of crop shares too, when a tenant farmer pays a proportion of crop harvest proceeds to the land owner for use of his farmland. This passive income is reported on Form 4835, *Farm Rental Income and Expenses.*

However, if a farmer *materially participates* in farming operations on the land he owns, the rent is considered farm income and is reported on Schedule F.

Special Rules for Estimated Taxes

Special rules apply to the payment of estimated tax by qualified farmers and fishermen.

If at least two-thirds of the business's gross income comes from farming or fishing activity, the business qualifies under the special rules for estimated tax, and the following rules apply:

- The taxpayer does not have to pay estimated tax if he files his return and pays all the tax owed by the first day of the third month after the end of his tax year (usually March 1).
- If the taxpayer must pay estimated tax, he is required to make only one estimated tax payment (called the "required annual payment") by the fifteenth day after the end of his tax year (usually January 15).

For the 2012 tax year only, the IRS announced an extension in the filing deadline for qualified farmers or fishermen. Many typically file by March 1 under the special rules that allow them to avoid making quarterly tax payments during the year. However, the late tax changes of the fiscal cliff legislation[132] affected the IRS's ability to process some of the forms farmers and fisherman use, particularly those for depreciation.

Because of this, the IRS will waive penalties for the 2012 tax year for those farmers and fishermen who miss the March 1, 2013 deadline, so long as they file their returns and pay the tax due by April 15, 2013.

Accounting Methods for Farming

Most small farming businesses operate using the cash method of accounting. However, since farming usually requires an inventory (of crops or livestock, for example), larger farming businesses are required to use the accrual method.

Farmers generally choose an accounting method when they file their first income tax return. They are allowed to use any of the following accounting methods:

- **Cash method**
- **Accrual method**
- **Special methods (the Crop method)**

---

[132] Formally called the American Taxpayer Relief Act of 2012, passed on January 2, 2013.

- The Crop method is a special inventory valuation method that is only allowed for farming businesses. If crops are not harvested and disposed of in the same tax year they are planted, with IRS approval a farmer may use the crop method of accounting. Under the crop method, the farmer may deduct the entire cost of producing the crop, including the expense of seed or young plants, in the year income is realized from the crop. This method is not allowed for timber.
- **Combination (hybrid) method:** The IRS allows businesses to use a hybrid combination of the cash method and the accrual method. For instance, companies may use the accrual accounting method to satisfy tax requirements and the cash basis method for all other transactions.

Example: Ernie is a self-employed farmer who uses the accrual method of accounting. He keeps his books on the calendar-year basis. Ernie sells grain in December 2012, but he is not paid until January 2013. Ernie must include the sale and also deduct the costs incurred in producing the grain on his 2012 tax return.

Example: Miguel is also a self-employed farmer, but he uses the cash method of accounting. Miguel sells livestock in December 2012, but he is not paid until January 2013. Since Miguel uses the cash method and there was no constructive receipt of the sale proceeds until 2013, he does not report the income from the livestock sale on his 2012 return. Under this method, Miguel includes the sale proceeds in income in 2013, the year he receives payment.

The accrual method is required for certain large farm corporations and partnerships. The following farming businesses must use the accrual method:

- A corporation (*other than* a family farming corporation) that had gross receipts of more than $1 million for any tax year
- A family farming corporation that had gross receipts of more than $25 million for any tax year
- A partnership with a corporate partner
- A tax shelter (of any size or income)

Special Rules for Family Farming Corporations

Farming businesses are required to use the accrual method if they reach a gross receipts' threshold of $1 million (since farming businesses typically carry inventory). However, a special exception is made for family farming corporations. Qualified family farming corporations are still allowed to use the cash method so long as their average annual gross receipts are $25 million or less.

To qualify as a family farming corporation, the business must meet at least one of the following requirements:

- Members of the same family must own at least 50% of the corporation's stock
- Members of two families must have owned, either directly or indirectly, at least 65% of the corporation's stock
- Members of three families must have owned, either directly or indirectly, at least 50% of the corporation's stock

> **Example:** Dave and Raymond are brothers. They are also the two sole shareholders of Da-Ray Farms Corporation, which is a qualified family farming corporation. Da-Ray Farms raises cattle, and in 2012 it has $20 million in gross receipts. Since Da-Ray is a qualified family farm, the entity is allowed to use the cash method of accounting.

Farm Inventory Methods in General

Farmers may use the same inventory methods that are available to other businesses, such as cost and lower of cost or market, which were covered in Unit Three under inventory methods. However, there are two other inventory methods that are unique to farming businesses:

- **Farm-price method**
- **Unit-livestock-price method**

Farm-Price Method: Under the farm-price method, each item, whether raised or purchased, is valued at its market price less the cost of disposition. The costs of disposition include broker's commissions, freight, hauling to market, and other marketing costs. If a farming business chooses to use the farm-price method, it must use it for the entire inventory, except that livestock can be inventoried under the unit-livestock-price method.

Unit-Livestock-Price Method: The unit-livestock-price method is an easier inventory method that allows farmers to group livestock together, rather than tracking costs of each individual animal. A farmer may classify livestock according to type and age, and then use a standardized unit price for each animal within a class. The unit price must reasonably approximate the costs incurred in producing the animal. If a farming business uses the unit-livestock-price method, it must include all raised livestock in inventory, regardless of whether it is held for sale or for draft, breeding, sport, or dairy purposes. This method accounts only for the costs incurred while raising an animal to maturity. It does not provide for any decrease in the animal's market value after it reaches maturity.

Livestock in Inventory

All livestock purchased primarily for sale must be included in inventory. If the livestock was purchased primarily for draft, breeding, sport, or dairy purposes, the farmer can choose to depreciate it, or include the livestock in inventory. Regardless of the method chosen, it must be consistent from year to year.

If a farmer values his livestock inventory at cost or the lower-of-cost or market, he does not need IRS approval to change to the unit-livestock-price method. However, if he values his livestock inventory using the farm-price method, then he must obtain permission from the IRS to change to the unit-livestock-price method.

All harvested and purchased farm products held for sale, such as grain, hay, or tobacco, must be included in inventory. Supplies acquired for sale or that become part of the items held for sale must be included in inventory. A business may expense the cost of supplies consumed in operations during the year.

Uniform Capitalization Rules (UNICAP)

Farming businesses are subject to the uniform capitalization rules (UNICAP).[133] A farmer can determine costs required to be allocated under UNICAP by using the farm-price or unit-livestock-price inventory method.

If a farming business uses the accrual method of accounting, it is subject to the following uniform capitalization rules:

- The rules apply to all costs of raising a plant, even if the pre-productive period of raising a plant is two years or less.
- The rules apply to all costs related to animals.

Included in Farm Inventory

Farm inventory includes all items that are held for sale, purchased for resale, and for use as feed or seed, such as the following:

- Eggs in the process of hatching
- Harvested farm products that are held for sale, such as grain, cotton, hay, or tobacco
- Supplies that become a physical part of an item held for sale, such as containers, wrappers, or other packaging
- Any livestock that is held primarily for sale or purchased for resale
- Fur-bearing animals, such as mink, fox, or chinchilla, that are being held for breeding
- Purchased farm products that are being held for seed or feed

Not Included in Farm Inventory

Farm inventory does not include real property, such as land or buildings, or depreciable equipment, such as tractors.

Currently growing crops are generally *not required* to be included in inventory. However, if the crop has a pre-productive period of more than two years, the farmer may have to capitalize (or include in inventory) the costs associated with the crop.

Also not included in inventory is most livestock held for draft, breeding, dairy, or sport. These are business assets, and as such are subject to depreciation and generally not included in inventory.

Sales of Farm Products and Farm Assets

When a farmer sells products raised on a farm, the entire amount is reported on Schedule F. This is similar to any other self-employed taxpayer who sells regular inventory and reports the sales proceeds on Schedule C.

When a farmer sells farm products bought for resale, his profit or loss is the difference between his basis in the item (usually cost) and any payment received for it.

---

[133] UNICAP was covered in Unit 3, *Accounting Methods.*

> **Example:** In 2011, Oscar bought 20 feeder calves for $6,000 for resale. He sold them in 2012 for $11,000. Oscar reports the $11,000 sales price, subtracts his $6,000 basis, and reports the resulting $5,000 profit on his 2012 Schedule F.

Income reported on Schedule F does not include gains or losses from sales or other dispositions of the following farm assets:

- Land
- Depreciable farm equipment
- Buildings and structures
- Livestock held for draft, breeding, sport, or dairy purposes (this is livestock that is not held primarily for sale)

The sale of these assets is reported on Form 4797, *Sales of Business Property*, and may result in ordinary or capital gains or losses.

Dispositions of Farm Property and Real Estate

When a farming business disposes of depreciable property (section 1245 property or section 1250 property) at a gain, the taxpayer may have to recognize ordinary income under the depreciation recapture rules. Any gain remaining after applying the depreciation recapture rules is a section 1231 gain, which may then be taxed as a capital gain. This is the same treatment as other businesses when they sell depreciable business property.

Section 1245: Part or all of the gain of the sale of section 1245 property is treated as ordinary income under the rules of depreciation recapture. Buildings and structural components are excluded under section 1245. However, "single purpose agricultural (livestock) or horticultural structures" are section 1245 property. So, for example, a barn that houses different animals and is used to store supplies would not be section 1245 property because it is not a single purpose facility. However, a greenhouse that is used only to grow plants would be single purpose, and thus section 1245 property. If a cash register is installed in the greenhouse so that a farmer can sell plants in addition to growing them there, the greenhouse would no longer be section 1245 property because it is no longer single purpose.

Other examples of farming-related section 1245 property include a grain silo, fencing for the confinement of livestock, and wells for providing water to livestock.

Section 1231 Transactions Specific to Farming Businesses

Gain or loss on the following farm-related transactions is subject to section 1231 treatment:

1. Sale or exchange of cattle or horses held for draft, breeding, dairy, or sporting purposes and held for 24 months or longer.

2. Sale or exchange of other livestock held for draft, breeding, dairy, or sporting purposes and held for 12 months or longer. Other livestock includes hogs, mules, sheep, and goats, but does not include poultry.

3. Sale or exchange of depreciable property used in the farming business and held for longer than one year. Examples include farm machinery and trucks.

4. Sale or exchange of real estate used in the farming business and held for longer than one year. Examples are a farm or ranch, including barns and sheds.

5. Sale or exchange of unharvested crops.

6. Sale from cut timber.

7. The condemnation of business property held longer than one year. Condemnations of business property usually qualify for nonrecognition treatment if replacement property is purchased within a certain time period, under the involuntary conversion rules.

Postponing Gain Due to Disaster Provisions

There are special rules for farmers regarding the postponement of gain due to weather conditions. If a farmer sells or exchanges *more* livestock (including poultry), than he *normally would* in a year because of a drought, flood, or other weather-related condition, he may postpone reporting the gain from the *additional* animals until the following year. The taxpayer must meet all the following conditions to qualify:

- The principal trade or business must be farming.
- The farmer must use the cash method of accounting.
- The farmer must be able to show that he would not have sold or exchanged the additional animals this year except for the weather-related condition.
- The area must be designated as eligible for federal disaster assistance.

The livestock does not have to be raised or sold in the affected area for the postponement to apply. However, the sale must occur solely because the weather-related condition affected the water, grazing, or other requirements of the livestock. The farmer must figure the amount to be postponed separately for each generic class of animals—for example, hogs, sheep, and cattle.

> **Example:** Yolanda is a calendar-year farmer, and she normally sells 100 head of beef cattle a year. As a result of drought, she sells 135 head during 2011 and realizes $70,200 from the sale. On November 9, 2011, because of drought, the affected area is declared a disaster area eligible for federal assistance. The income Yolanda can postpone until 2012 is $18,200 [($70,200 ÷ 135) × 35], which is the portion of the gain attributed to the additional animals that she sold over her normal amount.

A weather-related sale or exchange of livestock held for draft, breeding, or dairy purposes *may* also qualify as an involuntary conversion (in this case, this does not include poultry). Livestock that is sold or exchanged because of disease may not trigger taxable gain if the proceeds of the transaction are reinvested in replacement animals within two years of the close of the tax year in which the diseased animals were sold or exchanged. This would qualify as an involuntary conversion.

> **Example:** Paulo is a farmer who owns 3,000 head of cattle. In 2012, his herd is struck by viral disease and he is forced to send 1,500 to slaughter. His insurance reimburses his losses, and he promptly reinvests all the insurance proceeds into new livestock. This is treated as an involuntary conversion.

Postponing Gain from a Weather-Related Condition

To postpone gain, the farmer must attach a statement to his tax return for the year of the sale. The statement must have the following information for each class of livestock for which the taxpayer is postponing gain:

- A declaration that the postponement of gain is based on section 451(e) of the IRC
- Evidence of the weather-related conditions that forced the early sale or exchange of the livestock
- An explanation of the relationship of the area affected by the weather-related condition to the farmer's early sale or exchange of the livestock
- The number of animals sold in each of the three preceding years
- The number of animals the farmer would have sold in the tax year had he followed normal business practices in the absence of weather-related conditions
- The total number of animals sold and the number sold because of weather-related conditions during the tax year
- A computation, as described earlier, of the income to be postponed for each class of livestock

In order to postpone gain, the farmer must file this statement along with the tax return by the due date of the return, including extensions.

However, for sales that qualify as an involuntary conversion, the farmer can file this statement at any time during the replacement period. The replacement period for the sale of livestock due to weather-related conditions is four years, and up to five years if the property is subject to an involuntary conversion in a federally declared disaster area.

Crop Insurance and Disaster Payments

Insurance proceeds, including government disaster payments, are generally taxable in the year they are received. These payments are made as a result of the destruction or damage to crops or the inability to plant crops because of drought, flood, or other natural disaster.

The farmer can elect to postpone reporting the income until the following year if he meets all of these conditions:

- The farming business must use the cash method of accounting.
- Crop insurance proceeds were received in the same tax year the crops were damaged.
- Under normal business practices, the farming business would have reported income from the damaged crops in any tax year following the year the damage occurred.

A statement must be attached to the tax return indicating the specific crops that were damaged and the total insurance payment received.

In order to make this election to postpone income, the farmer must be able to prove that the crops would have been harvested or otherwise sold in the following year.

Sometimes, farmers choose to forgo the planting of crops altogether. These farmers may then receive agricultural program payments from the government. An agricultural program payment is reported on Schedule F, and the full amount of the payment is subject to self-employment tax.

Other Unique Tax Rules for Farmers

There are many other rules that are unique to farming businesses. Other examples of special tax breaks afforded to farmers are:

1. **Car and truck expenses:** Farmers can claim 75% of the use of a car or light truck as business use *without any records* (such as a mileage log) so long as the vehicle is used in a farming business.

2. **Soil conservation:** Farmers can choose to deduct as a business expense land-related expenses for soil or water conservation or for the prevention of erosion. Examples include leveling, eradication of brush, removal of trees, or planting of windbreaks. Normally, these expenses are capital expenses that are added to the basis of the land, but farming businesses may choose to deduct them instead.

3. **Net operating losses:** Farming losses qualify for longer carryback periods. The carryback period for farming losses is five years. Other businesses are allowed to carryback their losses only two years.

4. **Farm income averaging:** Certain farmers may average all or some of their current year's farm income by allocating it to the three prior years. This may lower a farmer's current year tax if the current year is high and his taxable income from one or more of the three prior years was low. Income averaging is only available to farming businesses that are sole proprietorships or partnerships. Farmers use Schedule J, *Income Averaging for Farmers and Fishermen,* to figure their 2012 income tax by income averaging.

5. **Excise tax credits:** Farmers may be eligible to claim a credit or refund of federal excise taxes on fuel used on a farm.

Unit 17: Questions

1. Isaac is a calendar-year, self-employed farmer on the cash basis. For purposes of the estimated tax for qualified farmers, all of the following statements are true except:

A. Isaac does not have to make any estimated payments if he files by April 15 and pays all his taxes with his return.
B. Isaac is a qualified farmer if at least two-thirds of his previous year's gross income is from farming.
C. The required annual estimated tax payment for farmers is due on the fifteenth day after the close of their tax year.
D. The required annual payment is two-thirds of the current year's tax or 100% of the previous year's tax.

The answer is A. If a farmer waits until April 15 to file his return, he must pay estimated taxes just like any other business. If the taxpayer is a qualified farmer, he can either:

•Pay all his estimated tax by the fifteenth day after the end of his tax year (this date is usually January 15)
•File his return and pay all the tax owed by the first day of the third month after the end of his tax year (usually March 1).

*Note: For tax year 2012, however, the IRS announced that it is waiving penalties for farmers and fishermen who miss the March 1, 2013 filing tax deadline, as long as they file their returns and pay the tax due by April 15, 2013. This is because of delays in IRS processing due to the last-minute tax changes of the fiscal cliff legislation. ###

2. Joel is a qualified farmer who usually sells 500 beef cattle every year. However, because of a severe drought, he was forced to sell 800 beef cattle. Which of the following statements is true?

A. Joel may choose to postpone all of the gain in this transaction.
B. Joel may choose to postpone a portion of his gain in this transaction.
C. Joel must use the accrual method of accounting in order to postpone gain.
D. Postponement of gain is not allowed.

The answer is B. Joel may postpone a portion of his gain to the following year. If a farmer sells or exchanges more livestock, including poultry, than he normally would in a year because of a drought, flood, or other weather-related condition, he may postpone reporting the gain from the additional animals until the next year. The farmer must use the cash method of accounting in order to postpone gain in this manner. ###

3. All of the following should be included in farming inventory except:

A. Farming equipment and machinery.
B. Livestock held primarily for sale.
C. Farm products held for feed or seed.
D. Supplies that become a physical part of items held for sale.

The answer is A. Farming equipment is an asset. Equipment is depreciated and therefore not included in inventory. ###

4. Which of the following statements about farmers is true?

A. Gross income from farming includes capital gains from the sale of equipment.
B. A farmer who is a sole proprietor may use income averaging to reduce his tax liability.
C. A farmer does not have to report income from crop insurance payments.
D. An individual who owns livestock as a hobby and grows a large garden can be considered a farmer for tax purposes.

The answer is B. Certain farmers may average all or some of their current year's farm income by allocating it to the three prior years. This may lower a farmer's current year tax if the current year is high and his taxable income from one or more of the three prior years was low. Income averaging is only available to farmers and fishermen who operate as sole proprietors or partnerships. It is reported on Schedule J, *Income Averaging for Farmers and Fishermen*. ###

5. All of the following are acceptable methods for valuation of farm inventory except:

A. Cost.
B. Harvest discount.
C. Farm-price method.
D. Unit-livestock-price method.

The answer is B. The harvest discount method does not exist. All of the other inventory valuation methods listed are allowed for farming businesses. ###

6. Jon owns a dairy business and has income from the following sources:

Income from milk production	$50,000
Sale of old dairy cows:	$20,000
Sale of feed:	$15,000
Sale of used machinery:	$4,000

What amount of income should be reported on Jon's Schedule F, *Profit or Loss from Farming*?

A. $50,000.
B. $65,000.
C. $74,000.
D. $85,000.

The answer is B. The farming income reported is from milk production and sale of feed ($50,000 + $15,000 = $65,000) Gross income from farming activity is reported on Schedule F, and includes farm income, farm rental income, and gains from livestock that were raised specifically for sale on the farm, or purchased specifically for resale. The sale of old dairy cows and the sale of used machinery do not qualify. The sale of depreciable machinery is not reported on Schedule F, and likewise, the sale of livestock used for dairy purposes results in a capital gain (or loss) and is not reported on Schedule F. Instead, these amounts should be reported on Form 4797, *Sales of Business Property*. ###

7. Hope is a qualified farmer who grows soybeans. In 2012, her soybean crop was destroyed by flood. If the crop had not been destroyed, she would have harvested it in 2013. Hope receives federal disaster payments in 2012. Which of the following is true?

A. Hope can choose to postpone the income from this disaster payment until 2013.
B. Disaster payments are not taxable income.
C. Hope must report the income on her 2012 return.
D. Hope may delay recognition of the gain for two years.

The answer is A. She can delay recognizing income on the payment until the following year. Payments for disaster relief may be included in income in the tax year following the year in which they were awarded. In order to make this election, the farmer must be able to prove that the crops would have been harvested or otherwise sold in the following year. ###

8. Oliver is a farmer and has decided to refrain from growing any crops in 2012. He receives agricultural program payments for this activity. How should these payments be reported?

A. As "other income" on the taxpayer's individual Form 1040.
B. On Schedule E, Supplemental Income and Loss.
C. As farm income, but not subject to self-employment tax.
D. As farm income on Schedule F, subject to self-employment tax.

The answer is D. An agricultural program payment is reported on Schedule F, and the full amount of the payment is subject to self-employment tax. ###

9. Luke is a qualified farmer. A bull calf was born on his farm on 2011. Luke raised the calf for breeding purposes. Luke spent $750 in feed for the calf and it was sold for $5,000 for breeding use in 2012. How much is Luke's gain from the sale of the bull calf?

A. $0.
B. $4,250.
C. $4,750.
D. $5,000.

The answer is D. The basis of livestock is generally cost. However, since the bull calf was born on the farm, the basis of the calf is $0. The cost of the feed is deductible and is listed on the return as a regular business expense and as a deduction from gross income. The cost of the feed is not added to the basis of the calf. The sale of livestock held for breeding is not included in regular farming income. Special rules apply to the sale of livestock held for draft, breeding, sport, or dairy purposes. In this case, the sale resulted in a capital gain of $5,000. Farmers report these sales on Form 4797, *Sales of Business Property*. ###

10. Andy owns 150 acres of farmland that he rents to other farmers. He does not actively participate in any of the farming activity. How should the income from this activity be reported?

A. As rental income on Form 4835.
B. As farming income on Schedule F.
C. As ordinary income on Schedule C.
D. As passive income on Schedule 4797.

The answer is A. The rent received for the use or rental of farmland is generally rental income, not farm income. If the farmer does not materially participate in operating the farm, the income is reported on Form 4835, *Farm Rental Income and Expenses*, and the income is not subject to self-employment tax. ###

11. To be eligible as a qualified farmer and not have to pay quarterly estimated taxes during the year, at least _____ of a farmer's gross income must be from farming.

A. Half.
B. Two-thirds.
C. Three-quarters.
D. 80%

The answer is B. An individual is a qualified farmer for 2012 if at least two-thirds of his or her gross income from all sources for 2011 or 2012 was from farming. ###

12. All of the following would be considered section 1245 property except:

A. A greenhouse.
B. A grain silo.
C. A wire chicken coop.
D. A barn that houses cows and horses.

The answer is D. Section 1245 typically excludes buildings and other structural components. However, there is an exception for single purpose agricultural or horticultural structures. A barn for cows and horses is not a single purpose structure so it would not qualify for section 1245 treatment. ###

13. Farm income averaging is computed on Schedule J, which may be filed:

A. For the current year when a taxpayer files Schedule F showing a farm loss.
B. For the current year, which includes a Schedule F showing net income from farming.
C. For the current year, along with Schedule C.
D. As an amended return showing the past three years of farming income.

The answer is B. If a farmer or fisherman elects income averaging, he must file Schedule J along with a Schedule F showing his net farming income for 2012. ###

14. Merle is a sheep farmer, and also has income from other sources. In 2012, he had the following total gross income amounts:

•Taxable interest: $3,000
•Dividends: $500
•Rental Income (Schedule E): $41,500
•Farming income (Schedule F): $75,000
•Gain (Form 4797): $5,000

Total income: $125,000
Total farming income: $75,000

Merle's Schedule D showed gain from the sale of sheep carried over from Form 4797 ($5,000) in addition to a loss from the sale of corporate stock ($2,000). Is Merle a "qualified farmer" according to IRS rules?

A. Yes.
B. No.
C. Only if his 2011 income was greater than his 2012 income.
D. Cannot be determined given the information provided.

The answer is B. Merle is not a qualified farmer for IRS purposes. The loss from the sale of corporate stock is not netted against the gain to figure Merle's total gross income or his gross farm income. His gross farm income is 64% of his total gross income ($80,000 ÷ $125,000 = .64). This means that Merle does not qualify for the special treatment for estimated taxes that is available to farmers and fishermen. An individual is a "qualified farmer" only if at least two-thirds (66%) of his or her gross income from all sources was from farming. ###

15. The carryback period for farming losses is _____:

A. Two years.
B. Four years.
C. Five years.
D. Farmers are not allowed to carryback their losses.

The answer is C. The carryback period for farming losses is five years. Other businesses are allowed to carry back their losses only two years. ###

Unit 18: Exempt Organizations

More Reading:
Publication 4220, *Applying for 501(c)(3) Tax-Exempt Status*
Publication 557, *Tax-Exempt Status for Your Organization*
Publication 4221-PC, *Compliance Guide for 501(c)(3) Public Charities*
Publication 598, *Tax on Unrelated Business Income of Exempt Organizations*

Nonprofit organizations may qualify for exemption from the requirement to pay income taxes, but they are still subject to certain filing and recordkeeping requirements under federal tax law. There are several different types of exempt organizations; all are tax exempt, but not all qualify to receive contributions that are deductible by the donor.

IRC Section 501(c)(3)

The majority of nonprofit organizations qualify for tax-exempt status under section 501(c)(3) of the IRC. These nonprofits are exempt from paying income tax in connection with their charitable activities, and they are eligible to receive tax-deductible charitable contributions. To qualify for these benefits, most organizations must file an application with the IRS to seek recognition as a 501(c)(3). There are three key components for an organization to be exempt from federal income tax under 501(c)(3):

- **Organization:** It must be organized as a corporation, trust, or unincorporated association, and its purpose must be limited to those described in section 501(c)(3). A nonprofit entity may not be organized as a partnership or sole proprietorship.
- **Operation:** A substantial portion of its activities must operate to further its exempt purpose. A 501(c)(3) organization:
  - must refrain from participating in political campaigns of candidates
  - must restrict its lobbying activities to an "insubstantial" part of its total activities
  - must ensure that its earnings do not benefit any private shareholder or individual
  - must not operate for the benefit of private interests such as those of its founder, the founder's family, or its shareholders
  - must not operate for the primary purpose of conducting a trade or business that is not related to its exempt purpose
- **Exempt purpose:** It must have one or more exempt purposes as listed under section 501(c)(3): charitable, educational, religious, scientific, literary, fostering national or international sports competition, preventing cruelty to children or animals, and testing for public safety.

Applying for 501(c)(3) Status

Before applying for tax exemption, the organization must be created using an *organizing document*. This document must limit the organization's purposes to those set forth in section 501(c)(3) and must specify that the entity's assets will be permanently dedicated to an exempt purpose. The organizing document should also contain a provision for distributing funds if it dissolves.

To request exempt status under section 501(c)(3), entities use Form 1023, *Application for Recognition of Exemption*. Organizations that do not qualify for exemption under section 501(c)(3) may still qualify for tax-exempt status by filing Form 1024, *Application for Recognition of Exemption Under 501(a)*.

In order to qualify for tax exemption, an organization must generally request exemption from the IRS by the end of the fifteenth month after it was created, with a 12-month extension available. A small organization is not required to file Form 1023 unless its annual gross receipts are more than $5,000.

An organization must file Form 1023 to request formal exemption within 90 days of the end of the year in which it exceeds this threshold. However, a private foundation is always required to request exemption, regardless of the amount of its gross receipts.

Example: An animal rescue organization that was created five years ago did not exceed the $5,000 gross receipts threshold until September 30, 2012. The organization must file Form 1023 to request formal tax exemption by March 30, 2013.

An organization that files its application before the deadline may be recognized as tax-exempt from the date of its creation. An organization that files an application after the deadline also may be recognized as tax-exempt from the date of the application by requesting exemption retroactive as of the date of creation.

The IRS will review an organization's application and determine if it meets the requirements for exemption. If the decision is affirmative, the IRS will then issue a letter recognizing the organization's exempt status and providing its public charity classification.

While an organization's Form 1021 is pending approval, the organization may operate as if it were tax-exempt. Donor contributions made while an application is pending would qualify if the IRS determines the entity should have 501(c)(3) status. However, if the application is not approved, these contributions would not qualify. The organization would also be liable for filing federal income tax returns unless its income is otherwise excluded from federal taxation.

Other Section 501(c) Organizations

Not all tax-exempt organizations are 501(c)(3) organizations. There are other organizations that qualify for tax-exempt status, but may or may not qualify to accept donor-deductible contributions.

Other examples of nonprofit entities that are not 501(c)(3) organizations include:

- 501(c)(4) Civic leagues and social welfare organizations

- 501(c)(5) Labor unions, agricultural, and horticultural organizations
- 501(c)(6) Business leagues
- 501(c)(7) Social and recreation clubs
- 501(c)(8) and 501(c)(10) Fraternal beneficiary societies
- 501(c)(4), 501(c)(9), and 501(c)(17) Employees' associations
- 501(c)(12) Local benevolent life insurance associations
- 501(c)(13) Nonprofit cemetery companies
- 501(c)(14) Credit unions and other mutual financial organizations
- 501(c)(19) Veterans' organizations
- 501(c)(20) Group legal services plan organizations
- 501(c)(21) Black lung benefit trusts
- 501(c)(2) Title-holding corporations for single parents
- 501(c)(25) Title-holding corporations or trusts for multiple parents
- 501(c)(26) State-sponsored high-risk health coverage organizations
- 501(c)(27) State-sponsored workers' compensation reinsurance organizations

To be exempt under IRC section 501(c)(7), a social club must be organized for pleasure, recreation, and other similar nonprofit purposes, and substantially all of its activities must be for these purposes.

Filing Requirements

Every exempt organization must file an annual information return on Form 990, *Return of Organization Exempt from Income Tax*, with the IRS, unless it is specifically exempt from the filing requirement. The organizations that are not required to file Form 990 are:

- Churches and their affiliated organizations
- Government agencies

Small tax-exempt organizations with gross receipts of $50,000 or less are required to file Form 990-N, *Electronic Notice for Tax Exempt Organizations Not Required to File Form 990*. This form is also called an "e-postcard" because it is filed electronically and is short. A small tax-exempt organization may also voluntarily choose to file a long form (Form 990) instead.

Exempt Entities: Financial Activity	Annual Information Return Required
Gross receipts normally < $50,000	Form 990-N (e-postcard)
Gross receipts < $500,000 and Total assets < $1.25 million	Form 990-EZ or 990
Gross receipts $500,000 (or greater), or Total assets ≥ $1.25 million	Form 990
Private foundation (must file every year, regardless of financial activity)	Form 990-PF
Churches and similar religious organizations	No yearly filing requirement, but may still be required to file payroll returns if the entity has employees

An exempt entity may choose to file on a fiscal year or a calendar year basis. The applicable annual information return is due by the fifteenth day of the fifth month after the year ends. For a calendar-year entity, the due date is May 15. If the organization has been dissolved, the return is due by the fifteenth day of the fifth month after the dissolution.

Extensions of Time to File

An exempt entity may request a three-month extension of time to file by filing Form 8868, *Application for Extension of Time to File an Exempt Organization Return*. The organization may also apply for an additional three-month extension, if needed, using the same form. When filing a request for the first three-month extension, neither a signature nor an explanation is required. However, when filing an additional three-month extension, both a signature and an explanation are required.

An organization must file Form 990 electronically if it files at least 250 returns during the calendar year and has total assets of $10 million or more at the end of the tax year. A private foundation is required to file Form 990-PF electronically if it files at least 250 returns during the calendar year.

Section 501(c)(3) organizations must make their application (Form 1023) and the three most recent annual returns (Form 990) available to the public. The IRS also makes these documents available for public inspection and copying.

Every tax-exempt entity must have an EIN whether it has employees or not.

Penalties for Late Filing and Failure to File

An exempt organization that fails to file a required return must pay a penalty of $20 a day for each day the return is late. The same penalty will apply if the organization provides incorrect information on the return. The maximum penalty for any year is the smaller of:

- $10,000, or
- 5% of the organization's gross receipts for the year.

However, for an organization that has gross receipts of more than $1 million for the year, the late filing penalty is $100 a day, up to a maximum of $50,000.

An organization's exempt status may be revoked for failure to file. Failure to file an annual information return for three years in a row will result in the automatic revocation of exempt status. In this case, the organization would be required to reapply for exemption. No penalty will be imposed if reasonable cause for failure to timely file can be shown.

Retroactive Reinstatement

If an organization's tax-exempt status was automatically revoked for failing to file a return or notice for three consecutive years, it must apply to have its tax-exempt status reinstated by filing either Form 1023 or Form 1024 and paying the appropriate fee.

In 2012, smaller organizations—defined as having annual gross receipts of $50,000 or less in their most recent tax year—that lost their tax-exempt status by failing to file the e-postcard were eligible for transitional relief. This relief included possible retroactive reinstatement and a reduced user fee.[134]

Employment Tax Returns for Exempt Organizations

The basic requirements for tax and wage reporting compliance, calculating withholding, making deposits, and keeping tax and reporting records apply to exempt organizations just like other businesses.

Even though some organizations (such as a church or other religious organization) are not required to file Form 990, any entity with employees must withhold and remit Social Security and Medicare taxes on its employees' wages, and some exempt organizations are also responsible for Federal Unemployment Tax (FUTA).

> **Example:** Trinity Methodist Church is not required to file an application for exemption in order to be recognized as tax-exempt by the IRS. Trinity applies for an EIN as an exempt entity and begins regular worship. In 2012, Trinity Church hires three employees: a part-time pastor, a Sunday child care worker, and a music leader. Although Trinity does not have to file Form 990, the church is still required to file employment tax returns and remit and collect employment taxes from its employees. In this way, the exempt organization is treated like every other employer.

Public Charity or Private Foundation?

Every organization that qualifies for tax-exempt status under section 501(c)(3) of the IRC is further classified as either a public charity or a private foundation. Tax-exempt entities are automatically presumed to be private foundations, unless they are specifically excluded.

For some organizations, the primary distinction between classification as a public charity or a private foundation is the organization's source of financial support. Generally, a public charity has a broad base of support while a private foundation has very limited sources of support.

This classification is important because different tax rules apply: the deductibility of contributions to a private foundation is more limited than deductibility of contributions to a public charity.

A private foundation is a charitable organization that is set up as a holding entity for donated assets. Private foundations receive less preferential tax treatment than public charities and religious organizations because they are not always seen as operating for the good of the public.

Some organizations are automatically excluded from being classified as private foundations. As listed in IRC section 509(a)(1), these organizations are not considered private foundations:

- Any church
- An educational organization, such as a school or college
- A hospital or a medical research organization operated in conjunction with a hospital

---

[134] IRS Notice 2011-43.

- Endowment funds operated for the benefit of colleges and universities
- Any domestic governmental organization
- A publicly-supported organization
- Organizations organized and operated exclusively for testing for public safety

Any exempt organization will not be considered a private foundation if it receives more than one-third of its annual support from its own members and/or the general public. All private foundations must file Form 990-PF, *Return of Private Foundation*, every year regardless of their income.

There is an excise tax on the net investment income of domestic private foundations. Certain foreign private foundations are also subject to a tax on investment income derived from domestic sources. This excise tax is reported on Form 990-PF, and must be paid annually or in quarterly estimated tax payments if the total tax for the year is $500 or more.

Unrelated Business Income Tax (UBIT)

Although an exempt organization must be operated primarily for a tax-exempt purpose, it may engage in unrelated income-producing activities so long as these activities are not a substantial part of the organization's regular activities. Income from unrelated business activity is subject to a federal tax called the unrelated business income tax (UBIT). For most organizations, an activity is considered an unrelated business and subject to UBIT if:

- It is a trade or business,
- It is regularly carried on, and
- It is not substantially related to furthering the exempt purpose of the organization.

An exempt organization that has $1,000 or more of gross income from an unrelated business must file Form 990–T by the fifteenth day of the fifth month after the tax year ends. An exempt organization must make quarterly payments of estimated tax on unrelated business income if it expects its tax for the year to be $500 or more.

Example: A university enters into a multi-year contract with a company to be its exclusive provider of sports drinks for the athletic department and concessions. As part of the contract, the university agrees to perform various services for the company, such as guaranteeing that coaches make promotional appearances on behalf of the company. The university itself is a qualified nonprofit organization, but the income received from the exclusive contract is subject to UBIT. The university is therefore required to file Form 990-T.

Example: A college negotiates discounted rates for the soft drinks it purchases for its cafeterias in return for an exclusive provider arrangement. Generally, discounts are considered an adjustment to the purchase price and do not constitute gross income to the purchaser. Thus, the amount of the negotiated discount is not includable in UBIT. The college is not required to file Form 990-T.

Unit 18: Questions

1. Which of the following organizations do not qualify for tax-exempt status?

A. A charitable organization.
B. A religious organization.
C. A private foundation.
D. An educational partnership.

The answer is D. A partnership does not qualify for exemption from income tax. A tax-exempt organization cannot be organized as a partnership or sole proprietorship. ###

2. Cat Rescue Inc. is a calendar year nonprofit organization that helps prevent cruelty to animals. It is required to file Form 990 in 2012. What is the due date of its tax return, not including extensions?

A. April 15.
B. March 15.
C. May 15.
D. October 15.

The answer is C. Since Cat Rescue is on a calendar year, its tax return is due May 15. Each tax-exempt organization is required to file by the fifteenth day of the fifth month after its fiscal year ends. ###

3. Which of the following statements is true?

A. Any exempt organization that qualifies for tax-exempt status with the IRS receives contributions that are fully deductible by the donor.
B. A church is not required to file an annual information return (Form 990).
C. A religious entity does not have to file payroll tax returns if it has employees.
D. A church may be organized as a sole proprietorship.

The answer is B. A religious organization is not required to file an annual information return. However, a religious organization with employees is still responsible for filing employment tax returns. ###

4. Most organizations seeking recognition of exemption from federal income tax must use specific application forms prescribed by the IRS. Which form must be filed in order to request recognition as a 501(c)(3) nonprofit organization by the IRS?

A. Form 1023.
B. Form 1024.
C. Form 1040.
C. Form 990.

The answer is A. The form required by the IRS to apply for 501(c)(3) status is Form 1023, *Application for Recognition of Exemption Under Section 501(c)(3) of the Internal Revenue Code.* ###

5. Which of the following exempt organizations is not required to file an annual information return?

A. A church with gross receipts exceeding $250,000.
B. An exempt literary organization with $6,000 in gross receipts.
C. A Chamber of Commerce with $26,000 in gross receipts.
D. A private foundation with income of less than $5,000.

The answer is A. Only the church would not be required to file a tax return. Tax-exempt organizations must file a Form 990 or Form 990-N (e-postcard) unless specifically exempt. Private foundations must file a Form 990-PF, regardless of income. ###

6. All of the organizations listed below would qualify for tax-exempt status under the Internal Revenue Code except:

A. A Christian church with only eight members.
B. A political action committee.
C. A trust for a college alumni association.
D. A local boys club.

The answer is B. A political action committee would not qualify. In general, if a substantial part of an organization's activities includes attempting to influence legislation, the organization's exemption from federal income tax will be denied. ###

7. The Blue Lake Sailing Club is a social club promoting the social activity of sailing. Which of the following is true?

A. The Blue Lake Sailing Club may apply and be recognized as exempt from federal income tax.
B. A social club cannot qualify for IRS exemption.
C. This type of organization only qualifies for exemption if it is organized as a religious organization.
D. None of the above.

The answer is A. The sailing club can apply for exemption from income tax. To be exempt under IRC section 501(c)(7), a social club must be organized for pleasure, recreation, and other similar nonprofit purposes and substantially all of its activities must be for these purposes. It should file Form 1024 to apply for recognition of exemption from federal income tax. Donations under 501(c)(7) are not deductible as charitable contributions. ###

8. The local Catholic church has two employees: Martha, who works as a secretary in the church rectory, and Jack, who is the church custodian. Which return(s) must the church file in order to fulfill its IRS reporting obligations?

A. Form 990.
B. Form 8300.
C. Employment tax returns.
D. Form 990-PF.

The answer is C. Exempt churches, their integrated auxiliaries, and conventions or associations of churches are not required to file information returns. However, every employer is responsible for filing employment tax returns. ###

9. Which of the following organizations may request exempt status under the Internal Revenue Code as a section 501(c)(3) organization?

A: A Catholic organization.
B: A Hindu organization.
C: A children's rescue organization.
D: All of the above.

The answer is D. Nonprofit organizations that are exempt from federal income tax under section 501(c)(3) of the Internal Revenue Code include entities organized exclusively for religious, charitable, scientific, testing for public safety, literary or educational purposes, fostering national or international amateur sports competition, or for the prevention of cruelty to children or animals. ###

10. A charitable organization has $2,000 in unrelated business income in the current year. How is this income reported?

A. The organization must file a business tax return for the unrelated business income.
B. The organization is required to file Form 990-T.
C. The organization will have its exempt status revoked.
D. The organization must file Schedule C to correctly report the business income.

The answer is B. An exempt organization that has $1,000 or more of gross income from unrelated business activity must file Form 990–T. ###

11. What does an organization that wishes to be recognized as a 501(c)(3) charity need to file with the IRS?

A. Form 990.
B. Form 990 and its organizing document.
C. Form 1023 and its organizing document.
D. Form 1023, its organizing document, a listing of its board of directors, and its bylaws.

The answer is C. Form 1023, *Application for Recognition of Exemption Under Section 501(c)(3 of the Internal Revenue Code*, must be filed with the IRS, along with the entity's organizing document. This document should contain the required information as to purposes and powers of the organization and disposition of its assets upon dissolution. ###

12. Which kind of organization is allowed to file an e-postcard?

A. A private foundation.
B. A nonprofit with gross receipts of $25,000 or less.
C. A nonprofit with gross receipts of $50,000 or less.
D. A nonprofit with gross receipts of $100,000 or less.

The answer is C. A tax-exempt organization with gross receipts of $50,000 or less may file the short "e-postcard" Form 990-N, Electronic Notice for Tax Exempt Organizations Not Required to File Form 990, instead of the longer information return, Form 990, if it so chooses. ###

Unit 19: Retirement Plans for Businesses

More Reading:

Publication 560, *Retirement Plans for Small Business*

Employers set up retirement plans as a fringe benefit for their employees. Self-employed taxpayers are also allowed to set up retirement plans for themselves. There are numerous forms of retirement plans that employers can choose; these include Simplified Employee Pension (SEP) plans, Savings Incentive Match Plan for Employees (SIMPLE) plans, and qualified plans.

The term "qualified" refers to certain IRS requirements to which the plan and the employer must adhere in order to qualify for tax-favored status. SEP and SIMPLE plans must also meet certain requirements, but they are much less complex than those that apply to qualified plans.

Deductibility Rules for Business

If retirement plans are structured and operated properly, businesses can deduct retirement contributions they make on behalf of their employees. Both the contributions and the earnings are generally tax-free to the employees until distribution.

The rules vary depending on the type of business. Any business, including a sole proprietorship or a partnership, can deduct retirement plan contributions made on behalf of employees, even if the business has a net operating loss for the year.

However, in the case of a sole proprietorship or partnership, if the owners of the business contribute to *their own* retirement accounts, they must take the deduction on Form 1040, and only if they have self-employment income. Self-employment income for the purpose of this deduction means net profits from Schedule C or Schedule F, or self-employment income from a partnership.

Example: Gemma is self-employed and reports her income and losses from her dress shop on Schedule C. She has a retirement account set up for herself and her five employees. In 2012, Gemma's dress shop showed a loss from operations on her Schedule C, and Gemma has no other source of taxable income. She made regular contributions to her employees' retirement accounts in 2012, and she may deduct these contributions as a regular business expense. However, Gemma cannot make a retirement contribution for *herself* in 2012 because she has no self-employment income. Since her business showed a loss, she has no qualifying income for purposes of her own retirement plan contribution.

Since an S corporation is a pass-through entity, shareholder-employees in an S corporation are also required to report these deductions on their individual returns.[135] However, as a C corporation is not a pass-through entity, the corporation deducts the expense on Form 1120, *US Corporation Income Tax Return,* whether it is made for an employee-shareholder, an officer, or a regular employee.

---

[135] In the case of an S corporation, this rule applies to employee-shareholders who own more than 2% of the S corporation stock.

Simplified Employee Pension (SEP)

A SEP plan provides the simplest and least expensive method for employers to make contributions to a retirement plan for themselves and their employees.

A SEP may be established as late as the due date (*including extensions*) of the company's income tax return for the year the employer wants to establish the plan. Employers must also make their contributions to the plan by the due date, including extensions. There is no requirement for a "plan document" such as those needed for qualified retirement plans. However, the employer must execute a formal written agreement to provide benefits to all eligible employees under the SEP. Except in certain circumstances, including when the employer also maintains a qualified plan, this can be done using IRS Form 5305-SEP. Using this form will typically eliminate the need to file annual information forms with the IRS and the Department of Labor. Contributions to a SEP can vary from year to year, so it is a very flexible option for small employers.

A SEP can be set up for an individual person's business even if he participates in another employer's retirement plan.

> **Example:** Mitch works full time for the post office as a mail carrier, and also runs a profitable catering business with his wife on the weekends. They have self-employment income from the business. Mitch may set up a SEP for himself and his spouse, even though he is already covered by the post office plan.

Under a SEP, employers make contributions to an Individual Retirement Arrangement (called a SEP-IRA), which must be set up for each eligible employee. The SEP-IRA is owned and controlled by the employee, and the employer makes contributions to the financial institution where the SEP-IRA is maintained. The SEP-IRAs are funded exclusively by contributions from the employer.

A SEP does not require employer contributions every year, but it cannot discriminate in favor of highly compensated employees (HCEs). This means that a business cannot choose to fund the SEP-IRAs of its highly-paid executives, while ignoring its other workers.

An eligible employee is one who meets all the following requirements:

- Has reached age 21
- Has worked for the employer in at least three of the last five years
- Has received at least $550 in compensation in 2012

If an employer sets up a SEP, then all the employees who are eligible employees must also be allowed to participate. An employer can use *less restrictive* participation requirements than those listed, but not *more restrictive* ones.

The following employees can be excluded from coverage under a SEP:

- Employees covered by a union agreement
- Nonresident alien employees who have received no U.S. source income from the employer

As with traditional IRAs, money withdrawn from a SEP-IRA (and not rolled over to another qualified retirement plan or account) is subject to income tax for the year in which an employee receives a distribution. If an employee withdraws money from a

SEP-IRA before age 59½, a 10% additional tax generally applies. Further, a participant in a SEP-IRA must begin receiving required minimum distributions by April 1 of the year following the year the participant reaches age 70½. However, unlike a traditional IRA, contributions can be made to participants over age 70½.

> **Example:** Quincy Company decides to establish a SEP for its employees. Quincy has chosen a SEP because its industry is cyclical in nature. In good years, Quincy can make larger contributions for its employees, and in down years it can reduce or eliminate contributions. Quincy knows that under a SEP, the contribution rate (whether large or small) must be uniform for all employees. The financial institution that Quincy has identified to be the trustee for its SEP has several investment funds for employees to choose from. Individual employees have the opportunity to divide their employer's contributions to their SEP-IRAs among these fund options.

SEP Snapshot

	Rules for Employers	Rules for Employees
Eligibility	Any business or self-employed individual may set up a SEP.	All employees aged 21 or older who have worked for the business for three out of the last five years and earned at least $550 in the current year.
Contributions	Vesting is immediate.	Only employers and self-employed individuals can contribute to a SEP. Employees cannot contribute to a SEP. Vesting is immediate.
Pros	Contributions can vary from year to year. Inexpensive to set up and administer.	Employers cannot prohibit distributions from a SEP, because vesting is immediate.
Drawbacks	A SEP must cover all qualifying employees. Employers cannot discriminate in favor of HCEs. Only employers can contribute.	Employees cannot contribute.

Contributions to a SEP

Contributions to a SEP must be made in cash; an employer cannot contribute *property* to a SEP. However, plan participants may be able to transfer or roll over certain property from another retirement plan account to a SEP-IRA. When employers contribute to a SEP, they must contribute to the SEP-IRAs of all participants who had qualified compensation, including employees who die or terminate employment before the contributions are made. A SEP-IRA cannot be a Roth IRA. Employer contributions to a SEP-IRA will not affect the amount an individual can contribute to a Roth or traditional IRA. The following SEP limits apply in 2012:

- For an employee: Contributions cannot exceed the lesser of 25% of the employee's compensation or $50,000.

- For a self-employed individual: Contributions cannot exceed the lesser of 20% of net self-employment income, after considering both the deduction for self-employment tax and the deduction for the SEP-IRA contribution, or $50,000.

Employees have control over their own SEP-IRAs, so employers cannot prohibit distributions from a SEP-IRA. Further, employers cannot make contributions conditional, or require that any part of the contribution be kept in the employee's account after the business has made its contributions.

SIMPLE Plan (IRA or 401(k))

A SIMPLE (Savings Incentive Match Plan for Employees) plan provides an employer and his employees with a simplified way to contribute toward retirement. SIMPLE plans have lower start-up and annual costs than most other types of retirement plans.

If a business has 100 or fewer employees who received $5,000 *or more* in compensation during the preceding year, it can establish a SIMPLE plan.[136] The business cannot maintain another retirement plan, unless the other plan is for a union workforce.

The business must continue to meet the 100-employee limit each year. However, if a business maintains a SIMPLE plan for at least one year and subsequently fails to meet the 100-employee limit, the business is allowed a two-year grace period to establish another retirement plan. Another exception may apply if the business fails to meet the 100-employee limit as a result of an acquisition, disposition, or similar transaction.

Employees can choose to make retirement plan contributions by allocating a portion of their salaries, and businesses can contribute matching or nonelective contributions. SIMPLE plans can only be maintained on a calendar-year basis. A SIMPLE plan can be structured in one of two ways: using SIMPLE IRAs or as part of a 401(k) plan (SIMPLE 401(k) plan).

SIMPLE IRA

Unlike a SEP, SIMPLE IRAs allow employee contributions and they mandate employer contributions.

A SIMPLE IRA must be set up for *each eligible employee*. An eligible employee is generally one who received at least $5,000 in compensation during any two years preceding the current calendar year and reasonably expected to receive at least $5,000 in the current calendar year, except for:

- Employees covered by a union agreement
- Nonresident alien employees who have received no U.S. source income from the employer

Prior to an election period (generally 60 days) preceding the start of the calendar year, employees must receive formal notice of their right to participate and

---

[136] For purposes of the 100-employee limitation, all employees employed at any time during the year are taken into account, regardless of whether all of them are eligible to participate in the SIMPLE plan.

make salary reduction contributions, and information regarding the employer's planned contributions.

During the election period, an employee may execute or modify a salary reduction agreement to defer a portion of his contribution (up to $11,500 for 2012.) Employees age 50 or over can also make a catch-up contribution of up to $2,500 (for a total of up to $14,000 for 2012). The salary reduction contributions under a SIMPLE IRA plan are elective deferrals that count toward an overall annual limit on elective deferrals an employee may make to this and other plans permitting elective deferrals.

Contributions to a SIMPLE IRA

Each year, the employer must choose to make either matching contributions or nonelective contributions. Employer matching of the employee's salary reduction contributions is generally required on a dollar-for-dollar basis up to 3% of the participant's compensation. The employer may elect to make matching contributions at less than 3%, but not lower than 1%, for no more than two years within a five-year period.

Instead of matching contributions, the employer may choose to make nonelective contributions of 2% of each eligible employee's compensation. An individual employee's compensation used for this contribution is limited to $250,000 in 2012. If the employer chooses to make nonelective contributions, it must make them for all eligible employees *whether or not* they make salary reduction contributions. The employer must notify employees of its choice to make nonelective contributions within a specified period prior to the employees' annual period for making their own salary reduction contribution elections.

An eligible employee may choose not to make salary reduction contributions for a given year, in which case the employee would accrue no employer matching contributions, but would receive an employer nonelective contribution if the employer elects to make this type of contribution for the year. No other contributions may be made under a SIMPLE IRA plan.

Employee and employer contributions are 100% vested—that is, the money an employee has put aside plus employer contributions and net earnings from investments cannot be forfeited, and the employee has the right to withdraw at any time, even though those withdrawals may be subject to tax.

Salary reduction contributions must be deposited with the applicable financial institution within 30 days after the end of the month in which they would otherwise have been paid to the employee. Matching or nonelective contributions must be made by the due date (including extensions) for filing the company's income tax return for the year.

An employer can set up a SIMPLE IRA plan effective on any date from January 1 through October 1 of a year, provided the employer did not previously maintain another SIMPLE IRA plan. A new employer may set up a SIMPLE IRA plan as soon as administratively feasible after the business comes into existence.

Example: Riley works for the Skidmore Tire Company, a small business with 75 employees. Skidmore Tire has decided to establish a SIMPLE IRA plan and will make a 2% nonelective contribution for each of its employees. Under this option, even if Riley does not contribute to her own SIMPLE IRA, she would still receive an employer nonelective contribution to her SIMPLE IRA equal to 2% of salary. Riley has a yearly salary of $40,000 and has decided that this year she cannot afford to make a contribution to her SIMPLE IRA. Even though she does not make a contribution this year, Skidmore must make a nonelective contribution of $800 (2% of $40,000). The financial institution partnering with Skidmore on the SIMPLE IRA has several investment choices, and Riley has the same investment options as the other plan participants.

Example: Rockland Quarry Company is a small business with 50 employees. Rockland has decided to establish a SIMPLE IRA plan for all of its employees and will match its employees' contributions dollar-for-dollar up to 3% of each employee's salary. Under this option, if a Rockland employee does not contribute to his SIMPLE IRA, the employee does not receive any matching employer contributions. Elizabeth is an employee of Rockland Company. She has a yearly salary of $50,000 and decides to contribute 5% of her salary to her SIMPLE IRA. Elizabeth's yearly contribution is $2,500 (5% of $50,000). The Rockland matching contribution is $1,500 (3% of $50,000). Therefore, the total contribution to Elizabeth's SIMPLE IRA that year is $4,000 (her $2,500 contribution plus the $1,500 contribution from Rockland).

Withdrawals from a SIMPLE IRA

Distributions from a SIMPLE IRA are subject to income tax for the year in which they are received. If a participant takes a withdrawal from a SIMPLE IRA before age 59½, an additional tax of 10% generally applies. If the withdrawal occurs within two years of beginning participation in the SIMPLE IRA plan, the additional tax is increased to 25%.

SIMPLE IRA contributions and earnings may be rolled over tax-free from one SIMPLE IRA to another. A rollover may also be made from a SIMPLE IRA to another type of IRA, or to another employer's qualified plan, but it will be tax-free only if it is made after two years of participation in the SIMPLE IRA plan.

A participant in a SIMPLE IRA plan must begin receiving required minimum distributions by April 1 of the year following the year the participant reaches age 70½.

A business cannot suspend its employer matching contributions mid-year or terminate its SIMPLE IRA plan mid-year.

The business must maintain the plan for a full calendar year (except in the year the business first establishes the plan). The employer is required to make the contributions that were promised to the employees.

A SIMPLE IRA plan may not require a participant to be employed on a specific date to receive an employer contribution. If a participant terminates employment during the year after making a salary reduction contribution, he would still be entitled to an employer contribution.

SIMPLE IRA contributions are not included in the "Wages, tips, other compensation" box of Form W-2, *Wage and Tax Statement*. However, salary reduction contributions must be included in the boxes for Social Security and Medicare wages.

SIMPLE IRA Snapshot

	Rules for Employers	Rules for Employees
Eligibility	Any employer with 100 employees or more who received $5,000 or less in the preceding year. The employer cannot maintain another retirement plan in addition to the SIMPLE IRA.	All employees who have earned over $5,000 in any two prior years and who is expected to earn at least $5,000 in the current year.
Contribution Thresholds	Employers may choose to make either matching contributions, at 1% to 3% of compensation for employees that make salary deferral contributions, or nonelective contributions at 2% of compensation for all eligible employees.	An employee can contribute up to $11,500 of his salary (or self-employment earnings, for a self-employed owner), plus an additional $2,500 if 50 or older for a total of $14,000.
Pros	Employees can make contributions. Vesting is immediate.	Employees can make contributions. Vesting is immediate.
Drawbacks	Employer matching is mandatory.	Employees with higher salaries may prefer a retirement plan option that allows them to contribute more.

SIMPLE 401(k) Plan

A SIMPLE plan can be adopted as part of a traditional 401(k) plan (see below) if the business meets the 100-employee limit discussed above for SIMPLE IRA plans and does not maintain another qualified retirement plan.

An employee can elect to make salary reduction contributions as a percentage of his compensation, but not more than $11,500 for 2012. An employee age 50 or over can also make a catch-up contribution of up to $2,500 (for a total of up to $14,000 for 2012).

Unlike a regular 401(k) plan, the employer must make either:

- A matching contribution up to 3% of compensation for each employee who makes a salary reduction contribution, or
- A nonelective contribution of 2% of compensation for each eligible employee who receives at least $5,000 of compensation from the employer that year.

Participants are fully vested in all contributions. SIMPLE 401(k) plans must file Form 5500 annually.

Qualified Plans

There are two basic kinds of qualified retirement plans, defined contribution plans and defined benefit plans, and different rules apply to each. An employer is allowed to have more than one type of qualified plan, but maximum contributions cannot exceed annual limits.

All qualified plans are subject to federal regulation under the Employee Retirement Income Security Act (ERISA). The federal government does not require an employer to establish any type of retirement plan, but it provides minimum federal standards for qualified plans.

ERISA mandates minimum funding requirements to ensure that benefits will be available to employees when they retire. For defined benefit plans, it also requires that plan funding be certified by an actuary. ERISA covers qualified retirement plans, as well as health and welfare benefit plans. Among other things, ERISA requires that individuals who manage plans (and other fiduciaries) meet certain standards of conduct. The law also contains detailed provisions for reporting to the government and for disclosure to participants. Further, there are provisions aimed at assuring plan funds are protected and participants receive their benefits.

ERISA also mandates that qualified plans meet specific requirements regarding eligibility, vesting, and communications with participants. The administrator of an employee benefit plan subject to ERISA must file an information return for the plan each year. Form 5500, *Annual Return/Report of Employee Benefit Plan*, must be filed by the last day of the seventh month after the plan year ends.

Defined Benefit Plans (Pension Plans)

A defined benefit plan (often called a traditional pension plan) promises a specified benefit amount or annuity after retirement. Most federal and state governments offer defined benefit plans to their employees. However, fewer companies now offer defined benefit plans because they are costly to administer and inflexible. The benefits in many defined benefit plans are protected by federal insurance.

Contributions to a defined benefit plan are not optional. Contributions are typically based on actuarial calculations. Contributions for self-employed taxpayers are limited to 100% of compensation. If the business does not have any income for the year, no contribution can be made.

Defined Benefit Plan Snapshot

Rule	Rules for Employers	Rules for Employees
Eligibility	Any business or employer.	All employees who have worked at least 1,000 hours in the past year.
Contribution Thresholds	There is no set limit for contributions to defined benefit plans. However, the annual benefit for a participant may be limited.	Employees cannot contribute to this type of plan.
Pros	Vesting is determined by the employer. Shareholder-employees of closely held corporations can contribute and deduct more per year than in a defined contribution plan.	Employees can be guaranteed a fixed payout after retirement.
Drawbacks	This plan can be expensive to administer. Annual reporting is required. Future benefits are dependent on contributions and investment performance.	Employer contributions can take years to vest.

Defined Contribution Plans

A defined contribution plan provides an individual account for each participant in the plan. It provides benefits to the participant based on the amounts contributed to the participant's account, and subsequent income, expenses, gains, losses, and, in some instances, allocations of forfeitures among participant accounts.

The participant, the employer, or sometimes both may contribute to the individual account on the employee's behalf. The value of the account will fluctuate due to the changes in the value of investments that have been made with the amounts contributed.

A participant's retirement benefits depend primarily on the amount of contributions made on his behalf, rather than upon his years of service with the employer or his earnings history. Examples of defined contribution plans include 401(k) plans, 403(b) plans, and 457 plans.

Traditional 401(k) Plans

A 401(k) plan is a defined contribution plan that allows employees to defer receiving a portion of their salary, which is instead contributed on their behalf to the 401(k) plan. Deferrals generally are made on a pretax basis, although some plans allow employees the option to make them on an after-tax basis.

Pretax deferrals are not subject to income tax withholding, and they are not included in taxable wages on the employee's Form W-2. However, they are subject to Social Security, Medicare, and federal unemployment taxes.

Sometimes the employer will make matching contributions. Employee deferrals and any employer matching contributions are accounted separately for each employee. Earnings on the retirement account grow tax-free until distribution. 401(k) plans can vary significantly in their complexity. However, many financial institutions administer 401(k) plans, which can lessen the administrative burden on individual employers of establishing and maintaining these plans.

Comparison of Defined Benefit and Defined Contribution Plans		
Rule	Defined Benefit Plan	Defined Contribution Plan
Employer Contributions	Employer contributions are required based upon actuarial calculation of amounts needed to fund benefits.	The employer may choose to match a portion of employee contributions or to contribute without employee contributions.
Employee Contributions	Employees generally do not contribute.	Many plans require the employee to contribute.
Managing the Investments	The employer must ensure that contributions to the plan plus investment earnings will be enough to pay the promised benefits.	The employee often is responsible for managing the investment of his account, choosing from investment options offered by the plan. For some plans, the plan administrator is responsible for investing the plan's assets.
Benefits Paid Upon Retirement	A promised benefit is based on a formula, often using a combination of the employee's age, years worked, and salary history.	The benefit depends on contributions made by the employee and/or the employer and investment earnings on the contributions.
Type of Retirement Benefit Payments	Traditionally, these plans pay the retiree monthly annuity payments that continue for life.	The retiree may transfer the account balance into an Individual Retirement Account (IRA) from which the retiree withdraws money. Some plans also offer monthly payments through an annuity.
Guarantee of Benefits	The government, through the Pension Benefit Guaranty Corporation (PBGC), may partially guarantee benefits.	No federal guarantee of benefits.

Prohibited Transactions

A prohibited transaction is a transaction between a plan and a disqualified person that is prohibited by law. A disqualified person may include the following:

- A fiduciary of the plan
- A person providing services to the plan

- An employer, any of whose employees are covered by the plan
- An employee organization, any of whose members are covered by the plan
- An indirect or direct owner of 50% or more of the applicable employer or employee organization
- A member of the family of anyone described in the bullet points above
- A corporation, partnership, trust, or estate of which any direct or indirect owner described in the bullet points above holds a 50% or more interest
- An officer, director, 10% or more shareholder, or highly compensated employee of the entity administering the plan

An initial 15% tax is applied on the amount involved in a prohibited transaction for each year in a taxable period. If the transaction is not corrected within the taxable period, an additional tax of 100% of the amount involved is imposed. These taxes are payable by any disqualified person who takes part in a prohibited transaction. If more than one person takes part, each can be jointly and severally liable for the entire amount of tax. Prohibited transactions include the following:

- A transfer of plan income or assets to, or use for the benefit of, a disqualified person
- Any act of a fiduciary by which plan income or assets are used for his own benefit
- The receipt of money or property by a fiduciary for his own account from any party dealing with the plan in a transaction that involves plan income or assets
- The sale, exchange, or lease of property between a plan and a disqualified person
- Lending money between a plan and a disqualified person
- Furnishing goods or services between a plan and a disqualified person

Example: A plan fiduciary had a prohibited transaction by investing in a life insurance company's group annuity contract, resulting in a 10% commission paid to his company on the investment. This is a prohibited transaction between a plan fiduciary and a retirement plan.

If a prohibited transaction is *not corrected* during the taxable period, the taxpayer usually has an additional 90 days after the day the IRS mails a notice of deficiency for the 100% tax to correct the transaction. This correction period (the taxable period plus the 90 days) can be extended if one of the following occurs:

- The IRS grants a reasonable time needed to correct the transaction.
- The taxpayer petitions the U.S. Tax Court.

If the transaction is corrected within this period, the 100% tax may be abated.

Required Minimum Distributions

A participant in a qualified retirement plan must begin receiving distributions by April 1 of the first year following the later of:

- The calendar year in which he reaches age 70½
- The calendar year in which he retires from employment with the employer maintaining the plan

However, the plan may require distributions by April 1 of the year after the participant reaches age 70½ even if he has not retired. Further, if the participant is a 5% owner of the employer, he must begin receiving distributions by April 1 of the year after the year he reaches age 70½.

Penalties for not taking required minimum distributions (RMDs) can be severe. Penalties are assessed if an account owner fails to withdraw an RMD, fails to withdraw the full amount of the RMD, or fails to withdraw the RMD by the applicable deadline. The penalty is 50% of the amount that is not withdrawn from the account when required.

Distributions from Qualified Plans

Generally, distributions cannot be made from a 401(k) plan until one of the following occurs:

- The employee retires, dies, becomes disabled, or otherwise terminates employment
- The plan terminates
- The employee reaches age 59½ or suffers financial hardship

Unless a distribution is properly rolled over into another retirement plan or individual retirement account, it will be subject to income tax upon receipt.

If a distribution is made to an employee before he reaches age 59½, the employee may have to pay a 10% additional tax on the distribution. However, the additional 10% tax would not apply in the following situations:

- Distributions are for the taxpayer's medical care, up to the amount allowed as a medical deduction.
- Disability or death.
- Distributions in the form of an annuity.
- Distributions are made because of an IRS levy on the plan.
- Distributions are made to a qualified reservist (an individual called up to active duty).

Even though these distributions will not be subject to the additional 10% tax, they will still be subject to tax at the taxpayer's applicable rate.

Example: Lauren, age 43, takes a $5,000 distribution from her traditional IRA account. She does not meet any of the exceptions to the 10% additional tax, so the $5,000 is an early distribution. Lauren must include the $5,000 in her gross income for the year the distribution is received and pay income tax on it. She must also pay an *additional* tax of $500 (10% × $5,000).

Overall Limits on Benefits and Contributions

For 2012, the following limits apply:

The annual benefit for a participant in a defined benefit plan cannot exceed the lesser of $200,000 or 100% of the participant's average compensation for his highest three consecutive calendar years.

A combined limit of $17,000 applies to each employee's elective deferrals and salary reduction contributions, other than catch-up contributions, to all defined contribution retirement plans and any SIMPLE IRA plan under which he is covered. If the limit is exceeded, the amount that would otherwise have been nontaxable must be included in the employee's gross income. Catch-up contributions are limited to $2,500 for each participant in a SIMPLE plan and $5,500 for each participant in other defined contribution plans.

Annual contributions to the account of a participant in a defined contribution plan cannot exceed the lesser of $50,000 or 100% of the participant's compensation.

An employer's deduction for contributions to a defined contribution plan cannot be more than 25% of the compensation paid or accrued during the year for the eligible employees. The maximum compensation that can be considered for each employee is $250,000.

Employer Credit for Pension Start-up Costs

Employers may be able to claim a tax credit equal to 50% of the cost to set up and administer the plan, up to a maximum of $500 per year, for each of the first three years of the plan.

Employers can choose to start claiming the credit in the tax year before the tax year in which the plan becomes effective. In order to qualify for this credit, the employer must have had 100 or fewer employees who received at least $5,000 in compensation for the preceding year.

Further, the employees cannot be substantially the same group covered by another retirement plan sponsored by essentially the same employer during the preceding three-year period. This credit is part of the general business credit, which can be carried back or forward to other tax years if it cannot be used in the current year.

Retirement Savings Contributions Credit

Retirement plan participants (including self-employed individuals) who make contributions to their own retirement plan may *also* qualify for the Retirement Savings Contributions Credit. The credit is 10% to 50% of eligible contributions up to $1,000 ($2,000 for MFJ). It is subject to specified limits on AGI.

Unit 19: Questions

1. Hurley Biomedical Corporation maintains a SIMPLE IRA for its employees. A former employee, Grace, quit her job on January 27, 2012, after the business had already deducted $75 from her wages based upon her election to contribute to its SIMPLE IRA plan. Hurley Biomedical makes a 3% matching contribution, and Grace had earned $2,000 in wages before she quit. How must Hurley Biomedical treat this $75 deduction from Grace's wages?

A. Hurley must return Grace's $75 salary reduction contribution.
B. Hurley must deposit Grace's salary reduction contribution in her SIMPLE IRA account. The company must also match Grace's salary reduction contributions up to 3% of her $2,000 compensation ($60).
C. Hurley must deposit Grace's salary reduction contribution in her SIMPLE IRA account. However, the company is not required to make a matching contribution for an employee who has terminated employment.
D. Hurley is required to remit the $75 to the U.S. Treasury.

The answer is B. Hurley Biomedical Corporation must deposit Grace's salary reduction contribution in her SIMPLE IRA account. The company must also match Grace's salary reduction contributions up to 3% of her $2,000 compensation ($60). An employer cannot return a salary reduction contribution after it has already deducted it from wages as a SIMPLE IRA plan contribution. A SIMPLE IRA plan may not require a participant to be employed on a specific date to receive an employer contribution. If a participant terminates service during the year after making a salary reduction contribution, he or she would still be entitled to an employer contribution, regardless of whether it is matching or nonelective. ###

2. "Prohibited transactions" are transactions between a retirement plan and a disqualified person. Which of the following is exempt from the prohibited transaction rules?

A. A fiduciary of the plan.
B. A person providing services to the plan.
C. An employer whose employees are covered by the plan.
D. A disqualified person who receives a benefit to which he is entitled as a plan participant.

The answer is D. It is not a prohibited transaction if a disqualified person receives a benefit to which he is entitled as a plan participant or beneficiary. ###

3. Sarah runs her own business, and sets up a new qualified defined benefit plan for her ten employees. In 2012, what is the maximum tax credit Sarah can receive for qualified retirement plan start-up costs?

A. $100.
B. $500.
C. $1,000.
D. $2,000.

The answer is B. The maximum annual credit amount is $500. Employers may claim a tax credit of up to 50% of the first $1,000 of qualified start-up costs if starting a new SEP, SIMPLE, or qualified plan. ###

4. Ram is a sole proprietor whose tax year is the calendar year. He made a contribution to his SIMPLE IRA on May 15, 2013. What is the earliest year for which he can deduct this contribution?

A. His 2013 tax return.
B. His 2012 tax return.
C. The contribution is not deductible on his tax return because it was made late.
D. None of the above.

The answer is B. Taxpayers can deduct contributions for a particular tax year if they are made by the due date (including extensions) of the federal income tax return for that year. Assuming the contributions made in May 2013 were within the applicable limits based upon his compensation for 2012, he could make deductible contributions until his extended due date of October 15, 2013 for his 2012 tax return. ###

5. What types of employers cannot establish a SEP?

A. A self-employed taxpayer without any employees.
B. A corporation with 90 employees.
C. A nonprofit entity with five employees.
D. All of the above can establish a SEP.

The answer is D. Any employer or self-employed individual can establish a SEP. ###

6. Brenda owns the Berry Company, a sole proprietorship with 150 employees. All of the following plans are available for Brenda's company except:

A. A qualified plan.
B. A defined benefit plan.
C. A SIMPLE IRA.
D. None of the above.

The answer is C. Brenda cannot set up a SIMPLE IRA for her employees, because her company exceeds the 100-employee threshold, unless at least 50 of the employees earned less than $5,000 in the prior year. ###

7. Maura, age 26, began participating in a SIMPLE IRA retirement account on March 10, 2011. She took an early distribution from the account on December 26, 2012. She does not qualify for any of the exceptions to the early withdrawal penalty. The distribution amount was $10,000. What is the amount of additional tax that Maura must pay on the early distribution?

A. $1,000.
B. $1,500.
C. $2,500.
D. $3,000.

The answer is C. Early withdrawals generally are subject to an additional tax of 10%. However, the additional tax is increased to 25% if funds are withdrawn within two years of beginning participation in a SIMPLE IRA. The answer is ($10,000 × 25% = $2,500). ###

8. Which of the following statements regarding a SEP-IRA is true?

A. Money can be withdrawn from a SEP-IRA by the employee at any time without tax or penalty.
B. Money can be withdrawn from a SEP-IRA by the employee at any time, but taxes may apply.
C. An employee must wait at least two years to withdraw money from a SEP-IRA.
D. An employee must wait at least three years to withdraw money from a SEP-IRA.

The answer is B. Although income tax may apply, including an additional 10% tax for withdrawals prior to age 59½, participants are allowed to withdraw money from a SEP-IRA at any time. Withdrawals can be rolled over tax-free to another SEP-IRA, another traditional IRA, or another employer's qualified retirement plan. ###

9. Marcelo owns Perez Body Shop and sets up a SEP-IRA for all of his employees. In his benefits handbook, he makes the following statements regarding the shop's SEP-IRA plan. All are correct except:

A. Only employees age 21 and older are eligible.
B. An employee cannot withdraw from his SEP-IRA while he is employed by Perez Body Shop.
C. A SEP-IRA will be set up for all eligible employees.
D. An employee must have worked for Perez for at least three of the last five years to be eligible.

The answer is B. Employers cannot prohibit distributions from a SEP-IRA. Employers also cannot make their contributions contingent on the condition that any part of them must be kept in the account. All of the other statements are correct regarding SEP-IRA plans. ###

10. The Azalea City Partnership has 15 employees and contributes to their retirement accounts. How is this transaction reported?

A. The business can take the deduction for its contributions to its employees' retirement accounts on Form 1065, Partnership Income Tax Return.
B. The business cannot take a deduction for its contributions to its employees' retirement accounts. Instead, the amounts contributed are added to the partnership basis.
C. The individual partners are allowed to deduct contributions to the employee retirement plans on their individual returns.
D. None of the above.

The answer is A. A partnership may deduct contributions to an employee's retirement plan, just as it would deduct any other ordinary business expense. However, the rules are different for contributions to the retirement accounts of the partners. Contributions made on behalf of the partners are passed through to each of them on Schedule K-1. ###

11. Huang Software, Inc. decides to establish a SEP for its employees. All of the following statements about Huang's retirement plan are correct except:

A. In good years, Huang can make larger contributions for its employees, and in down times it can reduce the amount.
B. Individual employees have the opportunity to divide the employer's contributions to their SEP-IRAs among the funds made available to Huang employees.
C. Under a SEP, the contribution rate can be different for each employee, based on length of service and sales performance.
D. Only employers and self-employed individuals can make contributions to SEPs.

The answer is C. Under a SEP, the contribution rate (whether large or small) must be uniform for all employees. Employers may contribute less when they have less income, but the plan cannot discriminate among employees. ###

12. Can a SIMPLE IRA plan be maintained on a fiscal-year basis?

A. Yes, if the business is on a fiscal year.
B. Yes, even if the business uses a calendar year.
C. Yes, but only if the business requests a 444 election.
D. No, a calendar year must be used.

The answer is D. A SIMPLE IRA plan may only be maintained on a calendar-year basis. ###

13. The Esslinger Carpet Company has started a SEP plan for its employees. The company currently has four employees. Which of the following employees is the company not required to cover under the SEP plan?

A. Faye, 45 years old, a full-time employee for the last five years.
B. Larry, 25 years old, a part-time employee for the last three years.
C. Randolph, 20 years old, a full-time employee for the last three years.
D. Mack, 42 years old, a seasonal employee for the last six years.

The answer is C. Randolph is not an automatically eligible employee because he is not at least 21 years old. For purposes of a SEP, an eligible employee is an individual who meets all the following requirements:

• Has reached age 21
• Has worked for the employer in at least three of the last five years
• Has received at least $550 in compensation

An employer can use less restrictive participation requirements than those listed, but not more restrictive ones. ###

14. Leah is a sole proprietor with two employees. She establishes a 401(k) SIMPLE plan. Leah has a net loss in 2012 on her Schedule C. Which of the following is true?

A. Because the business shows a loss, she is prohibited from contributing to her retirement account, as well as the retirement accounts of her employees.
B. Because the business shows a loss, she is prohibited from contributing to her retirement account, but she may contribute to the retirement accounts of her employees.
C. Leah may make a retirement contribution to her own retirement account as well as the accounts of her employees.
D. None of the above.

The answer is B. Leah is self-employed, so she must have compensation in order to contribute to her own retirement plan. However, she is not prohibited from contributing to her employees' retirement plan, even if the business has a loss. ###

15. All of the following are requirements of ERISA (the Employee Retirement Income Security Act) except:

A. ERISA requires that employers file an annual report on Form 5500 for their sponsored retirement plans.
B. ERISA requires employers to set up retirement plans for their employees.
C. ERISA requires minimum funding standards for retirement plans.
D. ERISA requires certain communications with plan participants.

The answer is B. ERISA does not require that employers set up retirement plans for their employees. No employer is forced to offer a retirement plan. All of the other answers are correct. ###

16. Theresa is a small business owner who maintains a SEP plan for her employees. Which of the following employees can be excluded from the plan, if Theresa chooses?

A. Stan, a 32-year-old part-time employee who has worked for Theresa for five years.
B. Aldo, a 42-year-old seasonal employee and U.S. resident alien who has worked for Theresa for three years.
C. Noel, a 21-year-old part-time employee who is also a union member.
D. Millie, a 55-year-old full-time employee who has worked for Theresa for four years.

The answer is C. Employers may choose to exclude employees covered by a union agreement. Since Aldo is a resident alien, he still qualifies to participate. Only nonresident aliens who do not have any U.S.-source income may be excluded. ###

17. Josie works full-time and participates in her employer's retirement plan. She also has her own graphic design business. She does not have any employees. Can Josie set up a SEP for self-employment income, even though she is already participating in her employer's plan?

A. Yes, Josie can still set up a SEP for her catering business.
B. No, Josie cannot set up a SEP because she is covered by an employer plan.
C. No, Josie cannot set up a SEP because she is a prohibited individual.
D. Josie can set up a SEP only if she hires employees.

The answer is A. Josie can set up a SEP. A SEP can be established for a person's independent business activity even if she participates in an employer's retirement plan. ###

18. What happens if an eligible employee entitled to a contribution is unwilling to set up a SIMPLE IRA?

A. Eligible employees may decline to participate in an employer's SIMPLE IRA.
B. Eligible employees may not opt out of a SIMPLE IRA.
C. Eligible employees may choose to set up a ROTH IRA in lieu of a SIMPLE IRA.
D. None of the above.

The answer is B. An eligible employee may not opt out of participation. However, any eligible employee may choose not to make salary reduction contributions for a year. In that case the employee would accrue no employer matching contributions for the year, but would still receive an employer nonelective contribution (if the plan provides for such contributions for the year.) ###

19. What are the penalties imposed on a disqualified person who takes part in a prohibited transaction?

A. 25% tax of the amount involved.
B. 50% tax of the amount involved.
C. An initial tax of 15% and an additional tax of 100% of the amount involved, if the transaction is not corrected within the taxable period.
D. An initial tax of 25% and an additional tax of 100% of the amount involved, if the transaction is not corrected within the taxable period.

The answer is C. An initial 15% tax is applied on the amount involved in a prohibited transaction for each year in a taxable period. If the transaction is not corrected within the taxable period, an additional tax of 100% of the amount involved is imposed. These taxes are payable by any disqualified person who takes part in a prohibited transaction. ###

20. All of the following statements are true regarding defined benefit plans except:

A. Employees receive a fixed payout upon retirement.
B. Generally, employers, not employees, contribute to defined benefit plans.
C. Defined benefit plans can be expensive to administer and have strict reporting requirements.
D. An employee must have worked 500 hours in the prior year to be eligible for the plan.

The answer is D. Under a defined benefit plan, an employee must have worked 1,000 hours in the prior year to be eligible. All of the other statements are correct. ###

21. A 401(k) is a type of _____:

A. SEP-IRA.
B. Government pension plan.
C. Defined contribution plan.
D. Defined benefit plan.

The answer is C. A 401(k) is a very common type of defined contribution plan in which employees contribute to their own accounts, generally on a pretax basis. Earnings grow tax-free until distribution. Employers often supplement or match employee contributions. ###

22. Under the rules for prohibited transactions, all of the following would be considered disqualified persons except:

A. A 5% shareholder of the entity administering the plan.
B. A fiduciary of the plan.
C. An employer whose employees are covered by the plan.
D. A person providing services to the plan.

The answer is A. A 10% or more shareholder of the entity administering the plan would be a disqualified person under the rules for prohibited transactions. ###

23. Channing, age 77, has not taken a required minimum distribution from his qualified retirement plan. What penalty, if any, does he face?

A. Nothing. He is allowed to let the retirement plan funds accumulate so his heirs can inherit the proceeds.

B. A tax of 15% on the amount not withdrawn from the account.

C. A tax of 50% on the amount not withdrawn from the account.

D. A tax of 50% on his balance in the account.

The answer is C. A participant in a qualified retirement plan must begin taking required minimum distributions by April 1 of the first year following the later of:

•The calendar year in which he reaches age 70½, or
•The calendar year in which he retires from employment with the employer maintaining the plan.

The penalty for failing to take an RMD is a tax of 50% on the amount that has not been withdrawn from the account as required. ###

Unit 20: Trusts and Estates

More Reading:

Publication 559, *Survivors, Executors, and Administrators*

Publication 950, *Introduction to Estate and Gift Taxes*

Publication 536, *Net Operating Losses (NOLs) for Individuals, Estates, and Trusts*

Estates and trusts are separate legal entities that are defined by the assets they hold. An estate is created when a taxpayer dies. The estate tax is imposed on certain transfers at death.

A trust is created while the taxpayer is alive or by a taxpayer's last will, and can determine how property will be distributed during his lifetime or at death. A trust can hold title to property for the benefit of one or more persons or entities. Estates and trusts are generally required to obtain an Employer Identification Number (EIN), just like any other legal entity.

Estates in General

For federal tax purposes, an estate is a separate legal entity that is created when a taxpayer dies. The deceased taxpayer's property may consist of items such as cash and securities, real estate, insurance, trusts, annuities, business interests, and other assets. A person who inherits the property from an estate is not taxed on the transfer. Instead, the estate itself is responsible for paying any tax before the property is distributed. However, if the estate's assets are distributed to beneficiaries before applicable taxes are paid, the beneficiaries can be held liable for the tax debt, up to the value of the assets distributed.

Requirements for the Personal Representative

After a person dies, a personal representative, such as an executor named in his will or an administrator appointed by a court, will typically manage the estate and settle the decedent's financial affairs. If there is no executor or administrator, another person with possession of the decedent's property may act as the personal representative.

The personal representative is responsible for filing the final income tax return and the estate tax return, if required.

The personal representative is also responsible for determining any estate tax liability before the estate's assets are distributed to beneficiaries. The tax liability for an estate attaches to the assets of the estate itself, so if the assets are distributed to the beneficiaries before the taxes are paid, the beneficiaries may be held liable for the tax debt, up to the value of the assets distributed.

Either the personal representative or a paid preparer must sign the appropriate line of the return. Current IRS requirements require that the following tax returns be filed:

- The final income tax returns (Form 1040) for the decedent (for income received before death);
- Fiduciary income tax returns (Form 1041) for the estate for the period of its administration; (if necessary) and
- Estate Tax Return (Form 706), if the fair market value of the assets of the estate exceeds the applicable threshold for the year of death.

> **Example:** James was unmarried when he died on April 20, 2012. His only daughter, Lillian, was named as the executor of his estate. James earned wages in 2012 before his death. Therefore, a final tax return is required for 2012. Lillian asks her accountant to help prepare her father's final Form 1040, which will include all the taxable income that James received in 2012 before his death. The accountant also helps Lillian with the valuation of her father's estate. After determining the fair market value of all her father's assets, they conclude that James's gross estate is valued at approximately $7 million. As this exceeds the threshold of $5,120,000 for 2012, an estate tax return (Form 706) is also required to be filed.

The Final Income Tax Return (Form 1040)

The taxpayer's final income tax return is filed on the same form that would have been used if the taxpayer were still alive, but "deceased" is written after the taxpayer's name. The filing deadline is April 15 of the year following the taxpayer's death, just like regular tax returns.

The personal representative must file the final individual income tax return of the decedent for the year of death and any returns not filed for preceding years. If an individual died after the close of the tax year but before the return for that year was filed, the return for that year will not be the final return. The return for that year will be a regular return and the personal representative must file it.

> **Example:** Stephanie dies on March 2, 2013. At the time of her death, she had not yet filed her 2012 tax return. She earned $51,000 in wages in 2012. She also earned $18,000 in wages between January 1, 2013 and her death. Therefore, Stephanie's 2012 and 2013 tax return must be filed by her representative. The 2013 return would be her final individual tax return.

On a decedent's final tax return, the rules for personal exemptions and deductions are the same as for any taxpayer. The full amount of the applicable personal exemption may be claimed on the final tax return, regardless of how long the taxpayer was alive during the year.

Income In Respect of a Decedent

Income in respect of a decedent (IRD) is any taxable income that was earned but *not received* by the decedent by the time of death. IRD is not taxed on the final return of the deceased taxpayer. IRD is reported on the tax return of the person (or entity) that receives the income. This could be the estate, the surviving spouse, or another beneficiary, such as a child. Regardless of the decedent's accounting method, IRD is subject to income tax when the income is received.

IRD retains the same tax nature after death as if the taxpayer were still alive. For example, if the income would have been short-term capital gain to the deceased, it is taxed the same way to the beneficiary. IRD can come from various sources, including:

- Unpaid salary, wages or bonuses
- Distributions from traditional IRAs and employer-provided retirement plans
- Deferred compensation benefits
- Accrued but unpaid interest, dividends, and rent
- Accounts receivable of a sole proprietor

Example: Carlos was owed $15,000 in wages when he died. The check for these wages was not remitted by his employer until three weeks later and was received by his daughter and sole beneficiary, Rosalie. The wages are considered IRD, and Rosalie must recognize the $15,000 as ordinary income, the same tax treatment that would have applied for Carlos.
Example: Beverly died on April 30. At the time of her death, she was owed (but had not yet received) $1,500 in interest on bonds and $2,000 in rental income. Beverly's beneficiary will include $3,500 in IRD in gross income when the interest and rent are received. The income retains its character as passive interest income and passive rental income.

IRD is includible in the decedent's estate and subject to estate tax, and may also be subject to income tax if received by a beneficiary. Therefore, the beneficiary may take a deduction for estate tax paid on the IRD. This deduction is taken as a miscellaneous itemized deduction on Schedule A, and is not subject to the 2% floor, as are most other miscellaneous itemized deductions.

IRS Form 1041, Fiduciary Returns

An estate is a taxable legal entity that exists from the time of an individual's death until all assets have been distributed to the decedent's beneficiaries. Form 1041 is a fiduciary return used to report the following items for a domestic decedent's estate, trust, or bankruptcy estate:

- Current income and deductions, including gains and losses from disposition of the entity's property;
- A deduction for income that is either accumulated or held for future distribution or distributed currently to the beneficiaries; and
- Any income tax liability.

Current income would include IRD, if it was received by the estate rather than specific beneficiaries. As investment assets will usually continue to earn income after a taxpayer has died, this income, such as rents, dividends and interest, must be reported. Expenses of administering the estate can be deducted either from the estate's income on Form 1041 in determining its income tax, or from the gross estate on Form 706 in determining the estate tax liability, but cannot be claimed for both purposes. Schedule K-1 is used to report any income that is distributed to each beneficiary and is filed with Form 1041, with a copy is also given to the beneficiary.

The due date for Form 1041 is the fifteenth day of the fourth month following the end of the entity's tax year, but is subject to an automatic extension of five months if Form 7004 is filed. The tax year may be either a calendar or fiscal year, subject to the election made at the time the first return is filed. An election will also be made on the first return as to method (cash, accrual, or other) to report the estate's income.

Form 1041 must be filed for any domestic estate that has gross income for the tax year of $600 or more, or a beneficiary who is a nonresident alien (with any amount of income).

Gross Estate

The estate tax is a tax on the transfer of property from an individual's estate after his death. It applies to the taxable estate, which is the gross estate less certain deductions. The gross estate is based upon the fair market value of the taxpayer's property, which is not necessarily equal to his cost, and includes:

- The FMV of all tangible and intangible property owned by the decedent at the time of death.
- The full value of property held as joint tenants with the right of survivorship (unless the decedent and spouse were the only joint tenants)
- Life insurance proceeds payable to the estate, or for policies owned by the decedent, payable to the heirs.
- The value of certain annuities or survivor benefits payable to the heirs.
- The value of certain property that was transferred within three years before the decedent's death.

The gross estate does not include property owned solely by the decedent's spouse or other individuals. Lifetime gifts that are complete (so that no control over the gifts was retained) are not included in the gross estate.

Deductions from the Gross Estate

Once the gross estate has been calculated, certain deductions (and in special circumstances, reductions to value) are allowed to determine the taxable estate." Deductions from the gross estate may include:

- Funeral expenses paid out of the estate.
- Administration expenses for the estate, including attorney's fees.
- Debts owed at the time of death.
- The marital deduction (generally, the value of the property that passes from the estate to a surviving spouse).
- The charitable deduction (generally, the value of the property that passes from the estate to qualifying charities).
- The state death tax deduction (generally, any inheritance or estate taxes paid to any state).

The following items are not deductible from the gross estate:

- Federal estate taxes paid.
- Alimony paid after the taxpayer's death. These payments would be treated as distributions to a beneficiary.

Property taxes are deductible only if they accrue under state law prior to the decedent's death.

Marital Deduction

There are special rules and exceptions for transfers between spouses. The marital deduction allows spouses to transfer an unlimited amount of property to one another during their lifetimes or at death without being subject to estate or gift taxes. The marital deduction is a deduction from the "gross estate" in order to arrive at the "taxable estate."

To receive an unlimited deduction, the spouse receiving the assets must be a U.S. citizen, a legal spouse, and have outright ownership of the assets. The unlimited marital deduction is generally not allowed if the transferee spouse is not a U.S. citizen (even if the spouse is a legal resident of the United States). If the receiving spouse is not a citizen, assets transferred are subject to an annual exclusion, which is $139,000 in 2012.

Basis of Estate Property

The basis of property inherited from a decedent is generally one of the following:

- The FMV of the property on the date of death.
- The FMV on an alternate valuation date, if elected by the personal representative.
- The value under a special-use valuation method for real property used in farming or another closely-held business, if elected by the personal representative.
- The decedent's adjusted basis in land to the extent of the value excluded from the taxable estate as a qualified conservation easement.

Property that is jointly owned by a decedent and another person will be included in full in the decedent's gross estate unless it can be shown that the other person originally owned or otherwise contributed to the purchase price. The surviving owner's new basis of property that was jointly owned must be calculated. To do so, the surviving owner's original basis in the property is added to the value of the part of the property included in the decedent's estate. Any deductions for depreciation allowed to the surviving owner on that property are subtracted from the sum.

If property is jointly held between husband and wife as tenants by the entirety or as joint tenants with the right of survivorship (if they were the only joint tenants), one-half of the property's value is included in the gross estate, and there is a step-up in basis for that one-half. If the decedent holds property in a community property state, half of the value of the community property will be included in the gross estate of the decedent, but the entire value of the community property will receive a step-up in basis.

Special Election for Decedent's Medical Expenses

Debts that were not paid before death, including medical expenses subsequently paid on behalf of the decedent, are liabilities of the estate and can be deducted from the gross estate on the estate tax return. However, if medical expenses for the decedent are paid out of the estate during the one-year period beginning with the day after death, the personal representative can alternatively elect to treat all or part of the expenses as paid by the decedent at the time they were incurred, and deduct them on the final tax return (1040) for the decedent.

Estates and Credits

Estates are allowed some of the same tax credits that are allowed to individuals. The credits are generally allocated between the estate and the beneficiaries. However, estates are not allowed the credit for the elderly or the disabled, the child tax credit, or the earned income credit.

Form 706: The Estate Tax Return

An estate tax return is filed using Form 706, *United States Estate (and Generation-Skipping Transfer) Tax Return.* After the taxable estate is computed, the value of lifetime taxable gifts is added to this number and the estate tax is computed. The tax is then reduced by the applicable credit amount. The applicable credit amount, formerly referred to as the unified credit, applies to both the gift tax and the estate tax. It equals the tax on the basic exclusion amount.

- For 2012, the basic exclusion amount is **$5,120,000**.
- The applicable credit amount is **$1,772,800**.

Any portion of the applicable credit amount used against gift tax in a given year reduces the amount of credit that can be used against gift or estate taxes in later years. For estate tax purposes but not for gift taxes, the unified credit amount may also include the tax applicable to the deceased spousal unused exclusion (DSUE). The DSUE is the unused portion of the decedent's predeceased spouse's estate that was not used against gift or estate tax liabilities. The predeceased spouse must have died on or after January 1, 2011 and the DSUE must have been reported on Form 706 filed on behalf of the first spouse's estate.

If required to be filed, the due date for Form 706 is nine months after the decedent's date of death. An automatic six- month extension may be requested by filing Form 4768. However, the tax is due by the due date and interest is accrued on any amounts owed that are not paid at that time.

The assessment period for tax is three years after the due date for a timely filed estate tax return. The assessment period is four years for transfers from an estate.

GST: Generation-Skipping Transfer Tax (Form 709)

The generation skipping transfer tax (GST) may apply to gifts during a taxpayer's life or transfers occurring after his death, called bequests, made to "skip persons." A skip person is a person who belongs to a generation that is two or more generations *below* the generation of the donor. The most common scenario is when a taxpayer makes a bequest to a grandchild.

The GST tax is assessed when a property transfer is made, including instances in which property is transferred from a trust. The GST tax is based on the amounts transferred to skip persons, after subtracting the allocated portions of the GST tax exemption. In 2012, the GST tax exemption is $5,120,000 and the GST tax rate is set at the maximum estate tax rate of 35%. The GST tax is imposed separately and **in addition** to the estate and gift tax.

> **Example:** Patrick sets up a trust that names his adult daughter, Helene, as the sole beneficiary of the trust. In January 2012, Patrick dies, and the trust passes to Helene. However, later in the year, Helene also dies, and now the trust passes to her children (Patrick's grandchildren). Patrick's grandchildren are "skip-persons" for purposes of the GST, and the trust fund property may be subject to the GST.

Any *direct* payments that are made toward tuition or medical expenses are exempt from gift tax or GST tax.

> **Example:** Gordon wants to help support his grandchildren, but he wants to make sure that his gifts are not subject to gift tax, GST tax, or estate tax. So, in 2012, he offers to pay his grandchild's college tuition in full. Gordon writes a check directly to the college in the amount of $25,000. There is no tax consequence for this gift, and no reporting is required.

Trusts in General

A trust is an entity created under the laws of the state in which it is formed. A trust may be created during an individual's life (an inter-vivos trust) or at the time of death under a will (a testamentary trust). The primary benefit of a trust is that it can be created to hold property for the benefit of other persons. A trust may also be created for the benefit of a disabled individual, or can be used to legally avoid certain taxes. The establishment of a trust creates a fiduciary relationship between three parties:

- **The grantor:** The person who contributes property to the trust.
- **The trustee (or fiduciary):** The person or entity charged with the fiduciary duties associated with the trust.
- **The beneficiary:** The person who is designated to receive the trust income or assets.

> **Example:** An elderly individual is having medical problems and decides to put his assets in a trust. He asks his attorney to create the trust and manage the assets. The elderly person then names his grandson as the beneficiary of the trust. In this common scenario, the elderly person is the **grantor**, the lawyer is the **trustee**, and the grandson is the **beneficiary**.

Sometimes, a trust is used to transfer property in a controlled manner. For example, a wealthy parent wishes to transfer ownership of assets to his child, but does not want the child to waste the assets or spend them unwisely. The assets could be transferred to a trust, with the parent as both the grantor and the trustee. The child would be the beneficiary. The parent still has control over the assets, and the child is prevented from using them all up.

The accounting period for a trust is generally the calendar year. The due date for a calendar-year trust is April 15. A trust must file IRS Form 1041, *U.S. Income Tax Return for Estates and Trusts* if it has:

- Any *taxable* income for the year (after subtracting the allowable exemption amount),

- Gross income of $600 or more (regardless of whether the income is taxable), or
- Any beneficiary who is a nonresident alien.

A trust calculates its gross income in a manner similar to an individual taxpayer. Trusts are allowed an exemption, but the amount varies based on the *type* of trust. A trust that must distribute all its income currently (a simple trust) is allowed an exemption of $300. All other trusts are allowed a yearly exemption of $100 per year.

Most deductions and credits allowed to individuals are also allowed to trusts. However, there is one major distinction: a trust is a pass-through entity that is allowed a deduction for its distributions to beneficiaries. The beneficiaries (and not the trust) pay income tax on their distributive share of income. Schedule K-1 (Form 1041) is used to report income that a trust distributes to beneficiaries. The income must then be reported on the beneficiaries' individual income tax returns.

Example: The Smith Family Trust has $400 in tax-exempt interest from municipal bonds during the year. There is no other income. Normally, the trust would not be required to file a tax return because the income earned by the trust is tax-exempt. However, the Smith Family Trust has a beneficiary who is a nonresident alien. Therefore, the trust is required to file a Form 1041.

Distributable Net Income of a Trust (DNI)

Taxable income earned by a trust is taxable to either the trust or the beneficiaries, but not to both. Distributable net income (DNI) is trust income that is currently available for distribution. If the beneficiary receives a distribution in excess of DNI, only the DNI is taxed. The income distribution deduction (IDD) is allowed to trusts (and estates) for amounts that are paid, credited, or required to be distributed to beneficiaries. The income distribution deduction is calculated on Schedule B (Form 1041) and is limited to the lesser of distributions less tax-exempt income or DNI less tax-exempt income.

Simple and Complex Trusts

With regard to income distribution, there are two types of trusts: a simple trust and a complex trust. The Internal Revenue Code defines a simple trust as a trust that:
- Distributes all of its income currently;
- Makes no distributions from principal; and
- Makes no distributions to charity.

Any trust that is not a simple trust is automatically a complex trust. A complex trust:
- Is allowed to accumulate income;
- Can make discretionary distributions of income;
- Can make mandatory (or discretionary) distributions of principal; and
- Can make distributions to charity.

A trust may be a simple trust one year, and a complex trust in another year. For example, if a simple trust fails to distribute all its income in the current year, it becomes a complex trust.

Trust Types (Grantor, Irrevocable, Tax shelters)

Grantor Trusts

A grantor trust is a valid legal entity under state law, but it is not recognized as a separate entity for income tax purposes.

The grantor (also known as trustor, settlor, or creator) creates the trust relationship and retains control over the trust. In the eyes of the IRS, the grantor is considered the owner of the trust for income tax purposes. The grantor establishes the terms and provisions of the trust relationship between the grantor, the trustee, and the beneficiary. These will usually include the following:

- The rights, duties, and powers of the trustee;
- Distribution provisions;
- Ability of the grantor to amend, modify, revoke, or terminate the trust agreement;
- The designation of a trustee or successor trustees; and
- The designation of the state under which the trust agreement is to be governed.

> **Example:** The John Doe Trust is a grantor trust. John Doe is the grantor. During the year, the trust sold 100 shares of ABC stock for $1,010 in which it had a basis of $10 and 200 shares of XYZ stock for $10 in which it had a $1,020 basis. The trust does not report these transactions on Form 1041. Instead, a schedule is attached to Form 1041 showing each stock transaction separately and in the same detail as John Doe (grantor and owner) will need to report these transactions on his Schedule D (Form 1040). The trust may not net the capital gains and losses; nor may it issue John Doe a Schedule K-1 (Form 1041) showing a $10 long-term capital loss.

Revocable Trust

A revocable trust is a trust in which the grantor retains the right to end the trust. The trust assets are subject to estate tax upon the grantor's death. A revocable trust is treated as a grantor trust for income tax purposes. This type of trust is generally created only to manage and distribute property. Many taxpayers use this type of trust instead of a will.

Revocable Living Trust

A revocable living trust is an arrangement created during the life of an individual and can be changed or ended at any time during the individual's life. A revocable living trust is generally created to manage and distribute property. Many people use this type of trust instead of, or in addition to, a will. Because this type of trust is revocable, it is treated as a grantor type trust for tax purposes.

Non-Grantor Trusts

A non-grantor trust is any trust that is not a grantor trust. A non-grantor trust is considered a separate legal entity from the individual or organization that created it. The trust's income and deductions are reported on Form 1041. If a non-grantor trust makes distributions to a beneficiary, in general those distributions carry any taxable income to the beneficiary.

1. **Irrevocable Trusts**: An irrevocable trust is a trust that cannot be revoked after it is created. The transfer of assets into this type of trust is generally considered a "completed gift" subject to gift tax.

2. **Disability Trust:** A qualified disability trust is a non-grantor trust created solely for the benefit of a disabled individual under age 65. In 2012, a qualified disability trust can claim an exemption of up to $3,800. This is a specific exception to the regular exemption of $600 for trusts.

3. **Charitable Trusts:** A charitable trust is a trust devoted to qualified charitable contribution purposes. Charitable trusts are irrevocable.

> **Example:** Hugo creates a charitable trust whose governing instrument provides that the Catholic Church (a qualified religious organization), and the SPCA (a 501(c)(3) charity) are each to receive 50% of the trust income for 10 years. At the end of the 10-year period, the corpus will be distributed to the Red Cross, also a 501(c)(3) organization. Hugo is allowed an income tax deduction for the value of all interests placed in trust.

Abusive Trust Arrangements

Certain trust arrangements purport to reduce or eliminate federal taxes in ways that are not permitted under the law. These are called abuse trusts. Abusive trust arrangements may use trusts to hide the true ownership of assets and income or to disguise the substance of transactions. These arrangements frequently involve more than one trust, each holding different assets of the taxpayer (for example, the taxpayer's business, business equipment, home, automobile, etc.) Some trusts may hold interests in other trusts, purport to involve charities, or be foreign trusts.

When trusts are used for legitimate business, family, or estate planning purposes, either the trust, the beneficiary, or the transferor to the trust will pay the tax on the income generated by the trust. Trusts cannot be used to transform a taxpayer's personal, living, or educational expenses into deductible items. A taxpayer cannot use a trust to avoid tax liability by ignoring either the true ownership of income and assets or the true substance of transactions. Participants and promoters of abusive trust schemes may be subject to civil or criminal penalties.

Termination of Trusts and Estates

Trusts and estates generally terminate when all of the assets and income have been distributed, and all of the liabilities have been paid. If a trust or estate's existence is unnecessarily prolonged, the IRS can step in and terminate it after a reasonable period for completing the final administration.

If an estate or trust has a loss in its final year, the loss can be passed through to the beneficiaries, allowing them a deduction on their returns. Losses cannot be passed through to beneficiaries in a non-termination year.

Unit 20: Questions

1. What is included in the gross estate?

A. The gross estate of the decedent includes everything the taxpayer owns at the date of death.
B. The gross estate of the decedent includes everything the taxpayer owns six months after the date of death.
C. The gross estate of the decedent includes everything the taxpayer owns at the date of death, including income that the taxpayer was owed but had not yet received.
D. The gross estate includes everything the decedent earned in the prior year, as well as income estimates for future years.

The answer is A. The gross estate of the decedent includes everything the taxpayer owns at the date of death. ###

2. The calculation of the gross estate includes all of the following except:

A. Life insurance proceeds payable to the decedent's heirs.
B. The value of certain annuities payable to the estate.
C. Property owned solely by the decedent's spouse.
D. The value of certain property transferred within three years before the taxpayer's death.

The answer is C. The gross estate does not include property owned solely by the decedent's spouse or other individuals. ###

3. What is the due date for Form 706 for a decedent who died in 2012?

A. April 15, 2013.
B. Nine months after the date of death.
C. Twelve months after the date of death.
D. Six months after the date of death

The answer is B. The estate tax return is generally due nine months after the date of death. ###

4. The Franklin Trust is required to distribute all its income currently. What is the yearly exemption amount for the Franklin Trust?

A. $0.
B. $100.
C. $300.
D. $600.

The answer is C. A trust that distributes all its income currently is allowed an exemption of $300. All other trusts are allowed an exemption of $100 per year. ###

5. All of the following are characteristics of a simple trust except:

A. The trust may distribute assets to charity.
B. The trust distributes all its income currently.
C. The trust makes no distributions from principal.
D. The trust makes no distributions to charity.

The answer is A. The Internal Revenue Code defines a simple trust as one that distributes all its income currently, makes no distributions from principal, and makes no distributions to charity. Any trust that is not a simple trust is automatically a complex trust. ###

6. All of the following are required to file Form 1041 except:

A. An estate with gross income of $600.
B. An estate with $700 in exempt income.
C. An estate with $200 in gross income and a beneficiary who is a nonresident alien.
D. An estate with $500 in gross income and a beneficiary who is a resident alien.

The answer is D. An estate with $500 in income and a beneficiary who is a resident alien is not required to file a tax return. Resident aliens (green card holders) are taxed the same way as citizens. An estate with a nonresident alien beneficiary would be required to file Form 1041, regardless of the amount of income earned. ###

7. What is the basic exclusion amount for an estate of an individual who dies in 2012?

A. $1 million.
B. $5 million.
C. $5,120,000.
D. $5,250,000.

The answer is C. For the estate of any decedent during calendar year 2012, the basic exclusion from estate tax amount is $5,120,000. ###

8. What is the amount of the applicable credit in 2012?

A. $100.
B. $600.
C. $1 million.
D. $1,772,800.

The answer is D. The applicable credit amount in 2012 is $1,772,800. A taxpayer must subtract the applicable credit amount from any gift or estate tax he owes. Any applicable credit used against gift tax in one year reduces the amount of credit he can use against gift or estate taxes in a later year. ###

9. What is the maximum estate tax rate for 2012?

A. 10%.
B. 25%.
C. 35%.
D. There is no estate tax in 2012.

The answer is C. The maximum estate and gift tax rate for 2012 is 35%. ###

10. Carlton's will provides that each of his ten grandchildren would receive $1 million. Assuming that none of his GST exemption amount has previously been used in connection with gifts to the grandchildren or other skip persons, what portion of the total amount distributed to the grandchildren after his death in 2012 would be subject to GST?

A. $8,700,000.
B. $5,120,000.
C. $10,000,000.
D. $4,880,000.

The answer is D. The aggregate portion of his estate distributed to his grandchildren ($10 million) would be reduced by his exclusion amount for GST ($5,120,000) and the remainder of $4,880,000 would be subject to GST. ###

11. Parker, a single taxpayer, died on March 3, 2012. Based on the following information, determine the value of his gross estate:

FMV on date of death	
Life insurance on Parker's life (payable to his estate)	$250,000
Parker's revocable grantor trust	$700,000
Liabilities owed by Parker when he died	$ 150,000

A. $250,000.
B. $800,000.
C. $950,000.
D. $1.1 million.

The answer is C. Life insurance payable to a trust and assets held in a grantor trust are included in a decedent's gross estate. Liabilities of the decedent are not included in the gross estate. However, they are an allowable deduction from the gross estate in determining the taxable estate. ###

12. Bianca, who is married, gave a vase worth $40,000 to her brother. Bianca's basis in the vase is $10,000. What amount will she report as the value of the gift on Form 709?

A. $10,000.
B. $20,000.
C. $30,000.
D. $40,000.

The answer is D. Generally, the value of a gift is its fair market value on the date of the gift. In this case, the value of $40,000 exceeds the annual exclusion amount of $13,000 for 2012. Even if Bianca and her husband took advantage of the gift-splitting option for purposes of the gift to her brother, the value would exceed their combined exclusion amount of $26,000, and would need to be reported on Form 709. ###

13. Luis died in March 2012. At the time of his death and when his estate was being settled, none of his basic exclusion amount was used to reduce or eliminate payment of gift or estate taxes. Form 706 was filed in October 2012, and the full amount of deceased spousal unused exclusion (DSUE) was reported thereon. His wife Jenna died in December 2012. As was the case with Luis, none of her basic exclusion amount had been used previously to offset gift taxes that would otherwise have been payable. What amount must Jenna's taxable estate exceed in order to be subject to estate tax?

A. $5,120,000.
B. $1,772,800.
C. $5,000,000.
D. $10,240,000.

The answer is D. When Luis died in 2012, his estate qualified for the full basic exclusion amount of $5,120,000. As a result of having reported the DSUE when Form 706 was filed for his estate, the amount of the DSUE is available in addition to Jenna's basic exclusion amount of $5,120,000. Therefore, the amount of her taxable estate would have to exceed $10,240,000 in order to be subject to estate tax. ###

14. Georgiana died on March 1, 2012. The executor of her estate has elected to file the estate's income tax return on a calendar-year basis. No distributions have been made by the estate. Based on the following, what is the taxable income (Form 1041) of the estate for the December 31, 2012 year-end before consideration of the estate's exemption amount?

•Taxable interest	$2,000
•Tax-exempt interest	$1,000
•Capital gain	$3,000
•Executor's fees	$300

A. $5,700.
B. $4,700.
C. $5,100.
D. $6,000.

The answer is B. Taxable income of $4,700 can be reported for the estate, determined as follows: Taxable interest of $2,000 plus capital gain of $3,000, less executor's fees of $300. The expenses of administering an estate can be deducted either from the estate's income on Form 1041 in determining its income tax or from the gross estate on Form 706 in determining the estate tax liability, but cannot be claimed for both purposes. The tax-exempt interest retains the character that would have applied if it had been reported by the decedent. The estate would be eligible for an exemption amount of $600 in determining its actual taxable income. ###

15. Roberto died on May 3, 2012. The estate's tax year ends on December 31, 2012. The estate had the following items of income during the year:

•Interest $250
•Dividends $150
•Stock-sale proceeds, net of broker's commission $10,000
•Basis of the stock $9,900

The estate made no distributions during 2012. Based upon the information provided, which of the following statements is true?

A. The estate is not required to file an income tax return.
B. The estate is required to file an income tax return.
C. The estate is required to file a return on Form 706.
D. Both B and C.

The answer is A. An income tax return (Form 1041) must be filed for any domestic estate that has gross income for the tax year of $600 or more, or a beneficiary who is a nonresident alien (with any amount of income). Roberto's estate has gross income of $500 ($250 + $150 + $100 gain from stock sale). Since the gross income is below the $600 exemption amount, an income tax return is not required to be filed for 2012. There is insufficient information to determine whether an estate tax return (Form 706) will need to be filed. ###

16. Shane, who had not given taxable gifts in any prior year, gave his five children the following gifts in 2012:

•Car to Pat $14,000
•Cash to Lizzie $12,000
•Stock to Adam $10,500
•Stock to Ben $9,500
•Cash to Kris $5,000

From the information above, determine the amount, if any, of taxable gifts given by Shane.

A. $0.
B. $1,000.
C. $6,500.
D. $41,000.

The answer is B. Only one of the children, Pat, received a gift in excess of the exemption amount of $13,000. The excess portion of $1,000 would be considered a taxable gift for purposes of filing a gift tax return. However, Shane can use a portion of his basic exclusion amount to avoid payment of gift tax in 2012. ###

Part 3: Representation

Tammy the Tax Lady ®

It's just easier this way... he's always in my pocket anyway!

Unit 1: Rules Governing Authority to Practice

> **More Reading:**
> Circular 230, *Regulations Governing the Practice of Attorneys, Certified Public Accountants, Enrolled Agents, Enrolled Actuaries, Enrolled Retirement Plan Agents, and Appraisers Before the Internal Revenue Service*
> Publication 947, *Practice Before the IRS and Power of Attorney*
> Publication 470, *Limited Practice Without Enrollment*

Overview of Part 3: Representation, Practice, and Procedures

Part 3 of the EA exam concerns the ethics and laws that regulate the tax profession: who is allowed to prepare taxes for compensation; who may represent taxpayers in appeals hearings before the IRS; what standards the tax profession is held to; what IRS procedures must be followed when it comes to assessing and collecting taxes; what rules guide the IRS in conducting audits; and what penalties tax preparers who violate the law face.

These issues and more are dealt with in detail in Treasury Department Circular No. 230,[137] which underwent a sweeping revision in 2011. The update of Circular 230 is part of a series of steps designed to increase oversight of federal tax return preparation. All enrolled practitioners[138] who represent taxpayers before the IRS are subject to the rules and regulations set forth in Circular 230.

"Practice before the IRS"

"Practice before the IRS" includes all matters connected with a presentation before the IRS, or any issues relating to a client's rights, privileges, or liabilities under laws or regulations administered by the IRS. "Practice before the IRS" is currently defined as:

- Communicating with the IRS on behalf of a taxpayer regarding his rights, privileges, or liabilities under laws and regulations administered by the IRS
- Representing a taxpayer at conferences, hearings, or meetings with the IRS
- Preparing and filing documents, including tax returns, for the IRS
- Corresponding and communicating with the IRS for a taxpayer
- Providing a client with written advice that has a potential for tax avoidance or evasion

> **Example:** Trina is a CPA. Her client, Samuel, has a large tax debt. Samuel does not wish to communicate directly with the IRS, but he wants to set up an installment agreement. Trina has Samuel sign Form 2848 giving her power of attorney and then she calls the IRS on his behalf and sets up the installment agreement for him. This action is considered "Practice before the IRS."

---

[137] Regulations governing practice are set forth in Title 31, Code of Federal Regulations, Subtitle A, Part 10, and are published in pamphlet form as Treasury Department Circular No. 230 on June 3, 2011.
[138] An "enrolled practitioner" is simply a tax professional who is allowed to represent taxpayers before the IRS. Usually, this is an EA, CPA, or attorney. See the following section for a detailed explanation of enrolled practitioners and some narrow exceptions to this rule.

U.S. citizenship is not required to practice before the IRS, and, in fact, many EAs, CPAs and attorneys work abroad helping expatriate taxpayers with their U.S. tax returns while they are living overseas.

Actions That Are Not "Practice Before the IRS"

"Practice before the IRS" does NOT include:

- Representation of taxpayers before the U.S. Tax Court. The Tax Court has its own rules of practice and its own rules regarding admission to practice.
- Merely appearing as a witness for the taxpayer is not practice before the IRS. In general, individuals who are not "enrolled practitioners" may appear before the IRS as witnesses—but they *may not advocate* for the taxpayer.

Enrolled Practitioners (§10.3 Who May Practice Before the IRS)

The following individuals who are not currently under suspension or disbarment may represent taxpayers before the IRS by virtue of their licensing. There are also some other individuals who may practice before the IRS because of a "special relationship" with the taxpayer, explained later in this unit.

Attorneys

Any attorney who is a member in good standing of the bar may practice before the IRS in all fifty states. A *student attorney* may also practice before the IRS by virtue of his status as a law student under Section 10.7(d) of Circular 230.

Certified Public Accountants (CPAs)

Any CPA who is duly qualified may practice before the IRS in all fifty states. A *student CPA candidate* may also practice before the IRS by virtue of his status as a CPA student under Section 10.7(d) of Circular 230.

Enrolled Agents (EAs)

Any enrolled agent in active status may practice before the IRS. An EA is a person who has earned the privilege of representing taxpayers before the IRS in all fifty states. Like attorneys and CPAs, EAs are unrestricted as to which taxpayers they can represent, what types of tax matters they can handle, and which IRS offices they can represent clients before. EAs are allowed to represent taxpayers in the U.S. Tax Court only if they have passed the U.S. Tax Court exam.

Enrolled Actuaries (Limited Practice)

Any individual who is enrolled as an actuary by the Joint Board for the Enrollment of Actuaries may practice before the IRS. The practice of enrolled actuaries is limited to certain Internal Revenue Code sections that relate to their area of expertise, principally those sections governing employee retirement plans.

Enrolled Retirement Plan Agents (Limited Practice)

Similar to an EA, an enrolled retirement plan agent (ERPA) is allowed to practice before the IRS. However, an ERPA's practice is limited to certain Internal Revenue Code sections that relate to their area of expertise, principally those sections governing employee retirement plans.

Registered Tax Return Preparers (DESIGNATION UNDER SUSPENSION)

Under the terms of Circular 230, any individual *other than* an attorney, CPA, enrolled agent, enrolled actuary, or ERPA who prepares a tax return and signs it as a paid preparer must be a registered tax return preparer (RTRP).[139] This provision was part of the major changes made to Circular 230 in 2011. The IRS wanted anyone who prepared tax returns for compensation to pass an IRS competency test and be subject to annual continuing education requirements.

However, under the terms of a district court ruling in January 2013,[140] the IRS is blocked from enforcing the regulatory requirements for registered tax return preparers. The court found that the IRS "lacks statutory authority to promulgate or enforce the new regulatory scheme for 'registered tax return preparers' brought under Circular 230."

The court ruling means that the new RTRP designation is currently under suspension. The RTRP regulations had been expected to affect many thousands of tax practitioners who prepare tax returns for a fee, without any professional certification, testing, or continuing education requirements. The IRS has announced it plans to appeal the district court's ruling. In the meantime, as of publication, the RTRP competency test is not being offered for 2013. It is unclear whether the IRS will choose to, or be allowed to, offer the test on a voluntary basis only, or whether Congress will step in and grant the IRS broader authority to regulate tax preparers.

Volunteer Students at Tax Clinics

Students volunteering in a Low Income Taxpayer Clinic (LITC) or a Student Tax Clinic Program (STCP) may represent taxpayers before the IRS. A taxpayer also may authorize a volunteer with VITA, Volunteer Income Tax Assistance, to represent him before the IRS. Under VITA, volunteer tax preparers offer free tax help to taxpayers who make $51,000 or less and need help preparing their own tax returns.

Practice During Special Circumstances (§ 10.7 limited practice)

There are some exceptions to the general rule regarding enrolled practitioners (CPAs, EAs, and attorneys). Because of a "special relationship" with the taxpayer, certain individuals may represent some taxpayers before the IRS.

This "limited practice" rule usually applies to representatives for a business entity, such as an officer of a corporation. However, a family member may also "practice" before the IRS on behalf of another family member.

An individual (self-representation): Any individual may always represent *himself* before the IRS, provided he has appropriate identification (such as a driver's license or a passport). Even a disbarred individual may represent himself before the IRS.[141]

Example #1: Gary was a tax attorney who was disbarred because of a felony conviction in 2011. An individual who is disbarred is not eligible to represent taxpayers before the IRS. Gary was audited by the IRS in 2012. Despite being disbarred, Gary may still represent *himself* before the IRS during the examination of his own return.

---

[139] Circular 230 §10.4(c).
[140] *Loving,* No. 12-385, U.S. District Court for the District of Columbia, 1/18/2013.
[141] See § 10.7(a), Circular 230.

A family member: An individual family member may represent members of his immediate family. Family members include a spouse, child, parent, brother, or sister of the individual.

> **Example #2:** Emily is an accounting student who is not an enrolled practitioner. The IRS is auditing her brother. Emily is allowed to represent her brother before the IRS, meaning she can "practice before the IRS" in this limited circumstance. Because of the family relationship, Emily's brother is not required to be present during the examination (Circular 230 Section 10.7(c)(1)).

> **Example #3:** Jim's mother is being audited by the IRS. Even though Jim is not enrolled to practice before the IRS, he is allowed to represent his mother because of the family relationship.

An officer: A bona fide officer of a corporation (including parents, subsidiaries, or affiliated corporations) may represent the organization he is an officer of before the IRS.

A partner: A general partner may represent the partnership before the IRS. *Limited partners* in a partnership are considered merely investors and may not represent a partnership before the IRS.

An employee: A regular full-time employee can represent his employer. An employer can be an individual, partnership, corporation (including parents, subsidiaries, or affiliated corporations), association, trust, receivership, guardianship, estate, organized group, governmental unit, agency, or authority.

> **Example #4:** Angelique is a full-time bookkeeper for her employer. She is not an enrolled preparer. During the year, the IRS sent her employer a notice regarding some unfiled payroll tax returns. Angelique may file a Form 2848 and speak with the IRS on her employer's behalf because of the employee-employer relationship.

A fiduciary: A trustee, receiver, guardian, personal representative, administrator, or executor can represent the trust, receivership, guardianship, or estate. In the eyes of the IRS, a fiduciary is considered to be the taxpayer and not a representative of the taxpayer.

> **Example #5:** Tony was named the executor of his mother's estate after she passed away. He is not an enrolled preparer, but he is allowed to represent his mother's estate before the IRS. Tony is considered the *fiduciary* for the estate.

Authorization for Special Appearances: Only in very rare and compelling circumstances will the Commissioner of the IRS or a delegate authorize a person who is not otherwise eligible to practice before the IRS to represent another person for a particular matter.

Return Preparer Office (RPO)

To better regulate preparers, the IRS has created a new department called the Return Preparer Office (RPO). The RPO has oversight for all matters related to the authority to practice before the IRS, including:

- Taking action on registration applications for enrollment and renewal; administering competency testing; approving continuing education (CE) providers and accrediting organizations; and ensuring that CE requirements are met by practitioners or those seeking practitioner status.

- Making preliminary determinations regarding denial or termination of practitioner registration or enrollment; making preliminary determinations with respect to revocation of status for CE providers and accrediting organizations.
- Receiving and processing complaints regarding alleged preparer or practitioner misconduct; initiating preliminary investigations, including data gathering and referring complaints to the Office of Professional Responsibility, the Treasury Inspector General for Tax Administration, or the Criminal Investigation Division for further action.

The Office of Professional Responsibility (OPR) used to handle many of the functions that have been delegated to the RPO. The OPR is now primarily concerned with initiating disciplinary proceedings and determining sanctions related to practitioner misconduct.

Mandatory Tax Preparer Registration

Under the revised regulations of Circular 230, the IRS now requires the following:
- All paid tax return preparers must register with the IRS and obtain a Preparer Tax Identification Number (PTIN).
- Tax preparers who register will be subject to a limited tax compliance check to make sure that they have filed their own personal and business tax returns.

In addition, the IRS plans to require that all tax return preparers be subject to verification of personal and business tax compliance every three years.[142] These requirements only apply to tax preparers who prepare returns for compensation.

Exception for Supervised Preparers

Supervised preparers are individuals who do not sign tax returns as paid return preparers but are:
- Employed by a law firm, EA office, or CPA practice, and
- Are directly *supervised* by an attorney, CPA, EA, ERPA, or enrolled actuary who signs the returns prepared by the supervised preparer as the paid tax return preparer.

Supervised preparers may NOT:
- Sign any tax return they prepare or assist in preparing
- Represent taxpayers before the IRS in any capacity
- Identify themselves as a Circular 230 practitioner

When applying for or renewing a PTIN, supervised preparers must provide the PTIN of their supervisor.

Exception for Non-Form 1040 Series Preparers

Non-Form 1040 series preparers are individuals who do not prepare or assist in the preparation of any Form 1040 series tax return or claim for refund, except a Form 1040-PR or Form 1040-SS, for compensation. Both these forms are only for residents of Puerto Rico. Non-Form 1040 series preparers may sign tax returns they prepare or assist in preparing. They may also represent taxpayers before revenue agents, customer service

---

[142]IR-2010-1, Jan. 4, 2010.

representatives or similar officers and employees of the IRS during an examination, only if they signed the tax return that is being audited.

Mandatory IRS PTIN Requirement

In 2011, use of the PTIN became *mandatory* on all federal tax returns and claims for refund prepared by a paid tax preparer.[143] The PTIN is a nine-digit number that preparers must use when they prepare and sign a tax return or claim for refund. Previously, PTIN use was *optional* in place of the preparer's Social Security Number.

Multiple individuals cannot share one PTIN. A PTIN is assigned to a single preparer to identify that he or she is the preparer of a particular return.

Any preparer who is compensated for the preparation of (or *assists* in the preparation of) a tax return must apply for a PTIN. This includes attorneys, CPAs,[144] and EAs. Failure to obtain a PTIN could result in the imposition of Internal Revenue Code Section §6695 monetary penalties, injunction, and/or disciplinary action.

All tax preparers with existing PTINs are required to renew their PTINs online each year and pay a fee to do so. Preparers who fail to list a valid PTIN on tax returns they sign are subject to penalties of $50 per return, up to a maximum of $25,000 a year.

Persons Who Are Not Considered "Tax Preparers"

If there is no prior agreement for compensation, an individual who prepares a tax return is not considered an "income tax preparer" for IRS purposes. This is true even if the individual receives a gift or a favor in return. The agreement for compensation is the deciding factor as to whether or not a person is considered a "tax preparer" for IRS purposes.

Example: Terri is a retired CPA who only prepares tax returns for her close family members. She does not charge her family to prepare their tax returns. Sometimes, a family member will give Terri a gift in return. This year, she received home-baked cookies from her sister and a sweater from her niece. However, Terri does not ask for any gifts or expect them. She is not a "tax return preparer" for IRS purposes, and she is not required to obtain a PTIN.
Example: Bob is a retired tax professional. He does not have a PTIN. Bob volunteers during the tax filing season at a VITA site, where he prepares individual tax returns for lower-income individuals for free. Bob is not a "tax return preparer" and he is not required to have a PTIN.

An individual will not be considered an income "tax return preparer" in the following instances:

- A person who merely gives an opinion about events that have not happened (such as tax advice for a business that has not been created).
- A person who merely furnishes typing, reproducing, or mechanical assistance.

---

[143] On February 1, 2013, the U.S. District Court for the District of Columbia modified its earlier court order to clarify that the injunction against registered tax return preparers does not affect the requirement for paid preparers to obtain PTINs. To comply with the earlier order of January 18, 2013, the IRS had suspended PTIN applications and renewals. It reactivated the system after the February 1 ruling.

[144] Under the authority of Section 1.6109-2(h), attorneys and CPAs do not need to obtain a PTIN **unless** they prepare federal tax returns. All EAs are required to obtain PTINs.

- A person who merely prepares a return of his employer (or of an officer or employee of the employer) by whom the person is regularly and continuously employed.
- Any fiduciary who prepares a tax return for a trust or estate.[145]
- An unpaid volunteer who provides tax assistance under a VITA program.
- An unpaid volunteer who provides tax assistance in the Tax Counseling for the Elderly program.
- Any employee of the IRS who is performing official duties by preparing a tax return for a taxpayer who requests it.

> **Example:** Thomas is a CPA. His neighbor, Ross, consults with Thomas about a business he is thinking about starting. Thomas gives Ross an opinion regarding the potential business and taxes. In this case, Thomas is not considered a "tax preparer" for the purpose of IRS preparer penalties. This is because Thomas is merely giving an opinion about events that have not happened yet.

> **Example:** Ginny is a bookkeeper for Creative Candies Corporation. She is a full-time employee, and she prepares the payroll checks and payroll tax returns for all of the employees of Creative Candies. As a full-time employee, Ginny is not considered a "tax preparer" for the purpose of IRS regulations. Her employer is ultimately responsible for the accuracy of the payroll tax returns.

> **Example:** Francisco is an EA who has a PTIN. He employs an administrative assistant, Claudia, who performs data entry during tax filing season. At times, clients call and provide Claudia with information, which she records in the system. Using the data she has entered, Francisco meets with his clients and provides tax advice as needed. He then prepares and signs their returns. Claudia is not a "tax return preparer" and is not required to have a PTIN.

Preparation of tax returns outside the U.S. is included in these rules. Tax preparers who work on U.S. tax returns overseas are still subject to Circular 230 regulations.

Employer of Tax Preparers

A tax preparer may employ other preparers. For example, if an enrolled agent owns a franchise that employs ten tax preparers, he or she, as the owner of the business, is the one who is primarily liable for any preparer penalties.

Any person who employs tax return preparers is required to retain records detailing the name, identifying number, and principal place of work of each income tax return preparer employed. The records of the income tax preparers must be made available upon request to the IRS. They must be retained and kept available for inspection for at least three years following the close of period for each tax return. The "return period" means the 12-month period beginning July 1 each year.

The "Substantial Portion" Rule

Only the person who prepares all or a substantial portion of a tax return shall be considered the "preparer" of the return. A person who merely gives advice on a portion or a single entry on the tax return is considered to have prepared only that portion. If more than

---

[145]Fiduciaries, as detailed by Section 7701(a)(36)(B)(iii) of the Internal Revenue Code, who file returns are not considered "tax return preparers" and are also not subject to the e-file mandate.

one individual is involved in the preparation of a tax return, the preparer is the person with the primary responsibility for the overall accuracy of the return and must sign the return.

In order to identify who is responsible for a "substantial portion" of the return, the following guidelines may be used. A portion of a tax return is not typically considered to be "substantial" if it involves only minor dollar amounts of:

- Less than $2,000, or
- Less than 20% of the adjusted gross income on the return.

Usually, a single schedule would not be considered a "substantial portion" of a tax return, unless it represents a major portion of the income.

Example: Greg and Eli are partners in a tax practice. In March, Eli finishes a few returns that Greg had started before he left on vacation. Later, one tax return comes up for audit, and it is determined that the return has a gross misstatement. Greg prepared Schedule C on the return, and Eli prepared the rest of the return. Schedule C represents 95% of the income and expenses shown on the return. Therefore, for the purpose of any potential penalty, Greg is considered the "preparer" of this return, since he prepared the schedule that represents the majority of the income and expenses on the return.

Forms Used For Representation

There are three forms that are used for representation. The first is Form 2848, *Power of Attorney and Declaration of Representative*, which authorizes an individual to represent a taxpayer before the IRS. The individual authorized must be a person eligible to "practice before the IRS."

The next is Form 8821, *Tax Information Authorization*, which authorizes any individual, corporation, firm, organization or partnership to receive confidential information for the type of tax and the years or periods listed on the form.

The last is Form 56, *Notice Concerning Fiduciary Relationship*, to notify the IRS of the existence of a fiduciary relationship. A fiduciary (trustee, executor, administrator, receiver, or guardian) stands in the position of a taxpayer and technically acts as the taxpayer, not as a representative. Because the fiduciary stands in the position of the entity, the fiduciary signs the Form 56 on behalf of the entity.

IRS Power of Attorney and Disclosure Authorization

When a taxpayer wishes to use a representative, he must fill out and sign Form 2848, *Power of Attorney and Declaration of Representative.* This form authorizes another person to represent a taxpayer before the IRS. The representative must be eligible to practice before the IRS in order to complete Form 2848. If a tax professional is disbarred or suspended, his power of attorney will not be recognized by the IRS.

Only "natural persons" may practice before the IRS, which means that an entity such as a corporation or partnership is not eligible. Any person representing a taxpayer must be qualified, and the duty may not be delegated to an employee. An EA who fills out Form 2848 on behalf of a client must list his own name as the representative, rather than the name of his business.

> **Example #1:** Caitlyn is an EA who operates Caitlyn Rivera's Accounting Corporation. When she prepares Form 2848 for a taxpayer, she must represent her client as an individual. Caitlyn is granted permission to represent her client, but her corporation is not.

A qualified representative can represent a taxpayer before the IRS *without* the taxpayer present, so long as the proper power of attorney is signed and submitted to the IRS. Any **authorized** representative can usually perform the following acts:

- Represent a taxpayer before any office of the IRS
- Record an interview or meeting with the IRS
- Sign an offer or a waiver of restriction on assessment or collection of a tax deficiency, or a waiver of notice of disallowance of claim for credit or refund
- Sign consents to extend the statutory time period for assessment or collection of a tax
- Sign a closing agreement
- Receive (but **never** endorse or cash) a tax refund check

A signed IRS Form 2848, *Power of Attorney and Declaration of Representative* (or other acceptable power of attorney, such as a durable power of attorney) is required in order for a tax professional to represent a taxpayer before the IRS.[146]

Form 2848 is used by:

- CPAs, enrolled agents, enrolled actuaries, and attorneys
- Other individuals, if specifically permitted, in limited circumstances (such as a family member representing a taxpayer, or an executor representing an estate)

A power of attorney is valid until revoked. It may be revoked by the taxpayer or revoked by the representative. A revocation statement must be submitted to the IRS in writing and must contain the taxpayer's identifying information, the representative's identifying information, and the specific tax and tax periods covered by the revocation. The statement should be signed and dated by the party desiring the revocation.

> **Example:** Nicola is an EA. She had a power of attorney on file for her former client, Edwin. Nicola fired Edwin for nonpayment, but she continued to receive IRS notices on his behalf. Nicola prepares a revocation statement and submits it to the IRS, notifying the IRS that she no longer represents Edwin.

A power of attorney is generally terminated if the taxpayer becomes incapacitated or incompetent. A power of attorney is automatically rescinded when a newer power of attorney is filed, *unless* the taxpayer *specifically requests* that the old power of attorney remain active.

A newly filed power of attorney concerning the same matter will revoke a previously filed power of attorney. For example, if a taxpayer changes preparers and the second preparer files a power of attorney on behalf of the taxpayer, the old power of attorney on file will be rescinded.

---

[146] A signed Form 2848 is not required when a taxpayer is deceased and is being represented by a fiduciary or executor.

Non-IRS Powers of Attorney (Durable Power of Attorney)

The IRS will accept a non-IRS power of attorney (such as a durable power of attorney[147]), but it must contain all of the information present on a standard IRS Form 2848. If a practitioner wants to use a different power of attorney document other than Form 2848, it must contain the following information:

- The taxpayer's name, mailing address, and Social Security Number.
- The name and mailing address of the representative.
- The types of tax involved and the tax form number in question.
- The specific periods or tax years involved.
- For estate tax matters, the decedent's date of death.
- A clear expression of the taxpayer's intention concerning the scope of authority granted to the representative.
- The taxpayer's signature and date. The taxpayer must also attach to the non-IRS power of attorney a signed and dated statement made by the representative.

Example: Ronald signs a durable power of attorney that names his neighbor, Erik, as his attorney-in-fact.[148] The durable power of attorney grants Erik the authority to perform all acts on Ronald's behalf. However, it does not list specific tax-related information such as types of tax or tax form numbers. Shortly after Ronald signs the power of attorney, he is declared incompetent. Later, a tax matter arises concerning a prior year return filed by Ronald. Erik attempts to represent Ronald before the IRS, but is rejected because the durable power of attorney does not contain required information. If Erik attaches a statement (signed under the penalty of perjury) that the durable power of attorney is valid under the laws of the governing jurisdiction, he can sign a completed Form 2848 and submit it on Ronald's behalf. If Erik can practice before the IRS, he can name himself as the representative on Form 2848.

IRS Form 8821, Disclosure Authorization

Form 8821, *Tax Information Authorization* (TIA), authorizes any individual, corporation, firm, organization, or partnership to receive confidential information for the type of tax and periods listed on Form 8821. Any third party may be designated to receive tax information.

IRS Form 8821 is used by tax preparers, banks, employers, and other institutions to receive financial information on behalf of an individual or a business.

Form 8821 is only a disclosure form, so it will not give an individual any power to represent a taxpayer before the IRS. Form 8821 only may be used to obtain information, such as copies of tax returns.

Representative Signing in Lieu of the Taxpayer

A representative named under a power of attorney is generally not permitted to sign a personal income tax return unless BOTH of the following are true:

---

[147] Durable power of attorney: A power of attorney that is not subject to a time limit and that will continue in force after the incapacitation or incompetency of the taxpayer.

[148] Attorney-in-fact: A person who holds power of attorney and therefore is legally designated to transact business and other duties on behalf of another individual.

- The signature is permitted under the Internal Revenue Code and the related regulations.
- The taxpayer specifically permits signature authority on the power of attorney.

For example, IRS regulations permit a representative to sign a taxpayer's return if the taxpayer is unable to sign for any of the following reasons:

- Disease or injury (for example, a taxpayer who is completely paralyzed or who has a debilitating injury)
- Continuous absence from the United States (including Puerto Rico) for a period of at least 60 days prior to the date required by law for filing the return
- Other good cause if specific permission is requested of and granted by the IRS

Example: Geoffrey is an EA. He has a client named Sally who travels extensively for business. Sally has signed Form 2848 specifically granting Geoffrey the right to sign her tax returns in her absence. Sally is currently traveling outside the U.S. for business and will not return until four months after the due date of her returns. Geoffrey is allowed to sign Sally's return (Publication 947).

When a tax return is signed by a representative, it must be accompanied by a power of attorney authorizing the representative to sign the return.[149]

Spousal Signatures: Exceptions

In the case of a joint return, both spouses must agree to sign the return. However, there are special circumstances in which a spouse may sign on behalf of the other spouse. One spouse can sign the return on the other spouse's behalf, **without** a power of attorney, in the following instances:

- Because of a medical or physical condition that makes the spouse unable to sign the return.
- If one spouse is mentally incompetent, the other may sign the return as a guardian.
- If one spouse is serving in a combat zone (or serving in a combat zone in "missing" status), the other spouse can still file a joint return and sign it. A joint return filed under these circumstances is valid even if it is later determined that the missing spouse died before the year covered by the return.

In any other circumstance, a spouse may sign for another spouse, but a valid power of attorney would be required.

In the case of a minor child, the parent or legal guardian may sign the return by signing the child's name, followed by guardian's signature and their relationship to the child, (such as "parent" or "guardian for minor child"). A parent or guardian does not need a power of attorney in order to sign on behalf of a minor child.

The Centralized Authorization File (CAF)

A Centralized Authorization File, or "CAF," is the IRS's computer database that contains information regarding the type of authorization that taxpayers have given representatives for their accounts.

---

[149] Regulations Section 1.6012-1(a)(5)

When a practitioner submits a power of attorney document to the IRS, it is processed for inclusion in the CAF. A CAF number is assigned to a tax practitioner or other authorized individual when a Form 2848 or Form 8821 is filed.

> **Example:** Josie is not a tax return preparer. In 2011, Josie's son, David, is audited by the IRS. David is 21 years old and does not wish to speak directly with the IRS. Josie files a Form 2848 and becomes the "authorized representative" for her son. She is issued a CAF number.

The issuance of a CAF number does not indicate that a person is either recognized or authorized to practice before the IRS. It merely confirms that a centralized file for authorizations has been established for the representative under that number.

> **Example:** Darren is an EA who recently submitted Form 2848 to the IRS on behalf of his client, Jennifer. He later called the IRS to check the status of Jennifer's tax refund. The IRS employee requested Darren's CAF number, which he provided. The IRS employee found Jennifer's power of attorney information in the CAF system and gave Darren the information about his client's refund.

A CAF number also enables the IRS to automatically send copies of notices and other IRS communications to a representative.

Summary of Tax Return Preparer Requirements
Quick Reference

Type of Preparer	PTIN	IRS Test	Continuing Education	Practice Rights
Enrolled Agent (EA)	Yes	Yes (EA exam)	72 hours every 3 years (16 hours and 2 hours of ethics per year)	Unlimited
Certified Public Accountant (CPA)	Yes	No	Varies by state	Unlimited
Attorney	Yes	No	Varies by state	Unlimited
Supervised Preparer	Yes	No	No	Limited

Unit 1: Questions

1. For taxpayers who want someone to represent them in their absence at an examination with the IRS, all of the following statements are correct except:

A. The taxpayer must furnish that representative with written authorization on Form 2848, *Power of Attorney and Declaration of Representative*, or any other properly written authorization.
B. The representative can be an attorney, CPA, or EA.
C. The representative can be any person who helped the taxpayer prepare the return.
D. Even if the taxpayer appointed a representative, the taxpayer may choose to attend the examination or appeals conference and may act on his own behalf.

The answer is C. Only certain persons are allowed to represent a taxpayer before the IRS. Usually, only an attorney, CPA, or EA may represent a taxpayer before the IRS without the taxpayer present. ###

2. Which of the following individuals does not qualify as an enrolled practitioner under Circular 230?

A. Certified public accountant.
B. Enrolled actuary.
C. Unenrolled student volunteer at a VITA site.
D. All of the above are considered enrolled practitioners.

The answer is D. All of the practitioners listed qualify to represent a taxpayer before the IRS, under certain circumstances. Student volunteers at a VITA site are given a special exemption to represent taxpayers before the IRS. VITA is the IRS's Volunteer Income Tax Assistance program, designed to help low-income taxpayers. ####

3. In order to practice before the IRS, attorneys and CPAs licensed to practice in a particular state must _____:

A. Be in good standing in that state and may practice before the IRS only in that state.
B. Be in good standing in that state and may practice before the IRS in any state.
C. Take the EA exam in order to practice outside the state in which they are licensed.
D. None of the above.

The answer is B. Any attorney or certified public accountant who is not currently under suspension or disbarment from practice before the IRS and who is licensed in good standing in any state, possession, territory, commonwealth, or the District of Columbia may practice before the IRS. Enrolled agents may practice in any state. ###

4. Which of the following statements is true?

A. A parent has authority to represent her child before the IRS only if the child is a minor.
B. A parent has authority to represent her child before the IRS without the child present.
C. A parent cannot represent her child before the IRS without an enrolled practitioner present.
D. None of the above.

The answer is B. A parent may represent her child before the IRS. The child is not required to be at the examination. A family member may represent, without compensation, a taxpayer before the IRS. ###

5. Denise and Gabriela are best friends. They are not family members. Gabriela must appear before the IRS for an examination. Denise wants to appear before the IRS on her best friend's behalf, though she is not an enrolled preparer. Which of the following statements is true?

A. Denise may represent Gabriela before the IRS without Gabriela being present.
B. Denise may advocate for Gabriela to the best of her ability.
C. Denise may appear before the IRS as a witness and communicate information.
D. Denise may not appear before the IRS in any capacity.

The answer is C. Simply appearing as a witness before the IRS is allowed and not considered "practice before the IRS." Individuals who are not practitioners may appear before the IRS as witnesses or communicate to the IRS on a taxpayer's behalf—but they may not advocate for the taxpayer. ###

6. Which of the following individuals is required to obtain a PTIN?

A. A CPA who does not prepare any tax returns.
B. An EA who works for a CPA firm, but does not sign any tax returns.
C. A tax attorney who only does representation before the Supreme Court.
D. A retired accountant who prepares tax returns for free for his family.

The answer is B. All EAs are required to obtain PTINs as a condition of their licensing (the PTIN must be included on Form 23, which is the application form to become an enrolled agent). Attorneys and CPAs do not need to obtain a PTIN unless they prepare tax returns for compensation. Someone who prepares returns for free is not considered a "tax return preparer" by the IRS and does not need a PTIN. ###

7. Matthew is a full-time employee for Parkway Partnership. He is not an EA, attorney, or CPA. Parkway requests that Matthew represent the partnership in connection with an IRS audit. Which of the following statements is true?

A. Matthew is allowed to represent the partnership before the IRS.
B. Matthew is not allowed to represent the partnership before the IRS.
C. Matthew is only allowed to represent individual partners before the IRS.
D. None of the above.

The answer is A. Matthew is a full-time employee for Parkway Partnership, so in that capacity he may represent his employer before the IRS. A regular full-time employee of an individual employer may represent the employer (Circular 230, §10.7). ###

8. Which of the following parties is allowed to act as an official representative for a taxpayer before the IRS?

A. An unenrolled tax practitioner who did not prepare the tax return in question.
B. A taxpayer's neighbor who is not a CPA, attorney, or EA.
C. A limited partner in a partnership.
D. A student attorney.

The answer is D. A student attorney who receives permission to practice before the IRS by virtue of his status as a law student under Section 10.7(d) of Circular 230 is allowed to practice before the IRS. ###

9. Barry helps his friend, José, who does not speak English fluently. Barry appears before the IRS and translates for José at an IRS examination. Which of the following is true?

A. Barry is practicing before the IRS.
B. José must sign Form 2848 authorizing Barry to represent him.
C. Barry is not considered to be "practicing before the IRS."
D. The IRS prohibits unrelated persons from being present at an IRS examination.

The answer is C. Simply appearing as a witness or communicating information to the IRS does not constitute "practice before the IRS." Barry is merely assisting with the exchange of information and is not advocating on Jose's behalf. An example of an individual assisting with information exchange but not practicing would be a taxpayer's friend serving as a translator when the taxpayer does not speak English (IRS Manual Chapter 25). ###

10. How long is a power of attorney authorization valid?

A. One year.
B. Three years.
C. Until it is revoked or superseded.
D. Until the due date of the next tax return.

The answer is C. A power of attorney is valid until revoked or superseded. It may be revoked by the taxpayer or withdrawn by the representative, or it may be superseded by the filing of a new power of attorney for the same tax and tax period. ###

11. A Centralized Authorization File (CAF) is _____.

A. An IRS computer file with information regarding the authority of an individual appointed under a power of attorney or person designated under a tax information authorization.
B. A file containing a practitioner's own personal tax return files, in order to assist with compliance regulation and monitoring of enrolled individuals.
C. An automated list of disbarred tax preparers.
D. An automated file of taxpayer delinquencies.

The answer is A. The CAF contains information on third parties authorized to represent taxpayers before the IRS and/or receive and inspect confidential tax information on active tax accounts or those accounts currently under consideration by the IRS. ###

12. Which of the following is considered a "paid preparer" under the Circular 230 regulations?

A. A full-time bookkeeper working for an employer who prepares payroll tax returns.
B. A retired attorney who prepares tax returns under the VITA program.
C. A person who merely furnishes typing, reproducing, or mechanical assistance.
D. A full-time secretary who also prepares tax returns for pay part-time from home during tax season.

The answer is D. A person who prepares tax returns for compensation is a paid preparer, even if the activity is only part-time. A person who prepares and signs a tax return WITHOUT compensation (such as for a family member or as a volunteer) is not considered a tax return preparer for the purposes of the preparer penalties. An employee who prepares a tax return for his employer or for another employee is not a "preparer" under Circular 230. The employer (or the individual with supervisory responsibility) has the responsibility for accuracy of the return. ####

13. "Practice before the IRS" does not include:

A. Communicating with the IRS on behalf of a taxpayer regarding his rights or liabilities.
B. Representing a taxpayer at conferences, hearings, or meetings with the IRS.
C. Preparing and filing documents for the IRS.
D. Representation of clients in the U.S. Tax Court.

The answer is D. Practice before the IRS does not include the representation of clients in the U.S. Tax Court. The Tax Court is independent of the IRS and has its own rules of practice and its own rules regarding admission to practice. ###

14. Khan is a CPA who employs Amy, an accounting student, to assist in the preparation of tax returns. Khan signs all of the tax returns. Which of the following statements is true?

A. Amy and Khan can share one PTIN.
B. Amy is required by law to sign the returns that she has prepared.
C. Amy is required to obtain a PTIN.
D. Amy cannot assist with the preparation of tax returns until she becomes a CPA.

The answer is C. Amy must obtain a PTIN. Every individual who, for compensation, prepares or assists in the preparation of a tax return or claim for refund must have his or her own PTIN. ###

15. Form 8821, *Tax Information Authorization*, may be used to authorize the following:

A. Any individual, corporation, firm, organization, or partnership to receive confidential information for the type of tax and periods listed on Form 8821.
B. Any designated third party to receive tax information.
C. Both A and B.
D. For unenrolled practitioners to indicate a representative relationship with a taxpayer and to authorize practice before the IRS.

The answer is C. Form 8821, *Tax Information Authorization*, authorizes any individual, corporation, firm, organization, or partnership to receive confidential information for the type of tax and periods listed on the form. Any third party may be designated by the taxpayer to receive confidential tax information. Form 8821 is only a disclosure form, so it will not give an individual any power to represent a taxpayer before the IRS. It may be used only to obtain information, such as copies of tax returns. ###

16. Willa is an EA with a signed Form 2848 from her client, who is currently under audit. Which of the following actions are not permitted?

A. Willa may record the audit meeting with the IRS examiner.
B. Willa may sign a consent to extend the statutory time period for assessment of tax.
C. Willa may receive and endorse a tax refund check on her client's behalf.
D. Willa may represent her client before the IRS appeals office, *without* the taxpayer present.

The answer is C. Form 2848 may be used by an enrolled tax practitioner to receive (but never endorse or cash) a refund check drawn on the U.S. Treasury. All of the other actions listed are permitted, so long as the tax practitioner is qualified to practice before the IRS. In this case, Willa is an enrolled agent, so her practice rights are unlimited. ###

17. Stan is an EA who already has a PTIN. What must he do to retain his existing PTIN?

A. Nothing extra is required after the initial application. Stan will be allowed to retain his PTIN so long as he is current in his enrollment status.
B. Stan must renew his PTIN every three years when he renews his enrollment status.
C. Stan cannot retain his existing PTIN. He must apply for a new PTIN every year.
D. Stan must renew his existing PTIN yearly, and a required fee must be paid.

The answer is D. The IRS now requires all paid preparers to have a Preparer Tax Identification Number (PTIN). Stan's PTIN must be renewed each year, and the required fee paid. Preparers must re-register using the new online system or Form W-12. In most cases, preparers will be issued the same PTIN, if they already have an existing PTIN. ###

18. Adele is a CPA with a bookkeeper, Ichiro, who assists in the preparation of returns. Ichiro has a PTIN and qualifies as a "supervised preparer" under Section 1.6109-2(h). He is not an EA or other enrolled practitioner. Ichiro may not:

A. Sign any tax return he prepares or assists in preparing.
B. Represent taxpayers before the IRS in any capacity.
C. Identify himself as a Circular 230 practitioner.
D. All of the above.

The answer is D. Supervised preparers may not:

- Sign any tax return they prepare or assist in preparing
- Represent taxpayers before the IRS in any capacity
- Identify themselves as Circular 230 practitioners

Individuals who apply for a PTIN under this provision are required to certify on their application that they are supervised by an attorney, CPA, or EA who signs the tax return. ###

19. What penalties can be imposed against tax return preparers who prepare tax returns for compensation, but refuse to obtain a PTIN?

A. None.
B. Censure by the IRS Office of Professional Responsibility.
C. Monetary penalties, injunction, and/or disciplinary action.
D. Automatic expulsion from the IRS e-file program.

The answer is C. Any individual who, for compensation, prepares or assists in the preparation of tax returns must have a PTIN. Failure to do so could result in the imposition of Internal Revenue Code Section 6695 monetary penalties, injunction, and/or disciplinary action. ###

20. Everett is an EA with a PTIN. His firm employs a bookkeeper named Fernanda. She gathers client receipts and invoices and organizes and records all information for Everett. Everett then uses the information that his bookkeeper has compiled and prepares all the tax returns. Which of the following statements is true?

A. Fernanda needs to have a PTIN, and she is required to become an EA because she assists in the preparation of returns.
B. Fernanda needs to have a PTIN, but she is not required to become an EA.
C. Fernanda is not a tax return preparer and is not required to have a PTIN.
D. None of the above.

The answer is C. Fernanda is not a tax return preparer and is not required to have a PTIN. An individual who provides only typing, reproduction, or other mechanical assistance, but does not actually prepare returns is not considered a "tax preparer" by the IRS. ###

21. A power of attorney may be revoked by _____.

A. The taxpayer.
B. The representative.
C. The U.S. Tax Court.
D. Both A and B.

The answer is D. A power of attorney may be revoked by the taxpayer or the representative. A revocation statement should be submitted in writing and must contain the taxpayer's identifying information, the representative's identifying information (name and CAF number), and the specific tax and tax periods covered by the revocation. ###

22. To determine which preparer is responsible for a "substantial portion" of a tax return, the following guidelines are used except:

A. Whoever has the primary responsibility for the accuracy of the return.
B. Whoever actually owns or manages the tax practice.
C. Whoever prepares the portion of the return that declares the greatest amount of adjusted gross income.
D. None of the above.

The answer is B. Ownership or management of a tax practice is immaterial in determining the substantial portion rule. The most important determination is whoever has the primary responsibility for the accuracy of the return. If several people are involving in preparing a return, the person who prepares the part of the return that declares the greatest amount of income would be considered the "preparer" who must sign the return. ###

Unit 2: Rules of Enrollment

> **More Reading:**
> Publication 947, *Practice Before the IRS and Power of Attorney*

Initial Enrollment

Enrolled Agent Licensing

There are two tracks to become an enrolled agent, which are outlined in Circular 230. An individual may receive the designation by passing a three-part exam, or may become an EA by virtue of past employment with the IRS.[150]

Track I: Exam Track

For the first track, an EA candidate must apply for a PTIN and register to take the Special Enrollment Examination (SEE, also known as the "EA exam") with the testing company Prometric, by filling out Form 2587, *Application for Special Enrollment Examination*. An applicant must be at least 18 years old. A candidate then must do the following:

- Achieve passing scores on all three parts of the SEE.
- File Form 23 to apply for enrollment within one year of the date of passing the exam. The IRS says it takes about six weeks to process applications.
- Pass a background check conducted by the IRS. The tax compliance check makes sure the applicant has filed all necessary tax returns and has no outstanding tax liabilities. The suitability check determines whether an applicant has engaged in any conduct that would justify suspension or disbarment.

> ***Note:** Do not confuse the form numbers. Applicants **apply** to take the EA exam by filing Form 2587, *Application for Special Enrollment Examination*. Candidates may also sign up online. Once the candidate passes all three parts of the EA exam, he must file Form 23, *Application for Enrollment to Practice before the Internal Revenue Service*, in order to obtain his Treasury card.

Track II: Previous Experience with the IRS

For the second track, an EA candidate must possess a minimum of five years of past service with the IRS and technical experience as outlined in Circular 230. Application must be made within three years from the date the employee left the IRS. Factors considered with this second track are the length and scope of employment and the recommendation of the superior officer. The applicant then must:

- Apply for enrollment on Form 23.
- Pass a background check, which includes tax compliance and suitability check.

---

[150] The IRS may waive the requirement for former IRS employees to pass the EA and ERPA exams, but will not waive the requirement for the enrolled actuary exam.

Former IRS employees who become enrolled agents without taking the EA exam may be granted limited or unlimited representation rights. The IRS's Return Preparer Office makes the determinations on applications for enrollment to practice.[151]

Denial of Enrollment

Any individual engaged in practice before the IRS who is involved in disreputable conduct is subject to disciplinary action or denial of enrollment.

Disreputable acts alone may be grounds for denial of enrollment, even after the candidate has passed the EA exam. Failure to timely file tax returns or to pay one's taxes may also be grounds for denying an application for enrollment. The Return Preparer Office must inform the applicant why he is denied an application for enrollment. If an applicant is denied enrollment, he may file a written appeal to the Office of Professional Responsibility within 30 days from the date of the notice. The appeal must be filed along with the candidate's reasoning why the enrollment application should be accepted.

> **Example:** Todd passed all three parts of the EA exam in 2012. He properly filed Form 23 requesting enrollment. Because he had failed to file numerous tax returns in the past, his application was denied. Todd filed an appeal with the Office of Professional Responsibility, explaining that he had been seriously injured years ago and therefore had failed to file his tax returns on time. He attached proof of his reasoning, along with copies of medical bills and a letter from his doctor. Todd also showed that all his tax returns had been properly filed after his recovery. The OPR accepted Todd's appeal and granted him enrollment.

IRS Roster of Enrolled Agents and Enrolled Retirement Plan Agents

The Return Preparer Office maintains a roster of EAs and ERPAs. The roster includes enrolled individuals whose status is inactive or retired. The roster has the following information:

- Current enrolled agents:
    - Who have been granted enrollment to practice
    - Whose enrollment has been placed on inactive status for failure to meet the continuing education requirements for renewal of enrollment
- Inactive enrolled agents:
    - Whose status is inactive due to retirement
    - Whose offer of consent to resign from enrollment has been accepted by the OPR
- Other individuals (and employers, firms, or other entities, if applicable) censured, suspended, or disbarred from practice before the IRS or upon whom a monetary penalty was imposed
- Disqualified appraisers
- Enrolled retirement plan agents (ERPAs):
    - Who have been granted enrollment to practice
    - Whose enrollment has been placed on inactive status for failure to meet the continuing education requirements for renewal of enrollment

---

[151] Similar rules apply to the ERPA exam. The applicant must pass an exam or qualifying experience as a former IRS employee.

This roster is available for public inspection as authorized by the Secretary of the Treasury.

Renewal of Enrollment

Enrolled agents must renew their enrollment status every three years. If an EA does not renew his enrollment, he may not continue to practice as an enrolled agent. The three successive enrollment years preceding the effective date of renewal is referred to as the IRS enrollment cycle. Applications for renewal of enrollment must be submitted between November 1 and January 31 prior to April 1 of the year that the next enrollment cycle begins. The last digit of a practitioner's Social Security Number determines when he must renew enrollment. If the candidate's SSN ends in:

- 0, 1, 2, or 3 – The next enrollment cycle begins April 1, 2013.
- 4, 5, or 6 – The next enrollment cycle begins April 1, 2014.
- 7, 8, or 9 – The next enrollment cycle begins April 1, 2015.
- EAs who do not have an SSN must use the "7, 8, or 9" renewal schedule.

As part of the application process, the IRS will check the candidate's filing history to verify that he has filed and paid all federal taxes on time. If the practitioner owns or has an interest in a business, the IRS will also check the tax compliance history of the business. In addition, the IRS will check that the EA has completed all necessary professional continuing education requirements.

Renewal Requirements

The IRS will send a reminder notice when an EA is due for renewal. However, failing to receive a reminder notice of the renewal requirement does not excuse the EA from the obligation to re-apply. An EA is expected to inform the Return Preparer Office of address changes within 60 days of a move to make sure he receives timely reminder notices. Preparers may lose their eligibility to practice before the IRS for the following reasons, among others:

- Failure to meet the yearly educational requirements for enrollment.
- Failure to renew a PTIN or pay required fees.
- Requesting to be placed on inactive/retirement status.
- Being disbarred by state regulatory agencies (in the case of attorneys and CPAs). An attorney or CPA who is disbarred from practice at the state level is also disbarred from practice at the federal level, and cannot practice before the IRS as long as their disbarment (or suspension) is active.

To renew, an EA must file Form 8554, *Application for Renewal of Enrollment to Practice before the Internal Revenue Service*, and submit the required nonrefundable fee. Even if an application is ultimately denied, the fee will not be refunded.

Inactive and Terminated EAs

The RPO will notify any EAs who fail to comply with the requirements for eligibility for renewal of enrollment. The notice via First Class mail will explain the reason for noncompliance and will provide the individual an opportunity to furnish the requested information, such as missing CE credits, in writing. An EA has 60 days from the date of the notice to respond to this initial warning. If no response is received, the EA will move to "inactive" status as of April 1.

To be eligible for renewal after missing one full enrollment cycle, an EA must pay a fee for both the prior and current renewal cycle and verify that the required CE hours have been taken.

Each year on April 1, the RPO will issue letters to all EAs who have missed two renewal cycles to advise them that their EA status is terminated. To have their termination status reconsidered, EAs must file a written protest within 30 days with the OPR and provide a valid reason for not enrolling timely. Reasons may include serious illness and extended travel out of the country.

Continuing Education (CE) for Enrolled Agents

During each three-year enrollment cycle, an EA must complete 72 hours of continuing education credit. A minimum of 16 hours, including two hours of ethics or professional conduct, must be completed during each enrollment year.

For new EAs, the month of initial enrollment begins the CE requirement. They must complete two hours of CE for each month enrolled, which must include two hours of ethics. Enrollment for any part of a month is considered enrollment for the entire month. When an EA's new three-year enrollment cycle begins, he will be required to satisfy the full 72-hour continuing education credit requirement.

Example: Don applied to become a new EA on September 30, 2012, which also happened to be the third year of his enrollment cycle. He is required to take two hours of CE a month prior to January 1, 2013, equaling eight hours total for the months of September, October, November, and December. Two of those hours must be on the topic of ethics. Since his initial enrollment came during the final year of his enrollment cycle, Don will be required to renew his enrollment status in 2013.

If a candidate takes more than two hours of ethics courses during a single year, the additional ethics courses will count toward the yearly requirement. However, an enrolled agent may not take additional ethics courses in the current year and neglect to take them in future years. Ethics courses must be taken *every year*.

Exception: If a practitioner *retakes and passes* the EA exam again since his last renewal, he is only required to take 16 hours of CE, including two hours of ethics, during the last year of his current enrollment cycle.

CE Coursework

In order to qualify as professional CE, a course must be designed to enhance professional knowledge in federal taxation or federal tax-related matters. Courses related to state taxation do not meet the IRS's requirement, unless at least 80% of the program material consists of a comparison between federal and state tax laws.

All individuals and companies who wish to offer continuing education to EAs must pay a registration fee and apply to be approved as providers, including accredited educational institutions. Providers approved by the IRS are issued a provider number and are allowed to display a logo that says "IRS Approved Continuing Education Provider." [152]

---

[152] The IRS contracts with a private company to maintain an updated list of qualified providers at https://ssl.kinsail.com/partners/irs/publicListing.asp.

Qualifying programs include traditional seminars and conferences, as well as correspondence or individual self-study programs on the Internet, so long as they are approved courses of study by approved providers.

All continuing education programs are measured in terms of "contact hours." The shortest recognized program is one hour. In order for a course to qualify for CE credit, it must feature at least 50 minutes of continuous participation. A qualified course may also be longer than an hour; for example, a course lasting longer than 50 minutes but less than 80 minutes still counts as only one contact hour.

Individual segments at conferences and conventions are considered one total program. For example, two 90-minute segments (180 minutes) at a continuous conference count as three contact hours. For a university or college course, each semester hour credit equals 15 contact hours and a quarter-hour credit equals ten contact hours.

A tax professional may also receive continuing education credit for serving as an instructor, discussion leader, or speaker on federal tax matters for approved educational programs. One hour of CE credit is awarded for each contact hour completed. Two hours of CE credit is awarded for actual subject preparation time for each contact hour completed as an instructor, discussion leader, or speaker at such programs.

The maximum credit for instruction and preparation may not exceed six hours annually for EAs. Individuals claiming this credit need to maintain records to verify preparation time.

CE Participant and Provider Recordkeeping Requirements

After completing CE coursework, an EA will receive a certificate from the course provider. Any programs that an EA has taken will be reported to the IRS by the approved course provider, using the PTINs of the individual participants. Course providers must renew their status every year.

In 2012, the IRS allowed PTIN holders to self-attest that they met the yearly CE requirement. However, beginning in mid-2013, the IRS says that tax professionals will be able to check their online PTIN accounts to see a display of the 2013 CE programs they have completed and reported by providers. (Hours from 2012 and prior years will not be included.)

Individuals applying for renewal of enrollment must retain their CE records for four years following the date of renewal. Records should include the following information:

- The name of the CE provider organization
- The location of the program
- The title of the program, approval number received for the program, and copy of the program content
- Written outlines, course syllabi, etc. required for the program
- The date(s) attended
- The credit hours claimed
- The name(s) of the instructors, speakers, or discussion leaders
- The certificate of completion and/or signed statement of the hours of attendance obtained from the continuing education provider

CE providers also are required to maintain detailed records for four years after coursework is completed. These records must include the first and last name and the PTINs of each participant, as well as the hours completed by program.

CE Waiver

A waiver of CE requirements may be requested from the RPO in extraordinary circumstances. Qualifying circumstances include:

- Health issues
- Extended active military duty
- Absence from the United States for employment or other reasons
- Other reasons on a case-by-case basis

The request for a waiver must be accompanied by appropriate documentation, such as medical records or military paperwork. If the request is denied, the enrolled agent will be placed on the inactive roster. If the request is accepted, the EA will receive an updated enrollment card reflecting his renewal.

Example: Cristian is an EA who is also an Army reservist. He was called to active duty in a combat zone for two years. During this time, he was unable to complete his CE requirements for his enrolled agent license. Cristian requested a waiver based on his deployment, which was granted by the RPO. Cristian was granted renewal of his EA license based on extraordinary circumstances.

Unit 2: Questions

1. Enrolled agents must complete continuing education credits for renewed enrollment. Which of the following describes the credit requirements?

A. A minimum of 72 hours must be completed in each year of an enrollment cycle.
B. A minimum of 24 hours must be completed in each year of an enrollment cycle.
C. A minimum of 80 hours must be completed, overall, for the entire enrollment cycle.
D. A minimum of 16 hours must be completed in each year of the enrollment cycle, including two hours of ethics.

The answer is D. A minimum of 16 hours of continuing education credit, including two hours of ethics, must be completed in *each year* of the enrollment cycle. An EA must complete a minimum of 72 hours of continuing education during each three-year period. ###

2. Each EA who applies for renewal to practice before the IRS must retain information about CE hours completed. How long must CE verification be retained?

A. For one year following the enrollment renewal date.
B. For four years following the enrollment renewal date.
C. For five years if it is an initial enrollment.
D. The individual is not required to retain the information if the CE provider has agreed to retain it.

The answer is B. Each individual applying for renewal must retain information about CE hours completed for four years following the enrollment renewal date. The CE provider must also retain records for four years. ###

3. What is the "enrollment cycle" for EAs?

A. The enrollment cycle is the year after the effective date of renewal.
B. The enrollment cycle means the three successive enrollment years preceding the effective date of renewal.
C. The enrollment cycle is the method by which the RPO approves exam candidates.
D. The enrollment cycle is the method by which Prometric chooses the exam questions for EA candidates.

The answer is B. The "enrollment cycle" means the three successive enrollment years preceding the effective date of renewal. After the initial enrollment renewal period, regular renewal enrollments are required every three years. This is known as an enrollment cycle. ###

4. EAs who do not comply with the requirements for renewal of enrollment will be contacted by the Return Preparer Office. How much time does the EA have to respond to the RPO?

A. 30 days from the date of the notice.
B. 60 days from the date of the notice.
C. 60 days from the date of receipt.
D. 90 days from the date of the notice.

The answer is B. Enrolled agents who fail to comply with the requirements for eligibility for renewal of enrollment will be notified by the Return Preparer Office through First Class mail. The notice will explain the reason for noncompliance. The enrolled agent has 60 days from the date of the notice to respond. ###

5. Nathan, an EA, teaches various continuing education courses in tax law. What is the maximum CE credit for instruction and preparation that Nathan can claim each year?

A. Two hours.
B. Four hours.
C. Six hours.
D. Eight hours.

The answer is C. The maximum CE credit for instruction and preparation is limited to six hours a year for enrolled agents. ###

6. All of the following are potential grounds for denial of enrollment except:

A. Failure to timely file tax returns.
B. Failure to pay taxes.
C. Felony convictions.
D. A candidate who is only 18 years old.

The answer is D. The minimum age for enrollment is 18, so anyone over 17 would not be denied enrollment based on his age. Failure to timely file tax returns, pay taxes, or felony convictions are all potential grounds for denying an application for enrollment. The RPO will review all of the facts and circumstances to determine whether a denial of enrollment is warranted. ###

7. Chris earned his initial enrollment in year three of his enrollment cycle, in the month of November. How many CE credits must he complete before the end of the year?

A. Four CE credits, of which two must be ethics courses.
B. Six CE credits, of which two must be ethics courses.
C. Sixteen CE credits, of which two must be ethics courses.
D. Two CE credits, of which one must be ethics courses.

The answer is A. Chris is required to complete four CE credits for November and December of the third year, of which two must be ethics courses. In his next renewal cycle, Chris will be required to complete a minimum of 72 hours of continuing education credits, which encompasses three calendar years. (Note: A minimum of 16 hours of continuing education credits including two hours of ethics or professional conduct credits must be completed during each enrollment year of an enrollment cycle.) ###

8. To maintain active enrollment to practice before the IRS, each practitioner is required to have his enrollment renewed. The Return Preparer Office will notify practitioners of their need to renew. Which of the following statements about renewal of enrollment is correct?

A. The RPO may charge a reasonable refundable fee for each application for renewal of enrollment.
B. Failure by a practitioner to receive notification from the RPO of the renewal requirement is not justification for the failure to renew enrollment in a timely manner.
C. Forms required for renewal may only be obtained from the National Association of Enrolled Agents.
D. The enrollment cycle is a three-year period, and all EAs must renew at the same time, no matter when they first became enrolled.

The answer is B. Application for renewal is required to maintain active renewal status. Not receiving notice of the renewal requirement does not excuse the EA from having to reapply. Failure to receive notification from the RPO of the renewal requirement will not be justification for the failure to renew enrollment in a timely manner. The renewal fee is nonrefundable, even if enrollment is not granted. ###

9. Andrea has been an enrolled agent for many years. Her records show that she had the following hours of qualified CE in 2012:

| January 2012, 7 hrs: General tax CE |
| May 2012, 1 hr: Ethics |
| December 2012, 9 hrs: General tax CE |

Has Andrea met her minimum yearly CE requirements?

A. Yes, Andrea has met her minimum yearly CE requirements.
B. No, Andrea has met her ethics requirement, but not the overall minimum requirement for the year.
C. No, Andrea has not met her ethics requirement.
D. None of the above.

The answer is C. The IRS enforces a 16-hour minimum per year, and requires two hours of ethics per year. Andrea has only completed one hour of ethics CE. She has met her yearly "general" CE requirement, but she has not met the ethics requirement for the year, so her minimum requirements have not been met. ###

10. A practitioner's status as an enrolled agent must be renewed every three years as determined by _____.

A. His last name.
B. The last digit of his Social Security Number.
C. The date of his initial enrollment.
D. The date that he passed the EA exam.

The answer is B. A practitioner's status as an enrolled agent must be renewed every three years as determined by the last digit of his Social Security Number. ###

11. Under Circular 230, an applicant who wishes to challenge the Return Preparer Office's denial of his application for enrollment is required to do which of the following?

A. File a written appeal with the Secretary of the Treasury.
B. File a written appeal with the Office of Professional Responsibility.
C. File a written appeal with the Commissioner of the IRS.
D. Resubmit another application within 30 days.

The answer is B. An enrolled agent who is initially denied enrollment and wishes to challenge the denial must file a written appeal with the Office of Professional Responsibility. ###

12. A minimum of how many hours of ethics education are required per enrollment cycle?

A. Seventy-two.
B. Forty-eight.
C. Eight.
D. Six.

The answer is D. In order to maintain their licenses, EAs must complete at least two hours of ethics education every year. Therefore, within a *three-year cycle*, an EA must complete at least six hours of ethics (minimum two hours per year). The IRS enforces a 16-hour CE minimum per year and requires at least two hours of ethics per year. ###

13. Chung, an EA, retakes the SEE in the second year of his renewal, and achieves passing scores. How many hours of continuing education must he take during the final year of his enrollment cycle?

A. Four.
B. Eight.
C. Ten.
D. Sixteen.

The answer is D. There is an exception to the mandated 72 hours of continuing education credit required per enrollment cycle. An enrolled agent who retakes the EA exam and has passing scores on each part only has to do 16 hours of CE during the final year of his enrollment cycle, including two hours of ethics training. ###

14. Jasmine applied for her initial enrollment during an enrollment cycle. How many continuing education credits must she complete?

A. Three hours of qualifying continued education credits per month, including two hours of ethics or professional conduct credits per year.
B. One hour of qualifying continued education credit per month, including two hours of ethics or professional conduct credits per year.
C. Two hours of qualifying continued education credits per month, including two hours of ethics or professional conduct credits per year.
D. Four hours of qualifying continued education credits per month, including two hours of ethics or professional conduct credits per year.

The answer is C. If initial enrollment occurs during an enrollment cycle, the EA is required to complete two hours of qualifying continued education credits per month, including two hours of ethics or professional conduct credits per year. When the new three-year enrollment cycle begins, he will be required to satisfy the regular 72-hour continuing education credit requirements. In order for an individual to maintain enrollment status, a minimum of 72 hours of continuing education credits must be completed during each enrollment cycle, which includes a minimum of two hours of ethics per year. ###

15. What action should an EA take if he chooses to appeal termination from enrollment?

A. Call the Office of Professional Responsibility to complain.
B. File a written protest within 30 days of the date of the notice of termination.
C. File a written protest within 60 days of the date of the notice of termination.
D. File a written protest within 90 days of the date of the notice of termination.

The answer is B. An EA who has been terminated from enrollment by the OPR should file a written protest within 30 days of the date of the notice. The protest must be filed with the Office of Professional Responsibility. ###

16. Eleanor failed to complete her continuing education requirements. She plans to request a waiver so that she can renew her EA license. All of the following are reasons the RPO will typically accept as it considers whether to grant her waiver except:

A. Financial hardship.
B. Absence from the United States for an extended period of time.
C. Back surgery that required lengthy rehabilitation.
D. Deployment to Afghanistan as a member of the Army Reserve.

The answer is A. Although the RPO will consider each waiver request on a case-by-case basis, it will typically grant waivers based on the following reasons: active military duty; absence from the U.S. for an extended period of time, provided the individual doesn't practice before the IRS during that absence; and health issues. Financial hardship is not generally considered a legitimate reason for someone not to complete her CE requirements. ###

17. When does a new EA's enrollment take effect?

A. On the date he applies for enrollment with the IRS.
B. On the date listed on his Treasury card.
C. On the date he receives his Treasury card.
D. On the first day of January after he receives his Treasury card.

The answer is B. An EA's enrollment becomes official on the date listed on his Treasury card, whether he has actually received the card or not. ###

18. Angela is taking a continuing education course that combines updates on new Kansas state law and on federal tax law. In order to satisfy the enrolled agent CE requirements, the following is true:

A. The course must be taken in person at a conference or workshop. An online self-study course is not allowed.
B. The course must be given by an approved CE provider who is a CPA.
C. The course must be given by an approved CE provider and must include at least 50% updates on federal tax law.
D. The course must be given by an approved CE provider and must include at least 80% updates on federal tax law.

The answer is D. All CE for credit must be given by an approved provider, whether in person, online, or in a self-study program. The course material must focus on federal tax law. If a course also deals with individual state law, at least 80% of the program material must consist of a comparison between federal and state tax laws. ###

19. Cameron is an EA whose Social Security Number ends with the number seven. When does the next cycle begin for him to renew his enrollment?

A. On the anniversary date of his initial enrollment.
B. Beginning April 1, 2014.
C. Beginning April 1, 2015.
D. Beginning April 1, 2016.

The answer is C. For EAs whose Social Security Numbers end in 7, the next enrollment cycle begins April 1, 2015. If the candidate's SSN ends in:

•0, 1, 2, or 3 – The next enrollment cycle begins April 1, 2013.
•4, 5, or 6 – The next enrollment cycle begins April 1, 2014.
•7, 8, or 9 – The next enrollment cycle begins April 1, 2015.

EAs who do not have an SSN must use the "7, 8, or 9" renewal schedule. ###

Unit 3: Tax Preparer Responsibilities

> **More Reading:**
> Publication 4019, *Third Party Authorization, Levels of Authority*
> Publication 947, *Practice Before the IRS and Power of Attorney*
> Publication 216, *Conference and Practice Requirements*

The Treasury Department's Circular 230 sets forth regulations that govern enrolled agents, CPAs, attorneys, and others who practice before the IRS. As of 2011, the rules of Circular 230 are applied to all paid tax preparers.

Circular 230 imposes professional standards and codes of conduct for tax preparers and tax advisors. It prohibits certain actions, requires other actions, and details penalties for ethical and other violations by tax preparers.

Central to the Circular 230 regulations is the mandate for practitioners to exercise **due diligence** when performing the following duties:

- Preparing or assisting in the preparing, approving, and filing of returns, documents, affidavits, and other papers relating to IRS matters.
- Determining the correctness of oral or written representations made by the client, and also for positions taken on the tax return.

Best Practices

Circular 230 explains the broad concept of "best practices." Tax advisors must provide clients with the highest quality representation concerning federal tax matters by adhering to best practices in providing advice and in preparing documents or information for the IRS.

Tax preparers who oversee a firm's practice should take reasonable steps to ensure that the firm's procedures for all employees are consistent with best practices. "Best practices" include the following:

- Communicating clearly with the client regarding the terms of the engagement.
- Establishing the facts, determining which facts are relevant, evaluating the reasonableness of any assumptions, relating the applicable law to the relevant facts, and arriving at a conclusion supported by the law and the facts.
- Advising the client of the conclusions reached and the impact of the advice rendered; for example, advising whether a taxpayer may avoid accuracy-related penalties if he relies on the advice provided.
- Acting fairly and with integrity in practice before the IRS.

The Duty to Advise (§10.21 Knowledge of client's omission)

A practitioner who knows that his client has not complied with the revenue laws or who has made an error or omission on his tax return has the responsibility to advise the client promptly of the noncompliance, error, or omission, as well as the *consequences* of the error.

Under the rules of Circular 230 §10.21, the tax practitioner is not responsible for fixing the noncompliance once he has notified the client of the issue. The tax professional is also not responsible for notifying the IRS of noncompliance by a client.

> **Example:** Jeremy is an EA with a new client, Monique, who has self-prepared her own returns in the past. Jeremy notices that Monique has been claiming head of household on her tax returns, but she does not qualify for this status, because she does not have a qualifying person. Jeremy is required to promptly notify Monique of the error and tell her the consequences of not correcting the error. However, Jeremy is not required to amend Monique's prior year tax returns to correct the error. Nor is he required to notify the IRS of Monique's claim of incorrect status.

The §10.21 obligations are not limited to practitioners preparing returns, so the discovery of an error or omission in the course of a tax consulting or advisory engagement will also trigger its requirements.

> **Example:** Gina is an EA who takes over another tax preparer's practice. She discovers that the previous preparer has been taking Section 179 depreciation on assets that do not qualify for this bonus depreciation treatment. Gina must notify her clients of the error and the consequences of not correcting the error. She is not required to correct the error.

A tax professional may rely on the work product of another tax preparer. A practitioner will be presumed to have exercised due diligence if he uses reasonable care in revaluating the work product of the other practitioner.

Other Duties and Prohibited Acts

Performance as a notary §10.26: A tax practitioner who is a notary public and is employed as counsel, attorney, or agent in a matter before the IRS or who has a material interest in the matter cannot engage in any notary activities related to that matter.

Negotiations of taxpayer refund checks §10.31: Tax return preparers must not endorse or negotiate (cash) any refund check issued to the taxpayer. A preparer faces a $500 fine for each time he improperly cashes a taxpayer's check.

No delay tactics allowed: A practitioner must not delay the prompt disposition of any matter before the IRS.

No employment of disbarred persons: A tax practitioner may not knowingly employ a person or accept assistance from a person who has been disbarred or suspended from practice. This restriction applies even if the duties of the disbarred or suspended person would not include actual preparation of tax returns.

Practice of law §10.32: Nothing in the regulations or in Circular 230 may be construed as authorizing persons not attorneys to practice law.

Confidentiality Privilege for Enrolled Practitioners

Enrolled practitioners and their clients are granted confidentiality protection. This confidentiality privilege applies to attorneys, CPAs, enrolled agents, enrolled actuaries, and certain other individuals allowed to practice before the IRS.[153]

---

[153]IRC Section 7525.

The confidentiality protection applies to communications that would be considered privileged if they were between the taxpayer and an attorney and that relate to:

- Noncriminal tax matters before the IRS, or
- Noncriminal tax proceedings brought in federal court by or against the United States.

The confidentiality privilege does not apply:

- In criminal tax matters
- To any written communications regarding the promotion of a tax shelter
- To the general preparation of tax returns
- In state tax proceedings

This confidentiality privilege cannot be used with any agency other than the IRS.

Conflicts of Interest §10.29

A tax professional may represent conflicting interests before the IRS only if all the parties offer their consent in writing. If there is any potential conflict of interest, the practitioner must disclose the existence of a financial interest and be given the opportunity to disclose all material facts.

A conflict of interest exists if:

- The representation of one client will be adverse to another client; or
- There is a significant risk that the representation of one or more clients will be materially limited by the practitioner's responsibilities to another client, a former client, or another third person.
- The representation of the taxpayer would be in conflict with the tax preparer's personal interests.

The consent must be obtained in writing and retained for at least 36 months from the date representation ends. At minimum, the consent should adequately describe the nature of the conflict and the parties the practitioner represents. The practitioner may still represent a client when a conflict of interest exists if:

- The practitioner reasonably believes that he will be able to provide competent and diligent representation to each affected client;
- The representation is not prohibited by law; and
- Each affected client waives the conflict of interest and gives informed consent, confirmed in writing.

Example: Christa is an EA who prepares tax returns for Jana and Brett, a married couple. In 2012, they go through a contentious divorce, and Christa believes there is a potential for conflict of interest relating to the tax advice she would give them. She prepares a written statement explaining the potential conflict of interest. Jana and Bret still want Christa to prepare their returns, so she has her clients sign the written consent. Christa must retain the record of their consent for at least 36 months.

Strict Privacy of Taxpayer Information: Section 7216

The IRS has enacted strict privacy regulations designed to give taxpayers more control over their personal information and tax records. The regulations limit tax professionals' use and disclosure of client information, and explain precise and limited exceptions in which disclosure is permitted.

Internal Revenue Code §7216 is a **criminal provision** enacted by Congress that prohibits tax return preparers from knowingly or recklessly disclosing or using tax return information. The regulations were updated in 2008 to clarify that e-file providers are among the return preparers who are bound by these privacy rules.

A convicted preparer may be fined up to $1,000, imprisoned up to one year, or both, for *each violation* of Section 7216. There is also a civil penalty of $250 for improper disclosure or use of taxpayer information, outlined in IRC §6713. However, this code does not require that the disclosure be "knowing or reckless" as it does under Section 7216.

Tax preparers must generally obtain written consent from taxpayers before they can disclose information to a third party or use the information for anything other than the actual preparation of tax returns. The actual consent form must meet the following guidelines:

- Identify the purpose of the disclosure.
- Identify the recipient and describe the authorized information.
- Include the name of the preparer and the name of the taxpayer.
- Include mandatory language that informs the taxpayer that he is not required to sign the consent, and if he does sign the consent, he can set a time period for the duration of that consent.
- Include mandatory language that refers the taxpayer to the Treasury Inspector General for Tax Administration if he believes that his tax return information has been disclosed or used improperly.
- If applicable, inform the taxpayer that his tax return information may be disclosed to a tax return preparer located outside the U.S.
- Be signed and dated by the taxpayer. Electronic (online) consents must be in the same type as the website's standard text and contain the taxpayer's affirmative consent (as opposed to an "opt-out" clause).

Unless a specific time period is specified, consent is valid for one year.

These updated privacy regulations apply to paid preparers, electronic return originators, tax software developers, and other persons or entities engaged in tax preparation. The regulations also apply to most volunteer tax preparers, for example, Volunteer Income Tax Assistance and Tax Counseling for the Elderly volunteers, and employees and contractors employed by tax preparation companies in a support role.

Allowable Disclosures

In certain circumstances, a preparer may disclose information to a second taxpayer who appears on a tax return. The preparer may disclose return information obtained from the first taxpayer if:

- The second taxpayer is related to the first taxpayer.
- The first taxpayer's interest is not adverse to the second taxpayer's interest.
- The first taxpayer has not prohibited the disclosure.

> **Example:** Zach is an EA with two married clients, Serena and Tyler, who file jointly. Serena works long hours, so she is unavailable when Tyler meets with Zach to prepare their joint tax return. Later, Serena comes in alone to sign the return. She also has a quick question regarding the mortgage interest on a tax return. Zach is allowed to disclose return information to Serena because the tax return is a joint return, both of their names are on the return, and Tyler has not prohibited any disclosures.

A taxpayer is considered "related" to another taxpayer in any of the following relationships:

- Husband and wife, or child and parent
- Grandchild and grandparent
- General partner in a partnership
- Trust or estate and the beneficiary
- A corporation and shareholder
- Members of a controlled group of corporations

A tax preparer may also disclose tax return information that was obtained from a first taxpayer in preparing a tax return of the second taxpayer, if the preparer has obtained written consent from the first taxpayer. For example, if an unmarried couple lives together and splits the mortgage interest, the preparer may use or disclose information from the first taxpayer to the second so long as the preparer has written consent.

The Definition of "Tax Return Information"

The IRS's definition of "tax return information" is broad and encompasses the following:

"All the information tax return preparers obtain from taxpayers or other sources in any form or matter that is used to prepare tax returns or is obtained in connection with the preparation of returns. It also includes all computations, worksheets, and printouts preparers create; correspondence from the IRS during the preparation, filing and correction of returns; statistical compilations of tax return information; and tax return preparation software registration information."

All of this tax return information is protected by §7216 and its regulations.

When Disclosure Permissions Are Not Required

A tax preparer is not required to obtain disclosure permission from a client if the disclosure is made for any of the following reasons:

- A court order or subpoena issued by any court of record whether at the federal, state, or local level. The required information must be clearly identified in the document (subpoena or court order) in order for a preparer to disclose information.
- An administrative order, demand, summons, or subpoena that is issued by any federal agency, state agency, or commission charged under the laws of the state with licensing, registration, or regulation of tax return preparers.
- In order to report a crime to proper authorities. Even if the preparer is mistaken and no crime exists, if the preparer makes the disclosure in good faith, he will not be subject to sanctions.

- Confidential information for the purpose of peer reviews.

A tax preparer may disclose private client information to his attorney or to an employee of the IRS, subsequent to an investigation of the tax return preparer conducted by the IRS.

> **Example:** The IRS is investigating a CPA named Harry for possible misconduct. Harry has an attorney who is assisting in his defense. In reality, Harry was the victim of embezzlement because his bookkeeper was stealing client checks. Harry discovered the embezzlement when the IRS contacted him about client complaints. Harry may disclose confidential client information to his attorney in order to assist with his own defense. Harry may also disclose confidential client information to the IRS during the course of its investigation.

A tax preparer may disclose tax return information to a tax return processor. For example, if a tax preparer uses an electronic or tax return processing service, he may disclose tax return information to that service in order to prepare tax returns or compute tax liability.

A tax preparer may also solicit additional business from a taxpayer in matters not related to the IRS (for example, if the preparer offers other financial services such as bookkeeping or insurance services). However, the tax preparer must obtain written consent from the taxpayer in order to make these solicitations.

> **Example:** Juliet is an EA who also sells life insurance. She obtains a written consent from her client, Manuel, and then sends him a solicitation by mail for her insurance services. This is allowed because Juliet obtained written consent from Manuel in advance.

Third Party Authorizations

A "third party authorization" is when a taxpayer authorizes an individual (usually his tax preparer) to communicate with the IRS on his behalf. A third party authorization is different from a regular power of attorney in a number of ways. Third party authorizations include but are not limited to:

- The Third Party Designee (sometimes referred to as "Check Box" authority)
- The Oral Disclosure Consent (ODC)
- The Oral Tax Information Authorization (OTIA)[154]

The third party designee authorization allows the IRS to discuss the processing of a taxpayer's current tax return, including the status of refunds, with whomever the taxpayer specifies. The authorization automatically expires on the due date of the next tax return.

---

[154] IRC 6103(e)(6) and (c) provide for disclosures to powers of attorney and other designees.

A taxpayer can choose a third party designee by checking the "yes" box on his tax return, which is why it is known as "Check Box" authority. The taxpayer then enters the designee's name and phone number and a self-selected five-digit PIN, which the designee must confirm when requesting information from the IRS.

Currently, the third party designee authorization is not recorded on the CAF system. Instead, during tax return processing, the authorization is recorded directly onto the taxpayer's account.

The designee can exchange verbal information with the IRS on return processing issues and on refunds and payments related to the return. The designee may also receive written account information, including transcripts upon request.

> **Example:** Rashid named his EA, Patty, as his third party designee on his tax return. A few months after filing his return, Rashid still had not received his refund. He asked Patty if she could check the status of his refund. Patty called the IRS and was given the information over the phone, because she was listed as a third party designee on Rashid's return. No further authorization was necessary for Patty to receive this confidential taxpayer information.

The third party designee authorization can co-exist with a power of attorney for the same tax and tax period. However, the authorization does not allow the designee to "represent the taxpayer." Although it is similar to the authority given by Form 8821, *Tax Information Authorization* (TIA), it is more limited. Unlike the third party designee authorization, Form 8821 can be used to allow discussions with third parties and disclosures of information to third parties on matters other than just a taxpayer's current return.

> **Note:** There is a significant difference between a third party designee and an "official representative." A power of attorney (Form 2848) allows a practitioner to represent and negotiate with the IRS on the taxpayer's behalf. An authorized representative (listed on Form 2848) may advocate for the taxpayer and may argue facts or law with the IRS. The appointee of a Tax Information Authorization (Form 8821 or third party designee) is only able to receive and exchange information with the IRS for purposes of resolving basic tax account issues.[155]

A taxpayer may give oral consent for the IRS to speak with a third party if necessary to resolve a federal tax matter.[156] However, oral consent does not substitute for a power of attorney or a legal designation, and the discussion is limited to the issue for which the consent is given.

The Oral Tax Information Authorization (OTIA) is the "verbal equivalent" of Form 8821 and is valid until revoked or withdrawn. The OTIA allows the taxpayer the ability to grant a third party, including friends and family, the authority to receive and inspect both written and verbal tax account information. The appointee must have a CAF number. The appointee may receive copies of notices and transcripts on open issues, but cannot receive IRS refund checks. The OTIA is recorded on the CAF.

---

[155] See Publication 4019 for a handy quick reference of third party authorizations.

[156] Public Law 104-168, commonly known as the Taxpayer Bill of Rights II, deleted the requirement that a taxpayer's request for disclosure to a third party be in writing. The change was not possible until Temporary Regulation 301-6103(c)-IT, effective January 11, 2001, which authorized the IRS to accept non-written requests or consents, authorizing the disclosure of return information to third parties assisting taxpayers to resolve federal tax related matters. The temporary regulation was made permanent by 26 CFR 301.6103(c) 1 (c).

The Oral Disclosure Consent (ODC) is a tax information authorization limited to specific notices and oral disclosure only. The ODC does not allow the appointee to receive any written information and does not allow the appointee to represent the taxpayer. It is not recorded on the CAF. It is recorded directly on the account.

When only requesting the disclosure of return information such as copies of tax returns, transcripts of an account to verify adjusted gross income, and wages earned for *nontax matter purposes* (such as income verification and loan applications), the taxpayer should use Form 4506, *Request for a Copy or Transcript of Tax Form*, and submit it to the IRS Return and Income Verification Services.

Summary: Types of Consents

1. **Third Party Designee Authorization** is submitted with the filing of a tax return for the purpose of resolving return processing, payment, or refund issues.

2. **Oral Disclosure Consent** is used when addressing a specific issue raised in a notice received from the IRS. This type of consent is usually done with the taxpayer over the phone.

3. **Oral Tax Information Authorization or Form 8821** is used when an examination of written account information is needed and the issues are related to the tax period versus a specific notice issue. In actual practice, this form is used most often to obtain taxpayer records or transcripts of prior returns.

4. **Power of Attorney (Form 2848)** is used when the authorization is for the purpose of allowing a tax professional (attorney, CPA, EA, etc.) to represent and act on behalf of the taxpayer, including negotiating with the IRS, signing returns, consents, and arguing facts or law. This is the most formal of all the consents. If properly authorized, Form 2848 allows enrolled practitioners unlimited practice rights to represent taxpayers.

IRS Information Requests § 10.20

Under Circular 230 §10.20, when the IRS requests information, a practitioner must comply and submit records promptly.

If the requested information or records are not in the practitioner's possession, he must promptly advise the requesting IRS officer and provide any information he has regarding the identity of the person who may have possession or control of the requested information or records. The practitioner must also make a "reasonable inquiry" of his client regarding the location of the requested records.

However, the practitioner is not required to make inquiry of any other person or to independently verify any information furnished by his client. The practitioner is also not required to contact any third party who might be in possession of the records.

Example: An IRS revenue agent recently submitted a lawful records request to Randall, an EA, for accounting records relating to a former client that was under IRS investigation. However, Randall had fired his former client for nonpayment and then returned his client's records. Randall promptly notified the IRS officer that he no longer had possession of the records. Randall also attempted to contact his former client, but the phone number was disconnected. Randall is not required to contact any third parties to discover the location of the requested records. Therefore, Randall has fulfilled his obligations under §10.20.

A practitioner may not interfere with any lawful effort by the IRS to obtain any record or information *unless* the practitioner believes in good faith and on reasonable grounds that the record or information is privileged under IRC Section 7525. A practitioner can also be exempted from these rules if he believes in good faith that the request is of doubtful legality.

If the OPR requests information concerning possible violations of the regulations by other parties, such as other preparers or taxpayers, the practitioner must furnish the information and be prepared to testify in disbarment or suspension proceedings.

Return of Client Records (§10.28)

A tax practitioner is *required* to return a client's records whether or not fees have been paid. Client records are defined as any original records belonging to the client, including any work product that the client has already *paid for*, such as a completed copy of a tax return.

The practitioner must, at the request of a client, promptly return any and all records that are necessary for the client to comply with his federal tax obligations. The practitioner must also allow the client reasonable access to review and copy any additional records retained by the practitioner that are necessary for the client to comply with his federal tax obligations. The practitioner may retain copies of the records returned to a client.

A fee dispute does not relieve the practitioner of his responsibility to return client records. The practitioner must provide the client with reasonable access to review and copy any additional records retained by the practitioner under state law that are necessary for the client to comply with his federal tax obligations.

Client records do not include the tax practitioner's work product. "Records of the client" include:

- All documents provided to the practitioner that pre-existed the retention of the practitioner by the client.
- Any materials that were prepared by the client or a third party at any time and provided to the practitioner relating to the subject matter of the representation.
- Any document prepared by the practitioner that was presented to the client relating to a prior representation if such document is necessary for the taxpayer to comply with his current federal tax obligations.

The term "records of the client" does not include any return, claim for refund, schedule, affidavit, appraisal, or any other document prepared by the practitioner if he is withholding these documents pending the client's payment of fees.

Example: Clara is an EA who does substantial tax work for a partnership, Greenway Landscaping. Greenway has been slow to pay in the past, so Clara asks that the owners of Greenway pay for the tax returns when they pick them up. Greenway refuses and demands the tax returns anyway. Clara decides to discontinue all contact with Greenway. Clara must return Greenway's original records, but she is not required to give Greenway work product that the owners have not paid for.

Example: Leroy, an EA, has a client, Samantha, who becomes very upset after he tells her she owes substantial penalties to the IRS in the current year. Samantha wants to get a second opinion, and she does not want to pay Leroy for his time. Leroy is required to hand over Samantha's tax records, including copies of her W-2 forms and any other information she brought to his office. Leroy returns her original records, but he does not give her a copy of the tax return he prepared, since she did not pay for the return. A practitioner is not required to give a client any tax return, claim for refund, schedule, affidavit, appraisal, or any other document prepared by the practitioner if he is withholding the documents because of a fee dispute.

Retaining Copies of Tax Returns

Tax preparers are required to keep a copy (or a list) of all returns they have prepared for at least three years. Alternatively, preparers may also keep copies of the actual returns. If the preparer does not keep copies of the actual returns, he is required to keep a list or card file of clients and tax returns prepared. At a minimum, the list must contain the taxpayer's name, identification number, tax year, and the type of return prepared.

***Note:** In actual practice, most preparers keep scanned, digital, or hard copies of client tax returns rather than simply a list of the returns prepared.

Signature Requirements for Preparers

A tax return preparer is required by law to furnish a completed copy of a return or claim to the taxpayer, no later than the time the return or claim is presented for the taxpayer's signature.

A paid preparer is required by law to sign the tax return and fill out the preparer areas of the form. The preparer must also include his PTIN on the return. Although the preparer signs the return, the taxpayer is ultimately responsible for the accuracy of every item on the return.

The preparer must sign the return *after* it is completed and *before* it is presented to the taxpayer for signature. If the original preparer is unavailable for signature, another preparer must review the entire preparation of the return or claim and then must manually sign it.

For the purposes of the signature requirement, the preparer with primary responsibility for the overall accuracy of the return or claim is considered the preparer, if more than one preparer is involved. The other preparers do not have to be disclosed on the return.

If a return is mechanically completed by a computer that is not under the control of the individual preparer, a manually signed attestation may be attached to the return. The signature requirement may be satisfied by a photocopy of the manually signed copy of the return or claim. The preparer must retain the signed copy. A valid signature is defined by state law and may be anything that clearly indicates the intent to sign.

A preparer may sign *on behalf of the taxpayer* in the client's signature area if certain standards are met. For example, a representative is permitted to sign a taxpayer's return if the taxpayer is unable to sign the return because of disease or injury, or continuous absence from the United States, including when a taxpayer is serving in a combat zone. When a return is signed by a representative, it must be mailed and accompanied by a power of attorney (Form 2848). A taxpayer may also assign another agent (such as a spouse or a family member) to sign his tax return, by completing a valid power of attorney.

Paid tax preparers are also required to sign payroll tax returns.

The preparer's declaration on signing the return states that the information contained in the return is true, correct, and complete based on all information the preparer has. This statement is signed under penalty of perjury. The signature requirements for e-filed returns are covered later.

Preparer Identification (PTIN Requirement)

Paid preparers must include their PTIN with every return filed with the IRS. Previously, paid preparers had the option of using their Social Security Number. With new regulations in force, all paid preparers are now required to have a PTIN in order to prepare tax returns for a fee.

Penalties Related to Tax Return Preparation

Under IRC §6695, the IRS lists the penalties that may be assessed when it comes to the preparation of tax returns for other persons. The penalty is $50 for each violation of the following:

- Failure to furnish a copy of a return or claim to a taxpayer
- Failure to sign a return or claim for refund
- Failure to furnish an identifying number (PTIN) on a return
- Failure to retain a copy or list of a return or claim
- Failure to file correct information returns

The penalty is steeper for a preparer who endorses, cashes, or deposits a taxpayer's refund check. A preparer may be assessed a fee of $500 for each check violation. The penalty is also $500 for each failure to comply with Earned Income Credit due diligence requirements (covered in detail later in Unit 5.)

The maximum penalty imposed by the IRS on any tax return preparer cannot exceed $25,000 in a calendar year or return period.

> **Note:** Specific penalties that may be imposed on both preparers and taxpayers are often tested on the EA exam. Test-takers should be familiar with each of these penalties listed, as well as others detailed in this study guide.

Identity Theft and Preparer Security

Identity theft occurs when someone uses another individual's personally identifiable information, such as his name, Social Security Number, or credit card number, without his permission in order to commit fraud or other crimes. Fraudulent refunds have become a major issue, with the acting IRS commissioner calling identity theft one of the "biggest challenges" facing the IRS today.

In February 2013, the IRS announced the results of a year-long enforcement crackdown targeting refund fraud caused by identity theft. Hundreds of suspects were arrested in a sweep of identity theft suspects. The IRS says aggressive enforcement stopped $20 billion in fraudulent returns from being issued in 2012.

One common source of fraud is when identity thieves file fraudulent refund claims using another person's identifying information, which they have stolen. To stop identity thieves, the IRS says it now has dozens of identity theft screening filers in place to protect tax refunds. To educate taxpayers, the IRS has added a guide to identity theft on its website.

As part of its crackdown, the IRS is issuing an Identity Protection Personal Identification Number (IP PIN) to any taxpayers who have:

- reported to the IRS they have been the victims of identity theft
- given the IRS information that verifies their identity
- had an identity theft indicator applied to their account

The IP PIN helps prevent the misuse of a taxpayer's Social Security Number or Taxpayer Identification Number on tax returns. It is used on both paper and electronic returns. If a taxpayer attempts to file an electronic return without his IP PIN, the return will be rejected. If it is missing on a paper return, there is likely to be a delay in processing as the IRS will have to validate the taxpayer's identity.

The IP PIN is only valid for a single year. A taxpayer will receive a new IP PIN every year for three years after the identity theft incident. If a spouse also has an IP PIN, only the person whose SSN appears first on the tax return needs to input his or her IP PIN.

Since practitioners are required to obtain and store client information, they have an important role to play in keeping this information secure. To help prevent identity theft, preparers should confirm identities and Taxpayer Identification numbers (TINs) of taxpayers, their spouses, dependents, and EIC qualifying children contained on the returns to be prepared. TINs include Social Security Numbers (SSNs), Adopted Taxpayer Identification Numbers (ATINs), and Individual Taxpayer Identification Numbers (ITINs).

To confirm identities, the preparer can request a picture ID showing the taxpayer's name and address, and Social Security cards or other documents providing the TINs of all individuals to be listed on the return.

Additional steps practitioners can take to guard against identity theft include the following:[157]

- File clients' returns early when possible.
- E-file returns to be notified of duplicate return notices more quickly.
- Consider truncating or masking SSNs on Forms 1098, 1099, and 5498.
- Let clients know that refunds may take longer in future years as additional system security steps are taken.
- Be very careful about confirming the identity of new online clients.

Practitioner Fees

The IRS prohibits practitioners from charging "unconscionable fees." Though that term has not been defined, it is generally believed to be when the fees are so grossly unethical that the courts would consider them as such.

---

[157] *Journal of Accountancy*, February 2013.

Strict Rules for Contingent Fees

A practitioner may not charge a contingent fee (percentage of the refund) for preparing an original tax return, amended tax return, or claim for refund or credit. A contingent fee also includes a fee that is based on a percentage of the taxes saved or one that depends on a specific result.

Additionally, a contingent fee includes any fee arrangement in which the practitioner agrees to reimburse the client for all or a portion of the client's fee in the event that a position taken on a tax return or other filing is not successful. The OPR says it will aggressively seek out and sanction tax preparers who are collecting unauthorized contingent fees.

The IRS does allow a practitioner to charge a contingent fee in some limited circumstances, including:

- Representation during the examination of an original tax return; an amended return or claim for refund or credit where the amended return or claim for refund or credit was filed *within 120 days* of the taxpayer receiving a written notice of examination; or a written challenge to the original tax return.
- Services rendered in connection with a refund claim or credit or refund filed in conjunction with a penalty or interest charge.
- Services rendered in connection with any litigation or judicial proceeding arising under the Internal Revenue Code.

Advertising Restrictions §10.30

Circular 230 covers preparer advertising standards. A practitioner may not use any form of communication to advertise material that contains false, deceptive, or coercive information. Under no circumstances may practitioners use official IRS insignia in their advertising.

Enrolled agents, in describing their professional designation, may not use the term "certified" or imply any type of employment relationship with the IRS. Examples of acceptable descriptions for EAs are "enrolled to represent taxpayers before the Internal Revenue Service," "enrolled to practice before the Internal Revenue Service," and "admitted to practice before the Internal Revenue Service."

Preparers are **prohibited** from using the following logos in any capacity:

Prohibited

A practitioner may not make, directly or indirectly, an uninvited written or oral solicitation of employment in matters related to the IRS if the solicitation violates federal or state law. Practitioners have the right to make solicitations involving IRS matters in certain cases. All of the following types of communications are allowed:

- Seeking new business from a former client
- Communicating with a family member
- Targeted mailings
- Non-coercive in-person solicitation while acting as an employee, member, or officer of a 501(c)(3) or 501(c)(4) organization (such as a door-to-door fundraiser for the SPCA or a church fundraiser)

Mail solicitations are allowed, so long as the solicitation is not uninvited. In the case of direct mail and e-commerce communications, the practitioner must retain a copy of the actual communication, along with a list of persons to whom the communication was mailed or distributed, for at least 36 months.

A practitioner may attempt to solicit new business from current or former clients, or a client's family. A practitioner may not continue to contact a prospective client who has communicated he does not wish to be solicited.

Practitioners may also send solicitations to other practitioners indicating the practitioner's availability to provide professional services (such as independent contractor bookkeeping or tax preparation services). The advertising and communications must not be misleading, deceptive, or in violation of IRS regulations.

Published Fee Schedules §10.30

A practitioner may publish and advertise a fee schedule. A practitioner must adhere to the published fee schedule for *at least* 30 calendar days after it is published.

> **Example:** Gracie is an EA who publishes an advertisement in her local newspaper. The ad includes a published fee schedule for preparing certain tax return forms at a deeply discounted rate. Gracie is inundated with calls and decides that the ad was a mistake. Regardless, she must adhere to the published fee schedule for at least 30 days after it was published.

Fee information may be published in newspapers, telephone directories, mailings, websites, e-mail, or by any other method. A practitioner may include fees based on the following:

- Fixed fees for specific routine services
- Hourly fee rates
- A range of fees for particular services
- A fee charged for an initial consultation

In advertising fees on radio or television, the broadcast must be recorded, and the practitioner must retain a record of the recording for at least 36 months (three years) from the date of the last transmission or use.

> **Example:** Travis is an EA who pays for a radio commercial about his services. It plays for four months during tax season. Travis is required to keep a copy of the radio commercial for at least 36 months from the last date that the commercial aired.

Unit 3: Questions

1. If an EA knows that a client has filed an erroneous tax return, the practitioner is legally required to _____.

A. Correct the error.
B. Advise the client about the error and the consequences for not correcting the error.
C. Do nothing if the practitioner was not the one who prepared the erroneous return.
D. Disengage from any further business with the client if the client does not agree to correct the error.

The answer is B. If an EA knows that a client has filed an erroneous tax return, he must advise the client to correct the error. The EA is not required to amend the return, but he must advise the client about the error and the consequences for not correcting the error. He is not required to notify the IRS about his client's error. ###

2. Dennis, an enrolled agent, wants to hire his friend, Brandon, who is also an enrolled agent. Brandon has just been disbarred from practice by the IRS for misconduct. Brandon correctly appeals the disbarment, and his disbarment is currently under review. Which of the following statement is true?

A. Dennis can still hire Brandon as a tax preparer, so long as Brandon does not represent any taxpayers.
B. Dennis can still hire Brandon, so long as he does not sign the tax returns.
C. Dennis cannot hire Brandon.
D. Dennis can hire Brandon while he legally appeals his disbarment.

The answer is C. Dennis cannot knowingly hire a disbarred practitioner, regardless of whether that person would be preparing tax returns or not. A practitioner may not knowingly employ a person or accept employment from a person who has been disbarred or suspended by the Office of Professional Responsibility, even if that person's case is under appeal. ###

3. Which of the following statements is correct regarding a client's request for his original records in order to comply with federal tax obligations?

A. The practitioner may choose not to return records to the client even if he requests their prompt return.
B. A fee dispute relieves the practitioner of his responsibility to return a client's records.
C. The practitioner must, at the request of the client, promptly return a client's records, regardless of any fee dispute.
D. The practitioner must, at the request of the client, return client records within three months of the request.

The answer is C. Records must be returned promptly upon client demand, regardless of any fee dispute. Records are defined as any original records belonging to the client, including any work product that he has already paid for, such as a completed copy of a tax return. However, unlike in the case of the client's original documents, the practitioner is allowed to withhold the return of his own work papers or preparer work product until the client has resolved any outstanding payment issues. ###

4. Circular 230 covers which of the following topics?

A. Taxpayer identification and security.
B. Individual taxation.
C. Corporate taxation.
D. Ethics and rules of practice for tax practitioners.

The answer is D. Circular 230 covers ethics and rules of practice for tax practitioners who are enrolled to practice before the IRS. ###

5. Which of the following statements is true regarding tax practitioners?

A. EAs cannot notarize documents of the clients they represent before the IRS.
B. EAs cannot be notaries.
C. Tax preparers cannot be notaries.
D. A notary who is also a tax practitioner will not be eligible for the e-file program.

The answer is A. Tax practitioners cannot notarize documents of the clients they represent before the IRS. However, they are not prohibited from performing notary services for clients in other matters. ###

6. Which of the following statements is correct?

A. Conflicts of interest do not apply to tax professionals, only to attorneys.
B. Tax practitioners may represent clients who have a conflict of interest if waivers are signed by both parties.
C. Tax practitioners may represent clients who have a conflict of interest if the taxpayer informs both parties by phone.
D. Tax practitioners may not represent clients who have a conflict of interest.

The answer is B. A tax practitioner can represent conflict of interest clients if the clients are notified and written waivers are signed by both parties. The notification must be in writing. A phone call is insufficient. ###

7. Enrolled agents may advertise their services in the following manner:

A. With the phrase "Certified by the IRS."
B. With the phrase "Enrolled to practice before the IRS."
C. With the phrase "An IRS-approved practitioner."
D. With the phrase "A Certified Tax Accountant."

The answer is B. An EA may state that he or she is "enrolled to practice" before the Internal Revenue Service. The other phrases are not allowed. ###

8. Franklin is an EA who decides to advertise his fee schedule in the local newspaper. Which of the following fee arrangements is prohibited?

A. Hourly fee rates.
B. Fixed fees for tax preparation.
C. Contingent fee for an original return.
D. A flat fee for an initial consultation.

The answer is C. A practitioner may never charge a contingent fee for an original return that is based on the refund amount. A practitioner may publish and advertise a fee schedule. All the other fees are acceptable. ###

9. Which does not constitute a "best practice" for tax return preparers under the guidelines of Circular 230?

A. Consulting other professionals when questions arise about a particular tax issue.
B. Acting fairly and with integrity in practice before the IRS.
C. Communicating clearly with the client regarding the rules of engagement.
D. Advising the client regarding the consequences of advice rendered.

The answer is A. Although it may be a good idea to consult with other tax professionals when particular tax questions arise, this is not listed as one of the "best practices" in Circular 230. Each of the other statements is called a "best practice" in the Circular 230 regulations.

10. All of the following statements regarding the signature requirements for tax returns are correct except:

A. A tax preparer may sign a taxpayer's return in lieu of the taxpayer, if the taxpayer cannot sign his own tax return due to a physical disability.
B. A tax preparer may sign a taxpayer's return in lieu of the taxpayer, if the taxpayer cannot sign his own tax return due to an extended absence from the United States.
C. A tax preparer is allowed to copy a taxpayer's signature if he has a signed power of attorney.
D. A tax preparer must have a signed power of attorney in order to sign on the taxpayer's behalf.

The answer is C. A preparer is never allowed to copy a taxpayer's signature. This is considered forgery. A preparer may sign in lieu of the taxpayer in certain situations. For example, rules permit a representative to sign a taxpayer's return if he is unable to do so himself for any of the following reasons:
•Disease or injury
•Continuous absence from the United States (including Puerto Rico) for a period of at least 60 days prior to the date required by law for filing the return
•Other good cause if specific permission is requested of and granted by the IRS
When a return is signed by a representative, it must be accompanied by a power of attorney authorizing the representative to sign the return. ###

11. When does the authorization for a "third party designee" expire?

A. Three months after the return is filed.
B. One year after the return is filed.
C. Three years after the return is filed.
D. On the due date of the next tax return.

The answer is D. A third party designee authorization expires on the due date of the next tax return. The designee may address any issue arising out of the tax return for a period not to exceed one year from the due date of the tax return. The designee may also receive written account information including transcripts upon request. ###

12. Ryan is an EA with a client named Hannah who has had significant income from a partnership for the past five years. However, Ryan did not see a Schedule K-1 from the partnership among the information Hannah provided to him this year. What does due diligence require Ryan to do?

A. Attempt to estimate the amount that would be reported as income on the Schedule K-1 based on last year's Schedule K-1 and include that amount on Hannah's return.
B. Call Hannah's financial advisor and ask him about Hannah's investments.
C. Nothing, because Ryan is required to rely only on the information provided by his client, even if he has reason to know the information is not accurate.
D. Ask Hannah about the fact that she did not provide him with the partnership's Schedule K-1, as she had in previous years.

The answer is D. A practitioner has a "duty to advise." This means that a practitioner who knows his client has not complied with the revenue laws or has made an error in or omission from any return, document, affidavit, or other required paper has the responsibility to advise the client promptly of the noncompliance, error, or omission. ###

13. Where is the third party designee authorization recorded?

A. On the CAF system.
B. Directly onto the taxpayer's account.
C. This authorization is not recorded by the IRS; it is recorded by the practitioner.
D. The taxpayer must record the third party designee in his own account.

The answer is B. During returns processing, the authorization is recorded directly onto the account of the taxpayer. Currently, the third party designee authorization is not recorded on the CAF system. ###

14. Darrell is an EA who has a third party designee authorization for his client, Annalise. All of the following actions are allowed with this type of authorization except:

A. Darrell can receive written account information on Annalise's behalf.
B. Darrell can receive Annalise's tax transcripts upon request.
C. Darrell can check the status of tax refund processing.
D. Darrell may receive Annalise's refund check.

The answer is D. In order to receive a tax refund check on a client's behalf, a Form 2848 must be filed. A third party designee authorization is not sufficient. With a third party designee authorization, Darrell can exchange verbal information with the IRS on return processing issues and on refunds and payments related to the return. Darrell can also receive written account information, including transcripts, upon request. ###

15. Under IRC §6695, the IRS lists the penalties that may be assessed relating to the preparation of tax returns for other persons. For these violations, what is the maximum penalty per year a preparer may face?

A. $10,000.
B. $25,000.
C. $50,000.
D. $100,000.

The answer is B. Under the terms of IRC §6695, the maximum penalty imposed on any tax return preparer cannot exceed $25,000 in a calendar year for these specific violations. ###

16. What penalty does a tax return preparer face if he improperly cashes a client's tax refund check?

A. Nothing. This is acceptable so long as the client has given permission to do so.
B. A fine of $50 for each violation.
C. A fine of $100 for each violation.
D. A fine of $500 for each violation.

The answer is D. It is prohibited for return preparers to negotiate (cash) taxpayers' refund checks. A preparer faces a fine of $500 for each violation. ###

17. All the following statements regarding confidentiality protection for enrolled practitioners are correct except:

A. The protection relates to noncriminal tax matters before the IRS.
B. The protection applies to communications that would be considered privileged if they were between the taxpayer and an attorney.
C. The protection is granted to CPAs, enrolled agents, enrolled actuaries, and supervised preparers.
D. The protection is not granted in state tax proceedings.

The answer is C. The practitioner privilege is granted to attorneys, CPAs, enrolled agents, and enrolled actuaries, but not to supervised preparers. ###

18. Which statement is true regarding the privacy regulations in Internal Revenue Code §7216?

A. The regulations do not apply to e-file providers.
B. The improper disclosure must be "knowing or reckless" for criminal provisions to apply.
C. A practitioner may be fined up to $500 and imprisoned for up to one year for each violation of this code.
D. Tax practitioners must obtain oral consent from taxpayers before they can use information for anything other than the actual preparation of tax returns.

The answer is B. Internal Revenue Code §7216 is a criminal code that limits tax professionals' use and disclosure of client information. "B" is correct because criminal penalties will apply only if the improper disclosure is "knowing or reckless," rather than simply negligent. The other answers are incorrect because regulations do apply to e-file providers; a practitioner may be fined up to $1,000, not $500, and imprisoned for up to a year for each violation; and written consent, not oral, is generally required before taxpayer information can be disclosed. ###

19. How long must a tax professional retain records relating to clients who have offered their consent for representation in conflict-of-interest cases?

A. One year from the date representation ends.
B. Two years from the date representation ends.
C. Three years from the date representation ends.
D. Five years from the date representation ends.

The answer is C. In conflict of interest cases, a preparer must obtain consent in writing and retain the records for at least 36 months (three years) from the date representation ends. ###

20. In what situation is a return preparer allowed to disclose information without first obtaining written permission from a client?

A. When he is issued a subpoena by a state agency that regulates tax return preparers.
B. When he is contacted by a newspaper reporter investigating a possible crime committed by his client.
C. When the information is requested by his client's uncle who helps support the client financially.
D. When the information is needed by a preparer who volunteers with VITA.

The answer is A. A preparer who is issued a subpoena or court order, whether at the federal, state, or local level, is not required to obtain disclosure permission from a client. In all the other cases, disclosure is not allowed, unless there has been prior written consent. ###

21. Which designation or form gives the appointed person the greatest rights to represent a taxpayer?

A. Third party designee, also known as "Check Box" authority.
B. Form 8821, *Tax Information Authorization*.
C. Oral Tax Information authorization.
D. Form 2848, *Power of Attorney and Declaration of Representative*.

The answer is D. Only Form 2848, *Power of Attorney and Declaration of Representative,* allows a third party to represent a taxpayer before the IRS. The other consents are much more limited and allow only a third party to receive or inspect written or oral tax account information. ###

22. All of the following statements regarding a tax preparer's responsibility to provide information requested by the IRS are correct except:

A. He must promptly turn over all records relating to the IRS request, no matter what the circumstances.
B. If the records are not in his possession, he must make a "reasonable inquiry" of his client about their whereabouts.
C. He is not legally obligated to contact any third party who might possess the requested records.
D. If he believes in good faith and on reasonable grounds that the requested material is legally privileged information, a preparer may choose to decline a records request.

The answer is A. Although Circular 230 dictates that a return preparer comply promptly with information and record requests, there are limited circumstances when records do not have to be turned over. A preparer may decline to do so if he believes in good faith that the request is not legal or if the information is privileged. ###

23. In which instance is a tax preparer allowed to charge a contingent fee?

A. When his regular fee is "unconscionable."
B. When the fee is based on a claim for refund only.
C. When the IRS rules that a certain position taken on a return is not allowed.
D. When the preparer renders services in connection with an IRS court proceeding.

The answer is D. There are very strict rules for when preparers are permitted to charge contingent fees (percentage of a refund). Only in very limited instances are these fees allowed, such as when a preparer offers services in connection with any IRC-related litigation or judicial proceeding. ###

24. What penalty does a preparer face for failing to sign a client's claim for refund?

A. A warning letter from the IRS.
B. A fine of $50.
C. A fine of $100.
D. A fine of $500.

The answer is B. Under IRC §6695, the IRS lists the penalties that may be assessed when it comes to the preparation of tax returns for other persons. The penalty is $50 for each violation of the following:
1. Failure to furnish a copy of a return or claim to a taxpayer
2. Failure to sign a return or claim for refund
3. Failure to furnish an identifying number (PTIN) on a return
4. Failure to retain a copy or list of a return or claim
5. Failure to file correct information returns

A preparer faces a maximum penalty of $25,000 per calendar year or return period for these types of violations. ###

Unit 4: Taxpayer Obligations, Fraud, & Penalties

More Reading:
Publication 583, *Starting a Business and Keeping Records*
Publication 552, *Recordkeeping for Individuals*
Publication 947, *Practice Before the IRS and Power of Attorney*

Basic Recordkeeping Requirements

There are some basic recordkeeping requirements expected of U.S. taxpayers that tax preparers need to be familiar with and make sure their clients understand. Various types of recordkeeping requirements are tested on all three parts of the EA exam.

Part 3 of the EA exam focuses on the substantiation of items and records retention. There are also specific recordkeeping requirements relating to the Earned Income Credit that are tested on Part 3. (The due diligence requirements for EIC claims are covered later in Unit 5).

Except in a few cases, tax law does not require specific kinds of records to be kept. Any records that clearly demonstrate expenses, basis, and income should be retained. Generally, this means the taxpayer must keep records that support an item of income or deduction on a return until the statute of limitations for the tax return runs out. The IRS recommends that taxpayers keep all sales slips, invoices, receipts, canceled checks, or other financial account statements relating to a particular transaction.

A taxpayer may choose any recordkeeping system that clearly reflects income and expenses. He must keep records as long as they may be needed for the administration of any provision of the Internal Revenue Code.

If a taxpayer or business decides to use a computer recordkeeping system, he or the business must still retain a record of original documents. However, these documents may be scanned or kept on a computer imaging system. The IRS generally does not require a taxpayer to keep original paper records (Rev. Proc. 97-22).

Statute of Limitations for Records Retention

A taxpayer should keep all relevant records until the statute of limitations for his tax return expires. For assessment of tax owed, this period is generally three years from the date the return was filed or the return was due, whichever is later.

For filing a claim for credit or refund, the period to make the claim generally is three years from the date the original return was filed or two years from the date the tax was paid, whichever is later.

Records relating to the basis of property should be retained as long as they may be material to any tax return involving the property. The basis of property is material until the statute of limitations expires for the tax year an asset is sold or disposed of. A taxpayer must keep these records to figure any depreciation, amortization, or depletion deductions, and to figure the asset's basis.

Example: Cory has owned a vacation home for eight years, but in 2012 he decides to sell it. In order to compute basis and his gain on the property, he should have the records relating to the purchase of the property, and any other events that would add or subtract from his basis. He reports the sale of the vacation home on his 2012 tax return. He must continue to retain the records relating to the sale of the home until the statute of limitations for the tax return expires, usually three years from the date of filing or the due date of the return, whichever is later.

There are longer record retention periods in some cases. If a taxpayer files a claim from a loss of worthless securities, then the period to retain records related to the transaction is seven years.

If a taxpayer fails to report income that exceeds more than 25% of the gross income shown on his return, the statute of limitations is six years from when the return is filed. There is no statute of limitations to assess tax when a return is fraudulent or when no return is filed.

Recordkeeping for Employment (Payroll) Tax Returns

A business is required to retain payroll and employment tax records for at least four years after the tax becomes due or is paid, whichever is later. Examples include: copies of employees' income tax withholding allowance certificates (Forms W-4), records of fringe benefits provided, and dates and amounts of payroll tax deposits made. This rule also applies to businesses that employ other tax preparers.

Example: Joelle is an EA who employs five other preparers in her office. She is required to keep the employment tax records relating to her employees for at least four years.

All employer tax records must be made available for IRS review. Necessary records include:

- Employer Identification Numbers (EIN)
- Amounts and dates of all wage, annuity, and pension payments, and amounts of tips reported (if applicable)
- The fair market value of in-kind wages paid
- Names, addresses, Social Security numbers, and occupations of employees and recipients
- Any copies of Form W-2 that were returned undeliverable
- Dates of active employment
- Periods for which employees were paid sick leave
- Copies of employees' and recipients' income tax withholding allowance certificates (Forms W-4)
- Dates and amounts of tax deposits
- Copies of all employment returns filed
- Records of fringe benefits provided, including substantiation

Statute of Limitations	
Type of Record/Return	**Minimum Retention Period**
Normal tax return	Three years
Omitted income that exceeds 25% of the gross income shown on the return	Six years
A fraudulent return	No limit
No return filed	No limit
A claim for credit or amended return	The later of three years or two years after tax was paid
A claim for a loss from worthless securities	Seven years
Employment and payroll tax records	The later of four years after tax becomes due or is paid
Fixed assets, real estate, other assets	Records should be kept until after the expiration of the statute of limitations for the tax year in which the asset is sold or disposed of

Test-takers should memorize these retention periods as they are often tested on the EA exam.

Tax Avoidance vs. Tax Evasion

The term "tax avoidance" is not defined by the IRS, but it is commonly used to describe the legal reduction of taxable income. Most taxpayers use at least a few methods of tax avoidance in order to reduce their taxable income and therefore lower their tax liability.

Example: Nate contributes to his employer-sponsored retirement plans with pretax funds. He also uses an employer-based Flexible Spending Account for his medical expenses, which reduces his taxable income by making all of his medical expenses pretax. Nate is using *legal* tax avoidance in order to reduce his taxable income.

Tax *evasion*, on the other hand, is an illegal practice in which individuals or businesses intentionally avoid paying their true tax liability. All citizens must comply with tax law. Although most Americans recognize their civic duty and comply with their tax obligations, the U.S. government estimates that approximately 3% of taxpayers do not file tax returns at all. Those caught evading taxes are subject to criminal charges and substantial penalties.

For each year a taxpayer does not file a return, the penalty can include a fine of up to $25,000 and a prison sentence of up to one year. If it can be demonstrated that the taxpayer deliberately did not file in an attempt to evade taxation, the IRS can pursue a felony conviction, which could include a fine of up to $100,000 and a maximum prison sentence of five years.

Exam takers should be familiar with the specifics of each of these penalties, as well as others detailed in this unit.

Penalties Imposed Upon Taxpayers

For individual taxpayers, the IRS can assess a penalty for those who fail to file, fail to pay, or both. The failure-to-file penalty is generally greater than the failure-to-pay penalty. If someone is unable to pay all the taxes he owes, he is better off filing on time and paying as much as he can. The IRS will explore payment options with individual taxpayers.

Failure-to-file Penalty

The penalty for filing late is usually 5% of the unpaid taxes for each month or part of a month that a return is late. This penalty will not exceed 25% of a taxpayer's unpaid taxes. The penalty is based on the tax not paid by the due date, without regard to extensions.

If a taxpayer files his return more than 60 days after the due date or extended due date, the minimum penalty is the smaller of $135 or 100% of the unpaid tax. If the taxpayer is owed a refund, there will not be a failure-to-file penalty.[158]

Failure-to-pay Penalty

If a taxpayer does not pay his taxes by the due date, he will be subject to a failure-to-pay penalty of ½ of 1% (0.5%) of unpaid taxes for each month or part of a month after the due date that the taxes are not paid. This penalty can be as much as 25% of a taxpayer's unpaid taxes.

If a taxpayer filed for an extension of time to file by the tax deadline and he paid at least 90% of his actual tax liability by the original due date, he will not face a failure-to-pay penalty so long as the remaining balance is paid by the extended due date.

The failure-to-pay penalty rate increases to a full 1% per month for any tax that remains unpaid the day after a demand for immediate payment is issued, or ten days after notice of intent to levy certain assets is issued. For taxpayers who filed on time but are unable to pay their tax liabilities, the failure-to-pay penalty rate is reduced to ¼ of 1% (0.25%) per month during any month in which the taxpayer has a valid installment agreement with the IRS.

If both the failure-to-file penalty and the failure-to-pay penalty apply in any month, the 5% failure-to-file penalty is reduced by the failure-to-pay penalty. However, if a taxpayer files his return more than 60 days after the due date or extended due date, the minimum penalty remains the smaller of $135 or 100% of the unpaid tax.

A taxpayer will not have to pay either penalty if he shows he failed to file or pay on time because of reasonable cause and not willful neglect.

Penalties are payable upon notice and demand. Penalties are generally assessed, collected, and paid in the same manner as taxes. The taxpayer will receive a notice that contains:

---

[158] Please note that the rules regarding failure-to-file penalties are different for entities (corporations, partnerships, trusts, etc.) In the case of partnerships and corporations, a late filing penalty may apply even if the entity shows a loss, or does not owe any tax.

- The name of the penalty,
- The applicable code section, and
- How the penalty was computed.

Accuracy-Related Penalties

The two most common accuracy-related penalties are the "substantial understatement" penalty and the "negligence or disregard of regulations" penalty. These penalties are calculated as a flat 20% of the net understatement of tax. In addition to other penalties, if the taxpayer provides fraudulent information on his tax return, he can be subject to a civil fraud penalty.

Penalty for Substantial Understatement

The understatement is considered "substantial" if it is more than the larger of:

- 10% of the correct tax, or
- $5,000 for individuals.

A taxpayer may avoid the substantial understatement penalty if he has substantial authority (such as previous court cases) for his position or through adequate disclosure.

To avoid the substantial understatement penalty by adequate disclosure, the taxpayer (or tax preparer) must properly disclose the position on the tax return and there must be at least a reasonable basis for the position.

Trust Fund Recovery Penalty (TFRP)

The trust fund recovery penalty is most commonly exacted on employers. It is also called the "100% penalty" because the IRS will assess a tax of 100% of the amount due.

As authorized by IRC Section 6672, this penalty involves the income and Social Security taxes an employer withholds from the wages of employees. These taxes are called "trust fund" taxes because they are held in trust for the government. They have been withheld from an employee's paycheck, so the employer is required to remit them to the IRS. Sometimes, when business owners have financial trouble, they neglect to remit these taxes to the IRS.

The trust fund recovery penalty can be assessed against anyone who is considered a "responsible person" in the business. This includes corporate officers, directors, stockholders, and even rank-and-file employees. The IRS has assessed the penalty against accountants, bookkeepers, or even clerical staff, particularly if they have authority to sign checks. In determining whether to proceed with assertion of the TFRP, the IRS must determine:

- Responsibility, and
- Willfulness.

A person must be both "responsible" and "willful" to be liable for an employer's failure to collect or pay trust fund taxes to the United States. This means that he knew (or should have known) that the payroll taxes were not being remitted to the IRS, and that he also had the power to correct the problem. Usually, this means that the individual had check-signing authority, but each case is evaluated by the IRS.

> **Example:** Shelly works for Wilsonville Construction as a full-time bookkeeper and processes all the payroll tax forms. She also has check-signing authority, so she can pay the bills when her boss is working off-site. In 2012, her boss has a heart attack, and his wife, Doreen, takes over the business in his absence. Doreen can't manage the business properly and Wilsonville Construction soon falls into debt. Doreen tells Shelly to pay vendors first. The business continues to withhold payroll taxes from employee paychecks, but does not remit the amounts to the IRS. Eventually, the business goes under and Doreen disappears. Shelly is contacted by the IRS shortly thereafter. Even though Shelly was "just an employee," the IRS can assess the trust fund recovery penalty against her because (1) she had check-signing authority, and (2) she knew that the business was not lawfully remitting payroll taxes to the IRS as required.

The trust fund recovery penalty may be assessed *in addition* to any other penalties, including the failure-to-file, failure-to-pay, or fraud penalties.

Other Penalties

Civil Fraud Penalty

If there is any underpayment of tax due to fraud, a penalty of 75% of the underpayment will be assessed against the taxpayer. The fraud penalty on a joint return does not automatically apply to a spouse unless some part of the underpayment is due to the fraud of that spouse. The injured spouse may request relief from joint liability in this case. Negligence or simple ignorance of the law does not constitute fraud. Typically, IRS examiners who find strong evidence of fraud will refer the case to the IRS Criminal Investigation Division for possible criminal prosecution.

Frivolous and Fraudulent Returns

Some Americans assert that they are not required to file federal tax returns or pay federal tax because they claim that our system of taxation is based upon voluntary assessment and payment. These arguments are considered "frivolous positions."

Some tax protesters maintain that there is no federal statute imposing a tax on income derived from sources within the U.S. by citizens or residents of the United States. They argue instead that federal income taxes are excise taxes imposed only on nonresident aliens and foreign corporations for the privilege of receiving income from sources within the United States.

In addition to tax protesters, there are many other ways taxpayers attempt to defraud the government by not paying their tax liability. All of the following are illegal schemes, and anyone participating in them or promoting them can be liable for civil and criminal penalties:

- Abusive home-based business schemes
- Abusive trust schemes
- Misuse of the disabled access credit
- Abusive offshore bank schemes
- Exempt organizations' abusive tax avoidance transactions

Failure to Supply Social Security Number

If a taxpayer does not include a Social Security Number or the SSN of another person where required on a return, statement, or other document, he will be subject to a penalty of $50 for each failure. The taxpayer will also be subject to the $50 penalty if he does not give the SSN to another person when it is required on a return, statement, or other document.

Any taxpayer who files a tax return that is considered "frivolous" may have to pay a penalty of $5,000, *in addition* to any other penalty provided by law. This penalty may be doubled on a joint return. A taxpayer will be subject to this penalty if he files a tax return based simply on the desire to interfere with the administration of tax law.

The IRS takes fraudulent returns very seriously. Should a taxpayer choose to participate in a fraudulent tax scheme, he will not be shielded from potential civil and criminal sanctions, regardless of whether or not he used a tax preparer.

A "fraudulent return" also includes a return in which the individual is attempting to file using someone else's name or SSN, or when the taxpayer is presenting documents or information that have no basis in fact.

A potentially abusive return also includes a return that contains inaccurate information that may lead to an understatement of a liability or the overstatement of a credit resulting in a refund to which the taxpayer is not entitled.

Alteration of the Jurat is Prohibited and Considered Frivolous

Some taxpayers attempt to reduce their federal tax liability by striking out the written declaration, known as the "jurat," that verifies a return is made under penalties of perjury.

The Jurat

Civil penalties for altering a jurat include:

- A $500 penalty imposed under Section 6702;
- Additional penalties for failure to file a return, failure to pay tax owed, and fraudulent failure to file a return; and
- A penalty of up to $25,000 under Section 6673 if the taxpayer makes frivolous arguments in the United States Tax Court.

Example: A taxpayer files Form 1040 for the 2012 tax year. The taxpayer signs the form but crosses out the jurat on the return and writes the word "void" across it. This return is now considered "frivolous" and is subject to penalties.

Client Fraud

The IRS encourages tax preparers to look for client fraud. Sometimes, the taxpayer is merely negligent or careless, or may have an honest difference of opinion regarding the deductibility of an expense. If fraud is actually taking place, there are some common "badges of fraud" that the IRS looks for. Examples include:

- The understatement of income or improper deductions
- Personal items deducted as business expenses
- The overstatement of deductions or taking improper credits
- Making false entries in documents or destroying records
- Not cooperating with the IRS or avoiding IRS contact
- Concealing or transferring assets
- Engaging in illegal activity
- Sloppy recordkeeping
- All-cash businesses

Some of these actions taken by themselves do not necessarily constitute fraud. However, consistent abuses or multiple red flags may be a reason to suspect taxpayer fraud.

Tax Practitioner Fraud

Tax professionals are sometimes guilty of preparer fraud. Preparer fraud generally involves the preparation and filing of false income tax returns with inflated personal or business expenses, false deductions, unallowable credits, or excessive exemptions on returns prepared for their clients. Preparers may also manipulate income figures to obtain fraudulent tax credits, such as the Earned Income Credit.

The preparers' clients may or may not know about the false expenses, deductions, exemptions and/or credits shown on their tax returns. Fraudulent preparers gain financially by:

- Diverting a portion of the refund for their own benefit;
- Increasing their clientele by developing a reputation for obtaining large refunds; and/or
- Charging inflated fees for the return preparation.

Preparer Penalties for Preparing Fraudulent Returns

All paid preparers are subject to civil penalties for actions ranging from knowingly preparing a return that understates the taxpayer's liability to failing to sign or provide an identification number on a return they prepare. Tax return preparers who demonstrate a pattern of misconduct may be banned from preparing further returns. Additionally, the IRS may pursue and impose criminal penalties against a tax return preparer who engages in severe misconduct.

For the purpose of preparer penalties, a preparer may rely in good faith upon information furnished by the taxpayer or a previous preparer, and is not required to independently verify or review the items reported on tax returns to determine if they are likely to be upheld if challenged by the IRS.

However, a preparer must make "reasonable inquiries" if the information appears to be incorrect or incomplete. A tax return preparer is not considered to have complied with the "good faith" requirements if:

- The advice is unreasonable on its face;
- He knew or should have known that the third party advisor was not aware of all relevant facts; or
- He knew or should have known (given the nature of the tax return preparer's practice) at the time the tax return or claim for refund was prepared, that the advice was no longer reliable due to developments in the law since the time the advice was given.

Example: Martin is an EA who conducts an interview with his client, Barbara. She states she made a $50,000 charitable contribution of real estate during the tax year when in fact she did not make this charitable contribution. Martin does not inquire about the existence of a qualified appraisal or complete Form 8283 in accordance with reporting and substantiation requirements. Martin reports a deduction for the charitable contribution, which results in an understatement of tax liability. Barbara's return is later audited, and the charitable deduction is disallowed. Because of his negligence, Martin is subject to a preparer penalty under Section 6694.

Example: Allie is an enrolled agent. She prepares her client's 2012 tax return and discovers certain expenses that are not deductible. However, the previous year, there was one District Court case where the court ruled in favor of the taxpayer, allowing the taxpayer to claim similar expenses. No other court cases are currently being litigated, and the IRS has not issued a statement of opinion on the case. Based on these facts, Allie will have a reasonable basis for claiming the expenses on her client's 2012 return. Allie will not be subject to the Section 6694 penalty as long as the position is adequately disclosed, because the position has a legal justification as a challenge to the current IRS position.

If a preparer willfully understates a client's tax liability, he is subject to penalties. Under IRS regulations, "understatement of liability" means:

- Understating net tax payable
- Overstating the net amount creditable or refundable
- Taking a position with no realistic possibility of success

Penalties for Understatement of Taxpayer Liability

There are two specific penalties when an income tax preparer understates a taxpayer's liability.

Understatement Due to an Unrealistic Position: If there is an understatement on a tax return due to an unrealistic position, the penalty is the greater of:

- $1,000 per tax return, or
- 50% of the additional income upon which the penalty was imposed.

This applies when a preparer knows, or reasonably should have known, that the position was unrealistic and would not have been sustained on its merits. However, if the position is adequately disclosed on a tax return, this penalty will not apply. In the case of a patently frivolous position (such as a tax protester position), the penalty will apply whether or not it is disclosed. A preparer may be excused from the penalty if he acted in good faith and there was reasonable cause for the understatement.

Understatement Due to Negligent or Willful Disregard: If a tax preparer shows negligent or willful disregard of IRS rules and regulations, and makes a willful or reckless attempt to understate tax liability, the penalty is the greater of:

- $5,000 per tax return, or
- 50% of the additional income upon which the penalty was imposed.

If a tax preparer is subject to a penalty for understatement of liability and this includes a change to the Earned Income Credit, then the preparer may be subject to additional penalties for failure to exercise due diligence while claiming the EIC.

A tax preparer may avoid these harsh penalties if he relied on the advice of another preparer in good faith. The penalty may also be avoided if the position is adequately disclosed on a tax return and is not frivolous. In this case, a tax preparer would bear the burden of proof.

Abusive Tax Shelter: Any tax preparer who organizes, sells, or promotes an abusive tax shelter will be subject to penalties of $1,000 for each activity, or 100% of the gross income derived from the activity, whichever is less.

Penalty Abatement

If a penalty is assessed against a tax preparer and he does not agree with the assessment, he may request a conference with the IRS officer or agent and explain why the penalty is not warranted. The preparer may also wait for the penalty to be assessed, pay the penalty within 30 days, and then file a claim for refund.

IRC Section 6694 states that the understatement penalty will be abated if, under final judicial decision, it is found that there is no actual understatement of liability. Sometimes this will occur when a tax court case is decided in favor of the taxpayer.

The Office of Professional Responsibility

As reorganized under the revisions to Circular 230, the OPR's mission is to "support effective tax administration by ensuring all tax practitioners, tax preparers, and other third parties in the tax system adhere to professional standards and follow the law."

Specifically, the OPR has the authority to exercise responsibility for all matters related to practitioner conduct, discipline, and practice before the IRS. This authority includes:

- Receiving and processing referrals regarding allegations of misconduct under Circular 230; initiating all disciplinary proceedings against individuals or entities relating to allegations or findings of practitioner misconduct consistent with the applicable disciplinary rules under Circular 230.
- Making final determinations on appeal from return preparer eligibility or suitability decisions; recommending and imposing all sanctions for violations under Circular 230 and accepting consents to be sanctioned under the same.
- Making determinations on whether to appeal administrative law judge decisions and reviewing and determining petitions seeking reinstatement to practice. [159]

---

[159] IRS Delegation Order 25-16, July 16, 2012.

Disciplinary Sanctions Against Practitioners

The OPR may impose a wide range of sanctions upon preparers:

1. **Disbarment from practice before the IRS**— An individual who is disbarred is not eligible to represent taxpayers before the IRS. Also, as a result of a suspension or disbarment, the practitioner will have his PTIN revoked.

2. **Suspension from practice before the IRS**— An individual who is suspended is not eligible to represent taxpayers before the IRS during the term of the suspension.

3. **Censure in practice before the IRS**— Censure is a public reprimand. Unlike disbarment or suspension, censure does not affect an individual's eligibility to represent taxpayers before the IRS, but the OPR may subject the individual's future representations to conditions designed to promote high standards of conduct.

4. **Monetary penalty**— A monetary penalty may be imposed on an individual who engages in conduct subject to sanction or on an employer, firm, or entity if the individual was acting on its behalf and if it knew, or reasonably should have known, of the individual's conduct. This fine may be in addition to or in lieu of any suspension, disbarment, or censure.

5. **Disqualification of appraiser**— An appraiser who is disqualified is barred from presenting evidence or testimony in any administrative proceeding before the Department of the Treasury or the IRS.

Preparer Incompetence and Disreputable Conduct

Circular 230 outlines many instances in which a practitioner might be sanctioned for disreputable or incompetent representation. These instances include:

- Conviction of any criminal offense under federal tax laws.
- Conviction of any criminal offense involving dishonesty or breach of trust.
- Conviction of any felony under federal or state law in which the conduct renders the practitioner unfit to practice before the IRS.
- Giving false or misleading information, or participating in any way in the giving of false or misleading information to the Department of the Treasury.
- Soliciting employment as prohibited under Circular 230 or making false or misleading representations with intent to deceive a client.
- Willfully failing to file a federal tax return, or willfully evading any assessment or payment of any federal tax.
- Willfully assisting a client in violating any federal tax law, or knowingly counseling a client to evade federal taxes.
- Misappropriating funds received from a client for the purpose of payment of taxes.
- Attempting to influence any IRS officer by the use of threats, false accusations, duress, coercion, or bribery.
- Disbarment or suspension from practice as an attorney, CPA, or actuary. (For example, if a CPA is disbarred at the state level, he would also be disbarred at the federal level).
- Knowingly aiding and abetting another person to practice before the IRS during a period of suspension, disbarment, or ineligibility of such other person.

- Contemptuous conduct in connection with practice before the IRS, including the use of abusive language, making accusations or statements knowing them to be false, or circulating or publishing malicious or libelous matter.
- Giving a false opinion knowingly, recklessly, or through gross incompetence.
- Willfully disclosing or using private tax return information; willfully failing to sign a tax return; willfully failing to e-file a return; willfully signing a tax return without a valid PTIN; and willfully representing a taxpayer before the IRS without appropriate authorization.

The IRS may sanction a practitioner for any of these violations, or for engaging in "reckless conduct." This is defined as an "extreme departure from the standards" a practitioner should normally observe. The IRS will look at a practitioner's pattern of conduct to see whether it reflects gross incompetence, meaning "gross indifference, preparation which is grossly inadequate under the circumstances, and a consistent failure to perform obligations to the client."

Judicial Proceedings for Preparer Misconduct

There are four broad categories of preparer misconduct, all of which may be subject to disciplinary action:
- Misconduct while representing a taxpayer
- Misconduct related to the practitioner's own return
- Giving a false opinion, knowingly, recklessly, or through gross incompetence
- Misconduct not directly involving IRS representation (such as a felony conviction)

The Secretary of the Treasury, after notice and an opportunity for a proceeding, may censure, suspend, or disbar any practitioner from practice before the IRS for misconduct. A practitioner who is disbarred may not practice before the IRS. A practitioner who is suspended may not practice during the period of the suspension.

A practitioner who is listed as "inactive status" or "retirement status" may not practice before the IRS. Inactive retirement status is not available to an individual who is the subject of a pending disciplinary matter.

> **Example:** Tim is a CPA who was disbarred by his state society and his license revoked for a felony conviction not related to his tax practice. Even though his CPA license was revoked for a separate issue, the OPR still considers this disreputable conduct. Since Tim has been stripped of his license, he is not enrolled to practice before the IRS. He can be permanently disbarred or censured by the OPR.

Conferences and Voluntary Consents

If the OPR has evidence or allegations of misconduct, the director of the OPR may confer with the practitioner, employer, firm, or other party concerning the allegations. A formal proceeding does not have to be instituted in order for the OPR to confer with other parties regarding the alleged misconduct.

A practitioner may offer consent to be sanctioned *in lieu of* a formal proceeding. The director of the OPR may, in his discretion, accept or decline the practitioner's consent to a sanction. The director may accept a revised offer submitted in response to his rejection or may counteroffer and act upon any accepted counteroffer.

Complaints Against a Tax Practitioner

The OPR can issue a formal complaint against a practitioner. In order to be valid, a complaint must:

- Name the respondent.
- Provide a clear and concise description of the facts.
- Be signed by the director of the OPR.
- Describe the type of sanction.

A complaint is considered sufficient if it informs the respondent of the charges so that the respondent is able to prepare a defense.

The OPR must notify the practitioner of the deadline for answering the complaint. The deadline may not be less than 30 days from the date of service of the complaint. The OPR must also give the name and address of the administrative law judge with whom the response must be filed, and the name and address of the employee representing the OPR.

Service of Complaint Against a Tax Practitioner

The complaint may be served to the practitioner in the following ways: Certified mail, First Class mail if returned undelivered by Certified mail; private delivery service; in person; or by leaving the complaint at the office of the practitioner. Electronic delivery, such as e-mail, is not a valid means of serving a complaint.

Within ten days of serving the complaint, copies of the evidence against the practitioner must also be served. The practitioner must respond to the complaint by the deadline outlined in the letter. A failure to respond constitutes an admission of guilt and a waiver of the hearing.

An administrative law judge is the one who will actually hear the evidence and decide whether the OPR has proven its case against a practitioner. If the practitioner fails to respond to the complaint, the administrative law judge may make a decision on the case by default without a hearing.

During a hearing, the practitioner may appear in person or be represented by an attorney or another practitioner. The director of the OPR may be represented by an attorney or other employee of the IRS.

If either party to the judicial proceeding fails to appear at the hearing, the absent party shall be deemed to have waived the right to a hearing, and the administrative law judge may make his decision against the absent party by default.

Within 180 days from the conclusion of a hearing, the administrative law judge should enter a decision in the case. He must provide a copy of his decision to the director of the OPR and to the practitioner or to the practitioner's authorized representative.

If there is no appeal, the decision becomes final. However, either party—the OPR or the practitioner—may appeal the judge's decision with the Secretary of the Treasury within 30 days. The Secretary of the Treasury, or his delegate, will then make a final determination on the case.

Disbarment vs. Suspension

When the final decision in a judicial proceeding is for disbarment, the practitioner will not be allowed to practice in any capacity before the IRS (except to represent himself). A disbarred practitioner may not:

- Prepare or file documents, including tax returns, or other correspondence with the IRS. The restriction applies regardless of whether the individual signs the document and regardless of whether the individual personally files or directs another person to file, documents with the IRS.
- Render written advice with respect to any entity, transaction, plan or arrangement having a potential for tax avoidance or evasion (tax shelter advice).
- Represent a client at conferences, hearings, and meetings.
- Execute waivers, consents, or closing agreements; receive a taxpayer's refund check; or sign a tax return on behalf of a taxpayer.
- File powers of attorney with the IRS.
- Accept assistance from another person (or request assistance) or assist another person (or offer assistance) if the assistance relates to a matter constituting practice before the IRS, or enlist another person for the purpose of practicing before the IRS.
- State or imply that he is eligible to practice before the IRS.

However, a suspended or disbarred individual is still allowed to:

- Represent himself in any matter.[160]
- Appear before the IRS as a trustee, receiver, guardian, administrator, executor, or other fiduciary if duly qualified/authorized under the law of the relevant jurisdiction.[161]
- Appear as a witness for the taxpayer.[162]
- Furnish information at the request of the IRS or any of its officers or employees.[163]

A practitioner may petition the OPR for reinstatement after a period of five years. The OPR may reinstate the practitioner if it determines that his conduct is not likely to be in violation of regulations and if granting the reinstatement is not contrary to the public interest.

---

[160] Authorized under Section 10.7(a).

[161] Authorized under Section 10.7(e). Fiduciaries should file Form 56, *Notice Concerning Fiduciary Relationship*.

[162] Authorized under Section 10.8(b) and Revenue Procedure 68-29, reprinted in pamphlet form as Publication 499.

[163] Authorized under Section 10.8(b)

Unit 4: Questions

1. Which of the following is true?

A. The IRS may not disbar a preparer without first seeking a legal criminal prosecution.
B. Even without bringing a criminal prosecution, the IRS may choose to disbar a tax return preparer.
C. A preparer is not liable for any preparer penalties if he diverts a portion of the refund to himself with the client's permission.
D. None of the above.

The answer is B. Even without bringing a criminal prosecution, the IRS may choose to disbar or prevent a tax return preparer from engaging in specific abusive practices. ###

2. What types of behavior would not subject a tax practitioner to be sanctioned by the OPR?

A. Misconduct while representing a taxpayer.
B. Misconduct related to the practitioner's own return.
C. When the practitioner is unable to pay his personal taxes due.
D. Misconduct not directly involving IRS representation.

The answer is C. Not being able to pay one's taxes on time would, most likely, not subject a tax practitioner to OPR sanctions. In general, the OPR defines four broad categories of misconduct, which may be subject to disciplinary action: (1) misconduct while representing a taxpayer; (2) misconduct related to the practitioner's own return; (3) giving a false opinion, knowingly, recklessly, or through gross incompetence; (4) misconduct not directly involving IRS representation. ###

3. All of the following statements regarding the fraud penalty are correct except:

A. If there is any underpayment of tax due to fraud, a penalty of 75% of the underpayment will be assessed against the taxpayer.
B. The fraud penalty on a joint return will automatically apply to a spouse.
C. IRS examiners who find strong evidence of fraud may refer the case to the IRS Criminal Investigation Division for possible criminal prosecution.
D. Negligence or simple ignorance of the law does not constitute fraud.

The answer is B. The fraud penalty on a joint return does not automatically apply to a spouse unless some part of the underpayment is due to the fraud of that spouse. ###

4. Glen is a CPA who prepares income tax returns for his clients. One of his clients submits a list of expenses to be claimed on Schedule C of the return. Glen qualifies as a return preparer and, as such, is required to comply with which one of the following conditions?

A. Glen is required to independently verify the client's information.
B. Glen can ignore implications of information known by him.
C. Inquiry is not required if the information appears to be incorrect or incomplete.
D. Appropriate inquiries are required to determine whether the client has substantiation for travel and entertainment expenses.

The answer is D. The preparer is not required to independently examine evidence of deductions. A preparer may rely in good faith without verification upon information furnished by the taxpayer if it does not appear to be incorrect or incomplete. However, the tax preparer must make reasonable inquiries about the validity of the information. ###

5. Which of the following types of disciplinary actions allow a practitioner to continue practicing before the IRS?

A. Disbarment.
B. Suspension from practice.
C. Public censure.
D. All of the disciplinary actions listed above will prevent a practitioner from practicing before the IRS.

The answer is C. A practitioner who is censured by the OPR is still eligible to practice before the IRS. Censure is a public reprimand. Unlike disbarment or suspension, censure does not affect an individual's eligibility to represent taxpayers before the IRS, but the OPR may subject the individual's future representations to conditions designed to promote high standards of conduct. ###

6. Melissa, an EA, was notified of a judicial ruling that she committed acts of gross misconduct and violated the rules of Circular 230, and, therefore, a decision was entered that she should be disbarred. Which of the following is true?

A. Melissa has a right to appeal the decision to the Secretary of the Treasury.
B. Melissa has a right to appeal the decision to the Office of Professional Responsibility.
C. Melissa has a right to appeal the decision to the Return Preparer Office.
D. Melissa has a right to appeal the decision to the Commissioner of the IRS.

The answer is A. An enrolled agent has a right to appeal the decision for disbarment to the Secretary of the Treasury. ###

7. Mario, an EA, prepared a client's tax return that contained a frivolous position which could not be defended under any circumstances. The examiner who conducted the examination made a referral to the Office of Professional Responsibility. After all procedural requirements have been met, who will make the final decision as to the appropriate sanction for Mario?

A. The OPR.
B. An administrative law judge.
C. IRS legal counsel.
D. The IRS examination division.

The answer is B. The OPR investigates complaints against preparers and then institutes judicial proceedings. However, if a hearing is required, an administrative law judge will make the decision regarding disbarment or other appropriate sanctions. ###

8. What types of sanctions will not be imposed by the OPR?

A. Disbarment.
B. Suspension.
C. Incarceration.
D. Censure.

The answer is C. OPR sanctions include disbarment, suspension, and censure. Although a tax preparer may be subject to criminal prosecution in some cases, the OPR would not be responsible for applying this penalty. ###

9. Following a disbarment, a tax practitioner may petition the OPR for reinstatement after a period of _____.

A. One year.
B. Five years.
C. Ten years.
D. Never. Disbarment is always permanent.

The answer is B. A practitioner may petition the OPR for reinstatement after a period of five years. ###

10. Carlos owns a business with three employees. How long is Carlos required to keep payroll tax records?

A. Three years.
B. Four years.
C. Six years.
D. Seven years.

The answer is B. A taxpayer or business is required to keep records relating to employment taxes for at least four years after filing the fourth quarter for the year. Employment and payroll records must be available for IRS review. Examples include copies of employees' income tax withholding allowance certificates (Forms W-4), and dates and amounts of payroll tax deposits made. ###

11. A suspended or disbarred individual may:

A. Appear before the IRS as a trustee, receiver, guardian, administrator, executor, or other fiduciary if duly authorized under the law of the relevant jurisdiction.
B. File documents on a taxpayer's behalf.
C. Represent a client at conferences, hearings, and meetings.
D. Execute a closing agreement for a client, so long as the practitioner has a valid power of attorney.

The answer is A. A disbarred practitioner may appear before the IRS as a trustee, receiver, guardian, administrator, executor, or other fiduciary if duly qualified/authorized under the law of the relevant jurisdiction. This is authorized under Section 10.7(e). Fiduciaries should file Form 56, *Notice Concerning Fiduciary Relationship.* ###

12. If there is substantial unreported income (over 25%), the IRS may audit tax returns for up to _____ after the filing date.

A. Three years.
B. Four years.
C. Six years.
D. Indefinitely.

The answer is C. In most cases, tax returns can be audited for up to three years after filing. However, the IRS may audit for up to six years if there is substantial unreported income (over 25% omitted). ###

13. Records for claim of loss from a worthless security should be kept for:

A. Three years.
B. Four years.
C. Six years.
D. Seven years.

The answer is D. Records relating to a claim for a loss from worthless securities should be kept for seven years. That is because a taxpayer can file an amended return to take a loss on a worthless security up to seven years after the filing date. ###

14. Colleen owns a business and has never filed a tax return. How long should she keep her records?

A. Three years if she owes additional tax.
B. Seven years if she files a claim for a loss from worthless securities.
C. For an unlimited period of time if she does not file a return.
D. None of the above.

The answer is C. A taxpayer must keep records as long as they are needed for the administration of any provision of the IRC. Taxpayers must keep records that support an item of income or deduction on a tax return until the period of limitations for that return runs out. If a tax return is not filed, there is no time limit. ###

15. All of the following statements are correct except:

A. If no other provisions apply, the statute of limitations for an IRS examination of a return is three years after the return was filed or the return was due, whichever is later.
B. If more than 25% of gross income has been omitted from the tax return, the statute of limitations is six years after the return was filed.
C. If a fraudulent return is filed, the statute of limitations is seven years.
D. If a tax return is not filed at all, there is no statute of limitations.

The answer is C. If a fraudulent tax return is filed, there is NO statute of limitations for collection. Under federal law, a tax return is "fraudulent" if the taxpayer files it knowing that the return either omits taxable income or claims one or more deductions that are not allowable. ###

16. Which of the following statements is true?
A. Tax avoidance and tax evasion are always illegal.
B. Taxpayers who commit fraud are subject to civil penalties only.
C. The IRS will assess a failure-to-file penalty or a failure-to-pay penalty but never both.
D. A felony conviction against a taxpayer who deliberately failed to file taxes could mean a fine of up to $100,000 and a prison sentence of up to five years.

The answer is D. It is correct that this is the maximum penalty and prison sentence in a tax evasion case. The other statements are false—tax avoidance is not illegal; taxpayers who commit fraud are subject to criminal penalties in addition to civil ones; and the IRS may assess both failure-to-file and failure-to-pay penalties. ###

17. What is the minimum penalty for failing to file a tax return more than 60 days late (assuming the taxpayer is not owed a refund)?

A. 10% of the unpaid tax.
B. $135.
C. The smaller of $135 or 100% of the unpaid tax.
D. A minimum of 25% of a taxpayer's unpaid tax.

The answer is C. The minimum penalty is the smaller of $135 or 100% of the unpaid tax. ###

18. Under IRS rules, which penalty is worse: failure-to-file or failure-to-pay?

A. The failure-to-file penalty.
B. The failure-to-pay penalty.
C. Both have the same penalties.
D. None of the above.

The answer is A. The penalty for filing late is usually 5% of the unpaid taxes for each month that a return is late. The penalty for not paying taxes by the due date is less—½ of 1% (0.5%). The IRS advises that if someone is unable to pay all the taxes he owes, he is better off filing on time and paying as much as he can. ###

19. What percentage of tax must a taxpayer pay if he is guilty of a "substantial understatement" penalty?

A. 5% of the net understatement of tax.
B. 10% of the net understatement of tax.
C. 20% of the net understatement of tax.
D. 25% of the net understatement of tax.

The answer is C. The substantial understatement penalty is calculated as a flat 20% of the net understatement of tax. A taxpayer may also face additional fraud-related penalties if he has provided false information on his tax return. ###

20. All of the following statements about the trust fund recovery penalty are correct except:

A. This is also referred to as the "100% penalty."
B. The IRS targets employees for this penalty.
C. This penalty involves payroll taxes withheld from the wages of employees.
D. The penalty can be assessed against anyone who is considered a "responsible person" and has failed to collect or pay trust fund taxes to the U.S. government.

The answer is B. This penalty is generally levied against employers, not employees, who have failed to pay the appropriate payroll taxes to the U.S. government. ###

21. What is the penalty for a taxpayer who has filed a return that is considered "frivolous"?

A. $500, plus any other penalty provided by law.
B. $1,000, plus any other penalty provided by law.
C. $5,000, plus any other penalty provided by law.
D. $10,000, plus any other penalty provided by law.

The answer is C. Any taxpayer who files a return found to be "frivolous" may be fined $5,000, in addition to any other penalty provided by law. This penalty may be doubled on a joint return. ###

22. What is not considered a potential "badge of fraud" by the IRS?

A. Sloppy recordkeeping.
B. Taking improper credits.
C. All-cash businesses.
D. Deductions for foreign travel.

The answer is D. IRS auditors are trained to spot common types of deception and attempts to defraud on tax returns. These acts are known as badges of fraud, and include deducting personal items as business expenses, the overstatement of deductions, and the understatement of income. Simply having deductions for foreign travel is not an indication of illegal behavior on the part of a taxpayer. ###

23. What is the penalty a preparer faces for understating income on a tax return due to an unrealistic position?

A. $1,000 per tax return or 50% of the additional income upon which the penalty was imposed.
B. $5,000 per tax return.
C. 50% of the understatement.
D. Nothing, so long as the preparer fails to adequately disclose the position on the return.

The answer is A. A preparer faces an understatement penalty of $1,000 per tax return or 50% of the additional income upon which the penalty was imposed. However, if the position is adequately disclosed on the return, the penalty will not apply. ###

24. All of the following statements regarding preparer penalties are correct except:

A. A preparer who has been assessed a penalty may request a conference with an IRS officer to dispute the fine.
B. A preparer who makes a "willful or reckless" attempt to understate tax liability faces a fine of $10,000 per return.
C. There may be additional penalties for understatement of income if the preparer has not exercised due diligence related to the EIC.
D. A tax preparer may avoid penalties if he relied on the advice of another preparer in good faith.

The answer is B. A preparer who makes a "willful or reckless" attempt to understate tax liability faces a penalty of $5,000 per tax return or 50% of the additional income upon which the penalty was imposed, whichever is greater. ###

Unit 5: The Ethics of the EIC

> **More Reading:**
> www.eitc.irs.gov
> Publication 596, *Earned Income Credit*
> Publication 4687, *EITC Due Diligence Requirements*
> Publication 4808, *Disability and EITC*

Earned Income Credit Extra Due Diligence Requirements

The Earned Income Credit (EIC)[164] is a refundable federal income tax credit for low to moderate income working individuals and families. When the EIC exceeds the amount of taxes owed, it results in a tax refund to those who claim and qualify for the credit.

The due diligence rules for tax preparers are more stringent for EIC returns. The number of individuals claiming the EIC is high, and the number of erroneous claims is also high. The IRS estimates an error rate of 21 to 26%, or $15 billion paid out in error in 2011.

Paid preparers must meet four additional due diligence requirements on returns with EIC claims or face possible penalties. IRS regulations clarify EIC due diligence requirements and set a performance standard for the "knowledge" requirement: what a reasonable and well-informed tax return preparer, knowledgeable in the law, would do.

The "Knowledge Standard" for EIC Returns

The "knowledge standard" requires a preparer to:

- Know the law and use his knowledge of the law to ensure he is asking a client the right questions to get all relevant facts.
- Take into account what his client says and what he knows about his client.
- Not know or have reason to know any information used to determine his client's eligibility for, of the amount of, EIC is incorrect, inconsistent, or incomplete.
- Make additional inquiries if a reasonable and well-informed tax return preparer would know the information is incomplete, inconsistent, or incorrect.
- Document any additional questions he asks and his client's answers at the time of the interview.

An in-person interview is required **every year** with each client who is claiming the EIC.

Example: Latonya is an EA. Mai is a new client who wants to claim the EIC. She has two qualifying children. She tells Latonya she had a Schedule C business and earned $10,000 in income but had no expenses. This information appears incomplete because it is unusual that someone who is self-employed has no business expenses. Latonya is required to ask additional reasonable questions to determine if the business exists and if the information about Mai's income and expenses is correct (Publication 4687).

---

[164] The IRS uses both the terms "earned income tax credit" (EITC) and "earned income credit." They are the same credit. For consistency's sake, we will refer to it as the earned income credit, or EIC.

EIC Due Diligence and Compliance Requirements

The four due diligence requirements for preparers related to the EIC are as follows:

- **Complete and submit the Eligibility Checklist.** A preparer must complete Form 8867, *Paid Preparer's Earned Income Credit Checklist*, to make sure he considers all EIC eligibility criteria for each return prepared. He must complete the checklist based on information provided by his clients. The form must be submitted either electronically or on paper, along with any returns or claims for refund.

- **Compute the credit.** A preparer must complete the EIC worksheet in the Form 1040 series instructions or the one in Publication 596, *Earned Income Credit*. The worksheet shows what is included in the computation (i.e. self-employment income, total earned income, investment income, and adjusted gross income.) Most tax preparation software has the computation worksheet, but the IRS emphasizes that software is not a substitute for knowledge of EIC tax law.

- **Knowledge.** A preparer must not know (or have reason to know) that the information used to determine eligibility for the EIC is incorrect. A preparer must ask his client additional questions if the information furnished seems incorrect or incomplete.

- **Keeping records.** A preparer must keep a copy of Form 8867 and the EIC worksheet, as well as any additional question/answers during the client interview. He also must keep copies of any documents the client gives to help determine eligibility for, or the amount of the EIC. In addition, a preparer must verify the identity of the person giving him the return information and keep a record of it. All records may be kept for at least three years in either paper or electronic format, and they must be produced if the IRS asks for them.

Example: A client states that she is separated from her spouse. Her child lives with her and she wants to claim the EIC as head of household. In reviewing the client's records it is apparent she earns a minimal income, which appears insufficient to support a household: pay rent/mortgage, utilities, food, clothing, school supplies, etc. The return preparer should ask appropriate questions to determine the client's correct filing status and determine how long the child lived with each parent during the year and probe for any additional sources of income.

Example: Judd is an EA. His new client, Thelma, 62, wants to take a dependency exemption for her son, Randy, who is 32. She also wants to claim the Earned Income Credit and the dependent care credit for her son. Since Randy is beyond the age limit for these credits, Judd makes reasonable inquiries and discovers that Randy is severely disabled and incapable of self-care. Therefore, Thelma may claim her son, and the credits will be allowed regardless of Randy's age. Judd has fulfilled his due diligence requirement by asking reasonable questions about an individual tax situation.

Paid preparers failing to meet their due diligence requirements face IRS penalties for filing incorrect EIC claims. The penalty is $500 for each failure to comply with the EIC due diligence requirements. (The penalty increased from $100 to $500 in 2011 as part of the IRS's campaign against fraudulent EIC claims.)

An employer also may be penalized for an employee's failure to exercise due diligence in the following situations:

- When an employer or principal member of management participated in or knew of the failure to comply with due diligence requirements.
- When the firm failed to establish reasonable and appropriate procedures to ensure compliance with EIC due diligence requirements.
- When the firm disregarded its compliance procedures through willfulness, recklessness, or gross indifference in the preparation of the tax return or the claim for refund.

Common EIC Errors

The IRS is always looking for abusive EIC claims. The three issues that account for more than 60 percent of all EIC errors are:

- Claiming a child who does not meet the age, relationship, or residency requirement. [165]
- Filing as single or head of household when married. [166]
- Incorrectly reporting income or expenses.

A common method of EIC fraud is the "borrowing" of dependents. Unscrupulous tax professionals will "share" one taxpayer's qualifying child or children with another taxpayer in order to allow both to claim the EIC.

> **Example:** Reggie has four children, but he only needs the first three children to receive the maximum EIC credit. The preparer lists the first three children on the first taxpayer's return and lists the other child on another return. The preparer and Reggie are "selling" the dependents and will then split a fee or split the refund. This is an example of tax fraud, both for the preparer and the taxpayer.

Since tax professionals prepare more than 70% of EIC claims, the quality of their work has a significant impact on reducing erroneous claims. Preparers who file high percentages of questionable EIC claims or returns with a high risk of EIC error may be subject to on-site audits. IRS agents will review preparer records to verify due diligence compliance, including whether they are meeting the knowledge standard. Penalties are assessed when noncompliance is identified. The IRS focuses on reducing EIC errors by:

- Ensuring experienced preparers who filed questionable EIC claims understand the law.
- Conducting on-site due diligence audits of preparers filing returns.
- Barring egregious preparers with a history of noncompliance from return preparation.

EIC errors may occur for many reasons, including:

- Lack of knowledge of EIC tax law

---

[165] A taxpayer may claim a relative of any age as a qualifying child if the person is totally and permanently disabled and meets all other EIC requirements. The tax law definition of totally and permanently disabled is "The person cannot engage in any substantial gainful activity because of a physical or mental condition. A doctor determines the condition has lasted or the doctor expects it to last continuously for at least a year (or lead to death)."

[166]Sometimes, married couples incorrectly split their qualifying children and both file as head of household to reap the benefits of the EIC. This is considered fraudulent. IRS uses both internal information and information from external sources such as other government agencies in order to research and flag these fraudulent EIC claims.

- Honest preparer mistakes
- Intentional or unintentional client misrepresentation of facts
- Disregard for EIC due diligence requirements
- Blatant disregard of tax laws to garner erroneous refunds

> **Example:** Esther is an EA. A new 28-year-old client wants to claim two sons, ages 14 and 15, as qualifying children for the EIC. Esther is concerned about the age of the children, since the age of the client seems inconsistent with the ages of the children claimed as sons. Esther discovers that the two boys are both adopted, which explains the age inconsistency. Esther has fulfilled her due diligence requirement and fulfilled the knowledge standard by asking probing questions to confirm the accuracy of the client's information.

> **Example:** Jeff is single and wants to claim his daughter, Charley, for the EIC. Jeff earned $14,500 and had no other income. Charley is 35 years old and unmarried, and Jeff says she is disabled and lived with him for the full year. Charley's mother is deceased. Both Jeff and Charley have valid Social Security numbers. Charley worked for part of the year and earned $5,200. Jeff states that Charley had an accident last May and sustained a disability from the injuries. Her doctor says she is totally and permanently disabled, not able to work, and the doctor does not expect Charley to recover. Jeff can claim the EIC using Charley as his qualifying child because her doctor determined Charley cannot work because of her disability and because her disability will last longer than a year.

The IRS is attempting to educate first-time preparers whose returns reflect EIC errors. Using a scoring system to determine the degree of future risk, the agency has sent informational letters to these preparers and, in some cases, stronger compliance letters. The compliance program enforces the following:

- Outlines EIC due diligence and preparer responsibilities
- Highlights recurring errors made by other EIC return preparers to help avoid common pitfalls
- Points to tools, information, and other resources on the IRS website
- Reminds preparers that tax software is a tool, not a substitute for knowing and correctly applying the tax law
- Educates experienced preparers by mail

In February 2013, the IRS emailed tax preparers to remind them to complete the EIC checklists, saying it had received a large number of returns with incomplete information. 2012 returns with information missing on Form 8867 will be suspended, causing a potential delay in refunds.

The IRS also announced it is asking tax software companies and electronic filers to ensure that the EIC checklists are complete and remind tax preparers they could face stiff penalties without the information.[167]

Penalties for Incorrect EIC Returns

The penalties for failing to exercise due diligence with EIC claims can be severe. Incorrect EIC returns affect both the preparer and the client. If the IRS examines a client's return and denies all or part of the EIC, the client:

---

[167] *Accounting Today,* Feb. 4, 2013.

- Must pay back the amount in error with interest;
- May need to file Form 8862, *Information to Claim Earned Income Credit after Disallowance*;
- Cannot claim the EIC for the next two years if the IRS determines the error is because of reckless or intentional disregard of the rules; or
- Cannot claim the EIC for the next ten years if the IRS determines the error is because of fraud.

Further, if the IRS examines an EIC claim that was prepared by a tax professional and it is determined that the practitioner did not meet all four due diligence requirements, the preparer can be subject to:

- A $500 preparer penalty for each failure to comply with EIC due diligence requirements for returns required to be filed after December 31, 2011. This penalty can be assessed against an individual preparer, as well as the preparer's employer. The penalty amounts are covered in IRC Section 6695(g).
- A minimum preparer penalty of $1,000 if a practitioner prepares a client return and the IRS finds any part of the amount of taxes owed is due to an "unreasonable position."[168]
- A minimum preparer penalty of $5,000 if a practitioner prepares a client return and the IRS finds any part of the amount of taxes owed is due to reckless or intentional disregard of rules or regulations.[169]

If a practitioner receives a return-related penalty, he may also face:

- Disciplinary action by the OPR
- Suspension or expulsion from IRS e-file
- Injunctions barring the practitioner from preparing tax returns

The IRS has streamlined procedures for faster referrals to the U.S. Department of Justice to prohibit preparers from making fraudulent EIC claims. These preparers could be permanently or temporarily barred from any type of federal tax preparation (Publication 4687, *EITC Due Diligence*).

Example: Stephanie is a return preparer working for a larger chain. She has knowingly prepared false EIC claims for several years. Eventually, the office is subject to an IRS audit, and the fraud is discovered. Stephanie is disbarred and fined. The employer is also subject to a fine under IRC § 6695(g), and can be assessed a fine for each fraudulent claim.

SSN Requirement for EIC Returns

A valid Social Security Number is required for EIC claims. If a primary taxpayer, spouse, (or both) have ITINs, they are ineligible to receive the Earned Income Tax Credit (EITC), **even if their dependents have valid SSNs.**

If a taxpayer and spouse (if filing jointly) have valid SSNs, only dependents with valid SSNs will qualify to receive EITC. In the case of a taxpayer who files a return using an ATIN (Adoption Taxpayer Identification Number), the EIC will be similarly disallowed for that dependent.

---

[168]For reference, see IRC Section 6694(a).
[169]For reference, see IRC 6694(b)).

Taxpayers are allowed to amend their original returns in order to claim the EIC, if they receive valid SSNs at a later date, as long as the taxpayer otherwise qualified for the EIC at the time the original return was filed.[170]

Summary of EIC Due Diligence Requirements for Paid Preparers	
Requirement	**Description**
1. Completion of eligibility checklist	• Make additional inquiries if a reasonable and well-informed tax return preparer would know the information is incomplete, inconsistent, or incorrect. • Document any additional questions the preparer asks and the client's answers at the time of the interview. The practitioner should also ask probing questions to determine correct eligibility.
2. Computation of the credit	• Keep the EIC worksheet that demonstrates how the EIC was computed. Preparers must complete and attach Form 8867, *Paid Preparer's Earned Income Credit Checklist*, and submit the form with all EIC refund claims. • The worksheet must show what is included in the computation: that is, self-employment income, total earned income, investment income, and adjusted gross income. Most tax software includes the computation worksheet.
3. Knowledge standard	• The preparer must know the law and use knowledge of the law to ensure he is asking the client the right questions to get all relevant facts. • He must take into account what the client says and what he knows about his client. • He must not know (or have reason to know) any information used to determine the client's eligibility for the EIC is incorrect, inconsistent, or incomplete.
4. Record Retention	• Retain Form 8867 and EIC worksheet. • Maintain records of how and when the information used to complete these forms was obtained. • Verify the identity of the person furnishing the information. • Retain all records for three years.

---

[170] To amend an original return to claim EIC, Form 1040X must be used.

Unit 5: Questions

1. Which statement is correct about the EIC?

A. Information obtained by the preparer may be discarded after the tax interview.
B. Interfering with IRS efforts to investigate EIC fraud is the best thing to do.
C. Incorrectly reporting income is okay so long as the client signs a release.
D. Preparers are required to ask additional questions if the information provided by a client appears incorrect, inconsistent, or incomplete.

The answer is D. During the EIC interview with a client, preparers are required to ask additional questions if the information appears incorrect, inconsistent, or incomplete. ###

2. The IRS can impose the following ban related to the EIC:

A. The IRS cannot ban a taxpayer from claiming the EIC.
B. Ten year ban for fraud.
C. Two year ban for fraud.
D. Permanent ban for fraud.

The answer is B. The IRS can impose the following types of bans related to the EIC:
- **Two year** ban for reckless or intentional disregard of EIC rules, or
- **Ten year** ban for fraud. ###

3. What is the penalty for preparers who fail to comply with due diligence requirements for the EIC?

A. A penalty of $500 for each failure.
B. A penalty of $1,000 for each failure.
C. There is no preparer penalty, but there is a taxpayer penalty for fraud.
D. A formal reprimand by the OPR, but there is no monetary penalty.

The answer is A. Any tax return preparer who fails to comply with due diligence requirements for the EIC can be liable for a penalty of $500 for each failure. ###

4. When must a tax preparer complete a client checklist for the EIC?

A. Every year.
B. With every new client.
C. Every six months.
D. The client interview is recommended, but not required.

The answer is A. For any client claiming the EIC credit, a preparer must either complete Form 8867 or an equivalent checklist every single year. The preparer is required to keep a copy of the checklist in his records for three years. ###

5. A client tells a preparer:

•She has no Form 1099.
•She was self-employed cleaning houses.
•She earned $12,000.
•She had no expenses related to the cleaning business.

What is the BEST course of action for the preparer in this case?

A. Refuse to prepare the return based on the client's information.
B. Ask probing questions to determine the correct facts and ask for proof of income or any expenses.
C. Accept the taxpayer's word so long as she fills out a legal liability release form.
D. Make the client swear to the truthfulness of her statements before an IRS officer.

The answer is B. The best course of action would be to ask probing questions and ask for proof of income. In some cases, the client may say she had no expenses when it is not reasonable to conduct the business without incurring expenses, or the expenses may seem unreasonably high. Again, the preparer may need to ask probing questions to determine the correct facts. ###

6. All of the following are EIC due diligence requirements except:

A. To evaluate the information received from the client.
B. To apply a consistency and reasonableness standard to the information.
C. To verify the taxpayer's information with the appropriate third parties.
D. To make additional reasonable inquiries when the information appears to be incorrect, inconsistent, or incomplete.

The answer is C. A tax professional is not required to verify a taxpayer's answers with third parties. The EIC due diligence requires a paid preparer to:
- Evaluate the information received from the client,
- Apply a consistency and reasonableness standard to the information,
- Make additional reasonable inquiries when the information appears to be incorrect, inconsistent, or incomplete, and
- Document additional inquiries and the client's response. ###

7. All of the following are common errors taxpayers make in claiming the EIC except:

A. Incorrectly reporting income or expenses.
B. Incorrectly claiming a child who does not meet the specific EIC requirements.
C. Filing as head of household when married.
D. Listing earned income for the year.

The answer is D. To qualify for the EIC, a taxpayer must have earned income during the tax period. Assuming it is reported correctly, listing earned income is not a common error made in claiming the EIC. The IRS cites the other three errors as common issues it sees with EIC claims. ###

8. All of the following are possible penalties for preparers who file fraudulent EIC claims except:

A. Suspension or expulsion from IRS e-file.
B. Criminal action undertaken by the OPR.
C. A ban from preparing tax returns.
D. A preparer penalty of $5,000 if the IRS finds any part of the amount of taxes owed is due to reckless or intentional disregard of rules or regulations.

The answer is B. The OPR may initiate disciplinary actions against preparers who violate rules related to the EIC. However, the OPR never initiates or prosecutes *criminal* cases. ###

9. Which is not one of the four due diligence requirements preparers are expected to follow for EIC claims?

A. Maintaining records for two years.
B. Completing the eligibility checklist.
C. Computation of the credit.
D. The knowledge standard.

The answer is A. Under the record retention portion of the due diligence requirements, records must be maintained for three years, not two. ###

10. Mack and Judy have valid ITINs. They have two children, both of whom have valid SSNs. Assuming they meet the income requirements, can Mack and Judy claim EIC?

A. They may claim the EIC for themselves and their children
B. They can claim EIC for their children, but not for themselves
C. They cannot claim EIC, regardless of whether their children have valid SSNs
D. Their dependents can claim EIC, but only if they file separate returns

The answer is C. If a primary taxpayer, spouse, (or both) have ITINs, they are ineligible to receive the Earned Income Tax Credit (EITC), even if their dependents have valid SSNs. ###

Unit 6: Covered Opinions

The Circular 230 requirements apply to all written forms of federal tax advice. There are especially strict rules for the written advice on "covered opinions," which are sometimes referred to as "tax shelter advice." The rules are extremely complex, and are in the process of being revised.[171]

Firms are required to have procedures in place to ensure compliance with the IRS regulations on covered opinions. Tax shelters themselves are not prohibited; some are fine. A pretax retirement plan, for example, is considered a legal tax shelter. However, some tax shelters are unlawful.

Covered Opinions (Tax Shelter Opinions)

Covered opinions relate to the advice a practitioner gives a client regarding a tax shelter. IRS regulations provide mandatory requirements for practitioners who provide covered opinions, which are defined as follows:

- Any transaction the IRS has determined is a tax-avoidance transaction.
- Any plan or arrangement that has tax avoidance as a principal purpose.
- Any plan or arrangement that has tax avoidance as a principal purpose if the written advice is either:
    - A reliance opinion
    - A marketed opinion
    - Subject to the conditions of confidentiality
    - Subject to contractual protection[172]

Reliance opinion: Written advice that is more likely than not (greater than 50%) of being sustained in the taxpayer's favor.

Marketed opinion: Written advice that is used by another person other than the practitioner in promoting, marketing, or recommending an investment plan to one or more taxpayers.

Under the rules, unless the advice contains a disclaimer,[173] the practitioner providing advice about a covered opinion must comply with ALL of the following requirements:

- The practitioner must use due diligence in fact finding.
- All pertinent facts must be separately stated and disclosed, and not be deemed unreasonable or immaterial by the practitioner.
- The opinion must relate the facts to applicable law standards without inconsistency.

---

[171] In September 2012, the IRS submitted proposed revisions to Section 10.35 of Circular 230. The revisions would revoke the complicated rules regarding covered opinions and substitute them with a single, basic new standard governing all written tax advice. As of publication, these new rules have not yet become final; thus exam-takers should study the current rules of Circular 230 covered in this unit.

[172] Circular §230(b)(2)(C), §230(C)(4)(i) and §230(C)(5)(I)

[173] In practical fact, many practitioners now routinely add a disclaimer to any written communication, including e-mails, regardless of whether the communication contains tax advice. According to the IRS, this practice may actually discourage compliance with ethical requirements because some practitioners believe a disclaimer allows them to disregard the current Section 10.35 standards governing written tax advice. This issue is one of the factors behind the IRS's proposal to overhaul the covered opinion regulations.

- All significant federal tax issues must be addressed and disclosed in the written advice.

The practitioner has a duty to also consider the impact of federal tax issues and provide a conclusion about whether the taxpayer's position on each issue is likely to prevail.

Requirements for Covered Opinions

General standards for practitioners who offer covered opinions are set forth in §10.35. Practitioners who provide covered opinions are required to:

1. **Know all the relevant facts:** A practitioner must describe a legitimate business purpose for the transaction, and he must use reasonable efforts to get the factual information correct.
2. **Relate law to the facts:** The opinion must relate law to the facts.
3. **Evaluation of significant tax issues:** The opinion must provide that the taxpayer will prevail (more likely than not) on the merit of the issues contained in the opinion.
4. **Overall conclusion:** The practitioner must provide an overall conclusion that the tax treatment is proper and give reasons for that conclusion.
5. **Practitioner competence:** The practitioner must be competent and knowledgeable about the issues addressed in the opinion.

When practitioners put tax shelter advice in writing, the following is expected under §10.37:

- A practitioner must not make *unreasonable* factual or legal assumptions.
- A practitioner must not have an *unreasonable reliance* on taxpayer information or third party information.
- The practitioner must consider all relevant facts and law.
- The possibility of an IRS audit cannot be a factor.

Excluded Advice (Not Considered Covered Opinions)

Some forms of written tax advice are not subject to the strict rules for covered opinions under Circular 230. Certain types of "excluded advice" that do not qualify as covered opinions include:

- Advice from in-house employees to their employers.
- Written advice solely for one taxpayer after the taxpayer has already filed a tax return.
- Written advice that does not resolve a federal tax issue in the taxpayer's favor. This is also called "negative advice," wherein an advisor tells a client a transaction will not provide the purported tax benefit.
- Written advice regarding qualified plans, state and local bonds, or SEC-filed documents.
- Any written advice if the practitioner is reasonably expected to provide subsequent written advice that satisfies the covered opinion requirements.

> **Example:** An accountant is working full-time as an employee for Baker's Dozen Corporation. The accountant gives incorrect advice to his employer regarding a tax shelter, and the employer is subject to penalties. The employee is not subject to Circular 230 penalties for covered opinions because he was acting as an in-house professional for his own employer.

Written advice will not be treated as a "reliance opinion" if the practitioner openly discloses that it was not intended to be used by the taxpayer to avoid penalties.

Reporting Requirements for Tax Shelter Activities

There are special types of tax shelter activities that must be reported to the IRS. If a taxpayer participates in any activity that the IRS has deemed to be a "tax avoidance" activity and a tax shelter, the activity must be disclosed on the taxpayer's return. Form 8886, *Reportable Transaction Disclosure Statement*, must be attached to a taxpayer's return for any year that he participates in a tax shelter.

Any taxpayer (individual or business) that participates in a reportable transaction must file Form 8886. Tax advisors also must disclose the transaction to the IRS. In addition, the tax practitioner is required to maintain a list of investors that must be furnished to the IRS upon request. Substantial penalties apply both to taxpayers and material advisors for noncompliance on either issue.

The fact that a tax shelter transaction must be reported on this form does not mean the tax benefits from such a transaction will be disallowed by the IRS. A taxpayer may also request a ruling from the IRS to determine whether a transaction must be disclosed.

A person who sells (or otherwise transfers) an interest in a tax shelter must provide the taxpayer the tax shelter registration number or be subject to a $100 penalty.

If a taxpayer claims any deduction, credit, or other tax benefit because of a tax shelter, he must attach Form 8271, *Investor Reporting of Tax Shelter Registration Number*, to the tax return to report this number. A taxpayer may have to pay a penalty of $250 for each failure to report a tax shelter registration number on a return.

Standards for Tax Returns and Documents §10.34

A practitioner may not willfully sign a tax return or claim for refund that the practitioner knows (or reasonably should know) contains a position that:

- Is frivolous
- Lacks a reasonable basis
- Is an unreasonable position as described in Section 6694(a)(2) of the Internal Revenue Code[174]
- Is a willful attempt by the practitioner to understate the liability for tax or a reckless or intentional disregard of rules or regulations

A tax professional cannot knowingly sign a frivolous return. A frivolous position is defined as one that the preparer knows is in bad faith and is improper.

---

[174] Section 6694(a) imposes penalties on paid practitioners who prepare returns reflecting an understatement of liability due to an "unreasonable position" if the practitioner knew (or reasonably should have known) of the position. No penalty is imposed, however, if it is shown that there is reasonable cause for the understatement and the tax return preparer acted in good faith.

The IRS will take into account a pattern of conduct in determining whether a practitioner acted willfully, recklessly, or through gross incompetence.

A practitioner may not advise a client to submit a document, affidavit, or other paper to the IRS:

- The purpose of which is to delay or impede the administration of the federal tax laws;
- That is frivolous; or
- That contains or omits information in a manner that demonstrates an intentional disregard of a rule or regulation unless the practitioner also advises the client to submit a document that evidences a good faith challenge to the rule or regulation (such as a disclosure statement).

A practitioner must make a reasonable attempt to determine if the taxpayer's position, especially a tax shelter position, will be sustained on its merits.

Advising Clients on Potential Penalties

A practitioner is required to inform a client of any penalties that are reasonably likely to apply to a position taken on a tax return if:

- The practitioner advised the client with respect to the position; or
- The practitioner prepared or signed the tax return.

The practitioner also must inform the client of any opportunity to avoid penalties by disclosure and of the requirements for adequate disclosure. This rule applies even if the practitioner is not subject to a penalty under the Internal Revenue Code related to the position or to the document or tax return submitted. A position is considered to have a realistic possibility of being sustained on its merits "if a reasonable and well-informed analysis by a person knowledgeable in the tax law would lead such a person to conclude that the position has a greater likelihood of being sustained on its merits."

A practitioner may still sign a return containing a position that does not meet the "more likely than not" standard so long as the position has a reasonable basis, is not frivolous, and is adequately disclosed. Positions taken by tax professionals on returns must meet certain standards. A position must meet at least ONE of these two standards:

- The position is "more likely than not" to be sustained on its merits, OR
- The position must have a "reasonable basis."

Example: Amanda is an EA with a client who has a very complex tax situation. She notices that the IRS publications reflect one position, but there is a recent court case that may allow a more favorable position for her client. There are also two other similar cases being litigated, but the outcome of those cases is currently unknown. Amanda believes that the position has a 20% chance of prevailing on its merits. Amanda thinks that the client's position has a "reasonable basis" and decides to disclose the position on the tax return. Even though the position is contrary to the IRS' current guidance, Amanda may take the position on the return, as long as it is disclosed. She should file Form 8275 along with the tax return stating the position, referencing the court case or any other basis she has for the position.

Definitions:

- **More likely than not:** There is a *greater than* 50% likelihood that the tax treatment will be upheld if the IRS challenges it. If a preparer is unsure that a position meets this standard, he may still avoid penalties by disclosing the position on the return. However, a disclosure statement will not protect the preparer if the position is patently frivolous.[175]

- **Reasonable basis:** A position is considered to have a reasonable basis if it is reasonably based on one or more of the authorities of the substantial understatement penalty regulations. "Reasonable basis" is a relatively high standard of tax reporting that is significantly higher than "not frivolous." The "reasonable basis" standard is not satisfied by a return position that is merely arguable. Under the "reasonable basis" standard, a preparer is required to inform the taxpayer of the penalties that may be assessed on the client under Section 6662.

Disclosure Statements

A practitioner must inform a client of the penalties reasonably likely to apply, of any opportunity to avoid any penalty by disclosure, and of the requirements for adequate disclosure. In the case of a tax return that requires a disclosure, the position should be disclosed to the IRS on either Form 8275, *Disclosure Statement*, or Form 8275-R, *Regulation Disclosure Statement*.

Form 8275 is used by taxpayers and preparers to disclose positions that are not otherwise adequately disclosed on a tax return to avoid certain penalties. It can also be used for disclosures relating to preparer penalties for understatements due to unreasonable positions or disregard of rules.

The disclosure can be used to avoid accuracy-related penalties so long as the return position has a reasonable basis (such as a recent court case in the taxpayer's favor). The penalty will not be imposed if there was reasonable cause for the position and the taxpayer (and preparer) acted in good faith in taking the position.

As detailed earlier in Unit 4, if there is an understatement on a tax return due to an unrealistic position, the preparer penalty is the greater of:

- $1,000 per tax return, or
- 50% of the additional income upon which the penalty was imposed.

This applies when a preparer knows, or reasonably should have known, that the position was unrealistic and would not have been sustained on its merits.

If a taxpayer files a frivolous income tax return, a penalty of $5,000 can be assessed under Section 6702. There are also penalties that can be imposed on preparers who file frivolous returns. The penalty for a frivolous position in the U.S. Tax Court is $25,000.

The "reasonable basis" rule does not apply to tax shelters. That is because a tax shelter must always be disclosed, regardless of any possibility standard.

---

[175] See Regulation 1.6694-1(e) for more information.

Reportable Transactions

A "reportable transaction" is a transaction that the IRS has determined as having a potential for tax avoidance or tax evasion. If a reportable transaction is not disclosed and results in an understatement of tax, an additional penalty in the amount of 30% of the understatement may be assessed. Reportable transactions must be reported on **Form 8886,** *Reportable Transaction Disclosure Statement.*

A separate statement must be filed for each reportable transaction. The following losses are not considered reportable transactions:

- Losses from casualties, thefts, and condemnations
- Losses from Ponzi schemes
- Losses from the sale or exchange of an asset with a qualifying basis
- Losses arising from any mark-to-market treatment of an item

Reportable transactions are also called "listed transactions." The rules for reportable transactions apply to all entities and individuals (including trusts, estates, partnerships, S corporations, etc.) Any entity that participates in a reportable transaction is required to file Form 8886.

Unit 6: Questions

1. Which of the following types of written advice would fall under the Circular 230 rules for "covered opinions"?

A. Advice from in-house employees to their employers.
B. Written advice solely for one taxpayer after the taxpayer has already filed a tax return.
C. Written advice that does not resolve a federal tax issue in the taxpayer's favor.
D. A plan or arrangement whose principal purpose is the avoidance of tax.

The answer is D. The rules regarding "covered opinions" include the written advice regarding a plan or arrangement whose principal purpose is the avoidance or evasion of any tax. ###

2. A tax professional cannot knowingly sign _____.

A. A tax return for a family member.
B. A tax return that is not prepared for compensation.
C. A tax return with a properly disclosed tax shelter position.
D. A frivolous return with a disclosure.

The answer is D. A tax professional cannot sign a frivolous return, even if the return has a disclosure. A frivolous position is defined as one that the preparer knows is in bad faith and is improper. ###

3. Reportable transactions are also called _____.

A. Listed transactions.
B. Loss transactions.
C. Tax transactions.
D. Government transactions.

The answer is A. Reportable transactions are also called "listed transactions."

4. What is the penalty for failure to furnish a tax shelter registration number on a return?

A. $150 for each failure.
B. $250 for each failure.
C. $500 for each failure.
D. $1,000 for each failure.

The answer is B. A taxpayer may have to pay a penalty of $250 for each failure to report a tax shelter registration number on a return. ###

5. Dylan is a client of Bethany's, an EA. Dylan wishes to claim a deduction for a large business expense. However, there is a question about whether the expense is "ordinary and necessary" for his business. If the deduction were disallowed, there would be a substantial understatement of tax (over 25%). Bethany researches the issue and tells Dylan that the position should be disclosed. Dylan doesn't want to disclose the position on the return, because he is afraid that the IRS will disallow it. What are the repercussions for Bethany?

A. None. All the penalties apply to the client.
B. Bethany may be liable for preparer penalties.
C. Bethany will not be liable for preparer penalties so long as she explains the potential penalties to the client.
D. None of the above.

The answer is B. If Bethany does not adequately disclose the position and the return is later examined by the IRS, she may be subject to a preparer penalty. The disclosure form is filed to avoid the portions of the accuracy-related penalty due to disregard of rules or to a substantial understatement of income tax. ###

6. A practitioner is required to inform a client of any penalties that are reasonably likely to apply to a position taken on a tax return if:

A. The taxpayer decides to self-prepare a return.
B. The practitioner gave the client professional advice on the position.
C. The IRS has the taxpayer under examination.
D. The taxpayer is deceased.

The answer is B. A practitioner is required to inform a client of any penalties that are reasonably likely to apply to a position taken on a tax return if:
- The practitioner advised the client with respect to the position; or
- The practitioner prepared or signed the tax return. ###

7. When it comes to professional tax advice, the IRS defines "more likely than not" as:

A. A tax treatment that has a reasonable basis and at least a 10% likelihood of being upheld in court.
B. A tax treatment that has at least a 50% likelihood that the position will be upheld if the IRS challenges it.
C. A tax treatment that has a greater than 50% likelihood that the position will be upheld if the IRS challenges it.
D. A tax treatment that is disclosed.

The answer is C. The IRS defines "more likely than not" as a position that has a greater than 50% likelihood that the tax treatment will be upheld if the IRS challenges it. A position is considered to have a realistic possibility of being sustained on its merits "if a reasonable and well-informed analysis by a person knowledgeable in the tax law would lead such a person to conclude that the position has a greater likelihood of being sustained on its merits." ###

Unit 7: The IRS Collection Process

More Reading:
Publication 594, *The Collection Process*
Publication 1035, *Extending the Tax Assessment Period*
Publication 971, *Innocent Spouse Relief*
Publication 556, *Examination of Returns, Appeal Rights, and Claims for Refund*
Publication 1660, *Collection Appeal Rights*

The IRS has wide powers when it comes to collecting unpaid taxes. If a taxpayer does not pay in full when filing his tax return, he will receive a bill from an IRS service center. The first notice will be a letter that explains the balance due and demands payment in full. It will include the amount of the tax plus any penalties and interest added to the taxpayer's unpaid balance from the date the tax was due.

This first notice starts the collection process, which continues until the taxpayer's account is satisfied or until the IRS may no longer legally collect the tax, such as when the collection period has expired.

The IRS has **ten years** from the date of assessment to collect a tax debt from a taxpayer. If a taxpayer does not file a tax return, the statute of limitations does not expire.

The statute of limitations on collection can also be suspended by various acts. The ten-year collection period is *suspended* in the following cases:

- While the IRS and the Office of Appeals consider a request for an installment agreement or an offer in compromise
- From the date a taxpayer requests a collection due process (CDP) hearing
- While the taxpayer is residing outside the United States
- For tax periods included in a bankruptcy

The amount of time the suspension is in effect will be added to the time remaining in the ten-year period. For example, if the ten-year period is suspended for six months, the time left in the period the IRS has to collect will increase by six months.

The IRS is required to notify the taxpayer that he may refuse to extend the statute of limitations. Filing a petition in bankruptcy automatically stays assessment and collection of tax. The stay remains in effect until the bankruptcy court discharges liabilities or lifts the stay.

Statute of Limitations for Collection and Refunds	
Claim for refund	Three years from the date the original return was filed or the return was due (whichever is later), or two years from the date the tax was paid, whichever is later.
IRS assessment	Three years after the due date of the return, or three years after the date the return was actually filed, whichever is later. There are exceptions for outright fraud, failure-to-file, extension by agreement, and substantial omission (over 25% of income).
Collection action	Ten years from the date of a tax assessment.

Actions the IRS Uses to Collect Unpaid Taxes

If taxes are not paid timely, the law requires that enforcement action be taken, which may include the following:

- Issuing a notice of levy on salary and other income, bank accounts, or property (legally seizing property to satisfy the tax debt).
- Assessing a trust fund recovery penalty for unpaid employment taxes.
- Issuing a summons to secure information to prepare unfiled tax returns or determine the taxpayer's ability to pay. IRS employees will prepare "substitute returns"[176] when taxpayers do not file voluntarily.
- Filing a notice of a federal tax lien.
- Offsetting a taxpayer's refund.

In addition, the IRS will apply future federal tax refunds to any prior amount due. Any state income tax refunds may also be applied to a taxpayer's federal tax liability.

Federal Tax Lien

The federal tax lien is a claim against a taxpayer's property, including property that the taxpayer acquires even after the lien is filed. By filing a notice of federal tax lien, the IRS establishes its interest in the property as a creditor. Liens give the IRS a legal claim to a taxpayer's property as security for his tax debt. A notice of federal tax lien may be filed only after:

- The IRS assesses the taxpayer's liability;
- The IRS sends a notice and demand for payment; and
- The taxpayer neglects to pay the debt.

Once these requirements are met, a lien is created for the amount of the taxpayer's debt. By filing notice of this lien, the taxpayer's creditors are publicly notified that the IRS has a claim against all the taxpayer's property, including property acquired *after* the lien is filed. The lien attaches to all the taxpayer's property (such as a house or car) and to all the taxpayer's "rights" to property (such as accounts receivable, in the case of a business).

Once a lien is filed, the IRS generally cannot release the lien[177] until the taxes are paid in full or until the IRS may no longer legally collect the tax (the statute of limitations runs out).

Notice of Levy and IRS Seizures

The IRS will send a notice of levy to a taxpayer before it confiscates his property. A levy allows the IRS to confiscate and sell property to satisfy a tax debt. This property could include a car, boat, or real estate.

The IRS may also levy wages, bank accounts, Social Security benefits, and retirement income. The IRS may also apply future federal tax refunds to prior year tax debt, or state income tax refunds may be routed to the IRS an applied to a tax liability.

---

[176] These substitute returns generally do not give credit for deductions and exemptions a taxpayer may be entitled to receive. Even if the IRS has already filed a substitute return, a taxpayer may still file his own return. The IRS will generally adjust the taxpayer's account to reflect the correct figures.

[177] See Publication 1450, *Request for Release of Federal Tax Lien*, for more information.

An IRS levy refers to the actual *seizing of property* authorized by an earlier filed tax lien. If a tax lien is the IRS's authorization to act by seizing property, then the IRS levy is the actual act of seizure. The following items are exempt from IRS levy:

- Wearing apparel and school books.
- Fuel, provisions (food), furniture, personal effects in the taxpayer's household, arms for personal use, or livestock, up to $8,570 in value for tax year 2012.
- Books and tools necessary for the trade, business, or profession of the taxpayer, up to $4,290 in value for tax year 2012.
- Undelivered mail.
- Unemployment benefits and amounts payable under the Job Training Partnership Act.
- Workers' compensation, including amounts payable to dependents.
- Certain annuity or pension payments, but only if payable by the Army, Navy, Air Force, Coast Guard, or under the Railroad Retirement Act or Railroad Unemployment Insurance Act. Traditional or Roth IRAs are not exempt from levy.
- Judgments for the support of minor children (child support).
- Certain public assistance and welfare payments, and amounts payable for Supplemental Security Income for the aged, blind, and disabled under the Social Security Act. Regular Social Security payments are not exempt from levy.

If an IRS levy is creating an immediate economic hardship, it may be released. A levy release does not mean the taxpayer is exempt from paying the balance.

IRS Seizures

An IRS seizure is the legal act of confiscating a taxpayer's property to satisfy a tax debt. There are special rules regarding IRS seizures. The IRS must wait at least 30 days from the date the notice of intent to seize is given before it can make a seizure. Typically, the IRS may not seize property in the following circumstances:

- When there is a pending installment agreement
- While a taxpayer's appeal is pending
- During the consideration of an offer in compromise
- During a bankruptcy (unless the seizure is *authorized* by the bankruptcy court)
- If the taxpayer's liability is $5,000 or less in a seizure of real property (real estate)
- While innocent spouse claims are pending

The IRS may not seize a principal residence without prior approval from the IRS district director or assistant district director. Judicial approval is required for most principal residence seizures. The IRS may still seize or levy property if the collection of tax is in jeopardy.

Collection Appeal Rights

A taxpayer may appeal IRS collection actions to the IRS Office of Appeals. The Office of Appeals is separate from and independent of the IRS Collection office that initiated the collection action.

The IRS ensures the independence of the Appeals office by adhering to a strict policy of no *ex parte* communication[178] with the IRS Collection office about the accuracy of the facts or the merits of each case without providing the taxpayer an opportunity to participate at that meeting. The two main procedures are "collection due process" and the "collection appeals program."

Collection Due Process Hearings (CDP)

A taxpayer who receives a notice may request a collection due process (CDP) hearing by completing Form 12153, *Request for a Collection Due Process or Equivalent Hearing,* and submitting it to the address listed on the IRS notice. Collection due process is available for the following notices:

- Notice of federal tax lien filing
- Final notice: notice of intent to levy
- Notice of jeopardy levy and right of appeal
- Notice of levy on a state tax refund
- Notice of levy with respect to a disqualified employment tax levy

After a taxpayer receives one of these notices, he has 30 days to file a request for a CDP hearing protesting the IRS's collection action. The taxpayer (or his representative) will then meet with an Appeals officer.

Many taxpayers will ignore IRS notices until they receive a final notice or a notice of intent to levy. Often, by the time this happens, it is too late to help the taxpayer solve these issues, and the IRS has already begun the collection process in earnest. Some of the issues that may be discussed during a collection due process hearing include:

- Whether or not the taxpayer paid all the tax owed
- If the IRS assessed tax and sent the levy notice when the taxpayer was in bankruptcy
- Whether the IRS made a procedural error in the assessment
- Whether the time to collect the tax (the statute of limitations) has expired
- If the taxpayer wishes to discuss collection options
- If the taxpayer wishes to make a spousal defense (innocent spouse relief)

After the hearing, the Appeals officer will issue a written determination letter.

If the taxpayer disagrees with the Appeals officer's determination, he can appeal to the U.S. Tax Court (or other court). No collection action can be taken against the taxpayer while the determination of the Appeals officer is being challenged in Tax Court.

Collection Appeals Program (CAP)

The collection appeals program (CAP) is generally quicker than a CDP hearing and available for a broader range of collection actions. However, the taxpayer cannot go to court to appeal if he disagrees with a CAP decision. CAP is available for the following actions:

---

[178]An "ex parte communication" occurs when a party to a case communicates directly with another party about issues in the case without the other party's knowledge. In this case, the IRS Collection office is prohibited from direct communication with the Appeals office. This allows the Appeals office to function independently of the collection arm of the IRS. Revenue Procedure 2000-43 has more information about Appeals' mandatory independence and ex parte communication, and is available at *www.IRS.gov.*

- Before or after the IRS files a notice of federal tax lien
- Before or after the IRS levies or seizes the taxpayer's property
- After the termination of an installment agreement
- After the rejection of an installment agreement

A taxpayer may represent himself, or the taxpayer may choose to appoint a qualified representative (attorney, CPA, EA, or spouse or family member). In the case of a business, the entity may be represented by regular full-time employees, general partners, or bona fide officers.

Taxpayer Advocate Service

The Taxpayer Advocate Service (TAS) is an independent organization within the IRS whose goal is to help taxpayers resolve problems with the IRS. A taxpayer may be eligible for TAS assistance when he is facing the following situations:

- Economic harm or significant cost (including fees for professional representation)
- A significant delay to resolve a tax issue
- No response or resolution to a problem by the date promised by the IRS
- Irreparable injury or long-term adverse impact if relief is not granted

The Taxpayer Advocate Service is free and confidential, and is available for businesses as well as individuals.

Example: Geraldine filed an amended return for 2012 over three months ago. She has an outstanding balance for the prior tax year and has been receiving IRS collection notices. Geraldine's expected refund would fully pay her balance due and leave her with a small refund. The official processing time for Form 1040X, *Amended U.S. Individual Income Tax Return*, is approximately eight to twelve weeks. However, she has been waiting more than three months for her refund to process. She has contacted the IRS numerous times about the delay, but was never given a reason for the delay. Geraldine may request intervention from the TAS.

Seeking Relief from Joint Liability

Many married taxpayers choose to file jointly because of certain benefits this filing status allows. In the case of a joint return, both taxpayers are liable for the tax and any interest or penalty even if they later separate or divorce.

"Joint and several liability" means that each taxpayer is legally responsible for the entire liability. Thus, both spouses are generally held responsible for all the tax due even if only one spouse earned all the income. This is true even if the divorce decree states that a former spouse will be responsible for any amounts due on previously filed joint returns.

In some cases, however, a spouse can get relief from joint liability. There are three types of relief from joint and several liability [179] for spouses who filed joint returns:

---

[179] **Joint And Several Liability:** This is when multiple parties can be held liable for the same act and be responsible for all restitution. For the IRS, this means that on a joint return, both spouses will typically be responsible for the tax, even if only one spouse has income or is responsible for the tax. One way for a taxpayer to avoid joint and several liability is to file for innocent spouse relief.

1. **Innocent Spouse Relief:** Provides relief from additional tax if a spouse or former spouse failed to report income or claimed improper deductions.
2. **Separation of Liability Relief:** Provides for the allocation of additional tax owed between the taxpayer and his spouse or former spouse because an item was not reported properly on a joint return. The tax allocated to the taxpayer is the amount for which he is responsible.
3. **Equitable Relief:** May apply when a taxpayer does not qualify for innocent spouse relief or separation of liability relief for something not reported properly on a joint return and generally attributable to the taxpayer's spouse. A taxpayer may also qualify for equitable relief if the correct amount of tax was reported on his joint return but the tax remains unpaid.

Requesting Innocent Spouse Relief

The taxpayer must meet ALL of the following conditions in order to qualify for innocent spouse relief:

- The taxpayer filed a joint return, which has an understatement of tax, directly related to his spouse's erroneous items.
- The taxpayer establishes that at the time he signed the joint return he did not know and had no reason to know that there was an understatement of tax.
- Taking into account all the facts and circumstances, it would be unfair for the IRS to hold the taxpayer liable for the understatement.

In order to apply for innocent spouse relief, a taxpayer must submit Form 8857, *Request for Innocent Spouse Relief*, and sign it under penalty of perjury.

A request for innocent spouse relief will be denied if the IRS proves that the taxpayer and spouse or former spouse transferred property to one another as part of a fraudulent scheme to defraud the IRS or another third party, such as a creditor, ex-spouse, or business partner.

If a taxpayer requests innocent spouse relief, the IRS cannot enforce collection action while the request is pending. But interest and penalties continue to accrue.

Example: Nancy and Allen are married and file jointly. At the time Nancy signed their joint return, she was unaware that her husband had a gambling problem. The IRS examined their joint return several months later and determined that Allen's unreported gambling winnings were $25,000. Nancy was able to prove that she did not know about, and had no reason to know about, the additional $25,000 because of the way her spouse concealed his gambling winnings. The understatement of tax due to the $25,000 qualifies for innocent spouse relief.

Requesting Separation of Liability Relief

To qualify for separation of liability relief, the taxpayer must have filed a joint return. Separation of liability applies to taxpayers who are:

(1) No longer married, or
(2) Legally separated, or
(3) Living apart for the 12 months prior to the filing of a claim. (A taxpayer also qualifies if he or she is widowed.)

"Living apart" does not include a spouse who is only temporarily absent from the household. A temporary absence exists if it is reasonable to assume the absent spouse will return to the household, or a substantially equivalent household is maintained in anticipation of such a return. A temporary absence may be due to imprisonment, illness, business, vacation, military service, or education. In this case, the taxpayer would not qualify for separation of liability relief.

The spouse or former spouse who is applying for separation of liability relief must not have known about the understatement of tax at the time of signing the return. An exception is made for spousal abuse or domestic violence, if the taxpayer had been afraid that failing to sign the return could result in harm or retaliation.

Requesting Equitable Relief

A taxpayer may still qualify for equitable relief if he does not qualify for innocent spouse relief or separation of liability relief. Equitable relief is available for additional tax owed because of:

- A reporting error (an understatement), or
- When a taxpayer has properly reported the tax but was unable to pay the tax due (an underpayment).

To qualify for equitable relief, the taxpayer must establish, under all the facts and circumstances, that it would be unfair to hold him liable for the understatement or underpayment of tax. The IRS also considers a taxpayer's current marital status, whether there is a legal obligation under a divorce decree to pay the tax, and whether he or she would suffer significant economic hardship if relief were not granted. According to the IRS, the following factors weigh in favor of equitable relief:

- Abuse by the spouse or former spouse
- Poor mental or physical health on the date the taxpayer signed the return or requested relief

This is a major shift in policy concerning equitable relief, which the IRS used to grant only in rare circumstances. Under new guidelines, the agency says it will be more likely to grant equitable relief when one spouse has abused the other or exerted "financial control" over money matters.

The agency also is no longer enforcing a two-year time limit for filing equitable relief claims, which is expected to greatly increase the number of claims granted. Starting in 2011, spousal requests for equitable relief are no longer required to be submitted within two years of IRS collection activity. Under this new provision, many taxpayers may even qualify for retroactive relief. A taxpayer whose equitable relief request was previously denied solely due to the two-year limit, may reapply using IRS Form 8857, *Request for Innocent Spouse Relief,* as long as the collection statute of limitations for the tax years involved has not expired. The IRS will not apply the two-year limit in any pending litigation involving equitable relief, and where litigation is final, the IRS will suspend collection action under certain circumstances.[180]

---

[180] For more information, see IRS Publication 971, *Innocent Spouse Relief.*

Example: Paula and Joshua were married in 2011 and filed a joint return that showed they owed $10,000. Paula had $5,000 of her own money and she took out a loan to pay the other $5,000. Paula gave Joshua the money to pay the $10,000 liability. Without telling Paula, Joshua spent $5,000 on himself. The couple was divorced in 2012. Paula had no knowledge at the time she signed the return that the tax would not be paid. These facts indicate to the IRS that it may be unfair to hold Paula liable for the $5,000 underpayment. The IRS will consider these facts, together with all the other facts and circumstances, to determine whether to grant Paula equitable relief from the $5,000 underpayment.

Injured Spouse Claims

"Innocent spouse relief" should not be confused with an "injured spouse" claim. These are completely different claims. A taxpayer may qualify as an injured spouse if he files a joint return and his share of the refund was applied against past due amounts owed by a spouse.

An injured spouse may be entitled to recoup only **his share** of a tax refund. In this way, injured spouse relief differs from innocent spouse relief. When a joint return is filed and the refund is used to pay one spouse's past-due federal tax, state income tax, child support, spousal support, or federal nontax debt (such as a delinquent student loan), the other spouse may be considered an injured spouse. The injured spouse can get back his share of the refund using Form 8379, *Injured Spouse Allocation*.

Example: Trudy and Brent marry in 2011 and file jointly in 2012. Unbeknownst to Trudy, Brent has outstanding unpaid child support and old delinquent student loan debt. Their entire refund is retained in order to pay Brent's outstanding debt and back child support. In this case, Trudy may qualify for injured spouse treatment. This means that she may be able to recoup *her share* of the tax refund. Brent's share of the refund will be retained by the IRS to pay the delinquent debt.

IRS Offer in Compromise Program

An offer in compromise (OIC) is an agreement between a taxpayer and the IRS that settles the taxpayer's tax liabilities for less than the full amount owed. Absent special circumstances, an offer will not be accepted if the IRS believes that the liability can be paid in full as a lump sum or through a payment agreement.

An offer in compromise can be applied to all taxes, including interest and penalties. A taxpayer may submit an OIC on three grounds:

Doubt as to Collectability

Doubt exists that the taxpayer could ever pay the full amount of tax liability owed within the remainder of the statutory period for collection.

Example: Elise owes $80,000 for unpaid tax liabilities and agrees that the tax she owes is correct. Elise is terminally ill, cannot work, and is on disability. She does not own any real property and does not have the ability to fully pay the liability now or through monthly installment payments.

Doubt as to Liability

A legitimate doubt exists that the assessed tax liability is correct.

*Note: If a taxpayer submits an OIC under "doubt as to liability," **no payment** is required with the submission.

Example: Sofia was vice president of a corporation from 2005 to 2011. In 2012, the corporation accrued unpaid payroll taxes and Sofia was assessed a trust fund recovery penalty. However, by 2012, Sofia had resigned from the corporation and was no longer a corporate officer. Since she had resigned prior to the payroll taxes accruing and was not contacted prior to the assessment, there is legitimate doubt that the assessed tax liability is correct. She may apply for an OIC under "doubt as to liability."

Effective Tax Administration

There is no doubt that the tax is correct and there is potential to collect the full amount of the tax owed, but an exceptional circumstance exists that would allow the IRS to consider an OIC. To be eligible for compromise on this basis, a taxpayer must demonstrate that the collection of the tax would create serious economic hardship or would be unfair and inequitable. It is extremely rare for the IRS to approve an OIC on these grounds.

Example: Brad and Stacy Snyder are married and have assets sufficient to satisfy their tax liability and also to provide full-time care and assistance to their dependent child, who has a serious long-term illness. The unpaid taxes were a result of the Snyders providing needed medical care for their sick child. They will need to continue to use their assets to provide for basic living expenses and ongoing medical care for the child. There is no doubt that the tax is correct, but to pay the tax now would endanger the life of their child and would create a serious hardship.

In order to apply for an OIC, a taxpayer must submit a $150 application fee and initial nonrefundable payment along with Form 656, *Offer in Compromise*.

For the initial payment, the taxpayer has two options:

1) The taxpayer may submit 20% of the total offer and wait for an acceptance from the IRS, and then pay the remaining balance of the offer in five or fewer installments.

2) The taxpayer can submit an initial payment with the application and continue to pay the remaining balance in monthly installments while the IRS is reviewing the offer. Once accepted, the taxpayer will continue monthly installments until the liability is satisfied.

The taxpayer may appeal a rejected offer in compromise within 30 days.

In 2012 the IRS published new guidelines for its OIC program, as part of its "Fresh Start" initiative to help taxpayers resolve delinquent federal tax liabilities. The new OIC guidelines change the way the IRS calculates a taxpayer's ability to pay. The changes are expected to significantly increase the number of taxpayers who qualify for an OIC.

Unit 7: Questions

1. All of the following are types of relief from joint and several liability for spouses who file joint returns except:

A. Innocent spouse relief.
B. Separation of liability relief.
C. Joint relief.
D. Equitable relief.

The answer is C. There is no such thing as "joint relief." There are three types of relief from joint and several liability for spouses who file joint returns: innocent spouse relief, separation of liability relief, and equitable relief. ###

2. A levy allows the IRS to _____.

A. Confiscate and sell property to satisfy a tax debt.
B. Publicly notify a taxpayer's creditors of a claim against his property.
C. Collect tax beyond the statute of limitations.
D. Sell property on behalf of the taxpayer.

The answer is A. A levy allows the IRS to confiscate and sell property to satisfy a tax debt. An IRS levy refers to the actual seizing of property authorized by an earlier filed tax lien. Answer "B" refers to a lien, which gives the IRS a legal claim to a taxpayer's property as security for his tax debt. ###

3. How does the IRS begin the process of collections?

A. With an email to the taxpayer as soon as he files his tax return.
B. With a certified letter to the taxpayer immediately after a tax return is processed and flagged for audit.
C. With a written examination notice when the taxpayer is notified of the possibility of an audit.
D. A first notice will be sent, which is a letter that explains the balance due and demands payment in full.

The answer is D. If a taxpayer does not pay in full when filing his tax return, he will receive a bill from an IRS service center. The first notice will be a letter that explains the balance due and demands payment in full. It will include the amount of the tax plus any penalties and interest added to the taxpayer's unpaid balance from the date the tax was due. ###

4. The IRS may accept an offer in compromise based on three grounds. All of the following are valid grounds for submitting an OIC to the IRS except:

A. Doubt as to collectability.
B. Effective tax administration.
C. Legitimate shelter argument.
D. Doubt as to liability.

The answer is C. The IRS may accept an OIC based on three grounds: doubt as to collectability, effective tax administration, and doubt as to liability. ###

5. All of the following statements about the IRS statute of limitations are true except:

A. The IRS generally has ten years following an assessment to begin proceedings to collect the tax by levy or in a court proceeding.
B. The IRS is required to notify the taxpayer that he may refuse to extend the statute of limitations.
C. The taxpayer may not choose to extend the statute of limitations.
D. IRS Form 872-A indefinitely extends the time that a tax may be assessed.

The answer is C. The taxpayer may choose to extend the statute of limitations by signing Form 872-A. The taxpayer also may refuse to extend the statute. If a taxpayer does not file a tax return, the statute of limitations does not expire. The statute of limitations on collection may also be suspended by various acts. ###

6. The statute of limitations on collection can be suspended by various acts. The ten-year collection period may be suspended in each of the following cases except:

A. While the IRS and the Office of Appeals consider a request for an installment agreement or an offer in compromise.
B. From the date a taxpayer requests a collection due process (CDP) hearing.
C. While the taxpayer is in prison.
D. While the taxpayer lives outside the United States.

The answer is C. The ten-year collection period is not suspended when a taxpayer is in prison. The ten-year collection period is suspended in the following cases:
- While the IRS considers a request for an installment agreement or an offer in compromise
- From the date a taxpayer requests a collection due process (CDP) hearing
- For tax periods included in a bankruptcy
- While the taxpayer is residing outside the United States

The amount of time the suspension is in effect will be added to the time remaining in the ten-year period. For example, if the ten-year period is suspended for six months, the time left in the period the IRS has to collect will increase by six months. ###

7. A taxpayer may qualify as an injured spouse if _____.

A. He files a joint return and his share of the refund was applied against past due amounts owed by a spouse.
B. He files a joint return and fails to report income.
C. He files a separate return and has the refund offset by past student loan obligations.
D. He files for bankruptcy protection.

The answer is A. A taxpayer may qualify as an injured spouse if he files a joint return and his share of the refund was applied against past due amounts owed by a spouse. The injured spouse may be entitled to recoup only his share of a tax refund. ###

8. Separation of liability relief does not apply to taxpayers who are _____.

A. Divorced.
B. Legally separated.
C. Widowed.
D. Single (never married).

The answer is D. In order to qualify for separation of liability relief, the taxpayer must have filed a joint return. That means that the taxpayer must have been married at one time. Separation of liability applies to taxpayers who are:
(1)No longer married, or
(2)Legally separated, or
(3)Living apart for the 12 months prior to the filing of a claim.
Under this rule, a taxpayer also qualifies if the taxpayer is widowed. "Living apart" does not include a spouse who is only temporarily absent from the household. ###

9. Ingrid requests innocent spouse relief in 2012. While Ingrid's request is pending, which of the following is true?

A. The IRS may still enforce collection action.
B. Interest and penalties do not continue to accrue.
C. Tax shelter penalties may apply.
D. Collection action must cease while the taxpayer's request is being considered.

The answer is D. If a taxpayer requests innocent spouse relief, the IRS cannot enforce collection action while the taxpayer's request is pending. However, interest and penalties continue to accrue. The request is generally considered pending from the date it is received by the IRS until the date the innocent spouse request is resolved. ###

10. Belinda and Neil file jointly. They report $15,000 of income and deductions, but Belinda knew that Neil was not reporting $3,000 of dividends. The income is not hers and she has no access to it since it is in Neil's bank account. She signs the joint return. The return is later chosen for examination, and penalties are assessed. Does Belinda qualify for innocent spouse relief?

A. Belinda is not eligible for innocent spouse relief because she knew about the understated tax.
B. Belinda is eligible for innocent spouse relief because she had no control over the income.
C. Belinda is eligible for injured spouse relief.
D. None of the above.

The answer is A. Belinda is not eligible for innocent spouse relief because she knew about the understated tax. She signed the return knowing that the income was not included, so she cannot apply for relief (Publication 971). ###

11. The IRS may legally seize property in which of the following circumstances?

A. During the consideration of an offer in compromise.
B. If the collection of tax is in jeopardy.
C. If the taxpayer's liability is $5,000 or less in a seizure of real property (real estate).
D. While innocent spouse claims are pending.

The answer is B. The IRS may still seize or levy property if the collection of tax is in jeopardy. Typically, the IRS may not seize property in the following circumstances:

•When there is a pending installment agreement
•While a taxpayer's appeal is pending
•During the consideration of an offer in compromise
•During a bankruptcy (*unless* the seizure is authorized by the bankruptcy court)
•If the taxpayer's liability is $5,000 or less in a seizure of real property (real estate)
•While innocent spouse claims are pending

Judicial approval is required for most principal residence seizures. The IRS may still seize or levy property if the collection of tax is in jeopardy. ###

12. Lena owes $20,000 for unpaid federal tax liabilities. She agrees she owes the tax, but she has a serious medical problem and her monthly income does not meet her necessary living expenses. She does not own any real estate and does not have the ability to fully pay the liability now or through monthly installment payments. What type of relief may she qualify for?

A. Doubt as to collectability.
B. Doubt as to liability.
C. Effective tax administration.
D. Collection advocate procedure.

The answer is A. Lena may apply for an offer in compromise under doubt as to collectability. Doubt exists that she could ever pay the full amount of tax liability owed within the remainder of the statutory period for collection. ###

13. A taxpayer may appeal IRS collection actions to the IRS Office of Appeals. The two main appeal procedures are:

A. Offer in compromise and doubt as to collection.
B. Collection due process and the collection appeals program.
C. Collection due process and the U.S. Tax Court Program.
D. Taxpayer Advocate Service and the collection appeals program.

The answer is B. The two main appeal procedures for IRS collection action are collection due process and the collection appeals program. ###

14. All of the following property is exempt from an IRS levy except:

A. Undelivered mail.
B. Child support payments.
C. Social Security payments.
D. Unemployment benefits.

The answer is C. Regular Social Security payments are not exempt from IRS levy. ###

15. Beverly wants to submit an offer in compromise to the IRS. In which of the following circumstances is she not required to send an initial payment along with her application?

A. Doubt as to collectability.
B. Effective tax administration.
C. Doubt as to liability.
D. An initial payment is always required, in addition to the application fee.

The answer is C. If a taxpayer submits an OIC under doubt as to liability, no payment is required with the submission. ###

16. Which statement is correct regarding the collection appeals process?

A. The decision in a collection due process hearing is final, and a taxpayer may not appeal even if he is unhappy with the determination.
B. A disposition in the collection appeals program is typically slower than in a CDP, but the taxpayer has the right to appeal if he is unhappy with a CAP determination.
C. Innocent spouse relief may not be discussed during a CDP hearing.
D. If a taxpayer disagrees with the Appeals officer's determination after a CDP hearing, he can appeal to another court.

The answer is D. In a collection due process hearing, the taxpayer retains the right to appeal, unlike in the collection appeals program where the determination is final. Innocent spouse relief may be a topic of discussion in a CDP, along with many other issues. ###

17. If a taxpayer believes the IRS is not handling its case in a timely and appropriate manner, he should contact the _____ for assistance.

A. The IRS Help Line.
B. The U.S. Tax Court.
C. The Taxpayer Advocate Service.
D. The IRS Appeals office.

The answer is C. Congress created the Taxpayer Advocate Service, an independent entity within the IRS, to help taxpayers resolve issues with the IRS and recommend changes that will prevent future problems. Every year, the TAS helps thousands of taxpayers find solutions to their tax issues. There is no charge to taxpayers to use the service. ###

Unit 8: The IRS Examination Process

> **More Reading:**
> Publication 556, *Examination of Returns, Appeal Rights, and Claims for Refund*
> Publication 1, *Your Rights as a Taxpayer*
> Publication 3498, *The Examination Process*

The IRS accepts most tax returns as they are filed, but selects a small percentage for examination.[181] In 2012, the IRS audited 1.03% of the total number of individual tax returns with a filing requirement, down slightly from the 2011 percentage. Higher income earners were audited much more heavily than those who earned less. The IRS reports the audit rate for returns with total positive income of $1 million or more was 12.14%.[182] Of the individual returns audited in 2011, nearly a third were for returns with EIC claims.[183]

An IRS examination is a review of an organization's or individual's accounts and financial information to ensure information is being reported correctly and according to the tax laws, and to verify the amount of tax reported is accurate. The IRS will contact a taxpayer by telephone or mail only, due to disclosure requirements. E-mail notification is not used by the IRS.

Selecting a return for examination does not necessarily suggest that the taxpayer has made an error or been dishonest. Filing an amended return does not affect the selection process of the original return. However, amended returns also go through a screening process and an amended return may be selected for audit.

The responsibility to prove entries, deductions, and statements made on a tax return is known as the "burden of proof." The taxpayer must be able to substantiate expenses in order to deduct them. Taxpayers can usually meet their burden of proof by having the receipts for the expenses.

A tax return may be examined for multiple reasons. After the examination, if any change to the taxpayer's return is proposed, he can disagree with the changes and appeal the IRS's decision. This is done through the appeals process, which we'll cover in Unit 9. In this study unit, we'll cover the examination process.

The IRS conducts most examinations entirely by mail. In these "correspondence audits,"[184] a taxpayer will receive a letter asking for additional information about certain items shown on the return, such as proof of income, expenses, and itemized deductions.

Correspondence audits occur typically when there is a minor issue that the IRS needs to clarify. Sometimes, the IRS is simply requesting proof that a particular transaction has transpired.

---

[181] Even though the IRS uses the term "examination" rather than "audit," the terms mean essentially the same thing.
[182] The Kiplinger Tax Letter, Vol. 88, No. 2.
[183] IR-2012-36, The IRS Data Book.
[184] In fiscal year 2011, 75% of all examinations were correspondence audits (IRS Data Book).

Example: The IRS sends Pete a notice about his 2011 tax return. He had disposed of a large number of stocks during the year, and the IRS wanted basis information on them. Pete requests a report from his stockbroker showing the basis and sends it to the IRS along with a copy of the notice. The issue is resolved without incident, and Pete receives a notice showing that no changes have been made to his tax return.

Example: The IRS selects Sarah's return for examination. Sarah had claimed her older half-sister as a "qualifying child" based on her permanent disability, and also claimed head of household status. The IRS asks for proof of disability and residency, and Sarah provides copies of doctors' records and additional proof that her sister lived with her full-time. The IRS accepts Sarah's documents and closes the case as a "no change" audit. Sarah never has to meet with the IRS auditor, as the entire audit is conducted by mail (Publication 3498).

Taxpayer Rights During the Examination Process

The taxpayer has a number of rights during the IRS examination process. These rights include:

- A right to professional and courteous treatment by IRS employees
- A right to privacy and confidentiality about tax matters
- A right to know why the IRS is asking for information, how the IRS will use it, and what will happen if the requested information is not provided
- A right to representation, either by oneself or an authorized representative
- A right to appeal disagreements, both within the IRS and before the courts

How Returns are Selected for Examination

The IRS selects returns for examination using a variety of methods, including:

- **Potential Abusive/Tax Avoidance Transactions:** Some returns are selected based on information obtained by the IRS through efforts to identify promoters and participants of abusive tax avoidance transactions.
- **Computer Scoring/DIF Score:** Other tax returns may be chosen for examination on the basis of computer scoring. A computer program called the "Discriminant Inventory Function System" (DIF) assigns a numeric score to each individual and some corporate tax returns after they have been processed. [185]
- **Information Matching:** Some returns are examined because payer reports, such as Forms W-2 from employers or Form 1099 interest statements from banks, do not match the income reported on the tax return. The return may also be selected for examination on the basis of information received from third-party documentation that may conflict with the information reported on the tax return.

---

[185] IRS computers automatically check tax returns and assign a "DIF score" based on the probability that the return contains errors, excessive tax deductions, or other issues. This does not necessarily mean that the return was prepared incorrectly. However, the computer is trained to look for aberrations and questionable items. If a taxpayer's return is selected because of a high score under the DIF system, the return has a high probability of being chosen for audit. The IRS does not release information about how it calculates a taxpayer's DIF score.

- **Related Examinations:** Returns may be selected for audit when they involve issues or transactions with other taxpayers, such as business partners or investors, whose returns were selected for examination.
- **Third Party Information:** A return may be selected as a result of information received from other third-party sources or individuals. This information can come from a number of sources, including state and local law enforcement agencies, public records, and individuals. The information is evaluated for reliability and accuracy before it is used as the basis of an examination or investigation.

Example: Perry is an EA with a client, Lila, who received an audit notice this year. Lila's tax return was selected because she had a very high number of credits and very little taxable income. However, her tax return was prepared correctly. Lila had adopted four special-needs children in 2012 and was able to take a large adoption credit. Perry provided proof of the adoptions to the examining officer, which resulted in a positive outcome for Lila and a "no-change" audit.

Example: Van embezzled money from his employer and was arrested in 2012 for felony embezzlement. The case was made public and the police shared their information with the IRS. The IRS then contacted Van and made an adjustment to all of his tax returns, assessing additional tax, interest, and penalties for fraud for failing to report the embezzled funds as income. This is an example of third party information that can trigger an IRS investigation.

Notice of IRS Contact of Third Parties

During the examination process, the IRS may contact third parties regarding a tax matter without the taxpayer's permission. The IRS may contact third parties such as neighbors, banks, employers, or employees.

The IRS must give the taxpayer reasonable notice before contacting other persons about his individual tax matters.

The IRS must provide the taxpayer with a record of persons contacted on both a periodic basis and upon the taxpayer's request. This provision does not apply:

- To any pending criminal investigation
- When providing notice would jeopardize collection of any tax liability
- When providing notice may result in reprisal against any person
- When the taxpayer has already authorized the contact

Example: Max's tax return was selected by the IRS for audit. The IRS suspects unreported income due to criminal drug activity. Max is also being investigated by the FBI. Because this is a pending criminal investigation, the IRS is not required to give Max reasonable notice before contacting third parties about his individual tax matters.

Repeat Examinations

The IRS tries to avoid repeat examinations of the same items, but sometimes this happens. If a taxpayer's return was audited for the same items in the previous two years and no change was proposed to tax liability, the taxpayer may contact the IRS and request that the examination be discontinued.

Representatives must have prior written authorization in order to represent the taxpayer before the IRS. Representatives may use Form 2848, *Power of Attorney and Declaration of Representative*.

The taxpayer may always represent himself during an examination. If during the audit he becomes uncomfortable and wishes to consult with a tax advisor, the IRS must suspend the interview and reschedule it. However, the IRS will not suspend the interview if the taxpayer is there because of an administrative summons.

On a jointly filed tax return that is selected for examination, only one spouse is required to meet with the IRS.

Limited Confidentiality Privilege

Taxpayers are granted a confidentiality privilege with any federally authorized practitioner (usually, a CPA, EA, or attorney). Confidential communications include:

- Advising the taxpayer on tax matters within the scope of the practitioner's authority to practice before the IRS,
- Communications that would be confidential between an attorney and the taxpayer, and
  - Relate to *noncriminal* tax matters before the IRS, or
  - Relate to *noncriminal* tax proceedings brought in federal court by or against the United States.[187]

The confidentiality privilege does not apply to communications in connection with the promotion of or participation in a tax shelter. A tax shelter is any entity, plan, or arrangement whose significant purpose is to avoid or evade income tax. The confidentiality privilege also does not apply to issues related to any other branch of government.

This privilege is not applicable to the preparation and filing of a tax return. Nor does the privilege apply to state tax matters, although a number of states have an accountant-client privilege.

The IRS must allow taxpayers to claim the confidentiality privilege in communications with a federally authorized tax practitioner. The taxpayer or representative must assert the confidentiality privilege; it does not arise automatically.

Recording the Audit Interview

The practitioner may record the examination interview. The practitioner must notify the examiner ten days in advance in writing that he wishes to record the interview. The IRS may also record an interview. If the IRS initiates the recording, the taxpayer and/or the representative must be notified ten days in advance, and the taxpayer may request a copy of the recording.

Suspension of Interest and Penalties Due to IRS Delays

The IRS has three years from the date the taxpayer filed his return (or the date the return was due, if later) to assess any additional tax. This rule applies even if a tax return is filed late. The IRS cannot assess additional tax or issue a refund or credit after the statute of limitations has expired.

---

[187] See IRS Publication 556.

The IRS must send a taxpayer a notice explaining any additional liability. However, if the taxpayer files his return timely (including extensions), interest and certain penalties will be *suspended* if the IRS fails to mail a notice to the taxpayer stating:

- The taxpayer's liability, and
- The basis for that liability.

Penalties and interest will not be suspended in the following cases:

- The failure-to-pay penalty
- Any fraudulent tax return
- Any amount related to a gross misstatement
- Any amount related to a reportable transaction (a tax shelter) that was not adequately disclosed
- Any listed transaction
- Any criminal penalty

The IRS will waive penalties when allowed by law if the taxpayer can show that he acted in good faith or relied on the incorrect advice of an IRS employee.

Requesting Abatement of Interest Due to IRS Error or Delay

The IRS will waive interest that is the result of certain errors or delays caused by an IRS employee The IRS will abate the interest only if there was an unreasonable error or delay in performing a managerial or ministerial act (defined below). The taxpayer cannot have caused any significant aspect of the error or delay. In addition, the interest can be abated only if it relates to taxes for which a Notice of Deficiency is required.

Managerial Act

The term "managerial act" means an administrative act that occurs during the processing of the taxpayer's case involving the temporary or permanent loss of records or the exercise of judgment or discretion relating to management of personnel. The proper application of federal tax law is not a managerial act.

Ministerial Act

The term "ministerial act" means a procedural or mechanical act that does not involve the exercise of judgment or discretion and that occurs during the processing of the taxpayer's case after all prerequisites of the act, such as conferences and review by supervisors, have taken place. The proper application of federal tax law is not a ministerial act.

Example: Calvin moves to another state before the IRS selects his tax return for examination. A letter stating that Calvin's return was selected for examination was sent to his old address and then forwarded to his new address. When he gets the letter, he responds with a request that the examination be transferred to the area office closest to his new address. The examination group manager approves his request. However, the original examination manager forgets about the transfer and fails to transfer the file for six months. The transfer is a ministerial act. The IRS can reduce the interest Calvin owes because of any unreasonable delay in transferring the case.

> **Example:** A revenue agent is examining Margaret's tax return. During the course of the examination, the agent is sent to an extended training course. The agent's supervisor decides not to reassign the audit case, so the examination is unreasonably delayed until the agent returns. Interest caused by the unreasonable delay can be abated since the decision to send the agent to the training class and the decision not to reassign the case are both managerial acts.

A taxpayer may request an abatement of interest on Form 843, *Claim for Refund and Request for Abatement.* The taxpayer should file the claim with the IRS service center where the examination was affected by the error or delay. If a request for abatement of interest is denied, an appeal can be made to the IRS Appeals Office and the U.S. Tax Court.

Special Rules for Partnership (TEFRA) Examinations

IRS audits of partnerships can be complicated since partnerships are regarded as pass-through entities, and do not pay tax on the income they report. Income, gain, loss, deductions, and credits are all reported on the partners' individual tax returns, not as a partnership as a whole.

When a question arises about the accuracy of a partnership return, it may be impractical for the IRS to audit each individual partner's return. Under the Tax Equity and Fiscal Responsibility Act of 1982 (TEFRA), the IRS will first audit the partnership as a single entity, with a "tax matters partner" (TMP) serving as the main contact.

IRS examiners will attempt to determine whether partnership losses were properly treated and recorded. If the IRS determines that losses were not properly treated, it will assess tax at the partnership level. The TMP would then decide whether to appeal the decision.

There is an exception under TEFRA for small partnerships consisting of ten or fewer partners. These partnerships may still elect, however, to be covered by the TEFRA provisions.

IRS examiners have strict procedures to follow during a TEFRA audit, including mandatory completion of check sheets to detail correct procedures.

Unit 8: Questions

1. Frank's tax return was chosen by the IRS for examination. He moved a few months ago to another state, but the IRS notice says that his examination will be scheduled in the city where he used to live. Which of the following statements is true about this issue?

A. Frank can request that his tax return examination be moved to another IRS service center since he has moved to another area.
B. Frank must schedule the examination in his former city of residence, but he can have a professional represent him.
C. Frank is required to meet with the auditor at least once in person in order to move the examination to another location.
D. None of the above.

The answer is A. If a taxpayer has moved or if his books and records are located in another area, he can request that the location of his audit be changed to another IRS service center. ###

2. On a jointly filed tax return that has been selected for examination, which of the following statements is true?

A. Both spouses must be present during an examination, because both spouses signed the return.
B. Only one spouse must be present.
C. Neither spouse must respond to the notice.
D. Neither spouse may use a representative.

The answer is B. For taxpayers who file jointly, only one spouse is required to meet with the IRS. The taxpayers can also choose to use a qualified representative to represent them before the IRS. ###

3. When a taxpayer is chosen for an IRS audit, which of the following statements is true?

A. The taxpayer must appear before the IRS in person.
B. A taxpayer may choose to be represented before the IRS and is not required to appear if he so wishes.
C. An audit case may not be transferred to a different IRS office under any circumstances.
D. If a taxpayer feels that he is not being treated fairly during an IRS audit, he cannot appeal to the auditor's manager.

The answer is B. The taxpayer is not required to be present during an IRS examination if he has provided written authorization to a qualified representative per Circular 230. ###

4. What is a DIF score?

A. A computer scoring process that the IRS uses to select some returns for audit.
B. A report that is transmitted with each filed return.
C. A score that an auditor gives to the tax practitioner.
D. An IRS scoring process for Tax Court procedures.

The answer is A. The Discriminant Inventory Function System (DIF) score rates potential returns for audit, based on past IRS experience with similar returns. IRS personnel screen the highest-scoring returns, selecting some for audit and identifying the items on these returns that are most likely to need review. ###

5. The IRS must give the taxpayer reasonable notice before contacting other persons about his individual tax matters. The IRS must also provide the taxpayer with a record of persons contacted on both a periodic basis and upon the taxpayer's request. This provision does not apply:

A. To any pending criminal investigation.
B. When providing notice would jeopardize collection of any tax liability.
C. When providing notice may result in reprisal against any person.
D. All of the above.

The answer is D. During the examination process, the IRS must give the taxpayer reasonable notice before contacting other persons about his individual tax matters. This provision does not apply:
- To any pending criminal investigation.
- When providing notice would jeopardize collection of any tax liability.
- When providing notice may result in reprisal against any person.
- When the taxpayer has already authorized the contact. ###

6. Taxpayers are granted a confidentiality privilege with any federally authorized practitioner. This is the same confidentiality protection that a taxpayer would have with an attorney, with some exceptions. Confidential communications include all of the following except:

A. Written tax advice.
B. Matters that would be confidential between an attorney and a client.
C. Participation in a tax shelter.
D. Noncriminal tax matters before the IRS.

The answer is C. The confidentiality privilege does not apply in the case of communications regarding the promotion of or participation in a tax shelter. A tax shelter is any entity, plan, or arrangement whose significant purpose is to avoid or evade income tax. ###

7. Does filing an amended return affect a tax return's audit selection?

A. Filing an amended return does not affect the selection process of the original return.
B. Filing an amended return always affects the selection process of the original return.
C. An amended return is more likely to be selected for an IRS audit.
D. An amended return is less likely to be selected for an IRS audit.

The answer is A. Filing an amended return does not affect the selection process of the original return. However, amended returns go through a screening process and an amended return may be selected for audit, just like any other return. ###

8. According to the IRS, tax returns are selected for audit based on a number of different reasons. All of the following are reasons a return may be chosen for audit except:

A. Potential abusive transactions.
B. Computer scoring.
C. Because the taxpayer is a foreign investor.
D. Information received from other third-party sources or individuals.

The answer is C. A taxpayer would not be chosen for audit simply because he is a foreign investor. The IRS selects returns using a variety of methods, including potential participants in abusive tax avoidance transactions; computer scoring; information matching (some returns are examined because payer reports such as Forms W-2 from employers or Form 1099 interest statements from banks do not match the income reported on the tax return); related examinations (related entities may be audited together); or local compliance projects (random audits). ###

9. In general, the IRS will not reopen a closed examination case. All of the following are reasons why the IRS would reopen a closed audit case except:

A. There was fraud or misrepresentation.
B. There was a substantial error based on an established IRS position existing at the time of the examination.
C. Failure to reopen the case would be a serious administrative omission.
D. The taxpayer filed a request for fast track mediation.

The answer is D. Requesting fast track mediation during the examination is not a reason for the IRS to reopen a closed audit case. In general, the IRS will not reopen a closed examination case to make an unfavorable adjustment unless:
- There was fraud or misrepresentation,
- There was a substantial error based on an established IRS position existing at the time of the examination, or
- Failure to reopen the case would be a serious administrative omission.

###

10. The IRS has begun an examination of Elaine's income tax return. The IRS would like to ask her neighbors questions related to the examination. There is no pending criminal investigation into the matter, and there is no evidence that such contact will result in reprisals against the neighbors or jeopardize collection of the tax liability. Before contacting the neighbors, the IRS must:

A. Provide Elaine with reasonable notice of the contact.
B. Make an assessment of Elaine's tax liability.
C. Ask the court for a third-party record keeper subpoena.
D. Mail Elaine a Statutory Notice of Deficiency.

The answer is A. Pursuant to IRC §7602(c), a third-party contact is made when an IRS employee initiates contact with a person other than the taxpayer. A third party may be contacted to obtain information about a specific taxpayer's federal tax liability, including the issuance of a levy or summons to someone other than the taxpayer. The IRS does not need permission to contact third parties, but it must notify the taxpayer that the contact with third parties will be made. ###

11. The IRS will close an audit in all of the following situations except:

A. When there's a recommendation of no change.
B. When the taxpayer disagrees with the IRS's conclusions and requests fast track mediation.
C. When the IRS contacts the county district attorney and recommends criminal prosecution.
D. When the IRS proposes changes and the taxpayer agrees.

The answer is C. An audit can be closed with "no change;" "agreed" (as in Answer D); or "disagreed" (as in Answer B in which the IRS proposes changes and the taxpayer disagrees. He may then ask for further review, request fast track mediation, or pursue an appeal with the IRS or the judicial system.) Answer C is incorrect. If criminal prosecution resulted from an IRS audit, it would not be pursued by a county district attorney and the audit would not be closed. ###

12. If a taxpayer or his representative wishes for an audit to be recorded, which of the following must he do?

A. Make a request the same day as the examination.
B. Notify the examiner ten days in advance, in writing.
C. Notify the examiner one week in advance, in writing.
D. Nothing. All examinations are automatically recorded by the IRS to ensure compliance of regulations by all parties.

The answer is B. If a taxpayer, his representative, or the IRS examiner wishes for an audit to be recorded, he must notify the other parties in writing ten days in advance. If the IRS records the interview, the taxpayer may request a copy. ###

13. When the IRS needs to examine the records of a partnership, it must do so under the rules of TEFRA. All of the following statements are correct except:

A. Partnerships with more than ten partners are exempt from the TEFRA rules.
B. Because TEFRA audits are so complicated, the IRS must follow special procedures when it initiates and conducts examinations.
C. A tax matters partner will be the main contact with examiners during a TEFRA audit.
D. Under TEFRA, the IRS will examine tax issues at the partnership level, rather than examine each individual partner's return.

The answer is A. "A" is incorrect because partnerships with ten partners or fewer are typically exempt from the TEFRA rules under a special small partnership exception. ###

Unit 9: The Appeals Process

> **More Reading:**
> Publication 5, *Your Appeal Rights*
> Publication 556, *Examination of Returns, Appeal Rights, and Claims for Refund*
> Publication 4227, *Overview of the Appeals Process*
> Publication 4167, *Appeals: Introduction to Alternative Dispute Resolution*

Because taxpayers often disagree with the IRS on tax matters, the IRS has an appeal system. Every taxpayer has the right to appeal changes on a tax return that is audited. Most differences are settled within the appeals system without going to court.

The Appeals Office is *independent* of any other IRS office and serves as an informal administrative forum for any taxpayer who disagrees with an IRS determination. Appeals is a venue where disagreements concerning the application of tax law can be resolved on an impartial basis for both the taxpayer and the government. The mission of Appeals is to settle tax disagreements without having to go to the courts and a formal trial.

Reasons for an appeal must be supported by tax law, however. An appeal of a case cannot be based solely on moral, religious, political, constitutional, conscientious, or similar grounds. If the taxpayer chooses not to appeal within the IRS system, he may take his case directly to the U.S. Tax Court. The tax does not have to be paid first in order to appeal within the IRS or to the U.S. Tax Court.

The taxpayer may opt to bypass both the IRS appeals process and the Tax Court and instead take his case to the U.S. Court of Federal Claims or a local U.S. district court. However, if the taxpayer chooses to go directly to the Court of Federal Claims or a U.S. district court, all of the contested tax must first be paid. The taxpayer must then sue the IRS for a refund.

Only enrolled preparers (usually, attorneys, CPAs, or EAs) are allowed to represent taxpayers before an appeals hearing.

Taxpayer Appeal Rights

During the IRS appeals and examination process, taxpayers have the right to:
- Disagree with their tax bill
- Meet with an IRS manager
- Appeal most IRS collection actions
- Have their cases transferred to a different IRS office if they have a valid reason, such as if they have moved to another city
- Be represented by an agent (such as a CPA, EA, or attorney) when dealing with IRS matters
- Receive a receipt for any payment made to the IRS

Starting the Appeals Process

At the beginning of each examination, the IRS auditor must explain a taxpayer's appeal rights. If the taxpayer chooses to appeal the examiner's decision through the IRS system, he can file an appeal at a local IRS appeals office, which is a separate entity from local IRS district offices. He will then receive a letter from the IRS, which sets a time limit to file for an appeal conference.

The appeals procedure varies based on the amount of the proposed tax. If the amount is less than $2,500, the taxpayer must only contact the IRS to initiate an appeal. If the amount is more than $2,500 but less than $10,000, a brief statement of disputed tax is required. If the disputed amount exceeds $10,000, then a formal written protest is required.

An IRS appeal does not abate penalties and interest on the tax due. They continue to accumulate until the balance of the debt is paid, or until the taxpayer wins his appeal and he is granted a no-change audit, meaning the IRS has accepted the tax return as it was filed, and no additional tax is due.

30-Day Letter and 90-Day Letter

Proposed Individual Tax Assessment: The 30-Day Letter

Within a few weeks after a taxpayer's closing conference with an IRS examiner, he will receive a Proposed Individual Tax Assessment (more commonly called the "**30-day letter**"). This letter includes:

- A notice explaining the taxpayer's right to appeal the proposed changes within 30 days
- A copy of the examination report explaining the examiner's proposed changes
- An agreement or waiver form
- A copy of Publication 5, *Your Appeal Rights and How to Prepare a Protest If You Don't Agree*

The taxpayer has 30 days from the date of notice to accept or appeal the proposed changes.

Statutory Notice of Deficiency: The 90-Day Letter

If the taxpayer does not respond to the 30-day letter or if he cannot reach an agreement with an appeals officer, the IRS will send the taxpayer a 90-day letter, which is also known as a "Statutory Notice of Deficiency." A Notice of Deficiency is required by law and is used to advise the taxpayer of his appeal rights to the U.S. Tax Court.

A Notice of Deficiency must be issued before a taxpayer can go to Tax Court. This means that the taxpayer must wait for the IRS to send him a "final notice" before he can petition the Tax Court to hear his case. The taxpayer will have 90 days (150 days if addressed to a taxpayer outside the United States) from the date of this notice to file a petition with the Tax Court.

If the taxpayer does not file the petition in time, the tax is due within ten days, and the taxpayer may not take his case to Tax Court.

If the taxpayer does file a petition in time and the case becomes docketed before Tax Court, his file will again go to an appeals office to see if it can be resolved before it goes to Tax Court. Over 90% of all tax cases are solved before going to Tax Court.

During the examination and appeals process, taxpayers always have the burden of proving their deductions and their income. However, with alleged "unreported income," the IRS has the burden of proof based on any reconstruction of income solely through the use of statistical information on unrelated taxpayers.

> **Example:** Ken owns a cash-only business and the IRS disagrees with his stated income. The IRS reconstructs Ken's income based on industry standards, but does not have actual proof that he misstated his income. During a court case, the burden of proof is on the IRS if it used a reconstruction of records solely to estimate Ken's liability.

Understanding Tax Law and the Courts

The Internal Revenue Code (IRC) is the main body of tax law of the United States. It is published as "Title 26" of the United States Code.

Other tax law is promulgated by individual states, cities, and municipalities. The IRS enrolled agent exam deals only with federal tax laws and not with the laws of any individual state or municipality.

Tax law is decided by all three branches of our federal government. The legislative branch (Congress) is responsible for the Internal Revenue Code and Congressional committee reports. The executive branch (the president) is responsible for income tax regulations, revenue rulings, and revenue procedures. The judicial branch (the courts) is responsible for court decisions.

Tax law is *primarily* decided by Congress, and it changes every year. Laws passed by Congress are the main source of IRC tax law.

The IRS is a federal agency that has the responsibility of *enforcing* tax law. It is the "collection arm" for the U.S. Treasury, which is responsible for paying various government expenses. The Department of the Treasury issues administrative pronouncements, including Treasury regulations, which interpret and illustrate the rules contained in the Internal Revenue Code.

In its role of administering the tax laws enacted by Congress, the IRS takes the specifics of these laws and translates them into the detailed regulations, rules, and procedures of the IRC.

Often, taxpayers and tax practitioners will disagree with the IRS's interpretation of the IRC. In these cases, it is up to the courts to determine Congress's intent or the constitutionality of the tax law or IRS position that is being challenged. There are many instances in which tax laws are either disputed or overturned. Court decisions then serve as guidance for future tax decisions.

The enrolled agent exam is based almost entirely on IRS publications, and exam candidates will not be tested on court cases unless the law has already made its way into an IRS publication. Likewise, if there is current pending tax law or legislation, the exam candidate will not be tested on any pending tax law; the exam will always be based on tax law from a prior year. However, EA candidates must understand the basics of tax law, the court system, and how it relates to the taxpayer.

The Court System

If a taxpayer does not agree with IRS appeals, the taxpayer may go to court. As mentioned earlier, a taxpayer may challenge the IRS in any of three courts: the U.S. Tax Court, the U.S. Court of Federal Claims, or the U.S. District Court.

Court precedent usually decides where the litigation should begin. The court system, for tax purposes, is organized as follows:

1. The U.S. Tax Court
2. District courts
3. Court of Federal Claims
4. Appellate courts
5. U.S. Supreme Court

If a taxpayer wishes to challenge the IRS in a U.S. district court (or any other court besides the U.S. Tax Court), he must pay the contested tax deficiency *first*. The taxpayer must then petition the court for a refund, essentially "suing the IRS" to have the disputed liability returned.

Example: The IRS chooses Peg's tax return for examination, which issues a deficiency of $45,000. Peg disagrees with the examiner's findings and does not wish to go through IRS appeals. Peg also does not wish to go to Tax Court. Instead, she wants to go straight to a U.S. District Court. In order to do so, she must first pay the contested liability and then sue the IRS for a refund.

If either party loses at the trial court level, the court's decision may be appealed to a higher court. In most cases, the burden of proof lies with the IRS during court proceedings, assuming the taxpayer has complied with all of the issues listed below:

- Adhered to IRS substantiation requirements
- Maintained adequate records
- Cooperated with reasonable requests for information from the IRS
- Introduced credible evidence relating to the issue
- Have tax liability of $7 million or less if the taxpayer is a trust, corporation, or partnership

The Tax Court is a federal court where taxpayers may choose to contest their tax deficiencies without having to pay the disputed amount first. The court issues both regular and memorandum decisions.

"Memorandum decisions" are court cases where the U.S. Tax Court has previously ruled on identical or similar issues. A "regular decision" is when the Tax Court rules on an issue for the first time.

The Tax Court has jurisdiction over the following **tax disputes** only:

1. Notices of deficiency
2. Review of the failure to abate interest
3. Notices of transferee liability
4. Adjustment of partnership items
5. Administrative costs
6. Worker classification (employee versus independent contractor)
7. Review of certain collection actions

The Tax Court has jurisdiction over the following **types of tax** only:

1. Income tax
2. Estate tax and gift tax
3. Certain excise taxes
4. Re-determine transferee liability
5. Worker classification

6. Relief from joint and several liability on a joint return
7. Whistleblower awards

This list is not exhaustive.

EAs and CPAs who want to represent taxpayers in Tax Court must be admitted to practice before Tax Court by first passing a separate exam specific to this purpose. Only licensed attorneys are not required to take the Tax Court exam before practicing before the court. However, any individual taxpayer may represent himself before the U.S. Tax Court.

Small Tax Case Procedure

Tax law provides for small tax case procedures (also known as S-case procedures) for resolving disputes between taxpayers and the IRS. A taxpayer may elect the small tax case procedure for cases involving up to $50,000 in deficiency per year, including penalties and other additions to tax, but *excluding* interest. Most taxpayers who elect the small tax case procedure are *"pro se"* litigants, (which means that the taxpayer has chosen to represent himself before the court).

The taxpayer and the Tax Court must both agree to proceed with the small case procedure. Generally, the Tax Court will agree with the taxpayer's request if the taxpayer otherwise qualifies.

Small tax cases are handled under simpler, less formal procedures than regular cases. Often, decisions are handed down quicker than in other courts.

However, the Tax Court's decision in a small tax case CANNOT be appealed by the taxpayer. The decision is final (the IRS is not allowed to appeal either, if it loses the case.) In contrast, the taxpayer and the IRS can appeal a decision in a regular, non-S case to a U.S. Court of Appeals.

Dollar limits for the Tax Court Small Case Division vary:

- For a "Notice of Deficiency": $50,000 is the maximum amount, including penalties and interest, for any year before the court.
- For a "Notice of Determination": $50,000 is the maximum amount for all the years combined.
- For a "Notice of Deficiency" related to a request for relief from joint and several liability: $50,000 is the maximum amount of spousal relief for all the years combined.
- For an "IRS Notice of Determination of Worker Classification": The amount in the dispute cannot exceed $50,000 for any calendar quarter.

A decision entered in a small tax case is not treated as precedent for any other case and a decision is not typically published.

Since the taxpayer cannot appeal a decision from the Small Tax Case division, he must consider if using the S-case procedure is worth the risk. A taxpayer who uses the regular U.S. Tax Court retains the right to appeal his case to a higher court. The IRS cannot attempt to influence a taxpayer to waive his rights to sue the United States or a government officer or employee for any action taken in connection with the tax laws.

IRS Acquiescence

The IRS may choose whether or not to acquiesce to a court decision. This means that the IRS may choose to ignore the decision of the court and continue with its regular policies regarding the litigated issue. The IRS is not bound to change its regulations due to a loss in court. The only exception to this rule is the U.S. Supreme Court, whose decisions the IRS is obligated to follow.

The IRS publishes its acquiescence and non-acquiescence first in the Internal Revenue Bulletin and then in the Cumulative Bulletin. The Internal Revenue Bulletin (IRB) is the authoritative publication for announcing official rulings and procedures of the IRS and for publishing Treasury decisions, executive orders, tax conventions, legislation, and court decisions.

The IRS does not announce acquiescence or non-acquiescence in every case. Sometimes the IRS's position is withheld.

Recovering Litigation or Administrative Costs

If the court agrees with the taxpayer on most issues in the case and finds that the IRS's position is unjustified, the taxpayer may be able to recover administrative and litigation costs. These are the expenses that a taxpayer incurs to defend his position to the IRS or the courts.

The taxpayer may be able to recover reasonable litigation or administrative costs if all of the following conditions apply:

- The taxpayer is the prevailing party.
- The taxpayer has exhausted all administrative remedies within the IRS.
- The taxpayer's "net worth" is below a certain limit.
- The taxpayer does not unreasonably delay any IRS proceeding.

The taxpayer will not be treated as the "prevailing party" if the IRS establishes that its position was substantially justified. The position of the IRS is not considered "substantially justified" if either of the following applies:

- The IRS did not follow its applicable published guidance (such as regulations, revenue rulings, notices, announcements, private letter rulings, technical advice memoranda, and determination letters issued to the taxpayer) in the proceeding. This presumption can be overcome by evidence.
- The IRS has lost in courts of appeal for other circuits on substantially similar issues.

The court will generally decide who the "prevailing party" is.

Net Worth Requirements for Recovering Litigation Costs

In order to request the recovery of litigation costs from the IRS, the taxpayer must meet certain net worth requirements:

- For individuals, net worth cannot exceed $2 million as of the filing date of the petition for review. For this purpose, individuals filing a joint return are treated as separate individuals.
- For estates, net worth cannot exceed $2 million as of the date of the decedent's death.

- For charities and certain cooperatives, the entity cannot have more than 500 employees as of the filing date of the petition for review.
- For all other taxpayers, net worth cannot exceed $7 million and the entity must not have more than 500 employees as of the filing date of the petition for review.

The taxpayer may apply for administrative costs within 90 days of the date of the mailing of the final decision of the IRS Office of Appeals regarding the tax, interest, or penalty.

Delay Tactics are Not Permitted in the Tax Court

If a taxpayer unreasonably fails to pursue the internal IRS's appeals system, if the case is filed primarily to cause a delay, or if the taxpayer's position is frivolous, the Tax Court may impose a penalty of up to $25,000.[188] "Frivolous positions" include those that contend that:

- The income tax is not valid,
- Payment of tax is voluntary,
- A person or a type of income is not subject to tax,
- Or espouse other arguments that the courts have previously rejected as baseless.

The Tax Court may also impose sanctions of up to $25,000 on those who misuse their right to a court review of IRS collection procedures merely to stall their tax payments.

This rule is basically targeted at taxpayers who do not have a legitimate complaint and are instead using the Tax Court simply to delay collection action in their case.

---

[188] The IRS makes public the names and cases of taxpayers who have been assessed these Section 6673 penalties by the Tax Court. The cases are published on the IRS website as well as in the Tax Court Historical Opinion area.

Unit 9: Questions

1. With an IRS appeal, which of the following statements is correct?

A. An appeal does not abate the interest, which continues to accrue.
B. A taxpayer must pay the disputed tax before filing an appeal with the IRS.
C. The IRS is prohibited from filing a federal tax lien if the taxpayer is outside the U.S.
D. Taxpayers who do not agree to the IRS changes may not appeal to the U.S. Tax Court.

The answer is A. An IRS appeal does not abate the interest, which continues to accrue until the balance of the debt is paid, or until the taxpayer wins his appeal and he is granted a no-change audit. A no-change audit means the IRS has accepted the tax return as it was filed. ###

2. The Statutory Notice of Deficiency is also known as:

A. A 30-day letter because the taxpayer generally has 30 days from the date of the letter to file a petition with the Tax Court.
B. A 90-day letter because the taxpayer generally has 90 days from the date of the letter to file a petition with the Tax Court.
C. An Information Document Request because the taxpayer is asked for information to support his position regarding liability for tax.
D. A federal tax lien.

The answer is B. The Statutory Notice of Deficiency, or 90-day letter, gives the taxpayer 90 days to file a petition in the U.S. Tax Court challenging the proposed deficiency. ###

3. Abigail received a Statutory Notice of Deficiency from the IRS. Abigail's permanent address is in Scotland. How many days does she have to respond and file a petition with the Tax Court?

A. 30 days.
B. 90 days.
C. 150 days.
D. 365 days.

The answer is C. The taxpayer normally has 90 days to respond to a Notice of Deficiency. However, a taxpayer is granted 150 days if the notice is addressed to a taxpayer outside the United States. ###

4. The IRS selects Aaron's return for examination. After the audit is concluded, he disputes the findings. He wants to go to appeals, but his tax return was prepared by an unenrolled practitioner. Aaron does not wish to be present during the appeals process. What are his options?

A. Aaron may only represent himself at IRS Appeals.
B. Aaron may represent himself or hire an enrolled preparer (CPA, attorney, or EA) to represent him at the appeals level.
C. Aaron may choose to forgo the appeals process and mail in his dispute.
D. Aaron may ask an IRS employee to represent him at IRS Appeals.

The answer is B. Aaron can appear before IRS Appeals by himself, or hire a qualified representative to appear on his behalf. If he wants to be represented by someone else, he must choose a person who is qualified to practice before the IRS. Only enrolled preparers (usually, attorneys, CPAs, and EAs) are allowed to represent taxpayers before an appeals hearing. ###

5. At the beginning of each examination, the IRS auditor must explain _____.

A. A taxpayer's appeal rights.
B. A taxpayer's right to a fair trial.
C. A taxpayer's right to remain silent.
D. A taxpayer's right to confidentiality.

The answer is A. At the beginning of each examination, the IRS auditor must explain a taxpayer's appeal rights. ###

6. Karl had his 2010 and 2011 income tax returns examined, resulting in adjustments. He has administratively appealed the adjustments through the IRS appeals process. Some of them were sustained, resulting in an income tax deficiency in the amount of $25,000 for 2010 and $27,000 for 2011. Karl now wants to appeal his case to the U.S. Tax Court. He will handle the case himself since he cannot afford a lawyer or other representative. Which of the following is true?

A. Karl has forfeited his rights to the small tax case procedure by going to appeals first.
B. Karl is entitled to invoke the small tax case procedure.
C. Karl is not entitled to the small tax case procedure because his disputed amount exceeds $50,000.
D. Karl must appeal to the U.S. District Court first.

The answer is B. A taxpayer may elect the small tax case procedure (also known as S case procedure) for cases involving up to $50,000 in deficiency **per year**, including penalties and other additions to tax, but excluding interest. Trials in small tax cases generally are less formal and result in a speedier disposition. However, small tax court cases may not be appealed. Decisions are final for both the taxpayer and the IRS. ###

7. Alyssa vehemently disagrees with the IRS examiner regarding her income tax case. Her appeal rights are explained to her, and she decides to go to Tax Court. Which of the following is true?

A. Alyssa must receive a Notice of Deficiency before she can go to Tax Court.
B. Alyssa must wait for the IRS examiner to permanently close her audit case.
C. Alyssa must request a collection due process hearing before going to Tax Court.
D. Alyssa cannot go to Tax Court unless she agrees with the auditor's findings.

The answer is A. A Notice of Deficiency (90-day letter) must be issued before a taxpayer can go to Tax Court. Once the taxpayer receives the Notice of Deficiency, she then has 90 days to respond and file a petition with the court. ###

8. What branch of government decides tax law?

A. Tax law is written by the Treasury Department.
B. Tax law is primarily written by the President.
C. Tax law is primarily decided by Congress.
D. Tax law is written by the Internal Revenue Service.

The answer is C. Tax law is primarily decided by Congress, and it changes every year. Laws passed by Congress are the main source of Internal Revenue Code tax law. ###

9. Morgan wants her income tax case to be handled under the Tax Court's small tax case procedure. All of the following statements regarding the small tax case procedure are correct except:

A. In tax disputes involving $50,000 or less, taxpayers may choose to use the IRS small tax case procedure.
B. The disputed amount must be paid before going to Tax Court.
C. The Tax Court must approve the request that the case be handled under the small tax case procedure.
D. The decision is final and cannot be appealed.

The answer is B. The disputed amount does not have to be paid before going to Tax Court. In tax disputes involving $50,000 or less, taxpayers may choose to use the IRS small tax case procedure, and the Tax Court must approve the request. The decision in a small tax case procedure is final and cannot be appealed. ###

10. Danielle owes a substantial sum to the IRS. She files a petition with the U.S. Tax Court. Her case is later determined to be frivolous, wholly without merit, and merely to cause delay. What is the potential repercussion of Danielle's actions?

A. The Tax Court may impose a penalty of up to $10,000.
B. The Tax Court may impose a penalty of up to $25,000.
C. The Tax Court may impose a penalty of up to $50,000.
D. The Tax Court may impose a penalty of up to $25,000 and one year in prison.

The answer is B. If a taxpayer unreasonably fails to pursue the internal IRS appeals system, if the case is filed primarily to cause a delay, or if the taxpayer's position is frivolous, the Tax Court may impose a penalty of up to $25,000. ###

11. The Commissioner of the IRS has decided to publicly non-acquiesce to a court decision. Where will this decision be published?

A. The Internal Revenue Bulletin.
B. The New York Times.
C. Only on the IRS website.
D. The Tax Court website.

The answer is A. The IRS publishes its acquiescence and non-acquiescence first in the Internal Revenue Bulletin and then in the Cumulative Bulletin. The IRS does not announce acquiescence or non-acquiescence in every case. ###

12. If a taxpayer wishes to challenge the IRS in a district court, the taxpayer must _____:

A. Pay the contested liability first, and then sue the Department of Treasury for a refund.
B. Pay the contested liability first, and then sue the IRS for a refund.
C. Pay a retainer to the IRS for a refund.
D. Go first to the U.S. Tax Court before appealing to the U.S. District Court.

The answer is B. In order to appeal in a district court, the taxpayer must first pay the contested liability and then sue the IRS for a refund. If either party loses at the trial court level, the court's decision may be appealed to a higher court. ###

13. Which of the following statements is true regarding IRS acquiescence?

A. The IRS may choose whether or not to acquiesce to any court decision.
B. The IRS must change its regulations due to a loss in court.
C. The IRS will announce acquiescence or non-acquiescence in every case.
D. The IRS is bound to follow U.S. Supreme Court decisions.

The answer is D. The IRS may choose whether or not to acquiesce to a court decision. The only exception to this rule is the U.S. Supreme Court, whose decisions the IRS is obligated to follow. The IRS is not bound to change its regulations due to a loss in court. The IRS does not announce acquiescence or non-acquiescence in every case. Sometimes the IRS's position is withheld. ###

14. Kevin and Javier are partners in a body shop business. Both had their individual returns examined and both disagreed with the IRS. Kevin decided to take his case to IRS Appeals. After the conference, he and the IRS still disagreed. Javier decided to bypass IRS Appeals altogether and go directly to court. Which of the following is true?

A. Both Kevin and Javier can take their cases to the following courts: United States Tax Court, the United States Court of Federal Claims, or the United States District Court.
B. Only Kevin may petition the U.S. Tax Court, because he went through the IRS appeals process first.
C. Neither may petition the U.S. Tax Court, because they chose to use IRS Appeals first.
D. None of the above.

The answer is A. Both Kevin and Javier can take their cases to court. A taxpayer is not required to use the IRS appeals process. If a taxpayer and the IRS still disagree after an appeals conference or a taxpayer decides to bypass the IRS appeals system, the case may be taken to the U.S. Tax Court, the U.S. Court of Federal Claims, or a U.S. district court. ###

15. Which tax professional is allowed to practice before the U.S. Tax Court without first passing a qualifying test?

A. Enrolled agent.
B. CPA.
C. Attorney.
D. Both B and C.

The answer is C. Only licensed attorneys are allowed to practice before the U.S. Tax Court without passing a qualifying test. EAs and CPAs must first take a separate exam that gives them the right to practice before the Tax Court. ###

16. Which statement is correct regarding the IRS appeals process?

A. No written statement is required for tax deficiencies of $10,000 or less.
B. If the disputed tax deficiency is more than $10,000, a taxpayer must file a formal written protest.
C. The local IRS Appeals office and local IRS district offices are the same entities.
D. The 30-day letter that is sent to a taxpayer details the date and location of an upcoming audit, and includes an agreement or waiver form.

The answer is B. In cases in which the taxpayer owes more than $10,000, a taxpayer must file a formal written protest. Only in cases of $2,500 or less is no written statement required, though the taxpayer is required to contact the IRS to initiate an appeal. When a taxpayer owes more than $2,500 and less than $10,000, he must include a brief statement of disputed tax. The IRS Appeals office is a separate entity from local IRS district offices. The 30-day letter is sent to a taxpayer after an audit is concluded and includes an agreement or waiver form and a notice explaining appeal rights. ###

Unit 10: IRS E-File and IRS Payments

More Reading:
Publication 3112, *IRS e-file Application and Participation*
Publication 1345, *Handbook for Authorized IRS e-file Providers*
Publication 4169, *Tax Professional Guide to Electronic Federal Tax Payment System*
Publication 4453, *IRS e-file for Charities and Nonprofits*
Publication 3611, *Easy Ways to Pay Electronically*

The IRS e-file program allows taxpayers to transmit their returns electronically. Last year more than 80% of American taxpayers filed electronically. According to the IRS, the processing of e-file returns is not only quicker but also more accurate than the processing of paper returns. However, as with a paper return, the taxpayer is responsible for making sure the tax return contains accurate information and is filed on time.[189]

The E-File Mandate

A law requiring most tax preparers to e-file income tax returns went into effect in 2011.[190] The mandate covers returns for individuals, trusts, and estates (fiduciary returns, Form 1041).

Any tax return preparer who anticipates preparing and filing 11 or more Forms 1040, 1040A, 1040EZ, and 1041 during a calendar year must use IRS e-file (with limited exceptions explained later.) Those who are subject to the e-file requirement are referred to as "specified tax return preparers."

The rules require tax firms to compute the number of returns *in aggregate* that they reasonably expect to file as a firm. If that number is 11 or more for the calendar year, then all members of the firm must e-file the returns they prepare and file. This is true even if, on an individual basis, a member prepares and files fewer than the threshold.

*Exceptions: Financial institutions and fiduciaries that file Forms 1041 as *a trustee or fiduciary* are not required to e-file and are not subject to the mandate.[191] The e-file mandate also does not apply to payroll tax returns.

Example: Caroline is an EA who works for a CPA firm. She also has a small side business doing tax returns from her home. For the coming tax year, Caroline expects to prepare and file five Forms 1041 (for estates and trusts) while working for the CPA firm. She also expects to prepare and file ten Form 1040 tax returns individually as a self-employed preparer. Since she expects to file 11 or more forms, Caroline is required to e-file tax returns. The number of returns must be considered *in aggregate*.

---

[189]The IRS e-file rules and requirements are included in Revenue Procedure 2007-40, throughout Publication 3112, and in other IRS e-file publications and notices on the IRS website.
[190] Internal Revenue Bulletin: 2011-17, April 25, 2011, T.D. 9518, *Specified Tax Return Preparers Required to File Individual Income Tax Returns Using Magnetic Media.*
[191]Fiduciaries, as described by Section 7701(a)(36)(B)(iii) of the Internal Revenue Code, that file returns are not considered tax return preparers and are therefore not covered by the e-file requirement.

Taxpayers may independently choose to file on paper. Even if a practitioner has prepared the return, a taxpayer may mail the return himself, if he includes a hand-signed and dated statement documenting his choice to file on paper.

A tax preparer may also request a hardship waiver from the IRS to be exempt from e-filing. IRS says it will grant waivers only in rare cases and usually not for more than one calendar year. It will deny waivers based solely on the fact a preparer doesn't have a computer or appropriate software, or prefers simply not to e-file.

Some returns are impossible to e-file for various reasons and are therefore exempt from the e-file requirement. The IRS also may grant administrative exemptions when technology issues prevent specified preparers from filing returns electronically. Whatever the reason for paper filing, preparers generally are required to attach Form 8948, *Preparer Explanation for Not Filing Electronically*, to clients' paper returns.

Authorized IRS E-File Provider

An authorized IRS e-file provider is a business authorized by the IRS to participate in IRS e-file. The business may be a sole proprietorship, partnership, or corporation. The applicant must identify its principals and at least one responsible official on its IRS e-file application. Each individual who is a principal or responsible official must:

- Be a United States citizen or a legal U.S. alien lawfully admitted for permanent residence;
- Be at least 21 years of age as of the date of application; and
- Meet applicable state and local licensing and/or bonding requirements for the preparation and collection of tax returns.

Applying to the E-File Program

To begin e-filing tax returns, a practitioner must first apply and be accepted as an authorized IRS e-file provider. There is no fee to apply to the IRS, and the process takes up to 45 days.

When a business is accepted to participate in IRS e-file, it is assigned an Electronic Filing Identification Number (EFIN), which is required to file electronically. EFINs are issued on a firm basis, with all preparers in a firm covered by the same number. So, for example, a tax preparation business that has ten employee-preparers in one location would all file using the same EFIN. Each preparer would then use his own PTIN on the returns that he individually prepares.

E-File Suitability Check

The IRS will conduct a suitability check on the applicant and on all principals and responsible officials listed on an application to determine their suitability to be authorized e-file providers. Suitability checks may include the following:

- A criminal background check
- A credit history check
- A tax compliance check to ensure that the applicant's personal returns are filed and paid
- A check for prior noncompliance with IRS e-file requirements

Denial to Participate in IRS E-File

An applicant may be denied participation in IRS e-file for a variety of reasons that includes but is not limited to:

- Conviction of any criminal offense under the revenue laws of the United States or of a state or other political subdivision
- Failure to timely file returns
- Failure to timely pay any federal, state, or local tax liability
- Assessment of penalties
- Suspension/disbarment from practice before the IRS or before a state or local tax agency
- Disreputable conduct or other facts that may adversely impact IRS e-file
- Misrepresentation on an IRS e-file application
- Unethical practices in return preparation
- Failure to sign the preparer's area of the tax return
- Stockpiling returns prior to official acceptance to participate in IRS e-file
- Knowingly and directly or indirectly employing or accepting assistance from any firm, organization, or individual denied participation in IRS e-file, or suspended or expelled from participating in IRS e-file

Large Businesses That Are Required to E-File

Certain corporations, partnerships, and tax-exempt organizations are required to e-file. Some other businesses are also required to e-file their tax returns. The IRS has long mandated this rule in order to improve accuracy and processing of complicated returns.

Partnerships with more than 100 partners are required to file electronically. This means that a partnership must file Form 1065 and the multiple Schedules K-1 electronically. Partnerships with 100 or fewer partners (Schedules K-1) may voluntarily file their returns electronically, but they are not required to e-file.

Large and midsized corporate taxpayers, including tax-exempt organizations with $10 million or more in assets that file at least 250 returns (information returns and others, such as Form 1099 and Form W-2), are required to e-file.

The e-file application must be current and must list all the form types (1120, 1065, 990, etc.) that the practitioner will transmit to the IRS. If the practitioner does not list a certain form on his application and later attempts to transmit that form, he will receive a rejection for return type.

Example: Karen is an EA. When she first applied to be an e-file provider, she only prepared individual returns. In tax year 2012, she wishes to prepare a partnership return. However, Karen forgets to update her e-file application. When she submits the partnership return online, it is rejected. Karen will have to update her e-file application in order to submit partnership returns electronically.

Resubmission of Rejected Tax Returns

All prescribed due dates for filing paper income tax returns also apply to electronic returns. If the IRS rejects an e-filed return and the preparer cannot rectify the reason for the rejection, the preparer must inform the taxpayer of the rejection within 24 hours. The preparer must provide the taxpayer with the IRS reject codes accompanied by an explanation.

If the taxpayer chooses not to have the electronic portion of the return corrected and transmitted to the IRS, or if the IRS cannot accept the return for processing, the taxpayer must file a paper return. In order to timely file the return, the taxpayer must file the paper return by the later of:

- The due date of the return; or
- Ten calendar days after the date the IRS gives notification that it rejected the e-filed return. This is called the "Ten-day Transmission Perfection Period," and it is additional time that the IRS gives a preparer and taxpayer to correct and resubmit a tax return without a late filing penalty.

The transmission perfection period is not an extension of time to file; it is additional time to correct errors in the electronic file.

Example: Russ is an EA who e-files a tax return for his client, Paravi. The e-filed return is transmitted on April 15, 2013. The next day, Russ receives a rejection notification from the IRS regarding her tax return. Russ properly notifies Paravi of the rejection within 24 hours. The issue cannot be corrected, so she must file a paper return. Russ gives Paravi a copy of the paper return on April 17, 2013, along with an attached statement explaining the rejection. The tax return will be considered filed timely, because the paper return was filed within ten days of the rejection and the original e-filed return was attempted in a timely manner.

After an e-file rejection, a taxpayer may want to file on paper. To ensure that the paper return is identified as a rejected electronic return and the taxpayer is given credit for timely filing, the following information must be included:

- An explanation of why the paper return is being filed after the due date
- A copy of the rejection notification
- A brief history of actions taken to correct the electronic return

The taxpayer should write in red at the top of the first page of the paper return:

REJECTED ELECTRONIC RETURN – (DATE)

The date should be the date of the first e-file rejection. The paper return must be signed by the taxpayer. The PIN that was used on the electronically-filed return that was rejected may not be used as the signature on the paper return.

It is important to note that the Ten-day Transmission Perfection Period does not apply to payments. If an e-file submission is rejected, a return can be corrected within ten days and not be subject to a late filing penalty. When a return is rejected on the due date, it is recommended that an electronic payment not be transmitted with the return, because the payment must still be submitted or postmarked by the due date.

Types of E-File Providers

There are many types of e-file providers. An e-file provider is not necessarily a tax preparer. Authorized IRS e-file providers can also be firms that develop tax software, transmit electronic returns to the IRS, and provide services to a multitude of taxpayer clients.

The roles and responsibilities of e-file providers vary according to a firm's activities. Once a firm applies for acceptance into the IRS e-file program, it selects its "provider option" at that time. Some providers may have more than one e-file activity. For example, an e-file transmitter may also be a software developer.

ERO Responsibilities

An electronic return originator (ERO) originates the electronic submission of tax returns to the IRS. An ERO is the person that the client entrusts with tax information for the purpose of filing income tax returns electronically in the IRS e-file program.

Although an ERO may engage in tax return preparation, and many of them do, tax preparation is a separate and distinct activity from the electronic submission of tax returns to the IRS. An ERO submits a tax return only after the taxpayer has authorized the e-file transmission. The return must be either:

- Prepared by the ERO; or
- Collected from a taxpayer who has self-prepared his own return and is asking the ERO to e-file it for him.

Example: Patrick is an EA who uses Ultra TaxPro software to prepare returns. Once he has completed a tax return, he gives a copy to the client, who then gives signature authorization to e-file the return. Patrick transmits the return to Ultra TaxPro, which is an authorized transmitter. Ultra TaxPro then transmits the return to the IRS. Most tax practitioners use this method; all the major tax preparation software companies have e-file transmission options.

In originating the electronic submission of a return, the ERO is required to:

- Timely submit returns.
- Provide copies to taxpayers.
- Retain records and make records available to the IRS.
- Accept returns only from taxpayers and authorized IRS e-file providers, and work with the taxpayer and/or the transmitter to correct a rejected return.
- Enter the preparer's identifying information (name, address, and PTIN).
- Be diligent in recognizing fraud and abuse, reporting it to the IRS, and preventing it when possible.
- Cooperate with IRS investigations by making documents available to the IRS upon request.

To become an ERO, an applicant must apply and be accepted into the program, and then receive an EFIN. All EROs must be fingerprinted.

Permissible Disclosures

Disclosure of client information between e-file providers is permissible, so long as the disclosures are for the preparation and transmission of the tax return. For example, an ERO may relay tax return information to a transmitter for the purpose of transmitting the forms to the IRS.

However, if tax return information is disclosed or used in any other way, a provider may be subject to IRS penalties or the civil penalties in Internal Revenue Code (IRC) §6713 for unauthorized disclosure or use of tax return information.

Electronic Signature Requirements

As with any income tax return submitted to the IRS, the taxpayer and preparer must both sign the tax return. If an electronic return does not have an appropriate signature, it will be rejected.

All e-file individual returns submitted to the IRS by tax practitioners must be electronically signed using a PIN. These requirements also apply to volunteers at VITA and TCE sites who provide free tax assistance and e-filing.

- **The Self-Select PIN** allows taxpayers to electronically sign their e-filed return by using a five-digit PIN to act as their signature. The IRS uses the taxpayer's prior year adjusted gross income or prior year PIN to validate the taxpayer's signature. This signature method is available if the taxpayer SELECTS and ENTERS his own PIN on the electronically filed return.

- **The Practitioner PIN** is another signature method for taxpayers who use an ERO. The ERO asks the taxpayer to choose a five-digit, self-selected PIN as his electronic signature. The ERO must then complete Form 8879, *IRS e-file Signature Authorization*, and include the *taxpayer's* self-selected PIN and his own *practitioner* PIN. The Practitioner PIN is an 11-digit number that includes the ERO's EFIN plus five other digits that he chooses. The ERO should use the same practitioner PIN for the entire tax year.

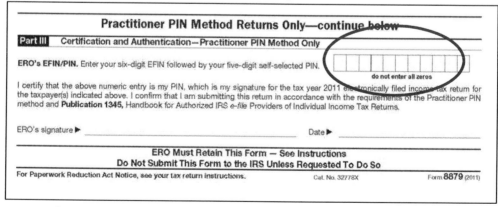

The ERO must sign and complete the requested information in the area provided: *"Declaration of Electronic Return Originator [ERO]."* An ERO may authorize employees to sign for him, but the ERO is ultimately responsible for all electronically-filed returns by its

795

firm. If the return was prepared for a fee, the ERO must also sign the jurat.[192] EROs may sign this form by rubber stamp, mechanical device (such as signature pen), or computer software program.

The ERO must retain copies of Forms 8879 for three years from the return due date or the IRS received date, whichever is later. EROs must not send Forms 8879 to the IRS unless requested to do so.

E-filed returns signed by a representative with power of attorney may be submitted to the IRS using Form 8453.[193] Form 2848, *Power of Attorney and Declaration of Representative,* is then submitted as an attachment. An e-filed return signed by an agent must have a power of attorney attached to Form 8453 that *specifically authorizes* the agent to sign the return.

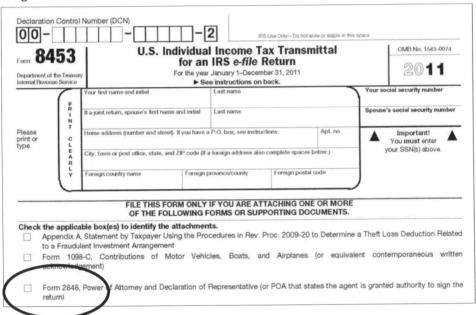

After Signing the Return

After the taxpayer signs the return, the ERO transmits the return to the IRS or to a third-party transmitter who then forwards the entire electronic record to the IRS for processing. Once received at the IRS, the return is automatically checked for errors. If it cannot be processed, it is sent back to the originating transmitter (usually the preparer) to clarify any necessary information.

After correction, the transmitter retransmits the return to the IRS. Within 48 hours of electronically sending the return, the IRS sends an acknowledgment to the transmitter stating the return is accepted for processing. This is called an "electronic postmark" and it is the taxpayer's proof of filing and assurance that the IRS has the return.

A tax preparer must retain a record of each electronic postmark until the end of the calendar year and provide the record to the IRS upon request. Most tax software

---

[192] Jurat: An affidavit in which the taxpayer and/or preparer attests to the truth of the information contained in the return and attached return information.
[193] See Publication 17 for updated procedures for attaching a power of attorney to electronically filed returns.

packages automatically retain a record of the return transmission report and electronic postmark.

EROs Who Make Changes to a Return

An ERO who originates returns that he has not prepared but only collected becomes an "income tax return preparer" when he makes "substantive changes" to the tax return. A "non-substantive change" is a correction limited to a transposition error, misplaced entry, spelling error, or arithmetic correction. The IRS considers all other changes "substantive," and the ERO *becomes* a tax return preparer when he makes these changes.

As such, the ERO may be required to sign the return as the preparer.

Example: Diana is an ERO. A taxpayer brings a self-prepared tax return for Diana to e-file. She notices gross errors on the tax return and talks with the client about the mistakes. The taxpayer agrees to correct the return, and Diana makes the necessary adjustments, in return for a small fee. Diana is now required to sign the return as a preparer.

Signature forms must be retained by the e-file provider for three years from the due date of the return, extended due date, or the IRS received date, whichever is later. Providers must make all these records available to the IRS upon request.

Providers may electronically image (scan) and store all paper records they are required to retain for IRS e-file. This includes signed documents as well as any supporting documents not included in the electronic record.

Providing a Copy of an E-filed Return to the Taxpayer

An ERO is required to submit an e-filed return to the IRS that is *identical* to the return provided to the taxpayer. The ERO is also required to provide a complete copy of the return to the taxpayer.

The copy given to the taxpayer may be in any media acceptable to both the taxpayer and the provider (for example, the taxpayer may request a scanned copy on disk or a paper copy.) The copy that is given to the taxpayer is not required to be signed by the preparer (only the copy that is filed with the IRS, whether electronic or on a paper return, requires a preparer's signature).

The taxpayer should retain this information for a minimum of three years from the due date of the tax return, extended due date, or the date the return was filed, whichever is later. This corresponds to the statute of limitations for that tax period.

E-File Advertising Standards

"IRS e-file" is a brand name, but acceptance to the IRS e-file program does not imply an endorsement by the IRS. A practitioner must not use improper or misleading advertising in relation to IRS e-file, including promising a time frame for refunds and Refund Anticipation Loans (RALs). If a practitioner advertises an RAL or other financial product, he and the financial institution must clearly describe the RAL as a loan, not as a refund. The advertisement on an RAL or other financial product must be easy to identify and in easily readable print.

Practitioners may not use the regular IRS logo (the eagle symbol) or IRS insignia in their advertising, or imply any type of relationship with the IRS. A practitioner may, however, use the IRS *e-file* logo.

A preparer may not combine the e-file logo with the IRS eagle symbol, the word "federal," or with other words or symbols that might suggest a special relationship with the IRS. A preparer's advertising materials must not carry the FMS, IRS, or any other Treasury seals.

The IRS e-file logo, which preparers may use

If an e-file provider uses radio, television, Internet, signage, or other methods of advertising, the practitioner must keep a copy and provide it to the IRS upon request. Practitioners must retain copies of any advertising until the end of the calendar year following the last transmission or use.

A practitioner may not advertise that individual income tax returns may be e-filed without using Forms W-2. In other words, a firm may not advertise that it can file a tax return using only "pay stubs" or "earnings statements."

E-file Revocations and Sanctions

The IRS may revoke e-file privileges if a firm is either:

- Prohibited or disbarred from filing returns by a court order, or
- Prohibited from filing returns by any federal or state legal action that forbids participation in e-file.

An authorized IRS e-file provider is not entitled to an administrative review hearing if e-file privileges are revoked because of a court injunction. If the injunction or other legal action expires or is later reversed, only *then* may the practitioner reapply to participate in IRS e-file.

Example: Steve was a CPA who was convicted of felony embezzlement. He was also disbarred and stripped of his license by his state accountancy board. The IRS revoked his e-file privileges without prior notice.

The IRS may also choose to sanction any practitioner that fails to comply with any e-file regulation. Before sanctioning, the IRS may issue a warning letter that describes specific corrective action the provider must take. The IRS may also sanction a provider without issuance of a warning letter.

Sanctions may include a written reprimand, suspension, or permanent expulsion from IRS e-file. The IRS categorizes the seriousness of infractions as Level One, Level Two, and Level Three. Level One is the least serious, Level Two is moderately serious, and Level Three is the most serious. For minor violations, the IRS will usually issue a written warning to the practitioner.

Suspensions make providers ineligible to participate in IRS e-file for a period of either one or two years from the effective date of the sanction. If a principal or responsible official is suspended or expelled from participation in IRS e-file, every entity listed on the firm's e-file application may also be expelled.

The IRS may list in the Internal Revenue Bulletin, newsletters, or other media the name and owner of any entity suspended or expelled from participation in IRS e- file and the effective date of the IRS action.

Practitioners who are denied or expelled from participation in IRS e-file usually have the right to an administrative review. Failure to respond within 30 days of the date of any denial or sanction letter irrevocably terminates the practitioner's right to an administrative review or appeal.

In order to appeal, practitioners must mail a written response within 30 days addressing the IRS's reason for denial or revocation and including supporting documentation. During this administrative review process, the denial of participation remains in effect.

In certain circumstances, the IRS can immediately suspend or expel an authorized IRS e-file provider without prior notice.

Refunds and Payments on E-Filed Returns

Taxpayers have several options for refunds and payments on electronically-filed returns. The IRS has attempted to make Direct Deposit[194] and automatic payments easier in order to encourage these methods.

Taxpayers often elect the Direct Deposit option because it is the fastest way of receiving their refund. Taxpayers may:

- Apply the refund to next year's estimated tax.
- Receive the refund as a Direct Deposit.
- Receive the refund as a paper check.
- Split the refund, with a portion applied to next year's estimated tax and the remainder received as Direct Deposit or a paper check.
- Use their federal tax refund (or part of it) to purchase U.S. Series I Savings Bonds by completing Form 8888, *Allocation of Refund (Including Savings Bond Purchases)*. Taxpayers can purchase up to $5,000 in bonds for themselves or others, such as a child or grandchild.

Direct Deposit

Providers are required to accept any Direct Deposit election to any eligible financial institution designated by the taxpayer. A provider may not charge a separate fee for Direct Deposit. The provider must not alter the Direct Deposit information in the electronic record after a taxpayer has signed the tax return.

Taxpayers can split their deposits in up to three different accounts. Most e-file and tax preparation software allows taxpayers to split refunds.

Refunds may be designated for Direct Deposit to qualified accounts in the taxpayer's name. Qualified accounts include savings, checking, share draft, or retirement accounts (for example, IRA or money market accounts). Direct Deposits cannot be made to credit card accounts. Qualified accounts must be in financial institutions within the United States.

---

[194]The IRS requires tax practitioners to capitalize the words "Direct Deposit" in their advertising, so we will use the same formatting here.

The provider must advise the taxpayer that a Direct Deposit election cannot be rescinded. In addition, changes cannot be made to routing numbers of financial institutions or to the taxpayer's account numbers after the IRS has accepted the return. Providers should verify account and routing numbers each year. Taxpayers will not receive Direct Deposit of their refunds if account information is not updated to reflect current information.

Refunds that are not Direct Deposited because of errors or any other reason will be issued as paper checks, resulting in potential refund delays of up to ten weeks.

Payments on Tax Returns

Taxpayers who have their returns filed electronically have several choices when paying any taxes owed on their tax returns, as well as any estimated taxes. The following methods of payments are accepted:

1. Direct debit
2. Credit card
3. Personal check
4. Installment agreement requests

Electronic payment options include:

1. Electronic Federal Tax Payment System (EFTPS)
2. Electronic funds withdrawal
3. Federal Tax Application (same day wire transfer)

Check Payments

Balance-due payments may be made by check. Payments do not have to be mailed at the same time an electronic return is transmitted. For example, the return may be transmitted in January and the taxpayer may mail the payment on a later date. So long as the payment is mailed by the due date of the return, it will be considered timely.

On all checks or money orders, the practitioner should write the taxpayer's Taxpayer Identification Number (EIN, TIN, or SSN), the type of tax return, and the tax year to which the payment applies. The check or money order should be made payable to the "United States Treasury."

Paying an IRS Debt with an Installment Agreement

Installment agreements are arrangements in which the IRS allows taxpayers to pay liabilities over time. A taxpayer who files electronically may apply for an installment agreement once the return is processed and the tax is assessed. Taxpayers must submit Form 9465, *Request for Installment Agreement,* in order to request payments in installments. The IRS charges a one-time user fee to set up an installment agreement.

The only agreements that may be granted are those that provide for full payment of the accounts (which means that the taxpayer must agree to pay the full balance due—the taxpayer cannot use an installment agreement to negotiate a lower tax liability). During the course of the installment agreement, penalty and interest continue to accrue. No levies may be served during installment agreements.

If a taxpayer owes less than $10,000 in taxes, he will be automatically approved for an installment agreement, provided that he is up-to-date on his filing responsibilities.

Installment payments are equal monthly installments, although the taxpayer may choose to pay more than the required monthly amount. Taxpayers may make their payments by check or by electronic withdrawal from their bank account.

A taxpayer with $25,000 or less in combined tax, penalties, and interest can use the IRS Online Payment Agreement and set up his installment agreement online. If a taxpayer owes more than $25,000, he may still qualify for an installment agreement, but a *Collection Information Statement*, Form 433-F, must be completed.

In accordance with law, each year the IRS mails Form CP-89, *Annual Installment Agreement Statement*, to every installment agreement taxpayer. The statement provides the dollar amount of the beginning account balance due; an itemized listing of payments; an itemized listing of penalties, interest, and other charges; and the dollar amount of the ending account balance due.

A late payment on an installment agreement will generate an automatic 30-day notice as to the cessation of the agreement, allowing the IRS to make changes to the installment agreement.

Electronic Federal Tax Payment System (EFTPS)

Balances due and estimated taxes can be paid year-round using the Electronic Federal Tax Payment System (EFTPS). Taxpayers and businesses enroll in EFTPS by using an online application.

Businesses and individuals can pay all their federal taxes using EFTPS. Individuals can pay their quarterly estimated taxes electronically using EFTPS, and they can make payments weekly, monthly, or quarterly. Both business and individual payments can be scheduled months in advance, if desired.

Businesses can schedule payments up to 120 days in advance of their tax due date. Individuals can schedule payments up to 365 days in advance of their tax due date. Domestic corporations must deposit all income tax payments by the due date of the return using EFTPS.

Refund Anticipation Loans (RALs): The Rules

A Refund Anticipation Loan (RAL) is a financial product offered by some tax offices. An RAL is not a tax refund. Instead, an RAL is a loan: money is borrowed by the taxpayer based on his anticipated tax refund.

The IRS is not involved in RALs or financial products. Tax preparers who assist taxpayers in applying for RALs or other financial products have additional responsibilities and may be sanctioned by the IRS if they fail to adhere to the following requirements. If a practitioner wants to offer RALs, he must:

- Ensure a taxpayer understands that by agreeing to an RAL or other financial product he will not receive his refund from the IRS but instead it will be sent to the financial institution.
- Advise a taxpayer that an RAL is an interest-bearing loan and not a quicker way of receiving his refund from the IRS.

- Advise a taxpayer that if a Direct Deposit is not received within the expected time frame for whatever reason, the taxpayer may be liable to the lender for additional interest and other fees.
- Advise a taxpayer of all fees and other known deductions to be paid from his refund and the remaining amount he will actually receive.
- Obtain the taxpayer's written consent to disclose information to the lending institution.
- Ensure that the return preparer does not have a "related party" conflict with the financial institution that makes an RAL agreement.
- Adhere to fee restrictions and advertising standards (explained earlier).

There are no guarantees that the IRS will deposit a taxpayer's refund within a specified time. For example, it may delay a refund due to processing problems or it may offset some or all of the refund for back taxes, child support, or other amounts that the taxpayer owes. The IRS is not liable for any loss suffered by taxpayers, practitioners, or financial institutions resulting from reduced refunds or dishonored Direct Deposits.

RAL and E-File Fee Restrictions

Providers may not base their tax preparation fees on a percentage of the refund amount or compute their fees using any figure from tax returns. A practitioner may charge an identical flat fee to all customers applying for RALs, meaning the fee cannot correspond to the amount of a refund for an individual client.

Unit 10: Questions

1. Which of the following is considered a "substantive change" to a tax return?

A. A correction in overall tax liability.
B. The correction of a spelling error.
C. The correction of a transposition error.
D. An arithmetic correction.

The answer is A. A correction that changes an individual's tax liability would be considered a "substantive change" to a return. A "non-substantive change" is a correction limited to a transposition error, misplaced entry, spelling error, or arithmetic correction. The IRS considers all other changes "substantive," and the ERO *becomes* a tax return preparer when he makes these changes.

2. Which of the following statements is true?

A. Separate fees may be charged for Direct Deposits.
B. E-file providers may not charge contingent fees based on a percentage of the refund.
B. E-file providers may not charge a fee for paper returns under any circumstances.
D. An e-file provider is not allowed to charge a fee for e-filing.

The answer is B. A practitioner may not charge a contingent fee (percentage of the refund) for preparing an original tax return. Separate fees may not be charged for Direct Deposits. However, a practitioner is allowed to charge a fee for e-filing. ###

3. An EA has a client who wishes to use Direct Deposit. Which of the following statements regarding Direct Deposit is correct?

A. An EA may not charge a fee for offering Direct Deposit.
B. An EA may advise the taxpayer to Direct Deposit to his credit card account.
C. An EA may advise the taxpayer to Direct Deposit directly into his bank account in Mexico.
D. An EA is not required to accept a Direct Deposit election from the taxpayer.

The answer is A. A practitioner cannot charge a fee for Direct Deposit. Direct Deposits cannot be made to credit card accounts. Qualified accounts must be in financial institutions within the United States. The practitioner is required to accept a Direct Deposit election by the taxpayer. ###

4. Taxpayers who have their returns filed electronically have several choices when paying any taxes owed on their tax returns, as well as any estimated taxes. Which method is not an acceptable method of paying an outstanding tax liability to the IRS?

A. Direct debit.
B. Credit card payments.
C. A U.S. Treasury bond note.
D. Installment agreements.

The answer is C. A bond note is not an acceptable method of payment. Taxpayers may pay their outstanding tax liability a variety of ways including direct debit, credit card payments, installment agreements, or payment by check. ###

5. If the IRS rejects the electronic portion of a taxpayer's return for processing and the reason for the rejection cannot be rectified with the information already provided to the ERO, what is the ERO's responsibility at that point?

A. The ERO is not legally required to notify the taxpayer.
B. The ERO must attempt to notify the taxpayer within 24 hours and provide the taxpayer with the reject code accompanied by an explanation.
C. The ERO is required to notify the taxpayer in writing within 72 hours.
D. The ERO is required to file the tax return on paper within 24 hours.

The answer is B. If the IRS rejects the electronic portion of a taxpayer's individual income tax return for processing and the reason for the rejection cannot be rectified, the ERO must take reasonable steps to inform the taxpayer of the rejection within 24 hours. The ERO must provide the taxpayer with the reject code(s) accompanied by an explanation. After receiving a rejection, the ERO is not required to file a tax return on paper. The ERO and the client should attempt to *correct* the e-file. However, if the return continues to be rejected, the taxpayer may be forced to file on paper. ###

6. All of the following statements regarding IRS installment agreements are correct except:

A. During the course of the installment agreement, penalty and interest continue to accrue.
B. A taxpayer who owes less than $10,000 in taxes will be automatically approved for an installment agreement.
C. The IRS charges a one-time user fee to set up an installment agreement.
D. IRS levies may be served during installment agreements.

The answer is D. No levies may be served during installment agreements. During the course of the installment agreement, penalty and interest continue to accrue. A taxpayer who owes less than $10,000 in taxes will automatically be approved for an installment agreement. The IRS charges a one-time user fee to set up an installment agreement. ###

7. Which logo may a practitioner use in his advertising?

A. The official IRS logo.
B. The IRS e-file logo.
C. The official seal of the U.S. Treasury.
D. The IRS eagle symbol.

The answer is B. A practitioner may use the IRS e-file logo, but may not use the IRS logo or insignia in his advertising, or imply a relationship with the IRS. A preparer may not combine the e-file logo with the IRS eagle symbol, the word "federal," or with other words or symbols that suggest a special relationship between the IRS and the logo. Advertising materials must not carry the IRS or other Treasury seals. ###

8. Mark is getting a tax refund this year. Which of the following methods is not available for Mark to receive his IRS refund?

A. Mark may apply the refund to next year's estimated tax.
B. Mark may receive the refund as a Direct Deposit to his retirement account.
C. Mark may use his federal tax refund to purchase U.S. Series I Savings Bonds.
D. Mark may Direct Deposit his refund to his credit card account.

The answer is D. A taxpayer may not designate a credit card account for Direct Deposit of his federal tax refund. ###

9. What happens when a taxpayer has a late payment on an installment agreement?
A. The late payment will generate an automatic 30-day notice.
B. The late payment will automatically increase the statute of limitations for collecting the tax.
C. The late payment will cause the installment agreement to default.
D. The IRS will file a Notice of Deficiency.

The answer is A. A late payment on an installment agreement will generate an automatic 30-day notice. It will not cause the installment agreement to default. ###

10. Electronic Filing Identification Numbers (EFINs) are issued _____.

A. On a firm basis.
B. On a preparer basis.
C. On a client basis.
D. Only to foreign firms.

The answer is A. Electronic Filing Identification Numbers (EFINs) are issued on a firm basis. All tax return preparers in the firm are covered by a single EFIN. Providers need an EFIN to electronically file tax returns. ###

11. Art owes more than $25,000 to the IRS. He would like to set up an installment agreement. Which of the following statements regarding his payment options is true?

A. Art may still qualify for an installment agreement, but a *Collection Information Statement*, Form 433-F, must be completed.
B. Art does not qualify for an installment agreement because he owes more than $25,000.
C. Art may still qualify for an installment agreement, but an offer in compromise must first be completed.
D. Art must enroll in EFTPS and have automatic withdrawals in order to have his installment agreement approved.

The answer is A. If a taxpayer owes more than $25,000, he may still qualify for an installment agreement, but the taxpayer will also need to complete Form 433-F, *Collection Information Statement*. ###

12. Which signature methods are acceptable for EROs to use for electronically filed returns?

A. The self-select PIN method.
B. The practitioner personal identification number method.
C. The scanned signature method.
D. Answer A and B are both correct.

The answer is D. Electronic return originators are required to use either the self-select PIN method or the practitioner personal identification number method to electronically file an individual tax return. ###

13. Which of the following tax preparers would be subject to the mandate that requires preparers to e-file their clients' returns?

A. Dean, a bookkeeper who prepares a tax return for himself.
B. Maria, an EA who only prepares payroll tax returns for her employer.
C. Scott, who files six individual tax returns and seven estate returns for compensation.
D. Chon, a CPA who files 100 returns for the Volunteer Income Tax Assistance (VITA) program.

The answer is C. Any paid preparer who files 11 or more individual or trust returns *in aggregate* in a calendar year is required to e-file. There are limited exceptions, such as for returns that cannot be e-filed (returns that require paper attachments, nonresident returns, etc.) The e-file mandate does not apply to payroll tax returns, volunteer preparers, or returns prepared under the Volunteer Income Tax Assistance (VITA) program. ###

14. A Refund Anticipation Loan (RAL) is
_____.

A. A refund from the Internal Revenue Service.
B. Endorsed by the Internal Revenue Service.
C. A financial product with no affiliation to the Internal Revenue Service.
D. A financial product offered by the Internal Revenue Service.

The answer is C. A Refund Anticipation Loan (RAL) is a financial product. It is not a tax refund. Instead, an RAL is a loan: money is borrowed by the taxpayer based on his anticipated tax refund. The IRS is not involved in RALs or financial products. ###

15. Which of the following is true regarding Refund Anticipating Loans?

A. Providers may compute their RAL fees using any figure from tax returns.
B. A practitioner may charge an identical flat fee to all customers applying for RALs.
C. A provider may accept a fee that is contingent upon the amount of the refund or an RAL.
D. The IRS has the responsibility for the payment of any RAL fees associated with the preparation of a return.

The answer is B. A practitioner may charge an *identical flat fee* to all customers applying for RALs, meaning the fee cannot correspond to the amount of a refund for an individual client. The practitioner must not accept a fee that is contingent upon the amount of the refund or an RAL. The IRS has no responsibility for the payment of any fees associated with the preparation of a return. ###

16. The IRS may excuse a preparer from the mandate to e-file in all of the following instances except:

A. Administrative exemptions due to technology issues.
B. An individual case of hardship documented by the preparer.
C. Lack of access to tax preparation software.
D. None of the above.

The answer is B. The IRS says it will grant e-file waivers due to hardship only on a rare, case-by-case basis, and typically only for a single year. An individual preparer's dislike of using a computer or not having appropriate software is not considered a legitimate reason to grant a hardship waiver. ###

17. The IRS may sanction providers who fail to comply with e-file regulations. It uses a specific system of categorizing how serious infractions are. Which is the most serious?

A. Level One.
B. Level Two.
C. Level Three.
D. Level Four.

The answer is C. Under the IRS system of rating e-file infractions, Level One is the less serious, Level Two is moderately serious, and Level Three is the most serious. There is no Level Four infraction. ###

18. Tammy is an EA who e-files a return for her client, Rick. However, Rick's e-filed return is rejected by the IRS. They cannot resolve the rejection issue, and the return must be filed on paper. In order to timely file Rick's tax return, what is the deadline for filing a paper return?

A. The due date of the return.
B. Ten calendar days after the date the IRS rejects the e-filed return.
C. Forty-eight hours after the date the IRS rejects the e-filed return.
D. Answer A and B are both correct.

The answer is D. In order to timely file a tax return, the taxpayer must file a paper return by the **later** of:
- The due date of the return; or
- Ten calendar days after the date the IRS gives notification that it rejected the e-filed return.

This is called the "Ten-Day Transmission Perfection Period," and it is additional time that the IRS gives a preparer and taxpayer to correct and resubmit a tax return without a late filing penalty. This is not an extension of time to file; rather, this is additional time that the IRS gives a preparer and taxpayer to correct and resubmit a tax return without a late filing penalty. The following steps must be followed to ensure that the paper return is identified as a *rejected electronic return* and the taxpayer is given credit for timely filing. The paper return should include the following:
- An explanation of why the paper return is being filed after the due date.
- A copy of the rejection notification.
- A brief history of actions taken to correct the electronic return. ###

19. How long must a tax practitioner retain Form 8879, *IRS e-file Signature Authorization?*

A. One year from the due date of the return or the date received by the IRS, whichever is later.
B. Two years from the due date of the return or the date received by the IRS, whichever is earlier.
C. Three years from the due date of the return or the date received by the IRS, whichever is later.
D. Three years from the due date of the return or the date received by the IRS, whichever is earlier.

The answer is C. The ERO must retain the form for three years from the due date of the return or the date received by the IRS, whichever is *later*. ###

20. Katie is an EA subject to the e-file mandate. She has power of attorney authority for her client, Timothy. What must she do to e-file Timothy's return?

A. Use Form 8453 and submit Form 2848, *Power of Attorney and Declaration of Representative,* as an attachment.
B. Use Form 8879 and submit Form 2848, *Power of Attorney and Declaration of Representative,* as an attachment.
C. Use the Practitioner PIN method as her signature requirement.
D. Katie is not allowed to e-file Timothy's return in this instance. She must file it on paper.

The answer is A. Katie must use Form 8453, *U.S. Individual Income Tax Transmittal for an IRS e-file Return,* and also submit Form 2848, *Power of Attorney and Declaration of Representative,* as an attachment. Form 8879, *IRS e-file Signature Authorization,* is used by EROs but only submitted to the IRS upon request. ###

21. Which individual or business is not required to e-file tax returns?

A. A partnership with 100 partners.
B. A corporation with $8 million in assets that files more than 500 information returns.
C. An EA who prepares ten Forms 1040EZ through VITA, five Forms 1040 for a small fee for neighbors, and six Forms 1041 through the tax firm she works for.
D. Both A and B.

The answer is D. A partnership with more than 100 partners must e-file. A partnership with 100 or fewer partners is not required to e-file, though it may choose to do so. A corporation with $10 million or more in assets must e-file if it files at least 250 returns. The EA in Answer C is required to e-file because she prepares 11 tax returns for compensation, which is the minimum number that triggers the e-file mandate. VITA volunteers are not covered under the e-file mandate. ###

Unit 11: IRS Documents and Pronouncements

For anyone not familiar with the IRS, the array of IRS guidance may seem puzzling at first glance. In its role of administering the tax laws enacted by Congress, the IRS must take the specifics of these laws and translate them into detailed regulations, rules, and procedures. The IRS Office of Chief Counsel fills this crucial role by producing several kinds of documents that provide guidance to taxpayers. There are **seven** types of common IRS guidance:

1. Treasury regulations
2. Revenue rulings
3. Revenue procedures
4. Private letter rulings
5. Technical advice memorandum
6. IRS notices
7. IRS announcements

The following is a brief explanation of these forms of IRS guidance.

Treasury Regulations

Treasury regulations are the Secretary of the Treasury's interpretations of the Internal Revenue Code. The IRC authorizes the Secretary of the Treasury to "prescribe all needful rules and regulations for enforcement" of the code. All regulations are written by the Office of the Chief Counsel, IRS, and approved by the Secretary of the Treasury. Regulations are issued as interpretations of specific code sections.

The courts give weight to Treasury regulations and will generally uphold the regulations so long as the IRS's interpretation is reasonable.

*Note: The IRS is bound by regulations, but the courts are not. U.S. Treasury regulations are authorized by law, but U.S. courts are not bound to follow administrative interpretations.

The courts also have the job of deciding whether a tax law challenged in court is constitutional or not.

There are three types of Treasury regulations:

- Legislative regulations
- Interpretative regulations
- Procedural regulations

Legislative Regulations

Legislative regulations are when Congress expressly delegates the authority to the Secretary or the Commissioner of the IRS to provide the requirements of a specific provision. A legislative regulation has a higher degree of authority than an interpretative regulation. A legislative regulation may be overturned if any of the following conflicts apply:

1. It is outside the power delegated to the U.S. Treasury.
2. It conflicts with a specific statute.
3. It is deemed unreasonable by the courts.

Interpretive Regulations

Interpretive regulations are issued under the IRS's general authority to interpret the IRC but are subject to challenge on the grounds that they do not reflect Congress's intent. An interpretative regulation only explains the meaning of a portion of the code. Unlike a legislative regulation, there is no grant of authority for the promulgation of an interpretative regulation by the IRS, so these regulations may be challenged.

Procedural Regulations

Procedural regulations concern the administrative provisions of the code. Procedural regulations are promulgated by the Commissioner of the IRS and not the Secretary of the Treasury. They often concern minor issues, such as when notices should be sent to employees, etc.

Proposed, Temporary, or Final?

Regulations are further classified as proposed, temporary, or final:

1. **Proposed regulations** are open to commentary from the public. Various versions of proposed regulations may be issued and withdrawn before a final regulation is made. Proposed regulations do not have authority.
2. **Temporary regulations** may remain in effect for three years, and may never be finalized.
3. **Final regulations** are issued when the regulation becomes an official Treasury decision.

Private Letter Rulings

Taxpayers who have a specific question regarding tax law may request a private letter ruling (PLR) from the IRS. A PLR is a written statement issued to a taxpayer that interprets and applies tax laws to the taxpayer's specific case. It is issued to establish tax consequences of a particular transaction before the transaction is consummated or before the taxpayer's return is filed.

A PLR is legally binding on the IRS if the taxpayer fully and accurately described the proposed transaction in the request and carries out the transaction as described. A PLR may not be relied on as precedent by other taxpayers or IRS personnel.

PLRs are made public after all the taxpayer's private, identifiable information has been redacted (the information is removed or "blacked out").

Technical Advice Memorandum

A technical advice memorandum (TAM) is written guidance furnished by the IRS Office of Chief Counsel upon the request of an IRS director, often in response to procedural questions that develop during an audit.

A TAM is issued in response to a technical or procedural question that develops during:

- The examination of a taxpayer's return
- Consideration of a taxpayer's claim for refund or credit
- A request for a determination letter
- Processing and considering non-docketed cases in an appeals office

Technical advice memoranda are issued only on closed transactions and provide the interpretation of proper application of tax laws, tax treaties, regulations, revenue rulings, or other precedents.

The advice rendered represents the position of the IRS, but only relates to the specific case in question. Technical advice memoranda are made public after all information has been removed that could identify the taxpayer whose circumstances triggered a specific memorandum.

Revenue Rulings and Revenue Procedures

The IRS issues both revenue rulings and revenue procedures for the information and guidance of taxpayers. Neither has the force of Treasury Department regulations, but they may be used as precedents.

A *revenue ruling* typically states the IRS position, while a *revenue procedure* provides instructions concerning that position.

Revenue Rulings

Revenue rulings are intended to promote uniform application of the IRC. The national office of the IRS issues revenue rulings, which are published in issues of the Internal Revenue Bulletin and the Federal Register. A revenue ruling is not binding in Tax Court or any other U.S. court. However, revenue rulings can be used to avoid certain IRS penalties.

The numbering system for revenue rulings corresponds to the year in which they are issued. Thus, for example, revenue ruling 80-20 was the twentieth revenue ruling issued in 1980.

Revenue Procedures

Revenue procedures are official IRS statements of procedure that affect the rights or duties of taxpayers or other members of the public under the IRC and related statutes or information that, although not necessarily affecting the rights of the public, should be a matter of public knowledge. A revenue procedure may be cited as precedent, but it does not have the force of law.

Example: A *revenue ruling* will announce that taxpayers may deduct certain automobile expenses. The *revenue procedure* will then explain how taxpayers must deduct, allocate, or compute these automobile expenses.

IRS Notices

An official IRS notice is a public pronouncement that may contain guidance involving substantive interpretations of the IRC or other provisions of the law. Information that is commonly published in IRS notices includes:

- Weighted average interest rate updates
- Inflation adjustment factors
- Changes to IRS regulations
- Presidentially Declared Disaster Areas
- IRS requests for public comments on changes to regulations, rulings, or procedures

IRS Announcements

An IRS announcement is a public pronouncement that has only immediate or short-term value. For example, announcements can be used to summarize regulations without making any substantive interpretation; to state what regulations will say when they are certain to be published in the immediate future; or to notify taxpayers of an approaching deadline.

Some examples of IRS announcements include:

- Availability of new or corrected IRS forms or publications
- Updated standard mileage rates
- Announcement of an IRS settlement program
- Correction of a typographical error in a previously published revenue ruling or revenue procedure

Freedom of Information Act Requests (FOIA)

The Freedom of Information Act (FOIA) is a law designed to ensure public access to U.S. government records. Upon written request, agencies of the U.S. government, including the IRS, are required to disclose requested records, unless they can be withheld under certain exemptions in the FOIA.

The FOIA applies to records created by federal agencies and does not cover records held by Congress, the courts, or state and local government agencies. Each state has its own public access laws.

Reasons Records May be Denied Under the FOIA

The IRS may withhold an IRS record that falls under one of the FOIA's exemptions or exclusions. The exemptions protect against the disclosure of information that would harm the following: national security, the privacy of individuals, the proprietary interests of business, the functioning of the government, and other important recognized interests.

When a record contains some information that qualifies as exempt, the entire record is not necessarily exempt. Instead, the FOIA specifically provides that any portions of a record that can be set apart must be provided to a requester after deletion of the exempt portions. Whenever a FOIA request is denied, the IRS must give the reason for denial and explain the right to appeal to the head of the agency.

A taxpayer may contest the type or amount of fees that were charged in the processing of the records request. A taxpayer also may appeal any other type of adverse determination under the FOIA, such as the failure of the IRS to conduct an adequate search for requested documents. However, a taxpayer may not file an administrative appeal for the lack of a timely response by the IRS.

A person whose request was granted in part and denied in part may appeal the part that was denied. If the IRS has agreed to disclose some but not all of the requested documents, the filing of an appeal does not affect the release of the documents that can be disclosed. There is no charge for filing an FOIA appeal.

Unit 11: Questions

1. Which of the following statements regarding revenue rulings is correct?

A. Revenue rulings cannot be used to avoid certain IRS penalties.
B. Revenue rulings can be used to avoid certain IRS penalties.
C. Revenue rulings are not official IRS guidance.
D. None of the above.

The answer is B. Revenue rulings can be used to avoid certain IRS penalties. Taxpayers may rely on revenue rulings as official IRS guidance on an issue to make a decision regarding taxable income, deductions, and also how to avoid certain IRS penalties. ###

2. What is a private letter ruling?

A. It is a private letter that a taxpayer writes to the IRS.
B. It is a private letter issued by the U.S. Tax Court.
C. It is a request by a taxpayer to the IRS to rule about a particular tax matter.
D. It is a request by the IRS to Congress about tax issues.

The answer is C. A private letter ruling is initiated by a taxpayer who has a question about a particular transaction. A taxpayer may request a PLR from the IRS. It cannot be used as a precedent by other taxpayers or the IRS. ###

3. Which is not a type of official IRS guidance?

A. Treasury regulation.
B. Private letter ruling.
C. Technical advice memorandum.
D. Tax Court memorandum opinion.

The answer is D. A Tax Court memorandum opinion is a pronouncement of the Tax Court and not of the IRS. ###

4. Which of the following choices is not a type of Treasury regulation?

A. Supporting regulation.
B. Interpretative regulation.
C. Legislative regulation.
D. Procedural regulation.

The answer is A. There are three types of Treasury regulations: legislative, interpretive, and procedural. There is no such thing as a "supporting regulation."###

5. Which of the following statements regarding the legality of revenue rulings and revenue procedures is correct?

A. Revenue rulings are binding in court, but revenue procedures are not.
B. Revenue rulings and revenue procedures are binding in court.
C. Revenue rulings and revenue procedures are not binding in court.
D. Revenue rulings and revenue procedures are binding in Tax Court, but not in U.S. District Courts.

The answer is C. Revenue rulings and revenue procedures are not binding in Tax Court or any other court. However, taxpayers may use revenue rulings and revenue procedures as official IRS guidance. ###

6. A legislative regulation has a higher degree of authority than _____.

A. The Internal Revenue Code.
B. A Supreme Court decision.
C. An interpretative regulation.
D. None of the above.

The answer is C. A legislative regulation has a higher degree of authority than an interpretative regulation. ###

7. When a Treasury regulation becomes "official," what happens?

A. A procedural regulation is issued.
B. A final regulation is issued.
C. A temporary regulation is issued.
D. A Tax Court memorandum is published.

The answer is B. A final regulation is issued when a Treasury regulation becomes an official Treasury decision. ###

8. A private letter ruling is *legally binding* on the IRS if _____.

A. The taxpayer fully and accurately described the proposed transaction in the request and carries out the transaction as described.
B. The IRS is notified of any discrepancies on a taxpayer's return.
C. The taxpayer goes to the Tax Court and requests a formal decision.
D. None of the above.

The answer is A. A PLR is binding on the IRS if the taxpayer fully and accurately described the proposed transaction in the request and carries out the transaction as described. A PLR may not be relied on as precedent by other taxpayers or IRS personnel. ###

Index

E&P. *See* earnings and profits

EA exam: application, 11; question format, 10; scheduling, 12; scoring, 10

early distributions. *See* distributions

early withdrawal penalty: as an adjustment to income, 142; from an IRA. *See* distributions

Earned Income Credit: in general, 224; preparer penalties, 237; qualifying child, 235

earnings and profits: AAA of an S corporation, 591; accumulated E&P, 569; accumulated earnings tax, 543; capital interest in a partnership, 513; distributions from E&P, 569; ordinary dividends, 568

economic performance, 407

education expenses: 529 plans, 99; education credits, 232; employer provided, 105; exception to the 10% IRA penalty, 327; job related education, 212

educational assistance, 439

educator expense deduction, 142

effective tax administration, 760

e-file: advertising restrictions, 704; authorized provider, 791; denial of participation, 792; entities required to e-file, 792; mandate, 790; rejected returns, 793; revocation, 798; suitability check, 791; types of providers, 794

EFIN: authorized e-file provider, 791; revocation, 798

EFTPS, 367, 409, 541, 801

EIC. *See* Earned Income Credit

elected deferrals, 108

Electronic Federal Tax Payment System, 801, *See* EFTPS

electronic return originator, 794

employee awards, 94

employee business expenses, 207

employee classification, 370

employee wages, 408

employer identification number, 359

employment taxes, 367, 419, 436

energy credit, 452

enrolled actuary, 662

enrolled agent: advertising restrictions, 704; assistance from disbarred persons, 693; best practices, 692; compliance for renewal, 682; confidentiality privilege, 693; conflicts of interest, 694; continuing education, 683; duty to advise, 692; employment records, 714; inactive and terminated EAs, 682; initial licensing, 680; performance as a notary, 693; recordkeeping requirements CE, 684; renewal, 682; signature requirements, 701; third party authorizations, 697

enrolled retirement plan agents, 662

enrollment: CE waiver, 685; continuing education requirements, 683; denial of enrollment, 681

entertainment expenses, 410, 412, 413

equitable relief, 758

ERISA, 630

estates: accounting period, 377; alternate valuation date, 259; as corporate shareholders, 573; bankruptcy estate, 340; basis and valuation date, 259; domestic production activities, 457; Form 706, 649; gross estate, 341, 648; in general, 338, 644; income in respect of a decedent, 645; right of survivorship, 342; the estate tax return Form 706, 343

estimated tax payments: C corporations, 542; farmers, 601; farmers and fishermen, 47; individuals, 46; on unrelated business income, 619; refund of corporate overpayment, 542; S corporations, 583

ethics: advertising standards, 797; delay tactics, 693; disreputable conduct, 724; duty to advise, 692; earned income credit, 735; e-filing, 792; performance as a notary, 693

examinations, 766; confidentiality privilege during, 693; contact of third parties, 768; determinations, 770; information matching, 767; location of the audit, 769; recording the audit, 771; repeat examinations, 768; TEFRA partnerships, 773

excess contributions, 330

excise taxes: credits for farmers, 608; health savings accounts, 441; imposed on a business, 419; trust fund recovery penalty, 368

executor, 338

exempt entities: filing requirements, 616; in general, 614; organizing document, 615; penalties, 617; unrelated business income, 619

extension requests, 378

failure-to-file, 44, 717

failure-to-pay, 44, 717

family farming corporations, 602

family partnerships, 513

farm debts, 99

farm income averaging, 608

farmers: estimated payments, 47; family farming corporations, 602; farm debts, 99; farm income averaging, 608; in general, 600; net operating losses, 608; qualified conservation easements, 185; rental income, 601; self-employment income, 100; treatment of disaster payments, 607

farm-price method, 603

federal tax lien, 753

federal unemployment tax: accountable plans, 444; employee wages, 590; in general, 369

fees: for RALs, 802; preparer advertising, 705

fiduciary: forms used for representation, 668; practice rights, 664

fiduciary returns, 340, 645

FIFO. *See* first-in, first-out

filing requirements: for dependents with income, 30; for individuals, 28

filing status, 56

final regulations, 811

financial statements, 366

first-in, first-out, 385

fiscal year: 52/53 week tax year, 374; exempt entities, 617; partnerships, 511; S corporations, 583

flexible spending arrangement, 103

foreign earned income exclusion, 122

Foreign Tax Credit, 238

franchise taxes, 419

fraud: civil fraud penalty, 719; EIC claims, 737; identity theft, 702; opening a closed audit, 770; statute of limitations, 716

Freedom of Information Act, 813

fringe benefits, 101; adoption assistance, 438; dependent care assistance, 439; educational assistance, 439; in general, 436; retirement plans, 623

frivolous positions: in general, 719; striking the jurat, 720; tax shelters, 746; using false documents, 720

standard deduction, 168
standard mileage rate, 415
start-up costs: C corporation, 548; capital expenditures, 473; for small employer pensions, 455; of a business entity, 422; partnerships, 514; qualifying costs, 422
state income taxes, 174
state tax refunds, 119
statute of limitations, 49; assessment, 752; collections, 752; employment records, 714; for keeping records, 714; fraudulent return, 716; payroll returns, 714
statutory employees, 370
statutory nonemployees, 371
stock distributions, 570
stock dividend, 116; basis of, 255; holding period, 261
stock options, 257
stock redemption, 571
stock split, 255, 261
stockpiling, 21, 792
straight-line depreciation, 476
student loan interest deduction, 153
Student Tax Clinic Program, 663
substantial portion rule, 667
substantial presence test, 33
supervised preparers, 665
supplemental wages, 110, 408
surviving spouse: filing status, 61; IRA rollover, 326; IRD, 339; marital deduction, 341; sale of home, 284
tax avoidance, 716
tax evasion, 716
tax home, 208
tax preparer: advertising restrictions, 704; authorized e-file provider, 791; best practices, 692; client fraud, 721; conflicts of interest, 694; contingent fees, 703; covered opinions, 746; disclosure of taxpayer information, 695; EIC ethics, 735; employer of preparers, 667; fees, 703; practitioner fraud, 721; published fee schedule, 705; signature requirements, 670, 701; substantial portion rule, 667; types of consents, 699
tax rates: capital gain distributions, 271; for dependents who file, 82; for self-employed persons, 100; individuals, 42
tax refunds. See refunds
tax returns: examination process, 766; frivolous return, 719; preparer identification, 702; rejected e-file, 793
tax shelter: reporting requirements, 746
tax shelter opinions, 744
tax year: 52/53-week year, 374; in general, 374; required tax year, 375; section 444 election, 376
taxable income, 91
taxes: as a business expense, 417; backup withholding, 368; employment taxes, 367, 419; excise taxes, 419; franchise taxes, 419; FUTA, 369; occupational taxes, 419; personal property tax, 419; real estate taxes, 463
taxpayer: allowable disclosures, 695; best practices, 692; civil fraud penalty, 719; conflicts of interest, 694; identity theft, 702; noncompliance, 692; penalty for tax evasion, 716; privacy of taxpayer data, 695; return of client records, 700; types of consents, 699
Taxpayer Advocate Service, 756
Taxpayer Identification Number, 27; misuse of, 703
taxpayer rights, 767
teacher credit. See educator expense deduction

technical advice memorandum, 811
TEFRA audits, 773
temporary regulations, 811
termination: C corporation, 572; of a partnership, 534; of S election, 581; relief from inadvertent termination, 582
TFRP. See trust fund recovery penalty
theft losses, 466
third party authorizations, 697
third party designee, 697
thirty-day letter, 779
Thrift Savings Plans, 108
tie-breaker rule, 76
time test, 145
tip income, 111
Title 26. See Internal Revenue Code
traditional IRA: deductible contributions, 152; excess contributions, 330; in general, 321; prohibited transactions, 330; rollover, 328
transmission perfection period, 793
transportation expenses: actual vehicle expenses, 416; as an employee fringe benefit, 443; for businesses, 415; listed property, 480; standard mileage rate, 415
travel expenses: accountable plan, 106; away from "tax home", 209; employee travel expenses, 208; from a home office, 211; military personnel, 210; related to rental activity, 310
travel expenses: for businesses, 411
travel expenses: per diem rate, 412
treasury regulations, 810
trust fund recovery penalty, 368, 718
trusts: abusive trusts, 653; accounting period, 650; domestic production activities, 457; in general, 650; non-grantor trust, 652; types of trusts, 652
tuition and fees deduction, 155
tuition reduction, 439
twelve-month rule, 381
U.S. Court of Federal Claims, 778
U.S. Tax Court, 780; appeals process, 778; memorandum decisions, 781; recovering litigation costs, 783; small case procedure, 782
unemployment compensation: repayment of, 157
UNICAP. See uniform capitalization rules
uniform capitalization rules: cost method, 388; exemptions from UNICAP, 390; farming businesses, 604; in general, 390
uniforms, 212
unit-livestock-price method, 603
unit-of-production method, 477
unrealistic positions, 722
unrelated business income, 619
valuation date, 259
VITA, 663
Volunteer Income Tax Assistance. See VITA
wages. See employee wages
wash sales, 274
withdrawal penalty. See distributions
work opportunity tax credit, 453
workers' compensation, 119
worthless securities: statute of limitations, 716
WOTC. See work opportunity tax credit

About the Authors

Collette Szymborski is a certified public accountant and the managing partner of Elk Grove CPA Accountancy Corporation. She specializes in the taxation of corporations, individuals, and exempt entities. Elk Grove CPA also does estate planning.

Richard Gramkow is an enrolled agent with more than sixteen years of experience in various areas of taxation. He holds a master's degree in taxation from Rutgers University and is currently a tax manager for a publicly held Fortune 500 company in the New York metropolitan area.

Christy Pinheiro is an enrolled agent, registered tax return preparer, Accredited Business Accountant, and writer. Christy was an accountant for two private CPA firms and for the State of California before going into private practice. She is a member of the California Society of Enrolled Agents and CalCPA.

Also Available from PassKey Publications

The Enrolled Agent Tax Consulting Practice Guide:

Learn How to Develop, Market, and Operate a Profitable
Tax and IRS Representation Practice

ISBN-13: 978-0982266045

Available in Kindle and Nook editions and as a paperback

22135286R00438

Made in the USA
Lexington, KY
13 April 2013